D0768535

Borneo
Sabah • Sarawak • Brunei

the Bradt Travel Guide

Tamara Thiessen

edition
3

www.bradtguides.com

Bradt Travel Guides Ltd, UK
The Globe Pequot Press Inc, USA

BRUNEI

Sabah

MALAYSIA

Sarawak

INDONESIA

N

Bradt

0 ——— 50km
0 ——— 50 miles

Gunung Kinabalu National Park: this ancient, sacred park is home to Mount Kinabalu, the island's highest peak at 4,095m
pages 203–11

Bandar Seri Begawan: exotic Islamic traditions intermingle with impressive modern architecture and spicy food in Brunei's capital
pages 144–57

SOUTH CHINA

SEA

Niah Caves: once occupied by prehistoric hunter-gatherers, these UNESCO-classified caves are archaeological treasure chests
pages 309–11

Bako National Park: this spellbinding, diverse national park contains 16 well-marked trails – perfect for spotting the proboscis monkey
pages 283–4

BRUN

Miri

Marudi

Lambir Hills National Park

Niah Caves

Niah National Park

Bintulu

Long Lan

MALAYSIA

Mukah

Belaga

Selangu

Rajang

Sarawak

Sibu

Sarikei

Kapit

Santubong

Bako National Park

Kuching

Semenggoh Nature Reserve

Bandar Sri Aman

Semenggoh Nature Reserve: an ideal day trip from Kuching, the Semenggoh Wildlife Rehabilitation Centre is home to semi-wild orangutans
pages 287–8

INDONESIA

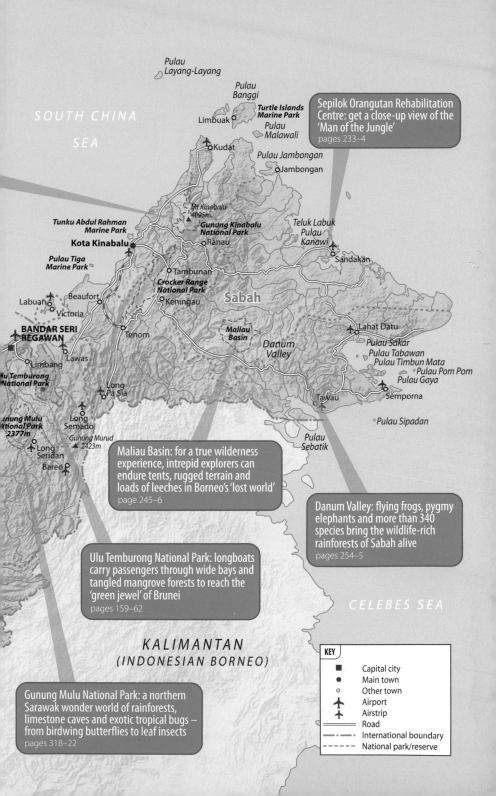

Pulau
Layang-Layang

Pulau
Banggi

SOUTH CHINA

Turtle Islands
Marine Park

Limbuak ○

Pulau
Malawali

SEA

○ Kudat

Pulau Jambongan

Pulau Jambongan

○ Jambongan

Sepilok Orangutan Rehabilitation
Centre: get a close-up view of the
'Man of the Jungle'
pages 233–4

Mt Kinabalu
4095m.

**Gunung Kinabalu
National Park**

Teluk Labuk
Pulau
Kanawi

**Tunku Abdul Rahman
Marine Park**

○ Ranau

Kota Kinabalu

Sandakan

**Pulau Tiga
Marine Park**

○ Tambunan

**Crocker Range
National Park**

Sabah

Labuan

Beaufort

○ Keningau

Victoria

**Maliau
Basin**

**Danum
Valley**

Lahat Datu

**BANDAR SERI
BEGAWAN**

Tenom

Pulau Sakar
Pulau Tabawan
Pulau Timbun Mata
Pulau Pom Pom
Pulau Gaya

Lawas

Limbang

lu Temburong
National Park

Long
Pa Sia

Tawau

Semporna

○ Pulau Sipadan

unung Mulu
tional Park
2377m

Long
Semado

Gunung Murud
2423m

Pulau
Sebatik

Long
Seridan

Bareo

Maliau Basin: for a true wilderness
experience, intrepid explorers can
endure tents, rugged terrain and
loads of leeches in Borneo's 'lost world'
page 245–6

Danum Valley: flying frogs, pygmy
elephants and more than 340
species bring the wildlife-rich
rainforests of Sabah alive
pages 254–5

Ulu Temburong National Park: longboats
carry passengers through wide bays and
tangled mangrove forests to reach the
'green jewel' of Brunei
pages 159–62

CELEBES SEA

**KALIMANTAN
(INDONESIAN BORNEO)**

Gunung Mulu National Park: a northern
Sarawak wonder world of rainforests,
limestone caves and exotic tropical bugs –
from birdwing butterflies to leaf insects
pages 318–22

KEY	
■	Capital city
●	Main town
○	Other town
✈	Airport
✈	Airstrip
═══	Road
—·—·—	International boundary
– – – –	National park/reserve

Borneo
Don't
miss...

Discover pristine coral reefs
The kaleidoscopic corals on the west and east coasts are a barometer of marine diversity
(ST) page 59

Explore Brunei's capital – Bandar Seri Begawan
The Gadong night market is an exciting place to try local cuisine at a fraction of the price of the restaurants
(JS/S) page 152

Take to the trees on a canopy walk for a birds' eye view of your surroundings
Here the canopy walkway in the Danum Valley
(AP/S) pages 254–5

Visit the Sepilok Orangutan Rehabilitation Centre
An orangutan-viewing hotspot in Sabah
(CM/FLPA) pages 233–4

Climb amidst the limestone pinnacles of Gunung Mulu National Park, Sarawak
Trekking, caving and longboat safaris are all options in this national park
(ST) pages 318–22

Borneo
in colour

left **Sarawak State Legislative Assembly building, Kuching** (DA) page 276

below **Sandakan, a city on stilts, is Sabah's second-largest town** (N/S) pages 223–9

bottom **The Sultan Omar Ali Saifuddien Mosque in Bandar Seri Begawan was built in 1958** (AFY/S) page 156

right   The Puu Jih Shih Buddhist Temple is adorned with gilded statues and painted columns (IB) page 228

below   Fresh Malay food served at the Gadong *pasar malam* (night market) in Bandar Seri Begawan (TT) page 152

middle   Detail from the Tua Pek Kong Temple in Lundu, Sarawak (DA) page 275

bottom   A river float parade on the Sarawak River in Kuching (DA) pages 259–60

above   The rural-style Tamu Tawau market has over 200 stalls selling everything from seaweed to traditional handicrafts (DK/SBT) page 244

left   Kek Lapis Sarawak is a traditional layer cake with intricate patterns (DA) page 110

below   Kuching lies on either side of the mighty Sarawak River and is studded with urban parks and colonial buildings (SWT) pages 259–78

AUTHOR

Tamara Thiessen is a freelance journalist and photographer from Australia, specialising in travel and cultural reporting. Between occasional bases in Melbourne, London and Paris, she considers her suitcase her real anchor and most recognisable landmark. With a background in radio and television journalism, since leaving for France on a journalism scholarship in 1996, she has reported news and current affairs for the Australian Broadcasting Corporation, SBS World News, Deutsche Welle Radio, European Parliament Radio Reports and Monocle Radio.

As a European correspondent, she has worked on international news desks such as Agence France-Presse, worked out of France, Italy and Germany, and written for newspapers including the *Toronto Globe & Mail*, *Montreal Gazette*, *Sydney Morning Herald*, *Melbourne Age*, *The Australian*, *Sunday Business Post*, *South China Morning Post* and *Singapore Straits Times*.

Her stories are published in leisure and business travel publications in London, Dubai, Brussels, Hong Kong, New York, Seoul and Sydney. As well as titles such as *National Geographic Traveller* (UK), *Business Traveller*, *Condé Nast Traveller*, *Islands Magazine* and *Monocole*, she writes for dozens of in-flight magazines worldwide.

A hotel addict, she spends about eight months a year in hotel beds of all kinds, and is a regular global correspondent for hotel industry and design magazines *Hotel News Now*, *Sleeper* and *Hospitality Design*. A contributing writer and photographer to the Eyewitness Travel Guides to Australia, France and Italy, and *Style City Europe* (Thames & Hudson), she is also the author and photographer of *Café Life Sydney* (Interlink) and *Chronicles of Old Rome* (Museyon). Tamara has fully updated and revised this third edition of her Borneo guidebook. You can keep in touch with (and contact) her on her website (*www.tamarathiessen.com*).

AUTHOR'S STORY

Born on the end-of-the-world island of Tasmania, far-flung, wild islands are an intrinsic part of my genetic make-up. Drawn inexorably to isolated places and their often otherworldly nature and culture, my childhood dreams of Borneo were fanned by forays into *National Geographic* magazine. In the mid 1990s they were rekindled during a chance encounter with a Malaysian in Melbourne. Quizzing him about the most beautiful places to visit in his country, he sketched Sabah and Sarawak on a paper napkin and told me how extraordinary but threatened Borneo's rainforests and animals were. Clutching that scrap of paper, the desire to visit simmered away for another couple of years. When I got there, it was just as he had described it – a land of astonishing wildlife and people, facing serious environmental threats.

One of the most intolerable tragedies of our times, I believe, is the irreversible destruction of the searing beauty and uniqueness of such places. As West Malaysia is consumed by a speedy, hyper-modern lifestyle, Borneo's natural beauty, cultural richness and traditional village lifestyles stand out even more. Those lucky enough to visit, will hopefully be inspired to help protect this extraordinary island of forested fantasies.

PUBLISHER'S FOREWORD   *Hilary Bradt*

The first Bradt travel guide was written in 1974 by George and Hilary Bradt on a river barge floating down a tributary of the Amazon. It was followed by *Backpacker's Africa*, published in 1979. In the 1980s and '90s, the focus shifted away from hiking to broader-based guides to new destinations – usually the first to be published on those places. In the 21st century, Bradt continues to publish these ground-breaking guides, along with guides to established holiday destinations, incorporating in-depth information on culture and natural history alongside the nuts and bolts of where to stay and what to see.

Bradt authors support responsible travel, with advice not only on minimum impact but also on how to give something back through local charities. Thus a true synergy is achieved between the traveller and local communities.

Third edition published January 2016
First published 2008
Bradt Travel Guides Ltd
IDC House, The Vale, Chalfont St Peter, Bucks SL9 9RZ, England
www.bradtguides.com
Print edition published in the USA by The Globe Pequot Press Inc,
PO Box 480, Guilford, Connecticut 06437-0480

Text copyright © 2016 Tamara Thiessen
Maps copyright © 2016 Bradt Travel Guides Ltd
Photographs copyright © 2016 Individual photographers (see below)
Project Manager: Claire Strange
Cover research: Pepi Bluck, Perfect Picture

The author and publisher have made every effort to ensure the accuracy of the information in this book at the time of going to press. However, they cannot accept any responsibility for any loss, injury or inconvenience resulting from the use of information contained in this guide. All rights reserved. No part of this publication may be reproduced, stored in a retrieval system, or transmitted in any form or by any means, electronic, mechanical, photocopying, recording or otherwise without the prior consent of the publisher. Requests for permission should be addressed to Bradt Travel Guides Ltd in the UK (print and digital editions), or to The Globe Pequot Press Inc in North and South America (print edition only).

ISBN: 978 1 84162 915 5 (print)
e-ISBN: 978 1 78477 128 7 (e-pub)
e-ISBN: 978 1 78477 228 4 (mobi)

British Library Cataloguing in Publication Data
A catalogue record for this book is available from the British Library

Photographs Daniel Austin (DA); Ulrike Bauer (UB); Scott Bennett (SB); Brunei Tourism (BT); Ian Butler (IB); Dreamstime: Bmlaarhoven (B/DT), Oriori; FLPA: Theo Allofs/Minden Pictures (TA/FLPA), Neil Bowman (NB/FLPA), John Holmes (JH/FLPA), Imagebroker (I/FLPA), Frans Lanting (FL/FLPA), Chien Lee/Minden Pictures (CL/FLPA); Natural Visions: Heather Angel (HA/NV), Jeff Collett (JC/NV), Anne Norris (AN/NV), Brian Rogers (BR/NV); Nature Picture Library: Edward Giesbers (EG/NPL); Sabah Tourism Board: David Kirkland (DK/SBT), Mewot (M/SBT); Sarawak Tourism Board (SWT); Shutterstock: alphonsusjimos (A/S), apple2499 (AP/S), Kim Briers (KB/S), Rich Carey (RC/S), James Harrison (JH/S), kkaplin (KK/S), Hugh Lansdown (HL/S), Natursports (N/S), Marcin Niemiec (MN/S), Nokuro (N/S), old apple (OA/S), Phil MacD Photography (PMP/S), Arnon Polin (AP/S), razmanrusli (R/S), Jan S (JS/S), Praiwun Thungsarn (PT/S), warmer (W/S), Ahmad Faizal Yahya (AFY/S); Tamara Thiessen (TT); Wikimedia Commons (W)
Front cover Male orangutan, Matang Wildlife Centre (EG/NPL)
Back cover Aerial view of Tun Sakaran Marine Park (R/S); Iban women (SWT)
Title page Blue-eared kingfisher (IB); Danum Valley, Sabah (KB/S); Malayan bush brown butterfly (IB)

Maps David McCutcheon FBCart.S; some maps include data © OpenStreetMaps contributors (under Open Database License)

Typeset from the author's disc by Ian Spick, Bradt Travel Guides
Production managed by Jellyfish Print Solutions; printed in India
Digital conversion by www.dataworks.co.in

Acknowledgements

My immeasurable appreciation goes to the tourism boards of Sabah and Sarawak for their huge assistance with travels in Borneo; to local tour operators for their generous on-the-ground support, fantastic guides and local knowledge; and innumerable hotels, resorts and guesthouses who offered me Bornean hospitality *par excellence* during my travels.

As well as local cultural organisations who assisted me with information, I would like to express my utmost gratitude to several notable Borneo experts who freely gave of their time and knowledge to make invaluable contributions to the guidebook: archaeologist Peter Bellwood for clarifying the complex and sometimes very confusing Bornean prehistory; Dr Glen Reynolds from the Danum Valley Field Center and eminent evolutionary biologist Sir Peter Crane for their insights into Borneo's natural history and conservation; archaeologist Huw Barton, the 'raider' of Niah's remarkable caves; and Heidi Munan for her insights into Sarawak craft.

I would also like to thank the wonderful Bradt team of editors for helping steer this *oeuvre* towards its third edition. Finally, thanks to everyone I have encountered on my travels in Malaysian Borneo and Brunei: the special friends I have made there and the people of the island whose culture, spirit and warmth – along with the heavenly natural world – make it the most memorable place in my privileged tally of world travels.

FOLLOW BRADT

For the latest news, special offers and competitions, subscribe to the Bradt newsletter via the website www.bradtguides.com and follow Bradt on:

- www.facebook.com/BradtTravelGuides
- @BradtGuides
- @bradtguides
- www.pinterest.com/bradtguides

Contents

LIST OF MAPS

KEY TO SYMBOLS

- International boundary
- State boundary
- Main road
- Other road
- 4x4 track
- Railway
- Airport (international/regional)
- Bus station
- Ferry (vehicular/other)
- Small boats
- Petrol station
- Tourist information
- Embassy/High Commission
- Museum/art gallery
- Theatre/cinema
- Historic building
- Statue/monument
- Bank
- Post office
- Hospital
- Hotel/guesthouse
- Camping
- Hut
- Restaurant
- Bar/wine bar
- Nightclub
- Internet café
- Church/cathedral
- Mosque
- Sikh temple
- Chinese temple
- Gardens
- Golf course
- Dive site
- Beach
- Cave
- Summit (height in metres)
- Stadium
- National park
- Urban park
- Urban market

Introduction

Borneo – the very name conjures up a sultry tropical island, brimming with mystery, maritime escapade and swampy, steamy jungle adventure. Situated at the junction of four seas, in the heart of Southeast Asia, the island's history is that of ferocious headhunters and pillaging pirates, long-haul ocean migrations and seafaring invasions. The name Borneo ostensibly comes from a European transformation of Bruni, a once-powerful Muslim trading post on the west coast of the island, known today as Brunei.

The world's third-biggest island after Greenland and New Guinea, Borneo is also the only isle on the planet shared by three nations – Brunei, Malaysia and Indonesia. This infuses it with an innate cultural and political complexity and myriad ethnic colours.

Throughout its intriguing past the island has been portrayed as remote and obscure, an aura fuelled by talk of pirate-ridden seas, savage natives, inhospitable landscapes and turbulent politics. Even today it evokes the promise of far-off adventure, owing to its indelible geographical isolation as much as the dense surviving jungles. It takes another two hours to reach Borneo, travelling by plane from mainland Malaysia. That remoteness, amplified by rich tribal vestiges and exotic otherworldly flora and fauna, makes Borneo a prime destination for those seeking cultural and natural authenticity.

With over 200 indigenous tribes – ancestors of ancient Chinese, Malayan and Javanese Empires – and large Chinese, Malay and Hindu populations, the island is a fascinating repository of ethnographic history. The two Malaysian states of Sabah and Sarawak, and the self-ruled Sultanate of Brunei, all covered in this guide, each has its own story to tell. Yet their history is also inextricably intertwined. All three came under British influence at some stage, and colonial influences endure in odd yet curious ways.

Borneo's natural wonders are undoubtedly its greatest and most famous asset. As a 'biodiversity hotspot', its variety and richness of life forms is unparalleled. Just 10ha of Bornean rainforest can support 700 species of tree – as many as are found across the whole of North America. The island boasts as many bird species as Europe, and the same mammal count as Australia. Foremost among them is Borneo's adorable yet endangered mascot – Asia's only great ape, the orangutan. Over 5,000 plant species and 500 animals are unique to the island.

Like many paradises, however, the very things that make Borneo so magical are under threat. Its extraordinary natural world and traditional cultures have been seriously eroded over the past half-century, with up to half of its tropical forests lost and much of its flora and fauna pushed towards extinction. In some cases it is too late to turn back the clock.

The urgency for conservation has not waned over the past three decades. In many ways, as the world awakes to what has been, and what is being, lost, it is spiralling. Local and international organisations, scientists, media and tourists have all helped turn up the heat on threats to Borneo's forests, assisting indigenous people who have long fought to save their island. As the consequences of environmental destruction and conservation of tropical forests and biodiversity gain prominence on the global agenda, hopefully Borneo's outstanding remaining natural treasures will be preserved for future generations.

HOW TO USE THIS GUIDE

MAPS
Keys and symbols Maps include alphabetical keys covering the locations of those places to stay, eat or drink that are featured in the book. Note that regional maps may not show all hotels and restaurants in the area: other establishments may be located in towns shown on the map.

Grids and grid references Several maps use gridlines to allow easy location of sites. Map grid references are listed in square brackets after the name of the place or sight of interest in the text, with page number followed by grid number, eg: [264 C3].

On occasion, hotels or restaurants that are not listed in the guide (but which might serve as alternative options if required or serve as useful landmarks to aid navigation) are also included on the maps; these are marked with accommodation (⌂) or restaurant (✖) symbols.

WEBSITES Although all third party websites were working at the time of going to print, some may cease to function during this edition's lifetime. If a website doesn't work, you might want to check back at another time as they often function intermittently. Alternatively, you can let us know of any website issues by emailing info@bradtguides.com.

FEEDBACK REQUEST AND UPDATES WEBSITE

At Bradt Travel Guides we're aware that guidebooks start to go out of date on the day they're published – and that you, our readers, are out there in the field doing research of your own. You'll find out before us when a fine new family-run hotel opens or a favourite restaurant changes hands and goes downhill. So why not write and tell us about your experiences? Contact us on ☎ 01753 893444 or e info@bradtguides.com. We will forward emails to the author who may post updates on the Bradt website at www.bradtupdates.com/borneo. Alternatively you can add a review of the book to www.bradtguides.com or Amazon.

Part One

GENERAL INFORMATION

BORNEO ONLINE

For additional online content, articles, photos and more on Borneo, why not visit www.bradtguides.com/borneo.

1

Background Information

GEOGRAPHY

Straddling the Equator between 4–7°N and 4°S, the remote island of Borneo lies in the humid, tropical zone of Southeast Asia, 1,500km east of continental Malaysia. Three times the size of Great Britain – at 743,294km² – it is the only island in the world to unite three nations within its shores: Malaysia, Brunei and Indonesia. Clustered in the north and down the northwest coast, the 'East Malaysia' states of Sabah and Sarawak, and Sultanate of Brunei, cover around a quarter of the island, while the Indonesian region of Kalimantan, not covered in this guide, occupies the rest.

Borneo's geography is one dipped in a melting pot of maritime forces. A generous-sized blob among dozens of island spots and specks, it is shored up by several straits and four oceans – the South China Sea to the northwest, Sulu Sea to the north, Celebes Sea to the east and Java Sea to the south. In shape, northern Borneo resembles a dog: ears pointing towards the Philippines, paw extending across the Makassar Strait to Sulawesi, tail jutting westward towards Singapore and feet dipping down towards Jakarta.

Wrongly imagined as extremely mountainous, waterlogged coastal areas less than 150m in elevation swathe more than half of the island; only 5% exceeds 3,000m (around 9,000ft), and most peaks average 2,000m (approx 6,000ft). Many of these lie near Gunung Kinabalu, the 4,095m mountain near the northwestern tip of Sabah. The tallest peak between the Himalayas and Papua New Guinea, Mount Kinabalu reigns high over Sabah. It's this colossal granite upsurge which qualifies Borneo as the 'sixth-highest island in the world'.

MALAYSIAN BORNEO The states of Sabah and Sarawak constitute Malaysian Borneo.

Sabah Sabah occupies the northernmost chunk of Borneo, forming the head of the 'dog'. Many rivers spring from 'its mountainous interior and surrounding hills are criss-crossed by an extensive network of river valleys. Nearer the coastal plains are lower-lying swampy hills. Sabah's chant *'negeri di bawah bayu'* ('land below the wind') comes from its location – just south of the typhoon belt, which all too frequently blights the Philippines – in the equatorial doldrums.

Sarawak Sarawak is a land of rivers. Rivers narrow and wide run through the countryside and cities, constituting an incredible navigable network of 3,300km. The state's 55 rivers provide a vital link between the coast and remote interior, and are still the only means of transport to some places.

BRUNEI A small enclave of a nation tucked between Sabah and Sarawak's frontiers, Brunei's 5,765km² territory accounts for less than 1% of Borneo. Despite the physical

BORNEO'S CLIMATE AT A GLANCE

Temperature Lowlands 23–33°C; Highlands 13–27°C. Steady throughout the year, varying by less than 2°C
Humidity 75–85% – can be uncomfortable; rainforest average 80%, up to 100% at night
Annual rainfall 2,500–4,000mm, usually 150mm minimum in most months

constraints, it's somewhat of a mini Borneo, geographically, composed of wide coastal mangrove plains, *nipah* and peat swamp, rainforest and hilly terrains. In comparison with Sabah's sizeable 1,600km coastline, and Sarawak's 720km shoreline, Brunei's South China Sea-face (the Laut China Selatan) is just 161km long.

POPULATION DENSITY AND DISTRIBUTION Sparsely populated by Asian standards, northern Borneo's average of 17 people per square kilometre compares with 74 on Peninsular Malaysia. About 5.9 million people – a third of Borneo's population of 16 million – live between Sabah, Sarawak and Brunei. Historically the population was split between coastal and inland dwellers, with most early human settlements concentrated along the coast and on riverbanks. Until the late 19th century, the hinterland was relatively uninhabited, while the coast and floodplains of major rivers were densely populated. Though these patterns still exist today, the distinction has faded with soaring urbanisation. In the mid 1970s, about 15% of Sarawak's population lived in towns and cities – today that figure is 50% and rising. The same goes for Sabah, where half the population now live in urban areas compared with 20% in 1970. This rapid evolution is having major repercussions on the environment, through urban waste problems and coastal and river pollution.

CLIMATE

Borneo's climate is equatorial-tropical, distinguished by marked wet and dry seasons: the wet season (or 'northeast monsoon') generally runs from November to March, the dry season (or 'southwest monsoon') from May to October. There is no official start and end point between seasons. In the wet season, there are usually daily rains, and sometimes violent storms, monsoon winds, flooding, landslides and torrential rains.

Half of the annual rainfall on Sarawak's west coast falls between December and March, while the hilly slopes of Sarawak's inland Kelabit Highlands receive the highest annual rainfall of the state – more than 5,000mm. The wettest months tend to be January and February, followed directly by the driest – March and April.

In more equatorial Sarawak, there is little variation in day length throughout the year – with only a seven-minute difference between the shortest and longest days.

The sun rises and sets at around the same time every day – between 06.00 and 18.00. Sunshine is bountiful, but a typical day will usually have some cloudy periods. Northern Borneo's great climatic exception is Mount Kinabalu, which has varying alpine microclimates, and can be quite chilly at the top.

See *Practical Information*, page 71, for more information on when to visit.

HISTORY

The following sections provide a brief summary of the island's history. For more reading, see the titles listed in *Further Information*, pages 331–4.

RAINFOREST TREASURES – EARLY TRADE WITH INDIA AND CHINA Evidence suggests that India was trading with Southeast Asia from as early as 290BC, with Chinese traders joining the continental market around AD1000. During this period of internationalisation, Borneo's tribes were gradually drawn into networks of trade in spices, camphor, precious woods and other exotic forest products.

The 11th to 13th centuries saw an explosion of trade between China and the Indo-Malaysian Archipelago in forest products, metals, gemstones and spices. A whole gamut of exotic export products came from the Bornean rainforests: beeswax for ointments, aromatic woods for incense, rubber, resin and rattan.

Some of the Chinese merchants settled in Borneo's ports. Excavations in the Sarawak River delta south of Kuching show evidence of a sizeable Chinese settlement in the 10th to 13th centuries. Other excavations in Brunei and Sabah suggest the Chinese were trading ceramics for spices even earlier than this.

In spite of the trading ties, the Hindu and Buddhist kingdoms of western Indonesia during the first millennium had little influence in Malaysian Borneo, which was already well under the spell of Malay culture.

MALAY CULTURE AND EARLY EMPIRES Malay culture was implanted in Borneo from the 7th to 13th centuries, propagated by links with major trading empires. At the time, the maritime empire of Srivijaya ruled supreme, controlling international sea trade across the Malay Archipelago. Originating in Sumatra, its influence extended through Borneo, with many Sumatran Malays purportedly settling on the island during this time.

In the 14th century, Srivijaya ceded to the Java-based Majapahit Empire. Borneo absorbed some Hindu influences, traces of which remain today. The Hindu empire in the Malay Archipelago started to topple at the end of the 15th century.

ENTER ISLAM It was around this time that Islam got a foothold in Borneo, though its presence had been felt since the 13th century, with Muslim trading states established in Sumatra, Java, Malacca and the Moluccas (the spice islands of Ternate and Tidore).

Malay language, culture and religion flourished along the coasts of what are today Sabah and Sarawak, as vessels from Malaya and Sumatra anchored in port. Traders, teachers and missionaries all played a hand in the implantation of Islamic civilisation in the region. Through the trading relationships with Muslim powers, Islam spread to Brunei. Sultanates blossomed in Brunei from the 14th century onwards, and it gradually became a centre of Islamisation for other parts of Borneo. Smaller Muslim–Malay states emerged all over the island during the 17th century, some converting purely for strategic and mercenary reasons, as they had done earlier to Hinduism and Buddhism. The Sultanate of Brunei ruled over much of northern Borneo until the 19th century – not without some significant territorial tugs of war.

As Muslim might snowballed, Borneo's economic influence was still marginal on a regional scale. The southern Philippines area of the Sulu Islands emerged as a powerful late 18th-century sultanate, and attempted to wrench parts of northern Borneo under its control. The Sultan of Brunei failed to honour an agreement to cede Sabah to Sulu; and the after-effect of these chronic territorial tensions persists today.

WHITE RAJAHS AND RANEES – EUROPEANS IN BORNEO The Portuguese were the first Europeans to set foot in Borneo, while the Spanish attacked Brunei in 1578, briefly occupying the port. Despite repeated attempts, no external power succeeded in gaining control over the island. Instead it was the Sultanate of Brunei that ruled over much of what is today Sabah and Sarawak, through a court of noble envoys, *raja* (princes) and locally appointed Malay chiefs.

The reign lasted throughout much of the 17th and 18th centuries, before the sultans' methods met with resistance. Faced with rebellion and piracy, Brunei's control over the region waned and colonial forces stepped in to fill the vacuum. The British saw power in Borneo as a way of protecting its shipping routes to China. In the early 19th century, Britain gained a foothold in northern Borneo through a series of naval coups waged on behalf of the weakened sultanate. From the mid 19th century, Borneo was carved up between European powers: the British in the north and Dutch in the south. Despite its formidable reputation as a home to headhunters, haunt for pirates and cesspool of tropical diseases, competition was fierce for the last available land in the area – what is today Sabah.

The foundations of Sabah Sabah at that stage did not exist – it fell within the Sultan of Brunei's territories. In the mid 1860s however, forced to relinquish several parts of its empire it could no longer control, the sinking sultanate struck a deal for a ten-year lease of Sabah with the American consul to Brunei, Claude Lee Moses. Sadly he did nothing more than run off to Hong Kong with the cession fees! British trading arrangements in Borneo had far more lasting repercussions.

The birth of the BNBC In 1875, Gustavus Baron Von Overbeck, the Austrian consul in Hong Kong, won the deeds to the American Trading Company. Austria wasn't interested in a colonial acquisition, so Overbeck turned instead to a London-based merchants' firm, run by Alfred Dent. With Dent's backing, they gained leases from the Sultan of Brunei for some 50,000km^2 of northern Borneo territory. A crucial deal with the Sultan of Sulu won them another chunk of land off Borneo's north coast, cementing the foundations of the British North Borneo Company (BNBC). Overbeck sold out to Dent and the company was officially baptised with a Royal Charter in 1881.

The BNBC had the freedom to administer as it saw fit, but heavy taxes on everything from rice to boats and birds' nests evoked widespread resentment and resistance from Sabahans. Despite concerted efforts, opposition to colonial authority was unsuccessful, and the BNBC administered the region of British North Borneo – today's Sabah – until 1888, when it became a British protectorate.

Meanwhile, in Sarawak... Brunei's need to seek outside support for protection was also the key to a decisive era in Sarawak's history. In 1839, Bengal-born James Brooke – a former British army officer and gentleman adventurer – sailed up the Sarawak River on his schooner *The Royalist*.

Here he met with Raja Muda Hassim, a consort of the sultan sent to suppress an uprising of exploited Malay and Dayak labourers. The coastal and river dwellers had been hit with excessive taxes, the men forced into working in antimony mines, and women and children into slavery. As the situation spiralled out of Brunei's control, the junior prince begged Brooke to help him regain order. Brooke complied and in 1841 was rewarded with land and the title of *rajah* – ruler – of Sarawak. Thus began a somewhat unlikely chapter in Sarawak's history, which was to leave a deep and lasting impression on the history of Borneo. For nearly a century, three generations of the Brooke family – hailed as the 'White Rajahs' – reigned over the state.

The Brooke empire spreads The Sultan of Brunei grew to be reliant on Brooke, and the British, to protect his sultanate. Brooke successfully fought off pirates who infested Sarawak's coastal and river areas, enabling him to secure increasing

RAJA, RAJAH AND RANEE

There are many contradictions about James Brooke's actual title and role in Sarawak. In Malay, *raja muda* generally denotes a junior or crown prince (*muda* literally means 'deputy' or 'young'). In the days of the first White Rajah, a *raja muda* may have been an heir to the Brunei sultan. *Rajah* means 'the Prince of all Princes', the ruler. *Ranee* is the title given to the wife of a *rajah*, a princess of kinds. The Brookes were not 'Kings' and 'Queens' of Sarawak as such, though they are often portrayed that way. They were undeniably luminous figureheads, with the British transmuting many frills of all that signifies from their own traditions and imposing them on a peculiar hybrid Malay British regal breed.

amounts of land under his control as he worked his way up the coast. Some pirate-quashing missions were excessively brutal, sparking disapproval from Britain and even a commission of inquiry, though Brooke was later acquitted. The Anglo-Brunei Treaty signed in 1848 guaranteed British control of trade along the northwest coast, and free trade and access to Brunei ports. It also prevented the sultan ceding territory to any other nation without British consent – giving the British a tight grip on authority in the region.

And spreads... From its origins as a small riverside settlement, by the 1890s the White Raj had expanded through much of Sarawak, devouring territories from Kuching south to the Indonesian border, and all the way north to Limbang. Even the BNBC ceded land to the Brookes. A lot of this expansion was driven by James Brooke's nephew, Charles, who succeeded him in 1868. As well as significantly extending the colonial Rajah's territory, no-nonsense Charles formed the Council Negari (State Council), boosted the economy and straightened out unruly tribes.

He in turn was succeeded by his son, Charles Vyner Brooke in 1917. Unlike previous family members, Vyner Brooke felt the Brooke dominion in Sarawak was something of an anachronism and chose to work in co-operation with a Supreme Council, diminishing the family's autocratic power. This decision was bitterly resented by the next in line, Anthony Brooke, who saw inheritance of his uncle's legacy as his birthright. Anthony stormed off to Singapore. The Brooke dynasty presided in Sarawak for over a century, until Japanese invasion on Christmas Day 1941.

For better and for worse, European presence had a major impact on tribal and Malay societies in Borneo. Most historians agree that the greatest positive fallout of colonial rule was the eradication of headhunting, bloody inter-tribal feuding, piracy and slavery. Over the first half of the 20th century, British rulers in Sabah

THE LAST GENERATION

In *The Daily Telegraph* in June 2007, author Philip Eade wrote of the third *rajah*, Charles Vyner Brooke: 'Vyner's career was encapsulated in one of the more impressive entries in *Who's Who*: "Has led several expeditions into the far interior [of Borneo] to punish headhunters; understands the management of natives; rules over a population of 500,000 souls and a country 40,000 square miles in extent."'

DEATH MARCH

Ten thousand leeches as big as pencils walking all over you... And big baboons [orangutans] screaming in the jungle of the night, wild pigs and crocodiles. And I'd think this is it, I'm going. You could feel yourself dying.

Comment by Australian POW Rex Blow at Memorial Park, Sandakan

Rex Blow was one of six Australian survivors of the atrocious Sandakan to Ranau 'death marches' of 1945, in which some 500 British and Australian POWs were forced to march 260km through hell, towards death, on the cusp of liberation.

and Sarawak promoted economic development, improved public welfare and introduced infrastructure, industry and territorial borders. Government and society were transformed with the introduction of Western transport, taxation, healthcare, education and legal systems.

WORLD WAR II IN BORNEO The Japanese invaded Borneo on Christmas Day 1941, and occupied parts of Sabah and Sarawak until liberation by Australian forces in 1945. Hundreds of British, Australian, Chinese and other Allied troops died a brutal death at the hands of the invaders. According to the Sandakan Memorial Park, 'The POWs under the Japanese suffered appalling living conditions, hard labour and death.'

Rebellion against the Japanese, led by the Chinese, showed some initial success, but the Japanese won with brute strength – guerrillas on the ground were no match for Japanese bombs. Headhunting was quickly resumed during the occupation. Some 1,500 Japanese heads were collected, *paranged* (a *parang* is a steel sword) with glee, and prized by the Dayaks (natives) for being 'nice round heads with good hair and gold teeth'. Though the Brooke regime had worked hard to extinguish this barbaric tradition, it was actually encouraged by Tom Harrisson (future curator of the Sarawak Museum), who famously parachuted into the jungle and recruited 1,000 Kelabit tribesmen to avenge the Japanese.

There are many recorded instances of bravery and humanity towards the Allied troops by Sabah's and Sarawak's indigenous populations. They built shelter for escapees, provided them with medical supplies and helped them across enemy lines.

The aftermath of war The towns and economies of northern Borneo were badly hit by the war, as was the tenability of colonial rule in North Borneo and the Brooke administration in Sarawak. The BNBC lacked the resources to rebuild after the devastation of the war, which levelled Sandakan and Jesselton (now Kota Kinabalu). It sold its assets to the British government and in 1946 the British Protectorate of North Borneo became a Crown Colony. Political parties sprang up, squabbled, then joined forces, resulting in the Sabah Alliance. Sabah actually became an independent country for 16 days before joining the Federation of Malaysia.

When the Japanese surrendered, Sarawak was placed under Australian military administration and Charles Vyner and Sylvia Brooke took exile in Australia. In return for a generous pension, he retired to England, but continued to have a say in Bornean politics. Upon his urging, the State Council voted in 1946 to cede Sarawak to Britain, and the old Raj became a British Crown Colony, remaining so until the formation of Malaysia in September 1963.

MERDEKA! Following Malaysia's independence from Britain in 1957, Tunku Abdul Rahman – prime minister of the freshly independent federation of Malayan states – pushed for a wider alliance to include Sarawak, North Borneo, Singapore and Brunei. Snubbed by Brunei, the new 1963 alliance was a ticket to freedom from foreign rule for Sabah and Sarawak. Singapore initially signed up to the Malaysian Federation in 1963, but quit two years later.

Throughout history, Brunei always opted to go its own way – in spirit if not entirely in practice. During the initial 'post-war years, it remained a British protectorate rather than cede to full outside authority as a British Crown Colony. In 1959, the country's first written constitution gave the sultan internal self-rule. Britain maintained responsibility for defence and foreign policy. On 1 January 1984, Brunei regained full independence, returning to sovereign rule as an Islamic Sultanate.

GOVERNMENT AND POLITICS

SABAH AND SARAWAK Sabah and Sarawak are among the 13 states which, together with three federal territories (the capital Kuala Lumpur, Labuan Island and Putrajaya), make up the Federation of Malaysia. Malaysia is a constitutional monarchy, with two chambers of democratic parliament – the *Dewan Negara* (State Council) and the *Dewan Rakyat* (People's Council). The East Malaysian states of Sabah and Sarawak elect their own state legislative assembly to decide on state affairs, but fall under national jurisdiction for all federal matters, and share the same king.

Monarchy The king, or *yang di-pertuan agong* (paramount ruler), of Malaysia acts as leader of the Islamic faith and official head of state. The latter role is largely

1

THE FALL OF AN EMPIRE

In *Sylvia, Queen of the Headhunters: An Outrageous Englishwoman and Her Lost Kingdom,* British author Philip Eade attributes the downfall of the Brooke dynasty in part to Ranee Sylvia, Vyner Brooke's wife. 'She did nothing to dispel the impression that Sarawak was populated by headhunters and lotus eaters, and saw to it that her position as Ranee remained enshrouded in myth. Her peculiar status and activities were endlessly celebrated by the press, but the Colonial Office had long regarded her as "a dangerous woman"'.

Drawing on Sylvia Brooke's 1940s autobiography, Eade's account is full of fascinating insights into the intrigues of the Brooke–Borneo relationship, from the couple's last night spent in a longhouse among rows of smoked Japanese heads, to their departure, when the Ranee wrote: 'hundreds of little boats lined the river banks, and behind the boats the crowds were so dense they looked like a forest of dazzling flowers with their golden sarongs and little coloured coats... I would have felt further from tears if some of them had denounced us and called down curses on our heads instead of invoking this gracious and merciful benediction, this unanimous affection.'

After the Brookes returned to London, writes Eade, and the Privy Council 'ordered the annexation of Sarawak to the British Crown' in July 1946, Sylvia somewhat tragi-nostalgically penned: 'shorn of our glory... [they were] faced with adjusting to a world in which we were no longer emperors but merely two ordinary, ageing people, two misfits.'

symbolic, and in reality, the king has little legislative control – similar to the British monarch. His powers include a say in appointing the prime minister and granting parliamentary dissolution, acting on the advice of the legislature. The *yang di-pertuan agong* is selected every five years by the nine hereditary sultans of Malaysia. The states without a hereditary sultan appoint their own state figureheads – Sabah and Sarawak both have a *yang di-pertua negeri* (head of state), appointed by the king, on the advice of the federal government. Those governors join the other states in the 'Conference of Rulers' to elect the *yang di-pertuan agong*.

Government   Loosely based on the British system, Malaysia has three levels of government: federal, state and local. In the federal sphere, executive power is vested in a prime minister who, along with (the two houses of) parliament, is elected every five years. The Senate-like *Dewan Negara* (State Council) is partly elected by the king, partly by the state parliaments, while the House of Representatives-style *Dewan Rakyat* (People's Council) is chosen by a national vote.

Legislative power is divided between federal and state governments. While the majority of political matters are decided at a federal level, Sabah and Sarawak (like the other 11 Malaysian states) have exclusive jurisdiction over matters of local government, land, forestry and agriculture. Sabah and Sarawak also enjoy particular autonomy from the federal government, akin to the special position of Northern Ireland in the United Kingdom's set-up. As well as its own head of state, each state also has its own constitution and elected assembly. The state assembly is led by a chief minister (*menteri besar*) and cabinet, and legislates on matters outside the federal parliament sphere.

Local government   At a local government level, the many tiers of administration are befitting of an English-inspired system of government. Sarawak's 13 state divisions are administered by district officers, and further divided and administered by Sarawak administrative officers. Beyond that, at the level of *kampungs* (villages), local affairs are taken in charge by the *ketua kampung* (village chief), also known as the *penghulu*.

Immigration   When Sabah and Sarawak surrendered the possibility of self-government to become part of Malaysia, one thing they both kept hold of was absolute power over their immigration laws. This means that even Malaysians from the peninsula have to produce passports and fill out immigration forms when entering Sabah and Sarawak. The bureaucratic hiccup is an intentional show of nominal autonomy in Malaysian Borneo. Trail-blazing prime minister of the 1990s, Dr Mahathir Mohamad, branded it totally out of step with the idea of a single nation. His contention over the immigration issue was just one of many thorns in the often prickly state–federal relationship between East and West Malaysia.

BORNEO'S GOVERNMENT AND POLITICS AT A GLANCE

Malaysia's prime minister (Datuk 'Seri) Najib Razak
Malaysia's king Abdul Halim Mu'adzam Shah
Sabah's chief minister (Datuk Seri) Musa Haji Aman
Sabah's governor (Tun Datuk Seri Panglima) Juhar Bin Mahiruddin
Sarawak's chief minister (Tan Sri) Adenan Satem
Sarawak's governor (Tan Sri) Abdul Taib Mahmud
Brunei's sultan and prime minister Hassanal Bolkiah

MERDEKA! MERDEKA! MERDEKA!

It features in the name of shopping plazas, football fields, hotels, hairdressers and banks throughout Sabah and Sarawak. *Merdeka*, meaning 'independence', was the cry echoing through what is now the Merdeka Stadium in Kuala Lumpur on 31 August 1957, when independence from British colonial rule was proclaimed with the raising of the Malaysian flag. The independence bid was led by Tunku Abdul Rahman Putra Al-Haj, who headed the delegation of Malaysian ministers that negotiated the deal through to completion.

While the relationship of Sabah and Sarawak with the federal government sometimes seems ambivalent, public enthusiasm for Malaysian independence and belonging to a Malaysian nation is clearly very strong according to the *merdeka*-count and frequency of crests, coats of arms, flags and other patriotic displays.

Political parties   Malaysia is governed by a coalition of 14 political parties, the Barisan Nasional (National Front), led by the predominant United Malays National Organisation (UMNO). The major Malayan group has held power since Malaysia's independence in 1957 – despite losing its cherished two-thirds majority for the first time ever in the 2008 general elections, it has produced all six Malaysian prime ministers. Other coalition parties all represent a different ethnic group, notably the MCA – the Malaysian Chinese Association – and the MIC – the Malaysian Indian Congress. The MCA is the largest of several Chinese parties; each represents a faction of the large and diverse Chinese community, which has been riddled for years by bitter squabbles.

BRUNEI   Constitutional sultanate or absolute monarchy... Where do you draw the line? Brunei describes itself as an independent 'constitutional' sovereignty, with the

FLAGS AHOY!

THE MALAYSIAN FLAG   The 14 red-and-white horizontal stripes on the flag represent the 13 Malaysian states, plus the federal entity. The flag is known as Jalur Gemilang – Stripes of Glory. The blue rectangle to the upper left is meant to unify these different states and people. Within it, there is a yellow star and moon crescent. The 14 points of the star again represent the federation, the crescent symbolises Islam, and the yellow is the dab of royalty and rulers.

THE FLAGS OF SABAH AND SARAWAK   Since 1988, Sabah has had its own flag with the state symbolised by a black silhouette of Mount Kinabalu, and its five divisions by the colours red, white, royal blue, zircon blue and icicle blue. Sarawak's flag, the Bendera negeri Sarawak, was also adopted by the state parliament in 1988. It uses the same colours as the Brooke Rajah flag – red, yellow and black – minus the Christian and monarchist symbols of a cross and a crown. The yellow star in the middle of the flag has nine points standing for the number of administrative divisions at the time (today there are 11). The flag was first raised at the National Day parade in Kuching in 1988. The unveiling of the flags marked a renewed sense of state pride, after 25 years in the Malaysian Federation.

1

sultan as self-elected, supreme executive authority. Constitutional would seem to imply some level of official checks and balances – by an independent legal authority – but Sultan Haji Hassanal Bolkiah reigns over both the constitution and the courts. He is not only sovereign ruler, but also prime minister, defence minister, finance minister and head of the Islamic faith. The '1959 constitution invested him with full executive authority, later amended to include full emergency powers. His brother, Prince Jefri Bolkiah, was finance minister until he caused a financial and personal scandal in the late 1990s, squandering millions on a line-up of playboy acquisitions – his super-yacht was called *Tits*, complete with two tenders, *Nipple I* and *Nipple II*! All that has long been forgotten and the siblings present as a happy family again.

It's hard to deny a nepotistic web at work in the machinations of the minuscule monarchy. The sultan's son – the crown prince and would-be 30th sultan Haji Al-Muhtadee Billah – is the senior minister at the prime minister's office, while another of the sultan's brothers holds the foreign affairs portfolio. Other ministerial posts are shared among a close group of allies, and personally handpicked by His Majesty. There are no elections. The sultan is advised on national policy by several councils, all of which he appoints – a Council of Cabinet Ministers, a Religious Council, a Privy Council, a Council of Succession and a Legislative Council.

Political parties Ever since a 1962 coup endeavoured but failed to woo political democracy to Brunei, the nation has been ruled by strict Sultan's decree. There is zero tolerance of political parties – albeit, they were countenanced for a few years in the mid 1980s, but outlawed again in 1988.

The Brunei Solidarity National Party (PPKB), first registered in 1985, has been largely inactive since; the Brunei People's Party (PRB) was banned in 1962; and the Brunei National Democratic Party lost its government registration in 1988. The sultan is allegedly making efforts to allow for democracy and public participation in political processes, recognising that less isolationism and better global relations are vital for economic and political survival. So far, there has been no major public call for dissident political parties to step forth and make themselves heard.

JUDICIARY AND LAW

SABAH AND SARAWAK In judicial affairs, both Sabah and Sarawak have a High Court that comes under the supreme jurisdiction of the Malaysian Federal Court and Court of Appeal. All these courts took a page out of the British judicial system. In Sarawak, James Brooke established a Court of Justice in 1841, while Charles Brooke launched a more developed court system in 1870, adding a Supreme Court, Magistrates' Court and Native Court.

Today, both states have special laws dealing with indigenous affairs, dealt with by the Native Courts. Various ordinances deal with Native Customary Rights (NCR) and claims of native communities to ancestral land. State governments have introduced many new laws to seriously curb (or 'tighten their claws' as one critic put it) Native Customary Rights. Well before the British set up courts, or the Malaysian Constitution was born, indigenous communities had their own complex body of customary law called *adat*, which governed their daily lives and socio-economic dealings. This was only recognised in a very limited manner by the NCR.

BRUNEI Brunei has a dual legal system, combining elements of English common law and court structure with Islamic Sharia law – known in Malay as *syariah*. In May 2014, a global outcry followed Brunei's 'adoption of Sharia law' into its penal code. (See pages 136–7.) Brunei has long had Sharia rules written into its system of governance (the Malay Islamic Monarchy or MIB). The 'Syariah Courts' coexist with the Supreme Courts and deal particularly with family law matters such as Muslim divorces, and questions of Malay–Muslim custom. They have done so since 1999. The latest move represents a strict toughening up of penalties for serious offences – an official enshrinement of Sharia laws in the penal code – and a vocal expression of those laws as a religious ethos unto the rest of the world.

The majority of legal cases until now have been handled by the Supreme Courts system, which includes a Magistrates' Court, High Court, Intermediate Court and Court of Appeals. The final court of appeal for civil cases can be made only through the Judicial Committee of the Privy Council, which sits in London. The new Sharia laws will usher in nearly 100 more offences, according to the *Brunei Times*, and transfer many existing crimes such as eating or drinking during Ramadan to the 'Syariah Penal Code Order'. As a result, the Sharia Courts will handle an estimated 250% more cases than they do currently.

ECONOMY

SABAH AND SARAWAK Historians claim Borneo was somewhat neglected during European presence. In Sarawak, the White Rajah did nothing to encourage large-scale private enterprise or capitalist investment, and the British government was not keen on outlays in their colonial possession. Sarawak and Sabah entered the Federation of Malaysia as disadvantaged, politically undeveloped and marginal territories. Since then they have become something of an 'offsite production centre' for Malaysian primary industry, producing timber, petroleum, palm oil, rubber and other raw materials for export.

Since the 1980s, Malaysia has transformed itself into a major industrial force and Southeast Asia's third-richest country. Sabah and Sarawak are developing at a much slower rate. Unlike Peninsular Malaysia, there is very little secondary industry though there is a slow shift to developing high value-added activities in the manufacturing, agriculture and service sectors, particularly in Sarawak. From biotechnology to wood-based industries, these endeavours hinge on the state's natural resources.

The differences of standards of living and earnings between Malaysian Borneo and the peninsula have lessened since the 1990s, when one-third of Sabah's residents lived in poverty. 'Despite its wealth of natural resources, economic growth and per-capita GDP in Sabah (RM19,000/US$5,800) is still well below the Malaysian average (RM34,500/US$10,500), nearly a quarter of that in Kuala Lumpur (RM74,000/US$22,500) and a shadow of that of neighbouring Brunei (B$51,000/US$38,500) (based on 2013 figures). Sarawak, on the other hand, is the richest Malaysian state, with the exception of the Federal Territory of Kuala Lumpur, with a per-capita GDP of about RM40,400/US$12,300. In Sabah, too, there are major signs of improvement. In 2012, it shed its 'poorest state in Malaysia' status, as average household income rose by nearly 30% compared with 2009 (RM4,000 per month up from RM3,100). Malaysian Prime Minister Najib Tun Razak attributed the swing to national poverty-tracking efforts and subsidies to rural areas. 'In 1963, probably more than 70% of the people could be said to be hardcore poor and destitute ... According to statistics, the average per capita income of Sabah now lies in the middle when compared to the richest and poorest states.' The PM also said: 'only about 7,000 people in Sabah now live in poverty – once that was 30,000.' This estimation differs starkly from government statistics which put Sabah poverty rates

1

in 2013 at 8.1% of the population – that's 240,000 – still well down from 19.7% (over half a million people) in 2009, but soaring over the national rate of 3.8%. The Malaysian government is aiming for a per-capita income of around RM50,000/US$15,000 by 2020. Sarawak seems well on course to reach that goal, but not Sabah, though the state government is pinning great hopes on the palm oil sector, oil and gas industry and biotechnology for economic miracles.

None of the wealth generated from agriculture and forestry is said to rub off on the chronically poor, particularly indigenous communities in rural areas.

Agriculture, forestry and fishing have underpinned Sabah' and Sarawak's economies for decades. However, since the early 2000s, tourism has been the fastest-growing sector of Sabah's economy, and the fourth foreign revenue earner after palm oil, crude petroleum and plywood. Tourism in Sarawak is also catching up.

In Sabah, agriculture provides about one-third of the state's GDP, a third of the jobs and a third of the state's export earnings. Palm oil, cocoa and rubber are the three biggest agricultural industries. Sabah State is Malaysia's biggest crude cocoa producer, providing 70% of the national crop, and rubber is the third most important commercial crop. Both rubber and cocoa beans are sent to Peninsular Malaysia for downstream processing into high value-added products.

For now and the foreseeable future, the timber industry is the backbone of Sarawak's economy. The annual value of Sarawak's wood products export was about RM7 billion in 2013, and the government announced it would be targeting RM54 billion of export value for the wood-based industry by 2020. So the state's forests continue to be exported *en masse* to traditional Asian markets, and of late, the Middle East.

The timber industry is also a major employer – in 2007 it represented 40% of total posts. Sarawak also grows 95% of Malaysia's black pepper, which sees the country ranked as the world's fifth-largest pepper producer with an annual yield of around 20,000 tonnes.

Palm oil In the past 15 years palm oil has overtaken forestry as the biggest export (and environmental issue) in Sabah (see box, page 224). Sabah produces over a quarter of Malaysia's palm oil and the controversial crop is the state's biggest earner, contributing over 40% or RM4 billion of its revenue.

In recent years, increasing numbers of farmers have converted their land to palm oil cash crops, with the promise of high yields and quick returns. The plantation expansion boom, and consequent deforestation, was further fanned by the promise of biofuel. Thwarted development of a thriving biofuel industry in Sabah, using palm oil as a potential renewable energy source, has nevertheless moved ahead, with some 30 biodiesel plants nationwide in operation or completed according to local reports in late 2014.

In Sarawak, where indigenous tribes were encouraged to convert their forested land into palm oil, plantations increased by 9.5% between 2009 and 2010, and the state now has 1.2 million hectares of the crop (up from 0.9 million hectares in 2012) compared with Sabah's 1.4 million hectares. The spreading menace is destroying tropical peat swamp forests (home to many species including proboscis monkeys and pygmy elephants), and may eliminate them by 2020, according to Wetlands International. 'Two-thirds of Sarawak's peat lands were until recently covered by thick, biodiversity-rich rainforest. Between 2005 and 2010 almost 353,000 of the one million hectares of peat swamp forests were deforested at high speed, largely for palm oil production. Within five years, almost 10% of all Sarawak's forests and 33% of the peat swamp forests were cleared. Of this, 65% was for conversion to palm oil production,' the organisation found in a 2011 study.

BRUNEI The people of Brunei enjoy a high quality of life. In 2014, the *Brunei Times* reported that the country's GDP per capita had hit an all-time high of US$74,397 – classing it among the world's richest economies along with Qatar, Macao, Kuwait and Luxembourg. According to the International Comparison Program (ICP), 11 global economies exceed the US$50,000 threshold for per-capita GDP.

A small nation with an intensively resource-based economy, Brunei's primary economic fuel and social lubricator are its extensive oil and gas fields. The oil-rich economy, says the government, affords its population high living standards, 'resulting in positive social indicators such as high literacy rates, longer life expectancy, and low unemployment and crime rates. The government provides for all medical services and subsidises rice and housing.' However, with life expectancies of the oil and natural gas resources as low as 25 and 40 years respectively, Brunei is under increasing pressure to find oil alternatives.

In its Asian Development Outlook report in 2011, the Asian Development Bank said Brunei urgently needed to diversify its economy away from a dependency on the oil and gas sectors, which account for 88% of the nation's exports and 50% of GDP (down from 75% in the 1970s). Proof of that came in 2014, with Brunei's Department of Economic Planning and Development reporting that the sultanate's GDP in the fourth quarter declined by 5.3% year-on-year due to a 16.7% decline in the oil and gas sector. The government's 'economic diversification program' is targeting international finance, tourism, transport, logistics and ICT as potential growth areas. Clearly it has a long way to go in assuring Brunei's future generations as high a standard of living as those of the oil-cushioned past. In a speech in 2010, leading Brunei businessman (founder chairman of Asia Inc Forum), Timothy Ong, said: 'In terms of HDI, which measures quality of life taking into account income per capita, mortality and education, Brunei is 30th in the world. The fact that we are behind three countries in Asia that have no natural resources... reminds us that we must make the transition from being just a resource-rich economy towards (also) being a knowledge-based economy.'

PEOPLE

ORIGINS AND PREHISTORY Midway between China, the Indonesian Archipelago and the Pacific region, Borneo is an ancient sea thoroughfare. Southerly migrations through the island began tens of thousands of years ago, leaving a deep footprint on its DNA. The island today is a human rainbow of racial influences and multi-hued traditions.

While the contemporary ethnic mosaics of Sabah and Sarawak are quite different in their intricacies, Borneo's Malay indigenes (known as *bumiputeras*) most likely originate from a common ancestral stock, together with the those of Sumatra, Java, Bali, Sulawesi Island, the Philippines and Malay Peninsula. Their ancestors possibly arrived in Borneo around the 15th century. Earlier tribes were wiped out by clan warfare or simply moved on to other shores.

Early hunter-gatherers Evidence dates human presence in Borneo as far back as 45,000 years. One of the most important archaeological finds of the 20th century occurred in 1958 on Sarawak's west coast, with the unearthing of a 40,000-year-old human skull, stone tools, animal bones and human burials at the mouth of the Niah Caves. The discovery confirmed the presence of prehistoric hunter-gatherers in Borneo; similar remains were found in caves in southeastern Sabah. Niah's caves have been nominated as the most important archaeological site in Asia. They have since been protected as a national park (see pages 309–11).

Austronesian migrations Despite evidence of such early *Homo sapiens* in Borneo, the linguistic ancestors of today's native populations are believed to have settled much more recently. Austronesians migrating through Taiwan and the Philippines from around 2500BC possibly settled in Borneo, the Philippines and Indonesia around 2000BC according to Professor Peter Bellwood from the Australian National University School of Archaeology and Anthropology; people with closely related Austronesian languages also settled the Malay Peninsula, other parts of the Malay Archipelago and the Pacific Islands, as far as Hawaii, New Zealand and Easter Island.

The story of the Austronesian-speakers tells of one of the most remarkable migrations in human history, from which people in the area of southern China 4,000–5,000 years ago set out and settled vast parts of Southeast Asia. Today, an estimated 300 million people speak Austronesian languages, populating a large chunk of the planet from Madagascar through to New Zealand and Hawaii. These people 'share over 1,000 related languages that derive from a common linguistic homeland in Taiwan', Professor Bellwood says in his 1997 book *Prehistory of the Indo-Malaysian Archipelago*. 'Before Christopher Columbus and the explosive expansions of Hispanic languages and English, the Austronesian language family was by far the most widespread in the world.'

The Austronesian-speaking migrants brought to Borneo the knowledge of 'weaving, bark-cloth making, pottery, pigs, dogs, rice, and finely polished stone tools', says Professor Bellwood. They originally settled lowland coastal areas, incorporating shifting agriculture and rice production into their culture. Only with the advent of metal use, iron in particular, were tribes able to penetrate the forests further inland.

Today There are now over two-dozen major ethnic groups living in Malaysian Borneo, and a handful of such groups in Brunei. Between them, they speak over 80 different dialects. Like Malaysia as a whole, Sabah and Sarawak have large contingents of Malay, Chinese and Indian populations, but stand out for their much wider variety of other ethnic groups. Brunei on the other hand has a big Malay majority.

ETHNIC GROUPS
Borneo's ethnic make-up is colourful and multi-layered, infused by myriad influences over the centuries. For every different type of landscape – highland, lowland, coast and interior – there are different indigenous tribes and dozens of sub-tribes. Some 70 different ethnic communities reside between Sabah and Sarawak alone. Brunei is predominantly Malay but also has Chinese, Indian and indigenous populations such as the Iban and Murut. The Malay people, too, are considered indigenous – *bumiputera* – 'sons of the soil'. Though the term ostensibly has been extended to include Borneo's other ethnic tribes, it is still largely identified with the Malays. As Willard Scott Thompson reports in *Ethnic Conflicts in Southeast Asia*, 'the indigenous/non-indigenous cleavage is compounded by a Malay/non-Malay bumiputera one mainly in Borneo states'. To avoid confusion, I've still chosen to separate the Malay people from Borneo's indigenous tribes.

Indigenous peoples
Sarawak Sarawak's population comprises 27 different ethnic communities, speaking 45 different languages and dialects. Around 50% of the population are indigenous races, 28% are Chinese and 21% Malay (*Melayu*).

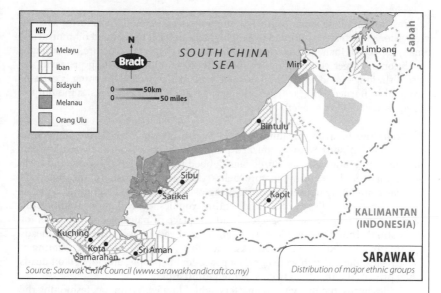

KEY

Melayu
Iban
Bidayuh
Melanau
Orang Ulu

N

SOUTH CHINA
SEA

0 ——50km
0 ——50 miles

•Limbang

Sabah

Miri•

Bintulu•

Sibu•
•Sarikei

Kapit•

Kuching•
Kota•
Samarahan• •Sri Aman

KALIMANTAN
(INDONESIA)

Source: Sarawak Craft Council (www.sarawakhandicraft.co.my)

SARAWAK
Distribution of major ethnic groups

Iban The major ethnic group of Sarawak migrated *en masse* from deep within the Kalimantan hinterland from the 16th century through to the 19th. A nomadic yet territorial group, the Iban successively annexed large parts of Sarawak, from the southern border region right up through the centre of the state, eventually reaching the coast. Around 30% of the Sarawak population today is Iban – a much smaller number also migrated to Brunei. The Iban were erroneously referred to by 19th-century Europeans as 'sea Dayak' (sea natives), when in fact they were inland, river-dwelling people. The term most likely arises from their superior boating skills, acquired from other tribes during years of commandeering the coast, and dabbling in piracy.

The name 'Iban' is synonymous with headhunting and hunter-gathering; various tattoos portrayed the success of an Iban man at these traditional activities. As shifting cultivators, Ibans originally built their homes near navigable rivers – and they were designed to last as long as their exploitation of rice farming in the area, before they moved on to new pastures. The first Iban settlements in Sarawak were at Lubok Antu, south of Kuching towards the Indonesian border. Many Iban still live in and around this area, sometimes several hours' boat journey from the

THE 'DAYAKS' OF SARAWAK

In Sarawak, the collective name 'Dayak' is given to all indigenous tribes (occasionally it is erroneously extended to include all indigenous people of Borneo). While its origin is debatable, the term has commonly been used to denote inland-dwelling tribes as opposed to the Malay coastal populations. The word 'Dayak' is not considered derogatory and is widely used in reference to indigenous issues and events. Settled Dayak farmers and forest nomads use it themselves to affirm their indigenousness politically and culturally, and to differentiate themselves from the rest of the population.

The closest equivalent in Sabah is the Kadazandusun, an umbrella term for the largest native population, which includes many ethnic subgroups and comprises about a fifth of the population.

nearest town. While some of today's longhouses sport modern luxuries such as televisions and fridges, afforded by employment in local timber and oil industries, many aspects of Iban life, from foraging for food to domestic structure, are strongly traditional. Larger communities count up to 20 families subsisting primarily on rice, fish, jungle food and a good dose of *tuak*, or rice wine. One thing is certain, from all of Borneo's diverse tribes, the upriver dwelling 'sea Dayaks' stand out for being as water-savvy as ever.

Bidayuh The Bidayuh, meaning 'people of the interior', live in the hinterland regions of southwest Sarawak, pushed progressively back from the coast by Iban invasions and pirate attacks. Europeans dubbed them the 'land Dayaks', and their gentle-mannered and timid nature belies their warrior past. In the Bidayuh's circular community houses or *baruk*, rising over a metre off the ground, skulls of their enemies were displayed as headhunting trophies. (Brave) guests traditionally slept out in the *baruk*, with severed heads in place of paintings on the walls for decoration! Thus their modern translation as 'head houses'. The trophy heads apparently followed retaliation attacks. Though it's hard to believe when staring at those heads, the Bidayuh were largely a peace-loving people, and lopped off heads when provoked rather than from sheer bloodthirstiness.

Besides heads, the Bidayuh are masters of building with bamboo, fashioning the dried stalks into a range of implements, from farming tools and cooking utensils to musical instruments. They also use bamboo for their ingenious watering system. This gravity-based system provides water for the longhouses, and waters the fields of rice and vegetables in times of little rain. Existing in just a small demographic sliver in the Samarahan District, the Bidayuh currently number 135,000 – about 8% of the population.

Orang Ulu The remaining population consists of various tribes, including the coastal **Melanau**, the **Kelabit** people in the highlands of northeast Sarawak near the Indonesian border, and several ethnic minorities in the interior. Collectively the upriver races are known as the **Orang Ulu**, literally 'people of the headwaters'. They number about 100,000 and account for 6% of Sarawak's population. The name 'Orang Ulu' was originally attributed to the larger **Kayan** and **Kenyah** tribes who live in the Upper Rejang and Upper Baram river areas, as well as smaller contiguous groups including the Kajang, Kejaman, Punan, Penan and Ukit. The term now embraces other mid- and lower-river people such as the Berawan and Murut, the Lun Bawang, Lun Dayeh and the Kelabits.

Kayan Another headhunting group who migrated from Kalimantan into Sarawak, the Kayan gradually moved, perhaps forcibly by other tribes, way up north. Some among the population of 15,000 still live in longhouses along the 400km Sungai Baram and its tributaries, and the lower Sungai Tubau in the Kapit Division. Kayan women have tattoos on their hands and legs – the men wear leopards' teeth in their ears. Though it is becoming increasingly rare to see, they once all had earlobes hanging down towards their shoulders extended with the help of brass and other metal weights. Like other tribes, their greatest skills grew from their river-dwelling lifestyle. The Kayan traditionally carved their boats from a single block of *belian* (ironwood) – the strongest tropical hardwood.

Kenyah The Kenyah people are closely related to their Kayan neighbours, and brutally rivalled the Ibans together as age-old allies. For centuries, both have also

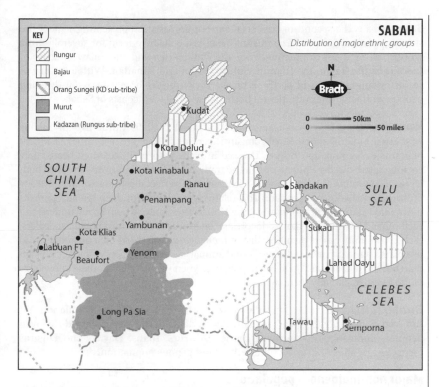

SABAH
Distribution of major ethnic groups

Rungur

Bajau

Orang Sungei (KD sub-tribe)

Murut

Kadazan (Rungus sub-tribe)

Kudat

Kota Delud

SOUTH
CHINA
SEA

Kota Kinabalu
Ranau
Penampang

Sandakan

SULU
SEA

Yambunan

Kota Klias

Labuan FT

Beaufort

Yenom

Sukau

Lahad Oayu

CELEBES
SEA

Long Pa Sia

Tawau

Semporna

practised shifting cultivation of dry rice in the upper parts of the Baram River. It's believed they could be the first of the aboriginal groups in Sarawak, preceding the Iban, after migrating from the Sungai Kayan (Kayan River) area of East Kalimantan where many of their cousins still live.

Sabah In Sabah about 39 different indigenous groups account for 50% of the population.

Kadazandusun This is the largest group, encompassing several distinct sub-tribes including the **Rungus** and the **Dusuns** of Tuaran, Ranau and Tambunan, all of whom speak very closely related dialects. With varying degrees of Chinese physical similarities, they most likely migrated from southern China thousands of years ago. Formerly known as Duson, meaning 'village' or 'orchard people', this was construed as an uncomplimentary name given by Malay coastal dwellers, and was changed to Kadazan in the 1970s. Once farming people – and fierce headhunters – the Kadazandusun communities are concentrated mainly along the west coast and in the hinterland areas of Penampang, Ranau, Tambunan and Keningau through to the Sarawak border. As Sabah's population rises, so the Kadazandusun's shrinks – in the 1970s they were a large majority at over 30% of the population. That has since fallen to around 19% of Sabah's three million-plus people.

Politically, the group refers to itself as Kadazandusun – sometimes written as Kadazan-Dusun – though some official population counts still separate them as the Kadazan and the Dusun. Many of the individual races would never identify with anything but their proper tribal name: **Dusun**, **Rungus**, **Lotud**, **Minokok**, **Tambanuo**, **Tindal** and **Orang Sungai** ('river people'), and it's far more courteous to do the same.

Bajau This is the second-biggest ethnic group in Sabah, representing 13% of the state population. Like Kadazandusun, Bajau is a collective term for several ethnic groups, all of them originating from the Philippines and the Sulawesi coast of Indonesia: the **Bajau**, the **Illanun**, **Suluk**, **Obian** and **Binadan**. With a history of seafaring migrations, and partly of piracy, they are still largely a coastal-dwelling people, with large communities on both the east and west coasts of Sabah.

Murut The third-largest indigenous group, about 50,000 Murut live in Sabah's west-coast hinterland and Kinabatangan River area. There are also tribes of Murut migrants in Sarawak and Brunei. Dressed in black with multi-coloured beads, they are longhouse-dwellers and many still live traditionally – close to rivers, and with high levels of community co-operation. The Murut are a perfect illustration of the intricacy of Borneo's kaleidoscopic culture. This relatively small slice of the population breaks down into 14 sub-ethnic groups speaking 12 dialects, some of whom do not understand each other. Living in and alongside forests, the Murut are seasoned botanical healers: each community has its own herbalist or *mongugusap*, wiser old men or women who use plants – roots, barks and leaves – and animals to cure a variety of ailments. From diarrhoea to diabetes and high blood pressure, when you have an intimate knowledge of the forest, apparently there's a natural cure for everything.

Brunei Indigenous tribes officially make up only 12% of Brunei's population. Yet the 'Malay' majority (73%) are actually descendants of the Melanaus and Kedayan people – indigenous to northern Borneo. **Muruts**, **Ibans**, **Dayaks** and **Dusuns** form the tiny slice of Brunei's other-ethnic indigenous population.

Major non-indigenous populations

Melayu (Malay) Originating from Yunnan, China, the Malay people first reached the Malaysian Peninsula around 2000BC. Owing to myriad influences from neighbouring areas like Java, Sumatra, the Indian subcontinent, China, the Middle East and the West, the cultures of the Malaysian Peninsula were constantly shaped and reshaped.

TATTOOING TRADITIONS

The Kayans, Ibans, Kenyah and Kelabits all have strong tattoo traditions. The Kayans are portrayed as the creative force behind most tattoo designs. Kayan men carved highly stylised designs of animals – hornbills, dogs, scorpions – on to wooden blocks that could be easily transferred on to skin and shared between villages. Tattoos were collected like passport stamps, as proof and souvenirs of journeys. It was the Kayan women, however, who traditionally applied the tattoos. These were usually made from soot or charcoal, and occasionally impregnated with special materials believed to make the tattoo more powerful, such as a piece of meteorite or animal bone. Women were adorned with their first tattoo as they passed into adulthood, although the most intricate designs were reserved for those of higher class and greater wealth. A design unique to the Kayan is the talisman (*lukut*) on the wrists, which prevents the soul from escaping the body. In Iban society, men applied tattoos, often after a successful headhunting expedition. Indeed, tattoos in all Dayak societies usually have more than a mere decorative purpose – they are symbols of spirits, status, success and wealth.

Owing to the presence of other large ethnic groups, Malays account for about 24% of Sarawak's population and just 10.8% in Sabah, compared with 62% nationally. The Malay population in Brunei is highest, at 73%. Malays started arriving in Borneo in the 15th century, from trading kingdoms in Sumatra (Indonesia). Nearly all of them settled on the coast and subsisted as fishermen. Today Malay *kampung* (villages) still cling largely to the seaboard. Some *kampung* in the Kuching area are even named after Javanese towns from where the locals sprang. The Malays are known for their gentle manner and rich arts heritage.

'The main defining characteristic of "Malayness" is the Islamic religion,' writes Victor T King in *The Peoples of Borneo*. 'One of the most important distinctions in Borneo is between those who are Muslims and those who are not.'

Not all Muslims, however, are Malay. Major ethnic groups such as the Bajau in Sabah and Melanau in Sarawak converted to Islam but still maintain their own cultural identity. Their conversion from Hinduism and Theravada Buddhism to Islam began in the 1400s, largely influenced by the decision of the royal court of Malacca.

The Federal Constitution of Malaysia defines a Malay as someone who practises Islam and Malay customs, speaks the Malay language and is the child of at least one

THE LAST OF THE HUNTER-GATHERERS

The Penan tribe have been making international headlines since the 1980s, when news of the devastation of Borneo's forests and indigenous traditions first started to break through island barriers. Many Penan were among those arrested for protesting against logging; despite being inherently shy people, having had little contact with the world beyond the forest until recent years, their determination to do something about the all-out war on their forest homes made them go public.

The Penan are among the only hunter-gatherers remaining in Southeast Asia, and the last tribe in Borneo still living this traditional lifestyle. They live in groups of 20–30 in the Upper Rejang River area and along the Sungai Baram in central Sarawak, and around Sungai Limbang in northern Sarawak. The Penan use blowpipes to kill deer and wild boar, moving to new areas when their supply of wild sago flour starch (which they make from sago palms) runs out; they supplement their diet with wild fruits, jungle roots and plants. Their shyness of the world outside the forest, and of sunlight, shows in the paler shades of their skin in comparison with other tribes. There is common confusion between them and the less numerous, dialectally distinct Punan.

Prince Charles caused outrage in Malaysia when he accused the country of collective genocide over the Penan. The Malaysian government maintained that it simply wanted the Penan to integrate with society for their own sake, attempting (unsuccessfully) to lure the hunter-gatherers to settle in luxurious longhouses; meanwhile, the logging continued.

The dispute continues, with Penan leaders maintaining that without the forests they 'become poor and lose our homes, with no hope of good jobs. Our children are robbed of their future and their heritage. We have the right to live in the lands of our ancestors, just as you do.'

According to Malaysian and international law, the Penan have clear land rights and must be consulted before any logging can proceed, but these rights are often openly violated.

parent who was born within the Federation of Malaysia before independence on 31 August 1957.

The question of 'Malayness' is quite a paradox, as many 'Malay' people in Borneo actually originate from 'indigenous tribes. Large numbers of the island's Malay population descend from Dayak tribes who converted to Islam from the 16th century onwards. Such a switch is called *maskuk Melayu* – to convert to Malay.

Chinese In Sabah, Sarawak and Brunei, the diverse Chinese communities represent the second-largest race of people and the largest non-indigenous group – 30% in Sabah and Sarawak and 15% in Brunei. Although evidence of Chinese settlements dating to the 10th and 11th centuries has been found, most of the ancestors of today's Chinese population came as settlers in the 18th century, during the early years of the British North Borneo Chartered Company in Sabah and the White Rajah's reign in Sarawak (see pages 6–7). Most of them were Hakka Christian farmers, and this is still the biggest Chinese race in Sabah. There are also populations of Cantonese, Mandarin, Teochew, Hokkien, Hainanese and Henghua, each with their own dialects.

From Sabah's east coast to Sarawak's west coast, the Chinese paint towns red with their festivities and urban and business acumen. In Sabah, many Chinese have intermarried with other races, in particular with the large Kadazandusun population; there are prevalent Sino-Kadazan and Sino-Dusun sub-cultures in Sabah, with people who practise both Kadazandusun and Chinese customs. Today, with typical industriousness, the Chinese prevail in the services and retail sectors and have turned small shops into multi-million-dollar businesses. Thousands of others operate coffee shops and restaurants.

LANGUAGE

Throughout Malaysian Borneo and Brunei, around 100 different regional and tribal dialects are spoken.

The official national language of Malaysia is Malay – *Bahasa Melayu*. A slightly different version is *Bahasa Malaysia*. Although mutually understandable, they are not entirely the same. There are also state variations of Malay – *Bahasa Sarawak* is Sarawakian Malay, spoken like a dialect with only a sprinkling of different words, but enough to surprise visitors from the peninsula. *Bahasa Malaysia* and *Bahasa Melayu* are similar to *Bahasa Indonesia* and can pretty much be understood from Sumatra to the Philippines.

While Malay may be the national language, it is far from being the true *lingua franca* in Malaysian Borneo. In Sabah, only a quarter of the population are Malay and more than half of the country's indigenous languages reside here. An estimated 39 ethnic communities speak some 55 different languages in 80 dialects: the four major linguistic families are Dusunic, Murutic, Paitanic and Sama-Bajau.

Note: '*Bahasa*' is Malay for 'language', so English is *Bahasa Inggeris*, French *Bahasa Perancis*, etc.

TRIBAL LANGUAGES Many tribal languages are thought to descend from the Austronesian and Malayo-Polynesian language family trees, due to the Austronesian settlement of the island in the third millennium BC. Even a minority group such as the Bidayuh in Sarawak has a dozen dialects, not universally understood across the race. Sabah's largest linguistic group, the Dusunic, is splintered into 14 dialects including Dusun, Rungus and Bisaya. Owing to imperial influence, Kadazans in

BIZARRE LANGUAGE

Born from the British military's time in Borneo when there was a need to find mutual comprehension with the Malay people and the indigenous tribes, a common linguistic ground was struck in what became known as 'Bazaar English'. This hybrid expression was so called because of its use in trading in small street bazaars and at markets (it was also useful on buses and riverboats). The hybrid tongue borrows words from many languages. With globalisation and the rise of the English language, it has grown into an increasing muddle of Malay, English, Chinese and Dusun words. People just mix it up as they like – it really should be called *Bizarre* English!

Sabah speak English more fluently than any other ethnic group. The same can be said of the Iban in Sarawak. With the decline of the Kadazan language and other tribal vernaculars, the Sabah state government have introduced policies to try to counter their extinction, such as encouraging public schools to teach indigenous dialects. The **Kadazandusun Cultural Association** (*www.kdca.org*) and **Kadazandusun Language Foundation** (*www.klf.com.my*) are both very involved in language issues, and their offices and websites are useful reference points for many other cultural links.

CONSERVING LANGUAGE AND CULTURE A study conducted in the mid 1980s showed that mass media, urbanisation, the education system, intermarriage and language prestige were all having their effect on the decline of indigenous languages in Sabah. Since then things have deteriorated, but the cultural vigilance has gained ground, as echoed in the following verse. It is written in Dusun dialect and kindly translated into English by Dr Benedict Topin from the Kadazandusun Cultural Association (KDCA).

Atagak o boros, atagak o koubasanan	Lose our language and we will lose our culture
Atagak o koubasanan, atagak o kointutunan	Lose our culture and we will lose our identity
Atagak o boros, atagak o pirotian	Lose our language and we will lose our understanding
Atagak o pirotian, atagak o puinungan, pisohudungan om pibabasan	Lose our understanding and we will lose our harmony, co-operation and peace
Atagak o pibabasan, atagak o piobpinaian	Lose peace and we will lose our brotherhood and sisterhood
Atagak o piobpinaian kopitongkiad o rikoton do rusodon.	Lose our brotherhood and sisterhood and we will be dispersed in our journey towards common destiny.

RELIGION AND SPIRITUALITY

Over the centuries, Borneo has been visited by many different traditional faiths and spiritual beliefs, just as it has by ethnic tribes, traders, explorers, migrations and missionaries. All these influences have brewed a rich religious life, which plays an integral part in culture and society. Under the official seal of Islam, there are other mainstream religions and many fascinating, though fading, rituals of tribal devotion to extensive spirit worlds.

RELIGIOUS HISTORY

Islam Across northern Borneo, Islam came to the trading states controlled by Brunei's rulers from the late 13th century. Within a couple of centuries, people were converting *en masse* to the religion of powerful Muslim merchants. Prior to that Buddhism and Hinduism were widely practised, as well as indigenous spiritual rituals.

In the 18th and 19th centuries, Islamic faith spread like wildfire into the hinterland areas of present-day Sabah and Sarawak, and many indigenous people converted. Religion reinforced the divisions between state-based and tribal society.

Christianity With the arrival of Europeans, Islam had a major competitor on its hands. The pressure of conversion to Christianity applied by colonists had profound effects on indigenous cultures. Thousands of Iban and Orang Ulu people including the Kelabits and Kayan ceded to various denominations of Christianity – and many of these former headhunters now celebrate Christmas Day.

Even the remotest ethnic communities were taken under the wings of Christianity. The same thing happened with Sabah's Kadazandusun peoples. In the process, some indigenous religions became extinct. Religious conversion was not just God-driven; it was used to improve law and order, to erode the power base of Muslim sultanates, reduce slavery and headhunting, and socialise people who were used to living in warring factions. As odd as it may seem today, headhunting was central to the spiritual beliefs of all those tribes who engaged in it.

RELIGION TODAY Islam is the official religion of Malaysia, enshrined in the Constitution. Buddhism and Christianity are also socially prevalent along with Hinduism, Taoism and tribal religions. Important dates on the Muslim, Buddhist and Christian calendars are nationally observed with public holidays, as are major spiritual celebrations of indigenous peoples. In Malaysian Borneo, Islam is less widespread due to the greater imprint of Christianity. Sabah and Sarawak are the only two Malaysian states to celebrate Easter – about a quarter of their populations are Christian, compared with just 2% of the population in western Malaysia; one-third are of Islamic faith and over 17% are Buddhists and Taoists. Mosques, Buddhist temples, Catholic and Anglican churches are seen in cities and in the countryside. Large numbers of indigenous peoples including the Kadazandusun in Sabah and Iban in Sarawak have converted to Christianity, and the Bajau in Sabah and Melanau in Sarawak to Islam. Many maintain their animistic and other traditional belief systems as well, in private, and in public celebrations. Death rituals, harvest festivals, effigies for healing and tattoos are all manifestations of such beliefs.

Islam in Borneo In Muslim-dominated cities and towns, the chants of Islamic prayer resonate through streets at dawn, and seep eloquently into skies at dusk. In Brunei, Islam is far more predominant – two-thirds of the population are practising Muslims. If you see the sign *KUDAT* in hotels, on the ceiling or table or in a bedside drawer, the arrow alongside it is not pointing out an emergency exit, but the direction of Mecca. One of the five pillars of Islam is that Muslims must make a pilgrimage – a *hajj* – to Mecca, the birthplace of the faith, once in their lifetime. By doing so, men are bestowed with the title *Hajji* and women *Hajja*. Such trips to Saudi Arabia are only possible for a relatively privileged few in poorer Southeast Asian Muslim countries. In Brunei there are many *hajji* and *hajja*. Naturally the sultan is the king of the country's *Hajji* – it's just one of the words in his seemingly endless title.

Religious harmony As freedom of religion heats up as a pointed social and political issue in Muslim-dominated western Malaysia, the situation in East Malaysia (ie: Malaysian Borneo) seems more progressive thanks to its inherent greater religious diversity. In general, the religious atmosphere is one of tolerance and inter-religious respect. The different cultures and religions are relatively harmonious and it is common for people to celebrate with those of different faiths privately and publicly. Often different religious beliefs coexist among different generations of one family. Various spiritual occasions are co-celebrated by different indigenous groups – prime examples are the Kadazandusun Tadau Ka'amatan (harvest festival) in Sabah, the Gawai Dayak (Iban harvest festival in Sarawak), not forgetting the Chinese New Year and end of Ramadan festivities. It's hard not to be touched by such a peaceful coexistence; Sabah is one of the few places left on earth where many faiths live together in such harmony.

TRIBAL BELIEFS

Iban Iban spirituality is professedly a centuries-old fusion of animism, Hinduism and Buddhism. Though hundreds of Iban converted to Christianity, they still parade their potent traditional beliefs for all to see through their festivals – the Gawai Dayak harvest festival, Gawai Kenyalang hornbill festival and Gawai Antu festival of the dead. The Iban dances – highly intuitive narratives – are punctuated by an array of mythical figures depicting relationships between the natural, spirit and human worlds. The *kenyalang*, or hornbill, is sacred to the Iban because the hornbill's nest, *tansang kenyalang*, is the abode of their supreme god of war Aki Lang Sengalang Burong – also known as 'the earth tremor which trembles and causes the full moon to fall'. In his earthly form, the Iban god takes the form of the eagle-like bird of prey, the Brahminy kite (*Haliastur indus*).

Orang Ulu The Kayan, the Penan and the Kenyah may wear cloaks of Christianity of varying denominations, but their animist beliefs live on in the supreme Bungan cult – an adaptation of their spirit-dominated worlds – and Bungan celebrations.

Melanau Old rituals remain vividly in the minds and practices of many indigenous folk. The Melanau in Sarawak are a good example – two-thirds of them at least have converted to Islam, yet still take part in feisty displays of animistic worship, and use carved wooden figurines to heal people. Journalist Diana Rose,

1

ANIMISM

Many indigenous spiritual beliefs fall within the world of animism, where souls and spirits are attributed to animals, plants and various objects. Some academics have rejected the term 'animism', as with paganism, accusing it of depreciating traditional belief systems as simplistic and illiterate, especially when applied to Africa. There is clearly no such adversity to the term in Borneo. People use both animism and paganism to describe complex belief systems and ceremonies hinging on spirits and souls, magic and myth, spells and charms, as well as symbolic rites linked with birth, harvest and death. Indeed, animism has apparently been more elaborated and intellectualised among the Ibans and related tribes of Borneo than anywhere else in the world. The beliefs are so varied, they actually defy a one-word definition. (See *Tribal beliefs*, above, for some brief descriptions.)

A common practice among the indigenous tribes of Borneo until the first decades of the 20th century, bands of young men ventured out to surrounding villages to collect the heads of enemies or other tribes. The freshly gathered heads were then skinned and dried, smoked over a fire or boiled and hung up on show in the longhouse. The dried skulls were believed to possess powerful spiritual properties, providing vital transfusions of energy for entire villages. The heads warded off evil spirits, disease and misfortune, while offering protection, fruitful crops and favourable weather. An unhappy head was capable of bringing terrible woes such as plagues, fires and droughts, so they were well looked after with offerings of food and blessings. Heads were the focus of much ritual, much of it ironically symbolising the procreative power of nature, and not the violent end of a life. The Kayan and Kenyah tribes in central-north Borneo regularly held large festivals to honour the heads.

Heads were held to lose their potency over time, so fresh heads were always required to replenish a village's spiritual energies. Although the practice has been all but eradicated, there are still the occasional reports of headhunting. Nowadays however, young male Dayaks are more expected to do a *bajalai*, or journey, to prove their worth rather than accomplish a successful headhunting mission. Many tribes still embrace and celebrate their headhunting histories, however, using replica heads made out of coconut shells.

who was born in the Melanau heartland of Mukah on Sarawak's west coast, says this: 'The original religion of the Melanau people was Liko, meaning "people of the river". In the Liko religion, life and the environment are one. Followers worship the spiritual world including the superior *tou* spirits and the lesser *belum* spirits that cause sickness. The pagan Melanau use effigies of sickness spirits when practising healing. Many Melanau today are Christian and Muslim, though they still celebrate traditional festivals, most notably Kaul.' (See page 302, for more information.)

Kadazandusun Among Sabah's major ethnic groups, the spirit world still reigns supreme. The best illustrations of this are the rituals of **Tadau Ka'amatan**, the rice harvest festival. The Kadazandusun believe that rice has a spirit, called Bambarayon or Bambaazon, which rejuvenates and ensures the bounty of next year's harvest. The thanksgiving festival is held to welcome the rice spirit back, to restore spirits that were lost in careless harvesting, to nourish the rice spirit with offerings of food, and for merrymaking and friendship. A legend about the need to fight off famine through worship, underpins the celebration.

Typical rituals carried out include the *bobohizan* (priestess) selecting seven stalks of the best rice from the paddy before the festival begins. These are then presented to the owner of the rice field after the harvest, and symbolise the homecoming of the rice spirit. The most important part of the festival is the Magavau ceremony, which takes place in the paddy under the first full moon after the harvest. Magavau involves a hunt for lost or strayed rice spirits who have been disturbed by mishandling of the crop or by pests. A sword-wielding male *bobohizan* leads the ceremony followed by a chain of female *bobohizans* who chant ritual verses to summon home the missing spirits. Triumphant, ear-piercing cries peel out over the paddy when a spirit is recovered. See *Public holidays and festivals*, page 115, for more on Tadau Ka'amatan.

EDUCATION The education system in Brunei is modelled on the British system, with Brunei-Cambridge GCE A-levels being used to prepare students for entrance to university and other higher education institutions in Brunei Darussalam and overseas. Government-provided overseas scholarships are a major concern, and Britain is the main destination for studies ranging from A-level to undergraduate (diploma, HND, degree), Master's and PhD studies.

The *Brunei Times* newspaper says within a century the Sultanate went from having a population among whom barely anyone could read or write romanised characters, to having one of the highest literary rates in the world – over 94% of its citizens in 2012 – the same percentage for school participation.

Educational improvements are a big focus of Brunei's current vision, 'Wawasan Brunei 2035' and its national development plan. Recognising the need to strengthen the education system, the Education Ministry has set about enhancing education structure, curriculum and assessment and providing more opportunities in the field of technical education. The need to provide skilled workers in diverse fields is sharpening as the oil dries up. The government is pouring substantial funds into the education sector, with the aim of becoming a knowledge-based economy. The emphasis on science, technology and innovation, with 60% of R&D funds dedicated to those sectors, compared with 40% going to humanities.

In Sabah and Sarawak the picture is, as often, in stark contrast to economic privileged Brunei. Moves are still under way to try and give control over education back to the state governments from Malaysian federal government administrators. In 2015, Sarawak's ministers again spoke out against the underprivileged education system of North Borneo – problems with funding and staff – and pinned it firmly on the biases of the national system.

While overall literacy rates in both states, according to 2010 statistics, do not lag too far behind national averages – 92.6% in Sarawak and 95.4% in Sabah compared with 97% countrywide – in areas such as computer literacy as in higher education levels, teacher training and culturally relevant curriculums, Sabahans and Sarwawakians are seriously underprivileged compared with most other Malaysian states.

CULTURE

Forget the opera, theatre and grand literary occasions. The performing arts of Malaysian Borneo and Brunei are found (often free of charge) in the streets. Costumes, crafts, dance and music are steeped in tradition. Far from being museum pieces, the traditional customs involving music, dance and rhythm are alive and kicking. Of course, there are also organised performances, festivals and orchestras, but they often lack the verve of raw performances.

MUSIC, SONG AND DANCE Everywhere you go in Borneo, each different culture sings out its own unique rhythm. Between all the various ethnic cultures – indigenous, Chinese and Malay – there is a rich tradition of instrumental music, song and dance performances. Music and dance usually go together; many dances are deeply symbolic and in some cases tied to spiritual worlds and ceremonies.

Gongs and other instruments Gongs are a big feature of cultural performance and music ensembles in Malaysia, in both indigenous and Malay music. There are many different types of gong.

Bruneians introduced the *kulintangan* into Sabah, which is played among ethnic groups of the Kadazandusun peoples on the west coast and the Muslim

1

Students from Seri Insan Secondary School in Kota Kinabalu provided the following insights into Sabah's musical landscape (they live up to being 'bright human beings' as the school's name proclaims). According to them, four main groups of instruments feature in Sabah's traditional musical culture: *membranophones* (drums), *idiophones* (bronze or brass gongs), *aerophones* (flutes), and *chordophones* (string instruments).

Like many other cultures, there are many types of vocal music including love songs, battle songs, epic tales and ritual chanting. Instrumental music is as rich and complex as vocal music, with a variety of solos and ensembles. Instruments are played by men and women.

Most gong ensembles have a drum to emphasise the main rhythmic patterns. Drums from the interior region around Tambunan are called *karatung*. Also known as *gandang* or *gondang*, these are usually cylindrical in shape with a single head of cowhide or goatskin bound to the body. The most common types of *idiophones* are bronze or brass gongs. Every gong has a name denoting its sound or the rhythm it plays. A gong ensemble consists of seven to eight gongs, depending on the community. One such ensemble is the *sopogandangan*, which is played as an accompaniment to *magarang* dancing in Tambunan, or *sumazau* in Penampang.

Sabah has a wide variety of traditional *aerophones*, including short bamboo end-blown mouth flutes called *suling*; longer nose flutes known as *turali*; jaw's harps named *turiding*; and *sompoton*, or mouth organs.

One of the *chordophones* used in Sabah is the *tonkungon*, a tube made either from a node or large *poring* bamboo. A large hole is cut in the back or in the top to enhance resonance and thin strips incised in the surface to form strings or chords.

Bajau on the east coast. It looks like a series of brass casseroles lined up – eight small knobbed gongs in xylophone-form which several players gong-chime away in turn.

Brunei's stringed lute, the *gambus,* is played to the beat of Malay dances such as *joget* and *zapin*. Its hollow body is made from *nangka*, which is covered with lizard or goatskin, the neck coated with a thin wooden veneer. Three pairs of brass or gut strings are traditionally plucked with the claw of an anteater. A Pesta Gambus festival is held every year on Sabah's west coast among the Bruneian–Malay community, and there are *pesta* gongs all over the place.

Song and dance in sickness and health Music and dance are central to Malay festivities. The most common is *joget*, a dance of lively tempo with lots of hand and leg movement, performed by couples in brilliantly coloured traditional silk dress. Its origins lie in Portuguese folk dance, which infiltrated Malay culture during the Malacca spice era. The dance is passionate, but graceful, and there are several regional variations and adaptations.

The Bajau of Sabah perform dance rituals such as the *magamboh* to offer thanksgiving, though this is now an extremely rare performance. Dance may also be used to heal a sick member of the community, sometimes accompanied by an elaborate bath, visits to the graves of ancestors and prayers for the sick person and their family. The whole community comes together during times of hardship and worry. After offering thanks and seeking blessing from the gods, the gong is struck and its resonant chime heralds the beginning of the dance.

Keeping the music alive While Western influences have had an altering effect (not all negative) on Dayak music and dance in Sarawak, efforts are under way to conserve traditional art forms. A big effort is being made to revive Bajau dance traditions among young people after it was realised that most of them could perform rap and hip hop, but not the traditional *tambawan* (performed by women only), the *lellang* (by men only), and the graceful *limbaian*.

Shamans and storytelling in dance and music Music is an important medium in many spiritualist ceremonies. The *kulintangan* is still used in some rituals presided over by the Kadazandusun *bobohizan* (or *bobolian*, depending on the tribe). Music and crafts are threaded together, too, as are music and storytelling. The traditional Iban women's dance – *ngajat indu* – is performed with costumes of woven *pua kumbu* cloths. Iban music and dance tells many stories of their past as virile combatants. In the *ngajat lesong* dance, the protagonist warrior displays his might by picking up a 20kg block of wood with his mouth, then dances round with it posed on his chin. The *ngajat pahlawan* is a dance to welcome the victorious warrior home after a successful week of headhunting.

Dances celebrate death, life and birth. The *datun julud*, an Orang Ulu dance, tells of the happiness of a prince when he was blessed with a grandson. From this grew a tradition; the Kenyah tribe, whose village consists of just one longhouse, perform it to welcome guests. The dancing is accompanied by the sounds of the *sape*, and much clapping and singing. 'A common aspect of the Kayan and Kenyah tribes is the singing of the *parap*, a folklore song relating expressions of love, happiness, loneliness and anger, while singing praises for the beauty of nature and all living things,' says the Sarawak Tourism Board.

Other tribes dance to appease spirits, to ask them for harvest blessings and for spiritual healing. Or, to pass legend and folklore through generations. In Malaysia's leading online newspaper *Malaysiakini.com*, Sim Kwang Yang wrote of Iban storytelling:

'They have a whole legion of folklore and myths... a myth of creation, and legends of heroes and titans which bear some resemblance to the ancient Greek myths. Since the Ibans have no written language, their myths and legends are handed down from generation to generation by word of mouth. The telling and retelling of stories, sometimes through the lyrical form of the *Sampi* recitals that go on for hours at a time, make the Ibans great orators... To call them merely animists is a little unfair. They certainly have a sort of pantheistic idea, in which the jungle and the land are alive with spirits.'

CRAFTS The cultural landscapes of Sabah, Sarawak and Brunei are woven in beads, fibres, fabrics and plants of many colours, shapes and forms. Every tribe has its

THE LEGEND OF HUMINODUN

The legend of Tadau Ka'amatan is that of Huminodun. Huminodun was the only daughter of the god Kinoingan, who sacrificed her (by cutting her up into many pieces) to end a great famine. It's her flesh and blood that are attributed to bountiful crops today – not only rice crops, but coconuts, maize and yams.

distinctive craft and skills: the Kadazandusun are known for their hand-woven rattan baskets and bamboo musical instruments; the Rungus and Kelabits for their beadwork; the Murut for their blowpipes; and the Bajau for their colourful woven mats and food covers, *tudung dulang*. Indigenous crafts often bear a strong allusion to local flora – a kind of geo-cultural identity. Whether they are made from forest woods or wickers, or the leaves or hard shells of tropical fruits, many could not be replicated anywhere else.

With the vegetative world as intensely varied as it is in Borneo, there has always been quite a range of construction and crafting materials – different woods are used for boats, houses, musical instruments, hunting objects and tools; rattan is woven into rope, baskets, birdcages, mats and crates; *nipah* palm fronds are used for thatched roofs; bamboo for musical instruments. Many of these 'functional' objects may appear to be quite simple – yet their often ingenious and attractive design qualifies them as traditional art, as much as the more intricate and embellished items made from precious materials.

Weaving Much of traditional life endures in Borneo; arriving in Melanau heartland in the region of Mukah, coastal Sarawak, you may see women sitting near the river weaving all kinds of basketry and traditional *terendak* sun hats from the fronds of sago palm – an economic staple and a cultural filament too.

Baskets are made by every tribe, invariably from rattan, bamboo, *nipah* leaves and pandanus (screw pines) fruits. The last are crafted into foodstuffs while their

BEAD CULTURE IN BORNEO

With input from Heidi Munan, cultural researcher and Honourable Curator of Beads at the Sarawak Museum, who has lived in Kuching for over 33 years.

The Dayaks of Borneo have a long, vibrant beadwork culture. Beads were held to impart their two salient properties – physical strength and brilliance – to the wearer. Small glass beads were brought by traders from distant lands, which added to their mystical value. The manufacture and use of bead-worked garments and ornaments was traditionally linked to a person's status within society. This applies particularly to the people of Central Borneo, where the most potent designs were restricted to the aristocracy. Beadwork itself was gender-defined in that only women threaded the beads, but men designed the patterns. Today, many old taboos and restraints have become obsolete. Not so the craft of beadwork – beadwork is produced for sale in the coastal towns; some young designers incorporate traditional design in their fashion creations. Much beadwork is still done for home use and at regional festivals; the young women are covered in more beads than their grandmothers ever dreamt of owning! The skills are passed from mother to daughter and materials are readily available. In sum, beadwork is flourishing in Borneo.

Bead culture is strong in Sarawak's Kayan, Kenyah, Bidayuh and highland Kelabit communities, and among Sabah's Rungus population. In her book *Beads of Borneo*, Heidi Munan explains that, excluding beads made from bone, teeth, seed and stone, many beads used in tribal crafts have long been imported. From as early as the 6th to the 12th century, trade with China and India brought beautiful, exotic beads. An ancient Kelabit headhunting song says that 'strangers came to buy pork and sell beads'. Later, Dutch and English explorers brought Venetian and Bohemian beads.

sheaths and fibre go into many household items – *tikar pandan* (pandan mats) for example, are made by the Kadazans of Papar on Sabah's west coast. Though probably more sober in the past, they are now being turned out in many colourful patterns, and woven into dining and drink mats to sell to tourists (with no loss of crafted quality and authenticity). The Kadazandusun also weave many rattan baskets, and purses covered in beads.

Fabrics Different cloths (*kain*) form the basis of diverse woven handicraft traditions. The Iranun, an ethnic minority originally from the southern Philippines who live in small pockets on the east and west coasts of Sabah, traditionally used *kain dastar* as headgear during festive celebrations. Now they use the heavily motifed fabrics to make *dastar* purses, sashes and more. The Iranun community in Kota Belud, two hours north of Kota Kinabalu, are said to have gone further – combining the *dastar* tradition with that of *songket*, which uses gold-coloured threads, to create *sampin songket dastar*, an amazing fusion of the gold-coloured threads and motifs. *Songket* originated among the Malayans of Brunei. There are lots of woven fabrics and cloth in Brunei; only here you may encounter real gold thread so make sure you have your purse with you. *Kain songket* ('cloth of gold') sarongs feature a woven cloth common to Malay cultures in Brunei, Sabah and Sarawak, which originates from the days when the Sultanate ruled over all these territories. The three-quarter or full-length sarongs featuring geometric or floral patterns are part of common daily dress

Beads of varying value were used to mark out social status between the indigenous aristocrats, and the middle and lower classes within tribes. Among the Kelabits, for example, lower classes were rarely allowed to wear beads or bear traditional motifs, says Heidi. 'Aristocrats would buy or exchange slaves with different families, using beads as a form of payment. If you were captured during tribal war, your family may have used beads as ransom payment.' With so much power accorded to these little gems, beads were also used in a spiritual sense – for example during agricultural rites to bless planting and harvesting of crops.

The Kelabits, both men and women, still live out the bead tradition and are busy handing it on to younger generations. Women regularly wear bead necklaces and belts made from peppercorn beads; on special occasions such as weddings, they don the bead caps called *pata* made from the noble *ba'o rawir* – drinking straw beads. Men sport *kabo* – red seed bead bobble – with their Sunday suits or *batik* shirts.

Beaded creations have become popular among tourists with a couple of major downsides – rising prices, fake productions and the loss of antique beads to far-off lands. 'Short of breaking the beads,' says Heidi, 'it's hard to tell the difference.' The proliferation of fakes is getting to the point where the Kelabits were even reported to be looking at a certification system, with the authenticity of bead creations authorised by the Pemanca or high chief of the Kelabit community.

Personally I don't care if the beads I buy are not old – I would rather those artefacts be kept among those who made them. However, I do not want cheap, machine-made replicas. A traditionally made creation hanging close to you is something to treasure.

New *pata* caps sell for around RM1,000 while an antique one can fetch well over RM20,000. Individual antique beads can cost from RM300 to RM1,000. Heirloom beads are priceless.

for many Malay people. Equally intricate and richly symbolic are the *pua kumbu* 'blankets' of Sarawak's Iban, whose abstract designs and motifs of plants and animals have a sacred link to important life passages, from birth to marriage and death.

COSTUMES Want to make a party statement? Think of donning a Kadazan outfit for the next special occasion. With their strikingly elegant black velvet dress, replete with elaborate trimmings and embroidery, the Kadazandusun stand out among the many beautiful costumes that accompany ceremony, dance and music in Borneo. According to the Kadazandusun Cultural Association, the men's jacket and trousers bear some Chinese influence. 'There are three different styles of blouses for the women. One is a blouse with short sleeves – *sinuangga* – worn by young ladies. Another is a blouse with three-quarter-length sleeves – *sinompukung* – worn by middle-aged ladies for daily or casual use. The third one – *kihongon* – is worn by elderly women and female ritual specialists or priestesses during ceremonies.' The blouses are worn over a long cylindrical black skirt – *tapi*. Traditionally it was a plain black cotton skirt but eye-catching renditions are trimmed with gold *siring*. The outfit is usually made with silk and velvet for ceremonial occasions and cotton for daywear. Mass-made versions now sell to tourists. Likewise the men's long-sleeved shirt, *gaung*, and black trousers, *souva*, have been dollied up with gold buttons, and trimming.

The men also wear some very fancy headgear: the *siga* is a conical hat made out of hand-woven cloth, *kain dastar*, folded or twisted in a number of distinctive ways including *hinopung* – python form – and *kinahu* – pot-holder style.

Like many cultures, the Kadazandusun top off their couture with lots of accessories: brass and silver spiral bracelets (*tiningkokos*); hairpins (*titimbak*) to decorate and fasten the hair bun of women's often very long dark hair; necklaces (*hamai*), earrings (*simbong*) and brooches made with gold coins (*paun*). The more *himpogot* or silver 'dollar belts' a person is wearing (usually anything from one to three around the waist and hips), the more wealthy they are. Men wear a black or coloured waist sash (*kaking*). As for the *bobohizan* priestess, her outfit is one of total feathered splendour. If you love costumes, customs and ethno-fashion, get hold of *An Introduction to the Traditional Costumes of Sabah* (see page 332).

The costumes of Borneo's tribes are a brilliant reflection of their ethnic diversity – the noble formality of Malay outfits, the simple black sarongs and bodices of the Rungus emblazoned in multi-hued black beads, and the strikingly beautiful, pom-pom-strung poncho and silver-feathered headdress of the Iban.

SEND US YOUR SNAPS!

We'd love to follow your adventures using our *Borneo* guide – why not send us your photos and stories via Twitter (@BradtGuides) and Instagram (@bradtguides) using the hashtag #borneo. Alternatively, you can upload your photos directly to the gallery on the Borneo destination page via our website (*www.bradtguides.com/borneo*).

2

Natural History and Conservation

Life on Earth is not evenly spread around our planet. Borneo – the world's third largest island – is one of its richest treasure-houses, full of an immense variety of wild animals and plants, all living in a magnificent tropical forest.
Sir David Attenborough, backing the WWF's Heart of Borneo project in 2007

BIODIVERSITY

Despite extensive destruction of its natural environment through forestry and agriculture, Borneo remains a paradise of tropical forests, filled with a staggering array of plants and animals. The world's 'biodiversity hotspots' cover less than 1% of the earth's surface but are home to over half of all the world's plant and animal species – Borneo is one of them, putting it on a par with the Amazon and equatorial Africa for species diversity.

Much of Borneo's flora and fauna is endemic – not found anywhere else. An estimated 5,000-plus flowering plants are unique to the island, as well as some 500 mammals, birds, reptiles and fish. This is just one of two places where the orangutan, Asia's only great ape, has survived. Just 10ha of Bornean rainforest can contain up to 700 tree species – more than found in the whole of North America. The total flora count of up to 15,000 plant species includes 6,000 endemics, more than 3,000 different trees and 2,000 orchids. The WWF says Borneo may have the highest plant diversity of any region on earth: since the mid 1980s, 422 new species have been discovered.

Likewise for animal species, scientific research in the decade up to 2004 alone upturned 260 new insects, 30 freshwater fish, seven frogs, five crabs, two snakes and one toad, to name a few. Those finds may be just the tip of the iceberg. In April 2010, three years after researchers began to probe the transnational forests at the centre of the island, known as the 'Heart of Borneo' (or HoB; see page 66), the WWF said 123 new species had emerged. Among them was a frog with no lungs, a 'ninja' slug which fires 'love darts' at its mates, the world's longest insect (the 57cm-long Chan's megastick), a bird called the spectacled flowerpecker, and a snake whose neck blazes bright orange colours to ward off predators. The research followed a conservation deal between the governments of Malaysia, Brunei and Indonesia to protect the 220,000km² rainforest zone. The WWF's 2010 report, *Borneo's New World: Newly Discovered Species in the Heart of Borneo*, says the Heart of Borneo is an 'island within an island', a mini biodiversity cosmos and home to ten species of primate, more than 350 birds, 150 reptiles and amphibians and 10,000 plants found nowhere else in the world. 'New forms of life are constantly being discovered in the Heart of Borneo. If this stretch of irreplaceable rainforest can be conserved for our children, the promise of more discoveries must be a tantalising one for the next generation of researchers to contemplate.'

Travelling the Malay Archipelago between 1854 and 1862, pioneering explorer and naturalist Alfred Russel Wallace made two vital discoveries.

After completing his travels around the Amazon Basin, Wallace set sail for Southeast Asia, documenting his travels and collecting species along the way. In eight years spent in the region, he assembled an astounding 125,660 specimens – 1,000 of which were entirely new to science. Through his observations of the region's flora and fauna, Wallace formulated groundbreaking theories about the environment and species evolution, similar to those of Charles Darwin. Unlike Darwin, Wallace failed to elaborate on his ideas or deduct a mechanism as to how evolution might occur. Subsequently, Darwin received the lion's share of credit for his work, with most history books citing him as sole author of the revolutionary theory.

Wallace nonetheless made another biological breakthrough during his time in the Malay Archipelago. On his island jaunts, he noticed a striking pattern of distribution of animal life across the archipelago, identifying a geological line separating two distinct groups of fauna of different origins. On one side, species were similar to those found in Southeast Asia; on the other they were clearly affiliated to Australasian fauna. Wallace had discovered the fault-line boundary dividing two vast continental plates that had drifted together over time, bringing two significantly different stocks of wildlife into close proximity. 'Wallace's Line' – at least – was consequently named in his honour.

GEOLOGY

Like all other islands, Borneo owes its isolation to tectonic plate movement and rising sea levels. Along with the Peninsular Malay and the islands of Java and Sumatra, the island is part of the Sunda Shelf, a stable continental shelf underlying the shallow South China and Java seas, as an extension of mainland Asia. Youthful on a geological scale, Borneo's foundations were set in place with the buckling of the earth's crusts around 15 million years ago. Over the next three million years, these underwater landmasses were forced above sea level by tectonic plate movement. When sea levels rose at the end of the last ice age, 12,000 years ago, Borneo was separated from Sundaland and the other territories with which it shares much common fauna.

Even today, most of Borneo's landmass lies at less than 150m above sea level. A marshy coastal belt – composed partly of rich alluvial (water deposited) soils, washed down from the mountains – girths much of the island, extending inland towards hills and valleys. The centre of the island, on the other hand, is dominated by mountain ranges. Concentrated in northern Sabah, a few isolated peaks of 1,500–2,000m rise along the Sabah–Sarawak and Sarawak–Kalimantan borders.

SABAH Separating the low-lying coast from the rest of Sabah, the 100km-long Crocker Range was formed 35 million years ago when ocean sediments were compressed into sandstone and shale, before coming to the surface with geological uplift. Most of the range lies 500–900m above the sea, with the great exception of Southeast Asia's highest mountain, 4,095m Mount Kinabalu, and Malaysia's second-highest peak, 2,643m Gunung Trus Madi. Several rivers spring from this mountainous core, including Sungai Kinabatangan, the nation's second-longest river, which flows east to the Sulu Sea.

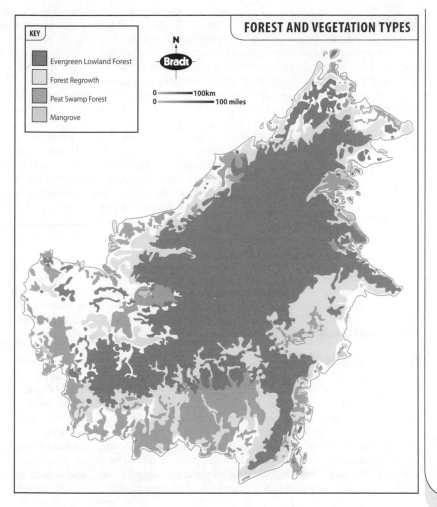

KEY

◼ Evergreen Lowland Forest

◻ Forest Regrowth

◼ Peat Swamp Forest

◻ Mangrove

N

Bradt

0 ▬▬▬ 100km
0 ▬▬▬ 100 miles

Rising high over the Crocker Range, Mount Kinabalu is not only Borneo's rooftop, but also the highest point between the Himalayas and New Guinea. It was formed 10–15 million years ago from a ball of molten granite beneath the earth's surface, which later hardened into a granite mound – known as a 'pluton'. The mass was forced upwards and burst through the Crocker Range relatively recently – one million years ago – making it one of the earth's youngest non-volcanic mountains. These forces are still at work, and Mount Kinabalu continues to grow by more than half a centimetre each year. The constant growing pains make it a challenge keeping up with its accurate height! Glaciers from recent ice ages carved the summit into the stunning form of sharp peaks, vertical cliffs and sheer valleys seen today.

Another geomorphologic wonder of Sabah is the Maliau Basin, a spectacular crater-like hollow with a diameter of over 20km and rugged rims reaching up to 2km in height. The basin was formed 15–20 million years ago, when much of Sabah was still underwater, then progressively shaped by elevation and buckling of the earth's crust.

SARAWAK Inland Sarawak hosts a spectacular array of limestone features including pinnacles, protrusions and mega caves. The world's largest cave chamber and cave passage, and Southeast Asia's longest cave, are all found at Gunung Mulu National Park. Sculpted by the corrosive action of water flowing through limestone and sandstone mountains, the immense subterranean system is continually transmuting; dripping water creates new features and rock is worn away by underground rivers.

BRUNEI Much of Brunei consists of low-lying coastal plains of alluvial soils, laced by mangrove-fringed river estuaries. Hills of sandstone and shale dominate the interior; together with clay and mudstone, they constitute the bedrock of both Brunei and West Sarawak. The Temburong District in eastern Brunei is more mountainous, with Bukit Pagon peaking at 1,843m. Brunei Bay – shared with Sabah and Sarawak – is heavily indented and features marine terraces cut by waves of the South China Sea.

ECOSYSTEMS AND FLORA

Borneo is often perceived as the archetypal jungle-covered island, yet it hosts a variety of other equally important habitats. The major ecosystem types fall into the following categories: tropical rainforest, montane forest, limestone forest, sub-alpine and summit forest, heath forest, coastal forests and wetlands. Note definitions for these habitats sometimes vary.

TROPICAL RAINFOREST Tropical rainforest covers 3% of the earth's surface, exclusively in a belt around the Equator. At one time as much as 90% of Borneo was under forest cover, but today that figure is much smaller – 50–60% in Malaysian Borneo. Much of this has been logged or left to regenerate as secondary forest – only pockets of primary 'old growth' rainforest remain. In Sabah, these are found in the central Danum Valley and Imbak Canyon region, Sepilok Forest and Tabin wildlife reserves on the east coast, and lower elevations of Mount Kinabalu in the Gunung Kinabalu National Park. Sarawak's primary rainforest occurs in some of the national parks – Kubah, Bako and Tanjung Datu in the south, and Similajau, Niah and Lambir Hills parks on the central and northeast coasts.

Life in the forest's layers Despite the apparent chaos of growth, tropical rainforest is actually organised into at least three overlapping vertical layers.

EMINENT BOTANIST'S VIEWPOINT   *Sir Peter Crane*

Climbing up into the rainforest canopy in Borneo at dawn is a terrifying experience: straight up the tall, ghostly grey trunk of a massive Koompassia tree to a platform 40m above the ground. And still you're not at the top. But from here, as the mist clears, the true grandeur of the lowland forest emerges. This is a precious place and home to some of the world's most charismatic animals.

Sir Peter Crane is Dean of the School of Forestry & Environmental Studies at Yale, and a former Director of the Royal Botanic Gardens, Kew, England. See pages 64–5 for more comments from him on conservation in Borneo.

Emergent (or overstorey) layer   These forest giants tower over the canopy layer, projecting through at heights of up to 90m. The towering slivery-grey Menggaris (*Koompassia excelsa*) is one such species with trunks up to 3m in diameter. The commonly named 'honeybee trees' are crowned by a mesh of horizontal branches where the giant bees (*Apis dorsata*) make their nests, safely out of reach of the honey-loving sun bear.

Canopy layer   Most of the productivity in a tropical rainforest occurs in the canopy. At a height of 25–45m, sunlight and rain are most available for exploitation by trees and plants.

Dipterocarp forest   Trees from the Dipterocarpaceae family dominate Borneo's rainforest canopy. The country is home to some 267 species – the greatest occurrence in Southeast Asia – an estimated 155 of which are endemic. Together, dipterocarps represent around 80% of tree species in Bornean forests. Sadly, they are also subject to the highest level of commercial logging activity: the 80% of Borneo, which was once covered in lowland dipterocarp forest, has been seriously whittled away.

Understorey and lower layers   Below the canopy, the understorey contains younger trees patiently waiting for a gap to appear above. When this happens, they suddenly spurt into accelerated growth to claim pole position at the top. Smaller trees and flowering bushes are also found in the understorey, including many plants from the Rubiaceae and Euphorbiaceae families (in places including the Danum Valley, these two species dominate the understorey). Euphorbiaceae is the second most common floral family in Borneo, with over 150 species from shrubs to creepers and wild fruiting plants. Aside from the omnipresent Dipterocarpaceae, other common families are Lauraceae (laurels), Ericaceae (heaths and heathers), and Annonaceae (custard apple).

Lauraceae   Borneo 'ironwood' (*Eusideroxylon zwageri*), locally known as *belian*, is a species of laurel that has been used by indigenous people for centuries to make roofs and a whole range of other sturdy things. *Belian* trees reach heights of up to 40m and live for several hundred years (and take almost as long to decay). They are one of the most common non-dipterocarp species in undisturbed forest canopies, though have become less prevalent due to overexploitation for their high commercial value. Extremely durable, *belian* timber is in great demand for heavy construction, roofing, agriculture and other uses.

As is sadly the case with many trees, *belian* is more threatened in Indonesian Borneo, and an endangered species in Kalimantan. With the gradual transformation of traditional to industrial agriculture, larger trees began to disappear at a faster rate. When farmers started using *belian* as support stakes in pepper crops in the 1970s, for example, numbers began to decline at a considerably high rate.

Fruit trees and palms   Hundreds of tree species with edible fruit and nuts are found in the rainforest and have provided indigenous people with a bountiful and varied diet for centuries. Commonly used plants include durian (Bombacaceae), mango (Anacardiaceae), and pawpaw (*Asimina triloba*). Several fruiting trees belong to the Moraceae family, including the jack-fruit-like *tarap* (*Artocarpus odoratissimus*), figs (*Ficus spp*), and lesser-known *peruput* (*Artocarpus rigidus*) and *timakon* (*Artocarpus lanceifolia*). One particular custard apple variety is the key ingredient

Dipterocarp trunks emerging from their huge buttress roots 'look like rockets on the launch pad'. This fitting description was made in *Natural History* magazine in 1999. 'Their spreading limbs provide platforms and runways more than a hundred feet in the air, enabling many kinds of animals to eat, sleep, and give birth without ever descending to the ground.'

The name 'dipterocarp' comes from the Greek, meaning 'two-winged seed' and describes the helicopter-style method with which the seeds are dispersed. The cyclical, sporadic and sudden flowering of Dipterocarpaceae trees, known as masting, determines the reproductive rhythm of the entire forest. Species from orangutans and gibbons to hornbills and bats are entirely dependent on this flowering and subsequent fruiting and the manner in which dipterocarps 'dictate bounty and scarcity in the rainforest'. 'Dipterocarps do not depend on animals or the wind to disperse their seeds. Flanked by two wing-like sepals, the seeds are heavy and gyrate to the ground close to the parent tree. Mature trees may not reproduce for three to ten years and then suddenly blanket the forest floor with their pea-to-walnut-sized seeds. Masting is not unique to dipterocarps, but nothing compares with what takes place here: a long hiatus in reproduction throughout the forest canopy, followed by a sudden and simultaneous fructifying.'

'Flowering of the Forest – Dipterocarp trees of Borneo', by Art Blundell was published in Natural History *magazine (US) in July 1999*

in a green, tangy drink called *sour sop*. Sago palms (*Eugeissona spp*) are a source of starchy energy, notably for the nomadic Penan who extract its fibrous pulp and turn it into flour.

Creepers and climbers

The understorey is a dense, delightful world bedecked with rich entangles of lianas, lichens, orchids and epiphytic plants. The last are among the shade-tolerant species that thrive in the rainforest understorey, having developed ingenious ways of surviving. **Epiphytes** grow on the surface of other plants without needing to embed their roots in the ground and include many kinds of lichens, liverworts, orchids, mosses and ferns. **Lianas**, woody climbers, are organic ladders – they start on the forest floor but use trees, and one another, to climb towards the canopy light to reproduce.

MONTANE FOREST

Montane forest occurs at altitudes above 900m. This habitat is further divided into lower montane forest (900–1,500m) and upper montane forest (1,500–3,300m).

Lower montane forest

In lower montane forest the density of trees thins out, forest canopies drop as low as 20m, and oak-chestnut trees (Fagaceae) gradually take precedence over rainforest varieties. Many orchids, both epiphytic and terrestrial, flourish in these cooler conditions, as well as climbers such as rattan palm. In Sabah, lower montane environments exist in the Crocker Range, the Tawau Hills Park and lower elevations of Gunung Kinabalu National Park near park headquarters. There are over 1,000 orchid species on Mount Kinabalu – 40% of all those found in Borneo.

Alfred Russel Wallace greatly admired wild durian (*Durio testudinarum*), dubbing the fruit 'the king of the forest' and the orange as queen. These large, green fruits are common in the rainforest. Their noxious-smelling flowers and fruits are produced directly from their trunks, a phenomenon known as cauliflory. In a letter to the then director of Kew Royal Gardens, Sir William Jackson Hooker, Wallace wrote:

The Durian grows on a large and lofty forest-tree, something resembling an Elm in character, but with a more smooth and scaly bark. The fruit is round or slightly oval, about the size of a small melon, of a green colour, and covered with strong spines, the bases of which touch each other, and are consequently somewhat hexagonal, while the points are very strong and sharp. It is so completely armed that if the stalk is broken off it is a difficult matter to lift one from the ground. The outer rind is so thick and tough that from whatever height it may fall it is never broken. As a tree ripens the fruit falls daily and almost hourly, and accidents not infrequently happen to persons walking or working under them. When a Durian strikes a man in its fall it produces a fearful wound, the strong spines tearing open the flesh, while the blow itself is very heavy; but from this very circumstance death rarely ensues.

Printed in volume 8 of Hooker's Journal of Botany *in 1856*

Upper montane forest In upper montane or **cloudforest** the spread of oak-chestnut trees is replaced by mossy forests rich in conifers, tea trees and pitcher plants. As altitudes rise, the vegetation becomes shrubbier in appearance and more stunted, the soils are thin and the canopy drops to 10m or less. Frequent cloud cover brings cool mists, which shower the understorey and propagate luxurious undergrowths of numerous species of lichens, mosses, ferns and orchids. Colourful rhododendrons thrive particularly well in the upper reaches (3,300m).

Within Sabah, this habitat type is restricted to Mount Kinabalu and the Trus Madi mountains, and supports many rare and restricted-range species. Studies of floristic diversity in the area have shown Mount Kinabalu's species density is greatest at altitudes of 2,500–3,000m rather than at lower elevations, as may be expected. Nine species of pitcher plant dwell on Mount Kinabalu, in the crossover of lower and upper montane forest, and in rare **ultramafic forest**, whose dark, metallic soils owe to mineral-rich ultramafic rocks.

LIMESTONE FOREST Composed of mostly small trees and shrubs, this type of forest is found growing on limestone hills and formations, including the Gomantong and Madai caves in Sabah, and the Niah and Mulu caves in Sarawak.

SUB-ALPINE AND SUMMIT FOREST Once you rise above 3,200m on Mount Kinabalu, the upper montane forest is replaced with scrubby sub-alpine vegetation made up of gnarled, stunted, wind-blown trees. Rarely exceeding 50cm, these denuded trees and shrubs often dwell in rock crevices, containing small patches of soil, which protect them from the elements – thus the reference to them as granite boulder flora.

HEATH ('KERANGAS') FOREST Though relatively rare, heath forest consists of small, poorly nourished trees growing in highly leached (nutrients washed away by rainwater) sandy soils. Found at the same altitude as lowland rainforest, they are concentrated around Sabah's and Sarawak's coastal and inland areas. In estuarine areas of Sarawak the Iban call the habitat *padang kerangas* – 'land where padi cannot be grown' – because rainwater cannot be retained to flood the land for planting rice crops. Rain falling on the open vegetation and poor soils encourages the growth of acid-loving plants such as rhododendron and the tropical she-oak *Gymnostoma*. Heath forest is low in diversity but rich in endemic plants adapted to nutrient-poor soils – pitcher plants, climbing epiphytes and, in Bako National Park, ant plants (*Clerodendrum*). *Kerangas* is also found in the Lambir Hills and Similajau national parks on the northern Sarawak' coast.

COASTAL FORESTS AND WETLANDS Sarawak, Sabah and Brunei contain a variety of wetland habitats. Wide coastal plains and marshy areas virtually surround the island, stretching up to 70km inland along the river system. Sabah's Wildlife Department classifies beach vegetation and mangroves, freshwater swamp forest and riparian riverine forest all under the umbrella of 'coastal forest'. These types of habitat are found at 0–30m above sea level.

Beach forests Dominated by coarse **casuarinas** coastal grass and **pandanus** palms, this kind of forest accounts for just a few percent of total vegetation. Coastal development has seen such habitats dwindle, or relegated to a 'decorative remnant'. Casuarinas are colonising species, thriving in strips along the coast in certain areas. *Casuarina equisetifolia* is the most common variety. Seen swaying in the wind at heights of 30–60m, they are joined by other mostly herbaceous plants and shrubs with waterborne seeds.

Only plant species that can cope with the harsh saline environment survive, thus plant diversity in beach forest is relatively low. Other species known as 'strand flora' have decamped back from the water line, occurring behind a casuarinas fringe and thin strip of mangroves. One such species is the common seashore screw pine (*Pandanus odoratissimus*). A culinary staple, featuring in many Sabah dishes, the flesh of its huge fruits is used to make green cakes, green coconut paste (*kaya*), green bread, sago and sweets.

Mangrove forests At the ecosystem frontier – where the worlds of sea and land meet – mangrove trees dominate. Their success in such a hostile environment, of high salt and low oxygen levels, owes to spectacular adaptive powers. As tides subside, their secrets emerge – arching, tangled roots protrude above the surface, allowing them to absorb oxygen from the air when exposed, and nutrients from the water when submerged.

Mangroves are the Roman legions of the natural world. They form important barriers from the sea, protecting coastal lands from the erosive actions of the tides and holding together unstable sandy soils. Many species of wildlife depend on them for nesting and breeding grounds, exploiting the sheltered, tangled root system to lay eggs and raise young. In Sabah, Sarawak and Brunei, mangroves are important breeding grounds for leaf monkeys, crocodiles, fish, large colonies of flying foxes, and wetland birds such as herons and egrets.

They usually grow in pure stands, often adjacent to lowland rainforest and coastal heath – a prime example is the Bako National Park in Sarawak. Despite being warriors for many of those with whom they cohabit, they themselves are under serious threat from man. Once widespread in low-lying coastal regions of Sarawak and along saline river estuaries, the forests now account for only a tiny proportion of the state's land area.

Durably harvested for firewood, building and crafts for centuries by tribal peoples, the real damage was done with extensive clearing of mangrove-covered state land for industrial and urban development, as well as for timber and wood-chipping. Though large-scale harvesting for export has almost been phased out, there's the new threat of urbanisation. A big belt of Kota Kinabalu City lies on former mangrove territory, with more set to be swallowed up by future construction of shopping malls, apartment complexes and hotels.

Brunei is the most mangrove-rich state, with around 4% of its surface area covered by intact mangrove forest. The mangroves in Brunei Bay represent one of Southeast Asia's largest, and relatively undisturbed, surviving tracts.

Nipah forests
Nibong (*Oncosperma*) and nipah (*Nypa fructitans*) palms are found mingling with mangroves; the former in the drier parts of mangrove forest, the latter in tidal reaches of rivers, such as along the Kinabatangan Estuary. Nipah palms are less salt tolerant than mangroves and often occur in pure stands of 'nipah forest'. Nipah leaves are used by coastal communities – Malay, Bajau and Melenau – for roofing known as *atap,* and for basketry and other crafts. Nipah sap was once used as a form of fuel. Certain areas in Sandakan were once known as 'energy plantations' because of the large tracts of nipah forest. Many of those areas are now planted with palm oil, used (controversially) as an alternative 'green' energy source. Brunei's riverbanks and estuaries are a good place to see nipah and nibong forest.

Transitional forest
The crossover area between mangrove, nipah or swamp wetlands and dry land is sometimes referred to as 'transitional forest'. This belt of vegetation is characterised by thorny nibong palms, rattan (Palmae) and brown-reddish tinged merbau trees (*Intsia palembanica*), a durable hardwood.

Swamp forest
According to the Sabah Forestry Department, swamp forest can be broadly separated into freshwater swamp and peat swamp. Freshwater swamps receive their water supply from streams and rivers, while peat swamps receive moisture solely from rainfall.

Freshwater swamp forests (riparian riverine forests)
When lowland rainforest is intersected by rivers, with an absence of tidal influences, specific riverine species of trees and plants flourish along the light-filled, water-lapped riverbanks. Shrubs, creepers and climbing plants such as rattan, bamboo, begonias, ginger and bright-yellow simpoh (*Dillenia excelsa*) grow in the fertile alluvial soils. Riverine forest plays an important role in absorbing floodwaters, protecting riverbanks and reducing soil erosion from hill slopes into rivers.

Peat swamp forests
Mostly seen in Sarawak, peat swamp forests lie further inland from the mangroves and nipah, woven within river deltas. The Maludam National Park in southern Sarawak is a prime example. The acidic environments form as deposits of organic matter, building up behind the mangroves. The rivers drain towards the coast. These mires are favoured habitats for proboscis monkeys and langurs; Sarawak's rare reptile, the false gharial; and aquatic species, including numerous wetland birds, some on long continental migrations. Peat swamp forest covers $15,000km^2$ of Sarawak's coastline, but have been so extensively exploited to feed Sarawak's sawmills that they are almost depleted of timber trees.

Rafflesias, orchids, pitcher plants and other unusual blooms have come to symbolise the extraordinary beauty of Borneo's forests and the botanical wonders that exist in them. Some feature on the endangered species list, but one hopes the awe and attention they attract as 'power flowers' will help to save them.

RAFFLESIA With its cabbage-shaped, riotous ruby-coloured blooms, the rafflesia isn't just an icon in Malaysian Borneo; it's an obsession. Also known as the 'corpse flower' for the rotting-flesh smell it emits when in bloom, the foul odour of this lowland rainforest and hill forest species has done little to dampen its popularity. Indeed, challenging smells in the botanical world (durian fruits are just as malodorous) seem to heighten interest. In 1928, Swedish entomologist Eric Georg Mjöberg described the smell as 'a penetrating odour more repulsive than any buffalo carcass in an advanced stage of decomposition'. The carcass smell attracts carrion flies in what has been described as 'pollination by deception'. Far from being a carnivore, the rafflesia is a parasitic plant that embeds and spreads its roots among Tetrastigma vines. The largest species in the rafflesia family is *Rafflesia arnoldii* (also known as the corpse lily in the US), which can produce flowers up to 90cm wide and 7kg in weight – it is the largest known flower on the planet.

The first European to report it was surgeon and lay-naturalist Joseph Arnold, after an expedition to the depths of Sumatra in 1818 with Sir Stamford Raffles. 'To tell you the truth, had I been alone with no witnesses I should have been fearful of mentioning the dimensions of this flower,' wrote Arnold. Long admired by indigenous people, they reportedly use the flowers for labour pains and post-natal fatigue, and as an aphrodisiac and fertility charm. Anglicised in 'Raffles's honour, the Rafflesiaceae family consists of 17 species, five of which are found in Malaysian Borneo: *R. keithii* and *R. tengku-adlinii* are found only in Sabah, while *R. arnoldii*, *R. pricei* and *R. tuan-mudae* can be seen in both Sabah and Sarawak. Rafflesia strongholds include Sabah's Crocker Range, Gunung Kinabalu National Park and Maliau Basin, and Sarawak's Gunung Gading National Park. Known collectively as *Bunga pakma*, they generally grow in hill rainforest but also lower montane forests at elevations of 400–1,300m.

The rafflesia bud – a darkish-brown lump the size of a large grapefruit – lies on the host vine for around nine months as it slowly swells in size. Upon its sudden opening, the giant flower heads have no leaves and virtually no stem, but five mammoth petals. Blossoming occurs over several days – during this time national parks and wildlife and tourism offices issue alerts, prompting a mad rush to see the flowers. Rafflesia are at their most beautiful during their first day or two of blossoming. After that they become covered in brown blemishes, and their flesh darkens and rots to reveal a 15cm-wide fruit full of thousands of tiny, hard-coated seeds. It still isn't known whether elephants, ants, squirrels or other animals disperse the seeds – a theory hypothesised by Arnold – or why the flowers are so large.

The need for protection of the rare rafflesia is high; the flowers are threatened by spreading urbanisation, trampling by animals and people, and damage caused by egg-laying wasps. As many as nine out of every ten buds never open, shrivelling and dying for inexplicable reasons.

Rafflesia have no specific breeding season – they can appear at any time, though blooms tend to be slightly more frequent between November and

January. A number of hotlines exist for checking on rafflesia status. Check with national park or tourism offices in the area you are travelling, though you may be as likely to smell the blooms before you hear about them!

For more information see the illustrated *Rafflesia of the World* (Natural History Publications, Malaysia, 2001) by Dr Jamili Nais, newly appointed Director of Sabah Parks.

PITCHER PLANTS Few plants capture the imagination more than the Hitchcock-ian carnivorous pitcher plants (genus: *Nepenthes*). These jug-shaped, open-mouthed pitchers are modified petioles (stalks) that grow along herbaceous vines and excel at luring, trapping and devouring insects and small animals. The insects are attracted to the anthocyanin pigments (the colourful cups are often flushed with maroon and pink) or lures of nectar around the rim. When they venture inside the trap, they slip on the mucus-lined walls and fall into the pool of liquid at the bottom, where they are dissolved by bacteria or enzymes secreted by the plant. Because the meat-eating plants derive their nutrients in this unlikely manner, they can survive in very poor soil.

Of the 30 species of *Nepenthes* found in Borneo, around half occur in Malaysian territory. The huge *Nepenthes rajah* is the largest of the genus, found only in Gunung Kinabalu National Park and near Gunung Tambuyukon. The largest-ever pitcher recorded contained a staggering four litres of liquid and a half-digested rat! Other species are endemic to the upper reaches of Mount Kinabalu, including *N. burbidgeae*, *N. villosa* and *N. edwarsiana*. Also known as 'monkey cups', the pitchers are used by some tribes to cook rice or carry water.

Prime pitcher-plant locations include the Gunung Kinabalu National Park and Maliau Basin in Sabah, and Bako, Gunung Mulu and Lampir Hill national parks in Sarawak. They are far less elusive than Rafflesia, though you have to climb to see them – most occur at 1,500–2,600m. Tham Yau Kong (e *thamyaukong@ thamyaukong.com; www.thamyaukong.com*) runs one-day to two-week *Nepenthes*-spotting tours in Sabah.

ORCHIDS Exquisitely delicate and intensely colourful, Borneo is said to house around one-tenth of the world's orchid species: that's 2,500 out of a documented 25,000 types in the Orchidaceae family. About 1,200 of these (including several endemic species) grow in Gunung Kinabalu National Park. The Rothschild's slipper (*Paphiopedilum rothschildianum*) exists only on Mount Kinabalu and is so rare that its specific location was kept secret for many years because of repeated attempts of smuggling. Now protected by law, its close relatives include four other 'slipper orchid' species, one of which – *P. dayanum* – is also classed as endangered.

Other orchid treasures, says Dr Jamili Nais, Director of Sabah Parks, include 'an amazing gigantic elephant-ear orchid (*Phalaenopsis gigantean*); peculiar species like the snake orchid (*Paraphalaneopsis labukensis*), which has rounded, cylindrical leaves looking like a snake; and the giant or tiger orchid (*Grammatophyllum speciosum*)'. About 120 Bornean orchids are on the IUCN's Red List – at least 70 of which are listed as critically endangered.

RHODODENDRONS Adding resplendent colour to rainforest and mountain environments, Borneo's 50 or so species of rhododendron range from ground-hugging shrubs to hanging epiphytes, with pink and red tubular flowers. Around 30 are found in Sabah, including 12 endemic species. Gunung Kinabalu National Park is a good place to see them.

LIPSTICK FLOWERS Various species of extravagant, multi-coloured 'lipstick flowers' (genus: *Aeschynanthus*; family: Gesneriaceae) are found in both Sabah and Sarawak. These Old-World epiphytes flourish in temperate, montane forest environments such as Mount Kinabalu. According to Anthony Lamb, British botanist and author of *The Lipstick Flowers of Sabah* and *The Lipstick Flowers of Sabah and Sarawak* (Singapore Botanic Gardens, 2003/2005), the name was originally applied to *Aeschynanthus pulcher* from Java, because the flower buds emerging from the cylindrical calyx tube look like ladies' lipsticks. Former director of Sabah's Agricultural Park, Lamb has catalogued some of the most rare and unusual species including *A. magnificus*, *A. speciosus*, *A. tricolour* and *A. siphananthus*. Of the 25 types in Sabah, ten inhabit Mount Kinabalu.

MARINE ECOSYSTEMS Coral reefs and seagrass beds are the two most important marine ecosystems in Borneo. The latter are important grazing grounds for dugongs (sea cows) and sea turtles, and provide vital nurseries for many species of fish. Coral reefs are equally vibrant ecosystems. Indeed, much of Sabah's east coast and surrounding islands touch on an area dubbed the 'Coral Triangle', which encompasses the Sulu and Sulawesi seas. Over 1,800 species of fish have been recorded here, including 400 species of algae, five of the world's eight species of sea turtle, 22 marine mammal species and over 450 types of coral.

However, the reefs also face several challenges: the large rivers of Sarawak deposit sediment around the coast hindering coral formation and many of Sabah's reefs have been damaged by the practice of dynamite fishing – using explosives to surface dead fish *en masse* – as well as coral bleaching, sedimentation, coastal development and overfishing. Serious conservation issues face the border-crossing area shared by Malaysia, the Philippines and Indonesia. Soaring populations and subsequent urban waste and pressure on resources, poaching and fishing piracy are all stressing the fragile ecosystem.

Malaysian grassroots organisations and international NGOs are engaging enormous efforts to work with local communities and help them protect the seas around Borneo. WWF Malaysia has several conservation programmes in the region, and many efforts are under way to expand the protected marine zones. The Marine Conservation Society has been working with Sabah Parks on the Semporna Islands project since 1988 to protect the marine biodiversity of the area and ensure a better future for the people who depend on its islands and reefs. The first milestone was the establishment in 2004 of the Semporna Islands Park (also known as the Tun Sakaran Marine Park) – Malaysia's largest marine park. Situated off the southeast coast of Sabah, it covers 340km² of sea and coral reefs, 10km² of land and eight islands. Since 2005, the UK-based Darwin Initiative, which helps countries safeguard their biodiversity by funding collaborative projects, has been backing conservation strategies in the park. Current activities are focused on raising awareness of marine biodiversity as well as working with local communities to promote alternative livelihoods that will alleviate pressure on reef resources.

MAMMALS Logging activities have shrunk Bornean forests, and the habitat of an estimated 222 mammal species, to half their original size. Displaced animals include elephants, rhinos and wildcats, and 44 endemic mammals, from iconic species such as the orangutan and proboscis monkey to lesser-known wonders including banded langurs, tree-climbing sun bears, giant squirrels and the Borneo clouded leopard. Smaller mammals include otters (hairy-nosed, oriental and small-clawed), porcupines, tree shrews, rats, bats and scaly pangolins. Nocturnal creatures include the 'flying lemur' or *colugo* (see box, page 56), bearded pig, the sambar deer and the world's smallest hoofed mammal – the lesser mouse deer.

The total mammal count rises sporadically with exciting new discoveries and 'mystery mammals' that baffle scientists. However, the depletion of Borneo's forests does not bode well for the survival of its mammals, especially endangered species like the Sumatran rhinoceros and pygmy elephant, which are rarely sighted.

Primates Some of the world's most interesting primate species are found on Borneo, and are relatively easy to see in the island's 'open' forests. Primates are characterised by their grasping hands with fingers rather than paws, fingernails over claws, and eyes on the front of the face enabling stereoscopic colour vision.

Borneo is home to two types of ape – orangutans and gibbons. Eight Old-World monkeys (family: Cercopithecidae) including macaques, langurs (leaf monkeys) and the peculiar proboscis monkey live here. The slow loris and extraordinary tarsier – a primate so strange that taxonomists still disagree on its classification – belong to the prosimian (a sub-order that most closely represents ancestral primates). Lorises and tarsiers are strictly nocturnal, while Borneo's monkeys and apes are active mostly during the day.

Apes

Orangutans (*Pongo pygmaeus*) With its innate magnetism and undeniable appeal, the 'man of the forest' – from the Malay *orang* for 'person' and *hutan* for 'forest' – has become a mascot of Borneo, which is home to 90% of the world's orangutans. The remaining 10% of the 'real ape' population exists in the tropical forests of neighbouring Sumatra. Asia's only great ape is actually of African origin, probably dispersed to Asia during the Miocene period.

Orangutans spend more time in trees than any great ape. Males reach up to 100kg, making them the largest arboreal animal on the planet. They sometimes descend to the forest floor to traverse gaps in the trees, moving on all fours. Owing to their large size, they use a form of locomotion known as quadrumanual climbing, rather than the brachiating technique used by many other primates (see page 49). This involves clambering through the trees grasping firmly with both hands and feet. They are surprisingly agile considering their size, aided by extremely long arms, which reach up to 2m in males. Neither swingers nor jumpers, 'orangs' rock branches back and forth until they reach the other side.

Females may be up to 50% smaller than males; sexual dimorphism is so extreme it led early European explorers to believe they were an entirely different species. Dominant males grow huge pads on their cheeks, and exhibit their superior rank by 'long calling' – a booming grunt that can be heard up to 2km away and may be accompanied by violent branch shaking. Unlike other apes, orangutans are largely solitary, spending much of their time travelling alone looking for food. Mothers are accompanied by their offspring until they become independent at around eight to ten

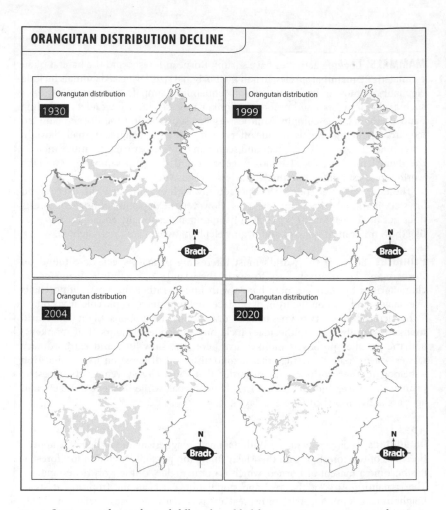

ORANGUTAN DISTRIBUTION DECLINE

Orangutan distribution
1930

Orangutan distribution
1999

Orangutan distribution
2004

Orangutan distribution
2020

years. Orangutans have a long childhood, suckled for up to six years. During this time, they keep a close watch on their mother, learning which foods are good to eat and how to process them. Wild orangutans enjoy a long life, some living up to 70 years.

Orangutans eat a diet of 100% fruit when available, though usually this constitutes 60% of their dietary intake. They move around the forest based on the availability of fruits, building a mental map to remember where and when trees are fruiting. Leaves, fungi, eggs, honey termites and small vertebrates supplement their diet. Great fans of figs, orangutans will stay in a laden tree for days on end, gorging themselves on the sweet fruits. They are the only species other than elephants that can crack open the sugar-rich durian fruit. As such, they are important dispersers of seeds through the forest.

Orangutans are mostly active during the day. Every evening, they construct a sophisticated nest high in the trees, weaving thin branches together to make a flat sleeping platform complete with a 'roof' for shelter. As well as being Borneo's most beloved creature, orangutans are an 'indicator species' – barometers of the well-being of the forest. Declining orangutan populations are a sign that the forest and all that live within it are in trouble.

WHY ARE ORANGUTANS ORANGE?

The long, shaggy, bright-orange body hair of the orangutan is immediately striking and unmistakable. Individual variation is great and may change with age, from bright orange in infants, to auburn and deep burgundy in adults. Why is the 'red ape' so vividly coloured?

Some say their distinctive colouring serves to announce their presence to other orangutans. On the other hand – while the fiery hues blaze in the sunlight, they virtually disappear in the shadows of the forest canopy. The dark skin underneath absorbs the light, obscuring the ape into an apparent blackness. This 'trick of the light' helps orangutans blend into their scenery, camouflaged from enemies but still visible to other members of the species.

Orangutan conservation The orangutan is a 'totally protected species' across Borneo – in Sabah, Sarawak and Kalimantan. That, however, has not put an end to the extreme dangers to the species' survival, with current numbers of orangutans living in the wild estimated at between 20,000 and 30,000 – less than a third of the population in the early 1990s, and down from 55,000 in 2005. In other words, the numbers have been rapidly declining, and continue to, even with the laws long in place.

In Sabah, the orangutan has been legally protected since 1958. The 1997 Sabah Wildlife Conservation Act imposes fines of up to RM100,000 and five years in prison for the illegal killing or rearing of orangutans. However, a huge problem remains, as these laws apply only to national parks and reserves. The majority of the surviving population in Sabah – estimated at around 11,000 – live outside of protected areas. As the *Orangutan Action Plan 2012–2016* by the Sabah Wildlife Department observes:

> A staggering 65% of the wild orangutans are surviving in non-protected forests that are prone to human exploitation. The vast majority of these animals are actually concentrated in forests managed for timber production by the Sabah Forestry Department and the Sabah Foundation... In Sabah, orangutan distribution and abundance decline are directly attributed to recent and drastic habitat losses mainly due to the conversion of large expanses of orangutan habitat (lowland mixed dipterocarp forests) to oil palm plantations and other crops. Other immediate threats include habitat degradation due to unsustainable and/or illegal logging practices, various forms of encroachments with protected forests, fires and poaching/killing (for bush meat, medicinal purposes and/or as a means of crop protection).

The WWF agrees: 'Only two Wildlife Reserves are reckoned to support viable orangutan populations and WWF surveys estimated that the majority of Sabah orangutans live outside protected forest areas, in land that is prone to exploitation.'

At current rates, the orangutan stands to become the first great ape of modern times, bullied, abused and pushed into extinction.

The fragmented nature of many small populations due to forestry and fires sounds their death knell. Overall, around 80% of orangutan habitat in Borneo has been radically degraded or destroyed – and orangutans without rainforest are like fish without a sea.

Their dependence on trees for food and shelter, slow breeding rate and need for large amounts of space, make orangutans extremely vulnerable to hunting and habitat loss. Females may not breed before they are 17, and with an inter-birth

Orangutans tug at the universal heartstrings for the plight they have endured. Adorable yet endangered, today they are famous as an international mascot for Malaysian tourism, but it hasn't always been that way. Nineteenth-century explorers and scientists depicted them as useless, dirty and dumb, write Gisela Kaplan and Lesely J Rogers in *The Orang-utans* (Allen and Unwin, Australia 1999).

Stories were told of orangutan males who abducted fragile English ladies and raped them in trees. The orangutan was too large and strong to be a pet and of limited use as a domestic helper. Their entertainment value when compared with the chimpanzee was poor; likewise for medical research. Capping off the long list of indictments, the orangutan was difficult to observe, boring to watch because of its 'sluggish' behaviour, and impossible to keep confined.

Based on their experiences with orangutans in Sabah, the authors saw just how far from dumb these animals were, particularly in the extent to which they are adapted to their rainforest environment.

The shrinking of that habitat seems all the more cruel when we understand how resourceful and flexible orangutans are. Just like humans, they are master generalists, performing well in everything they do. They are perhaps the fastest of the great apes in problem-solving, have excellent memories, and are superb imitators. They are also highly skilled trapeze artists – the largest mammal in the jungle canopy, negotiating this habitat requires developed cognitive abilities.

Orangutans are accomplished and innovative tool users, using leaves as hats or umbrellas when it rains, or as gloves to climb spiky-trunked trees. Sumatran orangutans craft termite-capturing 'fishing rods' from twigs, poking them into termite nests to collect the insects, just like chimpanzees. This intelligence goes beyond the confines of life in the rainforest. Orangutans fall within a cognitive circle once thought to include only humans: they can make fires, learn to play a guitar, wash clothes, use tools and imitate whatever humans do, simply by observing rather than being taught. 'In some areas a five-year-old orangutan may perform at about the same level as a four-year-old human child.' They are in fact 97% genetically similar to us, sharing a common ancestor 10–12 million years ago.

Orangutans are gentle, intelligent, complex and contemplative, often sitting for hours just gazing. As Willie Smits told *The Age* newspaper in 2004, 'The world would be a better place if humans were a bit more like orangutans.'

period of eight to nine years – the longest of any mammal – populations struggle to recover from losses.

Decades after the first orangutan rehabilitation centre opened in Sarawak in 1961 by pioneering conservationist Barbara Harrison, this incredible creature is still in dire straits.

The 1990s saw numerous campaigns and documentaries, bringing the orangutan into the spotlight as they captured the hearts of the world. Reports of cruelty and illegal transportation of orangutan babies made international headlines. One famous case was that of the 'Bangkok Six' in 1990, when six orangutans were transported from Borneo to Bangkok in wooden crates (one of which was upside down for the whole trip), without food and water. Photos of the frightened exhausted babies shocked and saddened readers worldwide. Though things ostensibly have greatly improved since, there is often cause to think not. In 2007, I opened a local newspaper in Sabah to read headlines of attempted smuggling of dozens of orangutans, including babies. They were found packed into a cage ready to be taken to the Netherlands for scientific tests, excreting on each other and even cannibalising each other. The sheer callousness was simply heartbreaking.

Illegal logging, conversion of the forest to plantations and the illegal pet trade are the main continuing threats. In some previously densely forested regions of Sabah and Sarawak given over to large plantations, the orangutan is considered a pest, and one that must be disposed of to save crops. The fact that hunting orangutans is illegal has not eliminated the practice. Human corruption and cruelty in these as other instances, does not recognise laws any more than it does moral values.

What can be done to help? At a political level, increasing foreign investment will allow Malaysia and Indonesia to rely less on their raw natural resources and manage them more efficiently. Introducing certification of ethically sourced (sustainable) palm oil and mandatory labelling of products on supermarket shelves, will allow consumers to avoid palm oil produced from unsustainable sources. The Indonesian and Malaysian governments need to ensure that laws are fully enforced, and that all forests on which orangutans depend – reserves or otherwise – are protected. On a personal people-power level, take positive action and stop buying products that are made with non-sustainably and unethically sourced palm oil (for your health and that of orangutans rule out palm oil food products all together). In 2014, Safeway became the latest US company to snub orangutan-killing and deforestation causing palm oil. 'It's time to peel back the label. … Look out for the often hidden ingredient, guised along with its derivatives on food labels,' urges the WWF, as: Vegetable Oil, Vegetable Fat, Palm Kernel, Palm Kernel Oil, Palm Fruit Oil, Palmate, Palmitate, Palmolein, Glyceryl, Stearate, Stearic Acid, Elaeis Guineensis, Palmitic Acid, Palm Stearine, Palmitoyl Oxostearamide, Palmitoyl Tetrapeptide-3, Sodium Laureth Sulfate, Sodium Lauryl Sulfate, Sodium Kernelate, Sodium Palm Kernelate, Sodium Lauryl Lactylate/ Sulphate, Hyrated Palm Glycerides, Etyl Palmitate, Octyl Palmitate, Palmityl Alcohol. 'As the most widely consumed vegetable oil on the planet, it is estimated that palm oil is in about half of all packaged products sold in the supermarket', says the WWF. Cookies, margarine, ice cream, packaged bread, pizza dough, shampoo, lipstick and detergent are high among them. You don't have to give up the goods if you don't want to – most are also produced in a sustainable way. Also look out for the labels RSPO and Green Palm for safe sustainable palm oil-based goods. For more details, visit www.worldwildlife.org/pages/which-everyday-products-contain-palm-oil.

Gibbons Gibbons are the smallest of the ape family – indeed they are often referred to as 'lesser apes' – and Borneo is home to two species: the **Bornean** or **Mueller's gibbon** (*Hylobates muelleri*), whose distribution extends throughout much of the island, and the **agile gibbon** (*Hylobates agilis*), found only in Indonesian Borneo. Both species inhabit dipterocarp forests, swinging with admirable ease through the high canopy using a form of locomotion known as 'brachiation'. This involves the gibbon hooking its long fingers over a branch and using a hand-over-hand, under-branch motion to effortlessly and gracefully swing through the trees at high speed like arboreal acrobats.

Gibbons live in family units consisting of two monogamous adults and two to three offspring. These pairs were thought to be faithful until studies revealed that mating with neighbours was common during inter-group encounters and some pairs will allow an extra adult to join them for short periods! Pairs do still mate for life though, and sing powerful duets at dawn to both strengthen the bond between them and announce their presence to the neighbours. The whooping song of the gibbon is one of the most evocative sounds of the forest, heard up to 2km away.

Old-World monkeys These fall into two distinct groups or sub-families: the generalist Cercopithecinae, and specialist Colobinae. Cercopithecinae, or 'cheek-pouch monkeys', have evolved pockets in their mouths which they fill with food before retiring to a safer place to eat. They also have 'ischial callosities': fleshy pads on their rear ends, which act as built-in cushions. The only Cercopithecines outside of Africa are the macaques, of which Borneo is home to two species. In contrast, the Colobinae are selective in what they eat, choosing only leaves. These are digested in bacteria-inhabited sacculated stomachs, which process the toxins found in the leaves. Borneo's five langur species (also known as 'leaf monkeys') and the bizarre proboscis monkey are all members of the Colobinae.

Langurs Langurs, or leaf monkeys, are nimble primate lightweights at just 5–7kg in weight and 200–600cm in length. 'Langur' means 'long tail', and they certainly live up to their name – their tails often exceed their bodies. Langurs are a diverse group found across Asia, and Borneo is home to five species.

The most widespread is the **maroon langur** (*Presbytis rubicunda*). Also known as the red langur, its fur is actually a fiery orange, and they have a ghostly blue-tinged face. Maroon langurs inhabit lowland rainforest in Sabah and Sarawak, and hill and mountain forests such as the Kelabit Highlands. **Hose's langurs** (*Presbytis hosei*) are found in the northwest of the island, and have a grey upper and cream lower body, with black hands and feet. Their pale-pink faces sport distinct black bands across the cheeks with a prominent black crest on top of the head. Hose's langurs (also known as grey langurs) live in the canopy of lowland and hill forests. Found exclusively in Sarawak, the inky **banded langur** (*Presbytis melalophos*) is so called for its distinctive black cheek bands. Colouring varies between black and white, black, red and white, and (in the case of the *Presbytis melalophos cruciger* – one of several recently identified types), burgundy with black markings. Adult males make a distinctive, loud '*ke-ke-ke*' call. Banded langurs live in lowland and hill forest including those in the Tanjung Datu and Maludam national parks. The **silvered langur** (*Presbytis cristata*) bears a physical resemblance to the banded variety, but lacks the bands on its face – instead it is entirely charcoal-coloured. The extremely rare **Miller's grizzled langur** is found only in some forests of East Kalimantan.

Macaques Macaques are one of the most successful primate genera, with a wider geographical range than any other primate except *Homo*. Unlike most other monkeys, they spend a lot of time on the forest floor and lower canopy levels, feeding on a variety of foods from fruit, leaves and seeds to insects, eggs, lizards and other small invertebrates. Borneo's **pig-tailed macaques** (*Macaca nemestrina)* have a short tail, carried half-erect, and resembling that of a pig – hence the name. They are mostly olive-brown in colour, with whitish underparts and brunette patches on the head and neck. Males reach up to 9kg, measure 500cm and can be quite intimidating with their stocky stature and bold nature.

Long-tailed macaques (*Macaca fascicularis*) are varying shades of grey and reddish-grey with fairer hair underneath. Many have prominent cheek whiskers

THE PROBOSCIS MONKEY

The proboscis monkey (*Nasalis larvatus*) lives only on Borneo and a few small islands close to its shores. Its most distinguishing feature is its nose: huge and fleshy in males, upturned and pixie-like in females. The male's pendulous nasal feature grows continuously, in a Pinocchio-like manner, and may reach a quarter of his body length! The function of this strange facial appendage is uncertain, though it is thought to act as both an 'organ of resonance', amplifying the male's strange '*kee-honk*' vocalisation, and a thermoregulatory device. Females also seem to prefer males with larger noses.

Together with their potbelly and swaggering gait, the large nose led locals to nickname them *kera belanda* ('Dutch monkeys') – a rather unkind reference to the Dutch plantation owners of colonial times. Their bloated belly contains bacteria used to digest toxin-containing leaves. Their appearance when at rest – the spindly legs dangling beneath corpulent bodies – was once likened to someone wearing 'a bomber jacket over ballet tights'.

Proboscis monkeys live near the waterways and coasts of Borneo, in mangrove, nipah, peat swamp and riverine forests. They can be seen catapulting themselves across expanses of water by swaying branches back and forth to gain momentum – or when a gap is too large, diving into the water and swimming across in single file. With partially webbed feet, they are accomplished swimmers. On land, they sometimes walk bipedally, swaggering and swaying from side to side on their hind legs.

Proboscis monkeys are threatened by habitat loss and fragmentation – they cannot cross plantations, thus isolating threadbare populations.

Some of the best places to observe them include Brunei's mangrove forests and riverbanks, Sarawak's Bako and Kuching Wetlands national parks, and Sabah's Kinabatangan River and Klias Wetlands. Proboscis monkeys now rival orangutans as the most popular primates to see in Borneo – and it seems their striking appearance may help to save them from extinction. If they continue to draw in economy-boosting tourists at such a rate, they may prove to be a viable alternative to cash crops.

and facial hair. Travelling in large troops of 20–30, they cover up to 1.5km between dawn and dusk and can be very noisy.

Both of Borneo's macaque species live in lowland rainforest and hill forest as high as 1,300m; the long-tailed macaque is also found on coastal wetlands, small islands, mangroves and beach forest. Macaques happily raid plantations and tourist lodges, so beware! I have had my fair share of run-ins, including one in the forest while pointing a camera lens too close at a pig-tailed macaque – not advisable. In my experience, the pig-tailed variety is far more menacing, the long-tailed simply mischievous.

Prosimians These are the forerunners of the monkeys and apes, 'prosimian' literally meaning 'before monkeys'. Of the two sub-orders of primates, prosimians make up the Strepshirhini, or wet-nosed primates. Primates within this sub-order, which include the lemurs of Madagascar, bushbabies of Africa and lorises of Asia, rely more heavily on olfactory (smell) communication and possess several anatomical differences from more visually oriented Haplorhini primates such as monkeys, apes and humans.

Slow lorises (*Nycticebus menagensis*) In contrast to the other fast-moving agile primates of Borneo, the nocturnal slow loris takes things at a much easier pace, creeping and clambering through the forests at night with slow, deliberate movements. Lorises can cling to branches for hours on end with their powerful grip, and communicate through the forest using olfactory and auditory – including ultrasonic – communication. Grey-brown to reddish brown in colour, with a dark strip down the spine towards the base of the short tail, lorises are among the least-studied of all primates. Their diet consists of slow-moving, often toxic, invertebrates. Lorises produce toxic secretions themselves, exuded from their underarms, which they lick to numb prey when biting into them. These prosimians can reach up to 28cm in length and weigh around 2kg. Protected under Sabah's 1963 Fauna Conservation Ordinance, they too are threatened with habitat destruction and hunting.

Western tarsiers (*Tarsius bancanus*) Named after their extended tarsus leg bone, Tarsiers are something of a bone of contention in primate taxonomy. Scientists cannot agree on which of the two primate sub-orders they belong to, with compelling evidence for their inclusion in both. The bizarre-looking nocturnal primate could easily line up as an extra for *The Lord of the Rings*. Its extraordinarily large buggy eyes outstrip those of any mammal in relation to body size, with each eyeball weighing more than its brain! Their long, powerful hind legs fold thrice into a zigzag at rest, but spring into action as the diminutive creature makes spectacular leaps up to 40 times its body length between trees. Tarsiers live in lowland rainforests across Borneo but are rarely seen. Occasionally they are spotted with torches on night-time wildlife excursions, but their low-reflective eyes help them to remain elusive. More often, they are heard, making distinctive high-pitched shrieks. Tarsiers are among the smallest primates in the world, 70–150cm in length and around 1kg in weight. Their carnivorous diet consists of large insects and lizards, even bats and birds. The best place to see them is Sabah's Danum Valley.

Large mammals

Borneo pygmy elephants Despite being known as a 'pygmy' species, the Borneo pygmy elephant is among the largest land mammals in Asia, with males reaching over 2m in height. They are nonetheless much smaller than their mainland Asian counterparts, which can stand at over 3m tall, while their African cousins are even larger. Their compactness gives them an endearing charisma, while their tolerant nature allows onlookers to get up quite close. The herbivorous pachyderms are an important part of the ecosystem, trimming vegetation and dispersing seeds throughout the forests. They are also lovers of durian, swallowing the fruits whole – spikes and all.

Genetic and archaeological evidence may have solved the riddle of the Borneo pygmy elephant's origins. Thought for many years to have been introduced from mainland Southeast Asia or Sumatra, the species has emerged as genetically diverse from other Southeast Asian elephants, strengthening the case for their protection as a distinct species. Since the 2003 studies (see box, page 54), some scientists have referred to them 'as an endemic species – *Elephas maximus borneensis* – yet more recent research claims there is no archaeological evidence of long-term elephant presence on Borneo. So where *did* they come from? The 'Borneo' pygmy elephant may well be the Javan elephant in disguise! That is, remnants of a sub-species long extinct on its native island of Java. The last Javan elephants supposedly disappeared shortly after the arrival of Europeans in Southeast Asia. The 1,500 or so remaining Bornean elephants are possibly descendants of two individuals introduced to

Borneo 300 years ago as a gift from the Sultan of Sulu (present-day Philippines). Their scarcity and rarity make it even more crucial to protect them from the habitat destruction, poaching and persecution that threaten them today.

Many of their traditional migratory routes have been converted to plantations, bringing them into conflict with humans when they continue to travel through them. Elephants can cause considerable damage traversing and foraging in farmers' crops. Yet the land traditionally belongs to them! Robbing them of it is no less a crime – an injustice and a perversion – than taking traditional tribal lands from indigenous tribes. Their footprint is limited to relatively small areas of lowland rainforest in eastern and central Sabah (Danum Valley and surrounding areas), spilling into Kalimantan. This range is forever being gobbled up by plantations, spreading like wildfire through once-densely forested lands. Whether purely Bornean, or partly Javanese, the most astounding thing about the elephant is their lack of protection. Despite being a clearly wondrous, special and endangered creature on a planet increasingly deprived of such wonders, they benefit from no official protection in Sabah. For a place that is increasingly living off its nature tourism dollar, that is both an economic and conservation travesty. The fallout of that was driven home in 2013, when 14 elephants were found dead, poisoned, in the Gunung Rara Forest Reserve, close to oil palm plantations.

Sumatran (Asian two-horned) rhinoceros (*Dicerorhinus sumatrensis*) The Sumatran rhinoceros is the smallest of the five extant species of rhino today – about 2.5m long, just over 1m tall and weighing around 800kg. Also known as the Asian two-horned or hairy rhinoceros, this is a tropical forest ungulate (hoofed, grazing animal), classified along with horses, zebras and tapirs as 'perissodactyls' – odd-toed ungulates – as they have three toes.

One of two sub-species (*Dicerorhinus sumatrensis harrissoni*) is found on Borneo; the other (*Dicerorhinus sumatrensis sumatrensis*) is native to Sumatra and Peninsular Malaysia. The patches of stiff, dark hair on their reddish-brown hide helps keep mud caked to the body, to cool the animal, and protect it from insects. Regular mud wallowing keeps the protective layer intact. Despite their thick skin, Sumatran rhinos are teetering on the edge of extinction after years of heavy poaching and habitat destruction.

'Rhinoceros' means '*nose-horn*', and the animals have been hunted for decades for their keratin-rich horns, which are used in Asian medicine. 'The creation of forestry access roads deep into the forest home of the rhino led to an influx of poachers who target rhinos, especially in the Tabin Wildlife Reserve and several areas adjacent to the Danum Valley Forest Reserve,' says the WWF. These are the areas where conservation efforts are being focused.

The Sumatran rhino is classified as 'critically endangered' on the IUCN Red List, though the WWF worryingly claim it to be 'possibly extinct' in Sarawak and Kalimantan, with 'fewer than 25 surviving in Sabah' (the IUCN on the other hand believe there could be up to 50). Once widespread throughout Borneo, numbers have plummeted in recent times, dropping by at least half in the last 18 years. The palm oil industry has joined the old threats of poaching and deforestation, as forests increasingly cede to plantations (see box, page 224).

Bornean clouded leopard (*Neofelis nebulosa diardi*) In 2007, Borneo's largest predator was recognised as a unique sub-species. Based on DNA research, scientists at the US National Cancer Institute concluded that the 1m-long wildcat – one of Asia's largest – differed from mainland species it was previously lumped with, to a similar

The WWF considers the three Asian rhino species as 'flagships' – 'charismatic representatives of the biodiversity of the complex ecosystems they inhabit'. By protecting them and their habitat, many other species benefit. WWF teams have been working on rhino conservation for decades. In 1998, WWF created the Asian Rhino and Elephant Action Strategy (AREAS), aimed at not only protecting specific areas but also reviewing land-use practices, strengthening anti-poaching efforts, monitoring trade of rhino horns and raising public awareness. The Sumatran rhino – *badak sumatra* in Malay – is a protected species within Sabah's national parks and reserves. According to the WWF, only two areas in Sabah – Tabin and Ulu Segama-Kuamut – contain rhino populations with prospects of long-term survival, 'if adequate protection and management is allowed'.

Amid serious forest loss, the Sabah government moved to protect the Tabin rhino population in 1984, with the establishment of the $1,225km^2$ Tabin Wildlife Reserve.

The rhinoceros of Ulu Segama-Kuamut District, says the WWF, are scattered through a vast zone of several contiguous forest reserves, 'probably centred on an area of less than $4,000km^2$ in the catchment areas of the Upper Segama and Upper Kuamut rivers'. The latter takes in the Danum Valley and Maliau Basin Conservation areas in the Sabah Foundation's 100-year logging concession.

In 2003, WWF and Columbia University researchers proved that Borneo's elephants are genetically distinct from other Asian elephants (see pages 52–3). Together with Sabah's Wildlife Department, surveys have been carried out on elephant populations, tracking them with satellite radio collars. Despite being endangered, they are not a protected species in Sabah and are extremely vulnerable to being hunted, shot at or electrocuted for 'trespassing' on oil palm plantations. The WWF calls them 'the least-understood elephants in the world'. What is sure is that they rely on having large open areas to live in – but their habitat is increasingly shrinking.

extent as other large cat species such as leopards and snow leopards. The species diverged around 1.4 million years ago, around the time Borneo separated from the mainland.

Separate studies of fur patterns also provided a key. Mainland leopards have large cloud-like markings on their skin – swirls of black around big tawny patches – whereas their Bornean cousins are the inverse: thin tawny cloud-linings, around many more speckled dark clouds and with much more black overall. The clouded spots provide effective camouflage, allowing the leopard to hide from its prey in the forest, pouncing on unsuspecting deer, wild pigs and monkeys. Their presence is an indication of forest health – the fact that they are rarely sighted today shows not only the effects of habitat loss and overhunting on their populations, but also how degraded the forests themselves have become.

Civets Of the several kinds of cat-like civets, the largely tree-dwelling and nocturnal binturong (*Arctictis binturong*) is perhaps the most fascinating – known as the 'bear-cat' because its stocky, dark-furred body gives it a bear-like appearance. Other civets include the masked palm civet (*Paguma larvata*) and common palm civet (*Paradoxurus hermaphroditus*), Malay civet (*Viverra tangalunga*) and Sunda otter-civet (*Cynogale bennettii*).

The clouded leopard, or *harimau dahan* in Malay, is a 'totally protected species' in Sarawak and in Sabah's parks and reserves. Listed as endangered by CITES and vulnerable by the IUCN, the WWF maintains an extensive leopard conservation operation, and puts Borneo's clouded leopard population somewhere between 5,000 and 11,000 individuals. Their 'last great forest home' is the Heart of Borneo area of Sabah and Kalimantan.

Extensive conservation and research work on this species is being carried out by the American Clouded Leopard Project, which provides this insight on the leopard's behaviour:

Clouded leopards are one of the best climbers in the cat family. They are able to climb upside down underneath tree branches and hang from branches with their hind feet. Several adaptations allow the leopards to achieve these amazing arboreal skills: their legs are short and stout, providing excellent leverage and a low centre of gravity while climbing; large paws with sharp claws allow them to gain a good grip on tree branches; and the tail is extremely long – up to three feet, the same length as its body – and is extremely important as a balancing aid.

Sun bear (*Helarctos malayanus*) Averaging 1m in length, the sun bear, or honey bear as it is also known, is the world's smallest bear species. Endemic to Borneo, the sun bear is largely arboreal and primarily nocturnal, feeding on insects in the rainforests at night. As their pet name suggests, they also have a taste for honey, using their long, sharp claws to reach beehives at the top of tall trees. Their dark fur makes them difficult to spot in the dark, though the V-shaped patch of lighter fur on its chest is a giveaway. The bear's intimidating 'bark' and hoarse grunts drive off potential threats – including many curious tourists! Sarawak Forestry classifies the sun bear along with the pygmy elephant, as one of the few potentially dangerous animals on the island, because of the 'unpredictability of its behaviour'. Listed by the IUCN as endangered, the *beurang*, as it is known in Malay, is threatened by habitat loss, and poaching for meat and medicinal purposes.

Giant squirrel (*Ratufa affinis*) This dark-furred squirrel, with a white underbelly and luxurious brush tail, is one of the world's largest tree-dwelling rodents, growing up to 50cm in length to the tip of the tail, and weighing up to 1.5kg. It feeds on leaves, shoots, birds' eggs, bark and insects during the day when it is most active and can make leaps of up to 6m between trees. Fiercely territorial, it defends its home patch with raspy chattering sounds.

Bearded pig (*Sus barbatus*) Much like a wild boar but with far more facial hair, this cumbersome creature can be rather formidable in appearance but is actually quite shy by nature. Their long, oversized heads are covered with a coarse beard of bristles all the way along the lower jaw, made even more ungainly by upward-pointing incisors that protrude from either side. Though they are primarily nocturnal, I have sighted them during the day lolling around the muddy environs of Bako National Park in Sarawak, foraging for earthworms, fallen fruits and seeds. The bearded pig's thick skin and lightly fuzzy coat colouration varies from grey to reddish brown, depending on how much wallowing it has been doing. The females make large nests on higher flood-free ground, out of piles of torn-off shrubs, saplings and plants.

THE FLYING LEMUR

'Flying lemur' is a double misnomer, for it is neither a lemur nor does it truly fly. Unlike true lemurs, the flying lemur is not a primate, though recent research suggests it may be the primate's closest living relative. Previous studies indicated it was more closely related to the Scandentia group, which includes tree shrews.

Flying lemurs (also known locally as *colugos* or *kubungs*) belong to the Dermoptera group. 'Dermoptera' literally means 'skin wings' and refers to the patagium, a flap of skin between its limbs and tail, which is used to glide – rather than fly – between the trees. The strange squirrel-like animal can reach distances of up to 70m using its 'wings', though is much less adept at climbing trees. During the daytime, *colugos* hang upside down much like bats, or cling to tree trunks. They come out at dusk and feed through the night on leaves, flowers and sap, scraping the latter from tree trunks with a 'comb' formed by the fusion of lower teeth.

BIRDS Borneo's forests are alive with birdsong. Of the island's 620 listed birds, 420 breed there and 51 are endemic. The rest exist throughout the Malay Archipelago. Bornean endemics range from eagles, falcons, pheasants and partridges through to much smaller wren-babblers, flycatchers, flowerpeckers and thrushes. Two-thirds of Borneo's endemic birds live only in montane areas, making Sabah in particular a birdwatcher's paradise.

The wonderfully named chestnut-crested yuhina, chestnut-hooded laughing thrush, Bornean treepie and Bornean whistler all occur above 1,000m, and are must-sees for ardent birdwatchers. 'Other mountain endemics are the Bornean stubtail, the Everett's thrush, the friendly bush warbler, the mountain blackeye, the eye-browed jungle-flycatcher, the Whitehead's trogon, the broadbill and the spiderhunter,' says Bornean bird specialist and guide C K Leong. 'Some lowland endemics of particular interest are the Bornean-banded pitta, the white-crowned shama, the white-fronted falconet, the yellow-rumped flowerpecker, the black and crimson pitta, the blue-banded pitta and the Bornean bristlehead (the only species in its family).'

Bulwer's pheasant (*Lophura bulweri*) The male Bulwer's pheasant is 'spectacularly handsome, with splendid blue facial wattles and a long, spreading, curved white tail,' says the Sarawak National Parks Office. Bulwer's pheasant is found only in the tropical hill forests of central and northern Borneo, where it nests and forages on the ground and roosts in trees. It is a poor flier but a fast and nimble runner, using a combination of darting runs and flurried bursts of flight to avoid predators. During the mating season, the male produces a shrill, piercing cry and performs a tail-spreading, wattle-raising dance for females. Though widespread in central Borneo, it has a low population density and is threatened by illegal hunting and habitat loss.

Hornbills Sarawak's list of 'totally protected species' contains 26 birds, including various egrets, eagles, pigeons and terns. The most coveted by far, however, are the hornbills, named for the large horn-like casques crowning their colourful beaks. There are eight species of hornbill, all of them protected and all with delightful names, from white-crowned, bushy-crested, wreathed, wrinkled and oriental pied varieties, to the two largest kinds, the helmeted hornbill (*Buceros vigil*) and rhinoceros hornbill (*B. rhinoceros*).

Though not endemic to Borneo, the rhinoceros hornbill is the symbol of Sarawak. The Iban people believe *kenyalang* are messengers from the spirit world. Their huge wings, which have a span of over 1m, make a distinctive whooshing sound as they fly past. Like most hornbills, the female builds her nest in the cavities of large trees and seals up the hole with mud, leaving just enough room for the male to pass fruit through as she broods. When the young hatch, the female leaves the nest and feeds the offspring through the hole, assisted by her partner. The hornbill is dependent on large trees for nesting places, but selective logging practices have limited their options. Sabah's diverse forests support an extraordinarily varied avifauna, and have been a magnet for ornithologists for over a century. A comprehensive reference guide and something of a birding bible is B E Smythies's *The Birds of Borneo* (see page 333). A more up-to-date and manageable field guide is the *Pocket Guide to the Birds of Borneo*, compiled by Charles M Francis (see page 333).

Top birdwatching spots To see the various Asian and Bornean riverine, lowland or montane birds, top birdwatching areas are **Gunung Kinabalu National Park** (see pages 203–11), **Danum Valley** (see pages 254–5) and the **Kinabatangan River** area (see pages 235–7). The 200 species in the Kinabatangan floodplain include all eight species of hornbills.

AMPHIBIANS AND REPTILES There are some 150 known endemic frog and reptile species across Borneo, with regular new discoveries. Prominent reptiles include several rainforest and mangrove snakes, the bizarre-looking monitor lizard (*Varanus salvator*), geckos, giant turtles, painted terrapins, and a couple of crocodiles.

Frogs According to WWF figures, Borneo is home to 150 known frog species. Within the past decade or so, at least seven frogs and a giant river toad have been discovered. *A Field Guide to the Frogs of Borneo* (see page 333) describes such gems as the Bornean horned frog, green paddy frog, jade tree frog, blue-spotted tree frog, greater swamp frog and Mjoberg's dwarf litter frog.

Snakes Of Borneo's 150 snakes, only a few are venomous and one truly lethal. Among several pythons is the reticulated python with its diagonal beadwork-like decoration in black, white and mustard. Other widespread snakes include the king cobra, common cobra and black spitting cobra, the Sarawak water snake and mangrove snakes. At Bako National Park in Sarawak, as well as Temburong National Park in Brunei, Borneo's only venomous dangerous snake is found: the triangular-headed Wagler's pit viper. The striking lime green and yellow creature with grey and cream crossbar markings is known as the temple viper in some other parts of Southeast Asia, as they are thought to bring good luck to Buddhist temples. The snakes can also be spotted by a keen eye in the canopy trees of the Temburong National Park forest in Brunei. It's encouraging to read in *Wildlife Watch in Brunei Darussalam* that a bite from one of these forest bullies seldom leads to death. 'The "pits" or heat-sensitive organs which lie between the eye and the nostril are used to detect prey. This is a venomous species, with powerful haemotoxins, however bites are rarely fatal.' On top of these sit-and-wait killer vipers, there are several other kinds of less dangerous (to humans at least), vipers in Borneo – including the Mock Viper in the Crocker Range National Park. They're almost the spitting image, with the typical viper's flat, triangular head. The big difference is in the bite.

Crocodiles The saltwater crocodiles (*Crocodylus porosus*) which inhabit the coastal swamps and rivers of Sarawak are nicknamed *bujang senang* ('happy bachelor') after one infamous 6m-long individual who went on a killing rampage in the Sungai Batang Lupar River in southeast Sarawak in 1993, before being shot dead. A lot more can be learnt about this bloodthirsty bachelor at **Jong's Crocodile Farm** near Kuching, where his skull is on display in a museum.

Care should be taken when visiting areas where there are crocodiles. To say you would be extremely ill advised to swim in the rivers where they dwell is an understatement. The warning from Sarawak Forestry makes no bones about the dangers: 'Adult crocodiles have a largely fishy diet, though sometimes develop a taste for dead or dying prey. Prey is taken alive and, unless very small, is generally left to rot before being eaten. They tend to be aggressive during mating season or when guarding nesting areas. They are territorial and will attack if you come on to their territory.'

Malayan false gharial crocodile (*Tomistoma schlegelli*) These crocodiles have long, narrow noses tipped by a bulbous form. They are residents of Sarawak's rivers, peat swamps and mangroves, normally nesting by the riverbank. Despite being described by the state as a 'taxonomically unique and harmless crocodilian species', human remains were found in the stomach of a 3m female in the 1990s. Though they feed primarily on fish, it is thought that this particular croc might have enjoyed some of the happy bachelor's leftovers.

Monitor lizards (*Varanus salvator*) Monitor lizards are decidedly antediluvian and reptilian in appearance. They live in all sorts of water habitats – even urban puddles – and can be seen lurking in tropical forests, mangroves, swamps, farmland and towns. Predatory and unfussy, monitor lizards will eat anything: young monkeys, snakes, lizards, birds, crabs, domestic chickens, carrion, human faeces and food waste. One species, the earless monitor lizard known as *cicak purba*, is a particularly bizarre, ancient-looking lizard. If you hear strange noises rising from the drains while walking about town at night, don't panic – the underworld presences in Bornean cities owes more to monitor lizards than the mafia.

FRESHWATER FISH Some of Borneo's most important recent natural discoveries have been freshwater fish, with 30 new kinds identified since the mid 1990s. Among them have been a couple of **catfish** displaying amazing adaptations to their environment. In 2010, the WWF announced news of a 'forest-walking catfish', so called because it can travel short distances over land. They are equally known as 'labyrinth catfish' due to a specialist gill – the 'labyrinth organ' – that allows them to take in oxygen from the air. Another species of catfish secretes poisonous mucus that causes instant death to other fish in the vicinity.

Documented much earlier, Sarawak's 'green arowana' or **dragon fish** (*Scleropages formosus*) is described as a 'living fossil' due to its ancient lineage. Known locally as *kelesa*, the large freshwater fish is found in 'rivers and lakes, preying on smaller fish, insects, worms, spiders, small lizards, small snakes and frogs.

INVERTEBRATES
Insects Lowland tropical rainforest harbours the greatest diversity of insect life on the planet, and the Bornean rainforest teems with insect life. There are over 100,000 species of beetles, hundreds of butterflies, stick and leaf insects, cicadas, cockroaches, dragonflies, termites, ants and mosquitoes. At Gunung Kinabalu

National Park, insects are said to represent 'the bulk of the fauna' with thousands of different species. Like much of Borneo's natural history, insects are understudied, but Sabah Parks has been collaborating with the German Society for Tropical Ecology to increase understanding of the insect world. Gunung Kinabalu National Park has some 300 **butterflies**, concentrated around the lowland rainforest and foothills areas as well as lower montane slopes. Over 50 are endemic to Sabah. The king of butterflies is the stunning Rajah Brooke's birdwing (*Trogonoptera brookiana*), with its cloak of black and jagged frill of metallic emerald-green triangles all along its wings. First catalogued by Alfred Russel Wallace in 1854, while gathering hundreds of insect specimens in Borneo – he named it after Rajah James Brooke who presented him with the specimen. Many butterfly specimens are contained in the 'Borneensis' collection, housed within the University of Malaysia in Sabah.

The website of the ASEAN Review of Biodiversity and Environmental Conservation (ARBEC; *www.arbec.com.my*) provides many good links to important studies and findings in entomology and other areas. One of the available documents is Dr J Holloway's *Moths of Borneo* (*www.mothsofborneo. com*), an 18-volume work cataloguing the larger **moths** of Borneo – currently estimated at some 4,500 species – all with colour illustrations. The Universiti Sarawak Malaysia, the Natural History Museum in London and ARBEC are responsible for publishing the entire tome online.

Crustaceans Lobsters, giant river prawns (*udang*) and crabs... The great variety of freshwater crustaceans in Borneo represent an important food source to the *orang sungai* river-dwelling populations. Mangroves especially have many interesting clawed critters, such as hermit crabs and fiddler crabs, which burrow into the mudflats among the mangroves. Male fiddlers are equipped with one overgrown, vividly coloured claw, which serves to attract females during the mating season and ward off male competitors trespassing on his mudpatch territory. The claw – called a *cheliped* – grows so big it can constitute 65% of his total body weight. The horseshoe crab, known in Sarawak as the *belangkas,* is not actually a crab but a descendant of an extinct marine arthropod lineage, the trilobites.

MARINE LIFE Coral reefs on the west and east coasts, particularly around the east-coast islands, support a huge variety of extravagantly coloured fish: lion fish with their 'mane' of chocolate brown and white frills, giant frogfish, hump head parrotfish, red and white clown fish, mandarin fish, snake eels and garden eels and many kinds of small colourful sand-dwelling gobies. There are also many molluscs, crustaceans and echinoderms including crabs, shrimps, giant clams, squid, blue-ringed octopus, cuttlefish, sea urchins, sea cucumbers and sea horses.

One of the fish to watch out for when diving is the clown triggerfish; it can bite, charge at you or chase you to the top of the water in mating season.

Corals Used as a barometer of marine biodiversity and coral health, the reefs of Sabah and Sarawak are home to hundreds of species of bright-banded and flecked butterfly fish. The corals themselves are kaleidoscopic in colour and variety – fern, stag horn, mushroom, cabbage and brain forms are all common. All hard and soft corals are protected species in Sarawak, but sadly many reefs are suffering from the effects of dynamite fishing.

Sharks There are quite a few sharks in Borneo's waters, though no deadly ones. It is common to see white-tip reef sharks when diving. In mid 2007, the Borneo shark

(*Carcharhinus borneensis*) – a species deemed extinct because there had been no sightings for over a century – was declared 'rediscovered' by Universiti Malaysia Sabah researchers. The shark can reach up to 20m in length and is brown on top with a white underside. The university's Borneo Marine Research Institute warned at the time that sharks could soon be extinct in Sabah because of the overharvesting of fins.

Dolphins All dolphins, porpoises and whales are protected in Sarawak and sightings of the following species are commonplace especially between March and September: the Irrawaddy, bottlenose, Indopacific humpback, finless porpoise and pantropic spotted dolphin.

Sea turtles I have been lucky enough to experience the wonder of swimming among sea turtles – *penyu* – several times in the aquamarine waters off Sabah's east coast. They seem such solid, wise and indestructible creatures, yet several species are seriously menaced by poaching (of both adults and eggs), habitat loss, pollution and accidental catch in fishing nets. Even without these added pressures life as a turtle is tough, owing to low reproduction rates and the slim chances of infant survival. Witnessing the plight of youngsters endeavouring to make their first peril-filled journey to the sea (see *Turtle Islands Marine Park*, pages 229–30) is distressing.

The Turtle Islands in Sabah have the world's largest remaining populations of **hawksbill turtles** (*Eretmochelys imbricata*). The name comes from their narrow pointed beak, reminiscent of a bird of prey, though locals call them *penyu sisik* – 'scaled turtle' – referring to their attractive shells. That shell is the beauty and bane of their existence. Market demand for tortoiseshell jewellery and curios covets the black and brown casing splashed with yellow – ironically intended as armour, it cannot protect them from man, and contributes to their critically endangered status.

Larger **green turtles** (*Chelonia mydas*) are a protected species in Sabah and Sarawak, though Sarawak's population of green turtles has halved since the 1970s. They are nevertheless still one of the most widely seen and the biggest of the marine turtles, reaching over 1m in length. Despite weighing over 150kg they can swim at speeds of 15–20km/h. Their name comes not from their carapace – this is olive or darker grey with swirled motifs – but the colour of their meat. Like all marine turtles, they are a traditional food source for local people.

Whether indigenous people have the right to continue customary practices of eating species now at risk of extinction is a controversial issue. The Suluk and Bajau Laut ('sea gypsies') eat marine algae, sea grass and large fish including barracuda, grouper and red carp of deeper waters. Some also eat dolphins and **dugong**. This tusked 'sea-cow' is a protected species and ocean heavyweight, reaching lengths of over 3m and touching on 600kg.

Ocean dangers This warning is issued to visitors of the Tanjung Datu National Park in western Sarawak, but applies to many other coral reefs around Borneo:

The reefs are home to several venomous creatures, including sea snakes, coral snakes, stonefish and cone shells. Marine snakes are generally harmless if undisturbed. Stonefish may conceal themselves in mud or sand around coral, especially at low tide, so do not walk or swim barefoot around coral reefs. Cone shells are highly venomous and should not be handled under any circumstances.

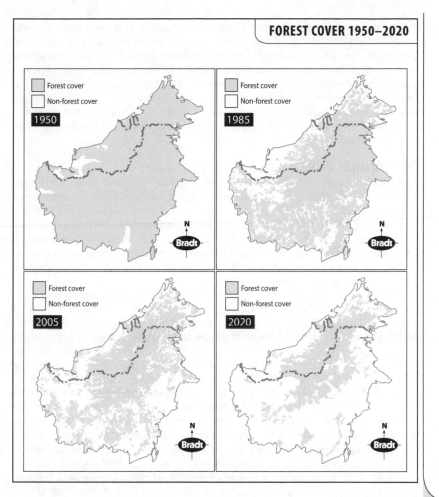

Forest cover
Non-forest cover
1950

Forest cover
Non-forest cover
1985

Forest cover
Non-forest cover
2005

Forest cover
Non-forest cover
2020

DEFORESTATION

Just a few centuries ago, over 90% of Borneo was carpeted in thick, luscious forests. The tendency to subjugate nature arrived with Europeans, developed with capitalism, and was fully unleashed with the dawn of industrial forestry practices. In the mid 1980s, 75% of the island's natural forest cover remained. Today that figure is 50% – a mere 7% of which is virgin lowland forest. While the situation is now most dire in Indonesian Kalimantan, which is years behind on the conservation front, irreversible havoc was wrought on Sabah and Sarawak's forests in three decades from the 1960s. Deforestation peaked in the 1980s due to the combined effects of an unchecked timber industry and exploitation of forests for agriculture. The immediate consequences of those practices were catastrophic: the rate of deforestation in Sarawak doubled between 1980 and 1990. Things have slowed significantly, but far from ceased. Between 1963 and 1985, 2.8 million hectares of primary forest in Sarawak was logged – today an estimated 850,000ha are lost each year. Tragically, the greatest fallout of past mistakes can't be undone. Half of all primary forest of both Sarawak and Sabah has been logged, either selectively or intensively, and effectively lost.

Decades of intensive logging for timber products and large-scale tropical hardwood exports, and mass conversion of forests for rubber, palm oil and cocoa plantations has incurred equally massive losses of biodiversity and indigenous ways of life. Many of the timber licences issued by the Sarawak government still concern traditional native lands. Since early 1987, indigenous people have been protesting about this encroachment, erecting blockades across timber roads in a desperate attempt to stop logging activities. Logging in dipterocarp forest continues to be excessive, with poor management of water catchments and poorly controlled logging operations.

THE SAWMILLS OF MALAYSIA Sabah and Sarawak have been described as the 'sawmills of Malaysia'. More than 70% of Malaysia's plywood mills are located in the two states, and they produce nearly all of the country's exported timber. Almost all trees felled are for export. Forestry underpins the economy and provides thousands of jobs – 40% of people in Sarawak are employed in the timber industry. The dipterocarp forests are subject to the most intense hardwood exploitation. Dipterocarp timber, however, is not of a very high quality, and most is used to produce plywood and sawn timber for construction – door and window frames, flooring, decking and other such uses.

Some 90% of logging licences ('forest concessions') in Sabah were ostensibly terminated in 2000. The industry claims logging in primary forest has been reduced to a trickle, but many logging operations are still carried out in government reserves, on large concessions that are still valid for decades to come. The woodchip industry in Malaysia apparently ceased activity in 1995, but hardwood exploitation has not.

Critics say that palm oil has simply taken up where logging left off, wreaking as much if not more environmental damage. The industry surpassed forestry as Sabah's biggest employer in the 1990s, and is now its biggest exporter, reaping 40% of state revenue, and over a quarter of Malaysia's palm oil.

Forestry remains the biggest industry in Sarawak, though palm oil is hot on its heels. The round-the-clock forestry practices that were rife in Sarawak in the 1990s have apparently eased, but there are still large timber-harvesting operations. Amid international criticism from NGOs of continuing bad forestry practice, misinformation in the local media is common. News reports in Sarawak boast of the state's 'green gold' – a lush tropical rainforest cover of 70% – with no mention of the extent of logging and losses. Such reports flagrantly permit the forestry industry to justify their activities, while turning the blame on traditional shifting cultivation practices. As one timber company representative asserted in a 2007 newspaper report: 'As soon as we open a forestry road the natives come running in to clear the land.'

FACING UP TO THE CONSEQUENCES

If the forests become too fragmented, their ability to function efficiently is compromised. Half a rainforest does not contain half the number of original species. It contains far fewer.

Wild Borneo, Nick Garbutt and Cede Prudente

As forest cover drops below 20%, many species are lost or become endangered. Scientific studies have shown logging in Sabah and Sarawak to have serious effects on the extent and intensity of reproduction of plant species, including dipterocarp trees. An international symposium on biodiversity conservation in tropical rainforests, held in Japan in 2006, heard that the continuing deforestation in

Malaysian Borneo was threatening 200 orchid species, 35 bird species, all rafflesia flowers and over 80% of primate species to the point of extinction.

In 2007, UNESCO joined the battle for Borneo's forests, with a chilling warning – illegal logging would soon see the island's rainforests decimated. According to Conservation International, if current deforestation levels and widespread logging in protected areas continue, lowland forests in Indonesian Borneo may soon disappear: 'Recent estimates show that Kalimantan's protected lowland forests declined by 56% between 1985 and 2001, primarily from logging, and that less than 33% of lowland forest and peat swamp remains across all of Indonesian Borneo.' Current predictions on the ultimate life expectancy for remaining lowland forests – the most biologically diverse habitat – stop at 2018.

A lot of the deforestation stems from illegal industry. In a report in the *Jakarta Globe* in April 2011, the Indonesian Forestry Ministry itself admitted that illegal logging, land clearance, forest fires and mining had devastated Indonesian Borneo and cost the country US$36.4 billion. Additionally, Maria Monica Wihardja from Jakarta's Centre for Strategic and International Studies says that illegal deforestation (resulting from crop plantations and mining activities) in East Kalimantan alone costs the government US$100 million in loss of revenue.

CONSERVATION

The riches of Borneo's forests were one of the first things to attract outside interest to the island. As early as the 10th century, Asian neighbours wanted a share in its natural bounties. The Chinese traded ceramic jars in exchange for jungle treasures. 'Luxury goods' were produced for the Asian market, using Borneo's turtles, birds, bark and wood.

The magnitude of Borneo's natural riches is not reflected in sufficient levels of protection. Things are changing. Bolstering of Malaysia's (1972) Protection of Wildlife Act aims to enable a more solid legal framework to safeguard flora and fauna at a national level. In 2003, the Sarawak Forestry Corporation was created to manage the forests and national parks of the state. The concept of sustainable forest management was virtually non-existent until the late 1990s. The Corporation has adopted the International Union for the Conservation of Nature (IUCN) recommended action that at least 10% of its land area should be in 'totally protected areas'. The dual management of forestry interests and national parks by the same authority continues, understandably, to raise serious questions as to the depth of environmental commitment.

SARAWAK One area in which Sarawak appears to be setting a precedent is the legal protection of its wildlife and flora. Commercial sale and capture of wildlife is outlawed under its 1998 Wildlife Protection Ordinance, which imposes severe penalties for offenders – a fine of RM50,000 and imprisonment is the going rate for killing a rhino. Hunting, on the other hand, was not banned, as 'it was recognised that rural communities depend on wild meat'. The ordinance safeguards 52 of Sarawak's rare and endangered mammals, birds and reptiles as 'Totally Protected Species' and another 40 as 'Protected Animals'. Only two plants are 'Totally Protected' – the various rafflesia species and the dipterocarp tree species *D. obloglofolius*. Another 46 plants, including many other dipterocarps and other tree species, are simply 'Protected'.

Those moves were the first signs of Sarawak moving towards adhering to international conventions in forest policy. The Protected Areas and Biodiversity

CONSERVATION IN BORNEO *Sir Peter Crane*

The rainforest of Borneo has been high on the international conservation agenda for decades. The reason is simple – Borneo is one of the world's most important centres of biological diversity and there is still time to make a difference. Over the past decade, significant help for conservation in the Borneo rainforest has come from many national and international initiatives, including the Darwin Initiative of the UK government. A key aim has been to help countries that are rich in biodiversity but relatively poor financially and in human resources, to develop innovative approaches to conservation and sustainability through international partnerships. An encouraging sign has been the 'Heart of Borneo' initiative that is supported by the governments of Brunei, Indonesia and Malaysia.

A primary target of national and international efforts in Borneo has been the conservation and sustainable management of the forests in Sabah, which has involved improving means to assess and manage plant diversity. A key partner in Borneo is Yayasan Sabah ('The Sabah Foundation'), a charitable foundation set up in the mid 1960s with the aim of improving education, health, welfare and other social services for the people of Sabah. Yayasan Sabah's income derives mainly from managing around a million hectares of tropical forest, of which about 15% is already devoted to primary forest reserves. These include the Danum Valley and Maliau Basin conservation areas, which are of global conservation importance.

The **Danum Valley Conservation Area** preserves some of the last remaining lowland rainforest in the whole island of Borneo. It is a pristine and more-or-less intact ecosystem of almost 450km^2, dominated by giant dipterocarp trees, legumes and other trees. It is also home to globally significant populations of large mammals, such as the Bornean pygmy elephant, the binturong (a type of arboreal civet), the sun bear and the Sumatran rhino. Danum and the surrounding areas also support more than 4,000 orangutans – the largest population of this primate in the world. First set aside by Yayasan Sabah, Danum is now designated as a Class I Protection Forest Reserve by the Sabah state government. As a result of a long-term partnership with the UK's Royal Society, it is well monitored from one of the most active of all research stations in Southeast Asia.

Conservation Unit, a section of the Sarawak Forestry Corporation, describes itself as the 'custodian of Sarawak's national parks', responsible for environmental protection and conservation activities throughout the state. Its vision is to be 'globally recognised as a leader in management of totally protected areas'.

SABAH Sabah has a dedicated Wildlife Department (*www.wildlife.sabah.gov.my*) in which its conservation goals and strategies are vested. The department falls within the Ministry for Tourism Development, Environment, Science and Technology.

Only 13 mammals, reptiles and plants make it on to Sabah's 'totally protected species' list, while under the state's 1963 Fauna Conservation Ordinance, species are only protected if they dwell within a national park or other protected area. (It doesn't pay to wander if you are an orangutan! Especially not from a national park into an oil palm plantation.) Since the late 1990s, the state has been showing a more concerted effort to implement CITES and other

In contrast to Danum, the **Maliau Basin Conservation Area** contains relatively little lowland rainforest, but it is nevertheless of great conservation importance. Covering nearly 600km², it is a remarkable block of tropical forest – virtually the entire catchment of the Maliau River – almost encircled by a dramatic escarpment that rises to over 1,600m in places. The basin includes spectacular waterfalls and vast tracts of forest. Again, this area was originally set aside by Yayasan Sabah and then formally upgraded to a Class I Reserve.

Then, in 2003, an exciting development for conservation came when Yayasan Sabah designated the **Imbak Canyon** as a new conservation area.

Exploratory expeditions, which included scientists from the UK and other countries, together with partners from Sabah and elsewhere in Malaysia, confirmed its truly exceptional conservation value. It is the last remaining significant area of unprotected lowland dipterocarp rainforest in Sabah and a crucial link between Danum to the southeast and Maliau to the southwest.

The conservation reserves at Danum Valley, the Maliau Basin and now the Imbak Canyon are a testament to the foresight of Yayasan Sabah in preserving large tracts of forest – for the people of Sabah, and also for the unique animals and plants that these areas sustain. It would be all too easy to harvest the timber and clear the land for oil palm plantations. Instead, watersheds are protected and key parts of the unique natural heritage of one of the world's most remarkable tropical islands have been secured for the future. The challenge now is how to manage the forest matrix in which the reserves are embedded in the best possible way. Well-developed buffer zones, and forest management systems that encourage the free movement of plants and animals among the three protected areas, will be crucial. If implemented effectively they will ensure that the outstanding conservation values of Maliau, Imbak and Danum are secure, and that the global significance of these remarkable places will continue to increase – rather than diminish – for many, many years into the future.

Sir Peter Crane, evolutionary biologist and former Director of the Royal Botanic Gardens, Kew, is Dean of the School of Forestry and Environmental Studies and Professor of Botany at Yale. He specialises in horticultural biodiversity and conservation issues.

international agreements on biodiversity. The Sabah Wildlife Conservation Enactment of 1997 was the first to seriously set aside and manage protected areas, and regulate wildlife exploitation.

THE FUTURE FOR BORNEO Since it hit world headlines – and the US supplied major funding – there's been a lot of talk of the 'Heart of Borneo' conservation project agreement between the island's three nations. Yet even this large core of surviving rainforest is threatened, says the WWF: 'Logging, land-clearing and conversion activities are considered to be the greatest threats. Today the conversion to oil palm plantations can be considered one of the biggest threats for the remaining rainforests in Borneo and the species that inhabit them.'

With such an apparently bleak outlook, can things be turned around? Experts in forest rehabilitation say the effects of selective logging on biodiversity are not necessarily irreversible. According to Dr Glen Reynolds, senior scientist at the Danum Valley Field Centre, 'even lowland rainforests which have been selectively logged still support the highest levels of biodiversity... It is the conversion of forests to plantations – particularly oil palm – that has the really disastrous impacts on biodiversity.'

THE HEART OF BORNEO – NOW OR NEVER As the forests of Borneo rapidly disappear, it is becoming apparent that the current fragmented network of protected areas does not have long-term viability. For forests to survive, they must be within a connected network, ensuring the inclusion of the most isolated pockets of forest.

Expanses of pristine rainforest teeming with life still exist in Borneo's hilly interior, but only parts are protected. As logging companies and plantation owners set their sights on the next lucrative schemes, in 2007 WWF stepped in with an ambitious project to save what is left.

The 'Heart of Borneo' (see *Biodiversity*, page 33) refers to a region the size of the United Kingdom – 220,000km² – in the central-northern region of the island, encompassing parts of Malaysian, Bruneian and Indonesian Borneo. The conservation zone is of undeniable biological importance, harbouring up to 6% of the world's biodiversity, a figure expected to rise with the discovery of new species.

According to the WWF, the threats to the Heart of Borneo – one of only two places where elephants, orangutans, rhinoceros and clouded leopards share the same territory – are enormous. 'Past experience shows us that the natural capital harbored within the Heart of Borneo is of great commercial interest... By the 1980s major commercial operations were eating away at the once untouchable and impenetrable forests of Borneo. The last 20 years of the century saw more timber cut and traded from Borneo than from the entirety of the Amazon and Congo regions. Timber companies, palm oil plantations, mining operations, hydropower and other infrastructure developments are all key players within the Heart of Borneo landscape.'

The WWF's tactic is to work co-operatively with the private sector, to try and head off threats: 'Our experience has shown that far greater results can be realised and sustained when business, government and civil society work toward a common goal.'

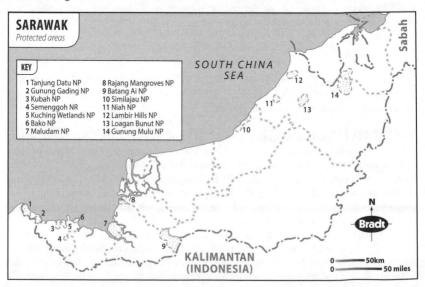

SARAWAK
Protected areas

KEY
1 Tanjung Datu NP
2 Gunung Gading NP
3 Kubah NP
4 Semenggoh NR
5 Kuching Wetlands NP
6 Bako NP
7 Maludam NP
8 Rajang Mangroves NP
9 Batang Ai NP
10 Similajau NP
11 Niah NP
12 Lambir Hills NP
13 Loagan Bunut NP
14 Gunung Mulu NP

SOUTH CHINA SEA

Sabah

KALIMANTAN (INDONESIA)

N

Bradt

0 — 50km
0 — 50 miles

PROTECTED AREAS

Sarawak Sarawak claims to have one of the most extensive sweeps of protected areas in Malaysia, encompassing 18 national parks, four wildlife sanctuaries and five nature reserves in a total area of 512,387ha. Only those national parks open to the public are listed below. All wildlife sanctuaries are closed to visitors – they exist to 'preserve and conserve vulnerable ecosystems or endangered wildlife'.

In a state nearly the size of England, reserved areas constitute less than 5% of the land. Nearly half of the state is 'Permanent Forest Estate', apparently for 'sustainable forestry', though critics would say this simply means logging.

Of the total 300,000ha of national park, the following are open to visitors:

Name	Area (ha)	Division	Date gazetted
Bako	2,727	Kuching	4 May 1957
Gunung Gading	4,196	Kuching	3 May 1988
Kubah	2,230	Kuching	11 May 1989
Tanjung Datu	1,379	Kuching	19 May 1994
Talang Satang	19,414	Kuching	4 November 1999
Kuching Wetland	6,610	Kuching	10 October 2002
Batang Ai	24,040	Sri Aman	11 May 1989
Similajau	7,064	Bintulu	20 April 1978
(Similajau Extension	1,932	Bintulu	2 June 2000)
Gunung Mulu	52,865	Miri	3 October 1974
Niah	3,138	Miri	2 January 1975
Lambir Hills	6,949	Miri	26 June 1975
Loagan Bunut	10,736	Miri	29 August 1991
Rajang Mangroves	9,373	Sibu	3 August 2000

The five **nature reserves** are:

Name	Area (ha)	Division	Date gazetted
Wind Cave	6.16	Kuching	4 November 1999
Sama Jaya	37.92	Kuching	23 March 2000
Semenggoh	653	Kuching	20 April 2000
Bukit Hitam	147	Limbang	22 June 2000
Bukit Sembiling	101	Limbang	22 June 2000

Sabah Things are different in Sabah, with just two national parks among eight areas gazetted under the 1984 Parks Enactment and managed by Sabah Parks. Three of these are terrestrial parks: Mount Kinabalu, the Crocker Range and Tawau Hills; and five are marine parks: Turtle Islands, Tunku Abdul Rahman, Pulau Tiga, Sipadan Island and Tun Sakaran Marine Park (also referred to as Semporna Islands Park). In total, they cover approximately 276,000ha. Another proposed park is the Tun Mustapha Park in the Kudat Peninsula and Kota Marudu districts.

Under the 1968 Forest Enactment (revised in 1984), there are seven classes of 'Protected Forest Reserves', ranging from 'Class I Protection Forest Reserve' to 'Class VI Virgin Jungle Reserve' and 'Class VII Wildlife Reserve'. Class II Forest – commercial forest – is not listed on Sabah Forestry's website yet amounts for the bulk of these reserves – 2,685,199ha.

According to *Discovering Sabah* (Natural History Publications, Borneo), only four of the seven classifications boil down to protected areas. The main function of Class I Protection Forests is to safeguard water supplies, soil fertility and

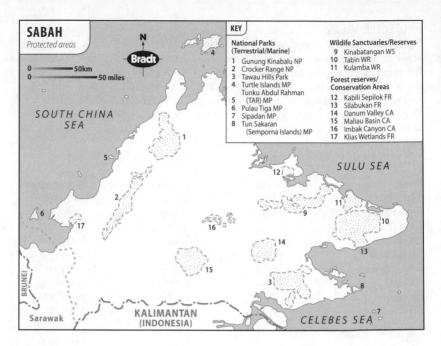

SABAH
Protected areas

N

Bradt

0 ———————— 50km
0 ———————— 50 miles

SOUTH CHINA
SEA

SULU SEA

BRUNEI

Sarawak

KALIMANTAN
(INDONESIA)

CELEBES SEA

KEY

**National Parks
(Terrestrial/Marine)**
1 Gunung Kinabalu NP
2 Crocker Range NP
3 Tawau Hills Park
4 Turtle Islands MP
Tunku Abdul Rahman
5 (TAR) MP
6 Pulau Tiga MP
7 Sipadan MP
8 Tun Sakaran
(Semporna Islands) MP

Wildlife Sanctuaries/Reserves
9 Kinabatangan WS
10 Tabin WR
11 Kulamba WR

**Forest reserves/
Conservation Areas**
12 Kabili Sepilok FR
13 Silabukan FR
14 Danum Valley CA
15 Maliau Basin CA
16 Imbak Canyon CA
17 Klias Wetlands FR

environmental quality. Danum Valley and Maliau Basin are two such reserves.
Class VI Virgin Jungle Reserves comprise some 50 relatively small areas intended
to provide undisturbed forest for research and the preservation of gene pools. The
fourth conservation class is Class VII Wildlife Reserves, which are for the protection
of wildlife. The core of the large Tabin Wildlife Reserve today falls under Forest
Class VII. In 1997, the Wildlife Conservation Enactment enabled the creation of
more protected areas.

Terrestrial and marine parks	Size (ha)	Protected forest reserve	Size (ha)
Lower Kinabatangan	27,800	Class I Protection	342,216
Sipadan	12	Class II Commercial	2,685,199
Kota Belud	12,200	Class III Domestic	7,350
Mantanani Kecil	61	Class IV Amenity	20,767
Kota Kinabalu	24	Class V Mangrove	316,024
		Class VI Virgin Jungle	90,386
Lankayan Billean Tegapil Marine		Class VII Wildlife Reserve	132,653
Conservation Area	30,000		
Kinabalu	75,370	**Marine parks (including coral reef)**	**Size (ha)**
Tawau Hills	27,927	Tungku Abdul Rahman	4,020
Crocker Range	139,919	Turtle Islands	1,740
		Pulau Tiga	15,864

Source: Discovering Sabah, Natural History Publications, Borneo

BRUNEI The government of Brunei Darussalam claims 'primary tropical jungle'
covers about 75% of the country, though also cites forestry as a major activity.
Thanks to oil, Brunei has had little need to cut down its forests for export to the
extent of its Malaysian neighbours, so the country's rainforests, peat swamp and
mangrove environments are among the better preserved in the region. Still its

record is not entirely clean: forestry is a major economic activity, mangrove woods have been culled to make charcoal, and mangroves are continually cleared to make way for urban and industrial developments. Urban pollution is another major environmental issue, with sewage from the capital's large water village – Kampung Ayer – running directly into the river and its ecosystems. Sustainable forest management is a relatively new concept in Brunei, but the country is aware of the need to preserve all that is left, and is positioning itself as a beacon of sustainability and ecotourism.

The Forest Act categorises forest reserves into five types: Protection Forest, Conservation Area, Recreational Area, Production Forest and National Park. There is just one national park, the 50,000ha **Ulu Temburong National Park**, created in 1988 within a huge forestry reserve. A further 32,000ha of reserves are classified for conservation purposes, and many urban and rural recreational areas underpin a visually green Brunei. A respectable 15% of Brunei's total land area is fully protected. The Forestry Department manages the reserves and has started to carry out some early day greening activities, such as rehabilitating degraded lands and raising public awareness. Talk of bolstering the Wildlife Protection Act, established in 1978, aims to give it more scope to create national parks and sanctuaries.

2

UPDATES WEBSITE

You can post your comments and recommendations, and read the latest feedback and updates from other readers, online at www.bradtupdates.com/borneo.

SEND US YOUR SNAPS!

We'd love to follow your adventures using our *Borneo* guide – why not send us your photos and stories via Twitter (@BradtGuides) and Instagram (@bradtguides) using the hashtag #borneo. Alternatively, you can upload your photos directly to the gallery on the Borneo destination page via our website (*www.bradtguides.com*).

3

Practical Information

WHEN TO VISIT

WEATHER Wet or dry season? There is no clear-cut best time to visit Borneo insofar as sunshine and warm weather are concerned (this is the tropics after all), but depending on the nature of your holiday, seasons may count considerably. Each has its advantages and drawbacks. The dry season (southwest monsoon) generally occurs from May to October, though huge downpours and floods can occur during that time, particularly in June and July. The wet season (northeast monsoon) reigns from November to April, and while monsoon rains may prove challenging, they are also atmospheric and can quickly clear to blue skies. As is the case for the entire planet, climate change is sparking increasing seasonal unpredictability.

For active and adventure holidays, the wet season is most likely to hinder your travel plans. Heavy rains and general bad weather may see flights to remote regions cancelled and likewise, disrupt boat travel. Trekkers should be prepared for short bursts of wet weather at any time of the year. During the northeast monsoon, open seas can be extremely rough; in January 2007, a tour company boat capsized off the north coast of Sabah due to a sudden change in weather conditions. On the other hand, low rainfall and river levels often affect boat travel. In hotter periods, upriver trips end up being partly self-propelled, with travellers required to hop out of longboats and help push them upstream.

CROWDS If crowds bother you, best avoid school holidays and major festive celebrations. Not only can it be hard to find accommodation during these busy periods, but hotels can be very noisy. The main school holidays usually fall between the last week of May and last week of June, and six weeks from mid-November through to the end of December. There are also weeklong holidays around mid-March and late August.

WHAT KIND OF HOLIDAY?

Whether setting out solo, with a family or group, on a package tour or independently, Borneo's variety can satisfy most holiday aspirations and needs. The high standard of hotels, health and safety, and ease of air, road and river transport generally enable a hassle-free holiday. The highlands, remote river areas and challenging peaks offer scope for the more adventurous traveller. Those who love sand and sun have the perfect beach-filled package holiday destination, with the significant add-ons of diverse culture and wildlife. A handful of operators offer high-end tailor-made tours combining the best of Sabah, Sarawak and Brunei. For independent travellers, the cost of voyaging between these places is relatively cheap – budget-dependent – by air, self-drive or bus. A serious possibility for budget or time-restricted travellers is to home in on one Malaysian state for your holiday: both Sabah and Sarawak offer ample scenic, natural and cultural variety for a complete, stand-alone holiday. For islands, diving and snorkelling Sabah is the ultimate culturally enhanced beach and watersport destination. For mountaineers, too, it is hard to look past Mount Kinabalu's heights and challenges (and those of neighbouring peaks).

Sarawak on the other hand stands out for incredible remote-river and highland trekking experiences – caves, caves and more caves (both geological and archaeological wonders) – and the sizzling cultural colour and Old-World charm of its cities and towns. It is very hard to favour either state for their flora and fauna wonders, as it really comes down to specific areas: Sabah's Kinabatangan River and Danum perhaps more so for overall wildlife encounters and birds; Mount Kinabalu definitely for orchid-lovers (and again birds); Sarawak's Niah National Park and Gungung Mulu for prehistory; and Bako National Park for proboscis monkeys. Brunei, the 'test-tube Borneo', has a bit of everything in a concentrated, easily accessible form, and is a fascinating destination in itself.

Those with more time or money might plan to take in more on a single visit, though more does not necessarily mean expanding the scope of the trip, but rather the depth. Greater time in one place is always better than skimming over things, so your luxury may simply be having longer to soak up individual places, whether you organise the transfers yourself or pay a tour company to do the work for you. If you have a special interest, be it diving, trekking or birdwatching, a good option can be a tailor-made tour, or designing your own trip using specialist local operators (see pages 78–80).

HIGHLIGHTS

FLORA AND FAUNA The flora and fauna hotspots of Borneo are so numerous and varied that it is impossible to categorise them, but below is a brief key to some major attractions and lesser-known wonders.

Ulu Temburong National Park, Brunei
Whether a day trip or overnight stay, the journey itself to the Temburong National Park, starting on the riverbanks of Brunei's capital, forms half the wonder of the trip. Meandering through a network of waterways, mangrove and tropical rainforest, you will enjoy a cultural immersion as you pass through the town of Bangar and witness the incredible boating skills of the Iban people. The walk to the suspension bridge in the park puts you at dizzying forest heights with views over Brunei and Malaysian Borneo.

Gunung Kinabalu National Park, Sabah
The steamy alpine world of Gunung Kinabalu can be enjoyed whether you climb to the peak or not. The complexity of vegetation in the 75,370ha World Heritage park reveals itself even on a shorter trek, through rainforest and lower montane areas around park headquarters, and other zones such as Poring Hot Springs. The butterfly- and bloom-filled park is designated a Centre of Plant Diversity for Southeast Asia by UNESCO, exceptionally rich in species.

Bako National Park, Sarawak
A wonderland mix of mangroves, peat swamp, heath and lowland rainforest, with epic coastal rock formations. On the fauna front, highlights include bright-green snakes, bearded pigs and the proboscis monkey. About 150 of the pendulous-nosed, pot-bellied creatures live in the national park (see page 283). The trails are excellent (as long as a tree doesn't fall on you, which is what happened to me when I visited!). It's virtually on the back doorstep of Kuching, about 40km away.

Danum Valley The closest you will come to the 'Heart of Borneo' (see page 66) without heading deep into the Maliau Basin. Wildlife sightings include gibbon, orangutan, long-tailed macaque, bearded pig, sambar deer, rhinoceros hornbill, maroon langur, western tarsier, clouded leopard, red leaf monkey and a diversity of birds. You will need to stay a few days to catch a glimpse of such a wide variety of animals, rather than just doing a one-hour night safari on the back of a (rather noisy) truck.

Orangutan encounters The huge appeal of this charismatic primate attracts many people to Borneo, and seeing one is often at the top of their agenda. Orangutan rehabilitation centres and sanctuaries (Sepilok in Sabah, and Semenggoh in Sarawak) are an easy option for quick sightings. Places to see them (and vast amounts of other wildlife) in the wild include the Tabin Wildlife Reserve on Sabah's east coast, the floodplain of the Lower Kinabatangan River and the Danum Valley Conservation Area.

Proboscis monkeys The proboscis monkey comes in a close second as the most popular primate to see in Borneo. They can be spotted in mangrove and peat swamp forests such as the Lower Kinabatangan and Klias Wetlands in Sabah, along Brunei's waterways and in the Bako National Park in Sarawak.

River safaris The boat journey along the Sungai Kinabatangan, Sabah's longest river, is awe-inspiring, with its searing sense of remoteness, natural richness and otherworldly beauty. For wildlife and birdwatching it is one of Borneo's most intense experiences, and the lodges along the river (in their varying degrees of rustic, or as of late, rustic chic) bolster the feeling of going deep jungle for a night or two. Late-afternoon boat trips lead up tributaries of the river to see shy proboscis monkeys and macaques. The global eco-significance of the area has unfortunately not protected it from forestry and palm oil invasion, though conservation and community development efforts are trying their best to turn the tide on the destruction. Staying with river-living (orang sungai) communities helps boost the local economy.

River trips in Sarawak stand out more as journeys into ethnography than nature – encountering tribes of the Batang Ai region in the southeast, or along the magnificent Sungai Rendang in central Sarawak, through to the remote outposts of Kapit and Belaga.

ISLANDS AND BEACHES As mentioned previously, for water-based fun and games or relaxation, the islands off Sabah's north and east coast are the go-to destination.

CITIES AND CULTURE Bandar Seri Begawan, Brunei's capital, offers an intense potpourri of Islamic faith, river tranquillity, royal riches, mosque silhouettes, Malay culture and indigenous cuisine. It is also bedrock of Bornean history, ethnic and religious. Kuching, Sarawak's main city, is mesmerising with its antiquated oriental airs, yet neighbourly and friendly. The Sungai Sarawak runs through the city, and indigenous Iban and Bidayuh cultures are woven through its watery fabric. Kota Kinabalu, Sabah's capital, is more the modern resort, a Côte d'Azur of Borneo, where people party late into the night and hang out at waterside bars. Cloaked in lush hills and framed by stilted villages and Chinese temples, the north-coast city of Sandakan (Sabah's original capital), exudes maritime charm. Nudging the Philippines, it is a historical ocean crossroads.

Cultural shows Dance performances at the **Sarawak Cultural Village** are an absolute highlight. A mainstream yet quality tourist attraction, the visit offers a joyous insight into a cross-section of Malay, Chinese and indigenous dance, as well as traditional housing. Similarly, the **Mari Mari Cultural Village** near Kota Kinabalu in Sabah provides an all-in-one cultural taste, well delivered and high quality. For ghoulish headhunting history, the House of Skulls (Siou Do Mohoing) at **Monsopiad Cultural Village** near Kota Kinabalu (see pages 190–1) is a must.

SCENIC DRIVES

East coast, Sabah The 'cowboy town' settlements along this stretch are more than a springboard to incredible islands and the Danum Valley. From thriving ports such as Tawau, buzzing with Chinese cafés and restaurants, to Malay outdoor markets and spicy flavours of Semporna, this road less travelled presents an offbeat and vivid cultural drenching. The seafood on the east coast is the best in Borneo.

Kudat Peninsula, Sabah Without a doubt, the whole region north of Kota Kinabalu offers one of the best opportunities for several days of leisurely travelling by car. Culminating in the Kudat Peninsula and the 'Tip of Borneo', the journey takes in markets and towns, coast and countryside. More difficult, but not impossible, is to do the journey by bus: regional services connect the towns.

Pan-Borneo Another off-the-beaten-track trip among tourist operators and independent travellers is the drive from Kuching in Sarawak, all the way up the coast to Brunei. The Pan-Borneo Highway unfurls between Kuching and Miri, before traversing the Bruneian border. You can also rely on a mix of coaches, buses and boats to do the trip. Highlights along the way are the Chinese city of Sibu, the Melanau' stronghold of Mukah, the Niah Caves – and the best sago and fish salads in the world.

SUGGESTED ITINERARIES

Decide what you most want to see in Borneo in the available time: culture and ethnic groups, jungle and wildlife, beaches and coast, highlands and islands, or a mix of all. This will help determine your itinerary, using the suggestions below as a guide, but maybe tweaking them to better suit your main interests. Given the ease and frequency of air travel, it is common for tour operators to propose weeklong itineraries that cherry-pick from the best of Borneo. Whatever you do, emphasise quality over quantity.

ONE WEEK If you only have a week, stick to just one Malaysian state. You could start with a one-day, one-night stopover in **Brunei**, visiting Temburong National Park, the water village and mosques on a packaged tour. Next, head to Sabah and spend a day wallowing in the watery charm of **Kota Kinabalu**. Don't miss the dawn-to-dusk markets – the fish and craft markets and evening pasar malam (evening food market) – held along the waterfront stretch of Jalan Tun Fuad Stephens. For the best view of the city climb to the top of Signal Hill. If your visit coincides, visit the Sunday market on Jalan Gaya, and eat seafood at the open-air Sri Selera food court. The next day, head off to **Gunung Kinabalu National Park** – the winding journey takes about two hours by car and passes vegetable markets and food and craft stalls in villages such as Kampung Nabalu. You can also take a taxi or bus to the park entrance from the Merdeka Field station. The 17km-return Summit Trail to the top of Mount Kinabalu includes an overnight stay *en route*, permits and a guide, and you need to book well ahead for both the trek and for park accommodation required before or after the climb. (The walk starts at the crack of dawn so staying the previous night is almost mandatory; most groups are back from the climb mid afternoon, so post-climb accommodation is less urgent.) From one of the park lodges, you can also spend two days soaking up the mountain scenery on unguided walks – first head to park HQ for a Mount Kinabalu Park Trails map – and visit the farmers' markets and World War II war memorial at nearby Kundasang. Many climbers end their walk with a night at Poring Hot Springs, part of the Gunung Kinabalu National Park, where rangers will post alerts on any rafflesia flowers in bloom (see box, pages 42–4).

Return to Kota Kinabalu for a flight to the coastal city of **Sandakan**: the views are ethereally beautiful over the rickety water village and harbour full of Old-World fishing vessels facing the Philippines and Sulu Sea. Head off to the afternoon feeding session at the **Sepilok Orangutan Rehabilitation Centre**, half an hour from town (you can also drop by the adjacent Sun Bear Conservation Centre), then later explore the sights of Sandakan by foot.

The next day, head off with a local operator along the 560km-long **Sungai Kinabatangan River** – the trip into the mighty yet blighted (by forestry and oil palm plantations) jungled interior of Malaysia's second-longest waterway comes close to being the most magical river journey in Borneo. Many tour operators, from budget to upmarket, offer packages including lodging, food and transport. In the mangrove and freshwater swamp environments of the Lower Kinabatangan Sanctuary, you will come in close contact with orangutans, proboscis monkeys, Bornean gibbons, pygmy elephants, Sumatran rhinoceros and pit vipers. Over 200 bird species reside here – eight types of hornbill alone, including the rare wrinkled hornbill.

Head south to **Lahad Datu**, gateway to some of the largest remaining areas of 'old growth' virgin rainforest, including the Tabin Wildlife Reserve, the Danum Valley Conservation Area, Maliau Basin and Imbak Canyon. Spend at least two full days taking in the flora and fauna. Danum and the surrounding forests are home to 4,000 orangutans – the world's largest population of the primate – yet there are serious concerns about the 438km^2 reserve being encroached on by a logging 'concession' area and oil palm plantations.

If you are a diver, you might want to switch (or shorten) the jungle experience for a couple of days' diving. The east coast's Bajau sea gypsy territory of **Semporna** is the springboard to Sabah's dive and snorkel islands: Pulau Sipadan, Mabul, Kapalai and Mataking. Purchase an all-inclusive stay on an island resort or stay in town, and use a budget operator for day trips.

TWO WEEKS In two weeks, you can spend time travelling between Sabah and Sarawak, via Brunei, and see some highlights in each. Your main consideration will be how much time to allot to different activities: do you want to tackle the mega-mountain (Mount Kinabalu), and/or do a longer jungle and river safari accompanied by some smaller cultural bites, or alternatively, get a bigger taste of Borneo's people, cities, countryside and villages and smaller glimpse of nature?

You could start with the weeklong itinerary outlined above, taking in the best of Brunei and Sabah. If you are travelling independently, however, you may want to travel by ferry from Brunei to Kota Kinabalu via the island of **Labuan**. You could also include in your Sabah itinerary a day or overnight trip north to the **Tip of Borneo** (Tanjung Simpang Mengayau), passing through the longhouse settlements, tamu (farmers' markets) and coconut plantations of the Kudat Peninsula.

Next, head to Sarawak for a mix of upriver adventure and rich ethnic immersion. With its airs of an old Chinese trading town, **Kuching**'s beauty emanates from the banks of the Sungai Sarawak River. Spend two days here and use the tambang (covered wooden boats) to cross over and eat in the restaurants of the Malay kampung by night, or charter one for an hour and float down the river past the Masjid Mosque, a perfect piece of Arabia on the Kuching skyline.

Allow time to see the museums and colonial buildings and shop for handicrafts along the waterfront Jalan Bazaar. One of Borneo's best places to see 'semi-wild' orangutans is the **Semenggoh Wildlife Rehabilitation Centre**, 20km south of the city. North of Kuching, accessed by speedboat, are the mangroves, amphibians and proboscis monkeys of **Taman Bako National Park** – worth a day trip at least, or stay overnight in basic park chalets after tackling one of the 16 walking trails. A more comfortable option is to stay at a resort at **Damai Beach**, on the neighbouring Santubong Peninsula.

The next day head to the **Sri Aman District**, which skirts the Indonesian border and is the heartland of Sarawak's most populous tribe, the Iban. Along the way, if you are self-driving, stop at **Serian**. The small market town is distinguished by its 'Big Durian' – the king of local fruits – and undercover tamu, whose stalls sell fruit and snacks such as pisang goring (fried banana).

Some 194km from Kuching, **Bandar Sri Aman**, on the Batang Lupar River, is a trading and transport hub, and gateway to the Batang Ai National Park. More traditional longhouse communities in the Batang Ai National Park can only be reached by boat, which leave from the jetty at the Batang Ai hydro-electric dam. The best thing is to book a trip with a Kuching-based operator, which includes a two-night stay in either the Hilton Batang Ai or a longhouse of varying standards.

Tweak this itinerary accordingly if you want to home in on one particular activity, such as diving, birding or trekking. Clearly if you want to spend four days diving on Sabah's east-coast islands, or flora fondling in Gunung Kinabalu's richly flowered environs, then something will have to go from this suggested schedule.

ONE MONTH A whole month's stay will enable you to taste the best of Brunei, Sabah and Sarawak – as outlined in the two-week journey above – with time for some major dabbling in pet activities. For example, you could enjoy a whole week of diving, birding or mountaineering (the best place for all of these is Sabah). Perhaps also pad out some of the visits, starting with an extra night's stay in Brunei's capital.

For a serious yet pricey side adventure in Sabah, head to the **Maliau Basin** – the so-called 'Lost World' – and endure nights in tents, rugged terrains and loads of leeches. Trips range from several days to a fortnight.

If you want the wildlife minus the hard adventure, spend more time in national parks and reserves – the Kinabatangan River, Tabin and Danum in Sabah, and Bako National Park in Sarawak.

Linger an extra couple of nights among the primates and birds of the Kinabatangan and an extra day among Sandakan's dilapidated but colourful water villages before heading south to the **Danum Valley**.

This is the closest you will get to the 'Heart of Borneo' (see page 66) without venturing into the Maliau Basin. Two to three days in Danum increases the chance of an impressive inventory of wildlife sightings: gibbon, orangutan, long-tailed macaque, bearded pig, sambar deer, rhinoceros hornbill, maroon langur, western tarsier, clouded leopard, red leaf monkey and a wondrous diversity of birds. (Though nearby Tabin is probably even better for birding.)

Down in Sarawak, **Bako** has a wonderland mix of mangroves, peat swamp, heath and lowland rainforest, and epic coastal rock formations. On the fauna front, highlights include bright-green snakes, bearded pigs and the proboscis monkey. About 150 of the pendulous-nosed, pot-bellied creatures live here (see box, page 51). Though lodgings are exceptionally basic, back-to-nature lovers will be happy to spend a couple of nights here exploring the excellent trails to hidden beaches and coves. Before or after a Bako visit, spend more time in fascinating Kuching.

Rather than doing the standard overnight trip to Batang Ai and its longhouse communities, opt for a real river adventure. Borneo Adventure organises 5–11-day treks on the arduous **Red Ape Trail**, mapped out with local Iban communities and endorsed by the Orangutan Foundation. Budget outfitters also touch on the region.

For an off-the-beaten-track rural adventure, drive or travel by bus from Batang Ai into Central Sarawak, whose lifeblood is the 760km-long Batang Rejang, Malaysia's longest river.

On the way to regional capital Sibu, break the journey in the town of **Sarikei**, in whose acidic soils pineapples, pomelo (large citrus fruits) and avocado thrive.

At the confluence of the Rejang and Igan rivers, 130km from the South China Sea, **Sibu** is a transport hub for the whole Rejang Basin. Explore its huge harbour, Chinese temples and gardens – and eat your heart out. Thanks to its population of Chinese, Melanau, Iban and Orang Ulu, Sibu has some of the most delicious, top-quality-and-value food in East Malaysia: spend at least a day and night at the markets and coffee shops sampling dishes such as mee udang (river prawns in a bowl of spicy broth) and mee sua (longevity noodles).

Stay in Sibu another night and visit a longhouse settlement on the Rejang, or take an express boat north to the coastal region of **Mukah** and experience the seafaring Melanau people's culture and zingy signature dish umai (a spicy salad of raw shredded fish marinated with lime, ginger and chilli). River enthusiasts might want to consider a boat cruise along the Rejang. If not, head further north along the Pan-Borneo Highway, stopping a few hours to see the remarkable prehistory-ridden caves at **Niah National Park**, before winding up in Miri. In this oil town turned resort town, you can either go diving or take a plane journey into the **Gunung Mulu National Park**, whose UNESCO-classified caves are geological and archaeological treasure chests.

TOURIST INFORMATION

SABAH AND SARAWAK The worldwide offices of **Tourism Malaysia** are invaluable for general travel information, while the websites of the Sabah and Sarawak tourism boards provide the most comprehensive, up-to-date information and are a good direct point of enquiry and feedback.

Sabah Tourism Board 51 Jln Gaya, KK; +6 088 212121; e info@sabahtourism.com; www.sabahtourism.com. Precise & highly visual information on attractions, events, tour operators, lodgings & other practicalities.

Sarawak Tourism Board 6th & 7th Floors, Bangunan Yayasan, Jln Masjid Kuching; +6 082 423600; e stb@sarawaktourism.com; www.sarawaktourism.com. Wow to the new website! Very bold & beautiful, highly visual, aesthetic & informative.

Tourism Malaysia (*www.tourism.gov.my*) The new website offers limited information but super slideshows of Borneo's top destinations. The 'contact us' link to overseas offices of the Malaysia Tourism Promotion Board has been obscured by the high-tech digital presentation. Some of the major overseas offices are listed on page 78.

Kota Kinabalu, the capital of Sabah, is universally abbreviated to KK, while Bandar Seri Begawan, the capital of Brunei, is shortened to BSB. These abbreviations are used widely throughout this guide, as in conversation.

Australia 355 Exhibition St, Melbourne; \+61 3 9654 3177; Ground Floor, MAS Bldg, 56 William St, Perth; \+61 8 9481 0400; e mtpb.perth@tourism.gov.my; e malaysia@malaysiatourism.com.au
France 29 Rue des Pyramides, Paris; \+33 1 42 97 41 71; e mtpb.paris@tourism.gov.my
Germany Weissfrauenstrasse 12–16, Frankfurt am Main; \+49 69 4609 23420; e info@

tourismmalaysia.de; www.tourismmalaysia.de
UK 57 Trafalgar Sq, London WC2N 5DU; \020 7930 7932; e mtpb.london@tourism.gov.my or info@tourism-malaysia.co.uk
USA 818 West Seventh St, Suite 970, Los Angeles; \+1 213 6899702; e mtpb.la@tourism.gov.my; www.tourismmalaysiausa.com; 120 East, 56th St, Suite 810, New York; \+1 212 7541113; e mtpb@aol.com

BRUNEI Information about travel in Brunei is best obtained through the central Brunei Tourism Office in Brunei itself. Overseas, Royal Brunei Airlines offices (*www.bruneiair.com*) and Brunei high commissions and embassies (see pages 83–4) are useful sources of information.

Brunei Tourism Jln Menteri Besar, BSB, Brunei Darussalam; \+673 2382822/32; e info@tourismbrunei.com; www.tourismbrunei.com. A stunning website with gorgeous visuals & excellent content design.

Royal Brunei Airlines 49 Cromwell Rd, London SW7 2ED; \020 7584 6660; e lonrba@rba.com.bn; Level 10, 45 William St, Melbourne; \+61 3 8651 1000; e melrba@rba.com.bn

TOUR OPERATORS

Go local! Whenever possible. There are advantages to using local tour operators: first and foremost, they provide in-depth local knowledge and add a strong personal touch; second, employing local people and companies helps the local economy, creates jobs and is far more energy efficient than a business run offshore. Familiarise yourself with the local operators in the areas you plan to visit – they can help organise special-interest tours for independent travellers or take the entire weight off your shoulders by providing a start-to-finish itinerary. What an international company might gain on sleekness, they can lose on authenticity and depth. Some international travel companies, indicated below, work with home-grown agencies, employing local guides rather than running the whole show themselves. Both the Sabah and Sarawak tourism board websites (*www.sabahtourism.com; www.sarawaktourism.com*) include directories of tour operators. Company details can also be found in the members' directory of the Malaysia Association of Tours and Travel Agents (MATTA) (*www.matta.org.my*).

BORNEO
Sabah and Sarawak
Amazing Borneo \+6 088 448409; e: info@amazingborneo.com; www.amazingborneo.com. Highly recommended KK-based travel agency. Many travellers pat them on the back for their

friendly professionalism. Trips Borneo-wide; very good day trips to the Tip of Borneo.
Borneo Adventure 55 Main Bazaar, Kuching; \+6 082 245175; e info@borneoadventure.com; www.borneoadventure.com. Upmarket ethical, this Sarawak-based company has wildlife-,

adventure- & culture-focused tours in Sarawak & in Sabah, as well as custom-made trips. It says it is 'dedicated to providing our clients with ethical tourism products that are sustainable', & steps that way with an ethnically diverse group of very professional guides (including many locals) & its own eco-lodges drawing strongly on local communities. The most comprehensive information on everything from climate, crime & suitcase essentials to health & leeches, on the FAQs section of its website. See ad on page 278.

Borneo Birds e ckleong@borneobirds.com; www.borneobirds.com. The website of resident Bornean bird specialist C K Leong provides a brilliant, photographic inventory of Bornean birds, from barbets & bee-eaters to whistlers & woodpeckers. In conjunction with TYK Adventure Tours, CK tailor-makes 1-day to 2-week birding trips, including a 12-day around Sabah tour taking in Manukan Island, Tabin Wildlife Reserve, the Kinabatangan River & Gunung Kinabalu National Park.

Borneo Divers 9th Floor, Menara Jubili, 53 Jln Gaya, Kota Kinabalu; +6 088 222226; e information@borneodivers.info; www.borneodivers.info. Longest-operating & extremely reputable operator with a training institute in Kota Kinabalu offering courses at all levels. Those who enrol for the PADI course reportedly get generous discounts on Mabul Island dive packages (dives, accommodation, etc).

Borneo Dream Travel & Tours F-G-1 Plaza Tanjung Aru, Jln Mat Salleh, Kota Kinabalu; +6 088 244064; e: info@borneodream.com; www.borneodream.com. Good reports on their Kota Kinabalu area snorkelling & dive day excursions.

Borneo Eco Tours Lot 1, Pusat Perindustrian, Kolombong Jaya; Mile 5.5, Jln Kolombong, Kota Kinabalu; +6 088 438300; e info@borneoecotours.com; www.borneoecotours.com. Launched in 1991 by eco-author Albert Teo, the group has 40 excellent guides/specialists, 15 AC vehicles, speedboats, riverboats & rafting equipment. Many awards to its name for its conservation & responsible tourism efforts. Vast choice of nature & cultural tours, treks & activities, all well outlined & easily booked on its site. Value packages & a budget corner. Operates the Sukau Rainforest Lodge & Borneo Backpackers in Kota Kinabalu.

Borneo Nature Tours Blk D, Lot 10, Ground Floor, Sadong Jaya Complex, Kota Kinabalu;

+6 088 267637; www.borneonaturetours.com. Adventure & nature tours with the operator of the Borneo Rainforest Lodge in the Danum Valley Conservation Area. Heading out from there, they organise adventure treks into the Maliau Basin Conservation Area, deemed the 'lost world' of Sabah.

Cede Prudente/North Borneo Safari +6 089 666196. Sandakan-based Cede Prudente has a long history in photography & nature touring in Borneo. The founder of North Borneo Safari & a highly acclaimed photographer, his shots have illustrated several iconic books including *Wild Borneo* (see page 333). Cede leads photo safari trips & nature photography workshops in Sabah's most wondrous parks & wildlife reserves.

Outdoor Treks +6 082 363344; m +6 012 8886460; e best@bikcloud.com; www.bikcloud.com. The kind of youthful, enthusiastic & down-to-earth company that draws in the film production crews & adventure travel programmes. They are familiar with a whole lot of mountain-bike trails within 1–100km from Kuching's central business district, as well as kayaking, guided nature treks, rock climbing & caving. Sarawak based.

Pulau Sipadan Resort & Tours 484 Bandar Sabindo, PO Box 61120, Tawau; +6 089 765200; e psrt@po.jaring.my; www.sipadan-kapalai.com or www.dive-malaysia.com. Packages based around their dive resorts on Lankayan & Kapalai islands, as well as their Sepilok Nature Resort. Very professional set-up, popular with families for their child-friendliness & fun.

SI Tours 10th Floor, Wisma Khoo Siak Chiew, Sandakan Town; +6 089 673502/3; e sales@sitoursborneo.com; www.sitoursborneo.com. Local company specialising in adventure, wildlife & cultural tours. Package itineraries & custom tours to Kinabatangan, Gomantong Caves & Turtle Islands National Park. Guides are passionately local & mostly well informed. The company is deeply committed to the environment & indigenous communities – & creating jobs for them.

Sticky Rice Travel 3rd Floor, 58 Jln Pantai, Kota Kinabalu; +6 088 250588; e: info@stickyricetravel.com; www.stickyricetravel.com. 'Young & ambitious global citizens, who dive, bike & trek... adventure is our middle name & conscious-travel is our style.' That's how the company describes itself & the ethos rubs off fast. They cover all of Sabah's nature playgrounds including the most off the beaten track – Maliau Basin, Mount Trus Madi, & the northern islands. Stunning big visual website where the pic's tell a thousand words & more of the adventures they offer. See ad, 3rd colour section.

Traverse Tours/Riverbug Lot 227–229, 2nd Floor, Wisma Sabah Jalan Tun Fuad Stephen; ☏+6 088 260501/2; e tours@riverbug.asia or sales@traversetours.com; www.traversetours. com. This 'indigenous' tour group has expanded its sustainable tourism offerings, from its traditional territory of whitewater rafting & river tours under the Riverbug tag (*www.riverbug. asia*). The group operates & runs tours to the Mari Mari Cultural Village near Kota Kinabalu (m *013 881 4921*), & the Mari Mari backpackers'/diver's' accommodation on Mantanani Island (m *013 883 4921*). They are professional, sensitive & highly enthusiastic.

TYK Adventure Tours Lot 38, 2nd Floor, Damai Plaza IV, Luyang; ☏+6 088 232821; e thamyaukong@gmail.com; www. tykadventuretours.com. Small, established & very highly rated operator with responsible travel written into their DNA. Based in west-coast Sabah, specialties include KK, Mount Kinabalu & the Crocker Range, Tenom coffee tours & homestays, the Sandakan Death March & Salt trails & North Borneo/Kudat Peninsula off-road & mountain biking. The multi-ethnic team from the director down is hands-on involved in tours, each with their own particular forte. Cycling & rafting trips, survival camps, village & longhouse stays & extended trekking. They also have a group of associated experts (eg: historians), increasing their local knowledge. They organise the Miki Survival Camp in the foothills of Mount Kinabalu (see page 213).

Brunei

Freme Travel Services Unit 403B, Wisma Jaya, Jalan Pemancha, Bandar Seri Begawan; ☏+673 2234280/1; e fremeinb@ brunet.bn; www.brunei-tours.freme.com. An established company with its head office in Kuala Belait, a big set-up in the capital & firm foothold nationwide. The team do excellent day or overnight visits to the Temburong district, where it has its own lodge, nudging the national park.

Sunshine Borneo Tours & Travel No 2 Simpang 146, Jln Kiarong, Kampung Kiulap, Bandar Seri Begawan; ☏+673 2446812/3; e sales@exploreborneo.com; www.exploreborneo. com. The local partner for Royal Brunei Airlines, sold overseas as Golden Touch Holidays through RBA offices (e *goldentouch@rba.com.bn; www.bruneiair. com*). A very Bruneian, highly conscientious, concerned & punctual operator, offering day trips & excursions within Brunei. They also have a branch in the lobby arcade of the Empire Hotel & Country Club in Jerudong (☏+673 2610578).

INTERNATIONAL

Gecko's Adventures (Peregrine Adventures) 380 Lonsdale St, Melbourne; ☏+61 3 8601 4444; German office +49 80 2447 44922; e websales@ geckosdventures.com or (Germany) kontakt@ geckosadventures.com; www.geckosadventures. com. Treks & safaris operated by the 'groovy young thing' part of Peregrine Adventures. Small groups, good prices & local guides.

Intrepid Travel ☏(UK) 01373 826611/0800 781 1660; (US & Canada) +1 866 847 8192; (Australia) +61 3 0036 4512; (New Zealand) +64 9 520 0972; e info@intrepidtravel.com; www.intrepidtravel. com. For environmentally conscious, independent travellers who want to travel in a group or on a budget. Intrepid offers several tours of Borneo: all are outlined on their website with itineraries, prices, trip notes & more. Based in Australia, with sales offices in New Zealand, UK, Ireland, US & Canada. The integrity of the company's green image is boosted with several responsible travel awards, & by achieving the goal of becoming carbon neutral by 2010. Women make up about two-thirds of its clientele.

National Geographic Expeditions ☏(US) +1 888 689 2557; www. nationalgeographicexpeditions.com. 11-day Borneo wildlife expedition, easy to moderate. Kinabatangan, Tabin, Danum Valley, Mataking Island. Group size 8–16, US$6,995 pp excluding airfare.

VENT (Victor Emanuel Nature Tours) ☏+1 512 328 5221; e info@ventbird.com; www.ventbird. com. America's largest specialist bird (& natural history) tour company.

WINGS Birding Tours ☏+1 520 320 9868; e wings@wingsbirds.com; www.wingsbirds.com. An Arizona-based bird tour group, their Borneo tour leader is Birds of Borneo author Susan Myers. They offer a 15-day tour at approx US$6,600.

World Expeditions (UK) 020 8545 9030; (Australia – Sydney office) +61 2 8270 8400; (US) +1 613 241 2700; (Canada) +1 613 241 2700; www.worldexpeditions.com. Adventure & outdoor travel with offices in the UK, US, Canada, Australia & New Zealand. They offer a 9-day 'Borneo Flora & Fauna' trip, plus Mount Kinabalu climbs & Red Ape Trail adventures in Sarawak.

UK AND IRELAND

Adventure Alternative 028 7083 1258/ 04870 831258; www.adventurealternative.com. For mountain adventure, this Northern Ireland-based ('the responsible adventure travel') company has a 14-day 'Roof of Borneo' adventure' that goes way off the overbeaten Mount Kinabalu climb to take in the Eastern Plateau & the North Ridge. This is only for the seriously mountain-at-heart – 12 days are spent climbing & camping, with highly experienced expedition leaders. They also do a 3-week 'Borneo Trilogy' adventure with trekking in the Kelabit Highlands in Sarawak. They also offer a 13-day 'Borneo Wildlife' adventure, from £1,995 for min 2 people, staying in lodges & homestays. Regional office in Kuching.

Audley Travel New Mill, New Mill Lane, Witney, Oxon; 01993 838000; www.audleytravel. com. The award-winning agency offers 'tailor-made journeys for the discerning traveller', run by specialists. Itineraries include the 15-day 'Borneo Headhunters' adventure & 18-day 'Borneo Uncovered', taking in the best of Sabah & Sarawak. The stunningly visual & eco-sensitive website includes a slide-show & interactive wildlife map.

Borneo Travel The UK arm of Borneo-based TYK Adventure Tours (see page 80), whose international operations are directed by Bob Jones; 0844 840 7777; e bob@travel-trading.demon. co.uk; www.borneo-travel.com. If you're looking for an adventure & outdoor holiday, this award-winning venture has survival, mountain-biking & trekking tours plus tailor-made tours for activities such as birdwatching, rock climbing & rafting.

Chaka Travel 98 University St, Belfast; 02890 232112; e mark@chakatravel.com; www.chakatravel.com. Golfing holidays in Sabah.

Cox & Kings 6th Floor, 30 Millbank, London; 020 7873 5000; e sales@coxandkings.co.uk; www. coxandkings.co.uk. Established high-end, culturally

in-tune UK group. Offers a 13-day 'Splendours of Borneo' tour', from £3,695 pp, 'exploring the cultural & natural attractions of Sabah & Sarawak'.

Exodus Holidays Grange Mills, Weir Rd, London SW12 0NE; 0845 863 9600; e sales@exodus. co.uk; www.exodus.co.uk. Family-friendly adventure holidays with small-to-medium groups under tour leaders & local guides. 14-day 'Trails of Borneo' tour requires good fitness, includes 3 days of walking, & a mix of hotels, lodges, camping & mountain huts.

Natural World Safaris (UK) 01273 691642; (US) +1 866 357 6569; e sales@ naturalworldsafaris.com; www. naturalworldsafaris.com. Tailor-made trips to see orangutans & more.

Nature Trek Mingledown Barn, Wolfs Lane, Chawton, Alton, Hants; 01962 733051; e info@ naturetrek.co.uk; www.naturetrek.co.uk. Wildlife tour specialist with 2 Borneo itineraries, focusing on orangutans, birds & the rainforest. Their 21-day tour, which they describe as a 'birdwatching extravaganza', takes in top birdwatching sites in Sabah: Kinabatangan, Mount Kinabalu & Danum Valley. Very good reviews of the trip. All their tours are guided by specialists trained as naturalists, environmental scientists & ecologists.

Regent Holidays 6th floor, Colston Tower, Colston St, Bristol BS1 4XE; 0203 588 6120; e regent@ regentholidays.co.uk; www.regent-holidays.co.uk. Regent has a selection of 8 different tours to Borneo including a 14-day tour specialising in Sarawak wildlife & culture & a 14-day Orangutan Experience tour. See ad on the inside front cover.

Saga Holidays 0800 096 0078; e reservations @saga.co.uk; www.saga.co.uk. Cushy package group holidays for the over-50s. Offer a 14-day 'Borneo Rainforest' adventure with a tour 'manager'. Save with online bookings.

The Travel Collection Kuoni Hse, Dorking, Surrey; 01306 744311 (sales), 01306 744319 (helpdesk); e tours@travelcollection.co.uk; www.travelcollection.co.uk. Part of the Kuoni Travel group, itineraries include an 8-night 'Wildlife of Borneo' holiday staying in high-end hotels.

USA

Go Borneo +1 888 359 8655; e info@ goborneo.com; www.goborneo.com. With extensive Borneo knowledge, & using local guides, the group offers adventure & family packages, & day tours.

Terra Incognita Ecotours 4016 West Inman Ave,

Tampa, Florida; ☎+1 855 326 8687; www.ecotours.com. Customised tours to Borneo.
World of Diving & Adventure Vacations 301 Main St, El Segundo, California; ☎+1 800 GO DIVING/800 463 4846; e mail@worldofdiving.com; www.worldofadventure.com. Specialises in diving trips to Sabah's east-coast islands with 7-day round trips from Los Angeles to Tawau all inclusive.

RED TAPE

VISAS AND ENTRY REQUIREMENTS

Malaysian Borneo If you have already passed through Malaysian customs in Kuala Lumpur, it is surprising to face passport control again on arrival in Sabah or Sarawak, but keeping control of their own immigration checks was one of the conditions for them joining the Federation of Malaysia in 1963. It's all just a formality, particularly for citizens of the UK, Australia, Ireland, the USA, Brazil, Canada, France, Italy, Germany, the UAE, South Korea, Japan, South Africa, Tunisia and a host of other western European, South American and Middle Eastern countries who do not need a visa to enter Malaysia for a visit of up to three months. It is mandatory, however, to be holding a passport valid for at least six months on arrival, as well as a return or onward ticket. An extension of up to two months is possible. Passport holders from countries which require a visa will be issued with a 30-day stay on arrival, which can in principle be extended for another 60 days at the Immigration Department in Kota Kinabalu. Citizens of countries including Costa Rica, Mexico, Lithuania and Ukraine require a visa for a stay exceeding one month. For more information on visa requirements for all countries, go to the website of the Malaysian Immigration Department (*www.imi.gov.my*).

Brunei No visa is required for residents of the USA (90-day entry), the UK, Ireland, Germany, Austria, New Zealand, Singapore, Malaysia, the UAE, Oman and South Korea (30-day entry), and residents of Belgium, France, Italy, Spain, the Netherlands, Luxembourg, Denmark, Norway, Sweden, Poland, Canada, Peru, Japan, the Philippines, Indonesia and Thailand (14-day entry). Australians are granted visas on arrival (30-day entry). A single-entry visa costs US$20 and lasts for ten days; a multi-entry visa lasts for 30 days and costs US$30; a 72-hour transit visa costs US$5.

If you require a visa and arrive into Brunei by road from Sabah or Sarawak, be aware that you must have Brunei dollars on you (which can be withdrawn from a bank in Malaysia) to pay the visa fee.

There are no ATMs at the immigration checks, and they do not take credit-card payments.

CUSTOMS The Malaysian customs department has enforced the green- and red-lane system for visitor arrivals nationwide. The green lane means nothing to declare; you will face hefty penalties if you are found carrying undeclared dutiable goods and should be in the red lane. Duty-free allowances per traveller include one litre of wine or spirits, 225g of tobacco, gifts and souvenirs valued at up to RM400 (excluding goods from duty-free islands Langkawi and Labuan, which must not exceed RM500). Customs duty on non-exempt items equals 30% of the overall value. See the Customs Department website for full details (*www.customs.gov.my*).

Brunei customs laws include particular rules relating to alcohol, which you cannot buy anywhere in the country. Non-Muslims over 17 years of age can bring in two bottles of liquor (about two litres) and 12 cans of beer, which has to be declared to customs upon arrival. Passengers over 17 can carry in 200 cigarettes, 60g of tobacco, 60ml of perfume and 250ml eau de toilette.

The trafficking of drugs in Brunei carries the death sentence.

EMBASSIES AND CONSULATES

ABROAD Embassy opening hours vary greatly and are generally from 08.00 to 16.30 Monday to Friday, but it is always best to ring ahead and check.

Malaysian diplomatic missions
Australia Malaysian High Commission, 7 Perth Av, Yarralumla, Canberra; +61 2 6273 1543; e malcanberra@netspeed.com.au
Canada Consulate General of Malaysia, Suite 1805, Terasen Centre, No 1111, West Georgia St, Vancouver; +1 604 685 9550; e mwvcouvr@axion.net; www.kln.gov.my
Ireland Embassy of Malaysia, Level 3A-5A, Shelbourne Hse, Shelbourne Rd, Ballsbridge, Dublin; +353 1 667 7280; e mwdublin@mwdublin.ie
New Zealand High Commission of Malaysia; 10 Washington Av, Brooklyn, Wellington; +64 4 3852439/8015659; e mwwelton@xtra.co.nz
UK Malaysian High Commission, 45 Belgrave Sq, London SW1X 8QT; 020 7235 8033; e ruzaidi@btconnect.com; www.jimlondon.net
USA Embassy of Malaysia, 3516 International Court NW, Washington, DC 20008; +1 202 572 9700; e malwashdc@kln.gov.my; Consulate General in New York: 313 East 43 St; + 1 212 490 2722; e malnycg@kln.gov.my. There is also a Consulate General in Los Angeles.

Brunei's diplomatic missions
Australia High Commission of Brunei Darussalam, 10 Beale Cr, Deakin, ACT; +61 2 6285 4500/1; e consular@brunei.org.au; www.brunei.org.au
Canada High Commission of Brunei Darussalam, 395 Laurier Av East, Ottawa, Ontario; +1 613 2345
UK High Commission of Brunei Darussalam, 19–20 Belgrave Sq, London SW1X 8PG; 020 7581 0521; e bruhighcomlondon@hotmail.com; http://ukinbrunei.fco.gov.uk
USA Embassy of Brunei Darussalam, 3520 International Court NW, Washington, DC; +1 202 2371 838; e info@bruneiembassy.org or washington.usa@mfa.gov.bn; www.bruneiembassy.org

IN MALAYSIA Foreign embassies are in Kuala Lumpur (see *www.kln.gov.my*). The British Council is on the ground floor of the Api-Api Centre in Kota Kinabalu.

Australia Australian High Commission, 6 Jln Yap Kwan Seng; +60 3 2465555
Austria Austrian Embassy, 7th Floor, MUI Plaza Bldg, Jln P Ramlee; +60 3 2484277
Belgium Belgian Embassy, 8A Jln Ampang Hilir; +60 3 2625733
Canada Canadian High Commission, 7th Floor, OFK Plaza, 172 Jln Ampang; +60 3 2612000
China Chinese Embassy, 229 Jln Ampang; +60 3 2428495
Denmark Danish Embassy, 22nd Floor, Wisma Angkasa Raya, 123 Jln Ampang; +60 3 2416088
France French Embassy, 192–196 Jln Ampang; +60 3 2484122
Germany German Embassy, 3 Jln U Thant; +60 3 2429666
Italy Italian Embassy, 99 Jln U Thant; +60 3 4565122
Japan Japanese Embassy, 11 Persiaran Stonor, off Jln Tun Razak; +60 3 2427044
The Netherlands Dutch Embassy, 4 Jln Mesra, off Jln Damai; +60 3 2485151
New Zealand New Zealand High Commission, 193 Jln Tun Razak; +60 3 2382533
Singapore Singapore High Commission, 209 Jln Tun Perak; +60 3 2616277
Sweden Swedish Embassy, 6th Floor, Wisma Angkasa Raya; +60 3 2485433
Switzerland Swiss Embassy, 6 Persiaran Madge; +60 3 2480622
UK British High Commission, 185 Jln Ampang; +60 3 2482122
USA US Embassy, 376 Jln Tun Razak; +60 3 2489011

The UK also has **Honorary British Consuls** in Sabah (Kota Kinabalu) and in Sarawak (Kuching).

E Sabah Mr Peter Mole; +6 088 253333;
e peter.mole@pekah.com

E Sarawak Mrs Valerie Mashman; Kuching;
+6 082 250950

IN BRUNEI   All the following embassies are along the riverfront area of Bandar Seri Begawan city centre (☉ *09.00–17.00 Mon–Fri*).

E Australia Australian High Commission, Level 6, Dar Takaful IBB Utama Bldg, Jln Pemancha; +673 2229435; e austhicom.brunei@dfat.gov. au; www.bruneidarussalam.embassy.gov.au
E Canada Canadian High Commission, 5th Floor, McArthur Building, No 1 Jln McArthur; +673 2220043; e hicomcda@ppl.brunet.bn; www.brunei.gc.ca
E New Zealand The New Zealand High Commission in Kuala Lumpur is accredited to Brunei, Level 21, Menara IMC, 8 Jln Sultan Ismail;

+673 20782533; e nzhckl@streamyx.com; www.nzembassy.com
E UK British High Commission, 2nd Floor, Block D, Kompleks Yayasan Sultan Haji Hassanal Bolkiah, Jln Pretty, Bandar Seri Begawan; +673 2222231; e brithc@brunet.bn; www.britishhighcommission. gov.uk/brunei
E USA Embassy of the United States of America, 3rd Floor, Teck Guan Plaza, Jln Sultan (corner of Jln McArthur); +673 2220384; e amembassy_ bsb@state.gov or http://bandar.usembassy.gov

GETTING THERE AND AWAY

BY AIR   The main international airports in Borneo are in Brunei's capital, Bandar Seri Begawan, or BSB as it is commonly known, Sabah's capital Kota Kinabalu – again, 'KK' for those in the know – and Kuching, the capital of Sarawak, which is less easily shortened. Clearly your choice of airline will be determined by your proposed itinerary. Sabah Tourism (*www.sabahtourism.com*) provides a summary and map of all international flights to Kota Kinabalu under its 'Getting to Sabah' section.

Good **travel metasearch sites** for fare comparing and other ticketing options are Mobissimo.com, Kayak.com, TravelSupermarket.com and Momondo.com. London's *Daily Telegraph* Travel section cited Adioso.com, Hipmunk.com, Kayak and Momondo as the most lateral-minded aggregators in 2014. Farecompare.com and Skyscanner.net are two others. Also, in a 2014 story, *USA Today* found Kayak came out top when price was used as the ultimate search criterion, as opposed to journey time, or other factors. 'Kayak was the only site to provide lowest fares in all three cases. Hipmunk and Momondo also performed well, when comparing strictly by price. But all of the lowest fares involved stops in at least one direction, while Mobissimo provided competitively priced non-stops.'

Flights from Australia, New Zealand and the Middle East

AirAsia (*www.airasia.com*) Perhaps AirAsia is destined to be just that. Unfortunately for travellers, the low-cost beyond-Asia forays were short-lived, with flights from Paris and London cancelled within a year. Emblazoned in its dynamic trademark red, Asia's leading budget airline hooks into many Asian destinations, as well as southern and northern India. There are direct flights to Kota Kinabalu from Kuala Lumpur, Penang and the southern Malaysian city Johor Bahru, and direct international flights to KK from Singapore, Ho Chi Minh City, Jakarta, and Clark in the Philippines. AirAsia also flies to Kuching from Kuala Lumpur and Singapore.

Royal Brunei Airlines (*www.bruneiair.com*) The only non-stop long-haul flights to Borneo are provided by Royal Brunei Airlines (RBA). The airline operates direct flights to Bandar Seri Begawan from the UK, Australia, New Zealand and the

Middle East. It has significantly upgraded its planes for its long-haul routes – the new Boeing 777s include 30 business-class seats that transform to full-length flat beds and 255 reclining economy-class seats.

From London, direct flights to BSB operate four-times weekly from Heathrow's Terminal 4, as well as three flights via Dubai.

Four weekly flights between London and Melbourne via Bandar Seri Begawan were introduced in 2011, expanding the Australian connections to Brunei, which already include direct flights from Brisbane and Perth. There are four flights weekly from Auckland, New Zealand.

Malaysia Airlines (*www.malaysiaairlines.com*) With a disappeared plane and a shot-down plane, Malaysia Airlines (MAS) had an *annus horribilis* beyond the worst imaginings in 2014, both disasters occurring within the space of four months, and many pundits forecasting the company's impending demise. Following the second of 'the twin tragedies', as they have come to be known, even usually faithful and discreet Malaysians were predicting the unlikely survival of their much-loved national airline, founded in 1972. The two catastrophes followed close on the heels of reports of MAS's deep financial strife. Yet within weeks, most of the negativity had fizzled, and people were snapping up MAS's hot domestic and international deals as though nothing had ever happened. Just as they ought, given the lack of direct airline fault in either of the massively unfortunate yet image-shaking ordeals. Whether MAS's solid brand ID and consumer following will be enough to shore it up in the long term is yet to be seen. In September 2014, the airline was embarking on the 'MAS Recovery Plan' – its fifth in a decade, and definitely its most critical. Meanwhile, thousands of people around the world were continuing, mostly without hangups, to hop aboard MAS and MASwings flights. The quality of the airline, and the good fares they offer, had almost overshadowed the cons.

Return ticket prices from AU$845 return Australia to Borneo direct are hard to beat on both price and journey time. MAS operates twice-weekly direct flights from both Sydney and Perth to Kuching, and from Perth to Kota Kinabalu.

Relatively seamless routes from many worldwide destinations transit the Malaysian capital Kuala Lumpur. MAS operates non-stop international flights to Kuala Lumpur from London, Amsterdam, Paris, Rome, Zurich, Frankfurt, Stockholm, New York, Los Angeles, Buenos Aires, Sydney, Perth, Adelaide, Brisbane, Melbourne, Auckland, Dubai, Cape Town and Johannesburg. Sometimes an overnight stay in Kuala Lumpur is necessary ahead of follow-on flights to Bandar Seri Begawan, Kota Kinabalu, Kuching, Labuan Island, and Sibu (Sarawak's second city).

From Kota Kinabalu, regional MASwings connects to Tawau, Lahad Datu, Sandakan and Kudat in Sabah, and Kuching, Miri, Mulu, Limbang, and Sibu in Sarawak.

Singapore Airlines (*www.singaporeair.com*) For quality and a seamless trip, this airline is a very good option for reaching Borneo. Planes fly non-stop to Singapore from London, Manchester, New York, Los Angeles, San Francisco, Moscow, Rome, Milan, Copenhagen, Paris, Frankfurt, Zurich, Athens, Brisbane, Sydney, Melbourne, Perth, Adelaide, Auckland, Christchurch, Dubai, Abu Dhabi, Johannesburg, Cape Town, Tokyo and Beijing. After as little as a one-hour transit, there are connecting flights to Kota Kinabalu, Kuching and Brunei with Singapore Airlines' subsidiary, Silk Air (*www.silkair.com*), or on code share with Malaysia Airlines.

Singapore Airlines also has flights in the UK from Aberdeen, Newcastle, Belfast, Glasgow, Edinburgh, Leeds/Bradford and Teesside, bypassing London.

Jetstar (*www.jetstar.com*) This Australian' low-cost airline, together with its offshoot Jetstar Asia, operates direct flights in both economy and business class between Kuala Lumpur and Melbourne, Kuala Lumpur–Auckland, New Zealand, Singapore–Perth, and indirect flights from Kuala Lumpur to Sydney, Hobart, Launceston, Adelaide and the Gold Coast, all via Melbourne.

Other carriers Passengers arriving in Hong Kong, either with Cathay Pacific from the US, BA from London, or Qantas from Australia, can then link with the daily direct flight to KK operated by Hong Kong-based **Dragon Air** (*www.dragonair.com*), part of the Cathay Pacific group. **Delta Airlines** (*www.delta.com*) have non-stop flights to Taipei in Taiwan, from where you can fly to KK with MAS. **China Southern Airlines** (*www.csair.com*) flies to Kuching from Guangzhou and Hong Kong. **Cebu Pacific** (*www.cebupacificair.com*) operates direct flights between KK and Manila. Lufthansa (*www.lufthansa.com*) flies to Kuching from Frankfurt.

Flights from Asia
Royal Brunei Airlines Regionally, Royal Brunei Airlines operates daily services from Bandar Seri Begawan to Singapore, Shanghai, Bangkok, Kuala Lumpur, Manila, Jeddah, Jakarta, Surabaya, Ho Chi Minh City and Hong Kong.
   There are about 17 weekly flights from Bandar Seri Begawan to Kota Kinabalu, and five flights to Kuching, assuring smooth regional connections throughout Borneo.

Malaysia Airlines Stepping up direct regional connections, MAS introduced several flights to Kuching from Japan (Tokyo and Osaka) and Korea (Incheon) in 2011, adding to its existing direct services to Kota Kinabalu from Japan, China (Hong Kong), South Korea (Seoul), and Taiwan (Taipei).
   MAS also has flights to Sabah and Sarawak from other Asian airports, including Hong Kong. MAS flies to Kota Kinabalu from Singapore, Seoul, Osaka, Tokyo, Hong Kong, Guangzhou, Taipei and Kaohsiung (Taiwan).

AirAsia AirAsia has revolutionised the Asian skies in the past few years, opening up travel almost for all. Its highly competitive prices, fun presentation and snappy service mentality frequently see it nominated as Asia's top low-cost airline. The airline has many direct connections from Kuala Lumpur to Kota Kinabalu, Sandakan, Miri and Kuching. It also has direct flights to Kota Kinabalu from Bangkok (allowing connections with Thai Airways, Qantas or British Airways flights among others).

Which airline? If sheer quality and comfort of service are your priorities, for long-haul trips it is (still) hard to beat Singapore Airlines and Malaysia Airlines, though Royal Brunei Airlines are making some major headway and offer very competitive prices. For price, Malaysia Airlines is very competitive. Upgrades to RBA's fleet have significantly notched up the comfort with larger planes, a new in-flight entertainment system and angled (as opposed to completely lie-flat) beds in business class. (For further details, see pages 84–5.) The cheapest flights on Just the Flight (*www.justtheflight.co.uk*) often turn up Malaysia Airlines, Air Emirates (via Dubai) and Qatar Airways (via Doha), so if you are not fussed about taking a direct flight – or are looking to enjoy an exotic stopover – the latter two could be entertained. Transit flights can also be taken via Bangkok (Thai Airways), Hong Kong (Cathay Pacific), Taipei, Kaohsiung, Manila, Cebu, Seoul, Singapore and Tokyo. These trips can be very tiring, involving two transfers, unless you use them expressly to stop over in a couple of interesting places. As a long-haul flight option for getting between Australia and Europe return, via Borneo, I find RBA's prices the best. The flight via Brunei and Dubai is intolerably long if you are just going from A to B. I make the most of the two stopovers and stay at least a few days in the UAE, following my usual weeks in Borneo.

For airline quality checks and star rankings in all brackets, from first class to budget airlines, see Skytrax (*www.airlinequality.com*).

The airline you choose should tie in with your itinerary. RBA makes it easy for an in-and-out of Brunei if coming from the UK or Australia. From there, internal flights are readily available to Sabah and Sarawak's capital cities.

HEALTH   *with Dr Felicity Nicholson*

PREPARATIONS   Preparations to ensure a healthy trip to Borneo require checks on your immunisation status: it is wise to be up to date on tetanus, polio and diphtheria (now given as an all-in-one vaccine, Revaxis, that lasts for ten years), typhoid and hepatitis A. Immunisations against hepatitis B, rabies and Japanese encephalitis may also be recommended. Hepatitis A vaccine (Havrix Monodose or Avaxim) comprises two injections given about a year apart. The course costs about £100, but may be available on the NHS; it protects for 25 years and can be administered even close to the time of departure. Hepatitis B vaccination should be considered for longer trips (two months or more) or for those working with children or in situations where contact with blood is likely. Three injections are needed for the best protection and can be given over a three-week period if time is short for those aged 16 or over. Longer schedules give more sustained protection and are therefore preferred if time allows. Hepatitis A vaccine can also be given as a combination with hepatitis B as 'Twinrix', though two doses are needed at least seven days apart to be effective for the hepatitis A component, and three doses are needed for the hepatitis B. This is only available for those aged 16 or over.

The newer injectable typhoid vaccines (eg: Typhim Vi) last for three years and are about 85% effective. Oral capsules (Vivotif) may also be available for those aged six and over; three capsules over five days lasts for three years, but may be less effective than the injectable forms if they are not absorbed properly. Vaccination against typhoid should be encouraged unless the traveller is leaving within a few days for a trip of a week or less, when the vaccine would not be effective in time.

Vaccinations for rabies should be offered to everyone, time allowing, but are even more important for travellers visiting remote areas, especially if you are more than 24 hours from medical help and always if you will be working with animals (see page 91).

Ideally you should visit your own doctor or a specialist travel clinic to discuss your requirements if possible at least six weeks before you plan to travel.

Good starting points for general health and safety advice are foreign embassies. See the travel advice on the British Foreign and Commonwealth Office website (*www.fco.gov.uk*). The International Society of Travel Medicine (*www.istm.org*), emedicine.com (*www.emedecine.com*) and The Travel Doctor (*www.traveldoctor.co.uk*) are also useful for medical and health information. Fit for Travel (*www.fitfortravel.scot.nhs.uk*) is another excellent website which uses the same information as the professional website Travax.

FIRST-AID KIT
- A good drying antiseptic, eg: iodine or Savlon Dry Antiseptic (don't take antiseptic cream)
- A few small dressings (Band-Aids)

3

- Suncream
- Insect repellent and bite treatment
- Aspirin or paracetamol
- Antifungal cream (eg: Canesten)
- Anti-diarrhoea tablets such as Imodium
- Rehydration sachets
- Ciprofloxacin, norfloxacin or rifaximin, for diarrhoea
- Tinidazole for giardia or amoebic dysentery (see below for regime)
- Antibiotic eye drops, for sore, 'gritty', stuck-together eyes (conjunctivitis)
- Alcohol-based hand rub or bar of soap in plastic box
- Condoms or femidoms

TROPICAL DISEASES

Malaria This is a serious and potentially fatal disease transmitted by mosquitoes, for which there is no vaccine. There are hugely differing estimates of the prevalence of malaria in Borneo, ranging from 'successfully eliminated' to 'widespread'. Most sources agree that the risk is greater in more remote areas and fairly low in urban and coastal regions.

Current recommendations for prophylaxis are Malarone, doxycycline or Lariam for those travelling to rural areas of Borneo; unless none of these tablets are suitable for you, then you would be advised to take them. Seek medical advice as to which is the most appropriate for you and follow the regime recommended carefully. That said, no malaria tablets are 100% effective and so you should always take precautions against mosquito bites. This includes wearing trousers and long-sleeved shirts particularly between dusk and dawn. Apply insect repellents containing around 50–55% DEET to exposed skin at the recommended intervals, and when necessary sleep under a permethrin-impregnated bed net. These may not be provided, so it is wise to take your own, especially if you are visiting remote areas.

Early diagnosis of malaria is essential for effective treatment, so if you suspect you or a companion has contracted the disease then seek medical help as soon as possible. Symptoms are flu-like and may include fevers, chills, muscle and joint aches, headache, tiredness, nausea, vomiting, and occasionally diarrhoea. The only consistent feature is a high temperature of 38°C or more and that alone should also make you suspect malaria. It can develop from as early as six to seven days after exposure, to up to as much as one year, so continue to be vigilant upon your return and seek medical advice if you develop flu-like symptoms.

For further advice and malaria information, see www.fitfortravel.nhs.uk/destinations/malaysia.htm, www.preventingmalaria.info, and www.traveldoctor.co.uk/malaria.htm.

Other diseases There are periodic outbreaks of **dengue fever** with peak transmission from June to November (for which there is no vaccination). This viral infection is spread by day-biting mosquitoes. It causes a feverish illness with headache and muscle pains like a bad, prolonged, attack of influenza. There may be a rash. Recurrent infections can be more serious so it is important to try and avoid the disease in the first place by using DEET containing insect repellents during the daytime as well as in the evening.

Japanese encephalitis is another viral disease transmitted by infected mosquitoes. Vaccination is recommended for those likely to be frequently exposed to bites during long stays, repeated visits or if staying in rural infected areas. The newer vaccine Ixiaro (two doses given ideally 28 days apart; if time is short then the

LONG-HAUL FLIGHTS, CLOTS AND DVT

Any prolonged immobility, including travel by land or air, can result in deep vein thrombosis (DVT) with the risk of embolus to the lungs. Certain factors can increase the risk and these include:

- Previous clot or close relative with a history
- People over 40, but greater risk over 80 years
- Recent major operation or varicose veins surgery
- Cancer
- Stroke
- Heart disease
- Obesity
- Pregnancy
- Hormone therapy
- Heavy smoking
- Severe varicose veins
- Being very tall (over 6ft/1.8m) or short (under 5ft/1.5m)

A deep vein thrombosis (DVT) causes painful swelling and redness of the calf or sometimes the thigh. It is only dangerous if a clot travels to the lungs (pulmonary embolus). Symptoms of a pulmonary embolus (PE) include chest pain, shortness of breath, and sometimes coughing up small amounts of blood and commonly start three to ten days after a long flight. Anyone who thinks that they might have a DVT needs to see a doctor immediately.

PREVENTION OF DVT
- Keep mobile before and during the flight; move around every couple of hours
- Drink plenty of fluids during the flight
- Avoid taking sleeping pills and excessive tea, coffee and alcohol
- Consider wearing flight socks or support stockings (see *www.legshealth.com*)

If you think you are at increased risk of a clot, ask your doctor if it is safe to travel.

second dose may be given no less than 24 days after the first dose of vaccine) has none of the more serious side effects of the older vaccines and therefore should be recommended for all rural travel if time and budget allow. This vaccine can be used in those aged two years and over. The disease is endemic, with small numbers of cases occurring year-round in East Malaysia (Sabah and Sarawak), but in addition epidemics occur following the start of the rainy season in Peninsular Malaysia (April to October) when mosquitoes are most active.

WATER In Malaysia water is treated, but it is still best to avoid drinking tap water. You would also be advised to clean your teeth with bottled water and to avoid ice in drinks.

AIR QUALITY Malaysia, and in particular Sarawak, periodically suffers from smoke haze pollution. Hazardous air-quality levels are reached due to extensive burning of forests in neighbouring Indonesia. The Malaysian Department of Environment (*www.doe.gov.my*) offers more information on this.

FOOD There are strict laws and health standards for food preparation, though this doesn't necessarily equate to high standards of cleanliness in coffee shops. Establishments with a grade A or B (see page 113) are usually of a good standard; anything of grade C or lower may be less than satisfactory.

TRAVELLERS' DIARRHOEA There is always a risk of getting a dose of travellers' diarrhoea; perhaps half of all visitors will suffer and the newer you are to exotic travel, the more likely that will be. By taking precautions against travellers' diarrhoea you will also avoid typhoid, paratyphoid, hepatitis, dysentery, worms, etc. Travellers' diarrhoea and the other faecal-oral diseases come from getting other people's faeces in your mouth. This most often happens from cooks not washing their hands after a trip to the toilet, but even if the restaurant cook does not understand basic hygiene you will be safe if your food has been properly cooked and arrives piping hot. The most important prevention strategy is to wash your hands before eating anything. You can pick up salmonella and shigella from toilet door handles and possibly bank notes. The maxim to remind you what you can safely eat is:

PEEL IT, BOIL IT, COOK IT OR FORGET IT

This means that fruit you have washed and peeled yourself, and hot foods, should be safe, but raw foods, cold cooked foods, salads, fruit salads that have been

TREATING TRAVELLERS' DIARRHOEA   *Dr Jane Wilson-Howarth*

It is dehydration that makes you feel awful during a bout of diarrhoea and the most important part of treatment is drinking lots of clear fluids. Sachets of oral rehydration salts give the perfect biochemical mix to replace all that is pouring out of your bottom but other recipes taste nicer. Any dilute mixture of sugar and salt in water will do you good: try Coke or orange squash with a three-finger pinch of salt added to each glass (if you are salt-depleted you won't taste the salt). Otherwise make a solution of a four-finger scoop of sugar with a three-finger pinch of salt in a 500 ml glass. Or add eight level teaspoons of sugar (18g) and one level teaspoon of salt (3g) to one litre (five cups) of safe water. A squeeze of lemon or orange juice improves the taste and adds potassium, which is also lost in diarrhoea. Drink two large glasses after every bowel action, and more if you are thirsty. These solutions are still absorbed well if you are vomiting, but you will need to take sips at a time. If you are not eating you need to drink three litres a day plus whatever is pouring into the toilet. If you feel like eating, take a bland, high carbohydrate diet. Heavy greasy foods will probably give you cramps. Some people like to take antibiotics at the first sign of traveller's diarrhoea. Rifamixin, ciprofloxacin or norfloxacin may be suggested. These are only available on prescription.

If the diarrhoea is bad, or you are passing blood or slime, or you have a fever, you will probably need antibiotics in addition to fluid replacement. Azithromycin is currently the treatment of choice for dysentery but is only suitable for those aged 18 or over. If the diarrhoea is greasy and bulky and is accompanied by sulphurous (eggy) burps, one likely cause is giardia. This is best treated with tinidazole (four x 500mg in one dose, repeated seven days later if symptoms persist).

prepared by others, ice cream and ice are all risky, and foods kept lukewarm in hotel buffets are often dangerous. That said, plenty of travellers enjoy fruit and vegetables, so do keep a sense of perspective. If you are struck, see box, page 90, for treatment.

Shellfish, crabs and some larger fish can be affected by 'red tide' – an algal bloom that produces harmful toxins. These can become incorporated into other sea creatures and may be harmful if consumed by humans. The Health Ministry issues warnings when this occurs, and restaurants follow their advice. Larger seafood restaurants in Borneo with their own tanks still trade during these periods.

RABIES Rabies is potentially carried by all warm-blooded mammals and is passed on to man through a bite, scratch or a lick of an open wound. More rarely it can be contracted by saliva getting into your eyes, nose or mouth. You must always assume any animal is rabid, even if it looks well, as there is a ten-day period where the animal is infectious but looks perfectly well. Scrub the wound with soap under a running tap or while pouring water from a jug for a good 10–15 minutes. The quality of the water is not important at this stage. If you have an antiseptic then use this next or an alcohol solution of spirits will do. Then get to medical help as soon as possible.

Pre-exposure vaccination for rabies is ideally advised for everyone, but is particularly important if you intend to have contact with animals and/or are likely to be more than 24 hours away from medical help. Ideally three doses should be taken over 28 days, though if time is short then 21 days will suffice. Contrary to popular belief these vaccinations are relatively painless. The main reason for having pre-exposure vaccine is to avoid the need for Rabies Immunoglobulin (RIG), which is a pre-formed antibody made from human (HRIG) or equine (ERIG) blood. It is hard to come by in a lot of countries and it is doubtful that Borneo would have any, meaning that you would have to evacuate to Singapore. Five doses of a cell-derived vaccine (HDCV, PEP or Verorab) are also needed on days 0, 3, 7, 14 and 28. If you have had the pre-exposure course of three doses of vaccine then the RIG is no longer needed and only two doses of vaccine are given three days apart. This is often easier to find locally and most often would not require evacuation.

If you are bitten, scratched or licked over an open wound by a sick animal, then post-exposure prophylaxis should be given as soon as possible, though it is never too late to seek help, as the incubation period for rabies can be very long. Tell the doctor if you have had pre-exposure vaccine, as this should change the treatment you receive. And remember that, if you do contract rabies, mortality is 100% and death from rabies is probably one of the worst ways to go.

DOCTORS There are two medical systems in Malaysia. Both public and private health care are widely available and of a high standard. Private health care is relatively inexpensive even as a traveller without local medical insurance. You can arrange to see a doctor easily at a medical centre or surgery, or ask your hotel to organise a doctor to visit you there. Though it is more expensive than public health care, but you are guaranteed a high level of service, and English-speaking staff. Medical staff administer most medication on the spot, so you shouldn't need to go to a pharmacy as well. Health centres and hospitals are listed in the relevant chapters. For a full list of hospitals and district health officers in Sabah and Sarawak, see the Malaysian government portal (*www.moh.gov.my/MohPortal/govhospPublic.jsp*).

BRUNEI Brunei is relatively free from malaria and other tropical diseases. It is outside the typhoon belt, has no active volcanoes and is not prone to earthquakes or other major natural disasters.

TRAVEL CLINICS AND HEALTH INFORMATION A full list of current travel clinic websites worldwide is available on www.istm.org. For other journey preparation information, consult www.nathnac.org/ds/map_world.aspx (UK) or wwwnc.cdc.gov/travel (US). Information about various medications may be found on www.netdoctor.co.uk/travel. All advice found online should be used in conjunction with expert advice received prior to or during travel.

SAFETY

British, US and Australian authorities periodically issue warnings against travelling around the coast of East Malaysia, particularly the Celebes/Sulawesi Sea islands off the southeast coast of Sabah. Those warnings have again come to a head after a dire couple of years for the region in 2013–14. Over a decade after the kidnappings in 2000, which saw all Sidapan Island resorts closed, and a bolstered and continuing Malaysian military surveillance in the area, there has been a recent spate of kidnappings by Filipino bandits, even the murder of one tourist. (See box, pages 248–51.) Furthermore, the regional political volatility and territorial disputes between Indonesia and Malaysia erupted in 2013 with the 'invasion' of Lahad Datu in Sabah by a group of armed Sulu rebels (see page 239). I personally am nervous about dipping myself into the diving region right now, until things seem more under control. At the time of writing in 2015, the FCO were advising against all but essential travel to all islands off the coast of eastern Sabah between Kudat and Tawau, including Lankayan, Mabul, Pom Pom, Kapalai, Litigan, Sipadan and Mataking. Check the FCO website (*www.gov.uk/foregn-travel-advice/malaysia*) for the current advice before booking your trip.

URBAN SAFETY AND CRIME 'There is a relatively low risk of being mugged or robbed', I wrote in the second edition of this guide, 'but always keep personal belongings close, and be on the lookout for pickpockets in markets'. Then came the horrifying events in August 2014, when two British medical students were murdered in Kuching – stabbed to death by frenzied criminals high on crystal meth. The 22-year-olds were on their way back to their hostel when four men attacked them, apparently after an altercation in a bar. The incident rocked the small city, and while the authorities presented it as an isolated attack, there have been reports of other aggressive behaviour against Irish medical students in a Kuching bar. No such headlines in Brunei, where the low crime rate owes largely to the severe penalties under Sharia law for stealing, aggression and other offences.

When driving in Sabah and Sarawak, keep an eye out for large cracks and holes in roads – some are very unkempt. Pedestrians too need to be careful on patchy streets and footpaths. Brunei's roads and footpaths are far better.

ANIMALS There are several poisonous snakes, both terrestrial and marine (see page 57), so caution must be taken at certain beaches. Crocodiles are a threat too in some coastal areas of Sarawak and rivers throughout Borneo. While there are no deadly mammals in the forest, jungle walks are safer in the company of a knowledgeable guide. Orangutans, though adorable-looking, can be ferocious particularly when goaded by ignorant tourists. Remember this is Asia's great ape – not a toy! Like all creatures, if it feels threatened or provoked it may attack. The pigtail macaques also can be very tetchy and aggressive.

WOMEN TRAVELLERS

After many years as a solo woman globetrotter, Malaysia probably stands out as the safest country in which I have travelled. Personal security, general public friendliness and political stability are all at a high. In September 2010, the Oxford Business Group identified the high levels of overall safety in Malaysia as one of the main reasons for it having 'strengthened its position as Southeast Asia's top tourism destination'. In Asia as a whole, Malaysia rated second only to China for its political and social stability. With the exception of one very high-profile murder case, the murder of a former prime minister's lover, no horrendous crimes against women immediately come to mind.

The sense of general personal security as a woman traveller is even greater in Borneo, because of the island's friendliness and its relatively small cities. In my frequent and lengthy travels in Brunei, Sabah and Sarawak, I have never once felt threatened by men; irritated occasionally by slightly juvenile attitudes to women in Malaysia, but not spooked. In the main cities – Kota Kinabalu, Kuching and Miri – I always feel safe walking around in key public areas, though poorly lit backstreets and more remote urban zones are best avoided at night. The fact that Malaysia is such a street-living society, with a density of people in public areas, boosts the overall feeling of safety.

In Brunei, the huge esteem shown for women makes it one of the safest countries in the world for female travellers. The incidence of crime is virtually nil – partly due to the penalties faced – and assaults against women are unheard of (though possibly go unreported).

The respect shown to me, and my own personal feeling of comfort, is no doubt heightened by my respect for Muslim customs and appropriate dress (longer skirts, blouses, no miniskirts or bare shoulders).

Muslim women in Brunei and Malaysia wear a tudong, a veil or scarf, on their head. While there is no expectation for foreigners to do the same, it is advisable to carry a light scarf in your bag to don at appropriate moments, such as visiting religious sites. While skimpier garments have become the norm amongst the clubbing classes of Kuala Lumpur, Borneo – particularly Brunei – is more conservative.

(See also page 126.)

DISABLED TRAVELLERS

A couple of major UK and US associations who deal with disabled travel have told me Borneo falls outside their radar. This is surprising and likely to change as tourist numbers increase. For the time being, travel on public transport, especially small town buses, would not be easy. Most four and five-star hotels claim to have facilities for the disabled including wheelchair access and 'adapted' rooms. The same can increasingly be said for independent hotels. The lack of dedicated disabled-friendly tours doesn't mean there is a lack of tour companies ready to create an itinerary, or hook in with local companies who have the right staff and vehicles. Use the various associations as your advocates so that they know there is a demand for such information. Also visit the websites of Mobility International USA (*www.miusa.org/ncde/intlopportunities/malaysia*), www.canbedone.co.uk, and www.disabledtravelers.com.

FAMILIES

Overall, Malaysian Borneo is safe, sunny and friendly and makes an inexpensive, educational, adventurous and exotic family holiday.

Far from just a sun-seeker's destination, it offers enriching opportunities such as volunteer family holidays, living and helping out in one of the villages, or working with wildlife.

Many city hostels – especially the 'lodge' kind – have family rooms from RM115 with breakfast included. With lounges, sun decks and other travellers for company, these often provide a more fun and instructive atmosphere than the cramped, sequestered environment of shoestring hotels, which offer family rooms from RM100 to RM150. If you have more to spend, and want more privacy and comfort, most mid-range to luxury hotels have family rooms or self-contained suites with separate living spaces and multi-bedrooms and bathrooms. Another good option is serviced apartments. Beyond the cities, beach resorts have larger rooms, or self-contained accommodation; or pay for several rooms to accommodate your brood. Mountain resorts often have self-contained chalet accommodation with equipped kitchens. Other options in rural areas are longhouse rentals and family-friendly homestays.

SINGLE TRAVELLERS

Many pros and cons of travelling solo in Borneo are common to all destinations. Particularly in luxury hotels, employees frequently grill me as to whether it is 'just one for breakfast?' 'I'm not hiding anyone' is my usual reply. A book or newspaper is a great refuge from indiscreet stares.

Financially, single travellers are heavily penalised with the lack of single-room rates: the difference in price between a single and double is either non-existent or negligible. Choose instead to stay in places where being single does pay – homestays, bed and breakfasts, hostels, budget or mid-range beach resorts, and the occasional hotel suite or apartment which offer rates suitably priced for the 'flash packer'. Even if you have the money for a more expensive hotel room, independently run or smaller-size accommodations can be more convivial, if it's company you are after. And many offer the possibility of upgrading to a bigger, more comfortable room. If you prefer a hotel environment, you can always go for the premium rooms or suites of budget city hotels, or serviced apartments. The same price bracket in some country hotels may get you anything from a superior room to a suite.

GAY AND LESBIAN TRAVELLERS

One of the most highly regarded gay and lesbian associations active in Borneo is **Utopia Asia** (*www.utopia-asia.com*). Its general advice for travellers in Malaysia is: 'Gay life in Malaysia as in other Asian countries is blossoming, despite conservative religion-based discrimination and outdated colonial era laws.'

Former deputy prime minister, Anwar Ibrahim, was famously ousted from office by a trumped-up sodomy conviction, overturned by Malaysia's High Court in 2004. The case is still making waves, as issues of homosexuality and discrimination are slowly (very slowly) brought out of the conservative closet. Islam is enshrined as the official state religion in the Malaysian constitution. Muslims, local and visitors, are thus subject to religious laws that penalise gay or lesbian sexual activity with flogging, and male transvestism with imprisonment, though this is rarely the case. The law does not in principle apply to non-Muslims. Yet homosexual citizens of any creed still face official discrimination. Police can arrest any person, Muslim or not, for having sex in a public place, such as cruise spots. That said, police rarely detain foreigners during raids on local gay businesses, focusing instead on ethnic Malay customers, almost 100% of whom by law are considered Muslim at birth.

Still, visitors should respect Malaysian law and customs while guests in the country, as is the general rule of thumb for all travel.

See Utopia Asia's *Utopia Guide to Malaysia*, which has listings for the gay and lesbian scene in 17 cities including Kota Kinabalu and Kuching. The guide, which can be ordered online (*www.utopia-asia.com/utopiaguide/utopiaguides. htm*), includes gay-scene city maps and listings of organisations, bars, discos, spas, accommodation and restaurants, with a special section highlighting venues that are particularly welcoming to women.

Kota Kinabalu is definitely Borneo's capital of camp. While there are no flagrantly gay hotels, some are discreetly so, while others are gay-friendly. There are also some well-known gay and lesbian bars and nightclubs in town. Kuching is more conservative; while Brunei takes the issue to a whole new level, or planet, of ethics. Overt tolerance of homosexuality is non-existent, and the gay community exists mostly 'undercover'. The result is a weekend exodus of Brunei's closet gays to the nearest place where they can show public displays of affection without the fear of being arrested – generally Miri in Sarawak. The former oil city has inadvertently developed a great future in gay tourism.

WHAT TO TAKE

What you take hinges on what kind of holiday you are planning as much as personal tastes. Rather than provide an exhaustive list, I have highlighted a few things you may not want to do without.

MAPS Basic town maps for tourists are about all the maps readily available in Borneo. Outside of that, it is best to bring your own, as detailed as required for individual purposes (see page 103), and especially important if you are travelling by car, embarking on trekking trips, or visiting national parks. Even at Gunung Kinabalu National Park, the maps provided are mediocre in scale and legend. **Periplus Publishing** (*www.peripluspublishinggroup.com*) produce travel maps of Sarawak and Sabah at a scale of 1:1,000,000, including Kota Kinabalu, Kuching and Bintulu city plans. Periplus also do good language books – various Behasa, Melayu-Behasa and Inggeris dictionaries, including a good pocket one.

CLOTHES Leave your jeans at home! No matter how addicted to your denim you are, it weighs a ton, dries slowly and is squirmingly uncomfortable in humid climates. My packing skills (and suitcase weight) have improved dramatically during recent trips to Borneo. The tropics are the best minimising agent: clothing layers are instantly shed, and the rest should be light, sleek and airy. My travel wardrobe always includes a pair of fast-dry, high-tech trousers, Bermudas or knee-length sportswear skirt for jungle trekking or boating. For city-wear, I favour smart waist-drawn three-quarter-length pants, and two casual cotton skirts, dresses or shorts, depending on your style. Finally, count on one evening skirt or dress and a pair of slinky night trousers. To mix-and-match with all of the above, I take two or three casual tops and two dressy ones, including a long-sleeved cotton shirt for general wear or over bathers, plus a light cardigan to survive the sometimes-polar temperatures in planes, buses and restaurants. This also comes in handy for cooler climates such as Mount Kinabalu – the only place where temperatures can drop to 15°C. Finally, I pack a flimsy jogging outfit – unfortunately jogging shoes always add bulk, which is why ideally you will also use them for hiking (unless you are headed for heavy-duty trails). Anyone planning to do outdoor activities needs a light waterproof jacket.

Aim exclusively for pure cotton, linen and silk clothing, or cotton-silk and cotton-nylon mixes. Avoid scratchy materials such as rayon or heavy, humid viscose-elastane combinations.

If you are planning an ascent of Mount Kinabalu or other peaks, you will need to take some thermal and waterproof clothing fit for near-zero temperatures (see box, pages 208–9).

Both sexes should try to keep the shoe count to a maximum four pairs, including walking or jogging shoes, flip-flops/thongs, practical sightseeing shoes and possibly a more chic pair of day/night sandals. Avoid confined or tight footwear as your feet will feel clammy and may swell up. Good walking shoes or sandals in breathable leather are great for walking around cities in the heat. Quality leather flip-flops are ideal for light city roaming and the beach. Higher-heeled versions double up for a tropical day and night, casual-chic look.

(See also *Women Travellers*, page 93.)

MONEY

EAST MALAYSIA

Currency The currency of Sabah and Sarawak is the Malaysian ringgit (RM). Notes come in denominations of RM1, 5, 10, 50 and 100. One ringgit comprises 100 sen. Coins come in 5, 10, 20 and 50 sen denominations. The exchange rate in October 2015 was: US$1 = RM4.1; €1 = RM4.89; £1 = RM6.66. Check exchange rates with the Malaysian newspaper *The Star Online* (*www.biz.thestar.com.my/business/exchange.asp*).

Exchanging and spending Foreign currencies and travellers' cheques are readily exchanged at banks and licensed money exchanges in larger cities, as well as hotels and some department stores. Credit cards (Visa, MasterCard, American Express and Diners Club) are widely accepted in hotels and bigger restaurants and stores, but not in small local shops. Payment by cheque is not accepted. Credit-card payment is increasingly difficult as you distance yourself from major cities; likewise for exchanging money and cashing travellers' cheques. ATMs are scarce in rural areas and some medium-sized towns.

Major national Malaysian banks with branches in Sabah and Sarawak include Bumiputera Commerce and RHB Bank. Bank hours are generally 09.30–16.00, Monday to Friday.

Until 2005, the Malaysian ringgit was equal in value to the US dollar (in response to the Asian financial crash). People still commonly quote in dollars in marketplaces and shops, so if you are quoted an unreasonably high price this could be the explanation. The difference between RM1 and US$1 is more than three-fold. Ask if you are unsure.

Brunei The Brunei dollar (BND) is equal in value to the Singapore dollar, which is also legal tender in Brunei. The dollar comes in 1, 5, 10, 50, 100, 500 and 1,000 denominations; coins in 1, 5, 10, 20 and 50 cents. All major credit cards are accepted throughout the country. Most Bruneian banks are government-sanctioned to handle travellers' cheques and currency exchange. In October 2015, the exchange rates were: US$1 = B$1.39, €1 = B$1.58, £1 = B$2.15 AU$1=B$1.01.

Carrying cash In both Malaysia and Brunei, it is advisable to always carry some cash, especially when travelling in the countryside. ATMs can be hard to come by and unreliable, even at key airports.

BUDGETING

Borneo caters pretty well for all budgets, and is particularly good value for those with less money to spend. Other parts of Southeast Asia may be cheaper, but tend to have a greater choice of 'high-end' products and services. Borneo has a wide range of budget accommodation and food. It is possible to live inexpensively whatever your budget. Hotels, car hire, tours and trips will be your biggest expenditures, other than flights. Still-abundant hotel deals, slashed internet prices, and inter-bleeding of accommodation categories between budget/mid range and mid range/upmarket, means you can easily upgrade for some hotel nights.

Some typical daily items and their costs are:

Loaf of bread	RM1.60–2
Street snack	RM1–3
Postcard/international postage up to 20g	RM1.20 Zone 1(Asia)
	RM1.40 Zone 2 (Asia Pacific) AU$0.48
	RM2 Zone 3 (Europe, US) £0.38, US$0.60
T-shirt	RM10–15
1.5-litre bottle of water	RM0.70–2.70 (plain/mineral)
1 litre of milk	RM6–7
1.5-litre soft drink	RM2.50
1 litre of petrol	RM2.30
Local bus fare	RM1–2

ACCOMMODATION
Upmarket Hotels which are truly five-star on an international par generally charge RM700–RM900 for their standard rooms, and RM1,000–1,600 for premium and club-level suites. These rates can drop by 30–40% with special offers, during low season and for long-term stays booked via the internet. In November 2014, for example, Shangri-La's Tanjung Aru Resort was offering 14-day packages at RM593 a night for stays through until the end of August 2015.

Generally, four-star hotels – and even some five-star properties – will offer prices well below their rack or published rates. Food in coffee shops, markets and food courts is among the most authentic available. If you prefer to dine in air-conditioned restaurants, there is plenty of choice. A daily spend of US$150–200 per person will allow for upmarket hotels with extras, top-range food and tours and car hire.

Mid range There are some very good deals for two- to three-star hotels, especially with online promotions. Many hotels offer deals such as a superior double room with breakfast, for two people over two nights for RM300; this works out to just RM75 (around US$20/£10) per person per night for bed and breakfast.

Remarkable upgrades to luxury accommodation are possible on a mid-range budget, especially if you plan ahead and book hotels independently, and online. Even five-star city hotels of the likes of Le Meridien and the Hyatt offer special rates of RM400–600 for a double room with breakfast.

By booking ahead, using local operators for day tours, and dining in hotel restaurants, an average daily budget might be US$80–100 per person. Add the occasional car hire, and count on a daily budget of about US$100–120 per person.

Budget/shoestring The best options on a tight budget are hostels, homestays and no-star hotels. Eat street food from stalls and markets and dine at coffee

Practical Information BUDGETING

3

97

shops. Take buses and ferries, and flights with AirAsia, and wing it on your own for sightseeing instead of guided tours. The food available at markets for RM1–3 is delicious. In coffee shops you won't need to dole out more than RM10 for a good meal including soft drinks. In Brunei, prices are around double that. In East Malaysia and Brunei, you can eat very well for US$5 at the markets.

If you are on a restricted budget but can go that extra bit further, budget/shoestring hotels are an option. A single/double room in a shoestring property (under RM150) can cost as little as RM60–75 in the major cities. In smaller towns and rural areas the same price might get you a better, bigger room in a budget-category hotel, usually classed as being over RM150 in this guide. With a bit more leeway, you can eat at coffee shops rather than survive uniquely on market food, and opt for the occasional half- or full-day excursion with a budget-oriented tour company. (Budget options are provided in each regional chapter.)

A daily budget of 'roughly RM150–200 (US$40–50) per person will allow you to travel without frills, but comfortably.

GETTING AROUND

BY AIR Though distances within each Bornean state are not particularly long, most people rely on air travel, not just for longer journeys, such as west-to-east-coast passages, but also between regional cities which are connected within two–three hours, such as those along the Pan-Borneo Highway. This is largely due to the abundance of cheap flights. Why spend six hours travelling by car when you can fly in 40 minutes? On top of that, there's the deterrent state of many roads. Low-cost airlines have popularised air travel in Borneo, as they have done throughout Asia. City-to-city and regional hops such as Kota Kinabalu to Tawau or Sandakan, are easier than climbing on a bus for a six–eight-hour journey. Likewise for metropolises on Sarawak's 1,000km coastline – several daily flights link up Kuching, Sibu, Bintulu and Miri in under an hour. If speed and convenience are what you are looking for, then flying is a good option. If you are concerned about the environmental effects of air travel, or want to take in the scenery between towns (and brave the roads), then read on for other options.

Established or no frills? With the slogan 'Now Everyone Can Fly' plastered all over their bright-red aircraft, AirAsia (*www.airasia.com*) is loved for liberating the skies and contributing to aviation democracy with affordable prices. They are also at times loathed for the frustrations caused by chronic delays, and a rather blasé attitude towards customers. The casualness is part of their brand image, and by no means equates with rudeness. Staff are far more friendly and professional than many low costs, and the planes more comfortable. In both respects, the airline is more on a par with the likes of Norwegian, Germanwings and easyJet than Ryanair or Jetstar. Malaysia Airlines were once considered far more reliable, and thus worthy of paying more. The tables have turned somewhat over the past couple of years, undoubtedly because of the low-cost competition for MAS, compounded by the company's more recent financial and security strife. These days, MASwings prices for regional Borneo flights (eg: Kuching–Miri), can occasionally be cheaper than AirAsia for the same routes, and they are generally very close. Similarly, AirAsia has raised its game on punctuality, and rates no worse than MAS or any other airline in this regard. The big enduring fare difference between AirAsia and MAS is on domestic routes between East and West Malaysia, and international flights to Borneo from other Asian airports, with fares from Kuala Lumpur usually at least 30–40% cheaper.

Things change quickly in the realm of the skies. In the second edition of this guide referring to MAS, I wrote: 'Their safety record and policy is unwavering... they allow 20kg for domestic flights compared with AirAsia's 15kg... they have on-board refreshments and assigned seats... and they allow ticket changes. If AirAsia cancels a flight on the other hand, you have the option of either taking another flight later that day or losing your ticket.' We all know what MAS has experienced since then, but I believe their reputation is gradually being restored, as people realise how little, if any, actual blame lies with the airline for the two disastrous incidents of 2014.

AirAsia has now lifted its baggage allowances, at a cost to the consumer for sure, but at least the choice is there. Flying from KL to BSB in Brunei recently, I checked in 20kg, and paid RM40 extra for that liberty. In all, my ticket price of RM147 was incredible for an international fare. Furthermore, looking at the fine print on the ticket regarding cancellations, I saw another welcome evolution in policy: instead of the shotgun approach of forcing you to take another flight immediately after the one you were booked on has been cancelled, the option is: '(b) should you choose to travel at another time, retain the value of your fare in a credit account for your future travel provided that you must re-book within three months.' Finally, AirAsia have built ticket changes into their more expensive flexible tickets, which are still much cheaper than MAS on extra-Borneo routes. Most travellers today, both domestic and international visitors to Malaysia, swear by them rather than at them! The overall choice provided by the two airlines is fantastic, and getting better every day.

Fares

Malaysia Airlines From Kuala Lumpur to Kuching, Miri, Kota Kinabalu and Labuan, MAS tickets can be as low as RM171 – but they are more often than not as high as RM600–800. AirAsia fares for the same routes are usually a third to a half of this. Where AirAsia and MAS prices do compete more is on the regional routes, operated by MASwings, such as those from Kota Kinabalu to Miri, Tawau and Sandakan, and from Kuching to Sibu and Miri. There are often massive price variations in internet fares from one day to another, so it pays to have flying flexibility and to book ahead. The same RM171 fare from Kuala Lumpur to Kuching may triple if you need to buy at short notice.

AirAsia AirAsia fares for a long time tended to be even lower, though MAS, as stated above, has been catching up with them under the heat of huge competition and an iffy future. AirAsia offers a fast and inexpensive means of getting around Sabah and Sarawak, if you time your bookings right. The airline offers journeys as low as RM20 for Sandakan–Kota Kinabalu, RM60 for Kuching–Kota Kinabalu, and RM53 for Kota Kinabalu–Tawau. The last journey in an express coach will take eight hours and cost RM70, so the company has helped revolutionise travel to and in Borneo.

Rural air services (RAS) All rural air services (RAS) in Sabah, Sarawak and Labuan are operated by MASwings, a subsidiary of Malaysia Airlines. Under the former operator, FlyAsianXpress (FAX) – a subsidiary of AirAsia – flights were frequently cancelled or delayed for repairs, breakdowns or bad weather. As one guide commented, 'some people say that FAX Airlines stands for Flight Always Cancelled!' Today, however, the number of MASwings fans is skyrocketing with their successful management of the new service. In November 2011, the *Borneo Post* reported the vital role the airline was playing for its 1.2 million passengers a year: flight frequency had more than doubled from 450 to 950 flights a week since 2007, and the old fleet of Fokker 50s had been replaced with sophisticated aircraft such as the ATR 72-500. MASwings's rural network covers some 21 destinations in Sabah and Sarawak; it also assures several weekly flights between remote regional centres in the two states. In 2012, its expanding regional network extended to Indonesia and the Philippines. Now MASwings wants to bolster the frequency of its services in Sabah and Sarawak. In May 2014, the airlines' CEO said he wanted them to become a shuttle service, much like buses, running every half an hour, 'without having to book tickets but simply walk over to our counter and purchase the ticket just before the flight. The regional fleet will continue to be upgraded with more of the better aircraft.

BY CAR The cost of car rental is similar to Western prices: around RM100–150 a day. Car journeys are particularly economical in Brunei, where petrol costs 53 cents a litre, so about B$20 to fill a tank. (Foreign-registered vehicles pay almost double that.) In Sabah and Sarawak, unleaded fuel costs around RM2.30 a litre (RM105 a tank). Petrol is the great exception – just about everything else is double the price in Brunei! Most national driving licences (UK, US, Australian) can be used in Malaysia for three months, beyond which you require either a Malaysian driving licence or an annually renewable International Driving Permit.

Roads All major roads are dual carriageways; there are no multi-lane expressways. The speed limit is 100km/h on open roads. Distances are now metric, but there are still some odd vestiges of the former imperial system. The major routes are all of decent (and improving) quality. Minor roads can vary enormously, and if you're driving around a lot you'll encounter some bumpy roads and unsealed sections as you travel between towns or through plantations and rural areas. Most routes leading into developing towns or rising tourist attractions are either undergoing roadworks or are earmarked for improvement.

Rules In Malaysia you drive on the left-hand side of the road and the cars are right-hand drive. Road signs are not brilliant – in their regularity or clarity, in cities or on highways. Things are better in Sarawak, where the British influence is more noticeable, and international signage is far more common on major routes, especially on the west-coast Pan-Borneo Highway. Two road signs you will see a lot are AWAS (slow) and Dilarang Masuk (private – no entry).

With the low population density it is easy to manoeuvre on the open road, though it is more difficult in cities – streets are small and quite congested. Owing to strict licence conditions and enforcement, road safety standards seem very high and the quality of driving is impressive. All licences have to be renewed annually and public service vehicles require a special licence. Expect police checks and roadblocks, especially in southeast Sabah towards the Indonesian border, where they are checking for illegal trafficking of people and general contraband.

Inter-state travel Travelling between states by car is possible; it depends on your itinerary, how much time you have, and whether you want to make the road trip part of your journey and get a feel for the landscape. The Pan-Borneo Highway (Lebuh raya Pan Borneo – also referred to as the Trans-Borneo Highway), links Sabah to Brunei and to Sarawak.

Although long road trips can be enjoyable, it is worth bearing in mind the practicalities of travelling between states, described here by a friend who tried it:

'It takes eight to ten hours to drive from Kota Kinabalu to Brunei town, which involves between three and five river crossings using a ferry – adding to the time and cost of the journey. And there is always the risk of having your passport taken at one of the numerous checkpoints.' If you are heading for Sarawak, you have to take this same route and travel through Brunei, a convoluted journey as there is no direct road once you reach Lawas through to Miri. Kota Kinabalu to Miri is a 12-hour drive; continuing south to Kuching would make it at least a 20-hour journey.

Immigration checkpoints Between Sabah, Sarawak and Brunei, these are found at Sindumin in Sabah to Merapok in Sarawak; Tedungan in Sarawak to Kuala Lurah in Brunei; and Sungai Tujoh in Brunei to Sungai Tujuh Miri in Sarawak. The Tedungan to Kuala Lurah checkpoint is one of the busiest, with waits of up to an hour. Sungai Tujoh (being the only place where holders of Frequent Traveller Cards can pass between Brunei and Sarawak) can also involve nightmarish waits as Bruneians head to the border for a weekend in Miri. Avoid it on long weekends when up to 1,500 cars will pass in a day. The Bruneian checkpoints in particular are not well staffed. There are also checks involved in the ferry crossing from Lawas in Sarawak to Labu in Brunei and from Puni in Brunei to Limbang in Sarawak.

Further road information, key distances and estimated driving times are included in the relevant chapters. Sabah Tourism also has an interactive distance chart online (*www.sabahtourism.com/distancechart/distancechart.html*).

BY BUS While buses provide a cheap, comfortable and potentially efficient form of transport, the urban bus system in both Sabah and Sarawak has historically been a bit of a shambles. Prevalent problems have been a maze of different bus companies, sometimes serving the same areas, a lack of a central bus terminal, and confusion over where to catch particular buses, at least for the uninitiated. The situation is improving in the capitals as infrastructure evolves. In smaller towns, buses may not be the best option, though I always find a bus journey – no matter how challenging (and perhaps even more so for that) – an incredible window on local culture and people. When the fascination factor wears off a little, or you are just too tired, taxis can be a cheap alternative for small distances. Indeed Malaysia is one of the rare places in the world where I feel I can genuinely afford them.

Town buses *Bas mini* (minibuses) ply city and suburban areas but also do some longer inter-city journeys. The vehicles are generally numbered rather than named, with a route diagram at key bus stops. Different bus companies usually operate within particular patches, serving specific towns and surrounding areas.

Long-distance buses Air-conditioned 'express buses' for long-distance trips leave from a different terminal to town buses. In bigger cities, these are usually located in the suburbs and referred to as the long-distance or express bus station. Several coach and express bus operators vie for longer journeys, both intra- and inter-state. All these choices don't necessarily mean travelling by bus is easy. Long-distance bus stations even in smaller towns can be inconveniently located, meaning you also have to take a minibus between the station and town centre.

Long-distance buses can be a very cost-effective (though not necessarily time-effective) way of travelling. For example, to cross Sabah from Kota Kinabalu to the east-coast city of Tawau (roughly 12 hours) the fare is RM50, including a meal.

Inter-state bus travel is more complicated. Travelling between Miri in northern Sarawak and Brunei's capital, Bandar Seri Begawan, involves four changes of bus and two river crossings by ferry. (See relevant chapters for more details.)

My advice is to limit bus journeys to five hours' maximum. Airfares of less than RM50 between Kota Kinabalu and Kuching (over 1,100km) make anything longer than this unnecessary on any budget. On the other hand, I understand totally the desire to immerse slowly in all the scenery skipped over with the butterfly-clip solution of air travel. In that case, consider stopping off several times along the way to break up the journey and deepen the experience. This is the in-depth way to go, for those with the time and inclination to do more than just get from A to B. For those on organised trips, tour operators use comfortable, 8–12-seat, air-conditioned recreational buses, for which they must have a licence.

BY BOAT

Ferries Ferries are an efficient and interesting way of travelling in Borneo. Some of the main links are Brunei to Sabah (via Labuan Island), Brunei to Limbang in Sarawak, Kota Kinabalu to Brunei (via Labuan), and Labuan to Menumbok in Sabah. Various operators, including passenger and car ferries, ply these routes. **Labuan Tourism** (*www.labuantourism.com.my*) is a good place to check timetables and prices. Labuan is a mandatory thoroughfare of ferry passage between Sabah and Brunei. There are no direct passages.

The journey between the two capitals takes about 4½ hours. Have your passport on hand for clearing immigration. If heading to Brunei, ensure you have the necessary money for the visa. There is a daily departure from Jesselton Point in Kota Kinabalu for Bandar Seri Begawan in Brunei via Labuan (*www.jesseltonpoint. com.my*); fares are around RM60–80, depending on the service and ticket class you take. Children are generally 30–40% less, about RM38.

There are also direct services between Labuan and both Limbang and Lawas in Sarawak, and Sipitang in southern Sabah (*www.labuanweb.com/gettferry.html* is a useful site). From Brunei, ferries to Limbang take half an hour. From there, you can continue by bus or car north to Sabah or south through Sarawak.

River transport Boats are an integral part of the public transport system, especially in Sarawak, with its 55 rivers. Here boats are used for journeying across urban rivers and bays, into jungles and to remote villages. Journeys such as those in Iban longboats (*temuai*) are a hugely enjoyable part of the trip. I would go further, and say a couple of such experiences have *been* the trip, taking you to the soul of the country and its culture.

Small fibreglass vessels, twin-engine motorboats and speedboats are used for river safaris and national park transfers, while large high-speed express boats are used for longer river trips, especially into central Sarawak. The latter vessels also represent the primary public transport between towns along Sarawak's west coast, and some regions of Brunei.

As regional air travel replaces once-obligatory extensive longboat trips to hinterland areas of Sarawak, such journeys are still an option for cashed-up independent travellers who can afford the wonder of a six-to-ten-hour river trip, or overnight custom-made adventure. That said, two-hour (partly motorised) longboat trips are a common feature of river safaris aimed at budget and upmarket travellers. If you are travelling independently, do everything you can to suss out the local public boat services for nearby towns, villages and islands. These are not always well publicised, but information can be found at tourism offices and public jetties.

MAPS For some reason, maps in Sabah and Sarawak are generally of poor quality and difficult to get hold of. The owner of an award-winning tour company in Sabah told me of his joy when he visited London in the 1990s and found the best maps of Sabah he had ever seen! Things have no doubt improved since then, but if the quality and availability of tourism maps are any indication, then you are well advised to bring your own road maps. For visiting the cities, the tourist maps will probably suffice, but if you want more detail or have a special interest – mountaineering, general touring, self-drive, nature-spotting – bring maps adapted to your needs.

The Kota Kinabalu city map provided by Sabah Tourism is reasonably useful, but those of other towns and cities in the state are inadequate or non-existent. Sarawak Tourism does a much better job. Their large foldout map of the state does not give adequate topographic detail fit for hiking, but shows rivers, mountains and small towns. On the reverse side, there is an excellent Kuching city map, city/town maps of Sibu, Miri, Bintulu, Kapit and Sarikei, and maps of the Damai Beach area and Gunung Mulu National Park. Pick one up from tourist offices in any of the towns mentioned above.

(See also page 95.)

DIRECTIONS Road signs are as elusive in Sabah and Sarawak as street names. In Kota Kinabalu and surrounds, there are few signs along major roads, and if you ask people (including local tour guides) which road or street you are on, they usually shrug their shoulders. The same goes for small towns; you may find that one street in the town has a name, but no-one ever uses it. Locals generally orient themselves in relation to a landmark – the name of a bank, a shopping centre or a business of some kind. So if you need directions, ask where a certain place is rather than which street it's in.

TOWN, VILLAGE AND ROAD NAMES A village of the likes of Kundasang, just south of Gunung Kinabalu National Park, is a *kampung*, sometimes spelt *kampong*. A small town such as Ranau, a few kilometres from Kundasang, is known as a *pecan*. A medium-sized town is a *bandar*, and a big city is a *bandarayar*. A village on water is a *kampung ayer* (pronounced 'eye-er'). A road is a *jalan* (abbreviated to jln). Lanes and pathways are *lorong* and avenues are *lebuh*. Note: a jalan can change name three times on a lengthy city strip. Tourism offices and locals confusingly switch between referring to streets in Malay and English. The main street in Kuching for example, erratically wavers between Jalan Bazaar and the anglicised version 'Main Bazaar', on maps as in conversation. It takes time to realise the reference is to one and the same place.

TOWN LAYOUTS AND ADDRESSES The town centres of Sabah, Sarawak and Brunei are built up around 'shop-lots'. Stores, bazaars, coffee shops and traders of all kinds occupy these wall-to-wall blocks of often open-fronted shops. Shopping centres too are composed of compartmentalised shop-lots. Addresses for hotels, restaurants and offices will often take the verbose format of, eg: 'Ground Floor, Block 3, Lot BG, 38 Kompleks Kuwasa, Jalan Karamunsing'.

Kompleks are commercial centres, and have a mix of businesses and shops. Some shopping centres and department stores are called wisma (eg: Wisma Merdeka).

Though kilometres are now the standard measure of distance, out-of-town addresses are often given in terms of miles from the nearest city or town. So 'Mile 8'

Sandakan means eight miles from the city centre. Nowadays this curious system has even passed on to metric – so one occasionally sees 'Km8' used for a locality.

ACCOMMODATION

HOTELS The Malaysian Tourism Ministry started toughening up criteria for national hotel ratings in 2011, after receiving many complaints from tourists about Malaysian hotel standards. While it's difficult to make blanket statements, one can assume that if there are problems on a national level, they are probably more acute in Malaysian Borneo where overall standards have lagged behind.

The 'Hotel Monitoring Team' of the Ministry of Culture, Arts and Tourism (MOCAT) keep an eye on the 992 registered hotels and more than 2,200 tourist accommodation premises nationwide. To receive any kind of rating, hotels must be MOCAT-registered. MOCAT also has another grading system, the **Orchid** classification, for lodgings that don't qualify for star ratings. This applies to budget hotels, family-owned 'resorts', homestays, bed and breakfasts, hostels and inns. You can expect a three-Orchid resort to be very comfortable and clean, perhaps with a pool, Wi-Fi and other facilities.

The **Malaysian Association of Hotels** (*www.hotels.org.my*) issues hotel star ratings. Some budget hotels have a no-star rating. You can check to see if they are registered or have any other classification – the **Malaysian Budget Hotels Association** (MBHA) website (*www.malaysiabudgethotels.com*) has an online booking system for all of its registered members. In Brunei, the **Brunei Association of Hotels** (*www.hotelsofbrunei.com*) issues star ratings to registered hotels. Its website has descriptions of and links to its members, from budget to luxury establishments.

In reality Accommodation choices and standards in Borneo are generally inadequate, despite the consistent rise in tourism numbers over the past decade. The current and continuing shakeup on the hotel scene in Sabah, Sarawak and Brunei is proof of that – as consumers demand better standards, operators strive for them, new hotels open to answer the call, and old ones fall by the wayside when they are not able to perform to market expectations. The local tourism industry has long openly admitted to the lack of a truly high-end product, relative to that in major Asian hubs. That situation has slowly changed, and the capitals such as Kota Kinabalu and Kuching have a few (though probably less than a handful between them), of truly top-class five-star hotels. Boutique budget and mid-range lodgings are starting to answer to the demand with style, but there is still way too much mediocrity. (Increasing demand will no doubt sieve out the underperforming establishments over the coming years.) Outside of the cities, just a couple of nature resorts stand out as truly exceptional, consistently so, in matching the quality of their services and lodgings to the magic location. At others, the standards waver way too much to be taken seriously – their operators need to wake up to reality. There are also a couple of extreme luxury rental properties and self-contained accommodations popping up in Sabah in particular, which are answering to a thirst for plush coastal hideouts with traveller glee. Privately run, they appear to be getting it right, on all levels, and this is new to Borneo.

Hotel choices in smaller towns or lesser-known places can be extremely limited. Researching this edition, I unfortunately perceived a perceptible degradation in the standard of some once-reliable and solid small-town and rural hotels, due to poor service and below-standard rooms and I had to delete them from the book. Hopefully if some are forced to close their doors, other better establishments will step in to fill the gap. For travellers, it often means no choice when travelling in rural areas. Day trips from the nearest big city are a good option in this case. If, on the other hand, you are happy to settle for simplicity and authenticity, no-star B&B's, rustic resorts and homestays in some regions will provide just that.

Back in the cities, in all categories, there are shortfalls in both facilities and service compared with international standards. Some 'five-star' hotels barely match a three or four star grade; and some three stars barely a one or two star.

The signs of change are definitely there; even (at last) in Bandar Seri Begawan, where there have been notable upgrades in a couple of high-end properties, and 'a' 'newcomer' on the luxury scene. Hopefully it is there to stay. Over the past decade, I have seen too many would-bes, in Kota Kinabalu in particular, set up and disappear within a couple of years, so always be sure to cross-check recommendations here with the most recent user reviews. In mid-sized cities such as Sandakan on the north coast of Sabah, there has been some positive change (but also some backsliding) in the upmarket sector.

However, overall the outlook is promising, for those who are in the business to survive, and thrive, by delivering the goods fit for traveller expectations.

In spite of the divergence in service standards, travellers in Borneo benefit from Asia's hallmark hospitality, amplified by the island's friendliness.

Rates Standards may be lower than those in many Asian capitals, but prices generally are too. Many hotel bargains are to be had, particularly in the well-supplied two- to three-star bracket, so you can shop around for the best deal. Rates quoted are usually inclusive of a standard 10% service charge and 5–10% government service tax. Good hotels will make this clear on their website; if not it pays to ask. Some hotels quote a 'weekend rate' of up to 30% less than the going rate, especially business hotels in smaller towns where they most need the weekend leisure clientele.

Booking The best deals are found on the internet, especially for independently run city hotels. Many of these offer promotional deals such as 30–40% cuts on published rates, or extra nights and services. If you are organising your own travels, it is advisable to book ahead, especially during the peak foreign visitor months (June–September), as well as Malaysian school holiday periods (see page 114).

HOTEL PRICE CODES

Accommodation listings are laid out in decreasing price order, under the following categories: Luxury, Upmarket, Mid range, Budget and Shoestring. Serviced apartments, hostels and homestays are grouped together and also listed in decreasing price order. The following key gives a further indication of prices which are based on the price of a double room with taxes in high season. See pages 97–8 for advice on choosing accommodation categories to suit your pocket.

		East Malaysia	Brunei
Luxury	$$$$$	RM600+	B$220+
Upmarket	$$$$	RM450–600	B$164–220
Mid range	$$$	RM300–450	B$109–164
Budget	$$	RM150–300	B$55–109
Shoestring	$	<RM150	<B$55

A couple of good domestic booking sites include the **Hotels Association** (*www. hotels.org.my*), though it tends to favour three- to five-star hotels and exaggerate some of the ratings. A good general Malaysian travel site with a reservations system is **CUTI** (*www.cuti.com.my*), endorsed by Tourism Malaysia.

Check-out In hotels, check-out time is generally noon. Be aware that if you are on a tour and have transfers by plane, boat and bus or excursions, local tour operators often start days very early, with check-out sometimes as early as 06.00 or 07.00. Check-in at hotels is generally from 14.00.

Payment Four- and five-star hotels, and some two- and three-star establishments, accept a wide variety of credit cards (American Express, Visa, MasterCard, Diners Club, etc). Expect to pay by cash or cheque for most jungle lodges, homestays and family-owned resorts.

Entertainment and internet For all hotels, a major new criterion being imposed by the MOCAT is Wi-Fi access on all floors of a hotel building. It's a big ask in Borneo, and the requirement is far from being met by mid-range hotels in particular, and even some luxury establishments. Unfortunately, the island seems to suffer from chronic problems with internet connection and speed, ubiquitous to all-star categories. It's a Borneo thing, everyone tells you. Slow internet speeds of 4–8 megabits per second (Mbps), very often throttled well below that, compare poorly with 50Mbps in Kuala Lumpur. Traveller complaints are rife – no doubt Wi-Fi woes are the most complained-about thing in Borneo hotel stays. Most four- and five-star hotels will have a 'high-speed' cable internet connection in rooms, and Wi-Fi in the lobby and public areas. Thankfully, only a few top-notch hotels continue to impose a charge for the service, whereas for hostels through to four-star hotels it is largely free. With-it budget hotels, backpackers, and two- and three-star business hotels' are far more likely to be connected than conservative small-town hotels. High-end hotels, an increasing number of mid-range hotels and exceptional one- and two-star establishments will have 'Astro' (satellite) television. Even when there is a large choice of channels, the BBC might not be among them, but five-star places should all have CNN, BBC, Discovery Channel, Disney and Cinemax Movies.

Room service Room service in Malaysia is generally very affordable if you are happy to eat like a local. You are likely to find several good-quality main-course Chinese and Malay dishes for RM7–10 in a three-star hotel, or RM15–20 in a four- or five-star establishment. Western food is much more expensive – pork chops or fish and chips may cost around RM30–40 in a mid-range hotel, whereas you can feast on rice, noodles and satay delicacies for half the price. Family hotels will invariably have a kids' menu.

Breakfast can often be disappointing in budget to mid-range hotels, with a 'spread' reduced to packaged white bread, an overcooked noodle dish and unripe fruit. While three-star hotels and up usually do a better Western-style breakfast, quality breads and cereals can still be sorely absent. A small number of luxury hotels offer little more than bread, cake and cereal on the breakfast buffet; the most reputable provide multi-ethnic smorgasbords of Asian and Western foods, homemade breads and cakes, on-the-spot cooked noodles, Indian staples, sushi, fruits and sweets.

Smoking in hotels As smoking rates in much of the rest of the world decline, in Malaysia they are forever on the rise, particularly among young people. Statistics show 50% of male adults and 30% of 12- to 18-year-old boys smoke. Malaysia has lagged behind on introducing and enforcing wide-reaching smoking bans and the hotel industry has been affected by this, with smoking permitted in many hotel lobbies and restaurants. In June 2010, however, the Malaysian government announced it would extend existing smoking bans to the private sector, which includes hotel lobbies as well as centralised air-conditioned offices, and that decision can now positively be seen in action in Borneo.

With regard to rooms, most four- to five-star hotels have dedicated non-smoking floors. Despite that, complaints (in hotel user reviews) of cigarette-smelling non-smoking rooms are way too common. There is an encouraging, though slow, uptake among part of the industry towards 100% non-smoking hotels. You know you are in a smoking country when a brand like Radisson has not introduced such a policy. The one area where there is a notable change is in hotel restaurants, lobbies and other public spaces. Finally the law is being enforced, and not too soon.

Sports facilities Gyms in hotels with less than a luxury rating are rare, so make the most of them when you get the chance if you are trying to keep fit while travelling. The heat and humidity make it tough to run outdoors. Mid-range to upmarket hotels, better homestays and beach lodges may have swimming pools. Other noteworthy fitness centres are included where relevant in the guide.

NATURE LODGES AND ISLAND RESORTS Most major tour operators specialising in nature and/or diving tourism manage their own lodges in key locations; other tour groups are affiliated with a particular lodge or resort. This creates something of a monopoly – with the accommodation on offer controlled by the same people running the tours. That only proves negative if the accommodation is not of an acceptable standard. On river and jungle safaris it tends to be rustic, from basic forest camp to clean and comfortable longhouse dwellings and lodges with generator-powered electricity. There is no ultra-luxury option, though a couple of high-end nature tourism operators have renovated their lodges to an eco-chic level in the last few years. Basic living conditions can also be seen as a vital part of an authentic experience, and budget travellers in particular seem to subscribe to that point of view.

Coastal and island resorts generally are more sophisticated than their jungle counterparts, with better food, services and accommodation. A handful are classified as luxury resorts: of those, a couple have quite sumptuous rooms and suites among their inventory.

National parks Accommodation in national parks in Sabah and Sarawak tends to be very basic. There are no cooking facilities, meaning a drive to a nearby town for food (not always possible if a boat trip is involved in reaching the park), or relying on the park cafés and restaurants if such facilities are available. Mount Kinabalu National Park is the great exception, with its plentiful food outlets and self-contained chalets.

LONGHOUSE STAYS The longhouses of some of Sabah's Rungus and Sarawak's Iban tribes welcome guests. In Sarawak, you can stay in quiet remote areas to experience local life. Longhouse accommodation is occasionally purpose-built, for those wanting to get a taste of tradition without living among a family. Most longhouse accommodation in Sarawak is in the Skrang, Lemanak, Batang Ai and Rejang river areas. Longhouses can be booked directly or through a tourist office. Many organised tours, such as hiking, river safaris and cultural trips include a longhouse stay.

3

Longhouse facilities are usually basic. A two-person room will include pillows, mattresses, mosquito nets, bed sheets, towels, blankets and slippers. A modern communal bathroom or traditional washroom facilities are provided for guests. Food will often be fish and vegetables, gathered fresh from the river and jungle. Activities may include hunting, fishing, jewellery making and cooking.

The threat of malaria is greatest in the remotest upriver areas. The Health Department carries out regular checks; if malaria is detected, tourism authorities are alerted and visits to affected areas suspended. For more information on malaria, see page 88.

HOMESTAYS It is also possible to stay in family homes as part of the 'homestay' programme. This is a very up-close-and-personal way of experiencing the lifestyle of local people and you may not have much privacy. Similar in principle to a bed and breakfast, homestays are run by individual families or the kampung (villages). Book through tourist offices in Kota Kinabalu, Kuching and Sibu. A homestay directory is available at http://travelmalaysiaguide.com/homestay.

Bed and breakfasts 'True' bed and breakfasts are rare in Borneo, as homestays have traditionally taken their place. There is, nonetheless, a bit of a trend towards B&Bs: a few are listed on www.insite.com. They can be as cheap as a hostel, with more services than a budget hotel (such as a pool).

EATING AND DRINKING

Food Borneo's mix of cultures creates a piquant culinary bouillabaisse. I hope this section will help you avoid the many tongue-tied moments I have experienced trying to order food, with no certainty of what I am about to eat!

Malaysians and Bruneians are nations of passionate eaters. While the two countries have distinct food, they also share many common Malay and (to a lesser extent in Brunei) Chinese dishes. Rice (*nasi*) and noodles (*mee*) are staples of Malay and Chinese cuisine – if you don't like either, be prepared to starve! The Chinese and Malay populations rely heavily on noodles in laksa and other soups, as well as main-meal dishes. Freshly made mee comes in various forms: large white or yellow ribbon wheat noodles, spaghetti thin noodles and clear vermicelli noodles. In coffee shops you can often choose your noodles from the masses hanging at a counter at the entrance. Then you have to decide on the style you want them cooked – the big differences being 'wet' (with sauce) or 'dry' (without); fried (*goreng*) or not fried; spicy or mild. Dried noodles are increasingly being used, so when you get the chance to taste the real thing then do so. Sedap dimakan! (*Bon appetit!*)

Malay food Malay cooking is spicy, salty and thick with flavour, in keeping with all the cultural influences that have infused it over the centuries. Sambal and satay are two staples of Malaysian and Bruneian cuisine. Satay comes in the form of marinated and barbecued skewers of chicken, beef or lamb, served on bamboo sticks. This typical Malay 'fast food' is eaten from street stalls and markets. In restaurants it's served with salad and peanut sauce. Sambal – chilli condiment – puts the spice in Malay food. Sweet (*sambal manis*), hot (*sambal olek*), or shrimpy (*sambal belacan*), the ground chilli pastes are flavoured with the gamut of typical Malay spices. Not for the faint-hearted, even the sweet sambal is fiery!

Rice (nasi) The most typical breakfast fare is *nasi lemak* – literally fat, or tasty rice, though it isn't nearly as fatty as it sounds. The rice is steamed, aromatised with coconut milk and pandan leaves, and garnished with spicy fried anchovies, sliced cucumber, peanuts and hard-boiled egg. At markets and roadside stalls it is often sold wrapped traditionally in a banana leaf. There are several other ubiquitous nasi dishes: *nasi kuning* (yellow rice with egg, coconut and cucumber); *nasi goring* (fried rice); *nasi ayam* (rice with slithers of steamed or roasted chicken); *nasi campur* (mixed rice); and if you are vegetarian, ask for *nasi dengan sayur* (rice with vegetables).

Noodles Popular Malay noodle dishes are *mee goreng* (spicy fried thick noodles), *mee mamak* (spicy-hot fried yellow noodles), and *mee rebus* (thick blanched noodles in a gooey, sweet and spicy sauce, served with hard-boiled eggs and green chillies).

Curry Typical fish, chicken and vegetable curries are *kari ikan, kari ayam*, and *kari sayur*, respectively. These are gently spiced and cooked with a light dose of coconut milk.

Meat Beef and chicken are ubiquitous meats. The first is the basis of the famous tangy coconut beef rendang, served with turmeric rice (*nasi kunyit*), while red cooked chicken, *ayam masak merah* is a casserole of chicken pieces in tomato.

Seafood Prawns (*udang*) and fish come in many forms. Whole grilled fresh fish is known as *ikan panggang*. The best places to eat seafood are small coastal restaurants where you order and eat barbecued fish, prawns and squid – *sontong panggang* – by the weight. Often it costs as little as RM2 per 100g, particularly in Sabah's east-coast towns. Prawns from the sea, or giant river prawns, are served whole and spicy in *sambal udang*, with lashings of shrimp and tamarind paste, chilli, garlic and shallots.

Vegetables There are many vegetable dishes in a typical Malay spread. *Sayur campur* (mixed vegetables) includes carrot, cabbage, broccoli, cauliflower and beans cooked in a light oyster sauce. The same vegetables stewed in coconut form *sayur lodeh*. Individual dishes of 'local vegetable', often roots collected from the jungle that morning, feature on many rural and urban tables. Most common are long bottle-green midin sprouts, dark-green fern tops *pucuk paku*, and *pucuk rajah* – emperor shoots. Cucumber and yam varieties also feature.

Fusion One of the most established culinary hybrids in Malaysia is Indian-Muslim *mamak* (uncle's) cuisine. The dishes are served up at food stalls and small Indian-Muslim eateries or 'Islamic (halal) restaurants', often around the clock. *Mamak* specials include tandoori chicken and fish-head curry. A famous fast-food delicacy is *roti canai* (after its origin, Chennai in India) – flaky, oily unleavened bread, cooked on an open grill. *Roti canai* (pronounced chan-eye) is often served with a side dish of curry for dipping the bread in – vegetarians can have it with dhal (split pulses). The *roti canai* translates into various other forms including *roti telur* – egg roti filled with egg and onion – again served with curry or dhal. *Murtabak* is wrapped *roti canai*, filled with minced meat, egg and onion. Vegetarians/vegans can order spinach- and onion-filled *Murtabak*, with or without the egg.

Nyonya (grandma's) cuisine is Malaysia's renowned fusion of Malay and Chinese food, with many regional variations notably from Melaka and Penang. It combines the spices of Malay food with marinated, sour Chinese flavours and results in dishes such as tangy, fishy *assam laksa*.

Chinese food With such a large and diverse Chinese population, many cities in Borneo have restaurants specialising in different kinds of Chinese food – Cantonese, spicy Szechuan, Teochew and Hakka. At traditional coffee shops and street stalls, meat dumplings, steamed sweet or savoury buns (*pau*) and rice porridge (*moi*) are served for breakfast, while dim sum are popular for lunch. One of the most delicious staple Chinese noodle dishes is *char kway teow*, flat rice noodles with beansprouts, egg, chilli and shrimp (or chicken). Monosodium glutamate is widely used in such dishes. To ask for your food without MSG, see box, page 112.

Soup Noodle soups are a lunch favourite. *Wantan mee* broth contains floating stuffed envelopes of prawn or pork, *mee suah* has fish balls or pork, and *tom yam* is a spicy shrimp soup. A famous Hokkien herbal soup is bak kut teh – literally 'pork bone tea' – acclaimed for its longevity properties. *Laksas* of many kinds are common at Chinese *kopi tiam* (coffee shops), served with prawn, chicken or egg. Fish and chicken clay pots with noodles are another popular choice.

Vegetarian There are many soybean-, soybean curd-, and tofu- (tau foo) based dishes in soups, noodle dishes, clay pots and curries.

Fish/seafood The Chinese do great fresh seafood. Small stalls, coffee shops and restaurants serve dishes such as sweet and sour fish, deep-fried fish with mango sauce, butter prawns, black pepper crab and oyster fried with egg.

Sweet stuff Look out for cake shops (*kedai kek*) making their own Chinese-baked goods. Favourites include *siew pao* (baked bun with chicken), yam pastry buns, egg custard tarts, steamed red bean cakes, lotus and red bean yeast buns, and hakka soybean cakes.

Indigenous foods Every ethnic group has its traditional cuisine tied closely to their way of life, inland or by the sea. Coastal cuisine features many sago and coconut dishes and marinated seafood salads, while people inland eat lots of rice and freshwater fish. Wild fruits and vegetables are used as much as home-grown crops. You will get to taste traditional indigenous dishes when visiting smaller towns and tamu markets, or at homestays and longhouses. Wonderful and weird specialities abound, such as the bamboo-shoot pickle – *bosou hobang* – of the Murut in Sabah. The Kadazandusun love their tangy pickles from mango and other fruits. And let's not forget fermented rice wine – called *tuak* by the Iban in Sarawak but also *lihing* among the Kadazandusun in Sabah. You will need to eat well to offset the effects of this!

Fruit The fruit bowl is always full with bananas (*pisang*) of many kinds (also try the *pisang goreng* – fried bananas – at the market); spiky red rambutan; jungle fruits such as the sweet, pulpy and aromatic tarap (*Artocarpus odoratissimus*); and *cempedak* – a cousin of the jackfruit – both are football-sized with thick, mustard-yellow husks full of pod-shaped fruits.

Vegetarian food Other than a few international diners, it's rare to see a menu with a dedicated vegetarian selection. Yet the huge variety and wide availability of vegetable dishes in Malay and Chinese eateries means vegetarians should never go hungry. Take it from an expert! Even in coffee shops where only meat and fish dishes appear on the menu, there are always vegetable side dishes to be eaten as mains with rice or noodles.

DRINK

Coffee-shop drinks The typical coffee-shop *harga minuman* (drinks list) may look something like this, with prices ranging from RM1 to RM3 in most places.

Kopi o	black coffee with sugar
Kopi o kosong	black coffee no sugar
Kopi c susu	coffee with condensed milk
Kopi-si	coffee with unsweetened (Carnation) milk
The o	black tea with sugar
Ping so kopi o ping	black sweetened iced coffee
Kopi o kosong ping	black iced coffee unsweetened
Kopi-si ping	iced coffee with unsweetened milk
Air limau	lemon water drink
Teh tarik	'pulled' tea: very strong and sweet, brewed black tea with condensed milk

Alcoholic drinks With Muslims accounting for over 60% of the population of Sabah and Sarawak, you will not find alcohol served in Malay-run cafés and restaurants, outdoor food stalls and open-air diners. The majority of Chinese-run *kopi tiam* are also restricted to food only, though a handful may serve beer. The main places serving alcoholic drinks are licensed bars and international restaurants – particularly those at hotels. Wine – given it is all imported – tends to be particularly expensive, as are spirits, while a pint of beer generally costs as much as it does in London's poshest pubs. Typical prices for a whisky or tequila shot is RM18, a pint of beer RM13, a bottle of wine RM100–120, and a glass of wine RM18.

Brunei rhymes with dry. Bring your own alcohol into the country according to regulations (for more details, see page 82). The sale and consumption of alcohol is prohibited in public places, though foreigners can carry in alcohol for their private consumption.

EATING OUT Food is readily available, often of exceptional quality in both freshness and flavour, and cheap. Market food can easily beat restaurant produce. Head to the nearest *pasar malam* night market or *taman selera* – literally an 'appetite park', full of open-air restaurants. Any formal or fine dining takes place in Western and international restaurants. The best thing is to eat local and eat fresh.

RESTAURANT PRICE CODES

Restaurant listings are laid out in decreasing price order, under the following categories: Upmarket, Mid range, Budget and Shoestring. Prices are based on the cost of a main meal per person.

		East Malaysia	Brunei
Upmarket	$$$$	RM60+	B$25+
Mid range	$$$	RM20–60	B$7–25
Budget	$$	RM10–20	B$4–7
Shoestring	$	<RM10	<B$4

SURVIVAL GLOSSARY

Tanpa perasa	no monosodium glutamate
Tanpa garam	without salt
Tambah	add
Sedikit	less or a little
Kurang	less (eg: *kurang manis* – less sweet)
Minyak	oil/fat
Tidak	no

If you don't want sugar in anything, just add *kosong* – empty. Though no-one apparently in their right mind would ask that of a *teh tarik* (very strong, sweet tea) – I have! You can always add a little sugar rather than swallow the copious amount served with it.

Coffee shops Lively open-air coffee shops are highly characteristic of Malaysian culture. Most started out serving coffee with morning dumplings and noodles. Today the *kedai kopi*, as they are called in Malay, also serve a long list of typical dishes and drinks. These open-fronted 'food and drink stores' – officially *kedai makanan dan minuman* – line city streets. Menus include various noodle, rice and curry dishes.

Chinese coffee shops – conversely known as *kopi tiam* – serve dumplings and soups, including *laksa* specialities cooked on the spot. On the whole, coffee shops provide good, cheap food and an authentic atmosphere. The best are full of locals, huddled around plastic chairs and linoleum tables. A tub of musk stick pink or tangerine chopsticks stands in the middle of the table, and a jar of homemade *lada* – a fiery soy, salt and chilli mix ready for piling on your food.

Larger hotel coffee shops are usually enclosed and air conditioned. Many have a strong local clientele and serve Malay and Chinese specialities. International luxury brands – think Hilton or Sheraton – tend to have a stronger Western touch, though Malaysian food may still count among the menu choices.

Food courts Nutritious, tasty food to go is available from shopping-centre food courts, usually located on the top floor. A dozen or two traders with open kitchens prepare all the standard local dishes. Most Chinese food such as noodles are cooked on the spot. Malay and Indo-Malay kitchens pre-prepare food and keep it warm in *bains-marie*. So it pays to arrive early lunch or dinner time to eat the food at its freshest. Typical spreads include chicken, fish, pork and vegetable curries or stews, roasted meats and steamed greens with chilli and prawn paste. Storekeepers ladle the dishes of your choice on to a plate of rice. They will also pop it on request in a polystyrene box for take-away (*bungkus*).

Restaurants Restaurants range from small, simple diners serving Malay, Indonesian, *mamak* or Chinese food, not much different from a *kedai*, through to air-conditioned fancier places. Hotels have several dining choices, from coffee shops to restaurants, offering both Western and local food. In bigger hotels, there will be several diners catering to local and Western tastes. Chinese restaurants can be large clamouring places, offering some of the best seafood in town. International establishments include restaurants, cafés and bistros. Fine dining often correlates with 1970s–80s style.

Smoking in restaurants While smoking in air-conditioned/enclosed restaurants in Malaysia has been banned for years, the law has been poorly enforced. That thankfully is beginning to change, and even since 2012, there has been a notable swing in hotel and other restaurants going fully non-smoking, generally with an outdoor area reserved for smokers. While the ban does not apply to open-fronted coffee shops, I have rarely been bothered by smoke at these eateries.

Western fast food Look out for the familiar logos – they are never far away in the main cities.

Halal There are hundreds of halal eateries in Malaysia, from street stalls to coffee shops and restaurants. These serve halal-only products – no pork, pork by-products (such as lard), or alcohol. All the food, including vegetables, spices and meats, must be produced in accordance with Islamic law. Brunei is developing a halal food export industry.

Street food *Gerai makan* (food stalls) are found all over the place, in the streets and at markets, along roadsides and highways, day and night. They sell noodle and rice dishes cooked on the spot, as well as pre-prepared packages of *nasi lemak* and other foods. Many smaller stalls have their specialities – *murtabak, roti canai, satays*, etc. Large open-air or covered spaces full of food stalls and semi-permanent kitchens set up daily in some towns. The kitchens of these *taman selera* – outside dining areas interspersed with tables and chairs – are somewhere between a stall and makeshift coffee shop. The *taman selera* often have a pleasant outlook, near the water or a park. The *pasar malam* night markets on the other hand are more a wander-and-eat affair, with stalls only, no tables or chairs.

Roadside stalls sell smoked meats, grilled corn on the cob, puding kelapa (a gelatinised coconut dessert), prawn crackers, nuts, bananas and drinks.

Markets (*pasar*) The nightly *pasar malam* are fantastic for fooding and atmosphere, with their dozens of *gerai makan*. The other big staples of market life are the wet markets, dry markets, central markets and rural tamu. Throughout the Ramadan month, *pasar* Ramadan serve delicacies for the public breaking of the fast. Wherever there is a central or tamu market there is food in multitudinous forms: fresh, dried, raw, cooked, pungent, wild, exotic; fruit and nuts; Chinese pastries and buns; and a huge array of produce for preparing at home. Usually a market will have some *gerai makan* food stalls pretty close by, if not under the same roof.

Eating-out practicalities

Cleanliness Local councils grade places as 'A', 'B' or 'C' class. The lowest-grade coffee shops and small restaurants are usually fine, though more 'fancy' restaurants with a C grade are best avoided. C-rated coffee shops can have filthy toilets but great food. Others pride themselves on having the cleanest loos in town. Food preparation, utensils and ingredients at the *gerai makan* stalls are all subject to strict food hygiene laws and active regulation.

Service As long as you can convey what you want simply, most Malay and Chinese will understand. Food is generally cooked as you watch – which is helpful if you are vegetarian or have allergies or special dietary needs.

Tipping Service charges are included in bills and tipping is not customary.

Prices Meal prices range from RM2 to RM3 at a market stall, double or triple that in a coffee shop, and from RM20 to RM50 for a main course in a snazzy or touristy seafood restaurant. The more you choose to dine in international hotels and tourist-pleasing or trendy eateries, the more the bill obviously increases.

PUBLIC HOLIDAYS AND FESTIVALS

Public holidays in East Malaysia generally fall into two categories, national and state, both of which embrace religious celebrations, cultural festivals and dates of major national importance. Brunei also has public holidays to mark significant state dates such as political independence, the sultan's birthday and religious occasions. Probably more important than the state occasions, and celebrated in a far more personal way, are the religious and ethnic celebrations – though these differ between East Malaysia and Brunei. The sultan is 'our Sultan' in Brunei – he is part of the people's daily lives, so his birthday is a big event. The same can't be said of the Malaysian king, who has less of an impact in Sabah and Sarawak than on the peninsula. Major state-wide celebrations mark important dates on the spiritual calendars of indigenous people, and of the Chinese, Malay and Indian populations, who observe Buddhist, Muslim, Hindu and Christian traditions. Festive rituals often combine a high level of spirituality and prayer, with colour, joy and feasting. That doesn't exclude commercialism. The general racial harmony that exists throughout Borneo extends to the festivals. People of different faiths celebrate with their friends on major holy days, and some specific inter-cultural celebrations are heartily enjoyed by all.

Some seven major religious and cultural celebrations are marked by public holidays in East Malaysia and Brunei. They are listed below, along with other public holidays for state occasions. Such holidays rarely cause business to come to a standstill, at least not shops. Banks and government offices close, but shopping centres will remain open for at least half the day, varying from place to place. Another advantage of being in multi-faith Borneo is that only the shops of those celebrating the day for their culture or religion will close. For others, it's business as usual. The shopping 'temples' are open all hours.

PUBLIC HOLIDAYS IN SABAH, SARAWAK AND BRUNEI
There is great regional and national variation between Sabah, Sarawak and Brunei for public holidays, even for the celebration of the same religious events and ethnic festivals. The following are an indication only, for often shifting holidays.

1 January	New Year's Day
3 January	Prophet Muhammad's birthday
February (variable date)	Chinese New Year (two-day holiday)
23 February	National Day Brunei
Good Friday	(Sabah and Sarawak only)
1 May	Labour Day
3 May	Wesak Day (height of Buddhist calendar)
30–31 May	Tadau Ka'amatan (Harvest Festival); thanksgiving to the rice spirits of the Kadazandusun (Sabah and Labuan only)
1–2 June	Pesta Gawai (Sarawak Dayak Festival)
6 June	Birthday of Yang di-Pertuan Agong, Malaysian king

15 July	His Majesty the Sultan of Brunei's birthday
July/August (variable date)	Hari Raya Aidilfitri or Hari Raya Puasa (two-day celebration for the breaking of the Muslim Ramadan fasting month).
31 August	National Day (Hari Kebangsaan); celebration of Malaysian independence, *Merdeka*, 1957
12 September (Sarawak only)	Birthday of Yang di-Pertua Negeri, Sarawak's head of state
October (variable date)	Hari Raya Haji or Hari Raya Qurban marks the end of the Muslim Hajj pilgrimage to Mecca.
5 November	Ramadan – end of Muslim fasting (Brunei)
November (variable date)	Deepavali – Hindu light festival (one day in the first half of the month)
October/November (variable date)	Awal Muharram (Ma'al Hijrah), the Muslim New Year and first day of Muslim calendar
25 December	Christmas Day

Chinese Lunar New Year The Chinese New Year is full of festivity and friendship, thanksgiving and hopes of prosperity – amid raucous cries of *Kong Hee Fatt Choy!* (Happy New Year!). After a month of preparation, in which homes are luridly decorated with lanterns, firecrackers and calligraphy, guests laden with gifts of mandarins and oranges arrive ready for much feasting and games of mah-jong. Celebrations also take place in Chinese temples, making this an ideal time to visit one. The dates vary from year to year according to the lunar calendar, beginning on the first day of the full moon and lasting for a fortnight. Like other Chinese festivals celebrated in Sabah, Sarawak and Brunei, the New Year festival is strong on symbolism and folklore, dance and colour – especially red. A highlight of the public festivities is the 'lion dance' – troupes of dragon-like figures prance through the streets to the beats of drums, warding off evil spirits, ushering in fortune and frightening the mythical lion away.

Wesak Day The most important date on the Buddhist calendar marks the birth, death and enlightenment of the Buddha. It is celebrated with prayers, offerings and chanting, and the release of doves and tortoises at Buddhist temples. Another magical time to head to a temple.

Tadau Ka'amatan (Harvest Festival) Each district of Sabah holds its own various festivities for this big event, the height of the indigenous calendar in Sabah. The celebrations can go on for the entire month of May, culminating during the Grand Finale on 30 and 31 May at the Kadazandusun Cultural Association Hall (KDCA) in Penampang, just south of Kota Kinabalu. *Tadau Ka'amatan* in indigenous tongue sometimes translates to *Pesta Kaamatan* in Malay. It is celebrated by the Kadazandusun and Murut communities in Sabah.

Deepavali The Hindu Festival of Light, a triumph of good over evil, is held on the seventh month of the Hindu calendar. Houses are decorated with lights, old debts settled, sweets sent to friends and new clothes purchased. All the Sikh temples (*Gurdwaras*) conduct prayer services and dish out vegetarian food.

Hari Raya Aidilfitri Also called Hari Raya Puasa, this is a day of celebration held at the end of the month-long Muslim fast of Ramadan (often spelt Ramadhan in Malaysia and Brunei). Fasting ends on the first sighting of the new moon, in the tenth month of the Muslim calendar, *Syawal*.

Hari Kebangsaan The Malaysian National Day marks Malaysian independence in 1957, when the Union Jack was lowered in Kuala Lumpur and the Malaysian flag hoisted to mark the end of colonial rule. It is celebrated with street parades in the main cities of Sabah and Sarawak, though less flagrantly than on Peninsular Malaysia.

SHOPPING

By far the most wonderful places to shop are the markets (*pasar*). A visit to a marketplace is possibly one of the most authentic cultural experiences you can have – experiencing the sights, sounds and smells of true local culture and an amazing range of produce, from fresh fruit and fish, jungle vegetables and speciality foods, to clothes and handicrafts.

Every region, city and town will have several markets: the *pasar besar* is the main market, held daily in larger cities and in towns, and once a week in some country districts. Larger, established pasar besar are often held undercover, and increasingly in new two- to three-storey buildings, incorporating several traditional markets: the 'wet market' (*pasar basah*), which sells fish and meats, the dry market, with other food and regional produce, and handicraft markets. The *pasar malam* night markets generally sell ready-to-go food only; others offer a mix of produce. Some places also have specific craft markets – *pasar pertukangan*. Larger ones in the cities are flooded with Filipino and Indonesian produce. You can always bargain in the marketplace.

You are more likely to find a priceless memento of your travels in rural markets. Some of the most beautiful and authentic items are woven textiles, bamboo and rattan baskets, beaded jewellery from shell, glass and plant seeds, pottery, carved wooden bowls and batik. In Brunei you will find more brass, gold and silver than beads and bamboo. (See page 154 for more on traditional handicrafts and markets.) Local shopping tips are included in the relevant chapters.

TAMU A rural market, the weekly *tamu* was apparently introduced by the British North Borneo Company to create a communal meeting place and ease ethnic tensions through trade. Both the name and the custom have spread to Brunei and to Sarawak, but *tamu* are still most common in Sabah where they are held on a varying day of the week from place to place. A growers' market, crafts market and commercial bazaar all in one, each one is unique, shaped by the cultural and agricultural environment. Farmers and fishermen bring their produce (including water buffalo). Traders pile their stalls high with an exotic array of strangely shaped and wonderfully coloured produce: kitchen and clothing wares; bric-a-brac; home-grown, homemade and jungle-reaped produce. The *tamu* remain a vital part of social and trading life rather than a tourist attraction – though some have become more tourist-oriented – and the best ones are often those with the fewest tourists. My best memories are those of Ranau, Kudat, and Tuaran in Sabah; Sibu, Serian and Miri in Sarawak; and Brunei's tamu. There is also a *tamu besar* – a major *tamu* – held once a year in the *tamu's* town of origin, Kota Belud.

General shopping Shopping plazas, supermarkets, electronic stores and pharmacies exist all over the cities and towns. Smaller kedai – food and retail stores, electronics and clothes shops – are often clustered in large blocks of 'shop-lots', along the street, around a public square or in multi-storey shopping centres. New plazas, malls and commercial centres (*kompleks*) are popping up in the capital cities and coastal towns. Between the dozens of city shop-lots and older shopping centres packed with shop-lots, you will find just about everything you need. However, neither Malaysian Borneo nor Brunei has the exciting department-store shopping or the modern emporiums that exist in Singapore, Hong Kong, Bangkok and Kuala Lumpur. There is little in the way of local or imported quality couture or food items, and department stores lack major pizzazz. Things are clearly changing, and Kota Kinabalu is moving the most in that direction. Some malls, especially older ones, are more like massive shop-lots, cluttered and not very attractive, yet relatively cheap. Major sales occur once yearly, but every day is a sale with the 'Buy One Free One' slogan applied to clothing, jewellery and food things.

Tax-free shopping   Labuan is a duty-free shopping and tax haven. The duty-free shops at major city airports are very good. Brunei is tax-free, too, but you won't find duty-free spirits and wine on the shelves there.

ARTS AND ENTERTAINMENT

The karaoke craze has not escaped Borneo, though it is now declining in favour of trendy, international **bars and clubs** in Sabah and Sarawak. These hip hangouts are also eroding the tradition of a hotel-based nightlife in Kota Kinabalu and Kuching. The **live music** scene is thriving, though music is a bit behind the international times. Traditional dance and music performances are one of the most heartening forms of entertainment. Brunei, being alcohol-free, has a quieter (some say non-existent) night scene. For those who consider cultural immersion exciting, there is much fun to be had at the night markets.

For anyone interested in the real cultures of Borneo, the best forms of art-based entertainment are the **festivals**, and dance and music performances. These are very regional – Sabah, Sarawak and Brunei organised – and local in nature. Each town and ethnicity will have cultural performances and pesta (festivals) celebrating dates and events dear to them. The local tourism offices are the best place to check for a list of upcoming events. Sabah and Sarawak tourism also have online events listings.

Museums in general are open seven days a week, but hours can vary from 09.00 to 16.30/17.00 to 10.00 to 18.00. Admission prices also vary greatly – some, including the Sarawak Museum, are free, others such as the Sabah State Museum cost a hefty RM15 with no reductions for students or children. (For more information on the arts, see pages 27–9.)

SPORTS AND OTHER ACTIVITIES

Borneo is better known for its wildlife than for extreme outdoor sports, but there is still plenty of adventure to be had in the natural world. Boasting Malaysia's three highest mountains, Sabah attracts mountaineers from near and far, though clearly these massifs are less of a challenge for climbers than other famous Indo-Asian peaks. Other adventures encompassing natural wonders can be experienced through diving, whitewater rafting, rugged jungle treks and off-the-beaten-path mountain climbing. Good locations include Sabah's Gunung Kinabalu National Park and Maliau Basin, and the Kelabit Highlands of Sarawak. A few local Sabah and Sarawak companies specialise in a mix of light- to medium-intensity outdoor adventure, such as mountain biking, rafting, trekking and rock-climbing excursions.

TREKKING   Because of Borneo's highly bureaucratic national parks and reserves, the arduously humid climate, and dangers of walking alone, it is better to use a tour organiser for established treks. They also offer the advantage of local knowledge and of transfers to and from the national parks. Permits, insurance and guides are obligatory in Gunung Mulu National Park in Sarawak and Gunung Kinabalu National Park in Sabah. Unfortunately, for those who prefer to be independent and unrestricted, you can't just turn up and trek. Unlike national parks in Europe, North America and Australia, guides are mandatory for the Kinabalu Peak Trail and the equivalent trail in Gunung Mulu. These must be booked in advance, along with trekker's accommodation. Outside of the major walks, neither park has an extensive network of trails; there are one or two major routes and a few shorter walks around park headquarters, which do not require a guide. Other national parks, such as Bako in Sarawak, stand out for a more extensive network of free-roaming trails. Beyond the national parks, in areas like the Danum Valley conservation area, there is the opportunity of solo trekking, along a couple of 'well-marked nature trails'. For a serious 'wilderness' adventure, head to the Maliau Basin – here you will get rugged terrain, sleeping in tents and lots of leeches, though it is costly, and only possible as an organised trip (see pages 245–6). Another relatively little-known area just north of Maliau is the Imbak Canyon.

There are plenty of other more relaxed places for trekking around Borneo. The Kelabit Highlands offers trekking through a hilly landscape and rich culture, permit and guide free, along an established tourist route. Other areas where you can go it alone include the Penrissen Highlands south of Kuching and Sabah's Crocker Range. (For details of where to obtain topographic maps, see page 95.)

Day hiking Many other parks and reserves offer easy- to medium-grade trails, where you can experience a good mix of lowland and hill rainforest on pleasant half-/full-day walks. These includee the Tawau Hills Park, Tabin Wildlife Reserve and Sepilok Forest Reserve, which are all located on the east coast of Sabah; and the Bako, Lambir Hills and Similajau parks in Sarawak. Nearly all of Sarawak's 18 parks (several of which are close to Kuching), have at least a couple of decent tracks. Both Bako and Lambir Hills have 10–12, though few routes exceed three or four hours in duration. Sarawak provides more for day hikers than Sabah; its national parks are well set up with good park information, maps, trails and rangers. The national parks website (*www.forestry.sarawak.gov.my/forweb/homepage.htm*) is also very user-friendly with details of every park and reserve, conservation and wildlife information and information on upcoming events.

Other areas outside of the parks are enjoyable to walk around. The Santubong Peninsula north of Kuching is one, with a few trails over the mountain, including the Mount Santubong Summit Trek (see page 282). This walk is quite challenging and requires good fitness levels. Pleasant walks amid mountain scenery can also be taken along country roads and through kampungs skirting national parks.

Jungle adventure treks Organised jungle adventures range from youth-oriented survivor-camps combining hiking with edgy activities such as eating snakes, to straightforward treks. The best take in the Headhunter's Trail in northern Sarawak, the Salt Trek in the Crocker Range, Mount Kinabalu National Park, and parts of the Sandakan-Ranau death-march trail. More costly trips probe the heart of Borneo and remote places such as the Maliau Basin. All local tour groups involved in outdoor adventure organise such trips.

Mountain adventure For more serious mountain adventures, see some of the tour operators listed on pages 78–81.

For really off-the-beaten-track Kinabalu climbs, hardcore climbers head to the Eastern Plateau, via Bowen's Route or Kotal's Route. Both were pioneered during

The following overview is intended to help you choose the dive location best suited to your level and interests. Further details on marine environments, dive operators and lodgings are found in the relevant chapters.

DIVE DESTINATIONS In Sarawak, you can dive off the coast around Miri, and further north in Brunei. Sabah, however, still tops the list of Borneo's best dive destinations. Good dive spots are found between the west-coast islands of Labuan and Layang Layang, at Lankayan off the north coast, and Sipadan, Mabul and Kapalai off the east coast. According to China-based writer William Moss, the diving attractions in Sabah include reefs, atolls and lagoons; shore diving and drift diving; and lots of pelagic life. 'The area off of Tawau and Semporna is particularly rich, featuring the islands of Mabul, Kapalai, and Sipadan. Any diver planning a trip to the area should divide their time between these locations – a week of dives will yield an amazing diversity of marine life of all sizes and shapes.'

The east-coast islands in the Sulawesi and Celebes seas have brought both fame and infamy to Bornean diving. Lying in territorial waters between Indonesia and Malaysia, the area is considered by some to be dangerous, and foreigners are often advised against visiting and diving in the area (see page 92). In April 2000, Sipadan made world headlines when an extremist Filipino Muslim group kidnapped a group of European tourists from the Borneo Diver's Resort. All accommodation on Sipadan has since closed, on both security and environmental grounds, and Sipadan is under constant military surveillance. Most diving accommodation is now found on other islands, but Sipadan remains a marine-lover's magnet.

DIVING SEASON Tough weather during the northeast monsoon season may affect diving conditions and ease of travel by boat. William Moss maintains that diving can be enjoyed all year round, though some inhabitants may be seasonal visitors, such as Layang Layang's hammerheads. Some say that April to July is the best time to dive.

DIVING CONDITIONS Surface water temperatures range from 24° to 31°C. A 3mm suit is sufficient for most diving conditions, though many people dive in skin-suits. Visibility averages around 20m but varies considerably, from 6–10m inshore to 15–30m-plus at offshore locations.

ACCOMMODATION Lodgings on several of the islands are managed by particular dive operators. Staying overnight on one of the islands is a memorable experience. The difference in price between doing so or choosing to stay on the mainland and make daily dive trips depends on the package you organise. If you pre-book your whole trip through an international dive operator, try and negotiate a price that includes all diving, equipment, accommodation, transfers and meals. Most of the local dive operators with island-based accommodation will offer this in any case. One of the best general-information websites to help make a selection is www.divetheworldmalaysia.com. It details dive sites, accommodation listings, and more.

the Royal Society expeditions on the mountain in the mid 1960s. Some adventure tour operators organise these routes.

Rock climbing and abseiling The granite peaks of Mount Kinabalu are the main attraction for rock-climbing enthusiasts in Sabah; in Sarawak, the limestone crags and sandstone environs of the Mulu Caves in the north, and the Fairy Caves near the town of Bau (40 minutes from Kuching) are popular for caving and climbing.

Cycling and mountain bikes Neither Sabah nor Sarawak is easy for road cycling. No dedicated cycle routes exist on main roads, either in the main cities or in the countryside. There are, however, some great off-road mountain-bike adventures. 'The Crocker Range is quite a challenge, and Kota Kinabalu to the east coast of Sabah makes a good one-week trip,' says Tham Yau Kong, adventurer-founder of TYK Adventure Tours, 'People think Sabah is easy for cycling, but don't underestimate how hard the humidity and heat can make it.'

Tham is well known and a good point of call for cycling enthusiasts (e *thamyaukong@thamyaukong.com; www.thamyaukong.com*). In the late 1990s he created the eco-friendly cycling business 'Eco Tourism on Pedals', and was one of the founders of the Mount Kinabalu International Mountain Bike Race and other cycling challenges. Along with his cycling associates, he claims to have entered the Malaysia Book of Records for being the first group to circumvent Mount Kinabalu by mountain bike, and believes mountain biking as a sports tourism activity will become big in Borneo.

In Sarawak, the Kuching area is excellent for mountain-bike adventure, as are the parks and rainforest reserves west towards Sematan and north towards the Santubong Peninsula and Damai Beach. The annual Rainforest Cup mountain-bike event is held in Damai each year, while the Battle of Borneo event takes place at Mulu. Brunei has several glorious reserves criss-crossed with mountain-biking trails, starting right in the city.

Rafting The two main rivers for rafting in Sabah are the Sungai Padas and Sungai Kiulu rivers in the hinterland of the west coast. According to operators, both are certified as Grade III and Grade II respectively in the international whitewater rafting grading system. Indigenous people, with their amazing water navigation skills, quickly caught on to whitewater rafting in the 1980s. The dry season is the best time for novices. Rivers can swell to Grade IV during the wet season, attracting the more experienced rafters. Outside of the wet season, the Sungai Kiulu is too low for rafting so the Sungai Padas gets most of the crowds at this time of the year. Kiulu rapids include 'Headhunter', 'Adrenaline Flow' and 'Merry Go Round'. Make sure you go with a licensed operator, some of which are listed on pages 78–81. The standard Padas excursion is a day trip, but longer trips can be arranged with accommodation at the Padas River Lodge in Rayoh. The basic trip provides a safety and technical briefing and life jackets. Experienced rafters can arrange for a custom-made trip. In Sabah, operators will arrange transport from Kota Kinabalu through the Padas Gorge. Bring a change of clothes, warm layers, a waterproof jacket and well-fitting shoes or diving boots. Spectacle-wearers should bring something with which to anchor glasses, while contact-lens wearers are advised to wear spectacles to avoid lens contamination.

Birdwatching 'In Sabah,' says Susan Myers, author of *Birds of Borneo* and *Field Guide to the Birds of Borneo*, 'birding is out of this world.' During a 17-day trip to five key sites, Susan once recorded 230 species. 'This included some highly sought-after *right*   Top nature watching spot at the Danum Valley Conservation Area, Sabah (FL/FLPA) pages 254–5

below   Mudskippers bask in mangrove mud at Bako National Park (DA) pages 283–4

bottom   The discovery of urns, textiles and tools has revealed that the spectacular Niah Caves were inhabited for thousands of years (SWT) page 237

left **Typical pom-pommed and woven costume of Iban in Brunei and Sarawak** (BT) pages 17–18

below **Iban tribeswoman raking through drying rice crop on the Lemanak River, Sarawak** (SS)

bottom **A traditional Iban longhouse** (SWT) pages 17–18

There are around 30 species of pitcher plant in Borneo of which half occur on Mount Kinabalu; see page 43.

The impressive *Nepenthes bicalcarata* is endemic to Bornean peat swamp forests. Unique among pitcher plants, it lives in close association with an ant species that helps to defend the plant against pest insects *(above left)*.

N muluensis growing in a thick carpet of moss on Mount Mulu, Sarawak *(above centre)*.

The large, vase-shaped pitchers of *N lowii* are not purely for trapping insects but attract tree shrews that use them as a toilet! *(above right)* (all UB)

There are 17 different species of the rafflesia or 'corpse flower' — so called for the whiff of rotting flesh they give off when in bloom — all of them endemic to Borneo. Indigenous tribes believe the species have aphrodisiac powers; see pages 42–3. Here a *Rafflesia pricei* *(left, SB)*, a *Rafflesia keithi* *(below left, KK/S)* and the bud of a *Rafflesia tuan-mudae* *(below right, DA)*.

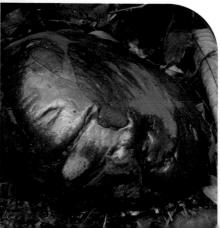

Aerial view of Pulau Gaya, home to several water
villages (IB) pages 193–5
Pictured below, the seven-tiered Maliau Falls
in Sabah's 'Lost World', the Maliau Basin
Conservation Area (M/SBT) pages 245–6

above left **Some 1,500 traders gather at Kuching's Sunday market** (A/S) pages 272–3

above right **The fishing village of Teluk Melano, in the Tanjung Datu Peninsula, Sarawak** (SS) page 285

right **An Iban fisherman throwing out a net** (SWT) pages 17–18

below **Stilted house of the Bajau people, Semporna** (N/S) pages 246–54

above   Illegal logging is devastating Borneo's rainforests. In the 1980s; 75% of Malaysian Borneo was covered in primary forest; today that has been reduced to 50% (RC/S) pages 61–3

left   NGOs and passionate locals do what they can to replace cleared areas (TT) pages 62–9

below   In recent years, forests have also been cleared for palm oil plantations resulting in huge losses in biodiversity and indigenous people's homes (SS) pages 61–3 species, such as the giant pita, storm's stork, Bornean bristlehead and Whitehead's trogon.' Local Bornean bird specialists offer one- to 12-day trips. There are several bird sanctuaries (run by the Wildlife Department) in Sabah, three or four on the west coast, and in Kota Kinabalu itself.

Golf Sabah's long, indented west coast is marked by several world-class golf resorts set spectacularly between Mount Kinabalu and the South China Sea. Sutera Harbour's Golf and Country Club in Kota Kinabalu has won awards as Malaysia's top course; to the north are the Dalit Bay Golf and Country Club in Tuaran, Nexus Golf Resort Karambunai, and Kudat Peninsula's Golf & Marina Resort. At 1,500m altitude, the Mount Kinabalu Golf Club is the highest in Sabah, while the Borneo Highlands Resort in Sarawak has received the most accolades as a cool-climate, ecologically minded golfing set-up. Brunei's top courses are the Royal Brunei Golf & Club, and the Empire Country Club course designed by Jack Nicklaus. Online UK magazine *Golf Today* (*www.golftoday.co.uk*) includes comprehensive details of these resorts on its world golf course guide.

Cultural history If archaeology, ethnography and anthropology are your main interests, then you should visit the Niah Caves in northern Sarawak, the Sarawak and Sabah state museums, the Islamic museums of civilisation and art, and the mosques and museums of Brunei. The whole of northern Borneo is one incredible outdoor ethnographic museum, with living cultural displays everywhere. There are also several brilliant local indigenous cultural associations mentioned in the guide worth contacting.

PHOTOGRAPHY

Taking photographs of **people** in Borneo, as anywhere else, is a deeply personal thing – different people react differently, and it's up to the photographer to be sensitive to individual wishes in this regard, and react accordingly. On the whole, I am greeted by spontaneous and willing subjects in both children and adults. People tend to interact with you as you take photos – it's a great joy, and a great privilege. Members of some ethnic groups are more timid than others – the Kadazandusun are often more extroverted and urban-wise, as are the Bajau, whereas the Rungus tend to be more shy and rural. It is best to ask permission before taking shots of individuals from close range, and this is a good general rule of respect. In rural areas, you will often end up the main source of fascination, as a tourist, and a photographer with a fancy camera. For street scenes and shots of crowds, you can comfortably take photos without prior permission or fear of adverse reactions. I have never incited the kind of angry reactions for taking crowd shots as I have done in Morocco.

So snap away to your heart's content, but with awareness of those Muslims who clearly do not warm to being photographed.

Buildings are another thing altogether. Government buildings, even shopping centres and other public or retail spaces, often have no-photo policies, generally enforced politely and discreetly. **Art galleries** and **museums** are 'a case-by-case affair; some state museums may allow you to take photos outside, but not within.

MEDIA AND COMMUNICATIONS

NEWSPAPERS Sabah, Sarawak and Brunei have their own newspapers, and there appears to be little demand for international newspapers. Even in luxury hotels in capital cities it is standard practice to hang a regional paper such as the *Sabah Times*, the *Daily Express*, the *Borneo Post* or the *Sarawak Tribune* on your door. Guests are rarely offered international papers. If you can't live without them, which I understand, you may find the *International Herald Tribune* in mixed bazaars of some towns, and a couple more choices in good English-language bookstores in the capitals, though they are likely to be back copies. Local newspapers sport a British-tabloid look, and are thin on content, especially foreign coverage. The *Daily Express* is considered Sabah's best newspaper. Sarawak's most prevalent English-language newspaper is the *Borneo Post*, which also has a section in Behasa Melayu, and by far the best foreign coverage. The weekend version is the *Sunday Post*. The Malaysian national English-language newspaper *New Straits Times* also circulates. Brunei has three daily papers: the Malay-language *Media Permata*, the English-language *Brunei Times*, and the top-rating *Borneo Bulletin*. A punchy, political online newspaper is *Malaysia Now* (*www.Malaysiakini.com*). The state-run Malaysian news agency is Bernama (*www.bernama.com*). An interesting Brunei blog is the Weekly Brunei Resources (*http://bruneiresources. blogspot.com*).

RADIO Radio stations in Sarawak seem to reflect the cultural diversity far better than television, with day-long or half-day services in Bahasa Malaysia, Mandarin, Hakka, Hokkien, English, Iban and Bidayuh, and half-day broadcasts in Kayan and Kenyah. Some of these are broadcast by WaiFM, others by the local radio station of Radio Television Malaysia (RTM). Sarawak FM has 24-hour Malay broadcasts. Sabah also has RTM radio and some English content on its FM stations – Hitz, Era and Mix FM. Radio Television Brunei (RTB) operates three radio stations – two in Malay, one switching between English, Mandarin and Hindustani programming. Commercial radio station Kristal FM is bilingual English–Malay and also operates cable television, Kristal Astro.

TELEVISION Two government-run (RTM) Malay television channels, TV1 and TV2, are broadcast in Malaysian Borneo as well as privately owned stations such as TV3, NTV7 (common in hotels), 8TV and TV9. Highly popular satellite server, Astro TV, provides channels such as CNN, BBC, Star World Movies, Cinemax Movies, Vision 4 (movies), Star Sport, and Japanese and Chinese channels. The choice of available channels varies and can be extremely limited in low-star hotels. Radio Television Brunei has one television station with largely Malay-language broadcasts.

TELECOMMUNICATIONS
Telephone dialling codes All local dialling codes in Sabah and Sarawak start with three digits, such as 088 for Kota Kinabalu. The Malaysian dialling code (covering Sabah and Sarawak) is +60. If calling from overseas, drop the first zero of local numbers (eg: +6 088 334567). When in Malaysia, dial the whole number if calling from outside of that town or region. Drop the local prefix only when in the town or city itself. The dialling code for Brunei is +673.

Public phones Malaysia's national telephone company is Telekom Malaysia Berhad (TM). Together with privately owned Citiphone, it provides payphone booths in the city and countryside. You can use either coins or the large variety of pre-paid phonecards. Calling cards, which function by code, are widely available from phone shops and street stores in RM20, 30, 50 and 100 denominations.

Telekom's iTalk is a good one, but it depends, as always, which country you are calling, so ask the vendor.

Mobile phones Called 'hand phones' in Malaysia, these are a national sport. On business cards the number is preceded by 'HP'. Most people have two or three hand phones, often ringing at the same time. There are telephone shops everywhere – plastered with flags and stickers of the companies they deal with. Major service providers are **Celcom**, **Maxis** and **DiGi**, which have expansive networks of stores and dominate roadside billboards. If you want to put a Malaysian SIM card in your phone (much cheaper for internal calls), it will cost RM10–30 depending on the provider. Celcom and DiGi offer pre-paid starter packs with SIM cards for RM8.50, which includes RM5 credit. Code-induced top-ups for whatever provider you are with can be purchased in shops or by phone. It is compulsory to register the SIM number with a name, so take your passport along. **Hot Link Maxis'** pre-paid mobile-phone cards are very popular and their rates are better than Celcom for overseas calls, providing '20 sen/min to 20 countries' (around US$0.06 per minute to many countries including the UK, US, France and Australia). However, it is not the best option for making domestic calls. If you are travelling in Malaysia, top up with RM100 before leaving; your account stays active for up to eight months.

INTERNET AND WI-FI Borneo has started to embrace the rest of Malaysia's enthusiasm for high-tech and internet communications, though the service is much slower than on the peninsula, generally 4–8Mbps maximum. The two major Malaysian internet service providers are TMNet and Jaring, the latter being more prevalent in East Malaysia. In large and small cities and towns it is usually easy to find internet cafés, charging RM2–4 per hour; some offer decreased rates for the second or third hour, and even a free drink. Increasing numbers of cafés and bars have free Wi-Fi for customers. (See page 106, for information on internet in hotels.)

BUSINESS

In Brunei Darussalam, contact the **Ministry of Industry and Primary Resources** (*One-Stop Agency, Ministry of Industry & Primary Resources, Bandar Seri Begawan;* \+673 2380026; *www.brunei.gov.bn/about_brunei/business.htm*) about all business opportunities.

In Sabah, contact the **Department of Industrial Development and Research** (*7th & 8th Floors, Block C, Wisma Tun Fuad Stephens, Karamunsing Centre, Kota Kinabalu;* \+6 088 215035; *www.sabah.gov.my/didr/english/WhySabah.htm*). Their website has a good section on doing business in Sabah.

LIVING IN BORNEO

Not all tropical destinations offer the combination of natural and cultural riches that Borneo does. The sunshine, islands, jungle, food and outdoor adventure are enough to tempt anyone to live there on a more permanent basis. But is it actually viable to realise such an exotic dream? There are many factors to consider and all are fairly personal decisions. A practical issue might be the climate – how well do you fare when humidity is high? Though I can survive happily in such conditions I do find that my sportier habits become somewhat subdued – sport should generally be done indoors to escape the heat. The isolation of living in more remote areas, and of living in such a different culture, may be a blessing or a curse for you.

3

There are sizeable expat communities in Brunei and Miri in Sarawak, working in the oil industry (oilfields and research). There may be scientific jobs available at forest research institutes and centres, and universities in both Brunei and Malaysian Borneo, as well as primary- and secondary-school teaching in foreign and Malaysian schools.

The attractions of living in Borneo include the simplicity of life, warmth of the people, rich culture and religious and cultural tolerance. Many colonially inherited English customs, and the common use of spoken English, make settling in relatively easy.

You may experience quite a cultural shock, but this in itself is an adventure just as travelling is. Many of the obstacles of settling into daily Malaysian Borneo life are as relevant today as when Heidi Munan, a Swiss-born, New Zealand-educated author, wrote *Culture Shock! A Guide to Customs and Etiquette, Borneo* in 1988 (revised 1992). It's a great book – personal and straight-talking. Expect some administrative frustrations: transport, roads and communication may not be up to the standard to which you are accustomed, though not enough to make life impossible. You will soon enjoy the easier-going pace and endless cultural fascination. Enriching as it is to immerse in other languages and cultures, English is widely spoken in the circles where you need it most: health, education and commerce.

MALAYSIA MY SECOND HOME (*Ministry of Tourism & Culture, Level 1, No 2, Tower 1, Jln P5/6, Presint 5, 62200 W P Putrajaya;* \ +60 3 8891 7424/27/34/39; e *mm2h@motac.gov.my; www.mm2h.gov.my*) Increasing numbers of people are being wooed to Borneo for the lifestyle. The 'Malaysia My Second Home' programme is a government initiative aimed at attracting foreigners to invest in Malaysia by buying a second house there. As well as the cheaper house prices, the programme promotes the low crime rates, political stability, favourable climate, low risk of natural disasters and access to quality education as tempting reasons to sign up.

The programme is open to foreigners of all races and religions. Those aged below 50 are required to make a minimum deposit of RM300,000; over-50s must put up RM150,000 or provide proof of a monthly offshore income of RM10,000. After a year, money can be withdrawn from the account for house purchase, education, medical expenses, etc, as long as a minimum balance of RM60,000 is maintained. You must also take out Malaysian medical insurance and provide a full medical report. If your application is accepted, the Immigration Department grants you a 'Social Visit Pass' and multiple-entry visa, which allow you to come and go as you please. These are initially valid for ten years but can be renewed thereafter. Since 2009, people have been able to apply to participate in the MM2H programme directly, without going through a third party. Alternatively they can use the services of licensed MM2H 'agents' – a list of which is available on the MM2H website. Over-50s wanting to live in Sabah or Sarawak can still apply directly to their immigration departments.

Immigration departments

Department of Immigration Sabah Tingkat 6, Bangunan Wisma Dang Bandang, Jln Tuanku Abdul Rahman, 88550, Kota Kinabalu; \ +60 088 80700; www.psupsabah.gov.my

Department of Immigration Sarawak Tingkat 1&2, Bangunan Sultan Iskandar, Jln Simpang Tiga, 93550, Kuching; \ +60 082 245661; www.sarawak.gov.my

Housing is available in both rural and urban areas and ranges from terraced and semi-detached houses and bungalows to chic flats and apartments. There are an increasing number of luxury apartment and condominium developments, especially in Kuching and Kota Kinabalu and nearby coastal areas, specifically aimed at foreign investors. Prices are therefore skyrocketing, but they are still relatively low. Look at the real-estate section of one of the online daily newspapers (see pages 121–2) to get an idea.

STUDYING IN BORNEO

There are many opportunities in Sabah, Sarawak and Brunei for pre-tertiary and tertiary studies, through student-exchange programmes, years abroad and short-term student tourism programmes. There is both a state education system and private schools, including international schools, universities, private colleges and expatriate schools (British, American, French and German).

MALAYSIAN BORNEO In Sabah, the Yayasan Sabah Group (*Tun Mustapha Tower, Yayasan Sabah HQ, PO Box 11623;* +60 88 326300; e *ysinfo@ysnet.org.my; www.ysnet.org.my*) is a progressive education foundation with information on secondary- and tertiary-level scholarships under its education development programme.

A website that posts student exchanges, study options and participating schools and institutions in Malaysia is www.studymalaysia.com.

Useful national education contacts with links to East Malaysia are the **Ministry of Higher Education** (+60 3 8883 5000; *www.mohe.gov.my*), which has a focused Department of Private Education; the **National Accreditation Board** (+60 3 7968 7002; *www.lan.gov.my*); and the **Malaysian Association of Private Colleges and Universities** (MAPCU) (+60 3 8656 9981; *www.mapcu.com.my*).

Major universities include the **Universiti Malaysia in Sabah** (*Locked Bag 2073, 88999 Kota Kinabalu;* + 60 8832 0000 e *crd@ums.edu.my; www.ums.edu.my*) and the **Universiti Malaysia in Sarawak** (UNIMAS) (*Jln Datuk Mohd Musa, 94300 Kota Samarahan, Sarawak;* +60 82 581388; *www.unimas.my*).

The **British Council** in Malaysia (*Wisma Selangor Dredging, 142C Jln Ampang, 50450 Kuala Lumpur; www.britishcouncil.org.my*) is a good point of contact for enquiries about secondary-school cultural exchanges. Australia's **Curtin University of Technology** (*www.curtin.edu.my*) also has a campus in Miri, Sarawak.

BRUNEI English-taught degree subjects offered at the Universiti Brunei Darussalam (UBD) (*www.ubd.edu.bn*) include education, mathematics and computer science; electronics and electrical engineering; geography/economics major; management studies; and public policy and administration.

CULTURAL ETIQUETTE

NAMES AND TITLES Malay people will address you by your first name, yet in a polite form, so I was immediately baptised 'Miss Tamara'. It comes across as both very respectful and warm. Most people are not offended if you call them by just their first name instead of adding the usual '*Encik*' (Mr/Sir) or '*Puan*' (Mrs/Lady). While there are many formalities in Malaysian society, the people are personable by nature and fairly laid-back about such things. It is appropriate, nonetheless, to address people formally in written correspondence and on formal occasions.

Chinese people on the other hand are called by their surnames, which appear in writing before their given names. So a lady named Chia Wei Li would be addressed as 'Ms Chia'. Many Chinese people have English names, such as a friend of mine Ivy Yap. Officially she would be 'Ms Yap', but everyone simply calls her Ivy. Chinese people are generally far more relaxed and unfussy about customs than the Malay. Again, it's only in official circles where formalities must be observed.

DRESS Women who visit Muslim Brunei are requested to dress modestly in keeping with local customs. The same applies to Muslim-dominated parts of Sabah and Sarawak. Elsewhere, many women wear a tudung (a hair scarf), while some bare their arms and legs. Wherever you are in Borneo, it is best to avoid baring too much flesh. (See also page 93.)

GREETINGS The customary Malay greeting is the *salam*: the person greeting you reaches out and grasps your hand gently while bringing their right hand to their chest. This graceful gesture means sweetly 'I greet you from my heart'. Hotel and restaurant staff and people in the streets and at marketplaces may greet you with an eclipsed version of this – just the hand to the heart bit. It is good manners, and greatly appreciated, to return the gesture. The reciprocated greeting is called bersalaman. Muslim members of the opposite sex do not generally touch in greetings. Chinese people tend to shake hands in the more traditional way. It is quite rare to see couples showing public displays of affection.

GESTURES It is deemed impolite to refuse food and drink (including rice wine!) by saying 'no' or shaking the head. If you can, accept a little; to refuse, touch the plate or glass lightly with the right hand. Use the right hand when giving and receiving objects or passing something, particularly food. The right hand is also used when eating with one's fingers. You should never point Western-style – instead curl the four fingers of your right hand inwards and point with the thumb.

BEHAVIOUR Malaysians are gracious, polite people who may be offended by boisterous behaviour; Chinese people are usually more outgoing. It is courteous to respect these cultures and behave appropriately. Avoid smoking in the streets.

ALCOHOL AND FOOD Muslims do not drink alcohol. It may be offensive to offer alcohol to a Muslim or drink it in their presence, though some restaurants and hotels openly encourage you to bring your own – but don't expect them to pull the cork for you! Discretion is the key.

During the Islamic fasting month of Ramadan, Muslims fast between sunrise and sunset (for about 12 hours). It is inconsiderate to blatantly eat and drink in their company during this time. If someone insists you do so, that's fine – this is Malaysian politeness at its highest. Muslims eat only halal food, and no pork.

MOSQUE DECORUM Mosques have strict non-Muslim visiting hours that avoid prayer times; these vary between places. Most mosques, temples and other places of worship ask all visitors to remove their shoes before entering. This also applies to Malaysian homes, homestays, guesthouses and public areas of some resorts. Some mosques provide robes and/or headscarves for female visitors. Remember to be respectful of rules and traditions. Avoid passing in front of a person who is praying, making lots of noise, or touching the Koran.

LONGHOUSE DECORUM Longhouse dos and don'ts vary between ethnic groups and even between individual communities. Remember that longhouses are people's homes rather than museums, and you are a guest. Enter a longhouse only when invited; don't enter or peep into sleeping quarters (sirang) or other private rooms unless invited to do so; do not enter a longhouse during times of mourning or as it is being built (this is considered to bring bad luck); never walk under a longhouse; upon your departure, say goodbye to everyone and thank them for their hospitality.

TRAVELLING POSITIVELY

The best way to 'give something back' can be done before you even arrive in Borneo, with your choice of holiday operators. As well as volunteer projects (outlined below), the tour operators you choose will dictate how 'responsible' your holiday can be, whether they are organising your entire trip or you are travelling independently. Using local tour operators does not guarantee local development, but several are committed to helping local communities. By choosing such responsible operators, you can directly help community development initiatives such as homestay programmes, or conservation efforts such as tree planting.

A good example of such responsible tourism is the work of **SI Tours** (see page 79) on Sabah's northeast coast. When you stay at their forest lodges or choose them as a day-trip host, they send RM1 to a local village. The money is used to help families buy school uniforms and bags for their children and improve their homes. SI Tours also source food and other products locally, boosting the local economy.

TYK Adventure Tours (see page 80) aim to demonstrate to local people that long-term benefits of tourism outweigh the short-term gains of cash crops, thus helping to change the 'slash and burn mentality' of communities and protect the environment. By involving indigenous communities in local tourist ventures such as native rafting and survival camps, the safeguarded environment becomes the livelihood.

If you book your trip with an international operator, ensure that they are working with local communities, operators and NGOs. Those that bear the stamp of responsible travel are usually legitimate. **Intrepid Travel** (*www.intrepidtravel.com*) are a shining example.

For more information and links, try **Responsible Travel** (📞 *01273 600030; www.responsibletravel.com*), a Brighton-based ecotourism travel directory that includes adventure travel, orangutan conservation tours and volunteer programmes.

CARBON OFFSETTING   Carbon emissions generated from your trip can be offset at www.atmosfair.de, a legitimate company recommended by BBC Wildlife magazine. The travel industry is the fastest-growing contributor of CO_2 emissions – mostly due to air travel. **Conservation International** (*www.conservation.org*) offers lots of helpful advice about carbon emissions, calculating your eco-footprint and reducing your negative impacts on the environment. Al Gore's (2006) film An Inconvenient Truth offers more information on the negative repercussions of travel, and ways of limiting them, as does the book The Weather Makers by Tim Flannery.

VOLUNTEER VACATIONS   There are many volunteer programmes to choose from in Malaysian Borneo, from conservation to teaching and village development. A good place to look for volunteer programmes in Sabah and Sarawak is Travel Tree (*www.traveltree.co.uk*). More student-oriented sites include www.realgap.co.uk and www.gapyearforgrownups.co.uk. In the US, I-to-I (*www.i-to-i.com*) runs Borneo summer camps and volunteer programmes for 16–19 year olds. Raleigh International (*Raleigh Hse, 3rd Floor, 2007 Waterloo Rd, London;* 📞 *020 7371 8585;*

e *info@raleigh.org.uk; www.raleighinternational.org*) calls itself an 'international development charity'. Its expeditions in Sabah call on volunteers from the UK, Malaysia and other countries, who get incredible life experience while working on community and environmental projects, as well as some real adventure.

NATURE CONSERVATION

Enormous conservation efforts are being made by several organisations. Leading the way is **WWF** (*www.panda.org*), with teams of international and Malaysian scientists active in dozens of projects for fauna and flora conservation. (See pages 65–6 for more information on WWF's 'Heart of Borneo' project.) They publish many invaluable reports on Borneo's biodiversity and work alongside international universities and research institutes. They are in constant need of funds – see their website for details of how you can help.

There are also many small Malaysian local groups making a big difference.

Other organisations, as well as general nature sites, post jobs on their websites. **Wildlife Extra** (*www.wildlifeextra.com*) is a British-based web wildlife magazine with links to wildlife volunteer and paid jobs, projects, wildlife holidays and lots of good causes and campaigns. The website www.greenvolunteers.com is a good guide and source of information on worldwide nature conservation volunteer programmes.

The UK's **Orangutan Foundation** (*7 Kent Terrace, London; www.orangutan.org.uk*) has a volunteer programme, usually with a six-week trip every year. Note these trips focus on the Tanjung Puting National Park in Kalimantan, Indonesian Borneo, but is nonetheless a very worthy cause in need of volunteers. Australia's **Orangutan Project** (*www.orangutan.org.au*) links in with them.

Sometimes the best way to help is with a donation to appeals such as the **SepilokOrangutan Appeal** (*11 Forest Hall, Lyndhurst Rd, Brockenhurst, Hampshire;* ✆ *01590 623443;* e *info@orangutan-appeal.org*) – you can adopt an orphaned orangutan at Sabah's foremost orangutan rehabilitation centre during orangutan caring week.

The **Malaysian Nature Society** (*Persatuan Pencinta Alam Malaysia;* e *mns@mns. my; www.mns.my*) has many conservation and community projects in Sabah and Sarawak. Its website links to grassroots organisations and their upcoming events and activities. To support them you can volunteer, join or donate.

Friends of the Earth Malaysia (*Sahabat Alam Malaysia (SAM);* ✆ *+60 42 276930; www.foe-malaysia.org*) carry out many grassroots community activities in Borneo and are involved in environmental and community issues. They have an office in Marudi, in the Baram river area in Sarawak, but their main office is in Penang.

Borneo is one of **Conservation International**'s biodiversity 'hotspots' (*1919 M St, NW Suite 600 Washington, DC 20036;* ✆ *+1 202 912 1000/800 406 2306;* e *hotspots@conservation.org; www.biodiversityhotspots.org or www.conservation. org*). There are plenty of suggestions about how you can help on their website.

Forests Monitor (*69a Lensfield Rd, Cambridge CB2 1EN; www.forestsmonitor.org*) is an NGO working with traditional communities of the world to lobby against activities destroying their habitats. You can donate to their appeals and volunteer with projects.

INDIGENOUS RIGHTS AND CULTURAL CONSERVATION

The **Borneo Project** (*2150 Allston Way #460*, Berkeley, California, CA 94703; ✆ *+1 415 341 7051;* e *info@ borneoproject.org; www.borneoproject.org*) is a major advocate for indigenous rights, rainforest protection and sustainable community development in Borneo. Established in 1991, they have helped indigenous people with native land claims, legal aid, reforestation and rural development primarily in Sarawak. A non-profit organisation sponsored by Earth Island Institute, it works closely with local groups who initiate and oversee various projects while a volunteer advisory board in the US gathers resources and educates audiences about the rainforests and people of Borneo. One recent reforestation scheme brought nine Penan, Kayan and Iban communities together: 'The villages share skills and strategies in reforestation of timber trees, coffee, pepper, rattans, medicinal plants, fruit trees, and vegetable gardening. Nine new nurseries have been constructed and are well on their way to rejuvenating degraded rainforests.' Other programmes focus on legal aid, community mapping (for claims to ancestral lands) and indigenous pre-schools.

The **Borneo Research Council** (*www.borneoresearchcouncil.org*) draws together a worldwide network of humanitarian field academics with an expertise in the history, language, culture, performing arts, etc, and is keen to recruit volunteers. The Sabah Museum and Sarawak Museum have many different research projects and departments in cultural heritage.

Survival International (*6 Charterhouse Bldgs, London EC1M 7ET;* ☏ *020 7687 8700;* e *info@survival-international.org; www.survival-international.org*) do a lot of work protecting indigenous peoples of the world, including those in Borneo.

PACOS (Partners of Community Organisations) (☏ *088 712518;* e *pacos@ tm.net.my*) is a community-based volunteer organisation in Sabah that supports indigenous communities. The **Borneo Resources Institute** (BRIMAS) (*brimas. www1.50megs.com*) works at a grassroots level in Sarawak, helping indigenous communities to defend their rights, and promotes community-based sustainable resource management and conservation.

Bruno Manser Fonds (BMF) (*www.bmf.ch*) is a Swiss-based environmental and human rights organisation, working to support the Penan people in Sarawak, as well as other indigenous peoples in their struggle to protect tropical rainforests from destruction.

The **Forest Peoples Programme** (FPP) (*www.forestpeoples.org*) works with forest-dwelling peoples worldwide, helping them to empower themselves build up their own organisations and negotiate with governments and companies on economic development and conservation on their lands.

The **Rainforest Foundation** (*rainforestfoundationuk.org*) supports indigenous rainforest-dwelling people in their efforts to protect their environment and fulfil their rights.

TROPICAL FOREST RESEARCH
The following research institutes and organisations are dedicated to unravelling the mysteries of Borneo's nature as well as conserving it. Many areas of Borneo's natural wonders remain unstudied and not fully understood. There is a great need for this research, and there may be opportunities for you to contribute your own knowledge.

The **Royal Botanic Gardens, Kew** (England) (e *info@kew.org; www.kew.org*) is a world leader in botany and plant conservation. At least one of its research teams works in Borneo; it also relies on 500 affiliated researchers, students and volunteers, collaborating in the UK and overseas to build the knowledge base. Information is beautifully presented, for both children and adults, on its website.

Local organisations
Organisations working on a local level are always in need of extra help, through volunteers and donations. Check out the **Institute of Biodiversity and Environmental Conservation** at Universiti Malaysia Sarawak (*www. ibec.unimas.my*), the **Institute for Tropical Biology** and the **Borneo Marine Research Institute** at the Universiti Malaysia Sabah (*www.ums.edu.my*). Sabah's **Wildlife**

Department (*www.sabah.gov.my/jhl*) carries out conservation projects all over the state with the university and NGOs; **Sabah Forestry** (*www.forest.sabah.gov.my*) and **Sarawak Forestry** (*www.sarawawforestry.com*) have various national-park activities and sustainable forest research programmes.

GIVING GIFTS Small gifts are a nice way of showing gratitude to hosts. These may be 'exotic' things from your own home country that are not available in Borneo. When visiting longhouses or other traditional communities, the custom is to present gifts to the village chief (*penghulu*) or longhouse chief (*tuai rumah*), who will share them around.

BEGGING Giving money to children is not encouraged. Begging is uncommon in Sabah and Sarawak. The main exceptions are some coastal towns with a lot of poor Filipino and Indonesian migrants. Children might cheekily extend their hands for money when parents are not looking.

UPDATES WEBSITE

You can post your comments and recommendations, and read the latest feedback and updates from other readers, online at www.bradtupdates.com/borneo.

Part Two

BRUNEI

Official name Negara Brunei Darussalam. 'State of Brunei, abode of peace' is the rather unwieldy name of the nation, but it is most commonly referred to as 'Brunei'.

International telephone code +673

Currency Brunei dollar

Exchange rate US$1 = B$1.39, €1 = B$1.58, £1 = B$2.15, AU$1=B$1.01 (October 2015)

Climate Humid; average daily temperature 28°C

Geography 5,765km²; situated on Borneo's northwest coast

Population 400,000; 73% Malay, 15% Chinese, 12% various indigenous tribes

Capital Bandar Seri Begawan (BSB)

Visa requirements Three-month visa-free stay US/UK and most European citizens; Australians granted 30-day visa on arrival (B$20) or three-day transit visa ($B5) (for further details, see page 82).

Language Official language Malay; Chinese and English also widely spoken

Emergency numbers Police 993; Fire 995; Ambulance 991

Banking/business hours 08.00/09.00–16.00/17.00 Monday–Friday, 08.00/09.00–11.00/noon Saturday

Shopping centre hours 10.00–22.00 daily

Government website www.brunei.gov.bn

Tourist board +673 238 2822; e info@tourismbrunei.com; www.tourismbrunei.com

BORNEO ONLINE

For additional online content, articles, photos and more on Borneo, why not visit www.bradtguides.com/borneo.

4

Brunei Darussalam

Being an inkblot of a nation has bruised neither Brunei's self-image nor its prosperity. The Islamic pride and sovereign swishness are embodied in the flag – regal, striking and strict all at once – the yellow banner with white and black diagonal stripes bears a red insignia of wings, umbrellas and masts signifying justice, peace and prosperity. A lofty sense of all three permeates the watery ambience of Brunei, along with the sounds of Muslim prayer time emanating from its golden-domed mosques. Brunei is the most strong-spirited Muslim place in Borneo – nearly two-thirds of its population is of Islamic faith, and the foundations of the national philosophy *Melayu Islam Beraja* ('Malay Islam Monarchy' or MIB) are deeply entrenched, even more so since the announcement of tough new Sharia laws (see box, pages 136–7). Despite those laws – and Brunei's tougher face to the world – the country remains moderately Islamic in practice.

Women are 'strongly encouraged' by state authorities to cover their hair with a *tudung* and men wear the traditional Malay cap, the *songkok*. However, this clothing is far more about cultural expression than it is a sign of oppression. The people of Brunei are smiling, warm people, washed over by gentle Malay-ness, albeit a little socially straightjacketed and undeniably parched when it comes to full individual freedom.

In the aftermath of the first Arab country uprisings in 2011, CBS News highlighted Brunei and Sultan Hassanal Bolkiah in a World Watch series programme dedicated to 'The world's enduring dictators'. Listing its 'most despotic acts' it claimed: 'Bolkiah's government is accused of arbitrary detention; limits on freedom of speech, press, assembly, and association; restrictions on religious freedom; discrimination against women; restricted labour rights; and exploitation of foreign workers, according to the US State Department.' While voices of dissent are negligible, the media is largely state-owned or controlled.

For their reverence to the monarchy and Muslim ideology, there are many rewards: people get free education and health care, tax-free salaries, cheap housing loans and many other incentives. There's virtually no crime, unemployment is below 5% and inflation hovers at around 0.5%. Duty-free imports account for the majority of goods consumed, from food to electronics, and most people have two newly imported cars. Driving around is a breeze on the uncongested roads and a high quality of life is also accorded by the low-density population and plenitude of gardens and other urban spaces. Brunei is ten times the size of Singapore with one-tenth of the population; it is also a youthful nation – 90% of its population is under 50.

The modern face of Brunei is still in the making. The Sultan-owned national carrier Royal Brunei Airlines only started to promote its realm to the world in the mid 1990s. It has recently swung from marketing Brunei as a 'stopover' to Sabah and Sarawak to being a destination in itself. The country is aware of its size limitations, yet Bruneians love their high quality of life and boast that they have jungle, sea,

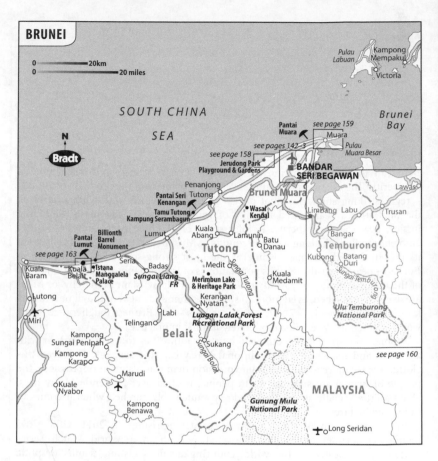

mosques and malls on their doorstep. As local DJ and television presenter Jenny Malai Ali says, Brunei is 'a magical little place that offers the luxuries of the new world against a rich and beautiful historical backdrop'.

HISTORY

Sultan Bolkiah is the 29th ruler of a 650-year-old unbroken Muslim dynasty. Prior to Islamic rule, ancient settlements in Brunei were a mixed bag of Malay, Chinese and Hindu influence. Chinese historical texts tell of thriving 10th-century trade with a region variably referred to as Puni, Po-li, Po-lo, Poni and Bunlai. In Arabic records, the early settlement was known as Dzabaj or Randj. In the 14th century, a Malay–Hindu–Buddhist settlement developed on the banks of the Sungai Brunei River. Folklore dictates that on discovering the area, newcomers exclaimed 'barunah!' – a Malay expression which roughly translates as 'this is it!'. Barunah later became Barunai, from the Sanskrit varuna – a nation of seafarers. In subsequent centuries, the name of the small trading post endured countless changes. Merchants, explorers and passers-by cited it as Bornei, Borney, Borneo, Bruneo, Burne and Bruni. The Chinese called it Wen-lai and Bun-lai.

The first Malay king to entertain Islam was Raja Awang Alak Betatar. He changed his name to Muhammad Shah and became the first sultan of Brunei, dramatically altering the course of history, and Brunei's cultural identity. Ever since his reign from 1363 to 1402, the long line-up of sultans represents the longest-lasting, though colonially interrupted, dynasty in the world.

Subsequent sultans ruled through an era which is widely known as Brunei's 'golden age', from the 15th to 17th century, when 'its control extended over the entire island of Borneo and into the Philippines. The kingdom was particularly powerful under the fifth sultan, Bolkiah (1473–1521). According to the *Brunei Times*, his successor, Sultan Abdul Kahar, continued through sea expeditions to expand Brunei's territories, 'which included the whole of Borneo, Palawan, Sulu, Balayan, Mindoro, Bonbon, Balabak, Balambangan and Bangi and Luzon... With the Brunei traders, Islam spread far including to the southern Philippines islands and Brunei was recognised as a centre of Islamic propagation.'

Brunei's expansion in the region provoked a showdown between Islam and Christianity. From the late 16th century, the Spanish used Manila as a trade centre and base from which to spread their religion. Fed up with Brunei proselytising on what they considered their territory, in 1573, a Spanish delegation was sent to Brunei seeking an audience with the seventh sultan, Saiful Rijal, to attempt to bring Brunei under Spanish protection and faith. They failed, and five years later they returned to Brunei with an armada of 40 warships, imploring the Sultan in a letter 'to send no preachers of the sect of Mohama to any part of these islands'.

The Spaniards attacked and burnt down the Great Mosque. Though they failed in their endeavours to bring the Philippines under Spanish sovereignty, they managed to minimise Brunei's regional influence. This marked the beginning of a period of decline for the sultanate, caught between internal rifts over royal succession and the rising influence of European colonial powers in the region.

From the 1830s, during the reign of the 22nd sultan, Muhammad Alam (1828–52), and the 23rd sultan, Omar Ali Saifuddin II (1852–85), the era of direct European involvement in Brunei began, starting with the arrival of James Brooke as the White Rajah of Sarawak. (See pages 6–7.)

The signing of the 1906 Brunei Treaty paved the way for a strong period of British influence in Brunei that has left a permanent mark on its royalist Islamic make-up. Executive powers were handed over to Britain through a British Residential System, by which a Brunei-dwelling British diplomat advised the Sultan on all state matters excluding Malay customs and religion. Throughout this period, the 25th sovereign, Sultan Hashim, had nominal powers. Honoured for his co-operation with the British authorities, with awards including Knight Commander of the Order of Saint Michael and Saint George, he died from malaria in 1924 at the age of 35.

In 1929, Brunei's fortunes took a positive turn when the only major onshore oilfield was discovered in the southern Seria District. Before the outbreak of World War II, British-administered Brunei was already enjoying many oil-export profits. At the end of Japanese occupation in 1945, retreating British troops sabotaged all oil infrastructure in Brunei and Sarawak to prevent them falling into enemy hands. Brunei Town was also bombed when the allies repossessed it. After the war, the British era in Brunei began to wane. In 1959, a constitutional agreement handed back more domestic rule to the sultanate. At around the same time, the Brunei Shell Petroleum Company started offshore drilling, striking oil for the first time in 1963 off the coast of Belait.

The 28th sultan, Haji Omar Ali Saiffuddien III (the father of the current Sultan), is widely regarded as the architect of modern Brunei. From his ascendancy in 1950 he used Brunei's oil revenues to finance a five-year development plan to bring some modernity and infrastructure to the country.

While it has long described itself as a moderate Muslim country, signs of severity had been creeping in well ahead of the dramatic headlines in April–May 2014 when the Sultan swept in Sharia law as an official state policy – the first Southeast Asian state to do so. His decision provoked an international outcry with celebrity boycotts of Sultan-owned Dorchester Collection hotels in LA, London and Paris by the likes of Virgin's Richard Branson, New Zealand actor Russell Crowe and star presenter Ellen DeGeneres, while Kate – the Duchess of Cambridge – famously broke it. The knee-jerk reaction by social media stars was not the only response to the news. The UN voiced 'deep concern' about the plan. Human Rights Watch called it 'a huge setback' for human rights in Brunei. 'It's an authoritarian move towards brutal, medieval punishments that have no place in the modern world of the 21st century,' said Phil Robertson, deputy director of the organisation's Asia branch.

The Sharia crackdown, which will be implemented over a three-year period from 1 May 2014, sets out punishments including the severing of limbs for theft, and death by stoning for adulterers. 'Today... I place my faith in and am grateful to Allah the almighty to announce that tomorrow... will see the enforcement of Sharia law phase one, to be followed by the other phases,' proclaimed the Sultan when announcing the decision.

Phase 1, reported the *Brunei Times*, means fines and prison sentences; Phase 2, amputations and whipping for crimes such as homosexual acts; and Phase 3, stoning for crimes including adultery and rape. The new Sharia law turns into stricter policy (if not practice), what has long been a principle in Brunei. The death penalty for drug possession, imprisonment for drinking alcohol, fines for not fasting, and corporal punishment with rattan canes, have existed for years, even if largely unenforced. The last execution in Brunei was in 1957. The last death by capital punishment (at the time of writing) in the US was in August 2015, where the death penalty is authorised in 37 states. So is Hollywood really qualified to judge Brunei so excessively from a distance?

Whether the official enshrining of these brutal penalties leads to more actual enforcement of those punishments remains to be seen. The 'Syariah Penal Code Order', written up in 2013, includes 'drinking intoxicating drinks' as one of the severely punishable crimes. It is highly doubtful in my mind, given the example of past decades, that a drinking offender will have a hand cut off, or that a Muslim man who doesn't attend Friday payers will be whipped, but the laws are there as a terrifying deterrent.

'The Penal Code lays out specific offences and punishments for crimes prescribed by the Al-Quran and Sunnah (tradition of the Prophet Muhammad),' said a document issued by Brunei Shell Petroleum/BSP. 'However, there are some offences and punishments that are not prescribed by the Al-Quran and Sunnah

Towards A Democratic Brunei? The British Gurkhas army of Nepalese troops are revered in Brunei today for helping bring to an end Brunei's last brush with democracy – a 1962 coup by the pro-democratic **Brunei People's Party** (PRB). The PRB and other political parties have been outlawed ever since. Brunei was the only Malay state to snub the Federation of Malaysia in 1963 through fear of losing the absolute monarchy's regal hold and oil wealth. It remained a British Protectorate until 1 January 1984, when it regained full independence.

that have been included in the Penal Code, such as making it mandatory for Muslim men to attend Friday prayers and the offence of disrespecting Ramadhan.'

The Sharia code will apply to non-Muslims for all offences bar those of a religious nature. So theft, rape and murder, but not for non-payment of *Zakat* or *Fitrah* – religious taxes. 'The law states that the Order shall apply to both Muslims and non-Muslims, except where expressly provided,' reported the *Brunei Times*.

'Non-Muslims could be implicated', according to the BSP document, in the case of 'adultery if committed with a Muslim'.

The move towards a strict enshrinement of Sharia in the penal code seems to have been welcomed in Brunei. Perhaps the Sultan is speaking for his people, by expressing a return to the deep roots of Islamic faith? Some observers say he is getting more religious and conservative as he gets older, with a need to affirm his faith. Others say that in doing so he is expressing a public wish, to bolster the national identity in a world of increasing Western and far-from-perfect ways. 'The Sultan himself is at a point where there is a need to come to terms with religious identity, both personally and for the country,' commented Joseph Chinyong Liow, a Singapore-based professor who specialises in Muslim politics.

On the other hand, pointed out Dr Chandra Muzaffar, a Muslim scholar and President of the International Movement for a Just World, surely there are better ways of affirming one's spirituality than by metering out punishment, even if under the Sharia code, that remains largely symbolic.

The Sultan has called Islam a 'firewall' against globalisation. Critics believe the firewall is being used as a mask for increasing orthodoxy, and an alarming move away from Brunei's supposedly moderate policies. A similar move is happening in certain Malaysian states such as Kelantan. In a *Deutsche Welle* report, social scientist and Islam expert Joshua Roose estimated overwhelming consent of the Sharia enforcement by Brunei's Muslim majority. 'Brunei has been a benevolent dictatorship for decades. It has been sheltered from the social unrest in the other Southeast Asian countries by its relative wealth,' he said.

Have the huge benefits of their system – the low or no taxes, free education and health care – rolled them into ready compliance, even with such heavy threats hanging over their heads for misdemeanours?

In the same DW report, Emerlynne Gil from the International Commission of Jurists in Bangkok said the sultanate has bought the compliance of its subjects. For her that boils down to growing self-censorship: 'For fear of retribution, people hold back their criticism of the new Sharia law.' Definitely, freedom of expression in Brunei was already deeply curtailed compared with the situation in neighbouring Muslim nation Malaysia. The paradox perhaps is that the people do not seem any unhappier for that.

In late 2007, the new B$62 million Legislative Council building was opened after being fast-tracked towards completion in just two years. Alleged to be part of a slow move towards increasing democracy, the Legislative Council members are, however, clearly in no hurry to acheive that end, despite the Sultan's awareness that his kingdom is something of a relic. At a conference on royalty hosted by His Majesty in 2006, he himself predicted the eventual demise of absolute monarchies. A declaration which makes his Sharia moves even more perplexing.

Once the world's richest man, Hassanal Bolkiah has fallen a few rungs to become simply one of the world's richest monarchs. *Forbes* place the oil-rich Sultan's US$20 billion fortune in second place to that of Thailand's King Bhumibol Adulyadej, who is worth US$30 billion.

Within his palace there are stables, a concert hall, helipads, several swimming pools, 200 bathrooms, a priceless art collection and many luxury 'toys' including Boeing airplanes and helicopters (the Sultan is a licensed pilot and did his military training at Sandhurst in England). A keen equestrian and car collector, he has 200 ponies and an automobile empire of some 2,000 cars, including Rolls-Royces, Ferraris, McLaren F1s, Porsches and Bentleys.

The perennially handsome, polo-playing Sultan is revered by his subjects, who call him Sultan *Kitani* (our sultan), and he is seen to share his riches around and have a genuine interest in the people. The seemingly down-to-earth manner with which he deals with the public contrasts with his own lavish lifestyle and privileged halo of friends. Honorary titles such as Dato and Pehin are handed out among this group on his birthday. While vast amounts of media space are given over to every detail of the royal family's official life, his private one is off-limits. At least it is to local press. Like many royal families, his seems to excel at creating and attracting spectacle: ex-wives who fall victim to phoney London fortune-tellers and have chronic gambling problems; bodyguards accused (yet cleared) of great diamond heists; multi-million-dollar marriage ceremonies of his children.

In 2010, his third marriage to Azrinaz Mazhar Hakim – a former broadcast journalist 32 years his junior – ended with the Sultan filing for divorce. Islam allows men to have up to four wives. The five-year marriage produced two children, bringing his total offspring to 12.

The Queen, or Raja, of Brunei is his first wife (and first cousin), Anak Saleha, whom he married in 1965. The Sultan's birthday is celebrated each July with three weeks of public partying, in which the palace dons a large shawl of fairy lights and big (booze-free) festivities take place.

GETTING THERE AND AWAY

Brunei is divided into four administrative divisions: **Brunei Muara**, which includes the capital Bandar Seri Begawan, **Tutong**, **Belait** and **Temburong**. Brunei is an eighth of the size of Switzerland, with the longest car trip in the country taking little more than three hours.

BY AIR

Brunei International Airport After more than two years and an outlay of B$150 million, the new-look arrival/departures hall at Brunei International Airport (*www.civil-aviation.gov.bn*) opened in October 2013, with 60% of work done on the overall expansion and renovation of the airport. Due for completion by around mid 2015, the modernisation will double annual passenger capacity from 1.5 million to three million. On top of the upgrades of the national carrier's fleet of planes, the move is a major sign of the sultanate flying towards the future after years of seeming reluctance to go global in its tourism infrastructure. The EU supported the overhaul as part of its ASEAN Air Transport Integration Project

BUDGETING

Visiting Brunei after Sabah or Sarawak, you might start out feeling the price tag of B$1 for many market items, a bus fare or bottle of water is on a par with the Malaysian states. The dollar, however, is double the value of the Malaysian ringgit, and you actually pay almost twice the price for many food items, transport, and even accommodation. If you are on a tight budget, eat at food stalls and coffee shops, and walk or take buses instead of taxis. Though hostel accommodation choices are limited, good deals can be struck in budget hotels. In the words of one traveller: 'Brunei may be a wealthy country but it is certainly affordable.' The great exception is petrol, which drops in price by almost half to 53 cents a litre. Bottled water, everyone jokes, is more expensive – a litre costs B$1.

– a move to create an aviation single market in Asia. Located in Berakas, 11km from the capital Bandar Seri Begawan, the hall comprises a new ticketing counter and computerised baggage system with security scanning devices, 40 additional baggage-handling counters and a car park for 600 vehicles. Though still relatively small, it will gradually incorporate more retail stores and cafés to the existing dearth. The urgently required introduction of ATMs will significantly simplify the arrival and visa processes. CCTV monitors and an entry monitoring system bolster security measures. Other gradual airport enhancements include new access roads in landscaped grounds, undercover aerobridges connecting terminals, parking for a total of 1,500 cars, special-needs lanes, and lifts and escalators. As this is Brunei, it is only natural that a spanking new, sparkling white *Surau* (prayer hall) was part of the transformation. Complete with domes and minarets, and big enough for 300 worshippers, it opened in March 2015. The airport is connected to worldwide destinations with Royal Brunei Airlines' direct services, and by Singapore Airlines, Thai Airways, Cebu Pacific Air, Malaysia Airlines and Dragonair through their respective hubs in Singapore, Bangkok, Manila, Kuala Lumpur and Hong Kong.

National carrier Royal Brunei Airlines (RBA) flies from Bandar Seri Begawan to 20 major cities in the Asia Pacific region, the Middle East and Europe. RBA has direct flights several times weekly between Melbourne, Brisbane, Perth, Auckland and Bandar Seri Begawan and flies from London Heathrow to Bandar Seri Begawan via Dubai three times a week. Connections in the Asia Pacific region and China are set to expand as Brunei's importance as both an economic hub and beyond-stopover destination grow.

Within Borneo, RBA have several daily flights between Bandar Seri Begawan and both Kota Kinabalu and Kuching. On the rise as Asia's third-biggest low-cost airline, Cebu Pacific (*www.cebupacificair.com*) flies between BSB and several Philippines' destinations via Manila. In December 2013, the Boeing 787-8 Dreamliner joined RBA's fleet of Airbus A320 and A319 aircraft as part of company plans to renew its long-haul fleet. New cabin-crew uniforms accompanied its launch. In April, the service was extended through to Melbourne. Operating on the London to Australia route via Brunei and Dubai, the Dreamliner lifts business-class capacity to 18 seats, has reclinable to fully flat-beds, and includes in-seat power and personal TV screens on all business (15in screen) and 236 economy seats (9in touch screen with USB charging capacity).

The first planes made of carbon fibre over aluminium, the Dreamliner promises to be better for airlines, passengers and the environment, with 20% more fuel

Brunei's population benefits from heavily subsidy-cocooned living standards. In a blatant test of those nanny oil state dependencies, in 2010, the government curiously decided to declare a 'No Fuel Subsidy Day'. Motorists were forced to pay commercial prices for gasoline. Instead of paying 53 cents a litre for unleaded petrol, they forked out 98 cents a litre – a price hike of 84%, hurting the well-lined Bruneian pocket. As the *Brunei Times* reported in 2012: 'The one-day campaign drew the ire of the public but was effective in reminding them of the impact the subsidy had on their daily lives. However, talks of extending the campaign to a week were not realised as "No Fuel Subsidy Day" was not repeated in 2011.'

Under the heading 'Financial prudence, subsidies hot topic', the story addressed the urgent need for citizens of the sultanate to tighten their belts and most of all, to stop 'wasting and abusing government subsidies'. According to the paper, locals and foreigners had been caught smuggling fuel over the border to sell in neighbouring Malaysia, where petrol prices are almost double.

'...Several customs officers are facing corruption charges for accepting bribes to turn a blind eye to the illegal activities', the paper reported. Water, like petrol, is heavily subsidised in Brunei, even if it is famously said to cost more than the latter. That is true in the case of a litre of bottled water purchased at the shop, however water for domestic use, considered undrinkable by most without being boiled (and few bother to do that), is unbelievably Third-World cheap: ...about 11 cents per cubic metre (1,000 litres) for the first 54 cubic metres and 44 cents for every cubic metre thereafter', wrote the *Brunei Times*. 'This bargain-basement tariff has made the sultanate the highest water consumer in Southeast Asia, with Bruneians guzzling water at a daily rate of 420 litres per head, compared with Singaporeans who use 150 litres daily at a rate of B$1.17 per cubic metre. Talk about fuel for thought.

efficiency, 20% fewer carbon dioxide emissions and fresher, more humid air drawn straight from outside. The cabins are more spacious with larger windows and lower air pressure.

Airline offices All are in Bandar Seri Begawan city centre. Most are open between 08.00–noon and 13.00–17.00, Monday to Friday.

✈ **Cebu Pacific Air** Either at Anthony Tours & Travel Agency, No 1, Lot 20171 Jln Laksamana Abdul Razak, Km2 Jln Tutong; ☎ 222 2666; or Pan Bright Travel Services, Suite 101-102, Bangunan Hj Ahmad Laksamana, 38-39 Jln Sultan; www. cebupacificair.com

✈ **Malaysia Airlines** Mezzanine Floor, Bangunan Hj Ahmad Bldg, Lot 38–39 Jln Sultan; ☎ 222 3074/1 (ticketing); 222 4097 (admin); www.malaysiaairlines.com

✈ **Royal Brunei Airlines** RBA Plaza, Jln Sultan; ☎ 221 2222/224 0500; www.flyroyalbrunei.com

✈ **Singapore Airlines** 5th Floor, Bangunan Hj Ahmad Bldg, Lot 38–39 Jln Sultan; ☎ 224 4901/2; www.singaporeair.com

Getting to and from the airport The **Central Line** buses pass the airport every 15–20 minutes and make several stops in the city district before arriving at the city bus terminal. The Northern Line 1 and 2 connect the airport and city via Berakas army camp. Some hotels have airport transfers. Average taxi fares to the city are B$15. The website of Brunei Tourism (*www.tourismbrunei.com/info/ground.html*) has a useful list of metered fares to dozens of destinations – hotels, city landmarks and attractions – with the airport taxi service.

BY CAR Apart from its northwestern seaboard, Brunei is hemmed in on all sides by the Malaysian state of Sarawak. The 'Pan-Borneo' Highway – a network of federal roads – connects Brunei with Sarawak and Sabah. It takes about 12 hours to drive between Brunei's capital and Kuching, and half that to Kota Kinabalu. An immigration checkpoint is located at Sungai Tujoh in northern Brunei. From Limbang in Sarawak to Bandar Seri Begawan, the trip time is 45 minutes and the checkpoint is in Kuala Lurah.

BY BOAT
To and from Sarawak A daily ferry service from Brunei to 'Utama Lawas in Sarawak departs at 09.30 from the Serasa Muara terminal, about 20km from the capital. It is prone to regular interruption so please check with Brunei Tourism (*www.tourismbrunei.com*) or the Marine Department (*www.marine.gov.bn/boat_schedule_arrival.htm*) for updates.

A daily speedboat for Sundar in Lawas leaves the riverside ferry terminal on Jalan Residency at 10.30.

To and from Sabah The new car ferry service between Brunei's Serasa ferry terminal and Menumbok in Sabah revolutionised international travel between Brunei and Sabah when it was introduced in 2009. The MV *Shuttle Hope* (*www.pkljaya.com*) has the capacity to carry 45 cars and 200 passengers. Travelling once a day from Brunei to Menumbok and vice-versa, the journey takes 2½ hours and costs B$70 per vehicle including driver, plus B$25 for each additional adult or B$12.50 for children. Foot passengers pay B$25 for a ticket, meaning budget travellers can make the journey from BSB to KK, buses included, for under B$35. The ferry cuts down the total bus travel time from 16 hours to five. Sailings are at 09.30 from the Serasa terminal, and 15.00 from Menumbok, though drivers must arrive an hour in advance.

To and from Pulau Labuan In 2010, the MV *Shuttle Hope* ferry company began a daily car ferry service between BSB and Labuan, leaving Serasa at 09.00 and Labuan at 16.00.

The two-hour trip costs B$55 for a small car including driver, B$75 for larger cars, vans and SUVs, B$15 for an adult, B$8 for three–12-year-old children, with no charge for under threes. Standard passenger ferry services continue several times a day with departures from Brunei at 07.30, 08.30, 09.00, 13.00 (Friday–Sunday), 13.30 and 15.30, and from Labuan to Brunei at 08.00, 11.00, 12.15, 14.00, 16.00 and 16.30. Daily ferries to Lawas leave Serasa at 11.30. To reach the terminal by bus, take the blue Eastern Line (No 33). Ferry schedules are subject to change and it is best to check the boat schedule online (*www.marine.gov.bn*) or by calling the **Shipping Office of the Marine Department** (✆ *277 3071 for services to Labuan & Lawas;* ✆ *224 4251 for services to Temburong & Limbang*). Brunei Tourism (*www.tourismbrunei.com*) also has updated ferry schedules on their website under 'Visitor Info', 'Getting Around'. Travel by ferry in Brunei is incredibly safe due to strict regulation. With typical Bruneian rigorousness you can count on, the authorities banned three Malaysian ferries in 2011 because of concerns over their maritime certification.

4

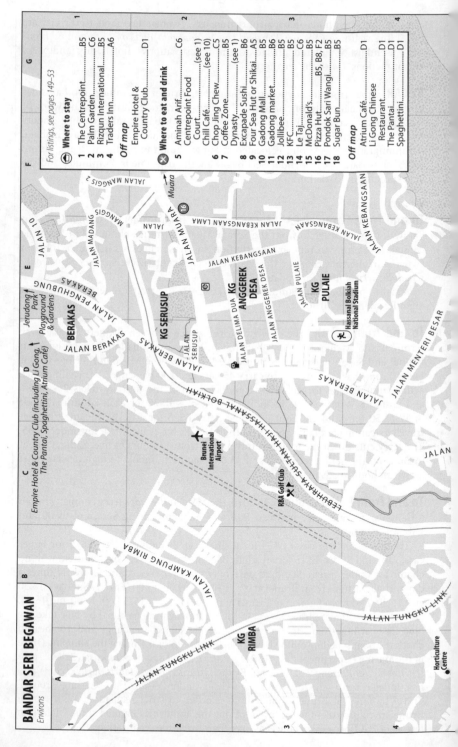

BANDAR SERI BEGAWAN
Environs

Empire Hotel & Country Club (including Li Gong,
The Pantai, Spaghettini, Atrium Café)

Jerudong ↑
Park
Playground
& Gardens

Muara ↑

JALAN MANGGIS 2

JALAN MANGGIS

JALAN MADANG

JALAN 10

JALAN PENGHUBUNG BERAKAS

BERAKAS

JALAN BERAKAS

JALAN BERAKAS

KG SERUSUP

JALAN SERUSUP

JALAN MUARA

JALAN MANGGIS

JALAN KEBANGSAAN LAMA

JALAN KEBANGSAAN

JALAN DELIMA DUA

KG ANGGEREK DESA

JALAN ANGGEREK DESA

JALAN PULAIE

KG PULAIE

JALAN KEBANGSAAN

JALAN KEBANGSAAN

Brunei
International
Airport

RBA Golf Club

LEBUHRAYA SULTAN HAJI HASSANAL BOLKIAH

JALAN BERAKAS

JALAN MENTERI BESAR

Hassanal Bolkiah
National Stadium

JALAN

JALAN KAMPUNG RIMBA

JALAN TUNGKU LINK

KG RIMBA

JALAN TUNGKU LINK

Horticulture
Centre

142

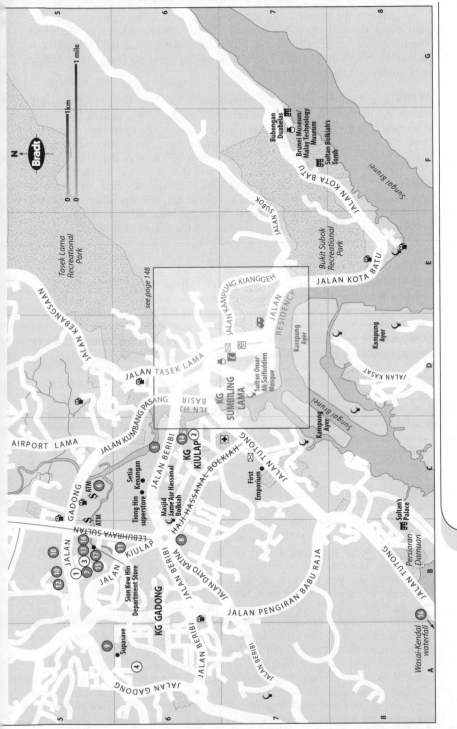

4

143

According to the *Brunei Times*, the recent new services are all part of moves to more integrated sea linkages between the east ASEAN (Association of South East Asian Nations) countries of Brunei, Indonesia, Malaysia, and the Philippines. A national development plan it reported will see improved port facilities including public toilets, car parks and weighbridges.

BY BUS Journeying by bus between Sarawak and Brunei is far from straightforward: it takes five hours, three buses and a ferry to cover the 120km to Miri. The choice of services over the past few years has been erratic with new operators entering the scene and leaving just as hastily. Borneo Explore Green (*www.borneoexploregreen. com*) now offers the only service twice daily from BSB to Miri, departing at 07.00 and 13.00, and from Miri to Brunei at 08.45 and 15.45. One-way tickets cost B$18. The same company connects Brunei and Kota Kinabalu with daily departures in both directions at 08.00 (*B$45*), and runs between BSB and several other locations including Limbang and Lawas in Sarawak (*08.00 departures; B$10/B$25 respectively*), Beaufort in Sabah (*08.00; B$40*), and Pontianak, Kalimantan (*15.30; B$80*).

LOCAL TOUR OPERATORS

Continental Yachting Tours 223 3200; e continentaltour@brunet.bn; www.onebrunei.com
Freme Travel Services 2234280/1; e fremeinb@brunet.bn; www.freme.com or www. brunei-tours.freme.com. Constantly evolving its offerings, & keeping in tune with global demands through its major outbound business, the 1971-established company has its head office in Kuala Belait, a major set-up in the capital & firm foothold nationwide. Highly recommended, the group has its own fleet of premium coaches, & is friendly & professional in dealings with clients.
Intrepid Tours Unit 105, 1st Floor, PGGMB

Bldg, Jln Sungai Kianggeh, BSB (opposite the tamu market & above express coach stop for Kota Kinabalu & Miri); 222 1685/6; e tours@ bruneibay.net; www.bruneibay.net
Mega Borneo Marketing Services 222 4026; e megaborneo@brunet.bn
Sunshine Borneo Tours & Travel No 2 Simpang 146, Jln Kiarong, Kampung Kiulap, BSB; 244 6509; 871 5863 (after hours); e sales@ exploreborneo.com; www.exploreborneo.com. Efficient choice for day trips & excursions; a 2nd branch is found in the lobby arcade of the Empire Hotel & Country Club in Jerudong 261 0578).

BANDAR SERI BEGAWAN

Few people have heard of Brunei's capital city before visiting, and it's hardly the catchiest of names. Fortunately, everyone calls it BSB. Known as Brunei Town – Pekan Brunei – up until 1970, the idyllic-sounding replacement of Bandar Seri Begawan (roughly translated as 'city of the glorious retiree') honours the 28th sultan, who took this title when he abdicated in 1967. It is a fascinating city – on the one hand, you feel you are in a place entrenched in trading history and Islamic exoticism, while on the other, is the emerging face of a 'modernised capital'. The much-publicised 'lavish adornments, gold towers, sparkling fountains and colourful mosaic tiles' are scattered about the city, from the riverbank area to the new modern districts. There is no historic mass of buildings as the old town and its colonial edifices were bombed by the Allies during World War II.

The city spreads out over 16km from the downtown area, which is hemmed in by riverside recreational areas, state-owned land, museums and ministries.

When the lights go out, so does most of the action. At 18.00 all public transport stops, and locals head for their favourite evening spot as the sun sets over the river. With the Muslim chants and the drone of cicadas resonating through the city, the country's full name becomes very fitting – Brunei Darussalam, 'Brunei, abode of peace'.

Once you get past the logistical challenges and locate the most animated *tamu* (markets), the museums and mosques, the gorgeous green spaces and nearby beaches, you can join the locals and enjoy a high quality of life for a few days as well as some rich cultural experiences.

ORIENTATION Bandar Seri Begawan has three districts: **Bandar**, the city centre or central business district (CBD) hedged around the riverfront; and **Gadong** and **Kiulap**, two neighbouring commercial districts on the western side of the river. Unless you intend to stay longer than the standard couple of stopover days, you will probably base yourself either in the CBD or in Gadong. Vibey Gadong is home to markets, malls, shop-lots, restaurants, cafés and a handful of hotels. Kiulap is an up-and-coming urban precinct, developing around an old village. The upmarket beachside suburb of Jerudong, 13km northwest of the city, is part of the Brunei Muara District (the Jerudong Playground theme park is located here). The northern part of Muara, known as Berakas, is the main administrative and government zone, which also has many sports facilities (stadiums, swimming pools, sports complexes, etc), and a couple of hotels. Muara's beaches lie north of the capital on Brunei Bay.

GETTING AROUND

By car Brunei's capital is not an easy place to get around by public transport. The main problem is not infrastructure, but limited availability. The last buses run at 18.00, so if you plan to be out after dark you have to rely on your feet, a taxi or a car. The key city sites are spread out over several kilometres, so the best option if you want to see as much as possible in a couple of days is to have your own car, or combine a day of car hire for the city sights with day or overnight tours to other places of interest. A litre of petrol costs around 53 cents – a tank is filled for around B\$20. Diesel is 31 cents a litre.

Car hire A list of car-hire agencies can be found on Brunei Tourism's website (*www.tourismbrunei.com/visitor-info/getting-around/ground*).

🚗 **Avis Rent A Car** 📞242 6345; e ncsbsb@ brunet.bn or davidgoh@brunet.bn; www.avis. com.bn. With service counters at the airport & the Sheraton Utama Hotel 📞222 7100), fleet manager David Goh assures an efficient service with 60 cars in various models & options including self-drive, chauffeur-driven, & airport to hotel transfers. Rates range from B\$75/day to B\$450/week for a Hyundai Accent, to B\$155/930 day/week for a Mitsubishi Magna, & B\$169/1,014 day/week for a 9-seater Ford Transit minivan.
🚗 **Azizah Car Rental** 📞222 9388
🚗 **Budget-U-Drive** 5th Floor, D'Anggerek Hotel, near the Convention Centre; 📞234 5573
🚗 **Hertz Rent-A-Car** 📞245 2244

By taxi Metered taxis can be hailed from most hotels, shopping centres, and the airport. In the capital, taxis are located at the Jalan Cator car park. Considering the low cost of petrol, taxis are expensive: about B\$1 per kilometre (B\$3 for the first kilometre, 20 cents per subsequent kilometre).

By bus The bus terminal for city and longer-distance routes is located on Jalan Cator [148 C3]. Six bus routes (with names such as **Northern Line**, **Western Line**, etc) serve Bandar Seri Begawan and the wider Muara District. They depart every 15–20 minutes from 06.00 to 18.00; average fares are B\$1. The two routes that stop

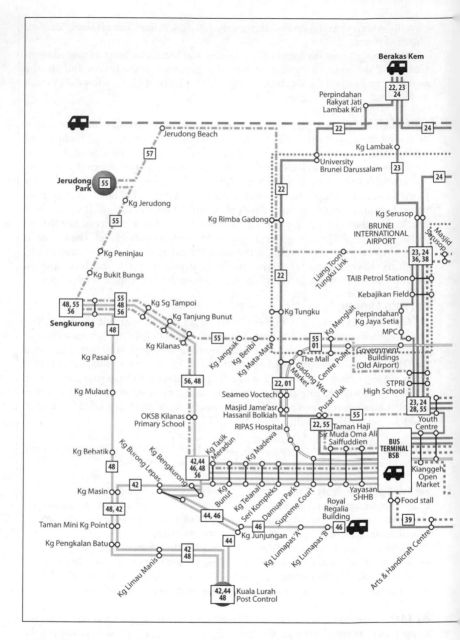

at the CBD, museums and other sites of interest are the **Central Line** and the **Circle Line**. The widely available Brunei Tourism map includes the essential public bus transport network map.

By boat

Water taxis These can be hailed from numerous docking ports and jetties along the banks of the river. They are the most common form of transport for

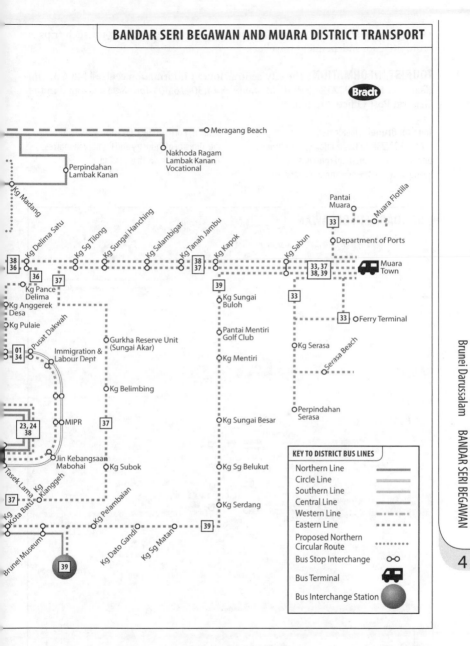

BANDAR SERI BEGAWAN AND MUARA DISTRICT TRANSPORT

Bradt

Meragang Beach

Nakhoda Ragam
Lambak Kanan
Vocational

Perpindahan
Lambak Kanan

Kg Madang

Pantai
Muara

Muara Flotilla

33

Department of Ports

Kg Delima Satu
Kg Sg Tilong
Kg Sungai Hanching
Kg Salambigar
Kg Tanah Jambu
Kg Kapok
Kg Sabun

38
36

36

37

Kg Pance
Delima

Kg Anggerek
Desa

Kg Pulaie

Pusat Dakwah

38
37

39

33, 37
38, 39

Muara
Town

Kg Sungai
Buloh

33

33 Ferry Terminal

Pantai Mentiri
Golf Club

01
34

Immigration &
Labour Dept

Gurkha Reserve Unit
(Sungai Akar)

Kg Mentiri

Kg Serasa

Serasa Beach

Kg Belimbing

23, 24
38

MIPR

37

Kg Sungai Besar

Jin Kebangsaan
Mabohai

Kg Subok

Kg Sg Belukut

Perpindahan
Serasa

Tasek Lama & Kg

37

Kota Batu

Kg Kianggeh

Brunei Museum

39

Kg Pelambaian

Kg Dato Gandi

Kg Sg Matan

Kg Serdang

39

KEY TO DISTRICT BUS LINES

Northern Line	
Circle Line	
Southern Line	
Central Line	
Western Line	
Eastern Line	
Proposed Northern Circular Route	
Bus Stop Interchange	∞
Bus Terminal	
Bus Interchange Station	

Brunei Darussalam   BANDAR SERI BEGAWAN

4

the Kampung Ayer (water village) area and prices are generally negotiable. The standard one-way fare for the river crossing to Kampung Ayer for residents is B$1. River tours (*30 minutes or 1 hour*), and trips to the Malaysian towns of Limbang and Lawas, cost anything from B$10 to B$30.

Longboats These are used in rural areas. When the waters are low, you might be required to get out and push! Prices for such trips are included in tour agent packages to destinations such as Temburong. The price of paying for such trips is prohibitive for independent travellers.

TOURIST INFORMATION The city centre's **tourist information centre** [148 C3] (*Jln Elizabeth Dua;* ☎2223734; ⊕ *08.00–noon & 14.30–16.30 Mon–Sat*) is located in the General Post Office Building.

Tourism Brunei (Jln Menteri Besar; ☎238 2822/238 2832; e info@tourismbrunei. com; www.tourismbrunei.com) has its headquarters in the government district of Berakas, north of the city centre, in the offices of the Ministry of Industry and Primary Resources. Their website is worth exploring.

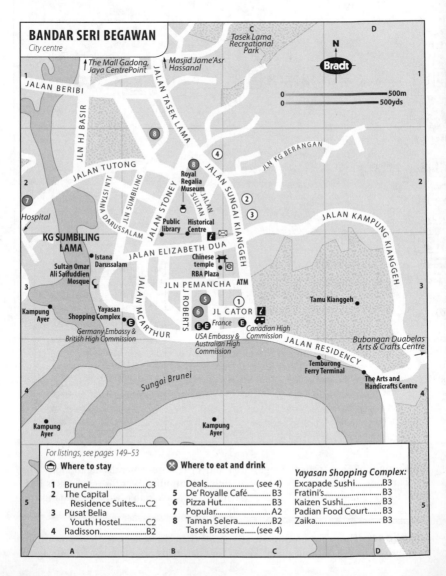

BANDAR SERI BEGAWAN
City centre

For listings, see pages 149–53

🛏 **Where to stay**

1 Brunei...........................C3
2 The Capital
   Residence Suites.....C2
3 Pusat Belia
   Youth Hostel.............C2
4 Radisson......................B2

🍽 **Where to eat and drink**

Deals......................(see 4)
5 De' Royalle Café............B3
6 Pizza Hut.......................B3
7 Popular..........................A2
8 Taman Selera................B2
Tasek Brasserie......(see 4)

Yayasan Shopping Complex:
Excapade Sushi..............B3
Fratini's..........................B3
Kaizen Sushi...................B3
Padian Food Court.......B3
Zaika...............................B3

148

Maps, pages 142–3 and 148, unless otherwise stated.

There are fewer accommodation choices in Brunei than you might expect for a country of its stature. Options include one- to five-star hotels, serviced apartments, guesthouses and hostels. Nearly 90% of the available accommodation is in the capital. Given the dispersed nature of the city, and generally poor public transport, be sure to pick your accommodation according to your priorities: CBD, retail and riverfront; nightlife and markets in Gadong; or groomed greenery, golfing and beaches in Jerudong. All of the hostels are in Bandar. Keep in mind it is sometimes possible to get better value for money by staying in a suburban hotel. The **Brunei Association of Hotels** website (*www.hotelsofbrunei.com*) provides links to its members, bringing together two-thirds of the country's hotels.

Luxury

Empire Hotel & Country Club [map, page 158] (423 rooms) Muara Tutong Highway, Jerudong (13km north of town); 241 8888; e sales@theempirehotel.com; www. theempirehotel.com. Fit for a sultan (or sultaness), the 6-winged hotel has swirled marble floors, stairway railings plated in 21-carat gold & wool carpets interwoven with gold thread. The stunning open-tiered lobby is actually on the 5th floor overlooking the sea; most rooms have ocean-facing balconies & the smallest suites are 30m². The swimming pools are Olympic-sized, fluid-formed & sand-based. Within the majestic grounds of the Country Club there are amazing sport & spa facilities. The dining alternatives (see page 151) rival those of a luxury shopping galleria & entertainment includes 3 cinemas. $$$$$

Rizqun International Hotel (168 rooms, inc non-smoking floor) Abdul Razak Complex Gadong; 242 3000; e info@rizquninternational. com; www.rizquninternational.com. An uplifting Muslim–Malay feel to this hotel, with its touch of palatial, huge marble & granite lobby, classical comfort & gracious staff. Deluxe rooms come with luxurious marble bathrooms, high-tech touches, ample lounge furnishings & work spaces. Excellent location close to city centre but in the heart of Gadong. Good Chinese/Malay/Indian/Western b/fast. Premier Club floor benefits include a club lounge (⊕ 06.30–23.00), complimentary b/fast & free 24hr internet access in rooms. Terrace swimming pool & fitness centre. $$$$$

Upmarket

The Centrepoint (216 rooms) Abdul Razak Complex, Km4 Jln Gadong; 243 0430; e info@thecentrepointhotel.com; www. thecentrepointhotel.com.com. Dated but large,

comfortable rooms with good facilities (AC, writing desk, minibar, satellite TV, kettle, swimming pool, gym). Very service-oriented & well staffed. Deluxe rooms, junior/executive/business suites & non-smoking floor. Dining choices in the hotel are plentiful & frequented by locals, especially Dynasty Restaurant (see page 151). Great shopping & nightlife location when compared with the CBD. Online prices often less than half the published rates (deluxe room for, eg: B$125 rather than B$280). $$$$

Radisson Hotel (142 rooms) Jln Tasek; 224 4272; e reservations.brunei@radisson. com; www.radisson.com. In 2012, the Radisson emerged from a 2-year refurbishment of the 29-year-old Sheraton Utama. The most centrally located upmarket hotel, 10–15mins' walk from the CBD, has a pleasant lobby, good dining choices, 2 meeting rooms & free high-speed Wi-Fi throughout. The spacious well-furnished, superior & executive deluxe rooms have high-tech features & ultra-comfy beds; ask for a pool-facing room if you don't want traffic noise. The staff are a particular asset – friendly, obliging & gentle-mannered. The hotel runs a complimentary shuttle service to Gadong's malls. The cool refreshments provided in the lobby & macaque-frequented pool offer welcome relief from humid sightseeing. $$$$

Mid range

Brunei Hotel (63 rooms) 95 Jln Pemancha; 224 4828; e reservations@thebruneihotel.com; www.bruneihotel.com. Brunei's top high-end budget to low mid-range hotel is bright, modern & cheerful, with a decidedly ready-for-business yet easygoing feel. It also has the best downtown location of all the hotels, close to shops, parks, bus terminal, markets and wharf, a 10min walk to the riverfront Jln Residency. Spacious rooms with fresh

& functional furnishings. AC, phone, cable TV, DVD, coffee/tea making, safe, complimentary minibar & Wi-Fi. Decent b/fast spread in the large lobby café. Book on the hotel's site for best deals. **$$$**

🏠 **The Capital Residence Suites** (18 rooms) Simpang 2, Lot 20127, Kg Berangan; 📞 222 0067; e reservations@capitalresidencesuites.com; www. capitalresidencesuites.com. Sleek professional & fresh approach from this new hotel, which I am yet to test drive. Apparently there's a friendly staff, good b/fast (local & Western mix), free airport shuttle service & excellent location, flanking the city centre, parks, jetty & tamu market. Smartly furnished rooms with remote AC, TV & complimentary Wi-Fi. Standard rooms actually fall into the budget category, while junior & executive suites sport lower-level upmarket price tags. Suites have microwave, fridge, toaster-equipped kitchens, living & dining rooms & up to 2 bedrooms & bathrooms. **$$$–$$**

🏠 **Palm Garden Hotel** (50 rooms) Lot 45328, Simpang 88, Kampong Kiulap; 📞 223 3448; e palmgarden@brunet.bn; www.palmgarden-hotel.com. In the Kiulap District, 10mins from the airport (B$25 hotel shuttle service), & about the same to the city (buses every 10mins, B$1 or B$10 taxi), the hotel is described as 'a good transit hotel' for its mix of airport-handy location, comfort & price. The zone has some shops & restaurants. Novel in its breezy style – the prefabricated curved-roofed building is emblazoned with palm trees; smart modern furnishings, incorporating

traditional materials, marble & wood. Gym, spa, beauty salon & 'Energy Kitchen' café for health-conscious West–East b/fast (noodles, veg juices, etc), lunches & dinner. **$$$–$$**

Budget

🏠 **Traders Inn** (84 rooms) Block D, Lot 11620, Jln Gadong (3km from CBD); 📞 244 2828; e traders@brunet.bn; www.tradersinn-bn.com. Budget business hotel on industrial edges of Gadong, with pleasant atmosphere, & market & coffee shops close by. The rooms are spacious & simple, but in need of refreshment. Business centre, free (but often unreliable) Wi-Fi, in-house coffee lounge (🕐 06.30–23.00), plus foot reflexology centre. **$$**

Shoestring

🏠 **Pusat Belia Youth Hostel** Jln Sungai Kianggeh; 📞 222 3936; e jbsbelia@brunet.bn. The only place to stay on a very strict budget in Brunei – don't expect huge service for your bucks. Cleanliness is not an issue (this is squeaky-clean Brunei!). However, lack of staff presence is a frequent complaint, perhaps linking in with another new phenomenon – that of alleged theft. Some users have complained of having laptops stolen from rooms, which can be broken into all too easily. Do the offenders know they have a death penalty hanging over their head? AC, 4-bed dorms with comfortable beds, good showers & access to a pool. **$**

✕ WHERE TO EAT AND DRINK *Maps, pages 142–3 and 148, unless otherwise stated.*

Brunei is no foodie capital when it comes to restaurants, but street food is amazing and among the most delicious and immaculately presented in Borneo. Indoors, there are many good coffee shops and casual restaurants; more sophisticated dining and international restaurants are chiefly found in four- and five-star hotels, though Brunei's modern dining scene is still in an embryonic stage. Gadong is the best place for multi-ethnic, well-priced food at small, family-run businesses, not forgetting the markets and mall food halls. New-wave cafés in the Kiulap District are home to East-meets-West flavours, trendy décor and a young, affluent crowd. Restaurants are not open as late as they are in Malaysian Borneo, with last orders from 21.00 to 22.00. (A number of 24-hour cafés and food stalls cater for night owls.) Given the dearth of but growing demand for chic eateries, it pays to make a reservation at hotel restaurants on weekends.

Malay/Bruneian

✕ **Aminah Arif** Unit 2–3, Block B, Ground Floor, Bangunan Haji Abdul Rahman, Simpang 88, Kg Kiulap; 📞 223 6198; e aminaharif.com.bn;

🕐 09.00–23.00 daily. In the Kiulap District, this is an institution among locals for the *ambuyat* (see box, page 152) & other classic Bruneian flavours. **$$$**

Chinese

✕ **Li Gong Chinese Restaurant** [map, page 158] Empire Hotel & Country Club, Tutong Muara Highway, Jerudong; ☎241 8888; ⊕ 11.00–14.00 & 18.00– 22.00 daily. Favourite local haunt for Sun brunches of dim sum & Cantonese roast duck. The interior is chic, with a semblance of a modern Chinese temple in its glass-walled form. $$$$–$$$

✕ **Dynasty Restaurant** Ground Floor, Centrepoint Hotel, Abdul Razak Complex, Gadong; ☎243 0430; ⊕ 08.30–14.00 & 18.00–22.00 daily. The most popular & established Chinese eatery in Brunei, famed for introducing halal dim sum & more recently for its rock melon *sago* dessert. Alongside the Centrepoint shopping mall in Gadong. $$$–$$

✕ **Four Sea Hut or Shikai** Unit 1, Block E, Sempurna Complex, Jln Batu Bersurat, Gadong; ☎245 6222; ⊕ lunch/dinner. High on rustic ambience, décor & food quality, this little place among suburban shop-lots serves Hong Kong-style roast duck & chicken dishes, plus a mix of Malay & Chinese noodle & soup staples. $$$–$$

Seafood

✕ **The Pantai** Empire Hotel & Country Club, Muara Tutong Highway, Jerudong; ☎241 8888; ⊕ evenings only. Reopened in 2013 after a major revamp is this sea-fronting restaurant with open kitchen at The Empire Hotel, 20mins from the city. The restaurant theme is 'south Asian seafood barbecue & grill'; guests can choose their seafood & have it sizzled before their eyes. Also prime cuts of meat & a salad bar. A new addition is the 22-seat 'restaurant within a restaurant' – **Zen** – an interactive dining experience of Japanese *teppanyaki* food. $$$$–$$

Indian

✕ **Le Taj** 2nd Floor, Seri Kiulap Complex, Jalan Kiulap; ⊕18.00–22.00 daily. Far from local shophouse Indian food – Roti Canai, Nasi Bryani, etc – a more upmarket, but still affordable choice, for excellent north Indian food. Some find food delivery is a bit slow – all the better if the time is being put into careful preparation. $$$$–$$

✕ **Zaika** G24 Block C, Yayasan Complex; ☎2231155; ⊕ 11.00–14.00 & 18.00–22.00 daily. For Indian delicacies in the city centre, excellent, stylishly antiquated décor. $$$–$$

✕ **Popular Restaurant** Ground Floor, Seri Complex, Mile 1, Jln Tutong; ☎222 1375; ⊕ 08.00–22.00 daily. Quality Indian savouries & sweets, samosas, *vadai* & many vegetarian dishes. Finish with the Indian twist on Malaysia's favourite tea, *the-tarek halia* (ginger-pulled tea). Cash only. $$

Indonesian

✕ **Pondok Sari Wangi Restaurant** Unit 12 & 13, 1st Floor, Block A, Abd Razak Complex, Jln Gadong; ☎244 5043; ⊕ 10.00–22.00 daily. Restaurant credited with starting an Ayam Penyet (literally 'smashed fried chicken') craze in Brunei. Indonesian classics – *ayam* (chicken) & beef rendang, *iga penyet* (beef ribs), *tauhu telur* (fried tofu with egg), *gado gado*, & *cendol* drink-desserts on its vast menu. $$$–$$

Japanese

✕ **Excapade Sushi** Ground Floor, Block A, Q-lap Complex, Kiulap; ☎223 4012; ⊕ 11.00–22.00 daily. Sushi-train restaurant – fast but high-quality Japanese food. $$

✕ **Kaizen Sushi** Kompleks Yayasan, Sultan Haji Hassanal Bolkiah, Jln McArthur; ☎222 6336; ⊕ 11.00–14.30 & 18.30–22.30 daily. New sushi joint conveniently located in downtown shopping centre. Well-noted for food & atmosphere; not such a good record on service & smiles. $$

Italian

✕ **Fratini's Restaurant** Yayasan Complex, BSB; ☎223 2555; ⊕ 10.30–22.30 daily. Brunei does very average Italian food, but the upper balcony of this franchise Italian restaurant overlooks the Sungai Brunei, with a great river-soaked ambience. Another branch at Centrepoint, Gadong; ☎245 1200. $$$

✕ **Spaghettini** Empire Hotel & Country Club, 6th Floor, Lobby Bldg, Jerudong; ☎241 8888; ⊕18.00–22.00 daily. A tiny place serving Italian food. $$$

Western

✕ **Deals** Radisson Hotel (see page 149); ⊕ noon–14.00 & 19.30–21.30 daily, 19.30–21.30 public holidays. Fine-dining restaurant with soft lights, nice décor; business lunch or formal dinner. $$$$

✕ **Atrium Café** Empire Hotel & Country Club, Tutong Muara Highway, Jerudong; ☎241 8858;

BRUNEIAN FEAST

Some Malay specialities are still sold from people's homes – you knock on the door to place your order, which is how *nasi katok*, 'knock rice', gets its name. Served in a cone of waxed brown paper and topped with a bit of fried chicken, beef or egg, and spicy sauce, it is the snack speciality à la Brunei. The famous *ambuyat* is a bowl of sago paste served with a variety of foods including beef jerky strips, fried fish, vegetable pickles, bamboo shoots, mango and chilli preserves. You can also eat these side dishes with rice if you prefer. For dessert, *kueh wajid* (pounded Temburong hill rice) is slow-cooked in palm sugar and coconut cream then wrapped in banana leaves and steamed until the sugar caramelises. Bruneians love their biscuits and cakes, collectively known as *kueh* or *kuih*. Green pandan-flavoured crêpes (*kueh gulung*) are filled with coconut and palm sugar. 'Each district of Brunei has its specialities, closely linked with agriculture. Tutong's savoury signature, *pulut panggang*, is grilled rolls of glutinous rice filled with shrimp or beef. *Chendol Temburong* is a dessert-drink made from droplets of green bean flour mixed with palm sugar, with or without coconut milk.

⊕ 06.30–22.30 daily. An impressive buffet spread & sublime location with floor-to-ceiling glass windows looking over the sea from up high. Alongside the rotating buffet of international, Malay & Indian specialities, there is a menu with local & Western dishes. $$$$–$$$

✕ **Tasek Brasserie** Radisson Hotel (see page 149); ☎ 224 4272; ⊕ 18.30–22.00 daily. Warm, woody setting & poolside eating. Excellent range of seafood & meats. BBQ evenings & good salad buffet. $$$

Market and street food Two of the most animated food markets are the Kianggeh market (*pasar Kianggeh*) and the Gadong night market (*pasar Gadong*). Held near the riverside along Jalan Residency, the **Kianggeh market** [148 D2] is a vestige of rural life in the city centre. Many of the gerai makan (food stalls) here are family-run, opening from around 15.30 and running through until late; a couple remain open all night. They serve satays and soups, noodle and rice dishes, fresh coconut juice and ketupat – origami-like pouches of rice wrapped in coconut palm or pandan leaves, served with peanut satay sauce.

The renowned **Gadong market** [143 B5] is a food-only, night-time affair – an outdoor eating theatre with the best range of food stalls in the city. The several-dozen stalls fire up from 17.00 until midnight. Held in a vast car park near the 'wet market' in the Gadong District, it is one of the best *pasar malam* (night markets) in the whole of Sarawak, Sabah and Brunei. Meticulously packaged portions of rice wrapped in banana leaves are a market mainstay; the trays of pyramid and finger-shaped *nasi lemak* contain rice filled with chicken, beef or anchovies and topped with spicy sambal sauce. *Nasi katok* is another popular rice dish (see box, above).

For those staying in the city centre, the **Taman Selera** [148 B2] (⊕ *17.00–as late as 02.00*) is an excellent night-time, food stall area. Set in a large car park zone between Jalan Tasek Lama and Jalan Kumbang Pasang, opposite the Radisson Hotel, the name literally means 'appetite park'. While it lacks the overall ambience of Gadong, some of the food is still very good, and the market is a godsend in this rather uneventful and dining-deprived zone. The **Bob U Me stall** [148 B2] is recommended for fresh seafood, cooked before your eyes, whichever way you like it.

As far as shopping-centre food courts go, the **Padian Food Court** [148 B3] in the city centre area – in the riverfront Yayasan complex – serves chicken, rice, laksa, Indian and Western food. In Gadong, there are two food courts – one on the ground-floor **Centrepoint Food Court** [143 B5], the other on the top floor of the more upmarket shopping centre, **The Mall** [143 B5]. Fast food is on the rise and the big international and domestic names – KFC, Pizza Hut, McDonald's, Sugar Bun and Jollibee – all have outlets in the city and at Jerudong Park. But why eat foreign fast food, when you can have nasi katok around the clock from the many coffee shops and stalls?

Cafés The most authentic Bruneian café award without a doubt goes to **Chop** (as opposed to 'shop') **Jing Chew** [143 B5] (*Simpang 5, No 10, Jln Gadong*) – located in a cluster of shop-lots near the river in Gadong. It's an experience filing among the tables of mostly men, and up to the counter of the city's oldest coffee shop, open since the 1940s, to buy freshly baked golden egg buns. The yeasty buns, eaten plain or toasted, are filled with coconut jam or *kaya*. Other favourites are *roti kacang kahwin* – buns with a centre of sweet ground peanuts, served with butter and *kaya* – and *roti cheese*, Jing Chew's answer to a cheeseburger, but without meat and with the mandatory *kaya*. Swallow them down with a sweet *teh tarik* – pulled tea now also referred to as 'tea latte'. Breakfast and around 15.00 are the best times to visit for fresh, out-of-the-oven buns. The place is a gem among an increasing number of chain outlets. There are **Coffee Bean & Tea Leaf** stores on the ground floor of the Bangunan Maya Puri Building on Jalan Sultan (*corner of Jln Permancha*), downtown Bandar Seri Begawan, and at Centrepoint, Gadong. A 24-hour meeting place, **De' Royalle Café** (ground floor of the Bangunan Haji Ahmad Bldg, 38 Jln Sultan), also has maverick charm. A clutter of books and cushions, and leopardskin pavement chairs, it is run by a veteran journalist and serves Illy espresso. In Gadong, **Chill Café** is at The Mall, while the **Coffee Zone**, near Centrepoint, serves espresso drinks and decent light food.

ENTERTAINMENT AND NIGHTLIFE In a place where there are no bars, where alcohol is banned and public transport ends at 18.00, you could be forgiven for assuming the nightlife is non-existent. Though not exactly the life and soul of the party, Brunei's capital has plenty to offer, especially in the way of family fun and theme-park entertainment.

The **Jerudong Park Playground and Gardens** [142 E1] (*Muara-Tutong Highway, 20mins from the city;* (☉ *17.00–midnight Wed–Fri, 17.00–02.00 Sat, 16.00–midnight Sun & public hols; B$1, day ticket B$15 adults, B$5 children; bus No 55*) is the sultanate's take on Disney, with 57 acres of gilt-lined roller coasters and marbled fun for everyone – 'including members of the Royal Family!', states the brochure. Despite the marble excess, the playground is reportedly a bit lacklustre (like many other faded urban theme parks of the world), but the night-time atmosphere is still lots of fun.

FESTIVALS Food plays the leading role in Brunei's festivals. Celebrated festivals include the **Chinese Lunar New Year** in late January and the month-long **Ramadan** (mid-September to mid-October), when government offices close for the day at 14.00 and food markets spring into action all over the city (see pages 114–15).

SHOPPING It may not be obvious that you are in a tax-free country, as the savings are pretty much offset by higher living costs compared with most of Asia. Still, there are savings to be had, with zero tax on clothes, food and (non-alcoholic) beverages; 5% tax on watches, jewellery, cosmetics, cameras, electrical equipment, furniture, photographic materials and electronics; and 20% tax on vehicles and car accessories.

Cultural buys Brunei's riches are revealed in its 'handicrafts' – not just beads and basketry, but silverware, brass artefacts (such as cannons), and most famously, the intricately designed brocades called kain tenunan, hand-woven with silver and gold threads. The gold thread is imported from Japan but the fabric is woven in Brunei: costing B$500–600 a yard it makes for quite an expensive sarong!

The riverside **Arts and Handicrafts Centre** [148 D4] on Jalan Residency may be an expensive place to purchase artefacts and fine handicraft items, but it is well worth a visit. For more affordable handicrafts and traditional souvenirs, head to the markets. At the **Tamu Kianggeh** [148 D3] in the city centre you can buy a keepsake *tudung dulang* – the decorative rattan food covers – or take home machete-like *pemarang* (though you may have trouble getting this through customs, depending on your country's particular rules). Many traditional handicrafts are made from bamboo, rattan and leaves, and are woven, waved and plaited. The best place to buy them is at city and rural tamu. For fabrics, head to Gadong – there are a couple of shops selling batiks, silk and sarongs near The Mall shopping arcades. Plant-lovers shouldn't miss the **Horticulture Centre** in Kampung Rimba, in the Gadong District. In the further-flung area of Serusop, 'Little India's' shops (Jln Muara, in the Berakas District), sell songkets in multi-gilded tones and bolts of bright silks. **Serusop** is an off-the-beaten-track shopping hub, and a favourite among foreign workers.

Markets The open-air market, **Tamu Kianggeh** [148 D3], is held every day in the village of Kampung Kianggeh, adjacent to the city centre. The stalls unfurl for half a kilometre along the banks of the Sungai Kianggeh (off Jln Residency). Water taxis ply the river waiting for a catch (to take tourists to the Kampung Ayer and around). From morning to evening, you can buy fresh and cooked food, handicrafts and baskets – all the typical things of a rural tamu. A **24-hour weekend market** is held along Jalan Sultan [148 B2] (⊕ *18.00 Sat–18.00 Sun*). On Friday and Sunday mornings, the Gadong marketplace blooms into a **flower market**, the *pasar bunga* [143 B5] (⊕ *07.00–noon*).

Shopping centres The largest shopping complex in Bandar Seri Begawan is the **Yayasan** [148 B3] (*CBD, riverfront*), another Sultan-owned business, billed as an 'upmarket array of shops and boutiques'. More serious retail activity is found in the Gadong and the Kiulap commercial districts. **The Mall** [143 B5] in Gadong (*bus Nos 55 & 01*) has a tad more ritz than glitz; it houses over 150 shops, including some international brands and boutiques. The neighbouring **Jaya Centrepoint Hypermarket** [143 B5] is lacklustre in presentation but has lots of cheap buys in jewellery, clothing and food.

Food/supermarkets The **Utama Grand** [143 B5] superstore on the ground floor of the Gadong Mall is the best supermarket for variety with a smattering of cool international products (Californian teas, Italian coffee, French cheese). **SupaSave** [143 A6] in Gadong has a huge range. The supermarket of the **Hua Ho** [143 B5/148 B3] department store has branches in the Yayasan complex and in Gadong and Kiulap, with fewer imports than the Utama Grand but loads of local and Asian produce. A chain store for food and other goods around Brunei is the **Milimewah**.

OTHER PRACTICALITIES
Hospital The Raja Isteri Pengiran Anak Saleha (RIPAS) Hospital [143 C7] (☏ *224 2424*) is on the corner of Jalan Tutong and Haji Hassanal Bolkiah.

BANDAR SERI BEGAWAN MUST-SEES

Sandra Bloodworth, Area Manager, Royal Brunei Airlines UK

Have you seen the proboscis monkey, been for an early-morning walk up the hill behind the Radisson Hotel, sat by the water fountain in the Yayasan shopping mall at 18.00 and watched the sun go down behind the mosque, or had a dinner cruise on the Brunei River? Another great place to watch the sun set is at the Empire Hotel – looking out over the South China Sea.

Internet Internet cafés are not as common in Brunei as they are in Malaysian Borneo. There are a couple of cafés in the city centre (see map, page 148), at the Yayasan complex [148 A3] and the RBA Plaza [148 A3]. There are more around the main shops of the Gadong District, and one in Muara town centre.

Money There are many licensed money exchanges in Bandar Seri Begawan city centre (see map, page 148), one at the airport and one in Gadong, but there are very few elsewhere so make sure you have enough money on you for excursions. The same goes for ATMs – you will find them in towns, but they are few and far between in rural areas.

Post office The General Post Office is located in the CBD on Jalan Elizabeth Dua [148 B2] (⊕ *07.45–16.30 Mon–Thu & Sat, 08.00–11.00 & 14.00–16.00 Fri*). There is also a post office in Muara Town.

WHAT TO SEE AND DO A full-day (six-hour) city tour, offered by many tour companies, usually takes in three or four sites, including museums, mosques and markets, plus a river trip to the water village, Kampung Ayer. Brunei Tourism's website (*www.bruneitourism.travel*, see page 132) has a list of all reputable tour operators, while Freme Travels (see page 144) gives a clear idea of overall tour possibilities.

Palaces and parliaments Built in 1984 at a cost of US$400 million, the **Istana Nurul Iman** [143 B8] – the Sultan's home – has 1,788 rooms and stretches over 0.5km along the riverbank, making it the largest residential palace in the world. The *Istana* (meaning 'palace') opens once a year to the public at the end of Ramadan, during the Hari Raya Aidilfitri celebrations. Thousands of Bruneians and foreigners queue for hours at its gates to get a peek inside. The open-house times are published in local newspapers, including the *Borneo Bulletin* (English-language) and *Media Permata* (Malay). At other times, the best exterior view of the palace and its 300-acre grounds is from a boat on the Sungai Brunei. On a night cruise, you will see it lit up like a true fairy-tale palace, thanks to some 55,000 light bulbs (the electricity is apparently very cheap, powered by gas turbines). Failing that, you can gaze at it from the public car park on Jalan Tutong, or from the adjacent park **Persiaran Damuan** [143 B8] (*Jln Tutong;* ⊕ *daily; free*). This 1km-long riverbank jogging haven has paved walkways and a series of sculptures by artists from the original six members of the Association of Southeast Asian Nations. The 'ASEAN-6' includes Indonesia, Malaysia, the Philippines, Thailand, Singapore and Brunei Darussalam.

On a river tour, you also get to see a rather different kind of palace. The **Istana Darussalam** [148 A3] is a modest, mint-coloured wooden home in Kampung Sumbiling – one of the many individual water villages that make up Kampung Ayer. It is here that the Sultan's father, the 28th sultan, was born – and where he returned to die.

If Brunei does one day become a democracy, the doors of the **Lapau** (Royal Ceremonial Hall) will probably be thrown open as a monarchical museum piece. For the time being, official permission is required to enter the gold-lined chamber where His Majesty was crowned on 1 August 1968. In the same neighbourhood, on Jalan Sungai Kianggeh, is the old **Dewan Majilis** (Legislative Council). The new home of the legislature is located well away from these city-centre landmarks, on Jalan Mabohai in the Berakas governmental district.

Mosques The most beautiful night-time views in Brunei come from the lights and bulbous forms thrown from its two very distinct mosques. The cream-and-gold **Sultan Omar Ali Saifuddien Mosque** [148 A2] (in the CBD, near the Central Bus Station; (⊕ *08.00–noon, 14.00–15.00 & 17.00–18.00 Sun–Wed*) is the older city mosque, built in 1958. It is a magical apparition of stained glass, Shanghai granite, chandeliers and Italian marble, surrounded by a lagoon on which a replica of the royal barge floats. The mesmerising gold dome contains 3.3 million fragments of Venetian mosaic, over a surface of 520m².

Despite it lacking any historic awe-factor, you will be struck by the opulence and strong sense of Islamic faith at the **Masjid Jame'Asr Hassanal Bolkiah Mosque** [143 B6] (⊕ *08.00–noon, 14.00–15.00 & 17.00–18.00 Sun–Wed, & Sat if no official ceremonies; bus Nos 1 & 22*). Gloriously ornamental, the edifice is a solid statement of the place of Islam in Bruneian life: architectural elements come in 29s. There are 29 golden domes, 29 steps and 29 pillars – the magic number represents the number of sultans that have ruled to date. Built to commemorate the 25th year of the current Sultan's reign, it is known as the Kiarong Mosque.

Kampung Ayer (water village) [148 D3] With 30,000 residents, this watery suburbia is actually composed of 28 individual villages, linked up by 8km of stilted walkways. One of the largest floating communities in the world, it has mosques, schools, markets and a fire station. The government has been trying to relocate the people on to land, but they refuse to abandon their spiritual home. Though it has burnt down several times, the origins of the water village pre-date the 16th century, when Italian historian Antonio Pigafetta described it as the 'Venice of the East'. The latest village addition, Kampung Bolkiah, is a high-tech set-up built from fireproof materials, with an eco-sewage system and houses spaced nearly 10m apart. In other words, the exact opposite of its predecessor!

Residents of 'KA' commute to work on a flotilla of water taxis, leaving their cars parked along Jalan Residency in town. To visit Kampung Ayer, you can take a water taxi from several points along Jalan McArthur and Jalan Residency to any location in the village, then walk about; the one-way fare is B$1–2. Alternatively, you can take a guided tour. For me, the water village is at its most mesmerising at night, viewed from the riverfront, as water taxis whizz past in trails of coloured lights ferrying people home.

River cruises Most local operators (see page 144) offer half-day trips, taking in the main city sights and the water village. Prices start from B$50 to B$70, depending on the market they work with. There are also night-time cruises on the river.

Museums All the leading museums are located in the Muara District, outside the CBD. During Ramadan, museum opening hours are usually shorter, closing at around 15.00 rather than 17.00.

The most interesting from a historical point of view is the **Brunei Museum** [143 F7] (*Jln Kota Batu;* 224 4545; *www.museums.gov.bn/bangunan.htm;* ⊕ *09.00–*

Between Brunei and Malaysian Borneo, expect constant variations in the spelling of *kampung* and *kampong*, both of which mean 'village'.

It's one of the maddeningly erratic things about Borneo – spelling discrepancies boil down to more than different dialects; they even occur within the same states and regions. Moreover, the spelling of an administrative entity, food or cultural dance can vary three times within as many pages of the same brochure and it is impossible to tell which instance is the correct version. Is it *kueh* (cakes) or *kuih*? *Chendol* or *chendul*? Once you get used to the frequent discrepancies, you can start ignoring them and appreciate the charm of such a fluid language.

17.00 Sun–Thu, 09.00–11.30 & 14.30–17.00 Fri, 09.45–17.00 Sat; free; bus No 39) with its bronze and brass artefacts, Chinese ceramics, jewellery and natural history displays, and chronicle of the oil industry. A real highlight is the Islamic art gallery, which contains exquisite jewellery and tapestries from around the world from the Sultan's private collection, dating from the 10th and 11th centuries. In a lovely, leafy riverside location just out of town, the museum is situated on an archaeological site in **Kota Batu** where Brunei's former settlements are still being unearthed. Ceramics and coins from the Tang dynasty have been found here. Nearby is the tomb of Brunei's fifth Islamic monarch, Sultan Bolkiah, who ruled from 1473–1521.

The **Malay Technology Museum** [143 F7] (*Jln Kota Batu, opposite the Brunei Museum;* ☏ 224 4545; ⊕ *09.30–17.00 Sat–Thu, 09.00–11.30 & 14.30–17.00 Fri; free; bus No 39)* uses rather unrealistic dummies in its exhibits – natives in their primitive Kampung Ayer stilt houses and Iban tribespeople in their longhouses. Nevertheless, it provides a fascinating insight into ancient housing and water-village cottage industries, including boatmaking technology, goldsmithing and fishing.

Celebrity attracts, and the **Royal Regalia Museum** [148 B2] (*Jln Sultan;* ☏ *223 8358;* ⊕ *09.30–16.30 Sat–Thu, 09.00–11.30 & 14.30–16.30 Fri; free)* is Bandar Seri Begawan's most visited museum. It puts on show the insignia, pomp and privileges relating to the stronghold sultanate, with a particular focus on the coronation of the present sultan in 1968. The large collection of artefacts includes royal family photographs, a replica of the throne from the royal palace, ceremonial armoury, the crown jewels, costumes and gold and silver chariots.

The oldest-surviving colonial building in Brunei, **Bubongan Duabelas** [143 F7] (*Jln Residency;* ☏ *224 4181;* ⊕ *09.00–16.30 Mon–Thu, 09.00–11.30 & 14.30–16.30 Fri)* is a timber house with a dozen peaked canopies (it's name literally means the 'house of 12 roofs'), balustraded porches and wide roof overhangs. Built in 1906, it was once home to the British Resident and British High Commissioner of Brunei.

Back closer to town is the **Arts and Handicrafts Centre** [148 D4] (*Jln Residency;* ☏ *224 0676;* ⊕ *08.00–17.00 daily; free)*, which conducts classes in making songkoks (traditional caps), weaving, woodwork, basketry and other age-old local skills, while revealing some of the cultural history of Brunei.

Urban reserves The major inner-city nature reserve is the **Tasek Lama Recreational Park** [148 C1] (*Jln Tasek Lama, about 2km north of the riverfront; Bus Circle Line)*, a protected pocket of urban rainforest with waterfall and lakes. On Jalan Residency, the hilly **Bukit Subok Recreational Park** [143 E7] (⊕ *07.45–18.00 daily; free)* is a more centrally located green oasis with views of the river and Kampung Ayer.

Brunei Darussalam BANDAR SERI BEGAWAN

4

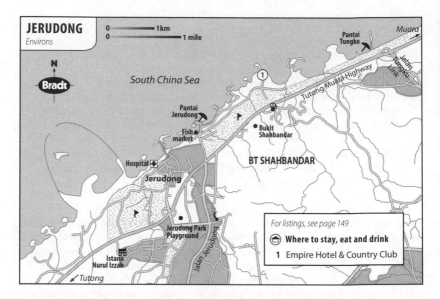

JERUDONG
Environs

0 ————— 1km
0 ————— 1 mile

South China Sea

Pantai
Tungku

Muara

Tutong Muara Highway

Jalan Tungku Link

N

Bradt

Pantai
Jerudong

Fish
market

Bukit
Shahbandar

BT SHAHBANDAR

Hospital

Jerudong

Jerudong Park
Playground

Jalan Jerudong

Istana
Nurul Izzah

Tutong

For listings, see page 149

Where to stay, eat and drink

1 Empire Hotel & Country Club

EXCURSIONS FROM BANDAR SERI BEGAWAN

Most other destinations in Brunei (and there are only two or three) are best done as day trips from the capital, or at a stretch with an overnight stay. Outside of the capital, the number of quality accommodations can be counted on the fingers of one hand. Thankfully, the short distances involved make day trips possible, but this does not mean you should rule out immersing yourself in beautiful Ulu Temburong National Park, or the oil district, for a night or two.

ISLANDS AND RESERVES If you want to go green for a day, morning or afternoon, several reserves within an hour's drive or boat trip of the capital offer nature trails for hiking and biking and picnicking spots.

Bukit Shahbandar (*15km from Bandar, along the Muara–Tutong Highway;* ⊕ *07.45–18.00 daily; free*) A 70ha hilly recreational park with a network of well-signed trekking paths, a mountain-bike trail, an observation tower with views over the capital and the Jerudong area, and resident long-tailed macaque monkeys. This is where the Brunei Marathon is held every December.

Wasai Kendal (*off Jln Tutong, the road running by the palace*) Thanks to its waterfall, this is a favourite forest retreat for family outings with its picnic facilities, trails, tropical flora and easy trekking. It is within 20 minutes' drive south of the capital, in Brunei Muara.

Pulau Selirong (Mosquito Island) A small mangrove-forested island with a plankwalk through tropical forest (a half-day tour). It's a 45-minute boat ride away from Bandar Seri Begawan, off Brunei Bay.

LEISURE AND SPORTS CENTRE
Hassanal Bolkiah National Stadium (*5km from city centre;* ⊕ *08.00–noon & 13.30–16.30 daily*) The Hassanal Bolkiah sports stadium in Berakas was built

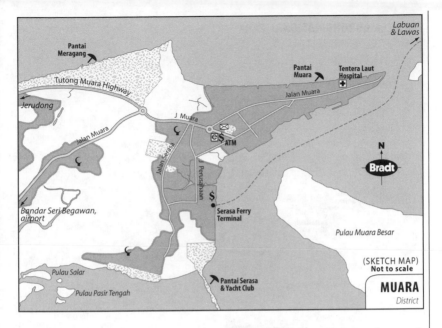

in 1999 for the SEA Games. It includes a high-tech sports medicine and research centre, indoor and outdoor stadium, an international swimming complex and track-and-field training facilities. A swimming pool and squash and tennis courts are open to the public.

BEACHES AND WATERSPORTS   Situated to the north of Bandar Seri Begawan, the Muara District is the most popular urban beach escape.

Pantai Serasa Beach   (*off Jln Serasa; bus No 33, Eastern Line*) A ten-minute drive from the CBD, Pantai Serasa is home to the Royal Brunei Yacht Club, the Royal Brunei National Windsurfing Association and the Serasa Water Sports Complex, so you can come here to sail, windsurf, kayak and water-ski, or just hang out. It's also frequented by those who like fishing – not just men, but women too.

Pantai Muara Beach   (*off Jln Serasa; bus No 33, Eastern Line*) Some 27km from the city, the beach has a long waterfront esplanade with picnic, playground and toilet facilities. On weekends, plenty of food and drink stalls set up around the headland. Bus No 57 heads northwest to Pantai Jerudong Beach where there are watersports, as well as seafood and other food stalls.

ULU TEMBURONG NATIONAL PARK   Referred to as the 'green jewel', the 50,000ha rainforest within the huge Batu Apoi Forest Reserve is Brunei's only national park. The park spills into the 'Heart of Borneo' conservation area, which sweeps in central forests of Sabah, Sarawak and Kalimantan (see pages 64–5). The Temburong District, in northern Brunei, is a major rice-growing area, producing nearly half the country's harvest. It is home to a multi-ethnic mix of Iban, Murut and Malay people. The journey to get there is more than half the fun – the boat speeds through wide bays and mangrove forests full of proboscis monkeys, then trespasses briefly on Malaysian territory before swinging back into Brunei.

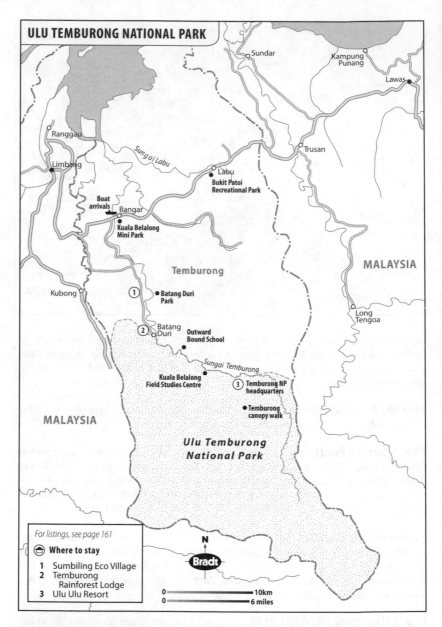

ULU TEMBURONG NATIONAL PARK

Sundar
Kampung Punang
Lawas

Ranggau

Limbang

Sungai Labu

Trusan

Labu
Bukit Patoi Recreational Park

Boat arrivals
Bangar

Kuala Belalong Mini Park

Temburong

MALAYSIA

Kubong

① Batang Duri Park

② Batang Duri

Long Tengoa

Outward Bound School

Sungai Temburong

Kuala Belalong Field Studies Centre

③ Temburong NP headquarters

Temburong canopy walk

MALAYSIA

Ulu Temburong National Park

For listings, see page 161

🏠 Where to stay

1 Sumbiling Eco Village
2 Temburong
    Rainforest Lodge
3 Ulu Ulu Resort

N

Bradt

0 ————————— 10km
0 ————————— 6 miles

Getting there and away

By boat From Bandar Seri Begawan, the journey to the national park requires a mix of speedboat, longboat and road transport. Express boats from the capital to Bangar, the main town in Temburong, leave regularly from the jetty on Jalan Residency between approximately 07.00 and 17.00. The 45-minute journey costs B$7.

From Bangar a vehicle transfer is necessary to **Kampung Batang Duri** where local Ibans navigate the 30–40-minute trip to the park in a temuai (longboat). The whole trip can be completed within a couple of hours, depending on water levels in the river, and the smoothness (or not) of negotiating more than a dozen rapids. A cost-efficient and comfortable option is to book the trip through a tour operator in Bandar Seri Begawan, as the longboat trip alone costs about B$100. The various tours offered range from day trips to overnight stays, with park accommodation.

By car If you opt for self-drive, you can continue as far as Batang Duri, then proceed upriver to the park.

Tours to Temburong
A day tour from BSB to the park, including all transport, a longhouse visit and lunch (*adult B$170, child B$128*), is available with **Sunshine Borneo Tours and Travel** and with **Freme Travel**. Count on double that price for an overnight stay at a park chalet. **Intrepid Travel** is good for groups and adventure tours; they do specialised rafting trips to Temburong, and say the Grade I–II rapids are ideal for beginners. Some operators offer student discounts.

Where to stay, eat and drink
Outward Bound Brunei Darussalam (OBBD) (*www.outward-bound.org*) operate in the Temburong National Park rainforest and there are opportunities for education groups and activities.

Several *kedai* and *restoran* along the main street of Bangar serve Chinese, Malay and Indian food. If you are heading for the park, stock up here as it's your last chance. For location of listings, see map opposite.

Ulu Ulu Resort 244 1791/244 6812; www1.50megs.com; sales@uluuluresort.com; www.uluuluresort.com. Some 45mins by boat from Temburong Town, the part-privatised venture of the National Park & Forestry Department has so far proved successful. The eco-lodge comprises 19 Malay-style villas & suites, sprawled along the riverbank, with natural furnishings, bright contemporary touches, AC & fans. Food at the large wood & rattan clad open-air restaurant ranges between good & excellent; the latter applying particularly to main meals of local dishes. A big evolution in the last couple of years is the availability of online bookings, with prices jumping simultaneously. (A day trip for 2 rose from B$270 in 2012 to B$326 in 2014.) The information centre & more basic park lodgings – hostel, self-contained chalets sleeping 2–4, & campsite – are still forestry-run. Connected by boardwalks, some lodgings are over 500m from the arrival jetty. The lodge is proudly sustainable & back to nature in spirit, providing guests with stainless-steel water bottles instead of plastic, no electronic or digital distractions, & no lights (generator-powered) after 22.00. The sheer silence, discounting a hullabaloo of insect drones, is a tremendous experience. Staff are both professional & incredibly friendly. The

canteen is not always open, so pack any can't-live-without snacks. **$$$$–$$$**

Sumbiling Eco Village 242 6923; e sales@borneoguide.com; www.borneoguide.com. This eco-village project is a joint venture with the Borneo Guide tour company & Ibans of Kampung Sumbiling Lama, in the Temburong District. A deep green jungle stay in every respect, from the environment through to conservation & recycling measures. Various packages from BSB include rainforest camping experience, tent accommodation, meals, treks & longhouse visits. **$$$**

Temburong Rainforest Lodge 223 4280/1; e fremeinb@brunet.bn; www.freme.com/bruneitours. A passion for Temburong among the crew at Freme Travel Services led them to open their own lodge, in a village approaching the entry to the park. The AC bunkrooms are clean & comfortable, staff are personable, & the watery setting of the Dining Terrace is sublime. Overnight packages from BSB includes return water taxis to Bangar, overland transfers, an early-morning longboat trip upstream to the park, rainforest canopy, jungle & waterfall trekking, return by raft, lunch, swim & afternoon tea. **$$$**

What to see and do   Bangar consists of the river jetty area and two or three streets. There is a daily market with fruit and other fresh produce, from wild ferns and bamboo shoots to handicrafts. There are some Iban longhouses in the area – if you want to visit for a traditional dance show, book through the Temburong Tourist Information Centre or request it as part of a day tour from Bandar Seri Bagawan.

The **Bukit Patoi Recreational Park** is 15km from Bangar in Kampung Labu. A 2½-hour trek takes in rainforest and waterfalls and every September the hilly area is the site of an International Challenge Run (15km).

Reachable only by a river trip, the park headquarters are situated in a big rainforest buffer zone at the confluence of the Sungai Temburong and Sungai Belalong rivers. The deep forest of the 'Heart of Borneo' is an extremely peaceful place where the evening conversation of cicadas and insects will drill through your hut walls. The variety of life is incredible; one entomologist discovered over 400 species of beetle on a single tree here.

By day you can bathe in the river, kayak and hike. The park has 7km of well-marked elevated boardwalks, with in-depth, intelligent and finely illustrated botanical interpretation. Built with funds from the Sultan-owned Shell oil company, the **Temburong canopy walk** is an out-of-this-world stainless-steel pathway through the treetops, 250m above the forest floor. The structure's five ladders, interlinked by metal bridges, take you to progressively greater king-and-queen-of-the-jungle heights. Don't let minor panic stop you from enjoying the breathtaking views and forest-top immersion. Best experienced as the dawn mist rises above the forest, it is reached after a 2km upward trek from the park HQ. If you do venture there on your own, as this author did on her last trip, do be wary of thunderstorms. After holing up for half an hour in one of the blessed undercover seating sections along the boardwalk, I eventually, trembling legs and all, made it to the top – and lived (again) to not regret it! Possible wildlife encounters along the way include Bornean gibbons, macaques, civets, sun bears, pit vipers, hornbills and Rajah Brooke's birdwing butterflies. On the return journey, take the standard jungle trail for an off-boardwalk real forest experience.

Temburong cultural experience   Also on this latest trip, I finally got to experience some Temburong beyond the jungle, during a day of tripping through its colourful ethnic kaleidoscope, undulating landscapes of rounded hills and rivers, and lush crops. Freme stands on its own in offering tailored as well as group excursions in this area. The trip will be sure to be broken up by spontaneous stops for Durian and Rambutan tasting direct from the trees, or proffered by exceedingly friendly locals. Intrepid Tours also do budget traveller trips to Temburong by day or with an overnight stay at their Batang Duri guesthouse.

The Kuala Belalong Field Studies Centre   On the way up the river to park HQ, you will pass an attractive building set into the rainforest – a series of dark timber houses with pike roofs and swerving balustrades; at night it glows like a beetle on stilts. The rainforest research base, run by the Universiti Brunei Darussalam, is an important centre for rainforest studies and it is not uncommon to bump into visiting scientists at night at park HQ further upstream. Researchers and students can enquire about studying here via the university's biology department (✆ 246 3001; e kbfsc@ubd.edu.bn).

TUTONG AND BELAIT DISTRICTS   The Tutong District is largely rural with hillier rainforest and lake reserves inland, with some longhouse territory bringing together people from the Dusun, Iban, Kedayan and Tutong tribes. Further south is the Belait District and Brunei's oil coast, centring on the towns of Seria and Kuala Belait.

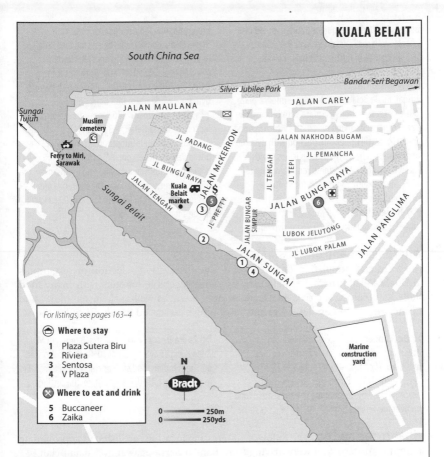

South China Sea

Bandar Seri Begawan

Silver Jubilee Park

JALAN MAULANA

JALAN CAREY

Sungai
Tujuh

Muslim
cemetery

JL PADANG

JALAN NAKHODA BUGAM

JL PEMANCHA

JL BUNGU RAYA

JALAN MCKERRON

JL TENGAH

JL TEPI

Ferry to Miri,
Sarawak

JALAN TENGAH

Kuala
Belait
market

JL PRETTY

JALAN BUNGAR SIMPUR

JALAN BUNGA RAYA

Sungai Belait

LUBOK JELUTONG

JL LUBOK PALAM

JALAN PANGLIMA

JALAN SUNGAI

For listings, see pages 163–4

Where to stay
1 Plaza Sutera Biru
2 Riviera
3 Sentosa
4 V Plaza

Where to eat and drink
5 Buccaneer
6 Zaika

Marine
construction
yard

N

Bradt

0 ———— 250m
0 ———— 250yds

Getting there and away

By car There are two roads heading to the Tutong and Belait districts – the coastal Muara–Tutong Highway and an inland route along the old road Jalan Tutong. From Seria to Kuala Belait (*17km*), the fast route is via the Seria bypass. The longer coastal road passes the Istana Manggalela, the Sultan's residence during his visits to town. The road leads to the Sungai Belait River, where there is a ferry to the village of Kampung Sungai Teraban. Coming from Sarawak you can arrive in Kuala Belait via the Sungai Tujuh checkpoint. Kuala Belait is about 90km from the capital, and 30km from Miri in Sarawak.

By bus There are hourly bus services between the main bus terminal in Bandar Seri Begawan (*Jln Cator*) and Seria – tickets are about B$6. Local buses travel between Seria and Kuala Belait – the 30km journey costs B$1. The Miri-Belait Bus Company runs five daily services between Miri's Jalan Padang bus terminal in Sarawak and Kuala Belait, with a change of bus at the Sungai Tujuh border checkpoint.

Where to stay   *See map, above.*

Plaza Sutera Biru (21 rooms) Lot 73, Jln Sungai, Kuala Belait; ☎ 334 7268; e info@psb. com.bn; www.psb.com.bn. The upmarket niche on the oil coast was filled in 2007 with this non-smoking hotel by the Belait River, 16km from Seria & 50km from Miri. High-tech, aesthetic rooms & kitchenette-equipped suites spread over 6 floors, with slim TVs, smart keys & AC. Sports Café specialises in northern Chinese cuisine. **$$$$$–$$$$**

🏠 **V Plaza** (82 rooms) Lot 1300, Jln Sungai, Kuala Belait; ☎ 334 7868; e info@v-plaza. com.bn or reservations@v-plaza.com.bn; www.v-plaza.com.bn. Spanking new 4-star which opened late 2014, & still under construction with gym due for completion by early 2015. Spacious rooms & suites, buffet b/fast, business centre, rooftop café, Wi-Fi. Many online room deals for multi-day & early-bird stays. **$$$$–$$$**

🏠 **Riviera Hotel** (30 rooms) Lot 106, Jln Sungai, Kuala Belait; ☎ 333 5252; e rivierahtl@

brunet.bn; www.rivierahotelkb.webs.com. Well-fitted, clean, comfortable beds, standard & deluxe rooms, AC, satellite TV, Shahryza Restaurant (⏱ 07.00–23.00), 3–4- star. Both this & the following hotel send clients on to nearby Harun's Gym for a workout (in DBB Bank). **$$$**

🏠 **Sentosa Hotel** (36 rooms) 92–93 Jln McKerron, Kuala Belait; ☎ 333 4341/2; e enquiry@bruneisentosahotel.com; www. bruneisentosahotel.com. AC, satellite TV, broadband internet, non-smoking rooms, mini fridge & safety-deposit box. The Syazana Café has good Malay & Indian food (⏱ 06.00–23.00). Recommended. **$$$–$$**

✗ Where to eat and drink   *See map, page 163.*

For a district population of just 60,000, there is a good selection of restaurants in Kuala Belait. There are daily fish, fruit and vegetable markets with many food stalls set up along the riverbanks and around town, as well as the usual Malay and Chinese dishes – noodles, laksa and spicy prawns – served in several coffee shops.

✗ **Buccaneer** Lot 94, Ground Floor, Jln McKerron; ☎ 333 0406; www.buccaneer. bn; ⏱ approx 11.00–14.00 & 18.30–22.30 daily. Formerly the Buccaneer Steakhouse, recommended by Western meat-eaters, good food but average service. $$$

✗ **Zaika Restaurant** Lot 308, Bangunan Maju, Jalan Bunga Raya; ☎ 334 7340. Good 'expat priced' northern Indian food such as chicken tikka masala in a wooden-tabled, warmly lit, restful setting. $$$–$$

What to see and do   The following interesting locations are listed in approximate ascending order if you were driving from Bandar Seri Begawan to Kuala Belait.

Tutong District   Barely 40km from the capital, the town of Tutong (also known as Kuala Tutong) lies among coconut palms near the Tutong River. (Kuala, by the way, means 'river mouth' and has nothing to do with Australian marsupials.) There are several kampung named Kuala along Brunei's estuary-specked coast. The **Tamu Tutong Kampung Serambagun** is a daily open-air market held 1km from the town centre, selling lots of local fruits, vegetables and handicrafts. Many vendors come from the rural hinterland to buy and sell their produce.

Pantai Seri Kenangan – 'the unforgettable beach' – is a popular recreation spot (fishing, swimming, picnics) five minutes' drive from Kuala Tutong Town. Located on a narrow spit of land between the South China Sea and the Tutong River, it has beach chalets, picnic pavilions, restaurant and food stalls. From here, you can also take a trip on the Sungai Tutong.

Situated 27km inland from Tutong Town, along mostly unsealed roads, is **Tasek Merimbun** (⏱ 09.30–15.30 Sun–Thu, 09.00–11.30 & 14.30–17.00 Fri, 10.00–15.30 Sat), a serpentine freshwater lake mirrored with blue sky and cloud reflections. Surrounded by peat swamp and grass marsh, the lake environment is both wildlife sanctuary, recreational park and research station, offering nature trails, an exhibition hall, butterfly garden, lakeside gazebos, rental boats and forest campsites Proclaimed an ASEAN (Association of Southeast Asian Nations) Heritage Park in

1984, some say it is the de facto first national park, though is not gazetted as one. A wooden walkway leads through the belly of the lake to an islet, Pulau Jalundung, which somewhat paradoxically has picnic-table facilities – given the crocodile warning signs alongside! Other resident fauna includes the clouded leopard, white-collared fruit bat, Bornean gibbon, giant squirrel, silver leaf monkey, pig-tailed macaque, sambar deer, honey bear, western tarsier, argus pheasant, hornbill, purple heron, pangolin and reticulated python.

Belait District Driving through Brunei you are never short of recreational and picnic spots and places to stretch the legs. On the coast side of the Muara–Tutong Highway is the **Sungai Liang Forest Reserve**, some 70km south of Bandar Seri Begawan (turn left at the Sungai Liang junction and proceed 450m along the Jalan Labi road to the park's entrance on the right). Here you will find a canopy walk and several other well-marked trails of varying grades through lowland rainforest. A further 25km or so along Jalan Labi is the **Luagan Lalak Forest Recreational Park**, whose alluvial freshwater swamp fills up like a lake in the wet season. From here, a steep 2km trek leads to the **Wasai Wong Kadir** waterfall. The Labi District is home to Iban people and there are chances to visit their longhouses along the way.

The oil coast starts in Seria: there is an **Oil and Gas Discovery Centre**, an interactive museum of oil history and technology, and the hard-to-miss **Billionth Barrel Monument** – a blend of Islamic tiles with industrial architecture. Kuala Belait is a town grown up on oil and a foreign workers' community, which has added a cosmopolitan touch to the place. Loved by expats, it has a bit of an R&B edge – someone even wrote a love song about Kuala Belait. Entertainment choices beat those found anywhere else outside of the capital, and locals enjoy a good quality of life. For jogging and family recreation, they head to **Pantai Lumut**, a secluded beach 10km from Seria off the coastal highway. Those looking for some serious partying should do as the locals do, and cross the border to the lively town of Miri for the weekend (see pages 311–17).

Brunei Darussalam   EXCURSIONS FROM BANDAR SERI BEGAWAN

4

UPDATES WEBSITE

You can post your comments and recommendations, and read the latest feedback and updates from other readers, online at www.bradtupdates.com/borneo.

SEND US YOUR SNAPS!

We'd love to follow your adventures using our *Borneo* guide – why not send us your photos and stories via Twitter (@BradtGuides) and Instagram (@bradtguides) using the hashtag #borneo. Alternatively, you can upload your photos directly to the gallery on the Borneo destination page via our website (*www.bradtguides.com*).

Part Three

SABAH

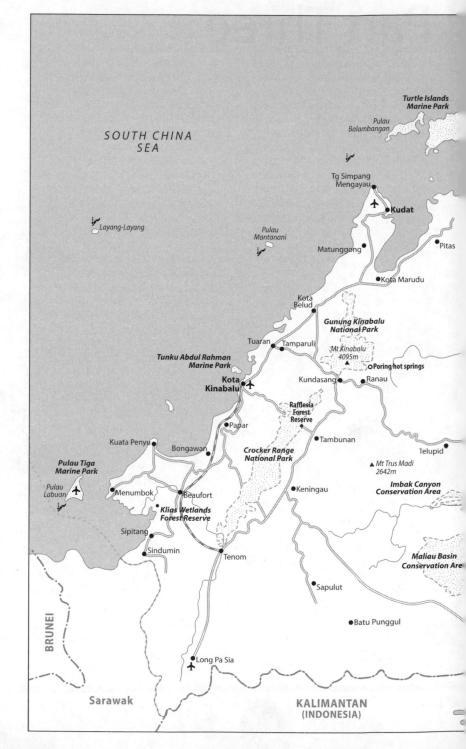

SOUTH CHINA
SEA

Turtle Islands
Marine Park

Pulau
Balambangan

Tg Simpang
Mengayau

Kudat

Layang-Layang

Pulau
Mantanani

Matunggong

Pitas

Kota Marudu

Kota
Belud

Gunung Kinabalu
National Park

Tuaran   Tamparuli

Mt Kinabalu
4095m

Poring hot springs

Tunku Abdul Rahman
Marine Park

**Kota
Kinabalu**

Kundasang   Ranau

Rafflesia
Forest
Reserve

Papar

Tambunan

Telupid

Kuata Penyu

Bongawan

Crocker Range
National Park

▲ Mt Trus Madi
2642m

Pulau Tiga
Marine Park

Imbak Canyon
Conservation Area

Pulau
Labuan

Menumbok   Beaufort

Keningau

Klias Wetlands
Forest Reserve

Sipitang

Sindumin

Tenom

Maliau Basin
Conservation Area

Sapulut

Batu Punggul

BRUNEI

Long Pa Sia

Sarawak

KALIMANTAN
(INDONESIA)

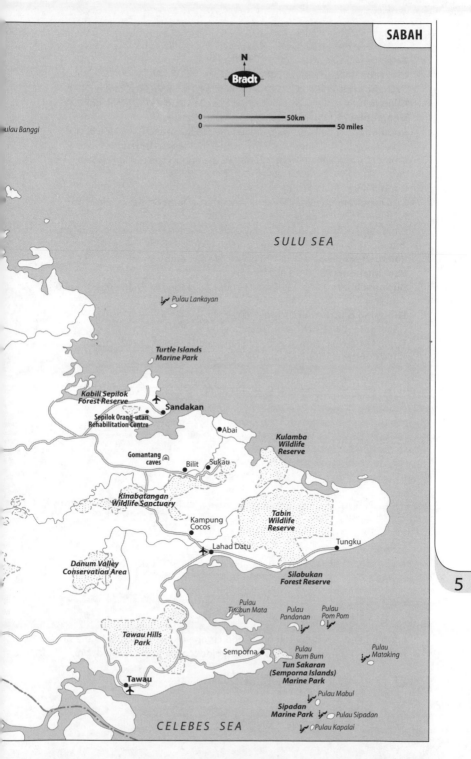

N

Bradt

0 — 50km
0 — 50 miles

SULU SEA

ulau Banggi

Pulau Lankayan

Turtle Islands
Marine Park

Kabili Sepilok
Forest Reserve

Sandakan

Sepilok Orang-utan
Rehabilitation Centre

Abai

Kulamba
Wildlife
Reserve

Gomantang
caves

Bilit   Sukau

Kinabatangan
Wildlife Sanctuary

Kampung
Cocos

Tabin
Wildlife
Reserve

Tungku

Lahad Datu

Danum Valley
Conservation Area

Silabukan
Forest Reserve

5

Pulau
Timbun Mata

Pulau
Pandanan

Pulau
Pom Pom

Tawau Hills
Park

Pulau
Mataking

Semporna

Pulau
Bum Bum

Tun Sakaran
(Semporna Islands)
Marine Park

Tawau

Pulau Mabul

Sipadan
Marine Park

Pulau Sipadan

Pulau Kapalai

CELEBES SEA

SABAH AT A GLANCE

Telephone area code +608
Currency Malaysian ringgit (RM)
Exchange rate US$1 = RM4.31, €1 = RM4.89, £1 = RM6.66 (October 2015)
Climate Humid; average daily temperature lowlands 30°C, highlands 22°C
Geography 76,115km²; situated in northern Borneo
Population 3.2 million; approximately 17.5% Kadazandusun, 13% Bajau, 12% Malay, 9.5% Chinese, 14% from other indigenous tribes, 5% Indian & others. Approximately one-quarter of the population foreigners (non-citizens).
Capital Kota Kinabalu (KK)
Visa requirements Visa-free three-month stay for most nationalities (for further details, see page 82)
Language Official language Malay (*Bahasa Melayu*); Chinese and Kadazan common community languages. English widely spoken.
Emergency numbers 999 for police, fire and ambulance
Banking hours 09.30–15.00 Mon–Fri
Business hours 08.00–13.00 and 14.00–17.00 Monday–Friday, 08.00–13.00 Saturday
Shopping centre hours 10.00–22.00 daily
Government website www.sabah.gov.my
Tourist board 51 Gaya Street, Kota Kinabalu; +6 088 21212; e info@sabahtourism.com; www.sabahtourism.com

FOLLOW BRADT

For the latest news, special offers and competitions, subscribe to the Bradt newsletter via the website www.bradtguides.com and follow Bradt on:

- www.facebook.com/BradtTravelGuides
- @BradtGuides
- @bradtguides
- www.pinterest.com/bradtguides

5

Kota Kinabalu

Emerald waters, bottle-green islands and a backdrop of lush, low-lying hills... The coastal city of Kota ('fort') Kinabalu may be a bit of an architectural hotchpotch, but its sea setting is sublime. Among the ramshackle shop-lots and piecemeal development sites, 'KK' has a palpable resort atmosphere – many locals take to the water after work and on weekends, enjoying the beach location to the full.

Levelled during World War II, some shabbier buildings are progressively being revamped, as mangrove swamps cede to shiny new shopping centres. From the top of Signal Hill, you can see how 70% of the town centre lies on a narrow belt of land, reclaimed from the sea in the 1920s. The Waterfront Esplanade – a buzzy strip of markets, hotels, seafood eateries, cafés and bars – hugs the shoreline. Off the coast, colourful cargo and fishing vessels fill the bay.

Of KK's 350,000 residents, 60% are a mix of Malay, Kadazandusun and Bajau, 35% are Chinese, 3% Murut and 1% Indian. Filipino and Indonesian migrants make up the remainder. Like a mini Kuala Lumpur, Kota Kinabalu has been gradually striving for a futuristic image. Modernistic superstructures are ruled out by low-flying air traffic, and there is a seven-storey limit on new constructions.

HISTORY

Like the stilted water villages on the city fringe of today, the earliest coastal settlements around KK were those of indigenous people. The first British presence came when the British North Borneo Chartered Company (BNBCC) set up a trading settlement in 1882 on Pulau Gaya, the largest of five islands in the bay. Before Europeans arrived, it was inhabited by the Bajau water-living tribe. Approval of the foreign administration was far from unanimous – the BNBCC was deemed insensitive to local customs and heavy-handed with taxes. One Bajau trader, Muhammad Salleh (popularised as Mat Salleh; see page 217), vehemently opposed a controversial tax on rice. In 1897, he and his supporters raided the British outpost on Pulau Gaya, burning it to the ground. Salleh and some 1,000 rebels were killed in a gun battle with the British police a few years later. By then the BNBCC had restored its headquarters at the small mainland settlement of Jesselton – named in honour of the company's vice chairman, Sir Charles Jessel. Locals referred to it as *Api-Api* – 'fire-fire' – apparently because of the frequent fires that blazed in water villages during firecracker-filled celebrations. A less politically correct version says the name actually arose from the sight of the BNBCC trading base on Pulau Gaya going up in flames. Jesselton was renamed Kota Kinabalu in 1968.

GETTING THERE AND AWAY

BY AIR
Kota Kinabalu International Airport (KKIA) (088 238555; *www.kotakinabaluairport.com*) Perched by the South China Sea, 8km from the city centre,

the airport's stunning views extend to the horizon over a vast blue stretch, dabbed with forested islands. In 2009, a five-year RM1 billion renovation project resulted in enhanced floor space, parking and interior design, new check-in counters and banking machines, and a dedicated low-cost terminal.

Terminal 1 serves international flights as well as **Malaysia Airlines** domestic flights, while Terminal 2 is home to **AirAsia**. The heavy investments saw little improvement to public services – though there are decent duty-free shops and food outlets, the airport is lacking internet stations, baggage lockers, transport shuttles and a decent individual website, all of which you might expect from Malaysia's second-busiest airport.

Royal Brunei Airlines flies between Brunei's capital Bandar Seri Begawan and Kota Kinabalu. **Malaysia Airlines** flies to/from Perth, Singapore, Seoul, Osaka, Tokyo, Hong Kong, Guangzhou, Taipei and Kaohsiung (Taiwan), as well as Kuala Lumpur, Labuan and other Borneo destinations – Sandakan, Tawau, Sibu, Miri and Kuching. **AirAsia** flies to/from KK and Singapore (and the neighbouring Malaysian city of Johor Bahru), Kuala Lumpur, Penang, Ho Chi Minh City, Jakarta and Clark in the Philippines, and regionally to Sandakan, Tawau, Miri and Kuching. **Cebu Pacific** operates direct flights between KK and Manila. Singapore Airlines's regional wing **Silk Air** (*www.silkair. com*) connects KK and Singapore in 2½ hours, and via there, many other Asian hubs including Delhi, Hong Kong and Ho Chi Minh City. **DragonAir** (*www.dragonair. com*), Cathay Pacific's regional offshoot, flies between KK and Hong Kong (one-way fares are as low as RM719/£137), hooking up with many other Asian destinations.

Airport–city transport Many hotels offer their own shuttle services. If you book a package, ensure transits are included. For taxis, buy a coupon in the arrivals hall – fares are around RM30 for up to four people. Though there is no official airport–city bus service, minibuses ply the route along the main road.

(For information on **visas**, see page 82.)

Airline offices Many airlines have an office in both Kota Kinabalu International Airport (most are on Level 2) and the city. Several city offices are clustered in the Kompleks Kuwasa (Jln Karamunsing) and Kompleks Karamunsing commercial centres in the south of Kota Kinabalu.

✈ **AirAsia** Ground Floor, KKIA, Terminal 2; ✆600 85 8888 (national inquiry number ☺ 09.00–18.00 daily); www.airasia.com. Book online for the best fares.
✈ **Malaysia Airlines** Ticketing Office, Level 2, KKIA, Terminal 1; ✆088 413676; ☺ 05.30–19.30

✈ **Royal Brunei Airlines** Ground Floor, Kompleks Kuwasa; ✆088 242193
✈ **Silk Air** Block L-69-5, 5th Floor, Times Sq, KK, off coastal highway; ✆088 485450/1/2

KOTA KINABALU – REVERED PLACE OF THE CHINESE WIDOW?

Named after the iconic mountain looming over the city, folklore holds that *Kinabalu* means 'Chinese widow' – *kina* being the Dusunic word for 'Chinese' and *balu* Malay for 'widow'. The story tells of a Chinese prince who came to the mountain in search of a pearl – closely guarded by a dragon at its summit. During his quest he married a local, but soon returned to China leaving her heartbroken.

The Kadazandusun people attest a more spiritual explanation: *Kinabalu* denotes 'revered place of the dead', derived from the term *Aki Nabalu* – *Aki* – that is 'ancestors' or 'grandfather', and *Nabalu*, the Dusun name for the mountain.

Kota Kinabalu to Mount Gunung Kinabalu National Park	88km
Kota Kinabalu to Kota Belud	75km
Kota Kinabalu to Kota Marudu	131km
Kota Kinabalu to Kudat	190km
Kota Kinabalu to Sandakan approximately	350km
Kota Kinabalu to Semporna	565km
Kota Kinabalu to Sindumin	158km

BY CAR There are four main highways in Kota Kinabalu. The Kota Kinabalu–Sandakan Highway (A4) connects the capital to the east-coast cities of Sandakan, Lahad Datu, Semporna and Tawau (via Tuaran, Tamparuli, Kundasang, Ranau and Telupid); although it is only 335km, the cross-state trip takes six or seven hours. The Kota Kinabalu–Kudat Highway (A1) heads north up the west coast to the Kudat Peninsula, via Tuaran, Tamparuli, Kota Belud, Kota Marudu and Pitas. The Kota Kinabalu–Sindumin Highway (A2) leads south towards the Bruneian border, and on to Sarawak, via Penampang, Papar, Beaufort and Sipitang. The Kota Kinabalu–Nabawan Highway (A3) steers southeast into the west-coast hinterland, via Penampang, Tambunan, Keningau and Tenom.

BY BOAT There are daily ferry services between Kota Kinabalu and Labuan, and on to Brunei – see page 102.

GETTING AROUND

ON FOOT The city centre is reasonably compact, though not particularly pedestrian-friendly with its sometimes narrow, messy pavements and chaotic traffic. Watch out at crossings, as cars tend to fly through them. Poorly lit, less-frequented areas well back from the waterfront are best avoided at night.

BY CAR The city centre is not hire-car friendly, with its disorderly, congested layout. For sightseeing beyond the CBD, however, a car is definitely handy. Sabah Tourism (*www.sabahtourism.com*) provides links to all **car-rental** companies statewide on their website.

🚗 **Extra Rent A Car** Head office, Lot 31, 1st Floor, Likas Sq Commercial Centre; ☎088 218160; also a desk at the Tune Hotel, 1 Borneo Hypermall; e admin@e-erac-online.com; www.e-erac-online.com. Highly recommended, established 1991.

🚗 **Kinabalu Heritage Tours & Car Rental** Lot E-2-7, 2nd Floor, Block E, Tanjung Aru Plaza, Jalan Mat Salleh; ☎088 318311; e info@sabahborneotours.net; www.sabahborneotours.net

🚗 **Kinabalu Rent A Car** 1st Floor, Kompleks Karamunsing; ☎088 232602; e jose_loh@

kinabalurac.com.my; www.kinabalurac.com.my

🚗 **KK Leisure Tour & Rent A Car** Lot 7, Block A, 1st Floor, Asia City, Jln Kampung Air 2; ☎088 234607; also a desk at KKIA, Terminal 1; ☎088 413550; e info@malaysiatour2u.com; www.malaysiatour2u.com

🚗 **KMT Global Rent A Car** KKIA arrivals level, Terminal 1; e info@kmtglobalrentacar.com; www.kmtglobalrentacar.com; also a city branch at Wisma Merdeka, Lot G02, Ground Floor; ☎088 223022

BY TAXI Taxis are generally cheap and plentiful, though fares vary, as they are largely unregulated. The only officially set fare (and thus meters officially not used), is the

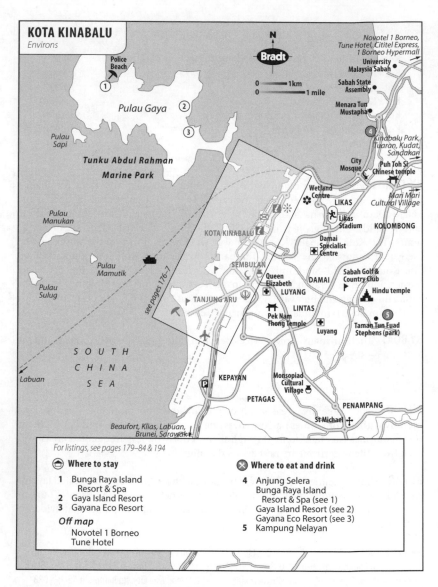

For listings, see pages 179–84 & 194

KOTA KINABALU
Environs

N

Bradt

0 ━━━ 1km
0 ━━━ 1 mile

Novotel 1 Borneo,
Tune Hotel, Cititel Express,
1 Borneo Hypermall

University
Malaysia Sabah

Sabah State
Assembly

Menara Tun
Mustapha

Police
Beach

Pulau Gaya (2)

(3)

Kinabalu Park,
Tuaran, Kudat,
Sandakan

*Pulau
Sapi*

City
Mosque

Puh Toh Si
Chinese temple

*Tunku Abdul Rahman
Marine Park*

Wetland
Centre

LIKAS

Mari Mari
Cultural Village

*Pulau
Manukan*

Likas
Stadium

KOLOMBONG

KOTA KINABALU

Damai
Specialist
Centre

*Pulau
Mamutik*

SEMBULAN

Sabah Golf &
Country Club

*Pulau
Sulug*

Queen
Elizabeth

DAMAI

LUYANG

Hindu temple

TANJUNG ARU

LINTAS

Pek Nam
Thong Temple

Luyang

Taman Tun Fuad
Stephens (park)

S O U T H
C H I N A
S E A

Labuan

KEPAYAN

Monsopiad
Cultural
Village

PETAGAS

PENAMPANG

St Michael

*Beaufort, Klias, Labuan,
Brunei, Sarawak*

see pages 176–7

Where to stay

1 Bunga Raya Island
  Resort & Spa
2 Gaya Island Resort
3 Gayana Eco Resort

Off map
  Novotel 1 Borneo
  Tune Hotel

Where to eat and drink

4 Anjung Selera
  Bunga Raya Island
  Resort & Spa (see 1)
  Gaya Island Resort (see 2)
  Gayana Eco Resort (see 3)
5 Kampung Nelayan

airport to the city. Outside of that, there are reports of unscrupulous practices. Some vehicles are not even equipped with meters. Fix the fare before you hop aboard! RM5–10 is a fair price for inner-city trips; double that at night. There are several ranks in the city: opposite the Hyatt Hotel on Jalan Datuk Salleh Sulong [177 G1]; at the post office on Jalan Tun Razak [177 F2]; and outside Centre Point shopping centre [176 E2]. A long-distance taxi station for trips to places such as Mount Kinabalu is located alongside the long-distance bus station at Padang Merdeka (Merdeka Field) [177 F2].

BY BUS With four different bus terminals, it's not always clear which one you should be using. Drop by Sabah Tourism (see page 175) for an updated list of departure terminals and destinations, schedules and prices.

Wawasan Bus Terminal [176 D2] (*corner Jln Tun Fuad Stephens & Jln Kemajuan*)
The main minibus depot is at Wawasan Plaza, at the south end of the waterfront. Buses
from here serve the city and outskirts and cost RM2–4. This is also where minibuses
serving the airport depart and arrive. They leave when all seats are taken, and are
marked with a route number, corresponding to destinations listed at the station.

City Park Terminal [177 F2] (*in front of city hall, Jln Pantai*) Buses to and from
Wawasan Plaza stop along the waterfront stretch of Jalan Tun Razak, and past the
city hall, court house and post office. Mid-distance buses for mostly south-of-the-
city destinations such as Beaufort, Kuala Penyu, Sipitang and Menumbok (for
Labauan Island ferries) also leave from here, as do long-distance coaches for Lawas,
Limbang, Brunei and Miri.

Pandang Bus Terminal [177 F2] Also known as the Merdeka Field Bus
Terminal, this chaotic station near the Merdeka sports field (Padang Merdeka),
serves Gunung Kinabalu National Park, and southern and northern Sabah. Air-
conditioned express buses, minibuses and vans head to Kundasang and Ranau via
Gunung Kinabalu National Park, as well as to Papar, Beaufort, Tenom, Keningau
and Tambunan. Northern destinations include Tamparuli, Tuaran, Kota Belud,
Kota Marudu, Kudat and Pitas.

City North Bus Terminal [177 H3] Located in the northern suburb of
Inanam, the city's biggest bus terminal is the hub for long-distance express buses,
predominantly to the east coast. Destinations include Sandakan, Lahad Datu,
Kunak, Tawau and Semporna. The journey to Sandakan takes about eight hours,
passing by Gunung Kinabalu National Park and Ranau. Minibuses link the city
with Inanam. Be prepared for ticket hustlers outside this station.

BY RAIL Sabah State Railway operates the only railway in Borneo, a 134km line
from Tanjung Aru (just south of Kota Kinabalu) to Tenom. Known by locals as
'the slowest train in the world', it takes three hours to cover the 93km to Beaufort
and another three hours to Tenom, after a lengthy stopover. The journey via Papar
and Beaufort is more a scenic tourist attraction than a viable means of public
transport. Schedules plus a distance/fare grid are available online (*www.sabah.gov.
my/railway*). The station is near the airport on Jalan Kepayan [176 A2] and there are
four trains each day. If you are considering doing the whole trip through to Tenom,
think of doing it in two stages with a stay over in Beaufort.

BY BOAT The jetty and ferry terminals lie on the northern edge of the waterfront
at Jesselton Point [177 H1]. Boats leave here to the islands of the Tunku Abdul
Rahman Marine Park, as well as to Labuan (see pages 220–1). There is a terminal fee
for all passengers of RM7.20 for adults and RM3.60 for children under 12. Various
tickets for one, two, three or four islands cost from RM20 to RM50; about 50%
less for children. The trip takes 15–20 minutes, weather dependent – the boarding
passes warn passengers to be prepared to get wet 'without complaining'!

TOURIST INFORMATION

**ℹ Sabah Tourism Board & Tourism
Information Office** [177 G2] 51 Jln Gaya;
☏ 088 212121

ℹ Sabah Tourist Guide Association (STGA) [177
G2] Lot 128, 1st Floor, Wisma Sabah; ☏ 088 242990;
e sabah_stga@hotmail.com; www.stga.com.my

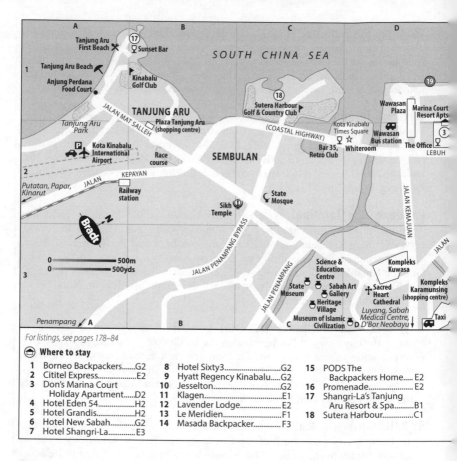

For listings, see pages 178–84

🛏 **Where to stay**

1	Borneo Backpackers.......G2	8	Hotel Sixty3............................G2	15	PODS The
2	Cititel Express...................E2	9	Hyatt Regency Kinabalu....G2		Backpackers Home..... E2
3	Don's Marina Court	10	Jesselton.................................G2	16	Promenade........................ E2
	Holiday Apartment.....D2	11	Klagen......................................E1	17	Shangri-La's Tanjung
4	Hotel Eden 54..................H2	12	Lavender Lodge.....................E2		Aru Resort & Spa..........B1
5	Hotel Grandis...................H2	13	Le Meridien...........................F1	18	Sutera Harbour................C1
6	Hotel New Sabah.............G2	14	Masada Backpacker..............F3		
7	Hotel Shangri-La..............E3				

ℹ **Tourism Malaysia** [177 E2] Sabah office, Lot 107, Ground Floor, Block 1, Lorong Api-Api 1 (in the Api-Api Centre); 📞088 248698; e enquiries@ tourism.gov.my; www.tourism.gov.my

🏠 **WHERE TO STAY** *Maps, pages 174 and 176–7*

Jalan Tun Fuad Stephens, which faces the waterfront promenade, is traditionally home to luxury and upmarket hotels, but lately a flourish of very competitively priced boutique budget to mid-range hotels have sprung up here. Shoestring hotels and hostels are concentrated around Jalan Pantai and Jalan Haji Saman. For those who prefer not to stay in the city, but still within easy reach, see page 192.

HOTELS Constant evolution – that is the current state of especially the **budget** to **mid-range** hotel industry in KK (whereas the **luxury** scene is little changed in terms of the key players). New hotels are opening quickly in response to market demand for more beds, but others are disappearing from the scene just as fast, either closing, or being left behind because of their tawdry service, appalling lack of cleanliness and a make-a-buck-quick mentality. These things do not wash in the modern world of savvy global travellers, whether budget- or luxury-conscious. The reshuffles will likely continue, for the city still has a lot of hotel-operating kudos to earn. Established hotels are also being

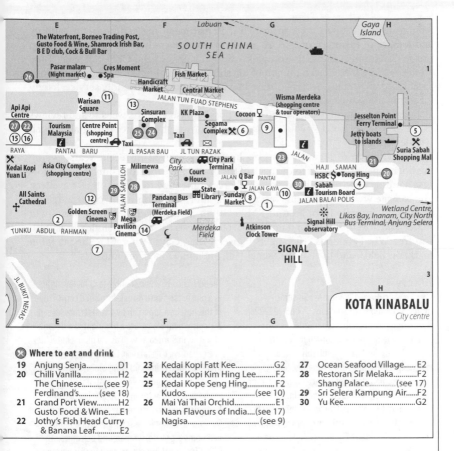

SOUTH CHINA SEA

Labuan

Gaya Island

The Waterfront, Borneo Trading Post,
Gusto Food & Wine, Shamrock Irish Bar,
B E D club, Cock & Bull Bar

Pasar malam
(Night market)
Cres Moment
Spa

Fish Market

26

Handicraft
Market
Central Market

Api Api
Centre

Warisan
Square
11

13

Sinsuran
Complex

KK Plaza

JALAN TUN FUAD STEPHENS

Cocoon

Wisma Merdeka
(shopping centre
& tour operators)

Jesselton Point
Ferry Terminal

27 22
15 16

Tourism
Malaysia

Centre Point
(shopping
centre)
25 24

Taxi

Segama
Complex
6

9

Jetty boats
to islands
5

Suria Sabah
Shopping Mall

RAYA   PANTAI   BARU

JL PASAR BAU

JL TUN RAZAK

JALAN

Kedai Kopi
Yuan Li

Asia City Complex
(shopping centre)

Milimewa

City
Park

City Park
Terminal

23

HAJI   SAMAN

HSBC $ Tong Hing

21

2

All Saints
Cathedral

12

Court
House

JALAN Q Bar PANTAI

Sabah
Tourism Board

30

4

20

Golden Screen
Cinema
2

JALAN SAPULOH

28

State
Library
Pandang Bus
Terminal
(Merdeka Field)

Sunday
Market

JALAN GAYA

8

10

JALAN BALAI POLIS

Wetland Centre,
Likas Bay, Inanam, City North
Bus Terminal, Anjung Selera

TUNKU ABDUL RAHMAN

Mega
Pavilion
Cinema
14

Merdeka
Field

Atkinson
Clock Tower

Signal Hill
observatory

7

SIGNAL
HILL

JL BUKIT NEHAS

KOTA KINABALU
City centre

Where to eat and drink

19	Anjung Senja...............D1	23	Kedai Kopi Fatt Kee...................G2	27	Ocean Seafood Village...... E2
20	Chilli Vanilla...............H2	24	Kedai Kopi Kim Hing Lee............F2	28	Restoran Sir Melaka.............F2
	The Chinese...........(see 9)	25	Kedai Kope Seng Hing............F2		Shang Palace.............(see 17)
	Ferdinand's..........(see 18)		Kudos....................................(see 10)	29	Sri Selera Kampung Air......F2
21	Grand Port View...........H2	26	Mai Yai Thai Orchid....................E1	30	Yu Kee....................................G2
	Gusto Food & Wine......E1		Naan Flavours of India....(see 17)		
22	Jothy's Fish Head Curry		Nagisa....................................(see 9)		
	& Banana Leaf.............E2				

pushed out by the competition, as a few bright young stars show the way to traveller satisfaction.

The city's many budget-priced hotels (see page 180) are classified locally as one-star. In reality, they vary too much in price and quality to be lumped together under a single rating. Some have very ordinary rooms at shoestring prices, yet good-value suites at budget prices. Others offer deluxe rooms at budget prices, and have services and facilities (coffee shops, restaurants, etc) befitting a higher-level establishment. The earth tremors in the budget-sector landscape are astounding in every sense. Exciting if they reap positive change and improvements, as opposed to just newness, scary for what it says about the serious shortfalls in quality of the existing offer – and even scarier for those constantly being swallowed up by the upheaval! Aside from the listings on page 180, a couple of additional untested ones you may want to investigate for yourself are **Horizon Hotel** (*www.horizonhotelsabah.com*) and **Dreamtel** (*www.dreamtel. my*), both centrally located.

Cheaper still, are usually star-less **shoestring hotels** (see page 180). The best you can hope for in this category will be a clean, modern and secure hotel with friendly staff, air conditioning, satellite television, efficient showers, and fridges. Price-wise, rooms cost on average under RM100, though fall as low as RM50 for a single/double. Some will offer family rooms for RM100–150, and there is usually the choice of 'upgrading' to a superior room, which may just mean the addition of a bathtub, and a piece of furniture or two. A couple of newcomers have or are springing up in the developing Asia City Kompleks shopping area of the CBD. AirAsia's Tune Hotels is something of a champion of the shoestring quality cause. The concept of a '5-star bed for 1-star price' is bolstered by 24-hour security, friendly service, handy locations and power showers.

If you are really after shoestring value, possibly also visit the website and reviews of the new **1 City Hotel** (*www.1cityhotel.com*), for which I cannot personally vouch – reviews waver.

A new bunch of forward-thinking **hostels** has arrived in recent years, edging mediocre operators out or to the back of the pack. I have included only those I know first hand or which have been personally recommended to me by other travellers. The website www.hostelworld.com provides information on many other lodgings, which vary in price from around RM20–30 for a dorm bed, RM60–80 for a twin share, and RM100–150 for family quarters. The tariff often includes breakfast, and free Wi-Fi abounds. The streets between Jalan Gaya (where the Sunday *tamu* market is held), and the base of Signal Hill, are home to a hive of hostels.

Luxury

🏠 **Le Meridien** (306 rooms) Sinsuran Complex, Jln Tun Fuad Stephens; 📞 088 322222; e lemeridien.kotakinabalu@lemeridien. com; www.lemeridienkotakinablau.com. My impression of this hotel is probably as dated as my experience of it, unfortunately. Smart, black-uniformed staff, yet service swinging from personal to poor, & cigarette smoke in the lobby have lingered in my mind for years since my stay. It seems things have massively improved under the current direction of hotel general manager, Fiona Hagan, Starwood's former regional sales & marketing director in Asia – also a coup for sexual equality in Sabah's hotel industry. Reports of enthusiastic & friendly staff are now common, with service befitting the buzzing, brilliantly central location & elegant, commodious public spaces & rooms. The sea change has brought repeat awards, including finalist as Malaysia's Leading Hotel in the 2013 World Travel Awards, TripAdvisor Certificate of Excellence Awards, & Traveler's Choice. Great deals for the Club Lounge/12th-floor rooms & suites – 42–84m²; sea views, lounge access, free Wi-Fi & b/fast from RM699/£132 a double. High-speed internet access & Wi-Fi in public areas. Fitness centre, steam bath, sauna & pool. That said, complaints sadly continue of cigarette-smelling non-smoking rooms. **$$$$$**

🏠 **Shangri-La's Tanjung Aru Resort & Spa** (492 rooms) 20 Jln Aru, Tanjung Aru (3km south of the city centre); 📞 088 327888; e tah@ shangri-la.com; www.shangri-la.com. My nights in a plush, turquoise & teak-furnished corner suite of this hotel, wrapped up by a vast terrace, ocean & tropical flora views, are a highlight of a decade of travels in Borneo as well as my global hotel life. The expansive coastal resort has 2 wings – the more luxurious Kinabalu Wing rooms have South China Sea & mountain views, elaborate furnishings in ebony, cherry & coconut woods, tapestries & ethnic artworks inspired by local vegetation. Sumptuous suites have separate sitting rooms, bedrooms & private, wraparound balconies. The 47m² Tanjung Wing rooms, each with a balcony, overlook the sea & flourishing gardens. Recent renovations have capped off the Kinabalu Wing with the Kinabalu Club. Its ultra-luxury rooms include personal check in-&-out, lounge access, complimentary beverages & bites, executive desks & other high-tech notes. A hotel's consistency of quality is largely determined by its management, & as often, the Shangri-La group ensures the sublime setting is matched by top-notch facilities, food & service (which frequently rake in Condé Nast Traveller & Smarttravelasia.com awards for top Asian resorts). The group also shows more than middling green commitment, with many measures for reduction of waste emissions. B/fast in the sweeping garden-&-sea-fronted Café TATU is a smorgasbord of Malay, Indian, Chinese & European tastes. Lovely breezy lobby area & bar, excellent spa, golf course, gym & entertainment facilities. The hotel's Sunset Bar lives up to its name & is undoubtedly one of the best places in KK to see this spectacle, in-house guest or not. (For details of the highly commendable Shang Palace Restaurant, see page 182.) $$$$$

🏠 **Sutera Harbour** (956 rooms) 1 Sutera Harbour Bd; ☎ 088 318888; e sutera@ suteraharbour.com.my; www.suteraharbour. com.my. A Disneyesque-cum-Dallas mega-resort, facilities here are second to none: glitzy restaurants, private marina with Marina Club & Kiddies Club, Olympic-size swimming pool, golf course, live entertainment & suites with marble-lined bathrooms & balconies. If you don't think size matched with sizzle & style is everything, it may not be your cup of tea. Spread over 150ha adjacent to the city, its distinct Pacific Sutera & Magellan Sutera wings are linked up by a shuttle service. The first is more business-oriented & calm; the second dedicated to luxury & family leisure. Between them, there is a plethora of dining choices, from dressy Chinese & Italian restaurants to bright, breezy family-oriented brasseries, pool bars, DJ clubs & lobby lounges. Surprisingly boring b/fast spread & slow Wi-Fi are repeat letdowns, however. The executive Pacific Club rooms & suites include personalised check-in, prime sea-views & lounge access. $$$$$

🏠 **Hyatt Regency Kinabalu** (288 rooms) Jln Datuk Salleh Sulong; ☎ 088 221234; e reservation. hrkinabalu@hyattintl.com; www.kinabalu. regency.hyatt.com. Hard-to-beat waterfront location, next door to Wisma Merdeka. The large, luxurious rooms have urbane furnishings, including smart though predictable 'artworks'. The 45m² sea view & club rooms are decked with ethnic-hued paintings & beige furnishings, & offer access to a private lounge. Good business & meeting facilities, gym & pool & popular entertainment outlets. Both the Chinese & Japanese restaurants are excellent (see page 182). Great-value deals on booking.com & other sites can reap mid-range prices on deluxe double & club rooms. $$$$$–$$$

Mid range

🏠 **Hotel Grandis** (188 rooms) Suria Sabah Shopping Mall, 1 Jln Tun Fuad Stephens; ☎ 088 522888; e info@hotelgrandis.com; www. hotelgrandis.com. In KK's newest mall on the main waterfront stretch, a business & leisure hotel (with meetings facilities, pool & gym, café, rooftop bar & piano lounge), LED TVs, safes, power showers & supposedly high-speed internet (a chronic problem

in Borneo). It's named after the *Ascidieria grandis* – an endemic Mount Kinabalu orchid. Room rates online are well below (30–40%) 'published' rates: a superior room for 2 from RM318 with b/fast as opposed to RM600; family rooms RM539 instead of RM800. The suite offerings are capped off by 150m2 premier suites – from RM1,288 online compared with the published rate of RM2,500. $$$ (suites $$$$)

🏠 **Hotel Shangri-La** (121 rooms) 75 Bandaran Berjaya; ☎ 088 212800; e rsvn@ kkshang.com; www.kkshang.com.my. Nothing to do with the famous Shangri-La brand, & many confuse them apparently when booking, which comes as a bit of a shock. This is a solid upper-mid range independent hotel, in presentation & services. Spacious, well-furnished, bright AC rooms with satellite TV, fridge & minibar & free internet, buffet b/fast in bright coffeehouse, decent gym & nice outdoor pool & relaxation area. Located away from the waterfront, but close to shopping centres, banks, long-distance bus terminal & restaurants of the SEDCO Sq area. Good-value deals include B&B for 2. Round-trip airport transfer for RM20 pp (07.00–17.00) to RM40 pp (17.00–07.00). Improved website needs some menu fine-tuning. $$$ (suites $$$$–$$$$$)

🏠 **Klagen Hotel** (208 rooms) Ground Floor, Block D, Warisan Sq, Jln Tun Fuad Stephen; ☎ 088 488908; e enquiry@theklagan.com; www. theklagan.com. Just as the Mercure Waterfront morphed in 2012 to the Imperial International, the latter quickly disappeared & has re-emerged in a slightly new skin. Design furniture pieces, added high tech & colour, good beds, free Wi-Fi, daily papers, minibar & safe. Standard, deluxe, family & suite rooms. $$ (suites $$$$)

🏠 **Novotel 1 Borneo** (266 rooms) 1 Borneo Hypermall, Jln Sulaman Highway (7km north of Kota Kinabalu); ☎ 088 529888; e info@ novotel1borneo.com; www.novotel.com. Located in Sabah's largest shopping centre, within a 20min drive of the airport, this hotel has spacious rooms starting at budget price deals through to top-dollar luxury suites. Restaurant & bar, high-speed paying internet, spa & meeting facilities for up to 1,200. 96 non-smoking rooms – about 30% – is a good indication of the public health v smoker's rights situation in the majority of Borneo hotels, even those international brands, whose overseas affiliates count many non-smoking properties.

Location chosen primarily by shopping tourists. **$$** (suites **$$$$**)

🏠 **Promenade Hotel** (451 rooms) Lorong Api-Api 3, Api-Api Centre; 📞 088 265555; e enquiry@promenade.com.my; www.promenade.com.my. Right in the commercial thick of things, this has long had a name as the best 4-star business hotel in the town centre, with good service & dining, elegant furnishings, gym & pool. Reviews started getting a bit patchy, but major renovations seem to be lifting them again. Rooms range from standard 25m² to 50m² executive suites with sea views; all have mod sleek black/white furnishings, wool carpets, internet & tea-/coffee-making facilities. Despite upgrades, a traditional feel reigns, with staff dressed in Kadazan-like, bold embroidered jackets & tunics. Internet special deals regularly available. Little price difference between standard & deluxe double rooms – both fall in the budget price bracket. **$$$$–$$**

🏠 **Jesselton Hotel** (32 rooms) 69 Jln Gaya; 📞 088 223333; e reservation@jesseltonhotel.com; www.jesseltonhotel.com. At last this hotel has come out of the dark ages of technology with a website – all the time retaining its Old-World charm! Opened in 1954 when Sabah was still British North Borneo, it promises guests the personalised service & impeccable attention to detail that delighted such illustrious colonial-era guests as Lady Mountbatten. Held in high esteem among business clientele, it has good service & a financial district location. Rates include b/fast & airport transfer. **$$$–$$**

Budget

🏠 **Cititel Express** (275 rooms) Jln Singgah Mata 1; 📞 088 521188 (hotel); 088 521311 (restaurant); e resvnbki@cititelexpress.com or infobki@cititelexpress.com; www.cititelexpress.com. Comfortable, clean, basic, friendly – these are the most common reports of this 2011-opened hotel. A 10min walk from downtown, with bright-coloured interiors, smiling staff, free parking, free Wi-Fi in public areas & rooms. Key cards, satellite TV, safes, tea- & coffee-making facilities in standard & superior rooms & 40m² studios. Complaints made of the small & windowless standard rooms – studios much better. **$$$–$$**

🏠 **Hotel Sixty3** (100 rooms) 63 Jln Gaya; 📞 088 212663; e stay@hotelsixty3.com; www.hotelsixty3.com. Another shooting-star budget

hotel in location-hot Gaya St. Since opening in 2014, it already rubs shoulders with top luxury hotels in user review ratings… For how long? Let's hope it lasts. My pessimism stems from seeing several highly lauded 'boutique budgets' born – then gone – since the previous edition of this guidebook. That's extremely short-lived compared with hotel industry norms in more mature markets. Though I am yet to sample Hotel Sixty3 for myself, its success is clearly based on a quality-price mix – 'unbeatable' according to a few. Clean, friendly, city-centre location – a flashpacker's dream. Also family rooms & 67m² suites sleeping 4.

The website is trying hard to be funky, but needs some technical fine-tuning. **$$$–$$** executive deluxe rooms & suites

🏠 **Hotel Eden54** (23 rooms) 54 Jln Gaya; 📞 088 266054; e stay@eden54.com; www.eden54.com. Described by 1 traveller as big 'bang for buck', this centrally located hotel has shot to the top of TripAdvisor's charts since opening in 2011, as overall No 2 hotel after Shangri-La's Rasa Ria Resort An impressive performance which comes down to its budget-chic attitude, self-declared 'luxury for less' urban style – spelt out in a tan, white & wooden palette – & astute service mentality. Stylish guestroom & studio interiors, free Wi-Fi, satellite TV, AC, complimentary water, guest lounge, kitchenette & common fridges. **$$**

Shoestring

🏠 **Hotel New Sabah** (25 rooms) Lot 3&4, Block A, Jln Pedas, Segama Complex; 📞 088 224590/873; e hotelnewsabah@yahoo.com; http://hotelnewsabah.showroom.sabahexpress.com; 'Open since 1977' & finally a website! Or rather, an online 'showroom' as the hotel describes it (& its rooms 'products'). Majority single bedrooms, a handful of doubles, all with queen-size bed, AC, Astro TV & bathrooms with hot shower. **$**

🏠 **Tune Hotel** (165 rooms) 1 Borneo Hypermall, Jln Suliman; 📞 03 7962 5888; e hotelnewsabah@yahoo.com. enquiry@tunehotels.com; www.tunehotels.com. Like a white & red Meccano block, AirAsia's minimalist budget hotel concept arrived in Kota Kinabalu in 2011, at Malaysia's largest hyper-mall – which has since become a destination in itself for many shopping travellers – not for nature & cultural trippers. For shoppers, this is a real bargain! For that, you get a clean room & efficient service –

absolutely no frills – even towels & toiletries are purchasable add-ons. Check-in is after 14.00, check-out at 10.00. The hotel offers a free shuttle service to the city centre. **$**

Hostels

🏠 **Borneo Backpackers** Jln Balai Polis; ☎088 234009; www.borneobackpackers.com. Newly run by Sticky Rice Travel & undergoing numerous upgrades perhaps will help this hostel regain its former accolades. 4-/6-/10-bed dorms, plus private rooms, free Wi-Fi, laundry, lounge & roof garden deck, fan & AC. The hostel's basement café-cum-wartime museum has become a bit of a landmark, loved for its yesteryear ambience. Styled as a traditional post-war coffee shop, the Borneo 1945 Museum Kopitiam is decked with copies of war memorial plaques, photos of 'unsung' wartime heroes – Australian & British – & antique furniture. **$**

🏠 **Lavender Lodge** No 6, Jln Laiman Diki, Kg Air; ☎088 217119; e lavend07@streamyx. com; www.lavenderlodge.com.my. Located in the Kampung Air zone, a 10min walk from the waterfront, the clean, comfortable hostel has AC dorm rooms, doubles, twin sharing & family rooms with bathrooms, free Wi-Fi & 24hr reception. **$**

🏠 **Masada Backpacker** No 9, 1st Floor, Jln Masjid Lama; ☎088 234954; e hotelnewsabah@ yahoo.com. masadabackpacker@gmail.com; www. masadabackpacker.com. 10mins' walk from the Gaya St market, Padang Merdeka bus terminal & the waterfront, the single, double & family rooms are topped off by common lounge & dining areas, free Wi-Fi & tea/coffee. The hostel, which sleeps 33, gets its name from an interesting play on the Malaysian expression *emas ada*, 'there is gold'. **$**

🏠 **PODS The Backpackers Home** 1-1-11, 1st Floor, Api-Api Centre, Jln Centre Point; ☎088 287113; e hotelnewsabah@yahoo. com. admin-kk@podsbackpacker.com; www. podsbackpacker.com. 'rest. assured' is the first thing I see on the website. Kind of cute – & confident. Following on from the first PODS in Kuala Lumpur, the 2nd PODS opened in KK in late 2014. It's new & making ripples. Perky in spirit as name, matched with its lime-green décor, cultural & digitally connected spirit. Simple double 'pod' rooms with mattresses on floor slats & small cupboards plus 6-bed bunkrooms – all with personal power/USB outlets & lockers. By most reports, great rates, very clean & secure with unexpected frills such as budget-version power showers. **$**

SERVICED APARTMENTS The proliferation of privately owned apartments for rent both via Airbnb and direct by owners on blogs and websites has clearly caused some confusion over the ID of certain accommodations in TripAdvisor and other reviews. The mix up no doubt owes to similarities in name and location (eg: Marina Court Resort). I have not tried any of the relatively new condos, but am dubious about the state of most of them. Note some apartments located in Marina Court currently boast sea views. According to Don from Don's place or rather Don's Condo, those views will soon be blocked out by a new waterfront hotel. This also means possible noise during stays throughout 2015 at least.

🏠 **Don's Marina Court Holiday Apartment** Unit B-01-04, 1st Floor, Block B, Marina Court Resort Condo, Api-Api Centre, off Lorong Api-Api 2; e don@marinacourt-sabah. com or marinacourt@outlook.com; http:// marinacourt-sabah.blogspot.com. 3-bed self-catering apartment in near-waterfront resort condominium. AC, lounge with TV & DVD, & well-equipped kitchen. With 2 pools, a gym, squash court, children's play area, lift, 24hr security, parking & Wi-Fi (RM10/24hrs) at residents' disposal, this represents a good-value alternative to hotels with a mid-range price tag. Balcony overlooks swimming pool. Book direct with owner. Airport pickup RM40 for up to 4; RM85 for 5–6. **$$$**

5

✖ **WHERE TO EAT AND DRINK** *Maps, pages 174 and 176–7*

While there are many food highlights to discover in Kota Kinabalu, there are also some things to watch out for. Flashy décor doesn't always mean good food, so don't look for shiny counters and dozens of Western faces as signs of a good place to eat. It is often the less polished places that serve the best food, at the best value. You can get a good meal of noodles with meat or seafood for as little as RM6.

RESTAURANTS Around 80–90% of KK's top restaurants appear to be of the international, European or hotel variety. As a true 'global gourmet' – that is someone who eats exclusively and voraciously local – I urge you to go nomad, get authentic, and eat in the street as much as possible. Do away with the frills and air-conditioning occasionally for the sake of some incredibly cheap and delicious Malaysian food – and buzzing local atmosphere. This does not mean snubbing hotel restaurants, as some offer among the best regional food on their smorgasbords. For those who are after (to quote one reviewer) 'a slice of Western food paradise' in KK, current in-places to try include **Chilli Vanilla** (*35 Jln Haji Saman*), **Kudos** at the Jesselton Hotel [177 H2] (*69 Jln Gaya*), and **Gusto Food & Wine** on the Waterfront [177 H2] (*Lot 17*).

Upmarket

✗ **Naan Flavours of India** Level 1, Garden Wing, Shangri-La Rasa Ria Resort, Pantai Dalit Beach, Tuaran; ☎088 797888; www.shangri-la. com; ⏱ 18.30–22.30. Excellent Indian food, from northern flavours to spicy Goa & Kerala, refined atmosphere, UK prices. Menu features seafood, meat & veg (also vegetarian set menus – unfortunately for min 2 diners), naan & tandoori breads, clay-oven specials, lassis & children's serves ('Little Gandhi'). Non-smoking policy. $$$$

✗ **The Chinese Restaurant** Hyatt Regency, Jln Datuk Salleh Sulong; ☎088 221234; www. kinabalu.regency.hyatt.com. The English name might not seem very original, but the Chinese calligraphy version rhymes with Hyatt! A favourite with local & visiting VIPs & business milieu, most dishes on the 9-page menu are Canton & Szechuan served in a classical Chinese-Empire setting of miniature teapots & hand paintings. Steamboats Wed & Sat nights. Meat, seafood, vegetable & noodle dishes served sizzling, spicy or wok-fried; signature dish Peking Duck; delicious vegetarian silken tofu, wok & clay-pot choices. $$$$

✗ **Ferdinand's Restaurant** Level 2, Magellan Sutera Resort, Sutera Harbour Bd; ☎088 318888; www.suteraharbour.com.my; ⏱ 18.00–23.00 daily. For those after candlelight romanticism & European fine dining, locals & foreigners appreciate the chance to eat excellent Italian food in a formal atmosphere, with stunning views & silver service. Clearly atmosphere levels have also soared here as the restaurant becomes busier. Pretensions persist in the alienating price tags

for wine, with nothing less than RM100/US$30. $$$$

✗ **Nagisa Restaurant** Hyatt Regency, Jln Datuk Salleh Sulong; ☎088 221234; www.kinabalu. regency.hyatt.com. Best Japanese food in Borneo, served from open kitchen in traditional-turned-modern décor of dark wooden tables & lattice screens. With set dinner menus, specials & à la carte dishes with European & New-World wines. Must-tries include *gindara* (cod fish) teriyaki & black sesame custard. Dining views of the sun setting over the South China Sea explain the restaurant's name: 'waterside'. The VIP rooms & sushi counter are perfect for solo diners. $$$$

✗ **Shang Palace** Ground Floor, Shangri-La Tanung Aru Resort, 20 Jln Aru, Tanjung Aru; ☎088 327888; www.shangri-la.com. Traditional food & elegant atmosphere. You can breakfast, lunch or dine on the renowned dim sum & sample other menu specials, from fried minced seafood salad to Shenzhen crispy roasted goose & deep-fried tempura mango ice cream. $$$$

Mid range

✗ **Grand Port View** Jln Tun Fuad Stephens (between the Customs Department & Marine Police, by Jesselton Point ferry terminal); ☎088 538178; ⏱ lunch & dinner. Along the redeveloping Jesselton Point Waterfront area. An AC, more upmarket version of Ocean Seafood, with more of a business clientele. $$$

✗ **Kampung Nelayan Restaurant** Taman Tun Fuad (15mins' drive east of town); ☎088 231003/5; ⏱ 11.30–14.00 & 18.30–23.00; dance performance 19.45–20.45. It may well be a tour-group magnet, but a special evening can be had at this antiquated floating 'seafood market restaurant' which opens on to the sea. Diners are treated to a cultural dance performance, seafood, & Chinese & Malay dishes (including many vegetarian options). Private VIP rooms have AC, karaoke, couch & washroom, though a less watery atmosphere. $$$

✗ **Mai Yai Thai Orchid** Lot 13, The Waterfront; ☏088 234841; ⏰ noon–22.00 daily. Traditional Thai favourites, lots of veggie choices & a pork-free menu in this simple, open-fronted hut restaurant. $$$

✗ **Ocean Seafood Village** 4 Lorong Api-api 3, Api-Api Centre; ☏088 264701; ⏰ lunch & dinner. Like a theme park of seafood dining, this place is famous countrywide & some see it as a destination in itself. If you don't mind the tour buses rolling into its car park, the food experience is excellent. Crabs, prawns, scallops, oyster & lobster are cooked by the kilo (min 300g) in whatever style you choose. You can pick your preferred catch straight from the eel-filled aquarium at the entrance & eat it in the part open-air (no AC), water-facing dining room. $$$

✗ **Sri Selera Kampung Air** Jln Kampung Air 4 (*next door to Golden Screen Cinemas*); ⏰ 17.00–22.00. In this evening-only complex, you can dine alfresco at a few casual seafood 'restaurants' with open kitchens. Seating up to 1,200 people, it has plenty of atmosphere & can be noisy. There's a rolling roof in case of wet weather. From the array of seafood on display in tanks, you can choose lobster, tiger prawns, elephant tusk clams, squid, crab & fish by weight & have it cooked up on the spot in the style you want – steamed, stir-fried, grilled, etc. Some eateries also have menus with

some meat choices & vegetable accompaniments – jungle ferns, spinach, cauliflower, broccoli. Critics fob the zone off as a tourist haunt, though it also attracts local customers. Its lack of ocean-facing views or other diversions means good seafood is its only selling point, though clearly there has been some major price-creep here over the past few years. **Twin-Sky** is getting good reviews for excellent, fresh, erring on expensive, seafood. **Hua Hing Seafood Restaurant** is another favourite with more reasonable prices. For coconut crab & butter prawns, try **Shuang Tain Seafood**. Prices at the square average RM40–50 pp, though it is cheaper to eat in a group, & alcohol adds a hefty sum to the bill. (Nearby gerai makanan food stalls & kedai makan coffee shop/restaurants provide cheaper options.) $$$

Budget and shoestring

✗ **Restoran Sir Melaka** 9 Jln Laiman Diki, Kampung Air; ☏088 224777; www.srimelaka.com; ⏰ 10.00–21.30 daily. Another inexpensive place for very good Nyonya & Malay dishes, such as the famous Malaysian fish-head curry. $$

✗ **Jothy's Fish Head Curry & Banana Leaf Restaurant** Ground Floor, Api Api Centre; ☏088 261595; www.jothyscurry.com; ⏰ 11.00–22.00 daily. Cheap but good southern Indian grub, in what the owner describes as a 'Karma Sutra setting' (though the place is famously child-friendly!). Many find the food is the highlight & the atmosphere lacking (surely true foodies would much rather that than the reverse). Its namesake dish, fiery hot fish-head curry, is served with a homemade blend of herbs & spices, & with brinjals, tomatoes & lady's fingers. Also popular is biryani fragrant rice served on banana leaf. $

WESTERN-STYLE CAFÉS AND ASIAN BAKERIES For local baked goods sniff out the **Southern Cake Shop** – there's one on Jalan Pantai, near the Sunday market area. The **Coffee Bean & Tea Leaf** have four outlets about town: in Wisma Merdeka, along the Waterfront Esplanade, in Kompleks Damai shopping centre, and in Kompleks Karamunsing. Despite the Westernised style and standardised sandwiches, salads and sweets, these cafés will quell your cravings for Arabica bean espressos and lattes or waffles and scones. Here you can sit and sip peacefully, with free Wi-Fi, then stock up on freshly ground coffee and speciality teas. Prices on the vast drinks menu average RM7–10, while snacks, sandwiches and pastas range from RM10 to RM15.

COFFEE SHOPS (*Kedai kopi* or *Kopi tiam*) Scattered all around the city's streets, and squeezed between shop-lots, coffee shops are open from breakfast through to dinner. At many of them you can down good-quality food and drink for RM5–10.

I have eaten excellent kway teow noodle dishes with prawns for RM3–4 from no-name coffee shops in the Kampung Air zone. Several others are clustered around the Sinsuran Complex, one street back from the waterfront stretch of Jalan Tun Fuad Stephen, on the corner of Jalan Sembilan Belas and Lorong Gomantong. Noodle dishes generally cost RM10 and below.

✕ **Kedai Kopi Fatt Kee** 28 Jln Baku, corner of Jln Haji Saman; ⏲ 11.00–22.00 daily. Not 'Ang's Hotel Restaurant' as wrongly cited in reviews, the budget hotel sits alongside this simple bustling *kedai kopi* – something of a Malay–Chinese hybrid in name & menu. Key dishes are chicken wings in oyster sauce, fish-head curry, tofu-&-minced-pork, pork knuckle, & sweet 'Sabah veggie' – *sayur manis* – a spinach-like veg cooked with oil, garlic, oyster sauce & dried shrimp *belacan* paste.

✕ **Kedai Kopi Kim Hing Lee** Block F, Lot 7, Sinsuran Complex. Good noodles, noodle soup & pork dishes. Renowned for one of Sabah's 'must do' dishes, *sang nyuk mian* – in Hakka this means 'raw meat noodles'. The Sabahan version is pork-based

& served either wet, with thin slices of meat on top of a bed of noodles & greens in a clear soup; or dry *Kon Loh Mee*, with fresh yellow Hokkien noodles, pork slices & leafy greens fried in dark soy sauce, sesame & peanut oil.

✕ **Kedai Kopi Seng Hing** Lot 10, Ground Floor, Sinsuran Complex; ⏲ 07.00–16.00 daily. A good basic noodle house & Chinese restaurant for *tom yam, tuaran mee*, etc.

✕ **Yu Kee** 74 Jln Gaya; ⏲ 16.30–23.00. Famous for its *bak kut the*, the herb & meat hotpot soup (about RM5 a bowl), which has a variety of meats in it. Apparently this dish 'attracts lots of ex-Hong Kong film stars' to the place!

STREET FOOD For quality food on the go, there are food stalls at several places in the city.

Night markets (*pasar malam*) The city's most accessible pasar malam is located on the waterfront, near the handicraft centre [177 F1]. *Gerai makan* food stalls set up here from late afternoon until midnight, serving grilled fish, satays, Malay and Indo-Malay fast (but good!) food. Try the Murtabak. Alongside them are traders selling fresh fruit, fish and vegetables. Another night market with a big choice of food can be found on Jalan Kampung Air, near City Park [177 F2]. Right at the back of town, towards the museum district, the **Kompleks Karamunsing** commercial zone [176 D3] has outdoor evening food stalls serving Malay and Indonesian food.

On the southern end of the waterfront, near the Promenade Hotel, the **Anjung Senja** [176 D1] – 'sunset deck' – is an outdoor feasting area with mostly Malay and Indonesian halal food. The **Anjung Selera** [177 H2], in Likas Bay, has food stalls and tables set up on a headland overlooking the sea.

Beaches Located 3km south of the city (in the direction of the airport), head to **Tanjung Aru Beach** for a beachy night atmosphere. **First Beach**, Tanjung Aru, holds a nightly barbecue where you can select a platter of seafood or meat and have it cooked and served with different sauces. A newly recommended casual restaurant at First Beach is **Sri Tanung Seafood Restaurant** (*Jln Aru;* ⏲ *11.30–14.30 & 16.30–22.30 daily*). Clearly targeting tourists, there are cultural shows of Bajau and Kadazan dance from 19.00 to 20.45 every evening bar Mondays.

SHOPPING-CENTRE EATERIES AND FOOD COURTS
Segama Complex [177 F1] Opposite Wisma Merdeka and crammed with ordinary shop-lots, retailers here include coffee shops and fast-food chains such as KFC.

Suria Sabah [177 H1] On the third floor of KK's newest shopping centre, at Jesselton Point, food-court and cafeteria eats come with water views. There are also plenty of fast-food outlets on the basement floor.

Warisan Square [177 E1] Less authentic than Malaysian food-court grub, this centre caters to international tastes with its cafés and restaurants spread over several floors. At ground level, you will find **Fish & Co** for 'Seafood in a Pan', while **Starbucks, San Francisco Coffee** and **Yoshima Japanese Restaurant** are all on the first floor.

Wisma Merdeka Food Court [177 G2] On the second floor of the landmark Wisma shopping centre in Jalan Tun Razak, there are at least a dozen different stalls. The fantastic range of food includes Malay, Chinese and Indian dishes, noodles, curries and laksas, and one vegetarian stall (**Healthy Vegetarian**). Count on as much as you can eat and drink for under RM12. For ready-made dishes served from *bains-marie*, it is best to arrive between 11.00 and 14.00, when the food is fresh and hot (anytime in shopping centre hours is fine for stalls that cook on the spot). The **Teatime Express** cake shop, located by the entrance, has pork-free pastries and sweets including English-style cakes, Chinese buns, avocado cake and mango puddings.

Anjung Perdana Food Court [176 A1] This food court has under-roof, open-air food kitchens and plastic tables and chairs. Aside from tasty, cheap and authentic food, it is a fun and vibey place to visit at night.

ENTERTAINMENT AND NIGHTLIFE

There's been a shake-up in the nightlife scene since 2012, with a couple of old-timers replaced by newcomers; in a couple of instances, they too have disappeared much quicker than their predecessors. Possibly a sign of a move to more dynamism in choices and quality, the upshot is an increasingly fun night out on the town. A lot of the action, bars and nightclubs exist along The Waterfront strip of Jalan Tun Fuad Stephen. Don't be fooled by the fancy name; the zone opposite Warisan Square is quite a raffish mix of souvenir shop, bar and café by day, yet with some hot clubbing spots. From twilight, the jumbled shop-lot look fades into the watery setting and often resplendent KK sunsets.

A few newer places such as the **Retro Club Pub & Bistro, Whiteroom** and **Bar 35** [all 176 C2] are also located just south of the city at the developing KK Times Square off Jalan Coastal, towards the airport. For a medium-sized city, Kota Kinabalu has a lively nightlife and thriving gay and lesbian scene. If you prefer musical and cultural events to clubbing, the best thing is to check with Sabah Tourism Board (℡ 088 212121; www.sabahtourism.com) for current shows and festivities. During major cultural celebrations, mid- to upper-star hotels organise daily music and dance performances. Drink prices vary between venues (as does the quality of mixed drinks and cocktails): RM13–18 for a beer, RM12–24 for a single shot of spirits, and RM14–29 for a glass of wine. Many bars have happy hours and even 'ladies' nights', serving free drinks to female customers.

♥ **B.E.D** [177 E1] Lot 1A, The Waterfront; ⊕ 20.00–02.00 Mon–Tue, to 03.00 Wed–Sun. 'Do you want to come to BED'... What a great line. B.E.D stands for 'Best Entertainment Destination', & this in the mind of its faithful clientele is just that. The club is a hit for live bands, dance & international DJs. For a mid-party snack, you can always duck out to the waterfront food stalls, open until 23.00, before heading back to party.

♀Cock & Bull [177 E1] Lot 3, Anjung Samudra, The Waterfront, Jalan Tun Fuad Stephen; ☉ 11.00–22.00 daily. A bar & bistro with live bands most nights.

♀Mosaic [177 G2] Jln Datuk Salleh Sulong; ☉ 10.00–23.00 daily. The Hyatt's sleek glass-walled café & wine bar is good for people-watching, with AC & modern dining.

♀Q Bar [177 G2] 15 Jln Gaya; ☉ approx 21.00–01.00 Mon–Thu, 20.00–03.00 Fri–Sat, 21.00–01.00 Sun. Many gay clubbers rave about the décor & friendly staff here. The venue is popular generally among those who like to party. With a DJ regularly on deck, Fri fun takes the form of a legendary crowd-pleasing show by the Q Bar Girls.

♀Shamrock Irish Bar [177 E1] 6 Anjung Samudra, Waterfront Esplanade; ☉ noon–01.00 Mon–Thu & Sun, until 02.00 Fri–Sat. Seafront Irish-themed bar with traditional Kelly-green décor, pool bar, DJ & live bands; serves Kilkenny, Tiger & Guinness draughts, good selection of wines, plus tasty meat stews, chips 'n' peas, burgers & 'Beef & Guinness pies'.

♀Shenanigans Fun Pub [177 G2] Jln Datuk Salleh Sulong; ☉ 17.00–01.00 Mon–Thu, until 02.00 Fri–Sat. The Hyatt's bar/disco is the most established watering hole & party place in the city. Locals come here to spend their savings on extravagantly priced drinks. 'Shani's', as they call it, pulls a mixed crowd, & is popular with the gay crowd.

♀Shenanigans Terrace [177 G2] Jln Datuk Salleh Sulong; ☉ 17.00–01.00 Mon–Thu, until 02.00 Fri–Sat. The calmer face to the fun pub, the seaside & poolside terrace is a great sunset-watching spot over a long, cool drink, if you are not bothered by the live sports screen. BBQ on the last Sat of every month.

♀Sunset Bar [176 B1] 20 Shangri-La, 20 Jln Aru, Tanjung Aru (3km south of city centre); ☉ 14.00–23.00 daily. The namesake sunsets here just keep turning them on spectacularly for the crowds. For the perfect sundowner cocktail or glass of wine, this is the most select & serene outdoor bar location in the city, with prices to match. Tucked on a tiny islet at Shangri-La's Tanjung Aru Resort, sunset falls between 17.30 & 18.30 depending on the time of year. The water-girthed gazebo is crowned by a massive Kadazan-like attap roof (thatched from palm fronds), with seating for 100.

FESTIVALS AND EVENTS

For further details on the following or other cultural celebrations and events, contact Sabah Tourism (e *info@sabahtourism.com*). Also pick up a copy of the bi-monthly Discover Sabah magazine.

TADAU KA'AMATAN (HARVEST FESTIVAL) Celebrations of the Kadazandusun and Murut communities happen during the month of May so look out for dance and other cultural performances at your hotel, or in the streets.

SABAH ART GALLERY During the month of May, watch out for the Patterns and Colours of Sabah, an annual month-long exhibition where craftspeople from Sabah's multi-ethnic communities show new samples of their intricate combinations of patterns and colours in their designs.

THE SABAH DRAGON BOAT RACE A traditional Chinese festival that attracts dragon boat teams from China, Japan, Brunei and Australia during the month of June. It is held at Likas Bay (also the site of Merdeka month – a month-long celebration to celebrate Malaysian independence, from mid-August).

MOONCAKE FESTIVAL Usually held in late September, and known as the mid-autumn festival, it marks the rebellion against the Mongols in 14th-century China and is celebrated with the eating of many moon cakes and with lantern parades.

RAMADAN BAZAAR (Spelt Ramadhan in Malay, as opposed to Ramadan in other societies.) Held sometime around mid-September to mid-October, Muslims fast for a month from sunrise to sunset. Amazing food is served at the sundown Ramadan bazaars held at various locations in Kota Kinabalu and organised by the Kota Kinabalu City Hall.

SHOPPING

HANDICRAFTS Handicrafts Sri Pelancongan [177 F2] (*Lot 4, Ground Floor, Block L, Sinsuran Complex, off Jln Chong Thian Vun;* e *kadaiku@sabathtourism.com*) is owned by Sabah Tourism and sells woven items, tapestries, paintings, books, musical instruments, T-shirts, beads, baskets, bookmarks, souvenirs and locally produced products such as Sabah tea and Tenom coffee.

The **Borneo Trading Post** [177 E1] (*Waterfront precinct, Jln Tun Fuad Stephens; www.borneotradingpost.com*) is an upmarket, online distributor of ethnic goods, with a Monsopiad warrior called 'Borneo Bob' as its mascot.

SHOPPING CENTRES Kota Kinabalu is not yet major high-street territory, but with new developments, the way is being cleared for luxury flagship stores. Glossy, glassy **Suria Sabah Shopping Mall** [177 H2] (*Jln Tun Fuad Stephen, Jesselton Point; www. suriasabah.com.my;* ⊕ *10.00–22.00*) is the new mall addition. Dubbed 'Suria KK' to distinguish it from big-sister Suria KLCC (in Kuala Lumpur City Centre), some 300 shops include the multi-storey department store Metro Jaya, The Times bookstore, and eight-screen GSC Cinemas. For many locals, the city-edge **Karamunsing Complex** [176 D3] (*Jln Nenas, 2km east of the centre;* ⊕ *10.00–22.00*) remains the favourite for clothing, beauty, and IT bargains.

Warisan Square [177 E1] on Jalan Tun Fuad Stephens has more upmarket brands – international, casual couture labels and Asian natural cosmetic brands. Overall, it's a chic shopping mall in a partly glass-roofed pavilion, with arcades of shops to each side (rather than the predominant wall-to-wall, sometimes unattractive and cramped, style of other shopping centres). The **Wisma Merdeka** [177 G2] on Jalan Tun Razak is more down to earth – the second-biggest shopping centre in Sabah has plenty of shops, restaurants and a food court. It is good for electronics and clothes, and many 'buy-one-free-one' offers. **Centre Point** [177 E2] on Lorong Centre Point is the choice for entertainment, electronics and photographic stores. **KK Plaza** [176 D3] on Jalan Lapan Belas is quite stuffy and dowdy, but it has a good hypermarket at basement level, cheap phone/electronic and clothing stores, and is open late.

South of the city centre, **The Asia City Complex** [177 E2] on Jalan Asia City is a shopping centre in progress, with a mix of shop-lots, offices, malls, restaurants, hotels, and clothing and accessory shops. The best supermarket if you want imports, foreign wines and liquor, or if you are pining for Lindt, McVitie's or Walkers Highland Oatcakes, is the **Tong Hing Supermarket** [177 H2] (*55 Jln Gaya;* ⊕ *08.00–22.00*). It also has a nice little Chinese bakery. Nearby, is **Milimewa** [177 F2] (*1 Jln Pantai*), the oldest supermarket chain in the state.

HYPERMALLS The largest mall in Sabah, **1 Borneo**, lies 7km north of the city [174 C1] (*Jln Sulaman Highway; www.1borneo.net*). Its 400 businesses include Malaysian department store Parkson, international- and Asian-brand leisure, food and entertainment outlets, and hotels.

MARKETS The CBD's main foreshore area along Jalan Tun Fuad Stephens is market row. Stretching over half a kilometre, side by side, are the handicraft market, the central market (*pasar besar*) and the fish market. A fresh fruit and fish market, interspersed with tables and chairs, is set up on the water's edge each afternoon opposite Le Meridien Hotel. By evening it transforms into a pasar malam (night market), full of food stalls. The main night market is held around the streets south of City Park. The 'handicraft market' seems to have been renamed as such to obscure the real name: *pasar Filipino*. With its flood of cheap Filipino produce, the large under-cover market has few genuine Sabahan crafts, but is still a vivid place to mingle. The **Sunday market** (also referred to as **Pesta Jalan Gaya** or the **Gaya Street Fair**), is held along Jalan Gaya every Sunday [177 G2] (⊕ *06.00–13.00*). Kota Kinabalu's take on the rural tamu sells remedial herbs, aquarium fish, baskets, bric-a-brac, crafts and potted plants. Refreshments include nasi lemak, all kinds of kuih cakes and coconut juice.

OTHER PRACTICALITIES

Ambulance/police ☎999; police hotline ☎088 221191. There are police stations on Jln Dewan (near the Atkinson Clock Tower) [177 G3] & at the southern end of town, along Jln Kemajuan [off map, 176 D3].

ATM's There are several banking machines around Jalan Gaya, and in shopping centres such as Centre Point.

Currency exchange Money exchanges can be found in major shopping centers including Wisma Merdeka, Suria Sabah and Centre Point, as well as at the airport though the latter outlets are renowned for poorer rates.

GPO/Pejabat Pos Besar Jalan Chong Thein Vun (off Jalan Tun Razak); ⊕ 08.00–16.30 Mon–Fri, 08.00–12.30 Sat.

Hospital Queen Elizabeth Hospital [176 C3] South, direction of airport; ☎088 218166. Public hospital.

Library Sabah State Library [177 F2] Jln Tasik, off Jln Maktab Gaya; ☎088 214828; www.ssl. sabah.gov.my; ⊕ 09.00–18.00 Mon–Fri, 09.00–14.00 Sat–Sun, closed public holidays

Medical centre Sabah Medical Centre Lorong Bersatu, off Jln Damai; ☎088 211333; www. sabahmedicalcentre.com. Private clinic.

WHAT TO SEE AND DO

Crammed between the ocean and hills, the city is concentrated around three main streets, which run parallel and span just a few hundred metres.

Along the waterfront, Jalan Tun Fuad Stephens is the hub of mid- to high-range hotels, shopping plaza and markets. It stretches from the Sutera Harbour area in the south to the Jesselton Point ferry terminal in the north. One block in, Jalan Tun Razak runs by shop-lots and shopping centres, and changes name several times along its course. Hugging closer to the foothills of Signal Hill, Jalan Gaya is a neighbourhood as much as it is a street, encompassing smaller boutique and budget hotels, hostels, banks, restaurants and the Sunday tamu market.

LOOKOUTS AND LANDMARKS
Signal Hill [177 G3] Signal Hill is the green belt that swathes Kota Kinabalu, and forms a leafy backdrop to the city. The view from the Signal Hill observatory takes in the entire city, coast and islands. Below, at Jalan Gaya 51, you can see the **Sabah Tourism building** [177 G2], dating to 1916, which is one of just three buildings to withstand World War II bombings. After minor restoration work, it was gazetted as a heritage structure and held many hallowed roles, including Government Printing Office, Treasury, Audit Office, District Office and Attorney General's Office, before the Sabah Tourism Board set up office there in 1991. At the other end of Signal Hill Road on Bukit Brace (Brace Hill) is another wartime

survivor, the **Atkinson Clock Tower** [177 G2], a quaint, white, wooden structure. It was built in 1905 by Englishwoman, Mary Edith Atkinson, in memory of her son, Francis George Atkinson, the first District Officer of Jesselton, who died of malaria aged 28.

Sabah's State Mosque (Masjid Negeri Sabah) [176 C2] (*visiting hrs change according to prayer times, but generally are mornings & afternoons, never around midday & after 16.00, with shorter hours Fri*) Lying south of the city centre in Sembulan, its towering minaret and pewter-coloured bulbous dome bear striking gold inlay motifs. Visitors must report to the on-duty information officer prior to entering, and are asked to dress appropriately.

Likas Bay [174 C2] Skirting parklands and mangroves, the coast road from the city around Likas Bay offers an edge-of-city nature and leisure strip, favoured for picnics and evening jogs. On one side is the ocean, with the Crocker Range foothills in the background, capped by Mount Kinabalu.

Wetland Centre [174 C3] (✆ *088 246955*; ⊕ *08.00–18.00 Tue–Sun, closed Mon; adult RM10, student RM5, under 6s free*) Set within a rare patch of mangrove forest, the former Kota Kinabalu City Bird Sanctuary morphed into this more educational and recreational centre, with 24ha of parklands, tree planting and other activities. Binoculars can be rented for RM5 to view the 80 different types of birds. To reach it by public transport, take bus No 1 (direction Likas), from City Hall or Wawasan Plaza stations, and alight at Likas Square.

Menara Tun Mustapah [174 C1] The modernistic tower looms over the foreshore of Likas Bay, 3km north of the city. The 30-storey building looks like a glass-windowed kaleidoscope – its walls are composed of 2,160 special reflective panels, which help it withstand winds of up to 272km/h. Despite its cylindrical appearance, the structure is actually a 72-sided polygon. The avant-garde landmark, built in the 1970s, stunningly reflects the silhouettes of surrounding mountains, mosques and sea.

City Mosque [174 D2] (*same visiting hrs as Sabah's State Mosque; see above*) Perched by a small lake near the water village of Kampung Likas, the mosque's white walls and blue bulbous dome shimmer in the sunlight. A fine example of contemporary Islamic architecture, built in 1997, the prayer floor can accommodate 10,000–12,000 people and houses three madrasas (Islamic religious schools). Take bus No 5A or a taxi for around RM12–15.

MUSEUMS
Sabah Museum Complex [176 C3] (*Jln Bukit Istana Lama;* ✆ *088 253199;* e *muzium.sabah@sabah.gov.my; www.museum.sabah.gov.my;* ⊕ *09.00–17.00 daily; RM15*) The cultural complex clustering the main city museums is located 4km from the city on Bukit Istana Lama (Old Palace Hill), where British North Borneo's colonial governor once resided. It houses the **State Museum**, the **Science and Education Centre**, **Sabah Art Gallery**, the **Museum of Islamic Civilisation** and a reconstructed 'heritage village' with traditional tribal houses and ethno-botanical gardens. Transport alternatives are bus No 13 (direction Penampang) – get off at the bottom of the hill and walk up – or a taxi for RM12–15. Photos can only be taken outside, not within the museum buildings.

The State Museum [176 C3] This has an exhibition hall on its ground floor with changing expos and six permanent galleries: the Islamic Civilisation Gallery; the Archaeology and History Gallery; Natural History Gallery; Art Gallery; Ceramic and Brassware Gallery; and Traditional Costumes Gallery.

The Science and Education Centre [176 C3] The centre houses the Geology Gallery, permanent exhibitions on the petroleum industry and copper mining in Sabah and other, temporary exhibitions.

BEACHES Some 3km south of the city centre, **Tanjung (Cape) Aru** [176 A1] gets its name from the rows of casuarina trees (aru) along the shoreline of its long, beach-rimmed headland. It's a peaceful, sand-lovers' escape from the city centre, yet with quite enough nightlife, shopping and dining (see page 184) of its own. Most upmarket resorts here offer bus-shuttle services to and from Kota Kinabalu city centre. Alternatively, take the bus marked Tanjung Aru Beach from City Hall Terminal. Ahead of the most spectacular sunsets, join locals running or walking along the shoreline through Tanjung Aru Park, previously named Prince Philip Park, which has a children's playground.

WELLBEING
Jari Jari Spa [177 H2] (*Suria Sabah Shopping Mall;* \ *088 487259; Lot 2.1, Block B, 2nd Floor, Tanjung Aru Plaza;* \ *088 272606;* e *sales@jarijari.com.my; www.jarijari. com.my*) With a new branch at the Suria Sabah mall, the company specialises in traditional Dusun massage – '*Dusun Lotud Inan*' – based on palm pressure, '*Palad*' and circulation-boosting '*Tanggara*' mountain massage. Treatments include the de-stress Manta Ray, Rafflesia massage, Karayam foot scrubs, the Bayu-Bayu ear candling therapy and facial, and Mato Nu O Dou after-sun remedy. Treatments range from 75 minutes to two hours, for singles, couples and kids, priced from RM175 to RM460.

EXCURSIONS FROM KOTA KINABALU

Some of the places included in the following chapter, West Coast Sabah, are also possible day trips from Kota Kinabalu. The following destinations are much closer to the capital (*30–35km*), and can either be enjoyed as half-day trips or used as an alternative accommodation base.

SOUTHEAST OF KOTA KINABALU – PENAMPANG The Penampang District is the nerve centre of Kadazandusun culture. Fringed by rice paddies and the Sungai Babujong/Penampang River, the region was once deep hinterland, but is now virtually within Kota Kinabalu's city limits. **Kampung Donggongon** is the heart of the district and the place to be every Thursday and Friday morning for the tamu. Starting from about 06.00 and continuing through to early afternoon, you will find everything from *lihing* (rice wine) to *butod* (sago worms) – the witchetty grubs of Borneo. There are a couple of places in town serving typical Kadazandusun food.

For a taste of mythical Kadazandusun culture, tribal warriors and headhunting, visit **Monsopiad Cultural Village** (MCV) [map, page 174] (\ *088 774337;* e *info@ monsopiad.com; www.sabahtourism.com/destination/monsopiad-cultural-village;* ⊙ *09.00–17.00 daily; adult RM75, teenager/student RM50, children free*). This major cultural tourist attraction is run by the artist-grandson of Sabah's most famous headhunter, Monsopiad. The crowd-pullers are cultural dances and the ghoulish House of Skulls (Siou Do Mohoing), where 42 'trophy' heads of the Dusun warrior hang from the rafters. The village comprises other traditional houses, including the tangkob, or granary, where the padi is housed, and a small museum with artefacts such as ceramic jars, padi grinders, bamboo items and bobohizan (high priestess) costumes. Admission includes a welcome drink, cultural performance (three daily), and guided tour (three daily).

A more staged, gee-whiz experience – authentic, not the least bit tacky – comes at the **Mari Mari Cultural Village** [off map, page 174] (*www.marimariculturalvillage. com; adult RM160, children 5–11 RM140*) in Kionsom, Inanam. Its success has seen prices rise by 20–40% in four years. Online booking includes transfers from various pickup points in KK, guide, meal and cultural performance. Expect a four-five-hour-total trip to link in with morning (*10.00*), afternoon (*14.00*), and evening (*18.00*) tours. You can also book via KK tour companies such as Traverse Tours (*www.traversetours.com*). Visitors are greeted by theatrically threatening headhunter types in various states of dress, who guide you around the different housing of the Bajau, Murut, Rungus and Dusun tribes, encourage you to taste traditional food cooked on the spot, and try out your skills with a blowpipe. They all demonstrate fire-starting and tattoo-making techniques, before treating you to a dance performance.

Getting there and away

By car Take Jalan Penampang from near the State Mosque just south of downtown Kota Kinabalu (in Sembulan), and head about 13km southeast to Donggongon. The MCV is another 2km from here.

By taxi The cost is RM35 one-way from Kota Kinabalu.

By bus Take the No 13 bus to Donggongon Town in Penampang from either the City Hall or Wawasan Plaza station. From here, board a minibus bound for Terawi and ask the driver to let you off at the MCV. The entire journey will cost less than RM3.

NORTH OF KOTA KINABALU – TUARAN Rivers and rural markets meet headland silhouettes and wispy beaches in the Tuaran District. While the coast is being built up, it is still far from a riviera – to reach it you will pass roadside food stalls selling *kelapa* (coconut pudding), mangrove swamps, lagoons and water buffalo in rice padi. The sprinkling of luxury and mid-range resorts in the area offer an alternative to the rush of Kota Kinabalu for families, beach- and nature-lovers, with the city still in close reach. From the Karumbunai Peninsula in Meggatal the beach continues 6km through to Pantai Dalit Beach in Tuaran, interrupted by a few lagoons.

Getting there and away
By car Tuaran is approximately 35km north of Kota Kinabalu, and 42km from Kota Kinabalu International Airport. The journey takes about 40 minutes along the northward-heading Kota Kinabalu–Kudat highway.

By bus From Wawasan Plaza, buses leave frequently for Tuaran between 07.30 and 17.00. Make sure to indicate to the driver where you want to get off. The trip takes about an hour and costs RM3.

🏠 Where to stay

🏠 **Nexus Resort & Spa Karambunai** (485 rooms) Off Jln Sepangar Bay (28km from KK), Meggatal; ✆088 411222; e info@nexusresort.com; www.nexusresort.com. In the midst of much-needed upgrades in late 2014, the hotel's once immaculately manicured appearance has fallen victim of late to seemingly dated presentation & service. Amid the spiralling competition, let's hope it lifts its game fast, and restores its once excellent name with maintenance & hospitality quality levels befitting its fabulous location. Symptomatic of the hotel's slide is the lack of awards it has won since 2009–10, when it raked in several for its green hotel standards & spa. The property includes a wing of 2-bed pool villas & 1–2-bed spa suites, 2km from the main resort, but connected with a free shuttle service. The self-contained duplex villas have kitchen & dining area, master & twin rooms, private garden & lap pool. Deluxe garden & ocean rooms occupy 2-storey villas; spacious at 42.5m², they have private balconies, local carved wood & Borneo rattan. The resort's public areas include a lobby-lounge, pool bars & dining choices galore. An 18-hole golf course & the Borneo Spa are topped off by several pools, a swimming beach (with jellyfish alerts), & dedicated kids' care & activities. **$$$$$–$$$$**

🏠 **Shangri-La's Rasa Ria Resort** (420 rooms) Dalit Bay Golf & Country Club, Pantai Dalit Beach, Tuaran (30km from KK); ✆088 797888; e rrr@shangri-la.com; www.shangri-la.com. Set in 400 acres of ocean-facing gardens, bordering a 64-acre nature reserve & orangutan sanctuary & Dalit Bay's green championship golf course. The sublime Ocean Wing, with its heavenly landscaping & artefacts, offers club-like intimacy, 90m² rooms with balcony tubs & an exclusive swimming pool & b/fast restaurant. Renovated in 2012, the Garden Wing rooms & suites have either gardened patios – in the case of ground-floor rooms – while upper floor rooms have a 2-level layout with daybed & balconies with rainforest or garden & sea views. Leisure facilities include a fitness centre with top equipment, spa, golf, watersports, horse riding, children's activities & nature walks. The dining choices (see below) span Western, Malay, Indian & Asian; entertainment includes evening traditional dance shows & resident musicians. Airport transfers range from RM240 in a 6-seater Nissan to RM450 in a Merc. **$$$$$–$$$$**

✖ Where to eat and drink

✖ **Coast Restaurant & Bar** Pantai Dalit, at the Rasa Ria Resort; ⊕ 06.30–10.30 b/fast, 18.30–midnight dinner (last order 22.30). If you're craving Mediterranean food, this stunning, glass-walled place which reflects the setting sun has décor extravagance & lights like neon octopus tentacles hanging over tables. The menu features lots of seafood, risotto & lasagne, bisques & consommés, salads, lamb & beef. Smoking permitted on outdoor deck only. **$$$$**

✖ **Gayang** Jln Sulaman Tuaran; ✆088 229066. A seafood restaurant in a mesmerising setting among mangrove forest & inlets, with fish straight from the aquariums if you wish. **$$$**

What to see and do The district township of **Pekan Tuaran** has a wistful river setting where you'll see people fishing from longboats. Smoke from the daytime gerai makan food stalls billows around its banks and you can get excellent cheap Malay food – grilled fish and meats and murtabak – and try the local noodle dish, tuaran mee, in the village coffee shops. Home of the Lotud tribe – part of the Kadazandusun – there is also a lively Sunday tamu market here (⊕ 06.00–14.00). There's also a tamu in neighbouring **Tamparuli**, about 5km further north, on Wednesdays. The *bambangan* condiment, made from a sour mango-like fruit, is delicious.

Dalit Bay Golf Club & Spa (e sales@karambunaigolf.com; ⊕ 07.00–20.00 daily) Situated in Tuaran, the club has an 18-hole course, designed by golf architect Ronald Fream, sculpted from a former mangrove swamp. There is also whitewater rafting on the Kiulu River, and there are equestrian centres for horseriding.

Kampung Mengkabong (4km from Tuaran) This is a satellite-dish-decked, yet dilapidated, Bajau village perched on the river that is perhaps a little overrated as a tourist attraction. Some locals welcome tourists and have crafts ready; others do not. The Mengkabong River estuary has many mangroves, and there are river cruises to go on. For watersports enthusiasts, the beach resorts offer them all, while **Lagoon Park** near Karambunai has skiing, jet-skiing, kayaking and windsurfing (and river cruises start from here too).

Rasa Ria Nature Reserve Established by Shangri-La's Rasa Ria Resort in collaboration with the Sabah Wildlife Department in 1996 as an orangutan sanctuary, the babies proceed to Sepilok when they reach a certain age. The reserve runs nature activities, birdwatching and nocturnal animal trips. Treks range from 20 minutes to two hours; the latter 'climb' reaches a 95m-high observation tower with good views over the Tuaran District.

WEST OF KOTA KINABALU – TUNKU ABDUL RAHMAN (TAR) PARK Off the coast
of Kota Kinabalu, the five islands of the TAR will accompany you through your journey in Kota Kinabalu and in coastal areas north and south of the capital. Pulau Gaya, Pulau Manukan, Pulau Sapi, Pulau Mamutik and Pulau Sulug make up a marine park, created in 1974 and named after Malaysia's first prime minister, the fiercely pro-independence (merdeka, merdeka!) Tunku Abdul.

Overseen by Sabah Parks, TAR takes in about 50km² of islands, coral reefs and ocean. The largest and most handsome, **Pulau Gaya**, is home to several kampong ayer, or water villages, with hundreds of houses precariously perched on stilts over the water looking back to the shores of Kota Kinabalu. The Bajau people were allowed to remain living in the park under native customary land rights. The original trading settlement of the British North Borneo Chartered Company was established here. The tiny (10ha) outcrop of **Pulau Sapi** was once connected to Pulau Gaya and you can still cross between the two by foot at low tide.

Water conditions in this marine park are not always in keeping with those of a marine reserve. Tourism is part of the problem, while educational campaigns are tackling the serious problem of rubbish in the water villages. The islands are contained by a fringe of reefs, particularly on the sheltered southern and eastern fronts facing the mainland. The beaches of **Pulau Manukan** and **Pulau Sapi** descend gradually into the reef drop-off, which can be seen quite clearly unless the winds are up. The ocean-facing western and northern coasts of the islands are more remote and marked by rocky cliffs and coral debris.

A shattered chain of lumps of sandstone and sedimentary rock, the islands broke off from the mainland during the last ice age. They are marked by honeycombed cliffs, caves, and a mix of coastal and strand flora including screw pines (Pandanus dubius), casuarinas and coconuts; big (really big!) monitor lizards and long-tailed macaque monkeys are among the terrestrial animals most commonly encountered. Along the trails, you may sight the weird, scaly anteater, or pangolin, or even a bearded pig.

Getting there and away Speedboats leave from Jesselton Point wharf in town about every half-hour from early morning until late evening. Local tour companies will arrange transfers, lunch, park entry fees, etc. If you are staying at one of the resorts on the islands, transfers are included. The trip takes 10–20 minutes. The conservation fees to Sabah Parks are RM10 for adults or RM6 for visitors below 18 years. Divers pay RM50 per person per day.

🏠 Where to stay, eat and drink *See map, page 174.*

🏠 Bunga Raya Island Resort & Spa
(47 villas) Pulau Gaya Island; ☎ 088 271000;
e info@bungarayaresort.com;
www.bungarayaresort.com. Top-rated sister
resort to Gayana Eco Resort, the timbered villas
are immersed in Gaya Island's jungle setting,
built into a hillside over a croissant-shaped
beach & bay. The villas range from rustic chic to
opulent 3-bed with wraparound decks, plunge
pools & private beach access. The secluded resort
offers activities such as diving, jungle treks &
the indulgences of a spa, which pairs traditional
Asian treatments with indigenous plants. Ferries
run to & from the island & Jesselton Point in Kota
Kinabalu 3 times a day. **$$$$$**

🏠 Gaya Island Resort (120 villas) Pulau
Gaya Island; ☎ 03 2783 1000; e travelcentre@
ytlhotels.com.my; www.gayaislandresort.com.
Mixed reports for this newcomer on a luxury
island enclave. The 47m² villas have flat-screen
satellite TV, large open bathroom with oversized
tub, veranda with day beds, & spacious bedrooms
with writing desks. For those arriving directly
from the airport, the resort provides return
private transfers between KKIA & its check-in

lounge at Sutera Harbour Marina (*1 Sutera Bd,
Sutera Harbour*). **$$$$$**

🏠 Gayana Eco Resort (52 villas)
Malohom Bay, Pulau Gaya Island; ☎ 088 380390;
e reservations@gayana-eco-resort.com;
www.gayana-eco-resort.com. Standing like
cormorants over the sea, the jetty, main pavilion,
villas, bars & restaurants are all built on water
stilts & connected by duckboards. Set between
jungle & coral reef, the design features natural
materials with some swish & exotic details.
The lagoon & forest-facing villas have private
balconies, AC & high-tech fittings, from DVD
players to power showers & free Wi-Fi. With
its own marine ecology research centre, vast
'Nature Pool', private 162ft luxury motor yacht
for cruising, & extravagant prices, the new
resort management is aiming for the luxury eco-
market. The open-air bar-lounges & restaurants
offer Chinese–Malay seafood & Western–Malay
fusion. **$$$$$**

Å Camping Sabah Parks (www.sabahparks.org)
runs campsites on Mamutik, Sapi & Gaya islands
for RM5 pp per night (RM2 under 18s).

What to see and do Many tourists don't see beyond the somewhat cattle-
herded barbecue buffet lunches offered by Sutera Sanctuary Lodge on **Pulau
Manukan**. This is fine for a packaged taste of the islands, but there are many
other marvellous things to do. In peak season, dozens of people descend on
these islands every day, but you can escape the crowds by planning a less
prescribed activity: sailing the park waters to a secluded cove; hiking to one of
the island interiors; or staying out on one of the islands overnight with just a
handful of people.

Trekking Pulau Gaya This is the largest island, covered in primary
rainforest that rolls its way voluptuously through creases and indents in the
landscape. The forest is said to be one of the few undisturbed coastal dipterocarp
forests left in Sabah. There are several trekking paths you can follow that
criss-cross the island, ranging from 20 minutes' duration to several hours.
One plankwalk leads inland to a mangrove forest. Pulau Manukan also
has several treks and there is a nice trail on Pulau Mamutik with cliff views over
the sea.

Yachting and private boat charter There are numerous secluded beaches
and bays that are reachable only by boat, including **Police Beach** on the northern
end of Gaya. This is the place for snorkelling, diving and swimming in the clear,
15m-deep, waters of the bay. Its western cove is a popular resting point for sailboats.
For island- or cove-hopping, boats can be chartered from the **Sutera Harbour
Marina** in Kota Kinabalu.

Diving and snorkelling

The fish are almost as numerous and even more colourful than the corals: spotted, striped and patterned in a variety of rainbow colours. Pink-and-green parrot fish, the turquoise moon wrasse, clown fish, sea cucumbers and star fish are all common. If you are very lucky, you might spot an ever-friendly whale shark!

Sabah Travel Guide.com

Pulau Mamutik The smallest island (just 6ha across) has the best reefs and coral, with clear, deep waters. It is Borneo Divers' dive station and frequently used for both novice and advanced PADI courses. It is also an access point to the more vibrant corals of the TAR marine park. The beaches, white sand and reefs start almost immediately in the shallows. The waters descend quickly on the eastern side facing Tanjung Aru on the mainland. Basic facilities include toilets, picnic shelters, tables and barbecue pits. Contact **Borneo Divers** to arrange diving trips (*9th Floor, Menara Jubili, 53 Jln Gaya;* ↘ *088 222226;* e *information@ borneodivers.info*).

Pulau Sapi ('Cow Island') The deep, crystal aquamarine channel between Pulau Gaya and Pulau Sapi has many reef patches for snorkelling and diving. Pulau Sapi has far more facilities than Pulau Mamutik, and far more tourists. It has a watersports centre and is also a big barbecue day spot, indented with gorgeous deep-blue pool coves. Its marine life is said to be good, towards the reef drop-off, on its sheltered eastern and southern sides.

Pulau Manukan I was very disappointed with the snorkelling off the main beach in Pulau Manukan. The waters are seriously stirred up by the day-tripping crowds and the island is also subject to strong currents and winds, though not as strong as the exposed north and western sides of the park. With a longer stay, you can discover Manukan's other long sandy strips and isolated bays.

Pulau Sulug At 8ha, Pulau Sulug is an island-beach, formed from a large sandbar and rimmed by coral reefs. It is the most remote and least-visited of the islands. The rocky northwestern side of the island provides interesting diving with many sightings of sea turtles and rays, and there is watersports equipment for hire on the island as well as decent facilities.

Borneo Reef World Pontoon A 20-minute catamaran ride from the Sabah Park Jetty, this reef pontoon floats above diversity-rich coral beds, off Pulau Gaya island. The reef offers various activities such as 'sea-walking' in an underwater observatory, diving, snorkelling and cruising in glass-bottomed boats. Packages (*from around RM200 per adult, RM150 children, group prices available*) include return boat transfer, light refreshments, a BBQ buffet lunch, the aquarium visit, changing room and shower facilities, snorkelling gear and 30-minutes of kayaking. Diving and other water sports are available at an extra cost. Various tour companies offer the trip including **Dynamic Holidays Cruise** (*Unit No G08, Wisma Sabah, Jalan Tun Razak;* ↘ *088 318777;* e *enquiry@borneoreefworld.com.my*) and **Amazing Borneo** (*Lot 1-39, Star City North Complex, 1st Floor, Jalan Asia;* ↘ *088 448409;* e *info@amazing-borneo.com*).

SOUTH OF KOTA KINABALU – KINARUT
The rural Papar District begins around Kinarut, and this area is another option for coastal accommodation, about 20km

from Kota Kinabalu. A car or taxi from the airport will have you at your lodging within 15 minutes. The taxi fare will be about RM40. Between visits to Kota Kinabalu you can take catamaran trips to nearby islands, go fishing or picnicking or head further south into Papar's padi fields, sago palms and Kadazan culture.

⌂ Where to stay

The reason I list Kinarut accommodations separately from Kota Kinabalu hotels, unlike some guides and review sites, is that it *is* a separate town – a small coastal settlement 17km from the city. A location in itself, it should not be considered by those wanting primarily to visit KK every day, but rather a place to take a relaxing break. Commuting prices/times to and from the capital make it unviable as a beachy base 'near' KK for repeat trips. As a place to land from the airport for a couple of days' rest it's ideal; likewise for a pre-departure beach stay.

⌂ **Langkah Syabas Beach Resort**
(18 chalets) Jln Papar Baru, Kampung Laut Kinarut, Kinarut; 088 752000; e info@langkahsyabas. com.my; www.langkahsyabas.com.my. Only 100m from the beach, with leafy surrounds, the chalets with swimming pool appease budget travellers & families who want it leisurely & laid-back. Food mostly Western. Australian-managed. **$**

⌂ **Seaside Travellers Inn** (23 rooms)
Km20, Jln Papar (Papar–KK Highway); 088 750555/0313/2067; e info@seasidetravellersinn. com; www.seasidetravellersinn.com.my. Friendly, family-run beach-house accommodation lapping the Kinarut seashore & South China Sea. Basic bungalows, 'deluxe' rooms with bathroom & family chalets dot the leafy cat-filled gardens, around a swimming pool. Free Wi-Fi, b/fast, kayaks & canoes, & also an in-house tour operator. The sea-balcony café serves b/fast, & simple Malay & Western dishes through the day. Some recent reports of the 'no-frills' accommodation being overly damp & tired. Easy minibus connections to town. **$**

UPDATES WEBSITE

You can post your comments and recommendations, and read the latest feedback and updates from other readers, online at www.bradtupdates.com/borneo.

West Coast Sabah

Between Kota Kinabalu, a series of undulating coastal plains and mountain ranges intersecting Sabah's interior, is Gunung (Mount) Kinabalu. The mountain presides over nearly all the west coast, with the exception of its northern and southern tips – the rocky coastline of the Kudat Peninsula and wetlands environment of Kota Klias. Traditional territory of the Bajau and Rungus tribes, the Kudat Peninsula blends forested and agricultural landscapes, culminating in Tanjung Simpang Mengayau – the Tip of Borneo. South of Kota Kinabalu, inland roads wind their way through the Crocker Range, lined with tapioca plants, rubber trees, rice paddy fields and water buffalo. The last are a common marriage dowry for the Kadazandusun.

KOTA BELUD AND KUDAT PENINSULA

Flagrantly promoted by Sabah Tourism as a day trip to 'Cowboy of the East' country, Kota Belud is the stronghold of the Bajau, renowned as expert horsemen and women. A predominantly Muslim town, the rural surrounds of Pekan Kota Belud are river-ribbed and picturesque, plaited with well-irrigated wet rice padi. Further north, some of the Rungus kampung are involved in tourism through homestays and cottage industries – the woven fabrics, beadwork and basketry are being sustained partly for and by tourists. Minority races including the Irranun and Suluk, originally from the Philippines, dwell on the Kudat coast.

It is possible to continue travelling as far as Sandakan on the northeast coast, via Kota Marudu, the Bengkoka Peninsula and Pitas. Be warned that both the roads and visitor facilities are poor – though this may add to the attraction of such a trip.

GETTING THERE AND AWAY

By car   Kota Belud is 75km north of Kota Kinabalu, along the KK–Kudat Highway; Kudat is 175km from KK; the Tip of Borneo 215km. If you are continuing around the coast of Sabah, it takes another 1½ hours to Kota Marudu from Kudat, and about seven hours to Sandakan. Several tour operators run day trips out of Kota Kinabalu to the Kudat Peninsula, from RM200 to RM300 per person. One highly recommended local travel agency is Amazing Borneo (♦ *088 448409;* e *info@ amazingborneo.com*). Their charges are approximately RM230 adult, RM200 child for two–three people minimum, taking in visits to three villages and their longhouse cottage industries, lunch, the Tip of Borneo, and hotel pickup and dropoff. The group also do two-hour helicopter tours of the tip, from Kota Kinabalu International Airport, from RM2,644 per adult/child.

By bus   Air-conditioned buses destined for Kudat, via Kota Belud, leave from Padang Merdeka at 06.30, 07.30, noon and 13.00. Buses leave from the City Bus Terminal North (Inanam) between 07.30 and 17.00. The trip takes three hours and costs approximately RM18.

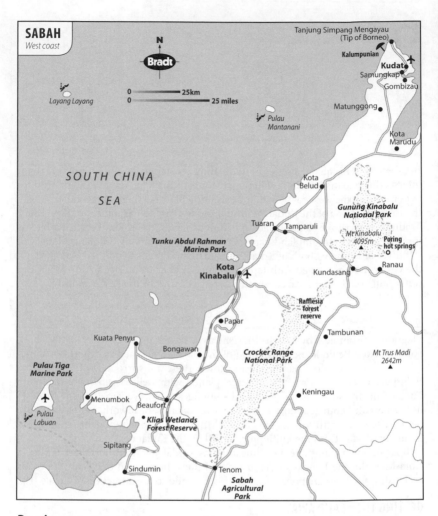

By air MASwings have a twice-weekly service, on Monday and Thursday, to Kudat from Kota Kinabalu in 19-seater Twin Otters. The 30-minute trip from Kota Kinabalu International Airport is quite bumpy. One-way fares start at RM850.

WHERE TO STAY The only three-star hotels are in Kudat Town, which also has over a dozen small hotels and guesthouses for under RM60 a double. Few of them are recommended on the basis of their cleanliness and safety standards. As for the Tip of Borneo, at last it is attracting some of the back-to-beautiful-nature lodgings it deserves, and allowing people to lie back and lap up the magical location for a couple or several days in a beach bungalow. There is, however, still room for massive improvement in the quality and consistency of services at those lodgings, but the building blocks are there.

Kudat Town

Kudat Golf & Marina Resort
(88 rooms) Off Jln Urus Setia; ☎ 088 611211;
e reservation@kudatgolfmarinaresort.com;

www.kudatgolfmarinaresort.com. In a commanding position over Marudu Bay, the hotel has slid towards the extremely mediocre, & needs some upgrading & better maintenance. Rooms are clean & light, but spartan, with kettle, fridge & TV. Spacious suites at mid-range prices. Small basic gym, swimming pool, tennis court, sauna, 18-hole golf course, Wi-Fi in lobby & a decent Chinese coffee house/restaurant which does better at lunch/dinner than the ordinary b/fast included in room prices. Poolside rooms can be noisy during holiday periods. **$$$–$$**

🏠 **Ria Hotel** (24 rooms) Jln Marudu, Ground Floor, Lot 3, Kudat; 📞 088 622794. In a bright tangerine-&-yellow cube-shaped building, this is the best budget hotel in town. For an increasing number of travellers, it is simply the best hotel in town, despite being basic. AC, TV, phone, minibar & kettle. The suites are even better value for money, spacious & with a kitchenette. Next door there is a café & 'Hawaii Internet Centre'. **$$–$**

Tip of Borneo

🏠 **Hibiscus Villa** m 019 895 0704; e info@hibiscusvillaborneo.com; www. hibiscusvillaborneo.com. Operated by James Burns, who also runs the Hibiscus Beach Retreat (below), this luxury getaway in tropical gardens with direct beach frontage sleeps 6–8. Fully equipped kitchen, AC & ceiling fans, flat-screen TV & DVD players, swimming pool, paddling pool, sun lounges & BBQ. No Wi-Fi. The rental cost includes daily servicing. **$$$$$**

🏠 **Hibiscus Beach Retreat** m 019 895 0704; e info@hibiscusbeachretreat.com; www. hibiscusbeachretreat.com. 5mins from the Tip of Borneo, on a small cliff top facing the South China Sea, is this 1-bedroom rental chalet for couples or small families. Describing itself as 'rustic chic', the white wood-walled, belian-roofed, glass-fronted chalet has a queen-size bed & sofa bed, stereo, basic kitchen facilities (fridge, toaster, kettle, coffee pod machine) & BBQ. B/fast is included in the rental cost. BBQs prepared by local chef & take-away service for lunch/dinner. As it is isolated (30mins from Kudat), bring all extras & goodies

with you. No internet or TV. The retreat arranges transfers from KKIA for RM350 each way. Other options are a hire car, a taxi from KK for about RM230, or take a MASwings flight to Kudat. **$$$$**

🏠 **North Borneo Biostation** (20 chalets) Kg Bak Bak, mile 7, Kudat; m 010 803 7310; e info@borneobiostation.com; http:// borneobiostation.com. Readers have recommended these self-catering chalets, built on 3ha near the coast. The inexpensive resort welcomes tourists & scientists who use the adjacent laboratory facilities for research in biology, ecology & hydro-physics. Run by 2 scientists, the pitched-roof chalets, scattered in a coconut grove, have a king-sized bed, table, fridge, AC & open-air hot shower. The restaurant serves a large choice of Western & Malaysian meals at budget–mid-range prices. PADI diving courses & trips to island dive sites. 15 minutes from Kudat Town; for those in a hire car, GPS co-ordinates are 06° 57 46.00"N; 116° 49 46.50"E. **$$–$**

🏠 **Kampung Bavangazo Rungus Longhouse** (10 rooms) 📞 088 621971. Also known as Meranjak Longhouse. Located in a valley a few kilometres off the main road to Kudat, signposted at the turn-off along Jln Tinangol, is this family-run venture consisting of 2 purpose-built longhouses made traditionally with split bamboo, beaten bark & rough-hewn wood. As well as rustic twin bedrooms (with mosquito-netted mattresses, an oil lamp & plenty of natural ventilation), there are double-bedroom chalets. Can be arranged through Sabah Tourism. **$**

🏠 **Misompuru Homestay** Kampung Minyak, 26km south of Kudat; m 013 872 1765; www. sabahhomestay.com. Co-ordinator Jeffry Yahya. A homestay network in the Kudat region, involving some 35 families who live in modern housing rather than longhouses, yet claim to offer a taste of traditional life through Rungus lifestyle & daily activities such as boat trips through mangrove forest, cultural dances, gathering wild food & fishing. **$**

✖ **WHERE TO EAT AND DRINK**

Kota Belud Day and night food stalls animate the riverbank. In town, amid the main block of shop-lots, **Kota Raya Restoran** is clean, bright and open-fronted with an excellent low-priced buffet.

Kudat Kudat seafood is excellent – shellfish, fish, squid, and prawns. A Hakka (northern Chinese) speciality is stuffed tofu with minced pork, *yong tau foo*. Adjacent to the *pasar ikan* fish market are a couple of shoebox-sized permanent food and drink stalls, opening on to a tree-lined car park used as extra seating space in the evenings. **Gerai Makan Dan Minum** (food and drink stall No 2,899) is very good. Just RM5–6 will get you a generous seafood noodle or rice dish and a drink – seaweed, coconut or sugarcane juice. Its neighbour, **Gerai Makan Sing Wang**, is also good. In the new part of town, **Sungai Wang Restaurant** is a popular Chinese restaurant with air conditioning and outdoor dining, standard Chinese food choices but seafood-heavy, with beer and soft drinks. **Ah Foo Coffee Shop** at the Kudat Golf Club is a Chinese seafood restaurant, good and open to the public.

A night market of Malay (halal) food stalls is held on Jalan Data near the Lembaga Bandaran; the open-air *gerai makan* stalls serve grilled meats and fish. No alcohol is served here. **Kedai Kopi Yu Hing** (ground floor at the rear of the Ria Hotel) has good, cheap breakfasts and lunches of *pau* (steamed buns), dim sum and noodles; it Is also good for local coffee or Chinese tea. Famous for its yong tofu is a small unnamed shop in a group of old shops along the main road (it's right beside the Siew Lan tailor shop and Jaja Trading).

WHAT TO SEE AND DO

Kota Belud Acclaimed home of the tamu tradition, Kota Belud ('hill fort') grew up around the site of the original market, held every 20 days as a meeting place for people from across the region. Today the Sunday market (⊕ *06.00–14.00*), unfurling on Jalan Hasbollah near the town *padam* (sports field), maintains that essential social flavour. Lots of handicrafts and food can be found among the rather jumble-sale produce. At the annual **Tamu Besar** in October, the once-straight-laced rural market turns into a showground complete with beauty pageant, water buffalo races and traditional dress parades.

Rungus Kampung (Kampung Gombizau) (*5min drive from the main Kudat road along Jln Kampung Gombizau, 43km from Kudat Town*) With its communal longhouse and local honey production, the village is commonly known as Kampung Madu, or 'honeybee village'. The Rungus also gather wild plants for use in traditional herbal medicines, and make many useful and decorative items, including brooms, bowls and wooden poles, from coconut husks and fibre. At neighbouring **Kampung Sumangkap**, the cottage industry is gong-making. There are 'nominal entry fees' to some of these villages and many tour operators in Kota Kinabalu will organise day visits to these longhouses. A visit to **Kampung Bavanggazo** costs RM35–40 for a welcome drink, cultural dance and handicraft item.

Tip of Borneo The Kudat Peninsula and Borneo itself end at **Tanjung Simpang Mengayau** or 'lingering junction'. One of the most magical, ambient places on the island without a doubt, on one side is the South China Sea, on the other the Sulu Sea, separated by Marudu Bay. Off the coast are the islands **Pulau Banggi** and **Pulau Balambangan**. The first-ever British settlement in Southeast Asia was a quickly thwarted effort to establish a trading post on the latter in 1773, to further the empire's developing trade with China. For all those foreigners complaining of no signs to the Tip of Borneo – they do exist – only, as pointed out in this guide, they read 'Simpang Mengayau' – that's Malay for 'one and the same thing'. On the main road heading to Kudat, 15km from the town, you will see the turn-off. Just keep following those signs. After a couple of initial turns and intersections, you are on to the final stretch. An 11km road leads to Simpang Mengayau, past Chinese plantation houses and coconut palms. This extensively pot-holed road was finally resurfaced in 2013, the sealed road unrecognisable from before. No longer do local innkeepers

Situated 300km northwest of Kota Kinabalu, Layang Layang is a manmade atoll, built as a Malaysian navy base and later developed into a dive resort – the **Layang-Layang Island Resort** (e *res@avillionlayanglayang.com; www.avillionlayanglayang.com*). Dive writer William Moss says:

Layang Layang is the summit of a huge seamount rising 2,000m from the ocean's abyssal depths. The submerged atoll spans over seven kilometres, encircling a vast lagoon. Its steep walls are a magnet for pelagics. The most famous residents are the scalloped hammerhead sharks --usually making an appearance from April to July, and gathering in their dozens or even hundreds. Other regular visitors include manta rays, schools of barracuda, dogtooth tuna, grey reef sharks, and leopard sharks. Spinner and bottlenose dolphins frequently follow the dive boats. Rarer sightings include whale sharks, orcas and melon headed whales. Isolation from the mainland keeps the reef pristine, and the small inhabitants are equally splendid. Dives at Layang Layang are often drifts and tend to be deep, so are best for experienced divers. There are sheltered waters in the lagoon, but divers with at least an advanced qualification will get the best of the atoll's pelagic majesty and 35–40m visibility. The resort is comfortable and has a great swimming pool. Layang Layang is reached by Twin Otters from Kota Kinabalu. The small aircraft have limited carrying capacity, so photographers or others carrying excess baggage should plan well ahead.

have to direct guests, 'Keep driving on this bad road...'. The rocky headland, with its sweeping stone pavements and giant pewter globe, is rimmed by glorious long beaches, such as **Pantai Kalampunian**. The best view of this 4km white sandy stretch is from Tomanggong Kurantud, the highest point of the Tip, named after a Rungus hero warrior who saved his people from a pirate attack in the 1880s. There are no guards on this beach, and the currents can be strong, so take care and don't let children swim alone. The lighthouse off the Tip came too late for the numerous ships that lie wrecked under this sometimes-treacherous stretch. Sunset at the Tip is so beautiful that there's a special festival every June to celebrate it – the Sunset Music Fest (*www.sunsetmusicfest.my*). Local and international artistes perform.

Kudat Named after the coarse *lalang* grass that grows between coconut and sago palms, until the 1970s the only access to this town was by boat along the river from Sikuati, 20km west – and it still feels marvellously isolated today. Despite its remote location, Kudat was British North Borneo's 'capital' from 1882 until 1884. In 1882, the chartered company wooed Christian Hakka families to Kudat from southern provinces of China to fill a labour shortage on farms and coconut plantations. The immigrants – and the coconuts – have had a long-lasting impact on the town. The **Pesta Kelapa** coconut festival is held every September. Declared the cleanest district in Sabah in 2003, Kudat is seaside relaxed with a 2km waterfront esplanade connecting the old and new towns. The former lies along Jalan Lo Thien Chok, with its fan-cooled kedai kopi and mixed businesses, temples and mosques. The **Tamu Kudat** is held here on Tuesdays and Wednesdays (⊕ *06.00–14.00*). The market is a great spot to mingle with local traders who sell Rungus handicrafts, such as beadwork and handwoven Tinohian cloth, vegetables, dried fish, tropical fruits and edible seaweed. This is a prime angling destination, and you can negotiate with local boat owners to hire fishing or cruising vessels down at the marina. From here,

West Coast Sabah KOTA BELUD AND KUDAT PENINSULA

6

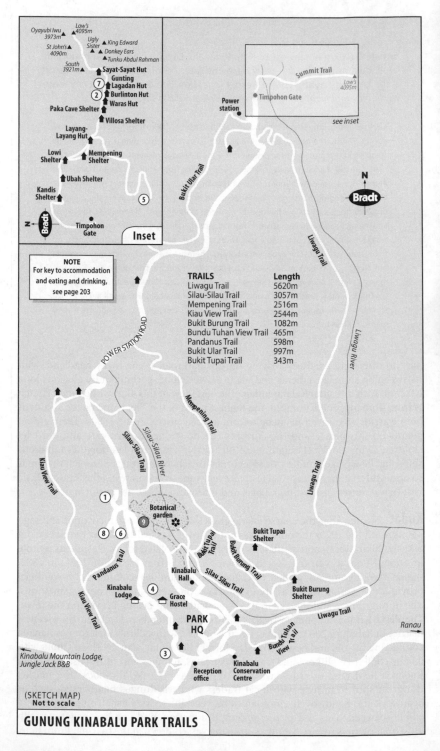

Inset

Oyayubi Iwu
3973m
Low's
4095m

St John's
4090m

Ugly
Sister

▲ King Edward
▲ Donkey Ears
▲ Tunku Abdul Rahman

South
3921m

Sayat-Sayat Hut
Gunting
Lagadan Hut
Burlinton Hut
Waras Hut

⑦
②

Paka Cave Shelter
Villosa Shelter

Layang-
Layang Hut

Lowi
Shelter

Mempening
Shelter

Ubah Shelter

Kandis
Shelter

⑤

Timpohon
Gate

Inset

Power
station

Timpohon Gate

Summit Trail

Low's
4095m

see inset

N
Bradt

Bukit Ular Trail

Liwagu Trail

Liwagu River

NOTE
For key to accommodation
and eating and drinking,
see page 203

POWER STATION ROAD

TRAILS | **Length**
Liwagu Trail | 5620m
Silau-Silau Trail | 3057m
Mempening Trail | 2516m
Kiau View Trail | 2544m
Bukit Burung Trail | 1082m
Bundu Tuhan View Trail | 465m
Pandanus Trail | 598m
Bukit Ular Trail | 997m
Bukit Tupai Trail | 343m

Mempening Trail

Silau-Silau Trail

Silau-Silau River

Kiau View Trail

Liwagu Trail

①

⑧ ⑥

Botanical
garden

⑨

Bukit Tupai
Shelter

Bukit Tupai Trail

Bukit Burung Trail

Bukit Burung
Shelter

Pandanus Trail

Kinabalu
Hall

Silau Silau Trail

Kinabalu
Lodge

④

Grace
Hostel

**PARK
HQ**

Kiau View Trail

Liwagu Trail

Ranau

Kinabalu Mountain Lodge,
Jungle Jack B&B

③

Reception
office

Kinabalu
Conservation
Centre

Bundu Tuhan View Trail

(SKETCH MAP)
Not to scale

GUNUNG KINABALU PARK TRAILS

GUNUNG KINABALU NATIONAL PARK TRAILS
For listings, see pages 205–7

🛏 **Where to stay**
1 The Hill Lodge
2 Laban Rata Resthouse
3 Liwagu Suite
4 Menggilan, the Rock Hostel
5 Mesilau Nature Resort
6 Nepenthes Lodge
7 Panar Laban hut
8 Rajah Lodge
Off map
   Jungle Jack B&B
   Kinabalu Mountain Lodge

❌ **Where to eat and drink**
   Balsam Café (see 3)
   Kedamaian (see 5)
9 Liwagu

an air-conditioned ferry leaves every day at 09.00 for **Pulau Banggi** (its main township is Kerakit) and returns mid afternoon. The **Kudat Golf Club** – Sabah's first – boasts of its historic links with St Andrews in Scotland.

Beaches The beaches in Kudat District are much cleaner than anywhere else in Sabah, largely because of the low population density. On the peninsula's west coast, the deeply indented, funnel-shaped bay of **Teluk Agal** – accessed via Kampung Bingolon – has a beach bookended by two rivers. Past Kampung Minyak – oil village – **Pantai Terongkongan** features a narrow cave carved into the rocky headland to the north. **Pantai Kelambu**, near the Tip of Borneo, has a sand spit leading to two small islands, with bays on either side – it's pleasant for picnics and swimming. The closest beach to Kudat is **Pantai Bak Bak**, 7km north. It's rocky rather than sandy, but rimmed with a picnic area. A few kilometres north is **Pasir Putih**, a good swimming beach with fine white sand true to its name.

Diving Kampung Kuala Abai, a fishing village 20km west of Kota Belud, is the departure point for the coconut-palm covered **Mantanani Islands**, about a 40-minute speedboat ride from the mainland. Accommodations on **Mantanani Besar**, the largest of Mantanani's three islands, have come and gone. Current options include diving and snorkelling day trips from Kota Kinabalu, operated by Traverse Tours, with the possibility of staying overnight at their island hostel. The **Mari Mari Backpackers Lodge** (☏ 088 2605011/2; (hotline) 📱 013 883 4921; 📧 sales@ mantananiisland.com or mantanani@traversetours.com; www.mantananiisland. com) has basic clean 'Sulap' cabins with private bedrooms and either shared or en-suite bathrooms (**$$** for two+ nights' stay), plus dormitory accommodation at the **Sayang Sayang Hostel** (**$$** bed linen provided).

The region is popular for wreck-diving, due to the numerous shipwrecks on the northwest coast close to the Pulau Kalampunian lighthouse

Traverse Tours says the 2.5km beach, shipwrecks and visibility up to 40m, offer a great diving experience: 'Blue spotted ray and marbled stingray flutter around amid large schools of fish. Muck diving is excellent, with imperial shrimps, jaw fish ribbon eels, seahorses, pink-eyed gobbles, the jaw-dropping blue ringed octopus and nudibranch of all sorts.'

Whether these new forays on Mantanani signal a flourishing of dive ventures here remains to be seen.

GUNUNG KINABALU NATIONAL PARK

Mount Kinabalu was sacred to local indigenous communities long before Gunung Kinabalu National Park gained World Heritage UNESCO status in 2000. For the Kadazandusun the mountain is the resting place of their ancestral souls, so indigenous climbers have always made an offering to avoid being cursed. Lower zones of Gunung Kinabalu National Park are scarred by forestry, mining and slash-and-burn agriculture. The UNESCO listing did not come too soon – and some would argue, not soon enough.

Spread over 754km², an area larger than Singapore, the park encompasses several distinct mountain environments and climate zones. The coolest place in Borneo, it is a botanical and ornithological paradise, with over 300 bird species, 5,000 flowering plants and a multitude of mosses, ferns and fungi. The floral inventory includes 26 rhododendrons, nine pitcher plants, over 80 fig tree species and more than 60 species of oak and chestnut tree. The 1,200 orchid species range in size from being as small as a pinhead to having 2m-long stems.

Ascending from 600m to 4,095m above sea level, Gunung Kinabalu passes through 12 climate zones. Such variety bears a wealth of biodiversity, and flora and fauna adapted to the altering conditions, from conifers and lowland rainforest to alpine meadows. The massif comprises 16 granite peaks of various heights, culminating in the 4,095m summit. It was baptised Low's Peak, after Sir Hugh Low, who led the first official expedition to the summit on 7 March 1851, when he was colonial secretary of Labuan.

At Panar Laban hut – 6km up the 8.5km trail – Low and his local guides performed the ritual sacrifice of a chicken to appease the ancestral spirits and seek safe passage. Two expeditions to explore the mountain's flora and fauna led by Professor John Corner on behalf of the Royal Society of London in 1961 and 1964 were also important steps to the creation of the national park in 1964. According to the UNESCO World Heritage Centre, a World War II prisoner of war also played an instrumental role. One of six survivors of the Sandakan to Ranau death march (see page 234), he formed the Kinabalu Memorial Committee hoping to 'preserve the Kinabalu area for the decency of man and a facility for the enjoyment of all of Sabah'.

The pride of Sabah, the park gets about 400,000 visitors a year. Most do not climb to Gunung Kinabalu's summit, preferring to soak up the sublime surroundings on the mountain's lower slopes. Many hopes are being pinned on tourism as a sustainable job creator, reducing the reliance on agriculture. In June 2015, a 5.9 magnitude earthquake hit Mount Kinabalu, killing at least 16 people including a group of schoolchildren climbers from Singapore. The natural disaster shook locals deeply. Officials blamed the quake on a group of foreign tourists, who allegedly desecrated the mountains' spirits by posing naked on the summit a few weeks earlier, and then posted their insensitivity on Facebook for all the world to see.

GETTING THERE AND AWAY
By car At 88km from Kota Kinabalu, the journey to the park takes approximately two hours. The second half of the drive passes vegetable markets, food stalls and craft stalls. At Kampung Nabalu, a few kilometres before the park, there is a *tamu* market every Thursday.

By taxi If you leave from the long-distance taxi rank near Merdeka Field, taxis charge around RM160 for up to four passengers, while the standard taxi fare from a hotel is RM300. You can reserve taxis at the park reception counter for the return journey.

By bus Take minibuses and vans heading to Kundasang-Ranau from the Merdeka Field station. Buses leave from 07.30 to 17.00, and a one-way fare will cost around RM18. Get off on the main road opposite the park entrance. Air-conditioned express buses between Kota Kinabalu's city north terminal and Ranau or Sandakan also pass the turn-off 100m from park HQ. Fares are around RM15.

Whether you are planning to visit Gunung Kinabalu National Park for a day trip, stay for a few days or plan to climb the mountain, the following information is essential. More climbing-specific information is outlined in the box *Climber's essentials*, pages 208–9.

CLIMATE Do not underestimate the cooler temperatures in Gunung Kinabalu National Park, which can vary considerably from those on the coast, and in nearby towns. Daytime averages at park HQ (1,563m altitude) are 21°C, but can drop to 8°C overnight. Have a thermal layer ready and trousers instead of shorts. The park is subject to intense downpours rather than prolonged rain. Between Poring Hot Springs on the southern edges of the park, to the summit, temperatures shift from a humid 25–28°C to 4–8°C and cooler.

ARRIVAL Gunung Kinabalu National Park HQ is the nerve centre for all people arriving in the park. Just off the main road, engulfed in a swirling mass of clouds, the glut of coaches and fumes around the parking area can put a dint in first impressions, but you don't have to venture far to feel the true beauty of the place.

ADMINISTRATION The park is very efficiently run, staffed by well-informed Sabah Parks naturalists, most of them locals with a passion for their culture and nature.

OPENING HOURS Offices, shops and restaurants are open for a minimum of 12 hours, restaurants up to 16 hours. The reception office operates from 07.00 to noon, when most visitors arrive in the park for day or overnight visits. Sabah Parks' operation counter is open 07.00–19.00, though it can be difficult getting assistance, and you must really insist on obtaining one of the scanty maps they provide. The Sutera Sanctuary reception has helpful staff, dressed in jungle greens. The souvenir shop is open 07.00–22.00.

PARK ENTRY (CONSERVATION FEES) Adult RM15; under 18 years RM10. NB: If you plan to visit Poring Hot Springs, hold on to your ticket stub as it entitles you to entry at the springs as well.

WHERE TO STAY *See map, page 202.*

Near the park A couple of places are starting to pop up on the borders of the park. The following, as is the 16-room **Kinabalu Mountain Lodge** (book via Agoda or HostelWorld) is about 1km before the park, approaching the mountain from Kota Kinabalu.

6

Jungle Jack B&B (2 dorms, 1 family room) Tenompok Bundu Tuhan junction, on the highway from Kota Kinabalu to Ranau, A4; ☎ 088 888036; m 010 947 7509; http://junglejack.weebly.com. Already a legend on the mountain within a few months of opening, Jungle Jack appears to be running a backpacker's dream. A local character,

he entertains & cooks for his guests. 4- & 6-bed mixed dorms, plus 1 double/family room, waking to views of Mount Kinabalu. Communal kitchen, dining, bathrooms & loos. Price includes 3 meals, snacks & non-alcoholic refreshments & Wi-Fi. Jack is also a happy tour & trekking guide, available for hire, including the summit climb. Scooters for rent. **$**

In the park Accommodation in the park consists of the lodges and chalets around park HQ, those at Mesilau Nature Resort and the mid-climb accommodation at Laban Rata. All are operated by **Sutera Sanctuary Lodges**, who have a contract from Sabah Parks to manage accommodation and eateries in the park. The sales office is in Kota Kinabalu (*Lot G15, Ground Floor, Wisma Sabah;* \ *088 308914/5/6;* e *info@ suterasanctuarylodges.com.my; www.suterasanctuarylodges.com.my*). It is always best to book ahead, especially in high season – around June–September and school holidays. Major mountain-climbing events and festivities such as the Chinese New Year are also very busy times (see pages 114–15, for important dates). Consider staying outside of the park (see pages 211–12), where there are a few budget to mid-range hotels and guesthouses and more expensive resorts.

Park accommodation consists of lodges including both hostel accommodation and chalet units of one to three bedrooms, heated showers and fireplaces (the first lot of firewood is included in the price), and in some cases television, kitchen and living room. The omnipresence of fireplaces gives an idea of the temperature drop you might experience from the coast region – especially at night (and still 2,500m from the summit of Mount Kinabalu).

Sutera Sanctuary Lodges, Gunung Kinabalu National Park
\ 088 889086; www.suterasanctuarylodges.com. There are 2 hostels & 8 lodges scattered through the forest near the park HQ. Lodges include those consisting of individual suites around common areas, as well as single-standing, self-contained chalets with 1 to 3 bedrooms. The key difference among these 'premier chalets' is size, & thus suitability for individuals, couples or families.

🏠 **Liwagu Suite** (4 units) Split-level units plunging into the forest, 1 double bedroom upstairs, living room & balcony downstairs. Tea-/coffee-making facilities, AC, TV. At busy times the beauty of this place can be marred by noise through thin walls & communal TV – the units are in the exhibition centre for the park, so there is quite a lot of traffic. **$$$**
🏠 **Nepenthes Lodge** (8 units) 2 bedrooms with 4 single beds, 1 queen, dining & living rooms. **$$$**
🏠 **Rajah Lodge** (3 bedrooms: 2 twin, 1 dbl) Dining & living areas, TV, kitchen, attached bathrooms. **$$$**
🏠 **The Hill Lodge** (10 units) Twin-bedroom chalets. Pleasant rooms, with rattan furnishings, lamps, desk, sofa & armchair. **$$**
🏠 **Menggilan, The Rock Hostel** (28 beds in dorms) & Medang, Grace Hostel (20 beds in dorms) have 48 beds between them in 4-/6-/8-bed dormitories. They provide a basic & clean place to sleep, in misty forested settings, with a communal lounge with TV, common bathroom & toilet facilities. **$**

Mesilau Nature Resort
🏠 **Mesilau Nature Resort** (3 rooms, 1 dorm) Jln Cinta Mata Mesilou, Jln Kundasang Kauluan, A4 road, Ranau; \ 088 871519; e info@ suterasanctuarylodges; www.mesilaunatureresort. com. In the eastern part of Gunung Kinabalu National Park on the Mesilau Plateau, this resort is the best bet for climbers taking the alternative Mesilau Trail to the summit & those who prefer a less-crowded, more secluded, forest environment. A misty mountain resort, situated 17km from park HQ (11km from the Kundasang turn-off), the venue is popular for scientific seminars & meditation retreats. Accommodation includes the 96-bed Bishop's Head Resthouse & 9 other split-level lodges with names such as Donkey's Ear

---

THE GROWING MOUNTAIN

The official figure of the summit height of Gunung Kinabalu varies between 4,095.2m and 4,102m, perhaps explained by the fact that the massif is still growing – some clearly haven't caught up with the latest growth spurts!

Peak Lodge & Ugly Sister's Peak Lodge. The latter lodges comprise a total of 16 3-bed chalets with heating, living areas but no kitchen, & 6 2–3-bed free-standing chalets with kitchens. It is surprising in such a noted place, with such noted operators (Sutera Sanctuary), that service levels are still so inconsistent, & the bane of many travellers. $$$–$$

Mid-climb lodgings
At 3,274m, Laban Rata is the acclimatisation spot for climbers who have started out from the Gunung Kinabalu National Park or Mesilau Nature Resort that morning. There are several rustic accommodations (`\ 088 872907`) where climbers & guides spend a few hours resting before resuming the climb to the peak the following morning at 03.00.

🏠 **Laban Rata Resthouse** (76 bunk beds, 2 units) At 3,274m, dorm accommodation, heated shower, room heater, restaurant area, & a common bathroom. Within the same building there is a heated unit, Laban Rata Buttercup 1, a twin-share room & bathroom, & the Laban Rata Buttercup 2, which has 2 twin-share rooms. There is also a restaurant. **$**

🏠 **Panar Laban Hut** (12 beds) At 3,314m Panar Laban, Waras Hut (12 beds) at 3,244m, & the Gunting Lagadan Hut (60 beds) at 3,324m all have basic cooking facilities, common bathroom & heated shower, though no room heater. **$**

✗ WHERE TO EAT AND DRINK See map page 202.
Whether you arrive at 07.00 or 17.00, getting quality food within the park is no trouble at several venues. The **Balsam Café** (⊕ 06.00–22.00 daily), down among the ferns near park HQ, serves buffet breakfasts and à la carte lunches with plenty of Asian, Western and vegetarian options. The daily climbers' briefing is held here at 18.00. At the **Liwagu Restaurant** a few hundred metres along from park HQ there is an à la carte menu and a set menu with higher (but still reasonable) prices. On the same site, there is a second **Balsam Café** (⊕ 06.00–22.00) which has a menu-breakfast, buffet lunch and à la carte options. The **Kedamaian Restaurant**, at the Mesilau Nature Resort, is much the same style as the Liwagu.

WHAT TO SEE AND DO
Mountaineering The summit peaks of the mountain are divided between western and eastern plateaux along a 16km-long chasm, which plunges over a kilometre into Low's Gully. Most people who attempt the 17km-return **Summit Trail** do so overnight, and with an average trekking duration of some 15 hours. The record return time is two hours and 37 minutes, set in 2003 by an Italian during the annual (October) Climbathon up the mountain. Some tour operators tackle the mountain along different routes to avoid the crowds.

Hikes Other than the summit climb, there are relatively few trails around the park. If you want a good hike, consider paying for a guide for the first leg of the mountain-walk return in a day. There are nine walks of varying lengths near park HQ (see map, page 202), for which you do not require a guide, though you can hire the services of a resident naturalist if you wish. The **Bukit Tupai Trail** is the shortest at just 343m; the **Silau Silau** is a very pretty trail of just over 3km through the nearby forest and back to the botanical garden. The longest is the **Liwagu Trail**, at over 5.5km. A daily guided walk also sets out from park HQ at 11.00.

Nature appreciation The parks run an **Interpretative Education Programme** – ask for a sheet with the current range of educational activities on offer (for both children and adults) at the Sabah Parks operation counter or Sutera Sanctuaries desk. Activities include a **Mount Kinabalu Botanical Garden Tour** (⊕ 09.00, noon &

West Coast Sabah GUNUNG KINABALU NATIONAL PARK

6

INFORMATION The new website for the official Mount Kinabalu climb booking and information office is www.mountkinabalu.com.

PERMITS All climbers are legally bound to obtain and pay for a climbing permit, mountain guide and insurance. Permits are available from the Sabah Parks counter at park HQ.

In high season (May–September), it is generally necessary to book ahead to climb Mount Kinabalu, otherwise you will arrive and be put on a waiting list, without any guarantee of making the ascent. Book through **Sabah Parks** (\ *088 889098;* e *info@sabahparks.org.my; www.sabahparks.org.my*). First- and second-class certificates include transport to and from Timpohon Gate (Power Station) or Mesilau Nature Resort. (See box, page 210, for a guide to prices.)

MOUNTAIN GUIDES If you plan to climb the mountain, a guide is mandatory rather than optional, not only for the safety considerations and expertise of local guides on the hiking routes, but also because of the sacredness of the park to indigenous peoples and the need to oversee climbers in both their hiking practice and general comportment. (See box, page 210, for a guide to prices.)

ACCOMMODATION For any accommodation in the park pre-, post- or mid-climb, you must book well ahead through Sutera Sanctuary Lodges; see page 206.

TRAILS There are two trails to the summit: the **Summit Trail** (8.5km) and **Mesilau Route** (10.2km). They intersect at Layang Layang, at 2,740m, 4km from the start of the Summit Trail (Timpohon Gate), and 5.5km from the Mesilau Nature Resort. There are shelters along the way of both trails. The Mesilau Trail started out in 1998 being used mostly by scientists and researchers. It is considered richer in plant and wildlife, not just altitude gain. It is tougher in parts, with 2km of unrelenting steps leading to the Tikalod Shelter. If you want to taste both trails, pay the fees to ascend the Summit Trail and descend the Mesilau or vice versa.

DURATION Though the hike can be done in a day, it is not advisable – many people have ended up with altitude sickness as a result. The best approach is a two-day overnight climb. On the Summit Trail, it takes four to five hours to reach Laban Rata (at the 6km mark); add an hour or two for the Mesilau Trail. The next morning, the final stretch to the summit (2.5km) takes two to three hours. There are ladders, hand railings and ropes to help you on your way. After taking in the scenery at the top, climbers return to Laban Rata or Panar Laban for breakfast, before the final four–five-hour descent to the park (the record slowest is 12 hours!).

ETIQUETTE This is a deeply sacred and special place. You should show the highest respect to the nature and to the local tribes who value it more than most. Shouting, fooling around and damaging the mountain environment should be avoided.

15.00 daily; RM4), daily screenings of the documentary Kinabalu Park – A Beacon of Biodiversity (RM2), and the **Mount Kinabalu Natural History Gallery** at Liwagu (⏲ *09.00–15.00 daily; RM2*). Flora from all over the park has been planted at the

PEAK TO PEAK Other peaks on the mountain include Donkey's Ear Peak (4,054m), St John's Peak (4,091m), and Victoria's Peak (4,090m) on the western plateau and King Edward Peak (4,086m) and King George Peak (4,062m) on the eastern plateau. Special permits are required from Sabah Parks to experience these more challenging climbs.

CLIMATE Be prepared for the cold. Temperatures at the top can drop to 0°C but average around 4–8°C in the morning. At Laban Rata and the other mountain resthouses (around 3,300m/10,800ft) the early-morning temperature hovers around 10°C (50°F). Wind, cloud and frequent rain (even when the weather is mild) must be expected, so waterproofs are essential to avoid a miserable ascent.

THINGS TO BRING
Clothing Suitable walking shoes, warm clothing, windbreaker, long-sleeved shirts, change of clothes, extra socks, hat, gloves.

Trail munchies Don't forget to bring some food. The canteens and lodges in the park organise packed lunches but they are pretty basic cheese sandwiches in a polystyrene container. It is best to bring your own trekking eats and drinks. Include drinking water and high-energy food (chocolates, nuts, raisins, glucose).

First-aid kit Headache tablets, sun block, lip balm, deep-heat lotion, plasters, insect repellent, mosquito oil.

Equipment Binoculars, camera, waterproof bag for camera, torch, towel/tissue paper, toilet roll.

Items available for rent Jackets, torches, blankets, sleeping bags and towels can be rented.

MEDICAL NOTE It is recommended that all climbers should have themselves medically checked before attempting any mountain climb. Sabah Parks advise people not to climb if you suffer any of the following ailments: heart disease, hypertension, diabetes, palpitations, arthritis, severe anaemia, peptic ulcers, epileptic fits, obesity, chronic asthma, muscular cramps, hepatitis (jaundice); or any other sickness, which may either hamper your climb, or be triggered by severe cold, exertion and high altitude.

DEPARTURE For safety reasons all climbers must depart from the Kinabalu National Park HQ by or before noon. There is also a horrific 03.00 start from the Laban Ratu hut the following morning, to avoid the cloud that quickly gathers at the peak.

Mount Kinabalu Botanical Garden or **Mountain Garden** (⊕ *09.00–13.00 & 14.30–16.00 daily; no admission charge*) not only beautiful ones, but those esteemed for their medicinal value by the local Dusun community.

CLIMBING FEES

Sabah Tourism has a full list of guide and porter fees on its website, under 'Destinations, Gunung Kinabalu National Park'. Inclusive of climbing fees, park entry, return transfers to the trailhead and trekker's overnight hut accommodation (RM50–60), it will cost you about RM300 to climb the mountain. That excludes optional extras such as porter fees.

CLIMBING PERMIT (Timpohon Gate/Mesilau Gate) Adult RM100; under 18 RM40.

CLIMBING INSURANCE RM7 per person.

MOUNTAIN GUIDE FEE The following prices are the total set fees payable for an overnight return trip, depending on route and group size. Halve the fee for a day trek:

Timpohon Gate–summit–Timpohon Gate One–three climbers – RM85; four–six climbers – RM100
Timpohon Gate–summit–Mesilau or Mesilau–summit–Timpohon Gate (starting and ending at a different point) One–three climbers – RM95; four–six climbers – RM1,150
Mesilau–summit–Mesilau One–three climbers – RM95; four–six climbers – RM120

PORTER FEE (OPTIONAL) Below are the total set fees payable for an overnight return trip for one to three climbers, staying at Laban Rata climbers' lodge *en route* with 10kg. For groups of four to six climbers, add 15–20% to stated costs.

Timpohon Gate return To Mount Kinabalu peak – RM80
Mesilau Trail return To summit – RM114

TRANSFER TO TIMPOHON GATE The trailhead is 4.5km from park HQ. Five people or fewer, RM15 per person one-way. Six people or more, RM4 per person one-way.

CERTIFICATE An optional take-home souvenir to prove that you have completed the climb:
• RM10 per person (full colour) to reach Low's Peak
• RM1 per person (black and white) before Low's Peak

The **Liwagu conference and exhibition centre** houses another small display on the park history and conservation, and there is a slide-show presentation held here (⊕ *14.00 & 19.00 daily except Wed & Sat; days & times are subject to change, however, so it is always best to check*) that introduces you to the park and its splendour.

In the vicinity of the **Mesilau Nature Resort**, wild orchids and the world's largest pitcher plant – the Nepenthes rajah, or Emperor – grow in abundance and there are guided nature walks (⊕ *09.30, 11.00 & 14.00 Mon–Fri, 07.30, 10.30 & 14.00 Sat & Sun*). Whether you are staying in the area or not, try to do some strolling or trekking around the **Mesilau Plateau** as it provides a very different picture of mountain ecology from park HQ, owing to the higher altitudes. At the Mesilau Gate, you will be welcomed by a rather loud sign: GRANITY MESILAU: YOU ARE NOW STANDING 2,000m AND INHALE 100% FRESH AIR FROM OUR HIGHLAND TROPICAL RAINFOREST. In the vicinity are conifers, climbing bamboos, Agathis trees, orchids and orange rhododendrons. Near the ridge crest, the forest becomes more stunted with rocks, tangled tree roots, spongy mosses and liverworts.

KUNDASANG AND RANAU

The first settlement after Gunung Kinabalu National Park is Kundasang, a village surrounded by conical hills like Chinese hats, dropping into a knife-cut in the valley. Crops cover the hills from head to toe. Kundasang is famous for its cool-climate vegetables – asparagus, spinach, broccoli, cauliflower, cabbage and mushrooms – and people come from Brunei and Sarawak to bulk-buy. The loss of forest habitat to intense cultivation has been high. There is still apparently no firm buffer zone between these communities and Gunung Kinabalu National Park – private land continues right up to its borders. The slippery-slide Kundasang road is lined every morning with wooden market stalls, selling local vegetable produce, lihing (rice wine), and honey. Ranau, an industrious yet relaxed town, is the commercial centre of the district. Its population of 50,000 is bloated every day by those who come to market to buy and sell. Sitting prettily in a basin of hills tipped with mountain mist, it's a great little place to absorb some local colour, eat at one of the noodle kitchens and wander about the market.

GETTING THERE AND AWAY Kundasang is 7km along the road from the Gunung Kinabalu National Park HQ, Ranau another 15km. From Ranau there is a road through to Tambunan, the Crocker Range and Tenom.

WHERE TO STAY

Mount Kinabalu Heritage Resort & Spa (formerly Perkasa Hotel Mount Kinabalu) Kampung Kundasang, Ranau; 088 889511; e perkasa@tm.net.my; www.mountkinabaluheritageresort.com.my or www.perkasahotel.com.my. Dated & shabby is the resounding verdict. Like some of its 'sister' Perkasa hotels in the region, the hotel has required better management & renovations for years, but there has been no headway despite the fancy name change, which does nothing but further belie the neglected truth of the place. The best thing it has going for it is the tremendous view; the Chinese red-&-white structure sits on the highest of Kundasang's conical hilltops, at about 1,500m above the valley. $$$

Kinabalu Pine Resort Kampung Kundasang (along the Kundasang–Ranau Highway); 088 889388; e reservation@kinabalupineresort.com; www.kinabalupineresort.com. The Dallas homestead-like entry is just on the right after the Kundasang market. Gorgeous nature-lodge setting in the forest, with attractive hardwood cabins. Consistently good reviews for the standard & deluxe rooms; all have satellite TV, intercom & Wi-Fi. A Malaysian Tourism Award for excellence, the site includes children's playground & BBQs. The halal Pines Restaurant has Western & local food & steamboats, & there's the ubiquitous karaoke lounge (⏲ 21.00–23.30). $$

Sabah Tea plantation Km18, Jln Ranau; (Ranau plantation) 088 876611; (res office, KK) 088 440882; e info@sabahtea.net; www.sabahtea.com.my. There are some twin-share cottages here as well as the Rungus longhouse accommodation, large family/group bungalows, & a campground. The longhouse sleeps about 25 & can be group-booked. The cottages have a bedroom, small lounge with TV, AC & ceiling fans. 4-bedroom bungalows sleep 10–15 (RM3,000/unit). The longhouse accommodation – mosquito nets, fans, wash basin, & shared bathrooms – costs RM120/room, sleeping 2–3. The Sapaon River-side campground costs RM10 pp or RM30 pp, with tent provided by Sabah Tea. The plantation has an on-site bar/restaurant (with Wi-Fi) & tea garden serving Western & Asian dishes from pancakes to butter prawns. Recent reports of middling accommodation & food standards. **$$–$**

🏠 **Slagon Homestay** (15 rooms) Kampung Silou, Ranau; ☎ 088 878187; e cruzellyn@yahoo. com; www.slagonhomestay.com. Guests at the Minudin family's home are told they can fruit-hunt & do mini jungle treks on this forest property. Twin/double bedrooms with & without bathroom & AC, chalets with kitchenettes. Meals served. Strangely enough, peak visitor season here is during the northeast monsoon, when Japanese people come & live for weeks to escape the cold at home. Some find the isolated location a pitfall, but it is precisely what others are seeking. From Ranau, take a minibus to Kampung Silou & ask to be dropped off at the homestay. **$$–$**

✗ **WHERE TO EAT AND DRINK** Ranau's dearth of accommodations is countered by a smorgasbord of food outlets, all crammed within a couple of streets. There are dozens of restoran and kedai makan dan minum (food and drink shops), serving Islamic, Malay and Chinese food. At the bottom of Jalan Persiaran there is a market every evening. Nearly all the Chinese shops are good (even if some toilets are best avoided) such as **Sung Fun Tong** (Jln Kibarambang), which serves great food. Next door is a good cake shop, **Kedai Kek Delicious**. Opposite there is a **food corner** with some open-fronted kedai kopi serving noodle and rice dishes. **Selan Kembera** near the market has Malay food.

WHAT TO SEE AND DO

The 'other mountain' Obscured by its big sister, **Gunung Tambuyukon** (2,579m) also lies within the Kinabalu National Park. It's about a two-hour drive from Ranau by 4x4 to Kampung Manggis, a vegetable-, chilli- and pepper-farming area and the closest village to the mountain's base. You will still need a climbing permit and insurance from the Sabah Parks Office at park HQ, though a guide is not compulsory. Local tour guides put the summit trek at three days and two nights, with two camps on the way up. There is a government-established homestay programme at Kampung Manggis, with a population of about 150. Some locals can be hired as porters for the trip. **TYK Adventure Tours** are experts on this climb, which takes in lowland dipterocarp and lower montane species of oaks, laurels up to 30m tall, mossy forest, pitcher plants, bright rhododendrons, and orchids.

Kundasang War Memorial (🕑 *09.00–17.00 daily*) At the Ranau end of the atrocious World War II 'death march' from Sandakan (see page 234), this memorial in landscaped gardens with ponds and pools and water features might look like a fort but is a stone-walled peace haven on the hilltop. The dichotomy of war and peace, horror and beauty couldn't be greater. Four interlinking gardens represent the homelands of soldiers: an Australian native plant garden, an English rose garden, a Borneo garden with wild flowers of the Gunung Kinabalu National Park, and a Contemplation garden with a reflection pool and pergola. Having fallen into a state of degeneration as a hangout for local youths, the memorial and gardens were restored in 2005, on the 60th anniversary of the end of World War II. Memorial services are often held here. Just a few metres from the memorial is the **Agro T Nursery** with flowers, fruit and vegetable plants – roses, orchids, hibiscus and tomatoes.

Nepenthes Garden The garden is within the Mesilau Nature Resort, on the eastern slopes of the Gunung Kinabalu National Park, a mountain slope covered with pitcher plants, including the giant Nepenthes rajah.

Mount Kinabalu Golf Course If you want to go golfing with your head in the swirling mists and massifs, this 18-hole course is nearby, at 1,500m above sea level in the Kundasang–Ranau area.

Pekan Ranau The undercover *pasar pekan* (town market) is at the bottom of Jalan Persiaran. This is a wet market with fish and meats. Alongside is the rainbow-coloured cultural and produce market, the **Pasar Terbuka Pekan Ranau**, an open-air market where Dusun and Murut people from the region sell myriad items, all fresh and fascinating. If you need supplies for the onward journey (or electrical items and car repairs), Ranau is the place. As well as fresh market produce, there is a Milimewa supermarket on Jalan Kibarambang, and a 'Superstore' 2km past the town on the right-hand side of the road.

Roadside rafflesia There are several private plots of rafflesia on the lower slopes of Mount Kinabalu, near Ranau and Poring Hot Springs. Look out for roadside signs in English announcing 'rafflesias blooming'. One such plot is found at Kokob Baru, 5km east of Ranau along the Ranau–Sandakan road.

Sabah Tea (*Km18, Jln Ranau–Sandakan, Kampung Nalapak;* \ *088 876611;* e *info@sabahtea.net; www.sabahtea.com.my*) Situated 18km east of Ranau on the Ranau–Sandkan road is the plantation and factory behind the prominent Sabah Tea label (which you will find in just about every hotel room and guesthouse in Sabah). In a blanket of 800m-high hills, the plantations produce both standard and organic (certified by a Dutch association) tea. Following a factory visit, you can sit at the tea house/restaurant with its wonderful views. The venture won the Malaysia Tourism Award's 2004 Best Tour Programme for Educational Tourism. **TYK Adventure Tours** (see page 80) organise a Sabah Tea Adventure – a strange brew of tea education with jungle survival skills, night treks and traditional longhouse immersion. The tour (including transfers, accommodation, etc) costs about RM550–650 per person for the package. They also run day tours to the plantation.

Hiking and biking The 2,500ha tea plantation is buffered by forest, and the trails through the tea bushels and surrounds of the Sapon Recreational Area are terrific terrain for mountain biking and hiking. Sabah Tea organise an annual mountain-bike competition in August. There is an easy two- to three-hour return trek to the top of the picturesque hill Bukit Kamunsu, through a condensed marvel of rivers, rafflesia, waterfalls and wild ginger.

Jungle survival camps Brothers Sadib and Maik Miki run **Miki Survival Camp** near the foothills of Mount Kinabalu in Kampung Kiau. Both are highly experienced Bornean trekkers and licensed mountain and cycling guides. During the camp they pass on skills from their Dusun ancestors. It's a three-day/two-night adventure in tents, about two hours' walk from Kiau. Others choose to visit Kampung Kiau for a big rice-wine party, held every Sunday. Contact **Maik Miki** directly (m *019 807 2814*) or via **TYK** (\ *088 720826; www.thamyaukong.com/miki*). **Intrepid Tours** do a homestay in the Kinabalu foothills area, sleeping in hammocks and staying with locals.

PORING HOT SPRINGS

Many climbers end their walk and ease their tired limbs and muscles with a near-direct descent into the hot springs. Poring is a Kadazandusun word for the bamboo that grows here. The lowland forests of Poring are part of Gunung Kinabalu National Park, located on its southern fringes at about 550m altitude in prime rafflesia territory – the park posts a notice if there is a rafflesia in bloom. Butterfly and birdwatchers are also in for a treat – both thrive amid the mixed dipterocarp forest of Menggaris 'bee trees' (*Koompasia excelsa*) and durians, mangoes and figs, adorned with epiphytic lianas, ferns and orchids. The eastern flank of Mount Kinabalu bears the scars of the Mamut copper mine, which was mined for decades after the creation of the national park, up until 1997. The health of local communities is still affected by pollution from the mine and its heavy metal run-offs. Plans have been mooted to convert the huge mining lease into an ecotourism resort, as the state tries, if a little tardily, to rectify errors of the past.

GETTING THERE AND AWAY The springs are 126km from Kota Kinabalu, 38km northeast of Gunung Kinabalu National Park HQ. Coming or going from Kota Kinabalu's city bus terminal north (Inanam), you must change in Ranau. (The terminal is near the market, and the springs are a further 15km from Ranau along the Ranau–Sandakan road.)

The buses operate between 07.30 and 17.00, and cost RM15 for the first leg of the journey, RM6 for the second. All long-distance buses plying the route between Kota Kinabalu and Sandakan also pass the springs, and there are several minibuses each day between Gunung Kinabalu National Park HQ and Poring.

WHERE TO STAY AND EAT

Sutera Sanctuary Lodges 088 878801; www.suterasanctuarylodges.com.my. With camping, a hostel, lodges & chalets, Sutera Sanctuary makes its mark in the park. The Palm Villa chalets are the *crème de la crème* of the lodgings with dining, living room & kitchen. The whopping rates of RM4,400/day for 6 people max includes a personal butler-prepared b/fast, lunch & dinner from either a buffet, steamboat or BBQ. **Enggang Cabin** has 3 bedrooms, a ceiling fan, dining & living rooms, bathroom & kitchen (**$$**). **The Rajawali Lodges** (2 units) have 3-bedroom chalets with AC, a dining & living area, bathroom & kitchen (**$$**). **The Tempua Cabin** has a double

bedroom, lounge, TV, kettle, lovely big bathroom, outdoor bath & harem-like bed. The cabin is great by night, but not ideal by day if you value your privacy & peace, as it's wedged between 2 car parks & the entry to the springs (**$$**). The campground accommodates 100 people. There are 2 hostels: the **Serindit Hostel 1** (24 beds), & the **Serendit Hostel 2** (48 beds), with common bathrooms & a sitting room & pantry (**$**).

Rainforest Restaurant 07.00–22.00 daily. An undercover wood pavilion by the springs. Serves Malaysian & Western dishes & drinks. **$$–$**

WHAT TO SEE AND DO

Poring Hot Springs and Nature Reserve (*Jln Lohan Bongkud, A4 road, Kampung Poring, 40km northeast of Kinabalu National Park;* 088 878801; 07.00–18.30 daily; adult RM15, children under 18 RM10) Operated by Sabah Parks, this sulphuric wonder-world by the banks of the Sungai Mamut River combines a series of hot sulphur baths with the park's other natural attractions. Once used by Japanese troops, the baths are five minutes' walk from the entrance down a gully and over a suspension bridge. The surrounding gardens brim with hibiscus, palms and ferns. As well as hot and cold pools (temperature-controlled from different sources), there are individual tubs and four indoor sulphur bathtubs (*RM15–20 per hour*) complete with living room, showers and toilet, and one with a jacuzzi. The conservation (entrance) fee should be paid at the visitor centre and park administration building, and includes access to an open-air bath, a slide pool,

PLANTS FOR LIFE

Over 70% of the local populations in the Crocker Range districts harvest wild plants and vegetables, mostly for their own consumption. The rest gather wild vegetables to sell at the marketplace. Studies have shown that the rate of harvest of these plants is not an environmental threat, with the exception of wild palms (many are used to make crafts for tourists). The Kadazandusun people here use over 50 plant species for treating minor wounds, skin diseases, diarrhoea, fever, coughs, malaria, hypertension and rheumatism.

rock pool and Gunung Kinabalu National Park. However, there are several add-on costs for activities around the springs, including camera and video fees. The springs are very busy during holidays and festivities. If you are lucky enough to have it to yourself if you stay overnight, you will better feel the wonder of the springs, which are now showing their age a bit in both upkeep and style.

Walks There are several treks starting from the springs. The jungle-walk attraction is the 150m-long **canopy walkway** (⊕ *09.00–16.00; adult RM5, children under 18 RM2.50*). Strung above the forest floor in 40m-high Menggaris trees, it provides an adrenalin-rushing view of the forest floor. A 1km hike leads to the small **Kipungit Waterfall**, a pretty picnic spot. The 3.3km Lanangan Trail leads to the highest waterfall in the Poring area, 120m-high **Langanan Waterfall**. Along the way, about 30 minutes from the entrance, is **Bat Cave** and a boon for botanists with frequent sightings of Rhizanthes – a parasitic flower and cousin of the rafflesia. The grounds also include a **butterfly farm** and **tropical garden** (*RM2–10*). The **Orchid Conservation Centre** has the largest collection of endemic wild orchids with all 1,200 species found in Gunung Kinabalu National Park represented.

TAMBUNAN TO TENOM

The Crocker Range – the backbone of Sabah – runs south from Gunung Kinabalu National Park en route for Tenom, skirting Tambunan and its large bamboo plantations, the small industrial town of Keningau, the Padas River, and the swamp forests on the Sarawak border. The journey is a wonderful one, through changing landscapes of lowlands and highlands, mossy forests and mountain mist, gorged river valleys, Kadazandusun communities and coffee crops. Taman Banjaran Crocker – the **Crocker Range National Park** – is the biggest park in Sabah. The mountain has been an integral part of the ethnographic history of the interior. Today, native land titles and conservation values are both weighed up seriously. Many locals are still hunter-gatherers, collecting forest vegetables and plants for food and medicine.

GETTING THERE AND AWAY
By car Tambunan is 65km southeast of Kota Kinabalu in the direction of Penampang. The Crocker Range National Park is 144km from Kota Kinabalu, and 13km from Keningau on the Keningau–Papar Highway (Jalan Raya Keningau-Papar); Tenom is 200km from Kota Kinabalu. This circuit can make a pleasant round trip from the capital, up over the Sinsuran Pass at 1,670m and back, with a slight detour to Tenom. If you are coming from Gunung Kinabalu National Park, there is a road from Ranau.

6

By bus Take the Keningau bus from the long-distance bus station, Padang Merdeka (Merdeka Field). Buses offered by various operators leave at 07.00, 08.00, 10.00, noon, 13.00, 16.00 and 17.00; the fare is RM16. One of the operators, Tungma Express, also runs buses from Merdeka Field to Tenom, via Keningau, departing at 07.00, 08.00, 10.00 and 16.00. The three-hour journey costs approximately RM17 and stops briefly in Keningau.

By train The Kota Kinabalu–Beaufort train (*07.45 daily departure Tanjung Aru; (Station Master Tanjung Aru) 088 262536; (Sabah State Rail) 088 254611*) is particularly scenic as it passes the Padas Gorge between Tenom and Beaufort.

WHERE TO STAY AND EAT Food is always available at coffee shops in the small centres of Keningau and Tenom (such as **Storkbill Kingfisher** café in the latter).

Hotel Juta Keningau (91 rooms) Peti Surat 25; 087 337888; e hjuta@tm.net.my; www. sabah.com.my/juta. Plain but clean rooms, with heavy tropical wood panelling, AC, TV, safe deposit, internet, room service. Restaurant & bar. **$$**

Perkasa Hotel Keningau (63 rooms) Jln Kampong Keningau; 087 331045; e keningau@ perkasahotel.com.my; www.perkasahotel.com. my. Established 3-star on the edge of town, & the best of the trio of Perkasa hotels in the region, yet still in need of overhaul & upgrades. 24hr reception, coffee house (Top Corner), Full Moon Restaurant, Peppermint karaoke lounge, & a health centre. **$$**

TAMAN BANJARAN CROCKER

The Crocker Range extends over more than 120km, separating Sabah's coastal region from the interior. Often nestled in rain cloud, its peaks undulate between 800m and 1,800m, covered in mixed lowland and hill dipterocarp, montane forest, primary and secondary forest. Indraneil Das from the Institute of Biodiversity and Environmental Conservation at the Universiti Malaysia in Sarawak says the Crocker Range is 'geologically and floristically' part of the same range as Mount Kinabalu. 'The altitudinal variation of this park is remarkable, in rising from near sea level to 1,670m and extending from the base of Gunung Alab to the town of Tenom. The higher slopes are dominated by moss forests and by a profusion of rhododendrons and orchids.' The largest protected area in East Malaysia, the 139,919ha national park was established in 1984, taking its name from William Maunder Crocker, a British administrator in the late 1800s under Rajah Brooke's Sarawak Civil Service.

The Crocker Range is bisected by the Padas Gorge and the rapids of the Padas River. Dozens of different studies are being carried out on the biodiversity of this large remaining slice of montane forest: on the many species of fish fauna in its upper rivers and mountain streams; its bats, birds, insects and small mammals; and its amphibian and reptile fauna. Over 200 kinds of vascular plants, 30 birds, 250 moths, 15 cicadas and 40 bat species have been found here, and high levels of deforestation of surrounding regions, particularly lowland rainforests, have sharpened the urgency to protect its primary forests. On its eastern side, the range cedes to the most densely mountainous parts of Borneo – from Gunung Trus Madi (2,643m) and thickets of highland montane forest to the peaks of the 'Heart of Borneo' (see page 66). Many rivers have their source in this area, including the mighty Kinabatangan.

right 90% of the world's orangutans are found in Borneo with the remaining 10% found in Sumatra (SS) pages 45–9

below The peculiar proboscis monkey is native only to mainland Borneo and a few of its small islands (CV/S) page 51

bottom The sun — or honey — bear is endemic to Borneo and is the world's smallest bear species (SS) page 55

left   Curious looking, the western tarsier is a nocturnal primate species and is among the smallest in the world at around 1kg (N/S) page 52

below left   The slow loris creeps and clambers through the forests at night and can cling to branches for hours on end with its powerful grip (W/S) page 52

below right   Borneo is home to two gibbon species, both of which inhabit dipterocarp forests, including the Mueller's gibbon pictured here (TA/FLPA) pages 49–50

bottom   The long-tailed macaque (*Macaca fascicularis*) is also commonly known as the crab-eating macaque. This one at Bako National Park is seen living up to its name by eating a horseshoe crab (DA) pages 50–1

above	The Malayan civet is one of several species found in Borneo (FL/FLPA) page 54
right	Fruit bats in Gunung Gading National Park (DA)
below left	A greater tree shrew eating katydid (FL/FLPA)
below right	Bornean mountain ground squirrels (*Dremomys everetti*) are easily seen at Mount Kinabalu (DA)

left   The Bornean clouded leopard is now a recognised subspecies (O/DT) pages 53–4

below   The Sumatran or Asian two-horned rhino is a tropical forest-dwelling ungulate (SS) page 53

bottom   Despite the name, the Borneo pygmy elephant is still one of Asia's largest mammals (TT) pages 52–3

right The bearded pig is quite a shy creature despite its formidable size (SS) page 55

below The lesser mouse deer is the world's smallest hoofed animal — weighing in at just 2kg (NB/FLPA)

bottom *Pangolin* is the Malay word for 'something that rolls up' — it is a nocturnal scaly anteater (CL/FLPA)

There are eight species of hornbill in Borneo including: rhinoceros (*above, BT*), oriental pied (*below right, N/S*), wreathed (*below left, AP/S*) and yellow-billed hornbills (*left, MN/S*). See pages 56–7.

above   **Olive-backed sunbird** (IB)

right   **Black-collared starling** (O/ S)

below right   **Temminck's sunbird** (NB/FLPA)

below   **Golden-naped barbet** (JH/FLPA)

above **Eastern grass-owl** (NB/FLPA)

below left **Crested serpent eagle** (IB)

below right **Oriental bay owl** (JH/FLPA)

above left **Blue-eared kingfisher** (IB)

above right **Striated heron** (HL/ S)

below left **Storm's stork** (JH/FLPA)

below right **Chinese pond heron** (NB/FLPA)

above   Chevron barracuda and big-eye jacks collide at Sipadan Island (SB)

The endangered green turtle (below left, AN/NV) and critically endangered hawksbill turtle (left, JC/NV) are both found in the pristine waters off Sabah's east coast page 60

below   The dugong is a protected species found in seagrass beds (I/FLPA) page 44

bottom   A resting white-tip shark casts a cautious eye over Sipadan Island (SB) pages 59–60

above   The tiny mandarin fish is one of the coral reef's most colourful residents (SB) page 59

right   A compliant black-tip grouper poses near Mabul Island, eastern Sabah (SB)

below left   A painted frogfish sits amid a cluster of tunicates at Kapalai (SB)

below right   A purple-gilled hypselodoris, one of the many species of sea slugs found at Mabul Island (SB)

bottom left   No bigger than a baby's fingernail, a pygmy seahorse is barely perceptible in its fan coral home near Mabul Island (SB)

above   The water monitor is a powerful lizard ranging from 20cm to nearly 3m in length (DA) page 58

left   A juvenile Wagler's pit viper (SB) page 57

below left   A crested agamid lizard perches astride a tree trunk at the Danum Valley (SB)

below   The five-banded flying lizard (*Draco quinquefasciatus*) has large skin flaps that allow it to glide from tree to tree (DA)

bottom   Though rare behaviour for crocodiles, the false gharial does not care for its young after birth (W) page 58

above   **Bornean horned frog** (SS) page 57
below left   **Wallace's flying frog** (SS)
below right **Harlequin flying tree frog** (B/DT)

above   A stunning species, the Rajah Brooke's birdwing butterfly is one of more than 50 endemics found in Borneo (FL/FLPA) page 59

left   A long-legged centipede waits for passing prey in the Danum Valley (SB)

below left   Tractor millipede (DA)

below   Atlas beetle (CL/FLPA)

bottom   Tiger leeches take great care to nurture their young — a trait which is rare among invertebrates (JH/S)

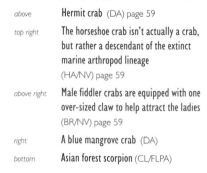

above	**Hermit crab** (DA) page 59
top right	**The horseshoe crab isn't actually a crab, but rather a descendant of the extinct marine arthropod lineage** (HA/NV) page 59
above right	**Male fiddler crabs are equipped with one over-sized claw to help attract the ladies** (BR/NV) page 59
right	**A blue mangrove crab** (DA)
bottom	**Asian forest scorpion** (CL/FLPA)

Mount Kinabalu is the highest point between the
Himalayas and New Guinea (PMP/S) pages 203–[ ]

BORNEO · explore responsibly

off the beaten path · tailor-made trips

meaningful adventures
STICKY RICE
TRAVEL

www.stickyricetravel.com

WHAT TO SEE AND DO

Mat Salleh Memorial (*Kampung Tibabar, Tambunan;* \ *088 253199;* ⊕ *09.00–17.00 daily; free*) Opened in 1999, this concrete igloo-like structure is a tribute to Sabah's rebel son and freedom fighter on the place where he lived and died. The bronze inscription outside the government-funded memorial to this local hero reads: 'This plaque marks the site of Mat Salleh's Fort which was captured by the North Borneo Armed Constabulary on the 1st February 1900. During this engagement, Mat Salleh, who for six years led a rebellion against the British Charted Company administration, met his death.' Under the umbrella of the Sabah Museum, which provides tour guides to this area on request, the memorial contains some photographs, weapons and other paraphernalia.

Rafflesia Information Centre (*KK–Tambunan road;* \ *087 774691;* ⊕ *08.00–15.00 daily*) This education and conservation centre is set up in a forest reserve along the main road. Rafflesia plots are planted all over the reserve between 1,000m and 2,500m altitude and can be reached within a 15–90-minute walk. Mandatory ranger-guides charge RM30 for a maximum of six people. Phone ahead to check if you have your hopes pinned on blooming buds.

Crocker Range National Park (*Taman Banjaran Crocker Park HQ, Keningau–Papar road;* ⊕ *08.00–19.00; adult RM10, under 18 RM6*) This is a very peaceful park to visit, especially after the masses of Gunung Kinabalu National Park. There are just a couple of short walking trails, including the 2km Crocker Trail, some rafflesia sites and educational facilities. Accommodation comprises a camping ground (*RM5 pp*), a 16-bed hostel (*adult RM20, under 18 RM10*), and a hut with two double rooms (*RM50 each*). Book through Sabah Parks' Kota Kinabalu office, or online.

Trekking, cycling, rafting The 40km **Salt Trail** traversing the Crocker Range has been used by locals for decades, originally to get to the tamu markets on the coast where salt was among the prized produce. The walk can be done in either direction, between Inobong in the Penampang District to Tikolod in Tambunan, in two to three days though tour groups usually do it over five days/four nights. The Sabah Parks **trail permit** (*adult RM80, under 18 RM40*) is compulsory; guides and porters are optional. TYK Adventure Tours and Borneo Eco Tours are both old hands at organising this trek, as well as trips to Gunung (Mount) Trus Madi. They and other specialists listed on pages 78–82 do cycling, hiking, camping and whitewater rafting trips throughout the Crocker Range, Tenom and Padas region.

Keningau Some 13km from the Crocker Range park HQ, squatted down among the timber factories, this is the largest town in Sabah's hinterland and home of the Murut peoples. The surrounding mountains and cultural colours of the region are the attraction rather than the town itself. The owners of Hillview Gardens resort say the area was built up on the timber industry – high-quality plywood and sawn timber – which is now being replaced by oil palm plantations as well as 'more sustainable agriculture and economic activities'.

Keningau's tamu on Sundays is a great place to see Kadazandusun traders from the region selling fresh produce and handicrafts.

Tenom This is a pretty area, interlaid with gorges, rivers, mountains and coffee crops. The so-called 'local coffee' you will drink in hotels and coffee shops

As Joseph Binkasan and Paskalis Alban Akim wrote in the *New Straits Times* after the opening of the Mat Salleh Memorial in 1999:

> The locals were unhappy due to alleged exploitation, and one man that stood up and led a rebellion against British rule was Datu Paduka Muhammad Salleh better known as Mat Salleh. To the British, he was a rebel but to locals, he was a warrior. He was killed in a gun battle with the British police on Feb 1, 1900... Also killed in the gun battle were about 1,000 of Mat Salleh's followers who fought from the neighbouring villages of Lotud, Tondulu, Piasau, Timbou, Kitutud, Kepayan and Sunsuron.

Mat Salleh and his followers were fed up with the British North Borneo Company's meddling in local law, especially the imposition of taxes on rice. Salleh was a voice for many angry people, but contrary to misconceptions, he was neither a lone crusader, nor the sole voice of dissent. Many others tried to throw off foreign rule in Sabah – each district seemed to have its warriors – and there is a smattering of memorials to them around the state, including the Ontoros Antanom statue of a Murut hero killed in a battle with the British in the Tenom District in 1915.

LOCAL HERO, LOCAL HISTORY In the heavily British-slanted telling of North Borneo's history, a non-colonial version is rare. It is therefore refreshing to read a fresh local slant as opposed to the top-heavy pro-colonial viewpoint. In a story about the new Mat Salleh memorial, published in the *New Straits Times* (9 March 2000), Sabah Museum director and Tambunan local, Joseph Pounis Guntavid, suggested the British had long bragged of downing Mat Salleh's rebellion to their rule. 'But a search and study on Mat Salleh's actions strongly indicated that he was not a rebel but a warrior who went against foreign rule, fighting for North Borneo's self-government,' he said. 'Mat Salleh initiated patriotism that led the people to fight for self-rule until Sabah gained her independence through Malaysia on 16 September 1963.'

throughout Sabah is from Tenom. Some of the factories are open for visits; most are Chinese-run. At the **Fatt Choi Coffee Factory** (*Jln Tenom-Kemabong*) you can sample the coffee, and also try iced coffee with durian ice cream (hold your nose as you drink). Tenom Kopi is mostly made from lower-altitude Robusta beans and is powder-fine, with a dark and muddy taste. The factories sell it for about RM10 per kilogram. Other than caffeine kicks, Tenom has several short forest trails passing streams and waterfalls. TYK Adventure Tours now organise a Tenom Farmstay Holiday hinging on visits to several farms in the region, with the possibility of overnight stays at organic farms – one of them run by TYK founder Tham Yau Kong (*www.tykadventuretours.com/farm.htm*).

Sabah Agricultural Park (*Taman Pertanian Sabah, 15km from Tenom;* ✆ *087 737952; e agripark@sabah.net.my*) Set among vast gardens and lakes, this is an agri-world with permanent living crop museums, bee centres, a native orchid centre, ornamental garden, agro-forestry and ethno-botany displays, as well as temporary expositions and events. A good family attraction, the grounds also contain forest trails, an animal park, picnic areas and a restaurant.

The **Klias Wetlands** region has recently become a top destination for nature lovers thanks to its large population of proboscis monkeys. Relatively secluded on a table-shaped cape and intersected by the Sungai Klias, the area is one of just a few remaining dabs of mangrove forest on the peninsula – most of it has been gobbled up by forestry, agriculture and coastal development. The wetlands are made up of a mix of habitats – tidal areas, rivers, swamps, mangrove and nipah forest. On the way to Klias through Papar and Beaufort, you will see a lot of sago palm (Matroxylon sagus or M. rumphii). Known locally as rumbia, the Kadazandusun and Bisayas use it for roofing, floor mats and baskets, and also produce the starchy food ambuyut from it (as Bruneians do). On the tip of the peninsula, Kuala Penyu is the launching point for the **Pulau Tiga Park**, a marine-and-reef park of more than 15,000ha, taking in three small islands about 10km offshore.

GETTING THERE AND AWAY

By car Beaufort is 95km from Kota Kinabalu, the Klias Peninsula around 110km.

By bus Take a minibus to Beaufort, then a connecting bus to Kuala Penyu. Contact the lodges below to arrange transport. Alternatively, book the whole thing through a Kota Kinabalu-based tour company (see pages 78–80) that also offers the wetlands as a day trip.

By train Trains run from Kota Kinabalu to Beaufort.

By boat Pulau Tiga Island is a 30-minute trip from the Kuala Penyu jetty. Boats leave at 10.00 and 15.00 and return 09.00 and 16.00.

WHERE TO STAY, EAT AND DRINK
Klias Wetlands/Kuala Penyu

🏠 **Borneo Proboscis River Lodge** Kota Klias (1km from the bridge over the Klias River); ☎087 209221; e lyndatang@pd.jaring.my; www.borneowildlife.org. Beautiful riverbank & traditional village setting, the nicest place to stay in Klias & very professional, friendly operators in Tang & Lynda Yeu. Rungus longhouses on stilts with bamboo walls & thatched-palm roofs & AC terrace-house room with attached bathroom. Also has good food & riverside dining. Excellent value. Overnight package with 5 meals, accommodation & 3 river cruises for RM400 a double in a longhouse room; RM500 in an AC room. **$$$–$$**

🏠 **Tempurung Seaside Lodge** (11 rooms) Putatan Point (off JKR Rd), Kuala Penyu; ☎088 773066; e info@borneo-authentic.com; www. borneo-authentic.com. Stunning, remote seaside location, on a forested hill above a beach. The wooden walkway-connected rooms, snuggled into lush native gardens, are simple & peaceful with bathrooms & AC. Good, inexpensive food

(& free Wi-Fi) at the open-air chalet-like restaurant. **$$$–$$**

🏠 **Naga Puri** (5 rooms, 1 chalet) Putatan Point Kuala Penyu; ☎087 884929; m 016 880 2357; e mail@nagapuri.com; www.nagapuri.com. A 'private hideout', this guesthouse looks out over the sea from the hillside opposite the above accommodation, & takes its name from that hill – Bukit Bukit Naga Aman Puri, or 'dragon's hill peaceful place'. For RM100 a night including breakfast, lunch & dinner, 'freeflow' tea, coffee & water, this is hospitality incarnated, with a personal, but chilled touch. The 2- & 3-night packages are just as good value & it would be a shame to stay here only a rushed night. **$$–$**

🏠 **Naga Puri Beach Retreat** (8 rooms) 1 Jln Bukit Naga, Kuala Penyu; ☎087 884929; e leongkheeheng@hotmail.com; www.nagapuri. com. A hip & homely place but shared bathrooms & no AC; just bed & beach. Owner-operated, above the beach with volleyball, archery & a small library. **$**

Pulau Tiga Island

🏠 **Survivor Lodge Pulau Tiga** Sipadan Dive Centre, 10th Floor, Wisma Shopping Centre, KK; ☎088 240584; e pulautiga@sdclodges.com; sdclodges.com. The survivor-island tag works, & most come away feeling they have had a crystal-watered island paradise to themselves. The downsides for many are tired & faulty lodgings (plumbing-wise), & masses of mosquitoes. Reports of thefts are alarming & I hope appropriate action is being taken. Operated by Sipadan Dive Centre/SDC Lodges, 12 standard & superior chalets with balcony, double or twin bed, fan or AC, as well as budget-priced longhouse (triple-share). PADI diving centre. Good to excellent buffet food & casual friendly atmosphere, games room & watersports. Overnight packages from Kota Kinabalu or Kuala Penyu include transfers, accommodation, meals & park entrance fees. $$$–$$

WHAT TO SEE AND DO For visits to the Klias Wetlands, boats leave the Kota Klias jetty late afternoon on river wildlife safaris. Other residents that may be spotted are macaques, crocodiles, monitor lizards, tree snakes and eagles. The night-time spectacle comes with a glowing performance by thousands of fireflies having a good feed out on the mangrove tree enzymes to impress their female friends.

Pulau Tiga (*adult RM10, under 18 RM6*) 10km offshore, it is possible to day trip here or stay overnight. Either way the boat trip part of the equation must be booked through a travel agent. So even though you can bus to Kuala Penya independently (*RM18; from Segama overhead bridge next to the post office in Kota Kinabalu*), there is little interest in doing so, as tours will include the return road trip ex KK. The crêpe-shaped island is 4.5km long and 1.5km wide and upholstered in old-growth rainforests, palms and volcanic outcrops. It shot to minor fame as a location for the US television series Survivor. The island is also famous for its therapeutic natural volcanic mud – and for its sea snakes.

In Kuala Penyu, there is a **Rumbia Information Centre** (*Kampung Kasugira;* ☎087 897078; ☉ *Mon–Fri (but closed lunchtimes)* & Sat am) with handicraft displays on things made with sago palm, and sago cooking demonstrations. Padas River whitewater-rafting trips set out from Panggi station near Beaufort.

WEST-COAST ISLANDS

PULAU LABUAN (*www.labuantourism.com.my*) Situated 10km off the coast of Sabah at the entrance to Brunei Bay, Labuan is a Federal Territory of Malaysia, a duty-free island and Brunei's main import–export hub. Its capital, Victoria, lies in a deep-sheltered harbour and is a centuries-old maritime crossroads. Part of British North Borneo, the township suffered grievous damage in World War II. In 1990, it was declared a tax haven to boost its development as an offshore finance centre. Historic landmarks include the War Memorial Cemetery and Surrender Point where the Japanese surrendered to Australia in 1945. The 98km² isle has a population of 55,000, made up mostly of Malay and Kadazandusun. An increasing pack of international retirees are also settling here, attracted by its relaxed lifestyle and safe-haven environment, with Brunei and Malaysia both within easy reach. With all those flunked ocean passages beneath it, Labuan has become one of Malaysia's wreck-diving hubs, and Borneo Divers have a PADI dive centre here.

Getting there and away

By air MAS and AirAsia each have one–two daily flights between Kuala Lumpur and Labuan. MASwings connects Labuan with both Kota Kinabalu and Miri.

By boat High-speed, air-conditioned ferries ply daily between Kota Kinabalu and Labuan. There is also a passenger and vehicle ferry wharf at Menumbok – just across from Labuan on the south coast of Sabah. Express Labuan services leave from Kota Kinabalu at 08.00 and 13.30, and from Labuan to Kota Kinablau at 08.30 and 13.00; the journey takes approximately three hours and costs RM21 for a child, RM34 for an economy adult, and RM39 for a first-class adult ticket. Check the Labuan tourism website for the latest fares and timetables: www.labuantourism.com.my.

Where to stay

Grand Dorsett Labuan (178 rooms) 462 Jln Merdeka; 087 422000; e info.labuan@granddorsett.com; www.dorsethotels.com/labuan. The top hotel for service & facilities has a lovely, elegant atmosphere & good management, investing significantly in refurbishments over recent years to keep it swish. Deluxe & spacious 8th-floor executive rooms are well furnished, with sea or city views, high-speed internet & other quality tech fittings. Walnut wood-fitted premier suites (75m²) have a dining area with kitchenette & separate living room. Lobby lounge, pub & Victoria's Brasserie (⊕ *06.00–22.30*), a good gym & pool. **$$$$$–$$$$**

Tiara Labuan (87 rooms) Jln Tanjung Batu; 087 414300; e reservations@tiaralabuan.com; www.tiaralabuan.com. Nice to find a relative newcomer hotel with such a friendly out-to-please attitude. The mod Chinese temple-style white-&-tan resort has been sweeping in awards for its service. Relaxing location about 3km from town, 2km from airport, in palm-swaying gardens between the coast & golf course. Complimentary return airport transfers & hourly shuttle service to town. Standard spacious rooms, suites & villas with ocean-facing balconies, warmly furnished with wood & rugs, large bathrooms. Free Wi-Fi, AC & fans, fridge & tea/coffee making. Gym, swimming pool, steam bath, squash court & business centre. Poolside café, pub, cocktail lounge & seafood restaurant. Internet specials include deluxe suites at about two-thirds the usual rate. **$$$$–$$**

SEND US YOUR SNAPS!

We'd love to follow your adventures using our *Borneo* guide – why not send us your photos and stories via Twitter (@BradtGuides) and Instagram (@bradtguides) using the hashtag #borneo. Alternatively, you can upload your photos directly to the gallery on the Borneo destination page via our website (*www.bradtguides.com*).

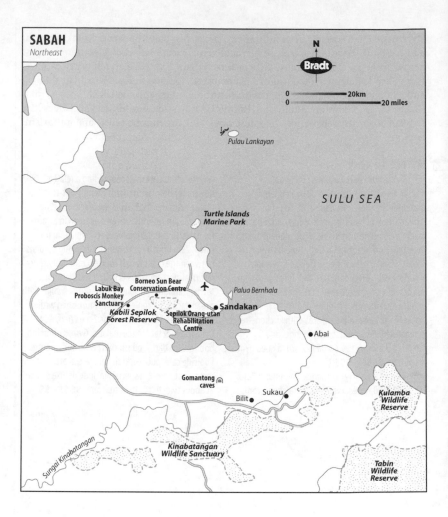

7

Northeast Sabah

SANDAKAN

A big belly of water dotted with islands, rickety fishing vessels and slanted cargo boats imbue Sandakan with an Old-World trading flavour captured in its nickname 'Little Hong Kong'. Its watery charm lies in the creaky water villages that throw rich hues and reflections of colourful roofs and paintwork over Sandakan Bay. Winds of other lands and people waft across the silvery harbour. The sea border with the Philippines, just 28km away, is visible across the bay, and hundreds of Filipinos are the latest in many exotic waves of migrants in the town. Capital of British North Borneo from 1883 until 1899, the town was nearly flattened by World War II bombings. Now Sabah's second-largest city, with a population of around 350,000, its economy is increasingly underpinned by the palm oil industry, in place of the export in tropical woods, which dominated its port from the 1930s.

Crowned by a swathe of lush hills, the name 'Sandakan' in Suluk tongue (the Filipino tribe who settled in the area) means 'the land that was pawned'. The town developed in the 1870s, when the Sultan of Sulu forfeited some land on the adjacent island of Pulau Timbang to Scottish adventurer and engineer William Clarke-Cowie, in return for ammunition and protection from Spanish conquerors. The area was subsequently leased by the BNBCC. Curious colonial leftovers include Edinburgh-style streets, English tea houses, Anglican churches and an Old Rex theatre. The modern sobriquet is 'nature city' because of Sandakan's strategic position as a gateway to many of Sabah's natural wonders: the Kinabatangan River, Gomantong Caves, and Sepilok's Forest Reserve and Orangutan Rehabilitation Centre. The slogan will soon ring hollow, if that nature continues to be swallowed up by ever-expanding industrial crops. While most people come to Sandakan to see the orangutans and the Kinabatangan, try to spend at least one night in this fascinating anchorage of maritime and migratory history.

GETTING THERE AND AWAY

By air Malaysia Airlines and AirAsia operate daily flights between Sandakan and Kuala Lumpur. Fares for the 2½-hour flight cost from RM204 with AirAsia; nearly double that with MAS. For Kota Kinabalu–Sandakan flights (*50 min*), fares start from RM164 with MASwings and RM84 with AirAsia. MASwings also has connecting flights from Sandakan to Tawau and Kudat. Both airlines have offices on the ground floor of the airport terminal building. The airport is 12km from the central business district (CBD), a 20–30-minute taxi ride (*around RM25*). There are no buses to town.

By car By road, Sandakan is 227km from Kota Kinabalu (a five- to six-hour drive), 91km from Lahad Datu. Tawau and Semporna are 177km away.

MONOCULTURE

Travelling the east coast of Sabah, you will be struck by the massive homogenous swathes of oil palm extending inland, over hillsides, and deep into areas once covered by forest. Soaring global demand for palm oil in food and cosmetics has seen Malaysia and Indonesia become the world's two leading producers, supplying over 80% of the market by using their Bornean states for large-scale monocultures of the high-yielding, thick-fronded *Elaeis guineensis* palms.

The reddish-brown oil extracted from the crushed fruit of the palm is riding high on the international commodities charts as a cheap crop that is easy to produce. In supermarkets, you will see 'palm oil' as an ingredient in a range of products including chocolate, biscuits, ice cream, bread, toothpaste, soap and body lotions. Pay attention to what you buy if you don't want to contribute to the spiralling deforestation and death of priceless native species. (For further information, see *Natural History*, pages 61–6.) Palm oil is also being eyed as a potential source of biofuel – supposedly a green fuel, but knocked by critics as 'deforestation diesel' because of the widespread forest clearing created by producers.

Oil palm plantations contribute about 5% of Malaysia's national GDP, and provide some 1.5 million jobs. Sabah is the biggest producer though Sarawak is quickly catching up. Since the end of the 1990s, production in Sabah has multiplied and the amount of land under plantation doubled from 700,000 to 1.4 million hectares – a staggering 20% of the state.

Sabah's favourable climate yields the highest palm oil crops per hectare, attracting a swarm of potential investors. Most plantations are found in the east where, according to the Sabah Institute of Development Studies, 'suitable agricultural land is available'. Much of that is actually destroyed forest, ruined by logging or oil palm practices.

In precious natural areas such as the Kinabatangan River, it is deeply troubling to see how much of the habitat of endangered species has been swallowed up by the industry. Orangutans that once lived in the jungle now live in plantations, where they are considered pests. The Palm Oil Council maintains these environmental encroachments are errors of the past, and that it is now seeking higher yields through seed technology rather than land clearing. Yet as the voracious appetite for palm oil and plantation space continues, the industry is charged with 'the genocide of the orangutan'. Many animals are killed during forest clearing, and many more lose their habitat.

Sarawak's increasingly common wholesale plantations are also said to be encroaching on the land of indigenous people, who repeatedly find themselves in confrontation with police called in by contractors. Instead of palm oil production being an answer to rural poverty, as the government claims it to be, critics see it as a gateway to misery, with indigenous races forced to abandon their homes and work for a pittance on plantations.

By taxi Taxis are relied upon a lot in Sandakan. The **Sandakan Taxi Association** (*Jln Leila, Hsiang Garden;* ✆ *089 222439*) charges about RM6 for around-town trips, RM25 to the airport, RM40 to Sepilok, and RM90 to Labuk Bay.

By bus Air-conditioned long-distance buses run to and from Kota Kinabalu, Tawau and Lahad Datu. The buses from Kota Kinabalu leave several times a day; the journey takes seven hours and costs RM43. From Tawau, it is a six-hour trip and costs RM19.50. All buses arrive and leave from Sandakan's long-distance express bus station terminal, 5km north of town in the commercial zone known as Taman Fajar (a RM10 taxi fare). There are also minibuses from the local bus station on Coastal Road near Centre Point Mall. Further along, on Jalan Pryer towards the central market, buses come and go all day, to Sepilok and Labuk Bay.

By boat Various companies operate boat trips from the jetty on Sandakan Bay to the islands and the lower Kinabatangan area. Outside the established tours, there are limited boat services, but that does not stop the adventurous chartering a speedboat (or even a fishing boat) as a water taxi and heading off to an island in the bay. The Sandakan Yacht Club is on the marina.

TOUR OPERATORS Established operators for excursions in the region are **SI Tours**, **Borneo Eco Tours** and **Wildlife Expeditions** (see pages 78–80, for details). All three can facilitate the excursions outlined in the **What to see and do section** (see pages 232–4 and 237), including day and overnight trips to the Kinabatangan River and the Turtle Islands. Other lodges organise their own transport and tours, including **Uncle Tan Wildlife Adventures** (see page 236). A newcomer is **Tropical Wildlife Adventures** (*Jln Tiga;* \ *089 271077; www.stwadventure.com*), which offers tours of Sandakan town, Sepilok's Orangutan Rehabilitation and Rainforest Discovery centres, and the Gomantong Caves.

🏠 **WHERE TO STAY** *See map, page 226.*
Sandakan Harbour Square is developing into a new hotel precinct, with a slow but sure widening of the city's offerings to include major international brands. Sadly both the Accor/Ibis Styles hotel and Best Western property were falling way short of their usual international standards in 2014. A cluster of budget and shoestring hotels are located about 1.5km along the coast in the Ramai Ramai commercial centre and Hsiang Garden districts. A new backpackers' lodge worth looking into is the **Harbourside Backpackers** (\ *089 217072; www.harboursidebackpackers.com*).

Upmarket and mid range

🏠 **Four Points by Sheraton** (299 rooms) Sandakan Harbour Sq; \ 089 244888; e reservations.sandakan@fourpoints.com; www. fourpointssandakan.com. The big arrival in 2014, connected to the Sandakan Harbour Sq Mall, Sandakan's already top-rated hotel continues to score high for room comfort & service; slightly less for food. Travel site/user-review performances it openly displays to visitors on its website, with a refreshingly modern & transparent attitude sure to shake up the town's hospitality industry. All rooms (many of them with harbour view) have the brand's comfortable bed, complimentary water & Wi-Fi, while larger rooms have coffee tables & sofa, & suites have a separate living room. Good-value Executive Club rooms & suites include lounge

access. Deli-café, lobby lounge, all day restaurant & beer bar; fitness centre, 13th-floor infinity pool & 9 meeting rooms. **$$$$–$$**

🏠 **Sabah Hotel** (120 rooms) Km1, Jln Utara (1km from city centre); \ 089 213299; www. sabahhotel.com.my. With standards at Sandakan's once top leisure hotel starting to slide dramatically, the hotel embarked on a much-needed renovation programme unfinished in late 2014. The 1970s building was showing its age; guests complain of damp rooms & indifferent service. The infrastructure if fully modernised could still make it a great hotel, thanks to its striking Chinese domino-like structure on the hilltop, in 5ha of garden overflowing into the rainforest. Spacious superior rooms (32m²) & executive suites (71m²). Business centre, swimming pool fed by a waterfall,

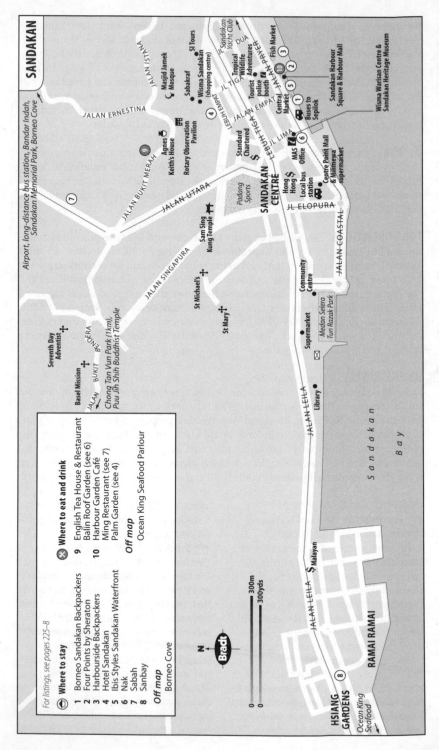

SANDAKAN

Airport, long-distance bus station, Bandar Indah,
Sandakan Memorial Park, Borneo Cove

JALAN ISTANA

JALAN ERNESTINA

JALAN BUKIT MERAH

JALAN SINGAPURA

JALAN UTARA

JALAN LELA

JALAN-LELA

JALAN-COASTAL

JL ELOPURA

JL TIGA

LEBUH EMPAT

LEBUH TIGA

JALAN EMPAT

JL LIMA

Masjid Jamek
Mosque

SI Tours

Sabakraf

Wisma Sandakan
(shopping centre)

Tropical
Wildlife
Adventures

Tourist
police
booth

Sandakan
Yacht Club

Fish Market

Sandakan Harbour
Square & Harbour Mall

Wisma Warisan Centre &
Sandakan Heritage Museum

Central
Market

Buses to
Sepilok

MAS
Office

Centre Point Mall
& Milimewa
supermarket

Hong
Hong $

Local bus
station

Agnes
Keith's House

Rotary Observation
Pavilion

Standard
Chartered

Padang
Sports

SANDAKAN
CENTRE

Sam Sing
Kung Temple

St Michael's ✝

St Mary ✝

Seventh Day
Adventist ✝

Basel Mission ✝

Chong Tan Vun Park (1km),
Puu Jih Shih Buddhist Temple

JALAN BUKIT BENDERA

Community
Centre

Supermarket

Medan Selera
Tun Razak Park

Library

$ Malayan

Ocean King
Seafood

HSIANG
GARDENS

RAMAI RAMAI

Sandakan Bay

② ③
① ⑤ ⑥ ④ ⑦ ⑧ ⑨ ⑩

For listings, see pages 225–8

Where to stay
1 Borneo Sandakan Backpackers
2 Four Points by Sheraton
3 Harbourside Backpackers
4 Hotel Sandakan
5 Ibis Styles Sandakan Waterfront
6 Nak
7 Sabah
8 Sanbay

Off map
    Borneo Cove

⊗ Where to eat and drink
9   English Tea House & Restaurant
    Balin Roof Garden (see 6)
    Harbour Garden Café
10 Ming Restaurant (see 7)
    Palm Garden (see 4)

Off map
    Ocean King Seafood Parlour

N

Bradt

300m
300yds
0

226

jungle jogging trail, fitness club & spa, buffet b/fasts & lunches, & a very good in-house Chinese restaurant. **$$$$–$$**

🏠 **Hotel Sandakan** (105 rooms) Block 83, 4th Av; ☎ 089 221122; e info@hotelsandakan.com.my; www.hotelsandakan.com.my. Excellent range of rooms & suites, switched-on service & technology & a resolute business beat. Save 30–40% on internet bookings. **$$$–$$**

Budget
🏠 **Ibis Styles Sandakan Waterfront** (former Swiss-Inn Waterfront Sandakan) (133 rooms) HS12, Sandakan Harbour Sq; ☎ 089 240888; e H9480-RE@accorhotels.com; www. accorhotels.com. Bright, mod-furnished hotel splashed with primary colours. Good-value rooms & suites with views over Sulu Sea, LCD TV, rain showers; business centre, car park, café. I hope the hotel picks up fast on a couple of shortfalls in food quality & maintenance, to do full merit to Accor's unique budget-with-style brand, & the great location. **$$**

🏠 **Sanbay Hotel** (58 rooms) Mile 1¼, Jln Leila; ☎ 089 275000; e sean@sanbay.com.my; www.sanbay.com.my. A couple of miles out of town with shuttle service to the city, 3-star with views over the bay. Good service & well-furnished spacious rooms with satellite TV/CNN, en-suite

bathrooms. AC throughout & generator-backed power. In-house Raja's café. **$$**

🏠 **Nak Hotel** (35 rooms) Jln Pelabuhan; ☎ 089 272988; e info@nakhotel.com; www.nakhotel. com. This shoestring boutique is a character-filled, family-run hotel, named after a former MP. Great value for money, though noisy. Pleasant roof garden-bar, clean comfortable rooms & old Chinese trading world aesthetic of reds & blacks. Standard singles & doubles, deluxe family rooms & 'suites'. **$$–$**

Shoestring
🏠 **Borneo Cove** (55 rooms) Lot 2, Mile 1½, Jln Buli Sim-Sim; ☎ 089 203777. About 4km north of the city centre, yet still deemed good value, with room promotions of RM95 with b/fast, & easy local bus connection to town. All rooms have AC, 32" LCD TV, Wi-Fi & bathrooms with rain showers. Also dormitory beds. **$**

🏠 **Borneo Sandakan Backpackers** (11 rooms) Lot 108, Block SH-11, Sandakan Harbour Sq; ☎ 089 221104; e enquiries@ sandakanbackpackers.com; www. sandakanbackpackers.com. Dorm, single/double rooms & 1 family room. No curfew; lounge & sundeck, internet, complimentary b/fast. Good for backpacker tours in the area. **$**

✕ **WHERE TO EAT AND DRINK** *See map, opposite.*
Sandakan has fantastic fresh seafood which can be enjoyed at food stalls and coffee shops selling it at a fraction of the price of seafood restaurants. Some good Malay, Chinese and Western eateries are found in hotels of all price brackets, usually with the choice of sitting outdoors or inside with air conditioning.

✕ **English Tea House & Restaurant** 2002 Jln Istana, adjacent to Agnes Keith Hse Museum; ☎ 089 222544; e info@englishteahouse. org; www.englishteahouse.org Very British, with its Bermuda grass & croquet lawns. The food is a rather bland fusion of Western & Asian, of sandwiches & *laksa*, but the gorgeous breezy hilltop location & viewpoint over the sea & city merit a cup of tea at least. Relatively expensive. **$$$$–$$$**

✕ **Ming Restaurant** In Sabah Hotel, Km1, Jln Utara; ☎ 089 213299. Large menu of Cantonese & Szechuan dishes including some interesting vegetarian 'chicken' & 'pork' meals (ie: sweet-&-sour tofu or honeyed soy). In the same hotel,

the poolside Plantation Café has excellent lunch & dinner buffets, including steamboats & BBQs. In-house breads (Chinese & European, white & sourdough) & pastries are sold in the lobby delicatessen. **$$$$–$$$**

✕ **Ocean King Seafood Parlour** Pasir Putih (White Sand). A 20min drive from the town centre on the coast, but worth the trip for the fresh seafood platter menu at very reasonable prices. Recommended by locals. **$$$**

✕ **Palm Garden** Hotel Sandakan, Block 83, 4th Av; ☎ 089 221122; (food served 06.30–23.00). Chinese restaurant specialising in Cantonese & dim sum delicacies. There is also a halal coffee shop – the Palm Café. **$$$**

✗ Balin Roof Garden The rooftop café-bar at the Nak Hotel (see page 227) is gaining some fans for its food & sympathetic breezy location. **$$$–$$**

✗ Harbour Garden Café Ground Floor, Sandakan Harbour Sq. Chinese café with great views & variable food. Johnny Lim from the Sepilok Jungle Resort says this: 'Came to the café because it was recommended by some tourists. Did not regret. Thoroughly enjoyed the chicken pau & dim sum. Best part was the friendly staff & the amazing waterfront view.' **$$**

Street food Head to the **central market**, and then to the adjacent **open market**, where you will find dozens of stalls with fresh and cooked food as well as coffee shops. Malay eateries are always set up between the waterfront Jalan Coastal and the Sandakan Community Centre.

ENTERTAINMENT AND NIGHTLIFE At Mile 4, about 5km from town towards Sepilok, **Bandar Indah** is a young, nouveau-riche suburb – a happening place with lots of bars, pubs and happy hours from 17.00 to 18.00. Live performances often follow, and things really start heating up at around 22.00 with karaoke and disco action. There is also some local nightlife for those staying in the **Ramai-Ramai** area, in the form of discos, bars and hotel entertainment.

SHOPPING The newest retail hub is the five-storey **Harbour Mall**, in the Harbour Square development (*www.shsquare.com.my*). The established shopping centre, **Wisma Sandakan**, is a multi-levelled mall at the back of town. Here you will find plenty of fast food, electronics, clothing and internet cafés in an uninspiring environment. The state-owned souvenir and crafts-shop chain, **Sabakraf**, is just behind this plaza. For books, the **South East Asia Bookstore** is located off Jalan Empat in the CBD. The **Centre Point Mall** off the waterfront's Jalan Coastal has a department store, supermarket and various shops and eateries.

OTHER PRACTICALITIES The **banks** district revolves around the visitor information centre – HSBC, Bumiputera Commerce and Standard Chartered. The **post office** and **library** are on the southwest edge of town, near Medan Selera Tun Razak Park.

WHAT TO SEE AND DO
Waterfront Sandakan is a port city and can be enjoyably explored on foot. The new shoreline development of **Sandakan Harbour Square** links with the 1.5km-long **Esplanade** to form a pleasant strolling stretch. In the middle of Harbour Square, the **fish market** and **central market** are situated in a modern three-storey complex, with the 'wet' and 'dry' markets on the ground level and clothing stores and shop-lots on the upper levels. The more rural tamu held here on Sundays is a cultural bouillabaisse of all the flavours ocean migrations have brought to Sandakan. Around the harbour, water villages are strung out on stilts; residents of the creaky, colourful, flower-potted Kampung Buli Sim Sim simply throw their fishing lines out of their windows to catch their dinner and enjoy the views of Sandakan's cargo boats and islands.

Temples and mosques Sandakan's velvety hills are covered with places of worship. **Sam Sing Kung** ('Three Saints Temple') is the city's oldest building, completed in 1887 – its three deities uphold righteousness, safety of fishermen and success in exams. A high spiritual, architectural and panoramic experience is the **Puu Jih Shih Buddhist Temple**, a red-shingled white-walled spectacle of writhing dragons and gilded Buddhas, perched on a hilltop a few kilometres north of the town centre. The temple was built in 1987 at a cost of RM7 million. Other holy places, including the **Masjid Jamek Mosque** and **St Michael's & All Angels' Church**, the latter built in 1893 from local granite and one of the only surviving pre-war buildings, lie along the **Sandakan Heritage Trail**. Pick up a map of the trail from the **visitor information centre** (between Lebuh Empat & Lebuh Tiga avs). In a 90-minute–two-hour loop walk, it links up 14 places of interest between the port and hilltop, via forested parkland and the **Stairs with a Hundred Steps** (warning: there have been reports of muggings in this area despite it being alongside a police station). Other sites of note include the **Chinese World War II Memorial**, more temples, and the **English Tea House**.

Museums Agnes Keith's book on life in pre-war Sandakan popularised the use of the old seafarer's name for Sabah – 'Land Below the Wind'. The American writer lived in a colonial wooden bungalow overlooking Sandakan Bay with her husband Henry Keith, the first forestry chief of British North Borneo. **Agnes Keith's House** (*Jln Istana;* \ *089 222679;* ⊕ *09.00–17.00 daily; RM15*) lies along the heritage trail, as does the more interesting local history depot, the **Sandakan Heritage Museum** (*Wisma Warisan Centre;* \ *089 222679;* ⊕ *09.00–17.00 daily*).

Memorials Within the Sibuga Forest Reserve, 12km north of the city, is the **Sandakan Memorial Park** (*Mile 7, Jln Labuk Utara;* m *016 822 1616;* ⊕ *09.00–17.00 daily*), just opposite the site of the original Sandakan prisoners of war camp. The 2,700 Australian and British POWs brought here in 1942 were used as a labour force to build a military airstrip, later destroyed by the Japanese. This is also where the dreadful Sandakan to Ranau 'death marches' set out from (see page 234). The memorial park's Commemorative Pavilion has a graphic display with an excellent, though heart-rending, interpretation of this appalling period. See also the **Chinese World War II Memorial**.

EXCURSIONS FROM SANDAKAN

ISLANDS For diving and turtle watching (or just playing Robinson Crusoe), there are several islands within and beyond Sandakan's beautiful harbour.

Pulau Berhala (Reached by charter boat or tour) Right in Sandakan Bay, the soaring red cliffs and dark forested clusters of Berhala Island are stunning. It was used as a POW camp during the war – and prior to that, a leper colony. Some Australian POWs used the old leper settlement as an escape route, swimming to the cliffs where they were helped by natives to freedom.

Turtle Islands Marine Park Situated 40km north of Sandakan in the Sulu Sea, the Turtle Islands Marine Park is part of a major nesting ground for green and hawksbill turtles. The turtle sanctuary, established in 1977 to protect the two species, encompasses the three small islands of Pulau Selingan, Pulau Bakungan Kecil and Pulau Gulisan. Pulau Selingan is the main nesting area for hundreds of green turtles, while the hawksbills are more attracted to the shores of Pulau Gulisan. Shaped like a musical note with a sandy rim and green core, it is less than 9ha in size.

Green turtles usually spend their time in shallow sea grass beds, but come ashore to lay their eggs. Each night during the nesting season, hordes of turtles drag themselves up the beach to deposit their unhatched offspring. An individual may spend hours choosing the right spot, before she commences digging a hole in the sand with her flippers. The best time to visit is between March and September (peak laying season and calm seas). Personally, I find the overcrowded spectacle quite upsetting. Rangers spotlight the scene with torches, revealing not only the egg laying but also the newly hatched youngsters making their way to the sea, for their first fragile hours in the big world. One can't help but feel that these creatures deserve the dignity of living out these moments in peace.

Getting there and away A boat leaves Sabah Parks's jetty on Jalan Buli Buli daily at 09.30. The trip to Selingan takes an hour. Sabah Parks has enlisted **Crystal Quest** (089 212711; e cquest@tm.net.my) to manage the park visits, trips and accommodation (**$$$–$$**). They have a presence at the Sabah Parks jetty on Jalan Buli Sim Sim. For overnight visits (the only way to witness the egg-laying exhibition), accommodation consists of simple but clean chalet rooms with bathrooms; expect sudden power cuts as electricity is provided by a generator. The rest of your time can be spent swimming in the crystal-clear waters.

Pulau Lankayan
The 80-minute speedboat trip out to Lankayan, across Sandakan Bay and into the Sulu Sea, is thrilling. Churned-up conditions have had my heart pounding as hard as the bottom of the boat on the waves, though boats will not leave if the weather is too bad. The 14 dive sites offer an ocean cocktail of reef, wreck and macro-pelagic diving. With increased protection (relying on observation by Malaysian and Filipino fishing vessels), large marine life to the surrounding reefs is said to be making a comeback – leopard sharks, marbled stingray, mimic octopus and giant grouper. 'Jawfish Lair' is home to yellow camouflaged jawfish. 'Lankayan Wreck' – a fish-poaching vessel put out of business – lies very close to shore. Though visibility was poor here when I dived, I still got to see stingrays, painted frogfish, harlequin ghost pipefish and schools of parrotfish.

Where to stay and eat Another one-island, one-resort set-up, operated by **Pulau Sipadan Resorts & Tours** (089 230782; e psrt@po.jaring.my; www.lankayan-island. com; **$$$$–$$$**), the 16 chalets nestle prettily at the water's edge or near the trees. Food served in the main lodge is simple but fresh. Take any extras you may require, as there are no shops. You don't have to be a diver to stay here – the seclusion and simple wooden chalets make a heavenly Robinson Crusoe-style break.

SEPILOK AND LABUK BAY
Sandakan would receive only a fraction of the visitors it does if it wasn't for Sepilok's famous orangutan sanctuary. Further west, Labuk Bay is a proboscis monkey sanctuary hedged in by plantations. A relative newcomer to Sepilok's sanctuary scene is the Bornean Sun Bear Conservation Centre.

Getting there and away Sepilok is 22km west of Sandakan, 11km from the airport, along Jalan Lintas Labuk. Labuk Bay is a further 25km in this direction. There are signs for both. **Minibuses** for both destinations depart from near the central market on Jalan Pryer. From Sandakan town centre bus station, take bus No 14 to the Sepilok Orangutan Rehabilitation Centre (*RM3*), which is 25km from Sandakan. Expect to pay RM35 for a 45-minute journey by **taxi**.

Where to stay
Sepilok Forest Edge Resort (16 rooms) Jln Rambutan (off Jln Sepilok, Mile 14); 089 533190; e sepilok@sepilokforestedge.com; www.sepilokforestedge.com. 9 standard, family & superior chalets (sleeping 5), plus a 7-room

backpacker longhouse (RM40–45 bed/RM85–95 double room). 'In farm environment' on edge of jungle, a 10min walk from Sepilok. **$$$–$**
Sepilok Nature Resort (17 twin rooms) Off Jln Sepilok, near the Orangutan

MIGHTY OR BLIGHTED KINABATANGAN RIVER?

Flowing 560km from its source near the Crocker Range east to the Sulu Sea, the Sungai Kinabatangan – Kinabatangan River – is Sabah's longest (and Malaysia's second-longest) waterway. The watery journey, deep into the jungled hinterland of northern Sabah, is one of the most magical experiences in Borneo, thanks to the contact with remarkable river creatures and people.

The boat sets out from Sandakan Bay into the Sulu Sea, before swerving up the estuary, through gaping floodplains and narrow straits.

Much of this area falls within the 28,000ha Lower Kinabatangan Sanctuary. Created in 1999, it provides a variety of habitats including freshwater swamp, mangrove, palms and bamboo – and is one of only two places in the world inhabited by ten species of primates. Four are endemic to Borneo – silvered, maroon and Hose's langurs, and the inimitable proboscis monkey. The Kinabatangan conservation area boasts the highest concentration of proboscis monkeys and orangutans in Malaysian Borneo. Other wildlife encounters may include long-tailed and pig-tailed macaques, Bornean gibbons, the rare slow loris, pygmy elephants and Sumatran rhinoceros. Over 200 species of birds are found here, including eight types of hornbill (among them the rare wrinkled hornbill), lesser fish eagles, stork-billed kingfishers, black and yellow broadbills, pitas and bulbuls.

The name 'Kinabatangan' comes from a combination of the words *Kina* – China – and *Batang* – large river. Evidence suggests there was a Chinese settlement on the banks of the river as far back as the 7th century, trading in birds' nests, beeswax, rattan and ivory. The Orang Sungai Kinabatangan river people who live along the riverbanks today are of mixed ancestry including Dusun, Suluk, Bugis, Bajaus and Chinese. A Chinese princess from the Kinabatangan married the first sultan of Brunei in the 15th century.

Oil palm plantations are encroaching on this beautiful river environment at an alarming rate. Decades of logging have cleared the riverbanks, opening the zone up for more exploitation. Electric fences shock pygmy elephants that try to feed on the plantations, which have replaced the forests they once roamed through freely. Meanwhile, villages that used to flank forests full of orangutans now see only agricultural estates. Despite the state government dubbing it a 'Corridor of Life' in 2002, and gazetting it as a Wildlife Sanctuary, the Kinabatangan's continually shrinking and disturbed habitat will remain seriously vulnerable until it is declared a national park. During the river rush hour of dusk wildlife tours, one can't help but wonder whether the intense tourist traffic is also upsetting the balance of nature. (See pages 127–30, for ways to minimise the negative impacts on the environment as you travel.)

Rehabilitation Centre; ☎089 673999; e sepilok@po.jaring.my; www.sepilok.com. A 10min walk from the orangutan viewings, the twin-bed chalets overhang a lake, festooned in rainforest species, orchids & ferns. This friendly, relaxed resort organises jungle treks & wildlife-spotting trips. Its rattan-roofed lodgings have AC, ample hot water & forest-viewing balconies. **$$**

Paganakan Dii Tropical Retreat
(6 rooms, 36 longhouse beds) Taman Hiburan Jalil Alip (Recreation Park); ☎089 532005; e info@ paganakandii.com; www.paganakandii.com. Nuts-&-bolts forest accommodation, calling itself a 'truly tropical retreat'. Loved by those wanting a bargain-basement jungle experience, yet with a tropical dream location. You get what you pay for lodgings-wise, but fans would say you also

get much more in the form of the Kadazandusun family friendliness & budget-jungle cool. Taxi from the airport RM35. $

🏠 **Sepilok Jungle Resort** (60 rooms) Km22, Jln Labuk; ✆ 089 533031; e info@sepilokjungleresort.com; www.sepilokjungleresort.com. In beautiful jungled gardens, Johnny Lim's resort is still far from reaching its potential, due to all-round tired décor, poor food, service & security. Despite ongoing upgrades (& the warning of possibly noisy stays) since late 2008, the 'accommodation blocks' (which are a bit cell-like rather than cosy), are still in a state of being dolled-up. The upside is the forest location, wild animals (orangutans & tarsiers are often seen in the gardens), & cheap prices for fan-cooled rooms. 'We are pampering you with the natural surrounding & the beautiful garden around the lodge,' says Lim. $

What to see and do

Rainforest Discovery Centre *(Jln Labuk, Sepilok;* ✆ *089 533780;* e *rdcsepilok@ yahoo.com; www.forest.sabah.gov.my/rdc;* ⊕ *08.00–17.00 daily; adult RM15, children*

BUILDING A BEAR'S PLAYGROUND

No sooner have a couple of volunteers performed acrobatic stunts to saw a tyre in two, than 'Mamatai' is clambering high and swinging happily from her forest swing. Mamatai is one of the female bears in the new bear house at Sepilok's Sun Bear Conservation Centre, which volunteers from around the world are helping build.

Making hammocks and swings for orphan bears and mucking out cub cages are all part of a day in the life of a volunteer here, I discover during a visit. After just a couple of days' work, Malaysian volunteer Hiu has quickly grown attached to the black, tawny muzzled Paddle Pop-pawed creatures. 'I wish they could go back to the wild and lead a normal life, and that the world was as clean and green and forested as it used to be.' With that, barely bear-sized Hiu hops inside a square metal cage in which poached animals are often kept prisoner for years. 'It's not fun to be in this small cage – trust me, you don't want to stay in here even for a minute under this sun.'

While Borneo remains a stronghold for the sun bear's survival, threats of deforestation, poaching and the illegal pet trade are ever-present. Named for the crescent-shaped patch of golden fur on their chests, the bears are hunted and their gall bladders, blood, bile and bones used for food and medicine. Sun bear paws are used to make a soup, considered a delicacy from Vietnam to Japan. Added to the International Union for Conservation of Nature red list in 2007, the IUCN Bear Specialist Group says the total sun bear population has declined by at least 30% in the last three decades.

'Baby sun bears are one of the cutest animals in the world, yet their habitats are being destroyed by deforestation and the bears are being brutally killed for commercial exploitation,' BSBCC founder Siew Te Wong tells me. After studying the conservation of the sun bear for a decade, the wildlife biologist steered the way to the centre's opening in 2010. On arrival, he gives all new volunteers a brief lecture on sun bear ecology, before venturing into the surrounding rainforest.

The 58ha patch of secondary rainforest – a mix of towering trees, fruit trees and streams – currently provides a haven for 28 rescued bears in varying states of rehabilitation. Siew compares it to a halfway house. 'Sadly, many of them have already spent too many years locked up in cages and are distressed, but day by day, we strive to improve their lives and eventually introduce them to the forest once again.'

RM7, children under 5 free) Adding to the long-established and at times overvisited orangutan rehabilitation centre, is this Sabah Forestry-run centre with its 147m-long canopy walk through Menggaris and other dipterocarp trees, 28m above the forest floor. The steel walk is punctuated by viewing towers – great for stealing a glimpse of the 250 resident birds, including the rare Bornean bristle heads, as well as hornbills, pittas, kingfishers and broadbills. The 800m rainforest discovery trail is a well-interpreted suspension-bridge stretch with possible sightings of flying squirrels, and, on night walks, tarsiers, mouse deer, large geckoes, stick insects and civets. While welcoming visitors, the centre's main role is as an environmental education centre for students, teachers and 'junior ranges'. All entry fees go into running the centre.

Sepilok Orangutan Rehabilitation Centre *(Jln Labuk, Sepilok;* \ *089 531180;* e *soutan@po.jaring.my; www.sabah.gov.my/jhl;* ⏰ *08.30–17.00 daily;*

The project is jointly run by the Malaysian NGO LEAP (Land Empowerment Animal People), which raises funds; the Sabah Wildlife Department, whose workers confiscate and relocate the animals and provide full-time bear care; and the Sabah Forestry Department, which allocated the land. But it's volunteers from the world over, young professionals and students, who have provided the vital backbone for the initiative, spearheaded by UK-based youth and sustainable development charity Raleigh International. Having built the original centre – enclosures, fencing and boardwalks – teams from Raleigh continue to join Malaysian volunteers and student zookeepers from Australia and the United States. They are busy building new bear enclosures – complete with playground – clearing jungle paths, and dragging logs and barrows of leaves. Teams of volunteers are helping transform the lives of these disenfranchised animals, by focusing on innovative concepts for 'environmental enrichment' of their physical habitat.

Despite the sadness of the bear's plight, observing them also brings many bear-bellied laughs, says another volunteer, Amanda. 'It's very entertaining watching the sun bears play with the enrichments we've helped make. One bear, Fulung did a Cirque du Soleil stunt while swinging on the rope of the tyre swing.'

'Sun bears are also powerful coconut breakers,' says another volunteer, Tommy.

'All these bear facts fascinate us... It was a privilege to be in such close proximity with these fluffies and a great joy to see the evolution of certain bears in my time here,' Amanda adds. 'I will never forget the moment when Rungus stepped outside of the fenced forest enclosure for the first time, followed by her friends Natalie, Julaini and Ah Lun. And when the youngest cub, eight-month-old Damai, started climbing tall trees and got used to sleeping in them. This nurtures their natural skills to survive in the wild again... At first I thought it was special to be one of the first locals to volunteer. Now I think everyone should do the same and learn about this amazing animal. Staff here are not only saving the sun bear's population, but giving them a second chance to live.'

Note: UK-based Raleigh International targets 18–35-year-old volunteers for two–three-month expeditions in Borneo which cost between approximately £1,200 and £1,900, and move around several projects in Sabah and Sarawak. On its website (*www.raleighinternational.org*), it suggests many ways for young people to raise the funds, which cover basic food, accommodation and journey costs.

adult RM30, children 18 & under RM15; video/photo fees extra) One of Borneo's orangutan-viewing hotspots, entry prices have soared here in recent years. 'SOURC' was set up in 1964 to rehabilitate orphaned orangutans who had lost their parents and their habitat through logging. The apes were brought here to be taught the necessary survival skills before returning to the wild. Operated by Sabah's Wildlife Department, it has now branched out into tourism and education, as well as conservation of other species. A boardwalk leads to the feeding platform, perched up in the trees about 25m from the viewing area. The number of orangutans to be viewed depends on luck – and whether the orangutan females' favourite 'Mr B' is there. Once the huge apes are full of bananas and vitamin shakes, they set off to have a swing and a play. Macaques and gibbons also come for a bite to eat. This is a great way to get a close-up view of the 'Man of the Jungle' and his primate cohorts. Feeding times are at 10.00 and 15.00 – the latter is generally quieter.

Bornean Sun Bear Conservation Centre (*Jln Labuk, Sepilok;* ✎ *089 534491;* e *info.bsbcc@gmail.com; www.bsbcc.org.my;* ⊕ *09.00–15.30 daily; adult RM30, children 17 & under RM15*) Also in Sepilok, right alongside the orangutan rehabilitation centre, a battle is on to save the world's smallest bear. The pint-sized Malayan sun bear or *Helarctos malayanus* is found only in Southeast Asia. On average, they weigh in at 70kg and reach 1m in height. The bear care centre, officially launched in October 2014, shares veterinary facilities, personnel, parking, access roads and ticket gates with the orangutan rehabilitation centre. (See box, pages 232–3 for more information on the centre's activities and volunteer programme.)

Kabili-Sepilok Forest Reserve Sabah's top tourist attractions – Sepilok's orangutans and the rainforest discovery centre – lies within an often-overlooked rainforest reserve. Most visitors watch the feasting frenzy and leave, but there is plenty to see in the reserve too. The 43km² of lowland rainforest contains 350 different tree species and almost 40% of the known Dipterocarpaceae flora in Sabah. There is also a 5km trekking trail to Sepilok Laut, through mangrove forest – for which you need to get a Forestry Department permit.

Labuk Bay Proboscis Monkey Sanctuary (*Mile 8, Bandar Sibuga Jaya, off Jln Lintas Labuk;* ✎ *089 672133;* e *labukbay@proboscis.cc; www.proboscis.cc; feeding times 09.30, 11.30, 14.30 & 16.30 daily; adult RM60, children 12 & under RM30*) This sanctuary offers an opportunity for proboscis monkey sighting and birdwatching for those who don't have time to travel up the Kinabatangan River for an overnight stay. Located in mangrove forest along the coast near Kampung Samawang, Labuk Bay, it's about an hour's drive from Sandakan (*48km*). The last 15km is along a gravel road through the centre of oil palm plantations. The best viewing times are apparently 10.30 and 16.30.

Deathly trek While some might find this hike through grim warring history too upsetting, TYK Adventure Tours (✎ *088 720826;* e *www.sandakantrack.com*) trace the steps of the chilling Sandakan–Ranau death march of World War II POWs, on a five- to seven-day trek. The trip is usually organised from Kota Kinabalu, and involves a flight to Sandakan and transfer to Tolupid (about three hours away) to begin the walk there, in order to avoid palm oil plantations. You could join the group in Sandakan rather than Kota Kinabalu if you prefer.

KINABATANGAN RIVER

Sukau A small settlement on the banks of the lower Kinabatangan River, Sukau is the jungle hub for those who want to dwell within the wildlife habitat of the Sungai Kinabatangan conservation area. Be prepared to go back to basics.

Getting there and away Travelling **by car**, Sukau is 80km from Sandakan and around 120km from Lahad Datu. The recent sealing of the last 42km of road from Sukau Junction has taken the bumps out of the ride (hopefully not with funding from the oil palm plantations, which dominate 90% of the scenery along this road). **Buses** operate from Sandakan market to Sukau. Local tour operators and river lodges use **speedboats** for transfers from Sandakan's jetty and the Sepilok area to the lower Kinabatangan. A few of these operators also run lodges, but will provide transport to a different lodge.

Where to stay and eat Accommodation options range from rustic lodges and jungle camps to more upmarket lodges with bungalow-style wood-panelled rooms, modern bathrooms and some individual chalets. Most offer packages that include accommodation, meals, transfers and excursions. The area is run on generator electricity, and offers an enriching back-to-nature experience. Tapping into the growing demand for more comfortable quarters and surrounds, Sukau Rainforest Lodge got the ball rolling with a major overhaul in 2010. Other lodges have also recognised shortfalls in accommodation standards and food, and have made significant upgrades in recent years. Food at the budget lodges can still be ordinary, so take some snacks and drinks and any special dietary foods you may require.

Sukau Rainforest Lodge (20 rooms) ☎088 438300; e info@borneoecotours.com; www.sukau. com. Reigning as the queen of the Kinabatangan lodges for 2 decades, Borneo Eco Tour's part solar-powered lodge has won various international prizes for its eco-approach & has been a pioneer in ecotourism since opening in 1995. Extensive renovations completed in 2011 brought new-look rooms, a lounge, a reception area, a restaurant, a jetty & sunset deck. It is an intimate stay alongside nature, with 4 bird- & wildlife-viewing decks & a 450m-long 'hornbill boardwalk' complete with 2 'elephant passes' to accommodate regular migrations of the animals through the lodge grounds. The river-facing restaurant & sunset deck is a scenic highlight to be savoured. The lodge uses electric boats for the river cruises to minimise wildlife disturbance. **$$$$$**

Abai Jungle Lodge & Restaurant (24 twin rooms) ☎089 213502; e sales@ sitoursborneo.com; www.sitoursborneo.com. Set in mangroves with a 300m boardwalk through the forest, the lodge is run by SI Tours as a rustic ecotourism experience with biodegradable products, rainwater & minimal electricity. The river-facing lodge is eco-rustic & beautiful. Twin rooms are spacious, with powerful fans, modern bathrooms & furnishings. An incredible wildlife immersion, there are 500–800m-long jungle trails made from belian (hardwood) & a bird-viewing tower. Silver langur, maroon langur, hose langur & orangutan are regularly spotted here – I slept with a snoring orangutan very close by! Clouded leopard & sun bear have been seen on the trails behind the lodge. Food is served from a simple but dedicated restaurant, with locally sourced produce. Get your hands dirty with tree planting & other local development activities. Prices have risen by about 25–30% in the past few years. **$$$$**

Kinabatangan Riverside Lodge (33 rooms) ☎089 213502; e info@sitoursborneo. com; www.sitoursborneo.com. On the banks of the Kinabatangan in a lush setting, also run by SI Tours. A new wing here has introduced more spacious & comfortable double/twin & family rooms, 12 semi-detached units & three 3-room chalets. The 2009 makeover also improved the jetty & added a lovely river-facing sun deck. I am yet to experience for myself the upgrades to the food, though secondhand reports say it has improved considerably. Elephants visit frequently & macaques, proboscis, hornbills, crocodiles & monitor lizards all hover close by. Staff are lovely & the atmosphere around the main lodge is fun. River excursions are a highlight, with knowledgeable guides. Packages approx RM500 for 2 days/1 night pp, including transfers, meals, accommodation & excursions. **$$$$**

🏠 **Abi Village Homestays** (approx 30 houses) Tour operators can arrange for you to stay in the Abi village in people's homes, instead of a lodge. **$$$-$$**

🏠 **Uncle Tan Wildlife Adventures** Mile 16, Jln Gum Gum, Sepilok; 📞 089 531639; e eugene@ uncletan.com; www.uncletan.com. If you don't mind sleeping with several people (& perhaps a monkey or 2), this now legendary set-up is basic, but with its heart in the right nature-loving place. On the edge of an oxbow lake of the lower Kinabatangan,

the quasi-bush camp is remote & offers greater chances of seeing wildlife in the 'backyard' than many other river lodges. The founder, 'Uncle Tan', has passed away, but his family still run the business & the guides are passionate about their work. Food, staff & safaris are all of an exceptional standard. Lodgings are open-fronted with just a mosquito net for protection. A bit of a rowdy place in the best sense, it's for those who like a party atmosphere – Tiger beers in the jungle, football, karaoke & a jungle disco! All-inclusive packages of 3 days/2 nights with transfers & 6 river & jungle excursions, start at around RM350 pp. Bring wellies, raincoat & torch. Pickup & transfers start from Uncle Tan's shoestring B&B on Jln Gum Gum. **$$**

Bilit Since 2009, the Kampung Bilit area has emerged as an alternative Kinabatangan River base to Sukau. Most of the new lodges around Kampung Bilit village have a very strong emphasis on conservation, and community. The accommodation is an interesting mix of eco-rustic and quality, eco-chic, sometimes with both options available within the same walls.

Getting there and away For **self-drive travellers** it's straightforward, though most lodges offer budget to mid-range packages, including transfers from Sandakan. For shoestring (dormitory accommodation) travellers, where transfers are not part of the deal, the lodge will arrange a pickup in Sandakan or at bus stops, for a fee. It's 122km from Sandakan to Kampung Bilit (roughly a 2½-hour drive), then a quick cross-river trip to the lodges. The Nature Lodge Kinabatangan advises **bus travellers**: 'For those coming by bus from Lahad Datu, Tawau or Kota Kinabalu, get off at Medan Selera, a coffee shop at Bukit Garam Kota Kinabatangan. We will arrange a pickup from this point at 13.30.'

🏠 ***Where to stay and eat***

🏠 **Nature Lodge Kinabatangan** (16 rooms) Kampung Bilit; 📞 088 230534; e sales@nasalislarvatustours.com; www. naturelodgekinabatangan.com. An eco-lodge that's proud to have almost no frills other than recently introduced electricity. 'Not so basic after all' says the website, with news of washroom upgrades & the extra creature comforts of the Agamid wing chalets: attached bathrooms, hot water, anti-mosquito mattress & windows with jungle view. The Civet Wing is more basic cabin or dorm accommodation. Widely reported as a budget & eco-friendly jungle-drenched lodge, this group clearly has its conservation heart in the right place. 3-day/2-night packages range from RM370 for dorm only, to a surprisingly steep RM1,250 for chalet accommodation with transfers from Sandakan included. The lodge also runs pick-up

vans 'for a minimum charge' from Sandakan (m 013 863 6263) to book. **$$$$-$$**

🏠 **Bilit Adventure Lodge** (24 rooms) Kampung Bilit; 📞 089 271077; e info@ stwadventure.com; www.stwadventure. com. Sandakan-based Sepilok Tropical Wildlife Adventure put a strong focus on local staff & conservation at their lodge. Travellers' expenditure on things such as snacks & leech socks, it says, go to staff earnings & their families. A friendly, homely place, albeit rustic with AC & fan-cooled rooms. 2-day/1-night packages including meals & transfers from Sandakan from RM630. **$$$**

🏠 **Myne Resort** (14 chalets) Kampung Bilit; 📞 089 278288/90; e myneresort@gmail.com. my; www.myne.com.my. Up close with nature experience, river cruises, amicable staff & guides are applauded. The let down for some visitors is the lack of upkeep of the lodge itself. Facilities & activities include lounge grill & riverbank

restaurant, mountain biking & jungle trekking. **$$$**

What to see and do

River excursions All of the lodges and tour operators probe the Kinabatangan and its tributaries to see the wildlife from fibreglass boats. The serpentine bends of the river meander through the floodplain and swell to bursting during the rainy season.

The Menanggol, a 26km offshoot heading towards the Gomantong Caves, is considered one of the best wildlife-spotting areas, taking in fig, orchid and rattan-entwined riverine environments and freshwater swamp forest. Boats leave most lodges at around 16.30 daily for 90-minute proboscis monkey-viewing trips. Other common sightings on these river excursions are pit vipers, macaques and gibbons. Orangutans are more commonly seen on the trip to and from Sandakan. SI Tours offer a day-long 'Kinabatangan River Safari' from Sandakan, setting out to Sukau by road, to hook up with a dusk-departing boat.

For quieter early-morning trips, try bird- and wildlife-watching on the **oxbow lakes**, starting out before 05.00. These tranquil, disconnected river bends are teeming with birdlife and afloat with water hyacinths.

Firefly spotting At night, float out on a boat for some tranquil firefly spotting. The 'bioluminescence' of the fireflies is produced to attract a mate, created in their abdomens by chemical reactions that emit light. The riverbanks are lit up like Christmas trees strung with garlands of fireflies; a beautiful sight to behold.

***Local* kampung** On a U-turn bend in the Kinabatangan River, **Abi village** lies on the other side of the water from the Abai lodge. It's about equidistant between Sukau and Sandakan, and can only be reached by a one-hour boat journey from either direction. On a visit here you might see the 60 village children studying in their longhouse school, or time your visit with the local Hari Guru festivity – a day of paying tribute to the village teachers. To celebrate, a day of fun, sport and music is held – such as a banana-eating competition, makan pisang – skin and all!

Tree planting Roll up your sleeves and get involved in local tree planting, with initiatives such as **Bandok Abai Jungle Tree Planting Kinabatangan Project**, a joint project between WWF, a local NGO and Sabah Tourism. I planted a mango tree, and will go back to check on it in a year's time.

Gomantong Caves The Gomantong Caves are the largest limestone outcrop in Sabah. Set within limestone forest in the lower Kinabatangan, the cave is home to some two million bats as well as two million swiftlets, which produce edible mossy nests from their saliva. Locals use rattan and bamboo ladders to collect the nests, which hang from the cave roofs. The dusk performance is a delight for bird enthusiasts, as bat hawks and peregrine falcons pursue the bats. Some 27 species of bat roost here, predominantly wrinkled-lipped bats. The nests sell for about RM2,000 per kilogram, though a top-grade white nest can fetch more than six-times that – as much as US$4,000 per kilogram in Hong Kong.

Getting there and away The caves are 95km from Sandakan along the sealed Sandakan–Sukau **road**, and 26km from Sukau. **By boat** you can visit from Sandakan, or Sukau and the Kinabatangan area. Driving from the south, the caves are about two hours from Lahad Datu.

SABAH
Southeast

Bilit • • Sukau
Kulamba
Wildlife Reserve

Kinabatangan
Wildlife Sanctuary

Imbak Canyon
Conservation Area

Kampung
Cocos

Tabin
Wildlife
Reserve

Lahad Datu

Tungku

Maliau Basin
Conservation Area

Danum Valley
Conservation Area

Silabukan
Forest Reserve

N

Bradt

0 ——— 30km
0 ——— 30 miles

Tawau Hills
Park

Pulau
Pandanan

Pulau
Pom Pom

Pulau
Mataking

Semporna

Pulau
Bum Bum

Tawau

Tun Sakaran
(Semporna Islands)
Marine Park

Pulau Mabul
Sipadan
Marine Park

Pulau Sipadan

Pulau Kapalai

CELEBES SEA

BORNEO ONLINE

For additional online content, articles, photos and more on Borneo, why not
visit www.bradtguides.com/borneo.

8

Southeast Sabah

Between the islands, lagoons and straits of southeast Sabah lurks a treasure chest of marine biodiversity. Along the coast, hilly hinterlands are interspersed with some of Borneo's biggest tracts of enduring rainforest. Cocoa, rubber and coconut crops thrive in the fertile volcanic soils – though the landscape is increasingly dominated by large oil palm plantations. The region is inhabited by the Bajau Laut – maritime nomads whose ancestors set out from the Filipino island of Mindanao over 1,000 years ago. Many have now settled in stilt villages along the shores of the mainland as well as offshore islands and reefs. The Bajau remain closely connected to the sea, living on the coast and making a living from fishing and seaweed cultivation. Several local and international initiatives are under way to save the eco-region of the Sulu–Sulawesi seas. National Geographic magazine named it as one of the most diverse marine communities on earth – with nine times as many stony corals as the Caribbean Sea, and over twice the number found in the Indian Ocean. Six of the world's seven species of sea turtles dwell here, along with whale sharks, massive manta rays, and an incredible abundance of fish species. Bordered by three densely inhabited nations, it is a region of socio-political volatility – the population is forecast to double within three decades, and ocean piracy, territorial tugs of war and terrorist attacks persist (see pages 248–9). Security in the region suffered a setback in February 2013, when a group of Filipino militants invaded the coastal area of Lahad Datu, leading to deadly and drawn-out clashes with Malaysian security forces. Under the tag of the Royal Army of Sulu, the group of some 180 warriors said they had come to claim Sabah from Malaysia, as descendants of the Sultan of Sulu. The southern Philippines sultanate ruled over parts of northern Borneo for centuries. The state of Sabah grew out of historic leaseholds from the sultan to colonials. Militants invariably demand the Malaysian government continue to pay them for that land, or return it to them. Some 60 people – 52 Filipinos and eight Malaysian police officers – died in the Lahad Datu standoff.

TAWAU

Spread around Sebuku Bay, the commercial port occupies a strategic sea and land location on the southeast frontier of Sabah, with Indonesia's border towns visible some 30km across the bay. Since the 1990s, the population of Sabah's third-largest town has doubled to about 250,000 due to the influx of illegal immigrants from the Philippines and Indonesia. With the fastest rate of development in the state, the government upholds Tawau as an agricultural beacon – the Malaysian leader in cocoa production, research and development, and hub of oil palm plantations. The port still maintains a lively timber trade, with significant logging imports coming from poorer Kalimantan, raising questions about Malaysian logging practices with its Indonesian neighbour.

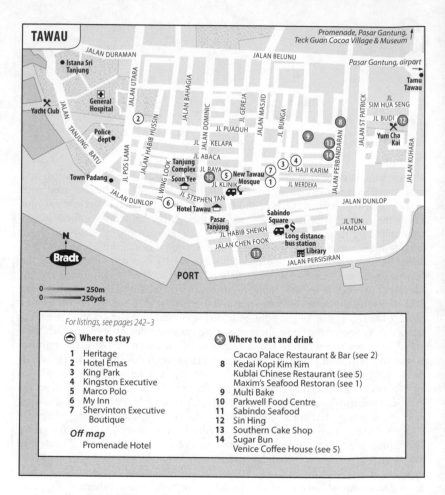

For listings, see pages 242–3

Where to stay

1 Heritage
2 Hotel Emas
3 King Park
4 Kingston Executive
5 Marco Polo
6 My Inn
7 Shervinton Executive
  Boutique

Off map
  Promenade Hotel

Where to eat and drink

Cacao Palace Restaurant & Bar (see 2)
8 Kedai Kopi Kim Kim
  Kublai Chinese Restaurant (see 5)
  Maxim's Seafood Restoran (see 1)
9 Multi Bake
10 Parkwell Food Centre
11 Sabindo Seafood
12 Sin Hing
13 Southern Cake Shop
14 Sugar Bun
  Venice Coffee House (see 5)

A small coastal fishing village in the 19th century under the Sultan of Sulu, Tawau was ceded to the British North Borneo Company in 1878, which established a rudimentary local government. In the 1890s, the population of 200 was made up largely of immigrants from Balungan and Tawi-Tawi, who had fled Dutch rule in Kalimantan. By the end of the 1930s, some 60 timber shop-houses, mostly Chinese-owned, lined the main street. During Japanese occupation in World War II, many locals were killed. British military administration continued until July 1946, when North Borneo became a Crown Colony and civil government was resumed. The noticeable religious diversity is an indication of its mixed roots and colourful history: there is a rather gaudy green-roofed, salmon-sided Buddhist lodge, a new mosque, the Basel Christian church and an Anglican church. Chinese make up about 15% of the population – Bajau and Malay peoples around the same – Indonesians nearly a quarter, while a mix of Kadazandusun and Murut comprise the rest. One Malay minority, the Bugis, are an exuberant seafaring people who have been migrating to Sabah for centuries from Sulawesi Island in Indonesia. As the main entry point for Indonesian traders and migrant workers, Tawau boasts a thriving barter-trade economy in cross-border products. Overlooking an immense stretch of sea, the tip of Tawau alone takes in 82km of coastline, 210 islands and 186 lagoons.

GETTING THERE AND AWAY
By air Tawau International Airport is located a lengthy 35km from town at Apas Balung – 70km from Semporna. As the transport hub for the southeast, most travellers to the nearby islands or Danum Valley area will pass by here. Rumoured plans for an airport in Semporna to handle island traffic have not materialised. MASwings has several daily flights to Tawau from Kota Kinabalu (*45 minutes*) and flights to/from Sandakan and Tarakan in Kalimantan (*promotional fares from RM135*). AirAsia connects Kuala Lumpur to Tawau in two hours and 40 minutes.

There are some buses from the airport to Tawau, operated by Kasah Transport. Some hotels operate shuttle services from the airport, charging around RM18 for a return journey. A taxi will cost RM40–60. If you are visiting the areas for diving, organise transfers with the dive package.

By car From Kota Kinabalu, take the east–west highway to Sandakan, then the east-coast highway to Semporna and Tawau. Tawau is also connected by major roads, such as the Tawau–Lahad Datu highway and the Tawau–Kunak highway.

By bus From Kota Kinabalu and Sandakan, express buses take eight hours and cost about RM60. From Lahad Datu the trip is 2½ hours. The long-distance bus station in Tawau is around Sabindo Square on the waterfront, between Jalan Dunlop and Jalan Chen Fook, adjacent to the mosque. Buses bound for Kota Kinabalu leave every evening at 19.45.

By ferry Ferry services operate several times daily between Tawau and the Kalimantan/Indonesian cities of Nunukan (*one hour away*) and Tarakan (*a three-hour journey*). Tawindo Express departs Tawau for Nunukan at 10.00 and 15.00, and from Nunukan to Tawau at 09.00 and 14.00. Tickets cost approximately RM40. The Tawindo Express sails between Tawau and Tarakan on Monday, Wednesday and Friday at 11.30, while the Indomaya express ferry departs Tuesday, Thursday and Saturday at 10.30. Tickets costs RM140. Note that for travel to Indonesia you must obtain a visa beforehand, as none is issued at the border. The visa-obtaining process in Tawau is famously fast; however, the Indonesian Consulate relocated in 2010 to an inconvenient location about 4km north of town (*Konsulat Republik Indonesia Tawau, Bangunan Yunwah, Mile 2.5, Jln Sin Onn, 91000 Tawau;* ☏ 089 772052/752969). Take a taxi to Jalan Sin Onn, and alight at the glass-towered Wisma Fuj building. The consulate lies to the right of this office/shopping building, a couple of hundred metres off the main street. Within an average two-hour wait a 60-day tourist visa is issued, costing RM160. Make sure you have two passport photos with you and proof of onward travel.

GETTING AROUND The best way to see the surrounding coast and hills is by car. The minibus station for local (and airport) buses is near the mosque. Taxis are easier and cost RM6–10 for most inner-town trips. The main town centre and wharf lies between Jalan Dunlop, Jalan Chen Fook, Jalan Stephen Tan and Jalan Chester. Kompleks Fajar commercial centre is the hub of many hotels, supermarkets, banks, ATMs and food outlets, near to the waterfront area around the Sabindo Complex.

🏠 **WHERE TO STAY** *See map, opposite.*
The mini budget hotel boom under way in Tawau three years ago has borne some fruit yet mostly with several new budget inns, guesthouses and hotels around city-central Jalan Haji Karim. As visitor numbers continue to rise, another handful of openings are forecast by 2020, concentrated in this zone and near the Fajar

shopping complex. While overall hotel service is on the rise as a result of the sharper competition and demand, it's happening mostly at the lower end of the hotel market. The mid-range to 'upmarket' hotels (Tawau has never had anything even approaching the luxury category) overall are lagging behind the times, and in need of some modernisation of furnishings and service.

In addition to the hotels listed below, another couple of newly opened inns you might want to check out are the **LA Hotel** (*www.lahotel.com.my*), with its shoestring-priced standard rooms and mid-range suites, and the bargain-basement **VS Guesthouse**, which has a Facebook page.

Upmarket and mid range

Promenade Hotel (180 rooms) 2nd Floor, Eastern Plaza, Jln Kuhara, Mile 1; 089 982888; e comm_tawau@promenade.com.my; www.promenade.com.my. 4-star sibling of the established hotel in Kota Kinabalu with large, excellently fitted rooms, though in need of overall refreshment. Good leisure & meetings facilities, modern décor & lighting, & a fine array of coffee shops, bars, nightclubs & restaurants. Prices are equally diverse, from the budget internet deals for standard rooms with b/fast, to top-notch executive suites. **$$$$–$$**

Heritage Hotel (88 rooms) 210–213 Jln Bunga, Fajar Kompleks; 089 766222; e info@ heritagehotel.com.my; www.heritagehotel.com. my. Inside the main shopping & commercial centre, a soberly stylish hotel with deluxe & superior rooms & suites, Wi-Fi, satellite TV, kettle. Overall good value & promotional rates online. **$$$–$$**

Hotel Emas (126 rooms) 2103 Jln Utara (North Rd); 089 762000; e emas@teckguan.com; www.hotelemas.com.my. An oldie but a goodie is this 3-star business hotel about 0.5km from the town centre, owned by Teck Guan cocoa company. In need of some overall lifting in décor & style, but very comfortable & hospitable. Deluxe rooms are good value with modern bathrooms, tea/coffee making, AC, TV & b/fast. Premier floor singles & twins with b/ fast still border on budget rates. Shuttle bus to airport RM15 one-way/RM18 round trip. The introduction of a website is a positive sign of evolution, but the shuffling pack-of-card images of rooms concept is a navigation disaster & symptomatic of the slightly 80s' approach here. **$$$–$$**

King Park Hotel (100 rooms) 30 Jln Haji Karim; 089 766699/767700; e kingpark@ streamyx.com; http://tawau.kingparkhotel.com. my. Reviews for this well-located 3-star hotel improved, yet now have slid since a 2010 makeover of its rooms & suites. Health centre, shuttle service, satellite TV, Wi-Fi & non-smoking floors. **$$$–$**

Budget and shoestring

Kingston Executive Hotel (30 rooms) Lot 3, Ground Floor, Jln Haji Karim; 089 769996; book via www.etawau.com. Great location amid cafés, shops & 24hr convenience stores. Double & twin rooms are bright & comfortable & the service is friendly & helpful. **$$–$**

Shervinton Executive Boutique Hotel Lot 1–4, Fajar Complex, Jln Bunga; 089 770000; e info@shervintonhotel.com; www. shervintonhotel.com. Bombastically calling itself an 'executive boutique hotel', this 2011-launched budget to mid-range hotel has standard, deluxe, family, twin rooms & large suites. All rooms have LCD TV, rain showers & free but often iffy-Wi-Fi. The good value has won fans, but the hotel's shortcomings are increasingly losing them. Persistent complaints of serious structural shortfalls (most apparent in smaller rooms), regarding soundproofing & thin walls. The website is an unaesthetically visual disaster & needs overhauling fast if the hotel doesn't want to lose customers battling with the faulty reservations menu. The site needs to clearly show room rates. **$$–$**

My Inn Hotel (68 rooms) TB 254, A/B Block 25, Jln Dunlop; 089 756699; e info@myinnhotel. com; www.myinnhotel.com. Plain but prim standard doubles, twins, family & triple rooms all for shoestring budgets. Clean, convenient, & good value. The much-promoted Wi-Fi (free, yet selected on booking) rarely works in-room. **$**

Out of town Eco-resorts and reef resorts near Tawau have come and gone or just slowly fizzled out due to poor management or quality. Another somewhat up-in-the-air project in late 2014 was the Sipadan Mangrove Resort (*http://sipadan-*

mangrove-tawau.h-rez.com). The Chinese-owned villa development has ostensibly opened in mangroves near to Tawau airport. The idea is clearly to cash in on the Sipadan diving crowd, with 30-minute boat trips from the resort to Sipadan. The lack of clear information on the hotel's status is not a good starting point for a 'high-end' resort. The website has room information, and directives about guest ID and credit cards required on checking in. Yet all my efforts to make a booking took me to an external website, stating rooms were not available during that period.

✗ WHERE TO EAT AND DRINK   *See map, page 240.*

Street food and markets Many people claim the best seafood in Malaysia is found in Tawau, and it's from here that Kota Kinabalu sources much of its fresh catch. Judge this for yourselves at the multitude of open-fronted *kedai kopi*, in under-cover markets and open-air food stalls all over town. The nightly food park **Sabindo Seafood** (*opposite the Sabindo Shopping Complex, Jln Chen Fook*) is a large open-air set-up with dozens of food stalls, and plentiful seating. At **Kam Ling Seafood**, a good dinner for two will cost under RM50. The larger **Good View Seafood** gets mixed reports. The whole area bustles with people from 18.00 to 23.00. There is also a seaside strip of evening food stalls selling fast Malay, Indian and Indonesian food – barbecued skewers and satays, *murtabak* and *nasi ayam, roti cani* – some serve *sulawesi soto makassar*, a Bugis buffalo soup dish.

Sabindo has plenty of casual eateries by day. Food courts are located in marketplaces and shopping centres, from the **Pasar Tanjung** central market to the Malay-oriented **Parkwell Food Centre** in the Parkwell supermarket (☉ *06.00–18.00*).

Coffee shops and restaurants The **Kompleks Fajar** has cheap eateries but also some air-conditioned restaurants, including **Maxim's Seafood Restoran** (*Jln Baru, Block 30 Fajar Complex;* ☎ *089 771800*). Locals refer to the area of Jalan Budi (*east of the Fajar centre*) as 'Yum Cha Kai' – Yum Cha Street. All the coffee shops here serve good food and drink; try **Kedai Kopi Kim Kim, Mui Lok** and **Sin Hing**.

Some hotel restaurants are good, with the added bonus of being off-street and air conditioned: **Cacao Palace Restaurant & Bar** in Hotel Emas goes a bit overboard on chocolate (including fish, soup and more!), but there is a good nightly steamboat buffet as well as à la carte.

Cake shops Tawau makes excellent *kedai kek*. For all sweet and savoury bakes and cakes, head to the area around the Fajar complex; the **Southern Cake Shop** is on Jalan Merdeka next door to the more average chain **Multi Bake**, and just opposite is a coffee shop-style branch of the **Sugar Bun** (*2 Jln Merdeka*) fast-food chain.

OTHER PRACTICALITIES There are several **banks and ATMs** in Tawau, concentrated around the main city blocks, including a CIMB Bank in the Fajar Kompleks commercial centre on Jalan Haji Karim, an Ambank ATM at 13 Jalan Dunlop, and Bank Simpanan Nasional at Sabindo Square. A Milimewa superstore is found in the Complex Cahaya Baru, Lot 257–261, Jalan Bunga. For **medical issues** (other than emergencies in which case dial ☎ 999), there is a major public hospital in Tawau, barely 1km west of the town centre on the coastal road (*Peti Surat 67, Jln Tanjung Batu;* ☎ *089 773533*).

WHAT TO SEE AND DO

Mosques Al-Kauthar, or **New Tawau Mosque** (*Jln Stephen Tan*), is the biggest mosque in Sabah. Completed in 2004, it cost RM31 million to build, can hold 17,000 people and has a library, seminar hall and offices.

Markets Tawau's markets are marvellous. The pastel-pink-winged **Pasar Tanjung** – the central market – on Jalan Dunlop is said to be the largest in Borneo, with 6,000 stalls selling fresh food and fish, salted dried fish (*ikan masin*), clothes, baskets and much more. The old central market is known as **Pasar Gantung** or 'hanging market', because all the items for sale (from clothing, handicrafts and handbags to house decorations) are suspended from the stalls. Most of the produce is Indonesian and Filipino. Colourful and relaxed, traders of all races mingle at the rural-style **Tamu Tawau** every Sunday morning on the corner of Jalan Apas and Jalan Kuhara. It has over 200 stalls laden with fruit, vegetables, handicrafts and clothing, as well as dried local specialities such as shark fins and seaweed. Running from 06.00 until early afternoon, it also has food stalls and a temporary eating area of tables and chairs.

Cocoa tours Tawau lets people taste its wares under the slogan 'Asia Cocoa City'. The **Teck Guan Cocoa Village** (*Quoin Hill;* \ *089 772277 ext 2254 to organise tours*) dubs itself 'Cocoa Kingdom' – a cocoa plantation up in the hills near Tawau. During a two-hour tour, you can enjoy cocoa breakfasts and lunches – with cocoa-flavoured noodles, porridge, prawn and banana rolls and fresh cocoa juice on the menu. A few minutes' drive away is a hiking trail that leads to a 9m-high waterfall, the **Culture Spring**. Teck Guan also operates the **Teck Guan Cocoa Museum** (*Mile 2, Tanjung Batu Laut;* \ *089 775566 ext 2601;* ⊕ *08.00–11.30 & 13.30–16.30 Mon–Fri; reservations necessary for guided visits*). The one-hour visit of the Majulah Cocoa Factory, guided by factory staff, includes a multi-media presentation of the history of cocoa, topped off by tastings of cocoa drinks and sweets. The tours are low-key and personable.

Festivals With a fifth of its population Chinese, February's **Chinese New Year Festival** paints the town red with fireworks, festivities and fun. A **Cocoa Festival** is also held, featuring colourful cocoa-inspired cultural dances.

EXCURSIONS FROM TAWAU

TAWAU HILLS PARK (TAMAN BUKIT TAWAU) (*24 km from Tawau; adult RM10, child under 18 RM6*) This rainforest and lower montane park of about 28,000ha was gazetted in 1979 to preserve the Sungai Merotai, Ulung Sungai Tawau and Sungai Balung rivers and their unique ecosystems. A small island of biodiversity within a region of limestone outcrops, rich alluvial volcanic soils, cocoa and oil palm crops, the park is a nice place for swimming, trekking, birdwatching and mountain biking. Over 150 flowering plants dwell here, among them the world's tallest tropical tree. Managed by Sabah Parks, it boasts hot springs, waterfalls (including the 30m-high Banjir Kilat), and several lovely trails including jungle treks to the tops of Gunung Magdalena and Gunung Maria. A special nature trail leads to the world's tallest tropical rainforest tree, the breathtaking 88.32m Seraya Kuning Siput (Shorea faquetiana), found in 2010. Alongside it, you will feel much like you are standing by the Empire State Building. On the trails, you can encounter monkeys, hornbills and orchids – and plenty of leeches, so it is advisable to wear leech socks. Park rangers are very helpful. Chalets, hostels and restaurants are operated by KOKTAS, the Sabah Parks staff co-operative. I can't personally vouch for the lodgings, but you must reserve for it ahead (\ *089 768719*). The campsite (*adult RM5, child RM2*) can accommodate up to 1,000, so you probably want to avoid Malaysian holiday times.

| | THE MALIAU EXPERIENCE | Sir Peter Crane |

A few days in the Maliau Basin provides a truly authentic tropical rainforest experience. All year round, day or night, the temperature rarely deviates more than a few degrees from its average of about 30°C. The humidity is always high, so dripping with sweat becomes a way of life. Torrential downpours are a regular occurrence – the region receives more than 3m of rainfall annually, which is about a metre more than the English Lake District receives in a typical year. Clothes and camera gear – and anything else – never dry out, and even the shortest journey involves slithering up or down precipitous slopes that always seem to end in sandstone cliffs or whitewater torrents. The ubiquitous leeches take every opportunity to gorge themselves on any passing mammal; leech socks are a must.

The exuberance and diversity of plant and animal life in Maliau more than compensate for the challenging conditions. In the valleys, dipterocarp trees dominate small patches of lowland rainforest containing incredible plants – such as the rafflesia with its enormous, malodorous flowers, and giant strangling figs. This is also the habitat of the greatly prized ironwood – one of the most dense and resistant of all tropical hardwoods.

Sir Peter Crane is a former Director of the Royal Botanic Gardens, Kew, England (see box, pages 64–5 for more information).

ASIA COCOA CITY TOUR (m *019 883 0173; adult RM550, child RM450*) Ivy Yap, local livewire and special project manager at Teck Guan Cocoa Company, organises four-day/three-night packages, taking in Tawau, the Balung Eco Resort, trekking, snorkelling and Semporna's Singamata Water Chalet.

MALIAU BASIN CONSERVATION AREA A 'protected forest reserve' once open to logging, Sabah's so-called 'Lost World' lies in south-central Sabah, about 40km north of the Indonesian border – an enclosed 390km² basin up to 25km across. The area is drained by tributaries of the Maliau River, one of which forms a stunning series of waterfalls, the seven-tiered **Maliau Falls**. It is a remarkable block of tropical forest – virtually the entire catchment of the Maliau River – almost encircled by a dramatic escarpment rising over 1,600m in height, insurmountable from most directions. The area was originally set aside by the Sabah Foundation and then formally upgraded to a Class 1 Reserve.

The basin has 12 different forest types, mostly Agathis tree-dominated lower montane, dry heath forest and lowland and hill dipterocarp forest. It is a faunal haven with over 1,800 species of plants and lots of wildlife including barking deer, banteng, sun bears, proboscis monkeys, clouded leopards, pythons and many species of birds including the rare Bulwer's pheasant, crimson-headed partridge and peregrine falcon. Only a couple of operators are allowed to visit this area – it is under tight wraps, and is very expensive – about RM4,000–6,000 for five days and four nights excluding airfares, less with a bigger group. It's also a tough trip – camping in tents, with lots of leeches around (including tiger leeches) and 06.00 starts. With long walking days in humid conditions, participants must be physically fit, and mentally prepared. There are about 12 licensed tour operators, both local and international, who can visit the area. **Borneo Nature Tours** (*Block 3, Ground Floor, MDLD 3285 Fajar Centre, on the edge of town near the airport;*

\089 880207; *www.borneonaturetours.com*) is one. Maliau treks start with pickup at Tawau Airport, followed by a five-hour drive in a 4x4 to the Maliau Basin Security Gate 180km away. The trip can also be done from Keningau on the west coast, with a six-hour drive in.

Those wanting to visit the Maliau Basin independently must get permits and written permission from the **Conservation and Environmental Management Division of the Sabah Foundation** (Yayasan Sabah) (*12th Floor, Menara Tun Mustapha Tower, Kota Kinabalu;* \ *088 326300;* e *mbca_kk@icsb-sabah.com.my*) or the **Maliau Basin Conservation Area** Tawau office (\ *089 759214;* e *maliau@icsb-sabah.com.my*).

The new **Maliau Basin Studies Centre** (MBSC) (\ *087 745100/101/103*) has a hostel, camping ground, exhibition hall, mini theatre, conference room and library.

IMBAK CANYON Just north of the Maliau Basin, this 300km² valley has only recently been set aside as a conservation area and looks set to become another magnet for rugged treks. It's a sweeping area of one of the largest contiguous lowland dipterocarp forests left in Sabah, enclosed by high sandstone ridges and canyon waterfalls. A vital link in the biodiversity corridor linking the Maliau Basin to the Danum Valley further east, it is also an important area for research and a botanical gene bank for forest rehabilitation projects. Visiting conditions are the same as for Maliau.

SEMPORNA

Semporna means 'perfect' in Bajau language, and that describes the seaside of Semporna far more than it does the town itself, though it is not lacking in cultural colour. At the end of the Semporna Peninsula, its feet bathing in the waters of the Celebes Sea, Semporna is a watery world: the bay is a whirr of engines, masts and boats of all forms. Bajau Laut, the indigenous population of the Bajau Sea, live along the coast in houses perched on stilts over shallow reefs. The high rate of conversion to Islam among the Bajau people explains the large proportion of Muslims – 90% of the 100,000-strong population in the Semporna area. Stone-Age tools found in the hills above Semporna show the area was a prehistoric pottery hub.

GETTING THERE AND AWAY Semporna is a 90-minute **drive** from Tawau Town, and an hour from Tawau Airport. A **taxi ride** from Tawau will cost RM100. **Express buses** from Kota Kinabalu leave daily at 07.30 and 19.30. It's a seven- or eight-hour trip and costs about RM60 with a meal included. Minibuses between Tawau and Semporna take close to two hours, with tickets costing RM15–20. Buses from Tawau arrive at the minibus station; those from Kota Kinabalu and Sandakan at the long-distance bus station. Both are in the town centre, though the latter is further back from the waterfront, to the side of the mosque.

⌂ WHERE TO STAY

⌂ **Seafest Hotel** (63 rooms) Jln Kastam; \089 782333; e info@seafesthotel.com; www. seafesthotel.com. Lovely end-of-pier waterfront location a few blocks away from town centre. By far the best hotel in town with its solid 3-star comfort & service, most of the standard & deluxe rooms & suites overlook the bay. Kettle, AC, ceiling fan & average buffet b/fast included. Health centre on site. **$$$–$$**

⌂ **Dragon Inn Floating Hotel** (65 rooms) 1 Jln Custom; \089 781088; e info@dragoninnfloating.com.my; www. dragoninnfloating.com.my. The atmosphere at this rickety inn on duckboarded stilts, extending into Sandakan Bay, is nothing less than magical. However, while you expect it in the longhouse lodgings, the standard double rooms of the wall-to-wall thatched roof chalets can also be very noisy (neighbour-dependent). The location can be enjoyed to the full from one of the 'VIP' rooms – the standalone chalets are a mix of greater comfort (AC, cable TV, heated showers) & rustic charm – the windows from the basic bathrooms open out to view passing boats heading to the local market. **$$$–$**

🏠 **Sipadan Inn** 2 Block B, Lot No B11–B14, Semporna Seafront; ✆089 784866; e sipadaninn2@gmail.com; www.sipadaninn.com. The rooms of the Sipadan Inn spill over into this neighbouring building & seem to be more popular as they are composed of the 'superior sea view rooms' & 'VIP sea view rooms'. **$$**

🏠 **Sipadan Inn** (32 rooms, inc Sipadan Inn 2) Block D, Lot No 19–24, Semporna Seafront; ✆089 781766; e sipadaninn@gmail.com; www. sipadaninn.com. Living up to its cheeky slogan of 'luxury budget accommodation', comfortable, clean but small rooms with colourful décor, AC, cable TV, drinking water & free internet. Boutique-style at budget prices; more spacious VIP & family rooms have a small lounge & fridge. The downside of the action-packed port location for some is the noise. Common complaints of late concern the rude receptionist which the hotel needs to act on to keep its good reputation intact. **$$–$**

✗ **WHERE TO EAT AND DRINK** Anjung Lepa (*Seafest Hotel, Jln Kastarn;* ✆ *089 7823333*) is a small open-air hut with plastic chairs, jutting over the water. Charcoal-grilled fish (*ikan panggang*), satay, and prawns and octopus by weight (RM2–4 per 100g, min 300g) are barbecued and served with rice and fresh melon juices – no alcohol is served. At the Seafest Hotel opposite, the **Lepa Café** serves buffet lunches and a lunch and dinner menu of Western and Eastern dishes. Day and night food stalls are dotted about town, near the market and in the area along Jalan Kastarn. The more pricey **Pearl City Restaurant** (*1 Jln Custom;* ✆ *089 781099*) is part of the floating Dragon Inn complex. The casual **Seafest Café** is on Jalan Kastarn, near the Seafest Hotel.

OTHER PRACTICALITIES Within a couple of streets, the town centre crams in accommodations, the wet (fish) and dry markets, a mosque and banks, but don't count on more than one or two ATMs. The Milimewa supermarket lies within the shop-lots of Jalan Datu Panglima Abdullah, along with coffee shops and a bakery.

WHAT TO SEE AND DO Semporna is small, and easily navigated on foot. In a matter of minutes you can journey from the pier to the bus station, markets, banks and hotels.

Semporna Ocean Tourism Centre (*1 Jln Custom;* ✆ *089 781077*) Locally called 'the floating', this is a source of local tourist information. It is built in Bajau water-village style on the pier, with a few bungalows, a hotel (the Dragon Inn), restaurant, bar and souvenir shops, all connected by duckboards.

Pasar Ikan The fish market is held in the beige pyramid-shaped structure right on the waterfront.

Semporna islands The largest in view is **Pulau Bum Bum** (pronounced 'Bom Bom'), and is bigger than Singapore – 1,000 families cultivate seaweed here. Speedboats (RM20) leave from the pier near the Seafest Hotel. **Sulawesi Sea Safari** (*Seafest Hotel, Jln Kastam;* ✆ *089 782318; www.sulawesiseasafari.com*) has an office here. Backed by local knowledge, it offers day and multi-day dive packages and Semporna–Sulawesi area touring, with accommodation at the Seafest. Personally I would opt for a tailor-made tour for a day of immersion into the culture of the Bajau Laut and Semporna Bay's remarkable sea world.

Semporna is the springboard to Sabah's famous dive islands: Pulau Sipadan, Mabul, Kapalai, Mataking and Pom Pom. In all, there are about 20 main dive sites clustered between Sipadan and Mabul. All the resorts offer beginners and advanced diving opportunities at these sites.

For the past two decades, the islands have been at the heart of a volatile, violence-struck region. The threats are not ever-present, but after a recent spate of 'incidents' in 2013–14, it would be remiss of me not to spell the dangers out in full.

The real troubles in paradise began on Easter Sunday 2000, when 21 people – nine Sabahans, two Filipinos and ten tourists from Europe, South Africa and Lebanon – were kidnapped by masked and heavily armed gunmen and whisked off to Jolo Island in Sulu Province. Eventually the hostages were released unharmed, but the kidnapping of both tourists and locals has continued. In the latter case, kidnappings generally go unreported, with the exception of the regional press. The militants responsible for these kidnaps for ransom (KFR) have since been linked with the Philippine Islamist group, Abu Sayyaf, which in turn has ties with al-Qaeda. 'In 2000, Abu Sayyaf raised US$15 million from kidnapping mainly foreign tourists from the Malaysian resort of Sipadan', the *Wall Street Journal* reported in 2013.

In 2004, Malaysian authorities closed all the dive resorts on Sipadan, in the wake of the kidnappings. Since then, the Sulawesi region and several island resorts have been under heavy military surveillance, but unfortunately not enough to prevent further attacks. The worst happened in November 2013, with the killing of a Taiwanese tourist and kidnapping of his wife at Pom Pom Island Resort. The group probably had their eyes set on several tourists, but escaped after the unplanned shooting. The woman was released months later.

In April 2014, a 29-year-old Chinese tourist and a Filipino worker were kidnapped from the Singamata Reef Resort, a couple of kilometres off the coast of Semporna. The *Straits Times* reported, 'they were being held on an island in the southern Philippines by Abu Sayyaf gunmen.'

Following those kidnappings, the chief of the Eastern Sabah Security Command (Esscom) released a statement saying some of the abductors were also involved in the Pom Pom Island and Sipadan Island affairs. 'We believe that this particular kidnap for ransom group is active and aggressive in the southern Philippines,' he said. Of further concern is the belief that the local Filipino community might have been involved, as informants, and several other staff members were arrested.

Tragedy struck again in July 2014, with the fatal shooting of a police officer during an ambush by eight Filipino gunmen at the Mabul Water Bungalows Resort, and kidnapping of his colleague.

The threats appear to be growing. In May 2014, the *Star* newspaper reported that the kidnap for ransom groups 'had become increasingly sophisticated and are now working in units that operate like a small army'. The militants are thought to have a network of spotters on the ground in Semporna, watching out for potential tourist prey and informing their warlords. Geography makes their mission easier – the guerrillas' nesting ground and kidnapping hideouts are 300km away.

Malaysian security forces have been reported in the national media as having foiled more recent abduction attempts .

There have been public and political calls for Esscom to set up a special anti-kidnapping squad to target the cross-border crimes, as current security measures fall way short of what is needed.

Meanwhile, the resorts need to be more transparent about the dangers. Pom Pom Island Resort does not advertise the tragedy that occurred there (even in their 'news' section), and some travellers have voiced disappointment on booking sites and forums that they were not forewarned on the resort's website. I believe the dive resorts should make clients aware of the ongoing threats on their websites. Honesty pays.

Furthermore, resorts involved in these incidents have been criticised in the Malaysian press and on travel review sites for tending to compromise security by trying to minimise the presence of heavily armed guards rather than prioritising the safety of tourists.

SIPADAN One hour by speedboat from Semporna, Pulau Sipadan looks like little more than a cluster of trees from above the water's surface. Formed by living corals growing on top of an extinct volcanic cone, it took thousands of years to develop and drops off 600m to the ocean floor. 'Sipadan's oceanic location keeps visibility at 30m or more, and marine life has thrived thanks to limits on the number of divers,' says dive journalist William Moss. 'Barracuda Point' is so called due to the incredible vortices of thousands of chevron barracuda that swirl through it. Close encounters with turtles and sharks (grey reef sharks, leopard sharks, scalloped hammerheads…) are common here and at the 'Pinnacle'. The drop-off is popular for shore and night diving. A Sabah Parks permit for Sipadan is RM40 per day.

For environmental and security reasons, there are no longer resorts on Sipadan. Dive operators visit there from the mainland and the other three islands, with enforced limits of 120 people per day. Since the kidnapping of divers on Sipadan in 2000, and with 'continuing threats', the British Foreign and Commonwealth Office (*www.fco.gov.uk*) and the Australian Department of Foreign Affairs (*www.smartraveller.gov.au*) have issued warnings against travelling to these islands (see page 92). The islands and surrounding waters are under constant military surveillance.

MABUL AND KAPALAI Sitting on the edge of the continental shelf, 45 minutes from Semporna, these islands have very different ecosystems, and visibility can be low – as little as 10m – because of the sandy bottoms, especially at Kapalai. However, their reefs 'host a dazzling array of odd and photogenic creatures including frogfish and leaf fish, ghost pipefish, anemone and cleaner shrimps, lionfish, octopi, venomous catfish, elusive mandarin fish, and a rainbow of nudi-branches,' says William Moss. Mabul is a beach-fringed atoll, part of a 200ha reef, and is popular for muck-diving. Kapalai sits further out to sea on the same reef, separated by a sand bar – the 'Jetty' dive has five wrecks, while the sloping 15m reefs of Kapalai are a highly photogenic place to dive.

MATAKING Mataking is a 40-minute boat ride from Semporna, for macro and pelagic diving with a 100m reef drop-off on the eastern shore.

RESORTS AND OPERATORS Most resorts offer two-, four- or six-night packages, including boat transfers from Tawau Airport to Mabul, three meals a day, accommodation, three boat dives a day, and most dive gear.

Continued overleaf.

Mabul

🏠 **Mabul Water Bungalows** (16 bungalows) 📞 088 486389; e info@mabulwaterbungalows. com or mabul@po.jaring.my; www.mabulwaterbungalows.com. This 4-star floating dive resort is owned by Sipadan Mabul Resort which also operates the Smart Divers Resort. The resort was marked in July 2014 by a terrorist attack, in which 1 police officer died. The water bungalows have AC, fans & balconies. Restaurant, shop, business centre, & dive centre. Sipadan is a 15min boat ride away. **$$$$$**

🏠 **Seaventures Dive Rig** (25 rooms) 📞 088 251669; e info@seaventuresdive.com; http:// seaventuresdive.com. A bit like a live-aboard but without the inconvenience of getting seasick, this former oil-rig platform, 0.7km from Mabul, 9km north of Sipadan, offers diving & nothing but deep blue diving. 'Live, dive, jump' is the resort's motto. A lift lowers divers directly on to the house reef below the rig! The allure of a working rig is still there, even in the basic room & bathroom facilities. This is the only major complaint – the diving instruction, the dives, the food & staff get top notes. Novelty comes at a top price, however – 4-day/3-night packages cost RM2,730 pp. **$$$$$**

🏠 **Sipadan Water Village** (45 chalets) 📞 089 751777; e info@swvresort.com; www.swvresort.com. This gloriously located resort spreads its stilted tentacles over the waters of Mabul Island. Bungalows built in Bajau style hover a metre above the water on a stilted walkway. Standard to deluxe chalets with ceiling fans, sliding doors & sun decks. 5-star PADI dive centre on site, dining hall & lounge-bar. Packages from Tawau include road & boat transfers, twin-share accommodation & buffet b/fast, lunch & dinner. **$$$$$**

🏠 **Smart Divers Resort** (40 chalets) 📞 088 486389; e info@sipadanmabulresort.com; www. sipadanmabulresort.com. Sipadan Mabul Resort or SMART as it is known by divers is a long-established name, & the sister company to Explore Asia Tours. Semi-detached bungalows, more comfortable standalone & suite chalets are scattered in a coconut grove, with beach/sea-facing decks, AC & tea- & coffee-making facilities. The resort has a restaurant, PADI TEC dive centre, Wi-Fi, swimming pool & jacuzzi. Packages include land transfers from Tawau, accommodation, buffet meals, 3 boat dives daily, unlimited house reef & night dives, & diving equipment. **$$$$$–$$$$**

🏠 **Borneo Divers Mabul Island Resort** (30 rooms) 📞 088 222226; www.borneodivers.info. A true diver's resort for diving excellence, but also a great nature island resort. Pretty wooden chalets with simple comforts & ethnic furnishings, AC & bathrooms, scattered in a tropical garden with pool. Good buffet meals & friendly, helpful staff. PADI dive centre. Promotional deals & good negotiating skills can result in 2-night packages of around RM1,000 pp, at least RM100 less for a non-diver. **$$$$–$$$**

Bukit Tengkorak Archaeological Site Museum (*Kampung Tampi Tampi, 5km from Semporna;* 📞 *088 253199;* ⊕ *09.00–17.00 daily*) The Department of Natural Heritage at Sabah Museum and university researchers found thousands of pottery residues here, with some specimens dating as far back as 8000BC. This suggests the area was one of the largest Neolithic craft centres in Southeast Asia and a major stop-off point on early Pacific trade routes.

Culture and festivities The *lepa*, a traditional wooden sailing boat with intricately carved embellishments, is an integral part of the life of the Bajau Laut people. Usually made of hardwoods, the *lepa* are flamboyantly decorated with a flotilla of red and yellow frilly sails (*sambulayang*) and small triangular flags (*tapis-tapis*). The Regatta Lepa is held in April with other traditional watersports including a rowing competition (*Lumba dayung*), in which rivals tug at the ropes of other boats, and races in small dugout boats (*kelleh-kelleh*). Traditional dances such as the daling daling – an upbeat courting dance – accompany the festivities.

🏠 **Scuba Junkie Mabul Beach Resort** (24 rooms) Block B, Lot 36, Semporna; e info@ scuba-junkie.com; www.scuba-junkie.com. This set-up's newly opened budget resort is getting great reviews thanks to the company's already well-established service mindset & affordable friendly prices. 8-bed dorm with balcony, at shoestring price tag, while basic wooden fan rooms, deluxe AC rooms with bathroom & balcony & 'VIP' rooms with private balconies & fridge cost between RM135 & RM460 depending on whether you are a diver or not, & the season. **$$$–$**

🏠 **Mabul Backpackers** (Office at entry to Dragon Inn Hotel Semporna); ☎ 089 782334; e info@ mabulbackpackers.com; www.mabulpackpackers.com. Clean, smart & comfortable it may well be, but reviews of the newly opened backpackers highlight plenty of room for improvement. I'm sure the much-needed lodge is all ears; the gap needed filling for a long time. Great location for budget travellers, with its ocean-viewing open deck; single, double & triple rooms. **$**

Kapalai

🏠 **Sipadan Kapalai Resort** (50 rooms) ☎ 089 765200; e psrt@po.jaring.my; www.sipadan-kapalai.com or www.dive-malaysia.com. Staying at this stilted sea resort is like staying in an aquarium. Built above the shallow sandbanks of the Ligitan Reefs, its boardwalks extend over coral beds, punctuated by thatch-roofed bungalows with private balconies & sea-facing bathtubs. The buffet restaurant has 360° sea views & a fish-gazing window at its centre. 2-night packages, starting at around US$500 & US$650 respectively for non-divers & divers, include 3 boat dives daily & unlimited home reef diving. Run by the same professional (Tawau-based) set-up that operates Sepilok Nature Resort & Lankayan Island stays. **$$$$$–$$$$**

Mataking Island

🏠 **Mataking Reef Dive Resort** (49 rooms) ☎ 089 770022; e sales@mataking.com; www. mataking.com. The thousands of coral reefs in the Celebes–Sulawesi eco-region are like paint splashes on the sea. The WWF describes the 600,000m² marine zone as a 'coral triangle' & 'hyper diverse underwater world', & it is this spectacular environment you will experience firsthand while staying at Mataking's magical resort. Individual chalets & high-end beach villas & spa are nestled in the trees off a forest boardwalk. The main open-sided restaurant is a focal point for good food & dining. This upmarket resort is popular with diving honeymooners & families & its PADI dive centre is run by proficient, friendly staff. **$$$$$–$$$$**

Diving The major 'dive islands' and their resorts are run by one operator or another (see box, pages 248–51). Some people stay in Semporna and go diving from there by day, finding it cheaper and/or more interesting. If you have arrived without a pre-booked package and want to go diving, beware of dodgy operations – there are at least a couple in town. Check blogs and reviews on major dive sites (such as www.scubatravel.co.uk and www.scubadiving-malaysia.com) – this is also an excellent way of getting feedback about different dive resorts and accommodation. Day diving is possible to many places, including Tampi Tampi, a dive resort ten minutes along the coast from Semporna.

People often ask how to get to the dozens of other small Semporna islands to dive. One answer is to eschew the dive operator/island resort packages; then you are free to cherry-pick. Some more budget-oriented Semporna-based operators visit such islands for day diving. Reputable operators for day dives include **Scuba Junkie** (*Block B, Lot 36, Semporna Seafront;* ☎ *089 785372;* m *019 584 657;* e *info@scuba-junkie. com; www.scuba-junkie.com; 1-day PADI Discover Scuba RM250, 3-day Open Water RM750, 3-day Advanced Open Water RM700*), who also organises outings to some

25 islands in the area. They are a young, business-driven operation, and take groups of 12 as a maximum. **North Borneo Dive and Sea Sports** (*Semporna Ocean Tourism Centre, Dragon Inn, Jln Kastam;* \ *089 942788/769950;* e *borneo_tours@hotmail. com*) also arranges diving in the area.

LAHAD DATU

Lahad Datu in Bajau language means 'a place of royals' – bestowed on the town by noble-blooded Bajau peoples who migrated from the Sulu Islands in the late 19th century. Facing over the Sulawesi Sea from the large inlet of Darvel Bay, palms and casuarinas line 'The Corso', which runs along the waterfront to the grubby old town centre. Here, the streets are packed with itinerant vendors, small shops, department stores, Islamic restaurants and food stalls. The large fish market, though a bit overbearing on the senses, is a captivating communal commotion.

The population of Bajau, Sulu islanders, illegal Filipino immigrants and minorities of 'river people' – the orang sungai sagama who live near the Sagama River – form an intriguing ethnic pool. Lahad Datu is trying to clean up its 'cowboy' image with a campaign driven by the local mayor. Results of the sprucing-up effort can already be seen around the 'new town', where more hotels and shopping centres are earmarked. Situated on the edge of town is a large immigrant kampung of 4,000, made up of Filipino and Indonesian migrants (the people underpinning the palm oil and construction industries with cheap labour).

GETTING THERE AND AWAY
By air MASwings flies to Lahad Datu direct from Kota Kinabalu and from Miri via Kota Kinabalu. One-way tickets from KK start at RM164.

By bus With all the cheap flight options it's best to avoid the lengthy bus journey from Kota Kinabalu to Lahad Datu. Between Sandakan and Lahad Datu, **Syarikat Chin** buses (m *019 883 4962*) leave from Sandakan's open-air bus terminal at Batu (2.5km from town) at around 07.30 – the 179km journey takes four to five hours and costs about RM20. **Sida Bus Express** (m *019 873 7808*) runs the same trip at 07.15. Pay for tickets on board for first-come-first-served seating. There is a single daily return trip from Lahad Datu to Sandakan, departing at 12.30.

By van/4x4 taxi Vans and 4x4 taxis run trips between Lahad Datu and Sandakan bus terminals, early morning (*about 07.00; RM20–25 pp*), leaving only when they are full – with about six passengers. If not, they may postpone the trip until the next day. Regular services also run between Lahad Datu and Semporna.

WHERE TO STAY Despite years of talk of new mid-market and five-star hotels coming to the town, the gap remains unfilled.

⌂ **Asia Hotel** (60 rooms) 639 Jln Teratai; \ 089 881771; e reservations@asiahotel.com.my; www. asiahotel.com.my. A 10-storey, recently renovated hotel with a competitive 3-star edge & constantly improving services. Secure parking & 24hr hotel security, business centre, boardrooms & free Wi-Fi. Rooms are light & well furnished, with AC, satellite TV, tea- & coffee-making facilities & safe.

Incredible online deals available for rooms/suites with b/fast & lunch included. **$$$–$$**

⌂ **My Inn Hotel** (96 rooms) Lot 256–271, Bandar Sri Perdana; \ 089 863388; e info@ myinnhotel.com; www.myinnhotel.com. Gloatingly declaring itself 'the latest luxury business class hotel in Lahad Datu' (one I am yet to try), the only reviews so far come from domestic travellers. The white Lego-set building is midway (10mins' drive) between the town centre & airport, among the shopping centres ('over 300 shop-lots') & boutiques of Bandar Sri Perdana. Rooms look sparse & boxy, but neat. All-inclusive family & executive suites have budget price tags & b/fast included. Possibly worth paying the RM228 for the latter for extra living room space. **$$**

🏠 **Perdana Hotel** (23 rooms) Block 31, Jln Seroja; 📞 089 881166; e ino@hotelperdana.com; www.hotel-perdana.com. The best of the basics by a country mile, with a pervading, out-to-please-all-tastes attitude. Even its executive rooms are budget-friendly. With its efficient, personable management, the hotel is constantly aspiring to offer even better value for money – key-card room security, shiny & clean presentation, brightly furnished restaurant bar, & free Wi-Fi. Standard rooms are small, but have good beds, DVD players & TV. Prices include b/fast & local newspapers, while laundry & 'butler service' are on offer! How could one ask for more at this price? **$**

✗ **WHERE TO EAT AND DRINK** Lahad Datu's split personality brings both new- and old-town eating. In the old town, a pasar malam is held along a paved strip in the middle of Jalan Mawar (directly opposite Emporium Ramai Ramai) – smoking, steamy stalls of skewers and satays, whole grilled fish (*ikan panggang*), chicken wings, roasted meats and sweets, among some tables and chairs. The other side of the street is full of late-night clothes shops and the **Restoran Islam**. There are also some stalls on Jalan Kastam Lama. In the 'new town', the pedestrian-only Jalan Panji leading up to the waterfront '*Corso*' has food stalls day and night, plus coffee shops and restaurants.

At **Sakura Seafood Restaurant**, a variety of fish and shellfish can be sampled for RM2–8 per 100g. There are also many Chinese dishes: noodles, dumplings and roasted duck, priced at about RM4. **Choi Kee** has good noodles, clay-pot dishes, roasted pork and duck; **Ah Seng** offers chicken rice; and opposite the Kedai Kopi, **San Hoi Pow** serves homemade noodles. For vegetarian food, try **Kedai Kopi Jeet Lee** (*Block 48, Lorong 1, off Jln Teratai opposite the Executive Hotel*). There is an international menu of snacks and dinners in the **Plantation Coffee House**. In the Kompleks Fajar, near the airport, the **Unicorn Vegetarian Restaurant** (*Jln Segama*) has a Chinese buffet and menu. Also here are two Malay–Chinese eateries: **Restaurant Dovist** (*Lot 73, Fajar Centre*), and **Restoran Serai Wangi** (its name comes from the citronella plant).

SHOPPING The **Emporium Ramai Ramai** (*Jln Bunga Raya;* 📞 *089 880151; www. ramairamai.com*) is a bustling supermarket on the main street near the fish market. It has a mix of Chinese and Asian produce, health and beauty products, and a good range of international brands of biscuits, confectionery, jams and alcohol. It is part of the multi-level **Wisma Ramai Ramai** shopping centre. The new RM128 million Darvel Bay Plaza in Jalan Teratai is the district's biggest shopping mall. Part of the overall Darvel Bay commercial centre development, it will eventually include hundreds of retail shop-lots, a supermarket, food court, house wares, IT, fashion stores and cafés which were still gradually getting off the ground in 2015.

OTHER PRACTICALITIES Intra Travel Service (📞 *089 274988;* e *enquiry@intra-travel.com.my; www.intra-travel.com.my*) offers budget to mid-range tours in the region, including Tabin. An excellent **pharmacy** is the well-stocked Guardian Chemist (*Hotel Mido, Ground Floor, Jln Teratai;* 📞 *089 880137*), which has many international brands (UK, US and Australian). A good **air-freight and transport company** with a Lahad Datu office is Kangaroo Worldwide Express (*Block A, Lot A4, Jln Kastam Lama; www.kangaroo.com.my*).

WHAT TO SEE AND DO Most people come to Lahad Datu to go diving, or to visit the Danum Valley and the surrounding region's natural attractions. The town appears grotty in places, but it still has a certain charm. A Sunday market is held in the town centre. A curiosity is **Kampung Cocos**, a village about 8km from town, populated by a large community of immigrants from the Cocos (Keeling) Islands in Australia. The 'Orang Cocos', as they are called in Malaysia, came here in the 1950s to work on the coconut plantations. With close to 4,000 residents, the population is six times bigger than that of their homeland (621 according to the Australian government census)!

EXCURSIONS FROM LAHAD DATU

DANUM VALLEY It is a bitter irony that one of the greatest 'protected areas' of Sabah, the Danum Valley Conservation Area (DVCA), exists alongside some of the most severe overlogging. The 438km² reserve is promoted as 'the largest remaining area of undisturbed virgin lowland rainforest in Malaysia', which has been set aside for research and education. However, as you drive into the 'untouched' area you will undoubtedly come across well-laden log trucks on the road, which can be upsetting. As Sabah Tourism declare candidly 'a vast timber concession area borders all around Danum Valley'. The road into the reserve passes through logged and regenerating forest areas – the DVCA is touched on every side by 3–100km of commercial forest, and beyond are oil palm plantations. Guides here express their heartbreak at what is happening, and what has already happened. Together with the Maliau Basin, Danum Valley is part of the huge 10,000km² timber concession of Yayasan Sabah (the Sabah Foundation). Since the 1980s, it has been a Class 1 Protected Forest Reserve and part of the foundation's long-term Forest Management Plan, to remain unlogged for the purpose of wildlife conservation, education and research.

Getting there and away Danum Valley is about 85km from Lahad Datu, a two-hour journey first along the Lahad–Tawau road, then on unsealed forestry roads.

🏠 Where to stay and eat

🏠 **Borneo Rainforest Lodge** (24 chalets) www.borneorainforestlodge.com. For its excellent food, staff & eco-luxury accommodation – but mostly for the magic of its rainforest setting & rare wildlife sightings – the lodge comes out top among Borneo's nature resorts. There's an uplifting welcome, with cool lemongrass tea & face towels. Handsome wood chalets elevated through the forest, amid a daily symphony of birds. Fan-cooled, en-suite bathrooms & river-fronting balconies with jacuzzi; also a tent camp for 2–6 people. Restaurant with good buffet food in red leaf monkey-observing main lodge. Prices of 2–3-night packages are prohibitive for many & penalise singles. Run by Borneo Nature Tours (for further details, see page 79). **$$$$–$$$**

🏠 **Danum Valley Field Centre** (DVFC) Block 3, Fajar Centre, Jln Segama, Lahad Datu; ☏ 089 881688/0441. Mostly for official researchers, but overseas students & scientists can visit with prior approval from the centre. 'Keen naturalists' can also apply to stay with written approval from the Danum Valley Management Committee (see www.ysnet.org for more information). VIP rooms, resthouse rooms, male & female hostels & campsite. **$$$**

What to see and do Lying on the upper reaches of the Sungai Segama (Sabah's second-longest river) and its tributaries, the area is one of undulating lowland tropical rainforest – hilly but not mountainous. Gunung Danum forms its apex at 1,090m. The 438km² conservation area is home to 120 mammal species including the rarest – Sumatran rhino, pygmy elephant, sun bear, clouded leopard and banteng (wild cattle), ten of eastern Sabah's primates and over 340 recorded species of bird. There are amphibians and reptiles galore too – from the rare Wallace's flying frog and Bornean horned frog, to turtles, geckos, pythons, vipers, cobras and coral snakes. Activities include guided jungle treks, night wildlife excursions, canopy walks, birdwatching and guided visits to the Danum Valley Field Centre.

Trekking There are many marked trails in the Danum Valley including self-guided trails, but most longer (especially overnight) treks require a guide. One such trek is to the highest mountain in the DVCA – Gunung Danum, at 1,090m. Starting from the Danum Valley Field Centre (see below), four hours into this possible day walk are the Sungai Purut River's seven-tiered waterfalls.

Danum Valley Field Centre The DVFC proclaims itself as 'probably the leading rainforest research centre in the Old World tropics'. Scientists come from all over the world to conduct research here – including work on the impacts of logging. All visitors must get a **permit** from the Sabah Foundation sales office in Lahad Datu (*Block 3, MDLD 3286, Ground Floor, Fajar Centre, Lahad Datu*), unless you are on an arranged tour, in which case that is likely to be taken care of. Self-drivers must get a vehicle pass from the office. Viewing-spot highlights include a suspension bridge over the Sungai Segama river and a 40m-high canopy observation platform.

TABIN WILDLIFE RESERVE The reserve lies on the Dent Peninsula, northeast of Lahad Datu, wedged between the lower reaches of the Segama River and the Silabukan Forest Reserve. The endangered trio – Asian elephant, Sumatran rhinoceros and clouded leopard – make another of their rare appearances in this 122,539ha reserve of primarily logged lowland rainforest reserve, which has been put aside to protect 75 mammals, including orangutan, proboscis monkeys, three wild cats, 220 birds and 45 reptiles. Contact the Wildlife Department Office in Lahad Datu (❧ *089 884416*) to check the current situation with permits.

Getting there and away It's 50km on a sealed **road** at first but then a very bumpy gravel road from Lahad Datu Town. A daily **bus** from Lahad Datu (destination Tomanggong) passes the entry to Tabin, a one-hour trip.

🏠 **Where to stay and eat**

🏠 **Tabin Wildlife Resort** (26 rooms) ❧ 088 267266: e enquiry@tabinwildlife.com.my; www.tabinwildlife.com.my. Even if the hope of an elephant sighting is unfulfilled, the nature immersion in this resort's jungle environment (with local leaf monkey & hornbill populations) is thrilling. By night, the eco-chic cabins with cathedral ceilings glow like insects in the forest & on the hillside. The bungalows, which are linked by boardwalks to a restaurant & games room, have warm woody furnishings, AC, private balconies & homely fittings. The birdlife here makes it one of the most popular itineraries for expert guides such as C K Leong (*see the Tabin blog on his website borneobirds.com*). The Sunbird Café (🕐 *07.00–19.00*) is a timber restaurant perched in the forest, with Western & local food. The website gives an idea of the nature-loving ethos of the excellent, award-winning operator, Tabin Wildlife Holidays, & the enthusiastic staff. Packages – including the 2-day/1-night Tabin Wildlife Encounter, & special-interest & educational tours – include transfers to & from Lahad Datu, meals & lodgings. **$$$$**

What to see and do Selected from the exploited areas of the Silabukan Forest Reserve, and protected as a Wildlife Reserve, a core of old-growth rainforest remains in Tabin, though most of it is disturbed – selectively logged and surrounded by oil palm plantations. There is also a wetland area to the northeast side, around the Segama River. The neighbouring Kulamba Wildlife Reserve, an area of 20,682ha hugging the east coast, has a quite different ecosystem of freshwater swamp forest, mangrove and beach vegetation. Sole access is by boat and there are no visitor facilities. The chances of seeing wildlife such as rhinos and elephants in Tabin Wildlife Reserve may be just as good as in the Danum Valley, with an estimated population of 300 elephants, 100 banteng and 20 rhino. The animals target Tabin's mud volcanoes – mounds of mud and clay – for their salt fix. An observation tower hovers over one of the muddy mounds, about 700m from the chalet. Tabin is also a special place for birdwatching, with eight species of hornbills, hawk-eagles and pink-necked green pigeons attracted by the abundance of fruit trees. The giant flying squirrel glides around at night – up to 70m between trees. Some animals are more likely to look for you – leeches are particularly abundant in the wet season.

UPDATES WEBSITE

You can post your comments and recommendations, and read the latest feedback and updates from other readers, online at www.bradtupdates.com/borneo.

Part Four

SARAWAK

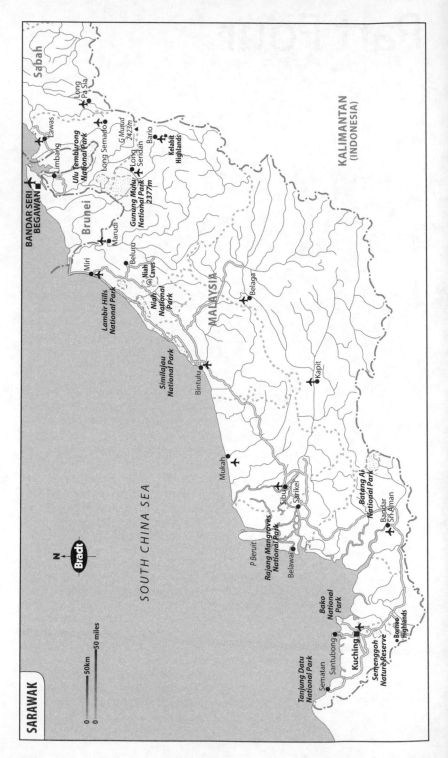

9

Kuching

The magic of Kuching, like much of Sarawak, emanates from the tremendous presence of water. The 120km Sungai Sarawak runs through the city, dividing it in two. The hustle and bustle of the old Chinese trading bazaar on its southern banks contrasts with the chants of Muslim prayer from the *kampung Melayu* (Malay villages) on the other side. Under the weight of soaring urbanisation, the waterway has been battling pollution, mostly from untreated sewage and accumulating rubbish. Things are improving, and Kuching's recent efforts to become cleaner and greener have won it a gold star from the World Health Organization. The city's cosy scale and mesh of urban parks, nature reserves and wetlands make it highly liveable, and likeable. The current Kuching Waterfront extension project plans to 'transform the city's golden triangle into a vibrant leisure and entertainment hub'.

The name *Kuching* is said to derive from the Malay word for cat, *kucing*. Though flagrantly promoted as 'Cat City' with its cat statues and museums, cats may actually have nothing to do with the name. Others put it down to the abundance of *mata kucing* – 'cat's eyes' – a lychee-like fruit growing on the riverbanks of the Sungai Sarawak. Or, possibly, the city was simply baptised Cochin – 'port' in Indo-Malay – by early Indian and Chinese traders. The indigo hues of Gunung Santubong provide

SARAWAK AT A GLANCE

International telephone code +608
Currency Malaysian ringgit (RM)
Exchange rate US$1 = RM4.31, €1 = RM4.89, £1 = RM6.66 (October 2015)
Climate Equatorial, humid; average daily temperature 28°C
Geography Largest Malaysian state, 124,450km²; northwest Borneo
Population 2.4 million; 31% Iban, 28% Chinese, 20% Malay, 8% Bidayuh, 6% Melanau, 5% Orang Ulu, 2% Indian Eurasian and minor ethnic groups
Capital Kuching
Visa requirements Visa-free three-month stay for most nationalities (for further details, see page 82)
Language Official language Malay (*Bahasa Melayu*); Iban and Chinese main community languages. English widely spoken.
Emergency numbers 999 for police, fire and ambulance
Banking hours 09.30–15.00 Monday–Friday
Business hours 08.00–13.00 and 14.00–17.00 Monday–Friday, 08.00–13.00 Saturday
Shopping centre hours 10.00–22.00 daily
Government website www.sarawak.gov.my
Tourist board +6 088 21212; e info@sarawaktourism.com; www.sarawaktourism.com

Kuching

9

a beautiful and mystical backdrop to the city skyline. The limestone massif rises up from the shores of the South China Sea 32km north. Unfortunately, the pretty and (generally) peaceful waterfront area has been tainted for tourists by tragic and sour notes, after the shocking murder of two young Britons in August 2014 (see page 92).

Though partly spared from World War II bombing, many older buildings had previously fallen as a result of a series of 19th-century fires and uprisings, and later from developers' bulldozers. Still with its generous sprinkling of colonial buildings and century-old Chinese remnants, Kuching serves up an evocative brew of the past. The odd neoclassical building and Corinthian columns add a quirky touch to the potpourri of Chinese shop-houses, mosques and Buddhist temples. Curiously, the city has two mayors – the Majilis Bandaraya Kuching Selatan (Kuching South City Council) is responsible for the south side, and the Dewan Bandaraya Kuching Utara (Kuching North City Hall) the north. The Old-World, but vibrant, city centre is set against the increasingly modern structures of its suburbs. All in all, greater Kuching's 580,000 residents represent a quarter of Sarawak's population.

HISTORY

Kuching's foundations were set in silt and on stilts, like so many of Borneo's river cities today. Before James Brooke sailed up the Sungai Sarawak in *The Royalist* (see page 6) in 1839, inklings of the water village – *kampung ayer* – existed in the same area as modern Kuching, with some 600 houses built from nipah palm thatch on the banks of the river. Kuching was the epicentre of control for the century of white rule in Sarawak – a period once described as an era of 'benign despots'. When James Brooke was conferred Governor and Rajah of Sarawak in 1841, roots of a colonial settlement were embedded, along with the earliest settlement on the southern banks of the river. In 1868, Brooke's nephew Charles took to the helm. More an administrator than an adventurer, under his rule a government was established and Kuching's streetscape took form with forts, courthouses and museums. From 1917, the third White Rajah – James's grandson Charles Vyner Brooke – expanded infrastructure and development. In 1941, he steered Sarawak towards democracy, ceding state legislative and budget issues to the Sarawak General Council. The empowerment of native chiefs and Chinese and Malay representatives was short-lived. The democracy gains were crushed within a few months with the onset of World War II and Japanese invasion. During the war, the last colonial ruler took refuge in Australia.

GETTING THERE AND AWAY

BY AIR
Kuching International Airport [off map, 264 B6] Modernised and attractive, Kuching International Airport is 11km from Bandaraya Kuching (Kuching City). There is a **Sarawak Tourism Board** information counter at the airport (⊕ *09.00– 13.00 & 14.00–18.00 daily*). There is no public bus service to and from the airport. A taxi to the city costs RM26 – buy a coupon at the taxi counter inside.

International flights Half-a-dozen airlines link Kuching directly with international destinations, including Brunei, Singapore and Indonesia. Malaysia Airlines (MAS), SilkAir, Tiger Airways and AirAsia all fly to/from Singapore; MAS has twice-weekly direct flights from Perth and Sydney; and Royal Brunei Airlines operate flights from Bandar Seri Bagawan in Brunei.

One-stop international routes include MAS and China Southern Airlines flights from Guangzhou and Hong Kong; MAS and Lufthansa from Frankfurt; and the new MAS routes linking Kuching to Tokyo Haneda Airport and to Osaka Kanei.

Domestic flights MASwings and AirAsia have direct flights between Kuala Lumpur and Kuching, Miri, Sibu and Bintulu in Sarawak, Kota Kinabalu in Sabah, and Labuan Island. Within Sarawak, both airlines fly from Kuching to Miri, Sibu and Bintulu.

Rural air services (RAS) From Kuching via Miri, MASwings operate flights to rural airstrips including Ba'Kelalan and Bario (Kelabit Highlands), Lawas, Limbang, Marudi, Mulu, Mukah, Long Akah and Long Lelang. Helicopter services are possible to other towns and more inaccessible areas in the Sarawak interior.

Airlines

✈ **AirAsia** Ground Floor, Arrival Level Kuching Airport; Ground Floor, Wisma Ho Ho Lim (shopping centre), Jln Abell

✈ **MASwings** Level 2, Kuching Airport

BY CAR The smooth-sailing Pan-Borneo Highway connects Sarawak with Brunei and Sabah – 842km from Kuching to Miri in the north, via Sibu (462km) and Bintulu (*644km*). The state road system is being upgraded constantly as traffic volume increases. There are excellent English-language interactive digital road maps for Kuching, Sibu, Miri, Mukah and Bintulu at http://sidra.sarawaknet.gov.my with free login.

BY BUS The new **Kuching Sentral/Express Bus Terminal** [off map, 264 B6] (*Jln Penrissen, Mile 6*) opened in March 2012 on Penrissen Road, some 10km from the city, but very close to Kuching International Airport. The three-storey RM55 million complex – a regional bus terminal-cum-shopping centre – took five years to build. The 14 bus companies operating some 80–100 buses from the terminal daily serve Kota Kinabalu, Tawau and Sandakan in Sabah, and Kalimantan, as well as Sarawak-wide destinations: Sarikei, Mukah, Bintulu, Sibu, Miri Limbang, Bakong, Batu Niah, Betong, Sri Aman, Simunjan, Engkilili, Lubok Antu, and Saratok. As hoped, Kuching Sentral is helping to alleviate the city's increasing traffic problems by streamlining bus services and better integrating them with regional lines. It also seems to be achieving its goal of becoming a major transport and retail hub for air and long-distance bus passengers, with 272,255 passengers filing through it in 2013. The taxi fare between the city and the terminal is about RM20.

Biaramas/Bus Asia (✆ *082 610111; Kuching booking office on Jln Khoo Hun Yeang, near Electra Hse;* ✆ *082 429418*) Despite being the major state-wide operator for inter-city and regional express services, the company website (*http://22.com.my/biaramas*) leaves much to be desired. A better alternative is to try their new 'micro-site' Bus Asia (*www.ba.my*) for bookings, though it's not that much better in terms of consumer-friendliness (you have to register even to see its fares).

Biaramas links Kuching with Sibu, Sarikei, Serian, Miri and Bintulu, as well as Bandar Seri Begawan in Brunei and Pontianak in Indonesia. Another useful website for their and other companies' fares is journeymalaysia.com. Biaramas's child fares are mostly 40–50% cheaper, except for international trips. While services for most of the above destinations are several times a day, there is just one daily bus to Pontianak via the Tebedu–Entikong border crossing, leaving at 07.45. (From Pontianak the bus leaves at 09.00.) The fare for the eight- to ten-hour journey is RM45 (or 140IDR).

Bintang Jaya Express Bus (082 531133; e bintangjayaexpress@gmail.com; www.bintangjayaexpress.com) Connecting Borneo from Sandakan in northern Sabah to Pontianak in Kalimantan via the home hub of Kuching. Offices/desks in all destinations. Book online – the best website of all the bus companies is gaudy, but unfortunately efficient. Yet they still manage to exclude Bandar Seri Begawan and Brunei from their routes.

Borneo Highway Express (082 453190) Tickets can be purchased at **Borneo Interland Travel** (*1st Floor, 63 Jln Bazaar;* 082 413595; www.bitravel.com.my).

EVA Express (082 576761) EVA operates buses between Kuching and Pontianak in Kalimantan, Indonesia.

PB Express Another long-distance bus company with business-class seats available, PB's Kuching sales counter is inconveniently located at 3.5 Mile, Jalan Kuching-Serian. There is, however, a ticket counter at the Saujana car park complex in Jalan Masjid, in downtown Kuching (082 244349). Note that some buses north to Sibu, Bintulu and Miri involve a change of bus or stopover in Sarikei, so make sure you are booked direct, if that is what you want.

SJS Super Executive (082 456999) This more upmarket coach service serves Pontianak from Kuching, with a daily service at 11.00 costing RM70.

Tebakang Express Kuching (082 456999) A subsidiary of Biaramas, operating the journey between Kuching and Pontianak in Indonesia.

BY BOAT A company called **Express Bahagia** ('express boat services') (082 410076) connects Kuching with other coastal cities and towns: Kuching–Sibu departs daily at 08.30. The 4½-hour journey costs RM40 (*RM45 first class*), stopping at Sarikei and Tanjung Manis. Tickets are sold at the wharf in Pending [off map 265 H3]. The taxi fare to the jetty is approximately RM10. From Sibu, boats to Kuching leave daily at 11.30, stopping at Sarikei and Tanjung Manis. Tickets are sold at the passenger terminal at Sibu's **Express Wharf** (084 319228; *RM40 (RM45 1st class)*).

GETTING AROUND

ON FOOT The city centre and waterfront areas are quite compact and easy enough to walk around. You will need to rely on other transport beyond that.

BY BOAT The traditional-roofed wooden boats, tambangs (the local version of sampans), are used for Kuching river crossings around the clock. A vital means of public transport around the waterfront area, they charge 50sen per person one-way, increasing to RM1 after 22.00. The journey takes less than five minutes. You can also charter one from any of the small jetties where they pull in, for about RM30 an hour. Ask them to take you anywhere you like, and to use either the motor or just to gently row the boat along the Sungai Sarawak.

BY BUS The main **city bus terminal** is on Jalan Masjid [264 B3] (*No 2, 1st floor*). This is the new axis for the gradually evolving **City Public Link** (CPL) bus service. Pulling together a number of different bus companies under one consortium, CPL will eventually serve over 40 city routes and 250 bus stops in Kuching. Spanking-new lime-green buses and a new bus routing system are part of the shakeup.

Buses are the main form of public transport in and around the city and offer plenty of character for the money, as well as reasonable efficiency and safety. The new system represents a big step away from the chaotic past. Though departure points still depend on the destination and company used, most inner-city services pass by Jalan Masjid. Beyond that, there is less duplication of suburban routes, and the companies serving them. All the city needs now is an online journey planner to simplify travellers' lives (and no doubt those of locals too).

The CAT system (playing on Kuching's city symbol) aims to improve transport infrastructure, reduce carbon emissions and integrate modern technologies such as electronic tickets and GPS. It uses route corridors and loops instead of the old point-to-point bus services. Over the coming years, it will be increasingly decentralised with a series of suburban hubs built in key residential areas.

Aside from City Public Link, there are several other major bus companies. **Sarawak Transport Company** (*STC; Jln Leboh Jawa*) [264 B2] (✆ *082 242967/451573/242579*) serves the Kuching area and southwest Sarawak. Their green-and-yellow buses depart from Leboh Jawa, with major bus stops at Jalan Mosque, the post office and Gambler Street. Bus No 3A goes to the long-distance bus terminal. **Petra Jaya City Bus** [264 B3] (✆ *082 429418*) serves Bako, Buntal, Damai and Santubong; their white-and-yellow buses depart bus stop No 1 on Jalan Leboh Jawa from the open-air market near Electra House. **Matang Transport Company's** [264 B3] yellow-and-orange buses depart from outside the Saujana car park and go to Matang and Kubah. **Bau Transport Company** (✆ *082 763160*) buses depart from the same place for Bau Town. **Chin Lian Long** (*Jln Gambier*) operates services to the city and suburbs with major bus stops on Jalan Gambier, as well as Jalan Masjid and outside the post office. Bus No 1 goes to the express boat jetty in Pending [off map 265 H3].

A kind of bus-hub area lies at the western end of the waterfront near the open-air market and Electra House, between Jalan Gambier and Jalan Mosque. Several bus companies operate in this area, each with their own station, serving distinct areas and marked with a bus symbol on the Kuching Tourist Map (available from most hotels and the tourism office in Kuching). You must have the correct fare on you as drivers generally do not give change. Trips within the city rarely exceed RM2.

BY BIKE There are some good mountain-bike trails close to Kuching, but the city generally does not lend itself to cycling. Bike rental can be arranged through many hostels and a couple of out-of-the-city-centre bike shops, such as **Thong Sen Cycle** (*5871B, Ground Floor, Kuching Garden, Jln Tun Razak; www.thongsencycle.com*), though the hostels are the best bet.

BY TAXI Taxi drivers in Kuching, like much of Sarawak, do not use the meters their taxis are installed with, so before you get into a cab, it is best to negotiate and agree on a price. Expect to pay about RM20 for the airport–city trip and RM5–10 for inner-city journeys.

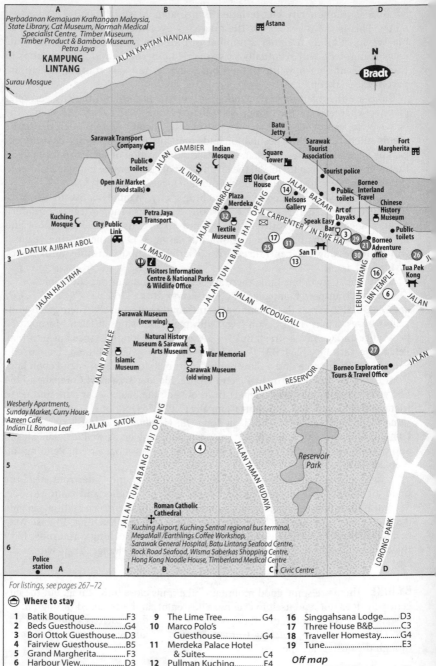

A Perbadanan Kemajuan Kraftangan Malaysia,
State Library, Cat Museum, Normah Medical
Specialist Centre, Timber Museum,
Timber Product & Bamboo Museum,
Petra Jaya

KAMPUNG
LINTANG

Surau Mosque

JALAN KAPITAN NANDAK

Astana

N

Bradt

Batu
Jetty

Sarawak Transport
Company

Public
toilets

Open Air Market
(food stalls)

Kuching
Mosque

City Public
Link

JL DATUK AJIBAH ABOL

JALAN GAMBIER

JL INDIA

JALAN BARRACK

Indian
Mosque

Square
Tower

Old Court
House

Plaza
Merdeka

Petra Jaya
Transport

Textile
Museum

JL MASJID

Sarawak
Tourist
Association

Tourist police

Nelsons
Gallery

JALAN BAZAAR

JL CARPENTER

Speak Easy
Bar

Art of
Dayaks

JN EWE HAI

17

25 31

13

San Ti

Public
toilets

29

21

30

Fort
Margherita

Borneo
Interland
Travel

Chinese
History
Museum

Borneo
Adventure
office

Public
toilets

26

JALAN TUN ABANG HAJI OPENG

Visitors Information
Centre & National Parks
& Wildlife Office

JALAN MCDOUGALL

11

LEBUH WAYANG

16

LBN TEMPLE

6

Tua Pek
Kong

JALAN HAJI TAHA

Sarawak Museum
(new wing)

Natural History
Museum & Sarawak
Arts Museum

Islamic
Museum

Sarawak Museum
(old wing)

JALAN PRAMLEE

War Memorial

JALAN RESERVOIR

27

Borneo Exploration
Tours & Travel Office

Wesberly Apartments,
Sunday Market, Curry House,
Azreen Café,
Indian LL Banana Leaf

JALAN SATOK

JALAN TUN ABANG HAJI OPENG

4

Reservoir
Park

JALAN TAMAN BUDAYA

LORONG PARK

Roman Catholic
Cathedral

Kuching Airport, Kuching Sentral regional bus terminal,
MegaMall /Earthlings Coffee Workshop,
Sarawak General Hospital, Batu Lintang Seafood Centre,
Rock Road Seafood, Wisma Saberkas Shopping Centre,
Hong Kong Noodle House, Timberland Medical Centre

Police
station

Civic Centre

For listings, see pages 267–72

264

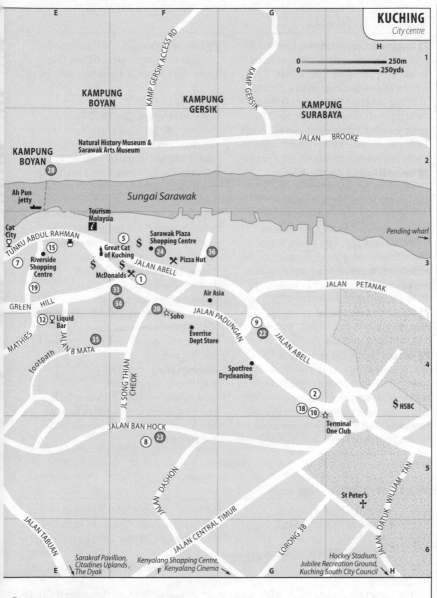

KUCHING
City centre

0 ——————— 250m
0 ——————— 250yds

KAMPUNG BOYAN

KAMPUNG GERSIK

KAMP GERSIK ACCESS RD

KAMP GERSIK

KAMPUNG SURABAYA

JALAN BROOKE

KAMPUNG BOYAN

Natural History Museum & Sarawak Arts Museum

28

Ah Pun jetty

Sungai Sarawak

Tourism Malaysia

Cat City

TUNKU ABDUL RAHMAN

15

7

Riverside Shopping Centre

19

5

Great Cat of Kuching

Sarawak Plaza Shopping Centre

24

Pizza Hut

36

JALAN ABELL

McDonalds

1

33

34

GREEN HILL

12

Liquid Bar

20

Soho

Air Asia

JALAN PADUNGAN

Everrise Dept Store

9

22

JALAN ABELL

JALAN PETANAK

Pending wharf

MATHIES

JALAN B MATA

35

JL SONG THIAN CHEOK

footpath

Spotfree Drycleaning

JALAN BAN HOCK

23

8

2

18 10

Terminal One Club

HSBC

JALAN DASHON

JALAN CENTRAL TIMUR

LORONG 3B

St Peter's

JALAN DATUK WILLIAM TAN

JALAN TABUAN

Sarakraf Pavillion, Citadines Uplands, The Dyak

Kenyalang Shopping Centre, Kenyalang Cinema

Hockey Stadium, Jubilee Recreation Ground, Kuching South City Council

Kuching GETTING AROUND

9

Where to eat and drink

20	Bing! Coffee Company......F3	30	Life Café....................D3
21	Black Bean Coffee &		Ling Loong Seafood.....(see 35)
	Tea Company................D3	31	My Little Kitchen...........C3
22	Chong Choon..................G4	32	Plaza Merdeka
23	Choon Hui......................F5		Food Court..................C3
24	H2O Food Court.............F3	33	Sin Min Joo....................F3
25	Indah Café Art Gallery......C3	34	Song Kheng Hai
26	James Brooke Bistro.........D3		Food Court..................F3
27	The Junk........................D4		Toh Yuen....................(see 7)
28	Kampung Boyan...............E2	35	Top Spot Food Court............E4
29	Kim Joo............................D3	36	Zhun San Yen Vegetarian.....F3

Off map

Azreen Café....................A5
Batu Lintang Seafood
Centre.........................B6
Curry House....................A5
The Dyak.........................E6
Earthlings Coffee
Workshop.....................B6
Hong Kong Noodle House.....B6
LL Banana Leaf.................A5
Rock Road Seafood............B6

TOURIST INFORMATION

ℹ️ Kuching Visitor Information Centre [264 B3] Sarawak Tourism Complex (Old Courthouse), Jln Tun Abang Haji Openg; ☎ 082 410944; e vic-kuching@sarawaktourism.com; ⏰ 08.00–17.00 Mon–Fri, closed Sat/Sun & public holidays. The best port of call for maps, hotel rates & bus routes. The office – along with the whole Sarawak Tourism Board – moved in 2011 from its offices in the Old Courthouse to this street near the mosque.

ℹ️ National Parks & Wildlife Office [264 B3] As for the visitor information centre above; ☎ 082 248088; http://ebooking. com.my. The place to obtain permits & book accommodation in the Bako, Gunung Gading & Kubah national parks & the Matang Wildlife Centre. Online booking service for parks state-wide available on the website. Park entry/conservation fees vary from park to park but are mostly adult RM10, children RM5.

ℹ️ Sarawak Tourism Board [264 B3] 6th & 7th floors, Bangunan Yayasan Sarawak, Jln Masjid; ☎ 082 423600; e stb@sarawaktourism.com

ℹ️ Sarawak Tourist Association (STA) [264 C2] Main Bazaar, Kuching waterfront near the Square Tower; ☎ 082 240620. Another very helpful outlet for recommending & organising tour guides in Kuching & for general visitor information. They prefer you to book weeks ahead for this service, either directly or through a tour agent, but last-minute arrangements are not out of the question.

ℹ️ Tourism Malaysia [265 E3] Kuching office, 2nd Floor, Bangunan Rugayah, Jln Song Thian Cheok; ☎ 082 246575; e mtpbkch@tourism.gov.my

TOUR OPERATORS

Borneo Adventure [264 D3] 55 Main Bazaar, Kuching; ☎ 082 245175; e info@borneoadventure. com; www.borneoadventure.com. One of the most notable tour companies in Borneo, Borneo Adventure targets an upmarket eco-trekking & cultural niche, with its innovative, personalised & insightful tours. It focuses on tapping into the ethnic communities & cultures, using the staff's local knowledge. They'll take you right to the source, in a sustainable manner, on set-theme & special-interest tours. See ad on page 278.

Borneo Exploration Tours & Travel [264 D4] 76 Jln Wayang; ☎ 082 252137; e chris@borneoexplorer.com.my; www. borneoexplorer.com.my. Recommended budget & independent travel group, can also help cut the costs incurred (ie: penalties & room price bias) for travelling alone.

Kuching Caving m 012 886 2347; e Kuchingcaving@gmail.com; www.kuchingcaving.com. Recommended by caving enthusiasts; speleological thrills & cave insects guaranteed. All equipment and specialist clothing is provided.

🏠 WHERE TO STAY *Map, pages 264–5*

The 'Golden Triangle' riverfront area around Jalan Tunku Abdul Rahman (which locals shorten to 'TAR') is still five-star forte, with a prime location matched by high prices (though still much cheaper than in Europe or the US). In the streets of adjacent China Town, you can get some excellent deals on mid-grade business and leisure hotels. Many budget hotels, and of late, B&Bs and homestays, are also located here.

The 'new town' vicinity of Jalan Ban Hock, a 1km walk from the waterfront, is a neighbourly hub of eating, nightlife and commerce, with several budget to mid-range hotels. There is still surprisingly little enforcement of total non-smoking bans in hotels, even in international chains with a strong American clientele. The exception is in hotel bars and restaurants, where non-smoking policies are being enforced.

HOTELS The upmarket hotel sector is in need of a bit more dynamism and competition, having remained largely stagnant for several years bar one or two new arrivals. Choices and newcomers abound on the other hand in the mid-range to budget categories. If you prefer less communal stays, then some small, mostly Chinese, hotels offer good value, with air-conditioned rooms and attached bathroom, television and free Wi-Fi.

Upgrade by moving away from the waterfront. Several hotels and inns in the area of Jalan Green Hill, Jalan Padungan and Jalan Nanas near the Sunday market provide a fan-cooled or air-conditioned room for RM70–90 double, and as low as RM110 for a family room.

Hostels are the best bet if you are seeking the company of fellow travellers or cheap family rooms. Nowhere has there been such turnover in the lodging market than in the shoestring sector, with a couple-of-dozen new **guesthouses**, **urban homestays** and **B&Bs** springing up since 2012, providing budget travellers with unprecedented variety. Dorm beds at hostels average RM25–RM35, while private rooms in hostels, guesthouses and B&B inns range from RM80 to RM90 double, and RM120 to RM140 for a family room, though individual rooms at no-frills places may be half these rates. Several minuscule highly personalised places are springing up – a result no doubt of the Airbnb private rental effect.

Luxury

🏠 **Hilton Kuching** (315 rooms) Jln Tunku Abdul Rahman; 📞 082 223888; e kuching@ hilton.com or sales_kuching@hilton.com; www1. hilton.com. Overlooking the river in the Golden Triangle area (ask for river-view room), the hotel is a bit dated but is solid & service-oriented. Spacious rooms & suites, including non-smoking floors, pool with faux waterfall setting, fitness & business centres, several top-notch eateries & entertainment outlets. This hotel consistently receives glowing reports (more so than any of the other luxury hotels). Mid-range prices possible on double rooms with internet specials & hotel promotions. Executive-floor rooms & suites include b/fast, Wi-Fi & access to executive lounge. **$$$$$–$$$**

🏠 **Merdeka Palace Hotel & Suites**
(214 rooms) Jln Tun Abang Haji Openg; 📞 082 258000; e info@merdekapalace.com or reserve@ merdekapalace.com; www.merdekapalace. com. There's lots of character at the Merdeka, though the 'palace' is dated in parts. Reviews vary between those who love the old-style comfort & others who loathe the lack of modernity. From my last stay, I find myself somewhere in between, wishing the gym & spa in particular were a little better maintained. Some standard rooms are a bit dowdy & cramped – best to opt for a deluxe room or even a huge apartment suite. Well located for museums & greenery, less so for waterfront attractions if you're averse to a 10min stroll. The location also means some degree of separation from city-centre noise. The

Wi-Fi is chargeable & there are a couple of non-smoking floors. Fitness centre, including gym & steam bath. **$$$$$–$$$**

🏠 **Pullman Kuching** (389 rooms) 1A Jln Mathies; 📞 082 222888; e H6332@accor.com; www.pullmankuching.com. Accor's 2011 arrival in Kuching's high-end market is going strong, with this striking modern hotel with wonderful hilltop views over the city & Sarawak River. The 'check-in, chill-out' ethos is reflected in high-tech rooms & suites with fitness gear & espresso machines, the groovy-lit bars & restaurants, & fitness centre & spa. There's a business centre & meetings facilities. It is in a good position, geographically, close to shopping malls & restaurants & only 10mins' walk from waterfront. **$$$$$–$$**

Upmarket

🏠 **Riverside Majestic** (241 rooms)
Jln Tunku Abdul Rahman; 📞 082 247777; e contact@rmh.my; www.riversidemajestic.com. As the name suggests, the Majestic occupies a prime location by the riverside, between major shopping centres, China Town & the old city. Some modernisation work is required, but it is good value & has great views, & service here comes with a smile. Spacious rooms with work desk & free internet, non-smoking floor & rooms/facilities for disabled guests. Excellent facilities include a roof pool, squash, tennis courts, gym, Malay, European & Thai restaurants, meeting rooms, business centre & executive lounge. **$$$$–$$$**

🏠 **Harbour View Hotel** (245 rooms) Lorong Temple; ☎ 082 274666; e sales@harbourview.com.my; www.harbourview.com.my. This 3-star, decent-value Chinese-run hotel has large, clean but plain rooms, yet a relaxed atmosphere & central location (opposite the Tua Pek Kong Temple). Free (though unreliable) Wi-Fi & b/fast included with all rooms. **$$$$**(suites)–**$$**

Mid range
🏠 **The Ranee** (24 rooms) 6 & 7 Main Bazaar; ☎ 082 258833; e reservations@theranee.com; www.theranee.com. Kuching's only new hotel in the mid- to upper-range category since 2011, the 'boutique suite' hotel in the main waterfront street is high on old China-Town airs, converted from 2 19th-century shop-houses & decked with colonial style, raw woods & natural fabrics. This establishment needs to do everything to ensure its service & staff match the boutique pretensions if it doesn't want to slip up. Various suites – Margaret, Sylvia, Leonora, etc – are either garden, river or inner-courtyard facing. Good b/fast included. Suites are spacious, with big bathrooms, 'sky garden decks', free Wi-Fi, fans & AC. Only the executive & extra-large suites creep into the upmarket price brackets; the rest rae mid-range Reading room, café & bistro. **$$$$**–**$$**

🏠 **Hotel Grand Continental** (192 rooms) Lot 42, Section 46, Jln Ban Hock; ☎ 082 230399; e kuching@ghihotels.com.my or reservation_kuching@ghihotels.com.my; www.ghihotels.com.my. In the new town business district. Spacious attractive rooms (including non-smoking & facilities for disabled), bargain-priced deluxe & family rooms, & nice rooftop swimming pool, spa & gym make this very good value. Executive Lounge rooms on the 12th–14th 'Continental Comfort' floors include complimentary daily paper & Wi-Fi. **$$$**–**$$**

🏠 **Batik Boutique Hotel** (15 rooms) 38 Jln Padungan; ☎ 082 422845; e talk2us@batikboutiquehotel.com; www.batikboutiquehotel.com. Quite funky & fresh in design, with warm-coloured mosaic bathroom floors, black terrazzo bathtubs, rain showers, silk duvets &, all in all, quality fittings. Spacious rooms & suites, quieter courtyard & city facing, with workspace & nice lighting fixtures. **$$$** (suites)–**$$**

🏠 **Grand Margherita** (288 rooms) Jln Tunku Abdul Rahman; ☎ 082 423111; e contact@gmh.my; www.grandmargherita.com. Excellent-value refurbished hotel with top management & staff. Comfortable, solidly furnished rooms, with work desk, complimentary water, safes, AC, ironing & coffee/tea facilities. All rooms from 'deluxe king' with river views to 'executive deluxe twins' with city or river views are budget-priced. Even junior & executive studios are lower mid-range prices, with access to the Executive Lounge, complimentary drinks, computer access, & speedy check-in. **$$$** (suites)–**$$**

Budget
🏠 **The Lime Tree Hotel** (50 rooms) Lot 317, Abell Rd; ☎ 082 414600; e info@limetreehotel.com.my; www.limetreehotel.com.my. As fresh as its name suggests, this boutique-style leisure & business hotel has pleasing touches throughout, with in-built universal sockets, LCD TV, Wi-Fi, rain showers, cushy bedding & zesty lime, white & beige décor from the rooms to restaurants. The café serves lime-inspired healthy foods (fresh from its own lime garden). The LimeLight rooftop lounge has become quite a popular drinks spot. Great internet specials such as the 'Sweet Suite Deal', including airport transfers & b/fast for 2. The 58m² executive & Limetree suites have a kitchenette. **$$$** (suites)–**$$**

Shoestring
🏠 **Beds Guesthouse** (12 rooms) 229, Lot 91, Section 50, Jln Padungan; ☎ 082 424229; e reservation@bedsguesthouse.com; www.bedsguesthouse.com. In the vibey Padungan China Town zone, this bright-pink guesthouse is popular with individuals & families seeking a more high-end hostel experience. Single, double, twin, quad rooms & 4-bed lofts, plus male/female dorms. Kitchen, bar, TV lounge, reading corners, 24hr reception. **$**

🏠 **Bori Ottok Guesthouse** (9 rooms) 94 Ewe Hai St. Dorm beds with sheets provided, clean, hot showers, welcoming local management, free Wi-Fi, common kitchen & basic b/fast – what more can you ask for? Also private & family rooms. **$**

🏠 **Fairview Guesthouse** (9 rooms) 6 Jln Taman Budaya; ☎ 082 240017; e thefairview@gmail.com; www.thefairview.com.my. Idiosyncratic & welcoming older guesthouse sits within a leafy tropical garden setting near Sarawak Museum & Reservoir Park. Accommodation includes fan-cooled dorm beds, plus plain but clean single, twin & triple AC rooms, a 3-bed 'master suite' with dressing room & a 5-bed family room. Shared kitchen, lounge & computers. **$**

🏠 **Marco Polo's Guesthouse** (4 rooms) 236 Jln Padungan; 082 246679. Looks can be deceptive & that's the impression some have before the bleak metal entrance of this hostel. Yet the popular hosts run a spic-&-span place with double to 8-bed rooms, shared bathroom, library, lockers, free Wi-Fi, outdoor terrace, linen to hire. Rates inclusive of b/fast. **$**

🏠 **Quiik Cat** (8 rooms) 12B Leboh Wayang. Tiny bright-painted hostel in 2-level 1930s' hop-house, a few mins' walk to the waterfront. Clean private rooms & dorm beds, hot reliable showers, kitchen, river stone foot massage. Welcoming (to pets too); free b/fast & parking, bed & bath linen. **$**

🏠 **Singgahsana Lodge** (22 rooms) Jln Temple 1; 082 429277; e info@singgahsana.com; www. singgahsana.com. An ethnic-hip budget boutique somewhere between backpacker & guesthouse, in a noisy city-centre location. Low-lit dorms & single/twin/double rooms decked out in tribal prints cater to a maximum of 30 travellers. The rooms seem to be a bit potluck – some find them dark & damp, or noisy – others have more privacy & are spacious & lighter. The lodge oozes the friendliness & local knowledge of its team of youthful staff & owners. Access cards, AC, bed linen (for dorms too, but not towels), continental b/fast included; non-smoking premises. **$**

🏠 **Three House B&B** (9 rooms) 51 Upper Jln China; 082 423499; m 019 885 3998; e info@ threehousebnb.com; www.threehousebnb.com. Absolutely bijou, opened in 2011; a bargain for its décor, location, friendliness & style, run by a Swedish woman. Modern Chinese tones of red & orange, silk & wooden furniture meet LCD TVs & Wi-Fi. There are cooking facilities, free lockers &

storage, & no curfews. Dorm beds, twin 'private dorms' & doubles. **$**

🏠 **Traveller Homestay** (5 rooms) 240 Jln Padungan; 082 414093. Home-sweet-home character guesthouse right by the Kuching cat. Good but noisy Chinatown location, preened décor & friendly attentive owner, Moi. **$**

🏠 **Tune Hotel** (135 rooms) Jln Borneo (off Jln Tunku Abdul Rahman); e enquiry@tunehotels. com; www.tunehotels.com. Rare for AirAsia's formula hotels to have such a great inner-city location, but it's one of the charms of a smaller city. Rooms include singles, doubles & twins. AC, towels, toiletries & Wi-Fi are all chargeable add-ons. Check-in 14.00, check-out 11.00 'sharp'. Non-smoking building, CCTV, 24hr reception. **$**

Serviced apartments

🏠 **Wesberly Apartments** (5 apts) Lot 2812, Block 195, Jln Rubber (West); 082 246197; e enquiries@wesberly.com.my; www.wesberly. com.my. Spacious & light 2- or 3-bedroom apartments with open kitchen-lounges, quality furnishings & fittings, washing machines & parking. Near the Sunday market, north of the city centre, the 110m² apartments with botanically inspired names are located above an art gallery & next door to Wisma Sandhu shopping centre. New infinity pool. **$$$**

🏠 **Citadines Uplands** (215 rooms) 55 Jln Simpang Tiga, Kenyalang Park; 082 281888; e enquiry.kuching@the-ascott.com; www. citadines.com. Being 4km from the city has not stopped the Ascott group property snowballing fans since opening in the government district in late 2012. Near the convention centre & shopping centres, not highly recommended for city-sights, but handy for the airport & business or shopping trips. For self-drive tourists too, the hotel offers good-value, budget-priced self-contained accommodation with fully equipped kitchenettes. Studios & 1–2-bedroom units, swimming pool, fitness room. **$$$–$$**

✖ WHERE TO EAT AND DRINK *Map, pages 264–5*

FOOD COURTS AND STREET FOOD The best places for on-the-go eating – easy on the pocket, with high-quality food and a bustling atmosphere. The indoor food courts are also good if you want air conditioning. An entertainment ground of eating, the **Top Spot Food Court** (*6th Floor, Taman Permata (car park), Jln Bukit Mata Kuching*; ⊕ *17.00–22.00 daily*), is one of the best places in Kuching for cheap, quality seafood as well as a huge variety of Malay and Chinese dishes. Located on the top of a multi-level car park, the 36 food stalls here offer a bevy of grilled fish, satays, chilli crab, clay-pot dishes, oyster omelette and curries. **Song Kheng Hai Food Court** (*off Jln Padungan, near cat statue*) is more of a no-frills snacking centre, with good noodle-heavy food stalls operating day and night. Head here for cheap *bee hoon* (rice vermicelli) satay noodles, Indian snacks and drinks such as iced kacang, cendol & coconut juice. On Level 3 of the **Plaza Merdeka** shopping centre is a food court, with many other cafés and fast-food outlets scattered throughout the mega-store.

FAST FOOD This can be found everywhere, but for sushi, burgers or KFC on the run, several fast-food chains are found at the **H20 Food Court** (*Jln Tunku Abdul Rahman;* ⊕ *10.00–21.30*), on the basement level of the Sarawak Plaza shopping centre.

CHINESE RESTAURANTS AND COFFEE SHOPS For cheap breakfasts or lunches, head to traditional coffee shops, where you can taste Sarawak noodle specialities, including *laksa*, for RM4–6. The price of such authenticity may be a bit of a wait, however, from 20 minutes up to an hour at peak times. Queues are usually a sign of quality. If, on the other hand, speed and predictability are what you are after, perhaps head to McDonald's.

✗ **Toh Yuen** Jln Tunku Abdul Rahman; ☏082 248200. The Hilton's sophisticated & relatively pricey Chinese diner, with fantastic décor & atmosphere where mahogany & red walls meet contemporary art. The dim sum luncheon buffet is highly recommended; the menu is a mix of Cantonese & Szechuan. $$$$–$$$

✗ **Hong Kong Noodle House** Wisma Saberkas shopping centre, Jln Tun Abang Haji Openg (3km out of town). Chinese locals & Westerners 'in the know' flock here for a cheap, quality lunch. Sweet, barbecued *char siew* is their speciality. $$–$

✗ **Chong Choon** Lot 121, Section 3, Jln Abell. An old-style b/fast institution where people read newspapers while eating bowls of steaming *kolo mee* & prawn-filled Sarawak *laksa*. Be prepared to share a table. $$–$

✗ **Choon Hui** Jln Ban Hock, near the Hindu temple. A b/fast hit for its *laksa* & *kolo mee* & *popiah* fresh spring rolls in unadorned surrounds. $$–$

✗ **Kim Joo** Jln Ewe Hye. Oodles of noodles, & good ones at that. Also soups, *char sui*, prawn omelettes & pork buns. Always abuzz with locals. $

✗ **Sin Min Joo/Noodle Descendants** Lot 18, Ground Floor, Jln Padungan. This little institution

got up & left its ancient location in Ewe Hai/ Carpenter St & is serving up their legendary homemade noodles & bowls of *kolo mee* from a China-Town location. (Fans still refer to it as 'Carpenter Street Kolo Mee'.) Very popular at b/ fast – you may struggle to get through the door! Not for impatient souls, some travellers complain about the long wait, but then in my mind, they are missing the point. The wait (of up to 45mins), according to the faithful flock, is well worth it for the quality. It also allows you time to soak up the local colour & charm. Join the queue! $$–$

Dayak

✗ **The Dyak** Sub Lot 29, Ground Floor, Panovel Commercial Complex, Jln Simpang Tiga; ⊕ 11.30–20.30 daily. 2km west of town in the Spring shopping mall/Swinburne University of Technology zone. Dayak or indigenous food served on traditional kitchenware. Jungle ferns, wild eggplant (aubergine), cooked durian & pandan; even *tuak* (rice wine) ice cream. Despite its location, the restaurant is clearly targeting the international (university students, etc) clientele with its prices. $$$$–$$$

INDIAN Over 1km from the waterfront, in the vicinity of the Sunday market, Jalan Rubber is the Indian-restaurant stamping ground – try the **Curry House** (*Lot 409, Section 10, Lorong 3A, Jln Rubber*), and the **Azreen Café** (*351 Lorong 12, off Jln Rubber*).

✕ LL Banana Leaf 7G, Lorong Rubber 1, Jln Rubber; ☎ 082 239404; ⏰ 07.30–21.00). With its very basic décor, cheap southern Indian food is served beautifully on a banana-leaf 'plate' at indoor & outdoor tables. It's also good for take-aways & vegetarian food. **$**

MALAY The best Malay food is cooked up in the kampung on the northern side of the river just near Fort Margherita – reached by a two-minute tambang ride from Ah Pun jetty to Encik Oman jetty.

Kampung Boyan [265 E1] is the first of four Malay villages along the riverbank, and there are several evening eating choices here including a few simple food kitchens and tables (**$**). These places are on temporary licences under a government programme to promote jobs for the *Melayu* (Malay) locals. Clean and simple, you couldn't ask for a better dining location for such cheap food. Opposite, there are a few more established Malay kedai with under-cover areas. All these restaurants are strictly halal, and not for party-goers or beer drinkers, but those who want to taste authentic Malay, and lap up the romance of Kuching water-crossings in an inky black setting at night. Have an aperitif before heading here.

SEAFOOD

✕ Ling Loong Seafood One of the better seafood diners at the TopSpot food centre for whole cooked fish by the kilo. **$$$–$$**

✕ Rock Road Seafood Mile 2, Jln Rock; ☎ 082 241575. A bit further along from Batu Lintang Seafood Centre (see next). You can select your catch here – fish or crustaceans – from tanks. **$$$–$$**

✕ Batu Lintang Seafood Centre Off Jln Batu Lintang (3km out of town, along Jln Tun Abang Haji Openg & into Jln Rock). Excellent cheap outdoor seafood, the kedai & stalls are open evenings only. **$$–$**

VEGETARIAN While many cafés and restaurants are vegetarian-friendly, the following are particularly good:

✕ Life Café 108 Ewe Hai/Jln Carpenter; ☎ 082 411754; ⏰ 11.00–22.00 Mon–Sat. This sweet paper-lantern-lit café serves many dedicated vegetarian dishes among its simple but spicy Szechuan fare, clay-pots, spicy noodles, pork/vegetarian dumplings. Dozens of different speciality coffees & teas served charmingly with traditional tea service, & iced & fruit teas such as mango, lychee & passion fruit in tumbler glasses. **$$–$**

✕ Zhun San Yen Vegetarian Lot 165, Jln Chan Chin Ann; ⏰ b/fast & lunch. Clean café with Chinese & Malay food, charged by the weight. Eggplant (aubergine) with ginger, sweet greens, sesame tofu. Fresh juices including cooling cucumber. Also à la carte noodle-veg choices. **$$–$**

INTERNATIONAL Fine and fusion dining in Kuching has proved a catastrophically fickle affair in recent years, and I am loath to add the latest in-places people head to, to eat what they can eat at home. However, to mention a few: **My Little Kitchen** at 56 Upper Jalan China for Swedish meatballs among other things; **James Brooke Bistro** in Jalan Tunku Abdul Rahman; and **The Junk** restaurant in Jalan Wayang for Italian and pizza.

COFFEE AND CAKES

✕ Bing! Coffee Company 84 Jln Padungan; ⏰ late. The only café in town that serves seriously European coffee & Illy is the bean. Young, lively, laptop-loving crowd. Wi-Fi. **$$–$**

✕ Black Bean Coffee & Tea Company 87 Ewe Hai/Jln Carpenter; ☎ 082 420290; ⏰ daytime only. An exquisite little boutique coffee roaster, ancient-Chinese infused with wooden pigeonholes. Inside this shoebox of a shop, you can sample or purchase freshly roasted pure Borneo coffee (Sarawak Liberica, Arabica & Robusta) & teas, including Chinese Green & Taiwan Oolong, among the vintage & contemporary accessories. The minimalist environment has just 1 table & a bow-sized counter. $$–$

✖ Earthlings Coffee Workshop Lot 45, Ground Floor No 1, CityONE MegaMall, Jln Song. The technical coffee craze has hit Kuching, though you have to go way out to the MegaMall (towards the airport) to try these wares. Worth keeping in mind if you are about to hit the shops, or simply craving a good single-origin, barista-made brew. $

✖ Indah Café Art Gallery 38 Upper Jln China. Art, cheesecake, coffee. A new concept in Kuching, this art-space café lies off Jln Carpenter in a small side street. $

ENTERTAINMENT AND NIGHTLIFE

Kuching's nightlife is constantly evolving towards the more sophisticated. The epicentre of late-night café-bars and clubbing lies between the waterfront strip of Jalan Tunku Abdul Rahman, Jalan Padungan and Jalan Bukit Mata. Increasing urbanity has seen a decline of the once-prevalent karaoke culture.

Head to the venues on Jalan Padungan for unwinding, a few drinks, and for clubbing. According to Gustino Basuan from the Sarawak Tourism Board, 'They are Kuching's most fashionable entertainment outlets, playing dance-oriented music and catering to a more mixed crowd.' **Soho's** [265 F3] (*64 Jln Padungan*) name says all that it is striving to be: a hip bar for Latin and jazz music, dancing and cocktails. **Terminal One/T1 Club** [265 G4] (*Lot 348–352, Jln Padungan Utara;* ⊕ *17.00–01.00 Mon–Thu, until 03.00 Fri–Sat*) is a big disco/dance venue with an upmarket crowd.

For sophisticated Martinis and acid jazz, **Senso** [265 E3] at the Hilton Kuching has a mood-lit lounge-bar with a mix of live music and resident DJ, plus a good cocktail list. **The Club Lobby Lounge** [265 E3] (⊕ *17.00–01.00*) at the Riverside Majestic offers a cosy drink spot minus the loud music. Poolside **Liquid** [265 E4] (⊕ *09.00–21.00 Sun–Thu, 09.00–midnight Fri–Sat*) on the second level of the Pullman Kuching is a nice place to sip a cocktail, warming up to dance and DJs on Friday and Saturday nights. A new wine bar in the old town for music and snacks is **Speak Eazy Bar** [264 D3] (*61 Jln Ewe Hai;* ⊕ *16.00–01.00 Mon–Thu, until 02.00 Sat–Sun*).

FESTIVALS

GAWAI DAYAK This important Iban festival venerates rice, and is held every June at the end of the harvest. It has developed into a state-wide celebration among the Dayak community with many dance and cultural performances.

THE INTER-CULTURAL MOON CAKE FESTIVAL (30 Sep–6 Oct) This is more of a friendship festival between the Malay and Chinese cultures of Kuching.

GERAI RAMADAN If you are in Kuching during mid-September–October, don't miss the atmosphere at one of the Ramadan bazaars such as Gerai Ramadan, held for the breaking of the month-long dawn-to-dusk fast. Around 400 stalls are held around the city serving curries, barbecued meats and satays. The most easily accessible bazaar unfurls on Jalan Satok, with another across the river in Jalan Semarak, Petra Jaya. Stalls are open 13.00–19.00.

SHOPPING

MARKETS The **Sunday market (Pasar Satok)** [264 A5] (which strangely enough starts on Saturday), is held along Jalan Santok, north of the city centre (*stalls* ⊕ *13.00–01.00/02.00 Sat, 06.00–noon Sun*). Take bus No 4A/4B from outside the post office, catch a taxi, or walk – it takes around 20 minutes. Some 1,500 traders gather here to sell food and fruit, Dayak handicrafts, forest produce such as wild honey, clothing, pets and plants. Saturday evening is a good time to go to eat, otherwise Sunday morning to see it in full swing. Be on the alert for pickpockets.

HANDICRAFTS Among the copious souvenirs and carbon-copy handicrafts found along Jalan Bazaar, there is some good and inexpensive basketry, some carved objects and textiles, and some more expensive, but authentic, objets d'art. The area is a treasure chest to be explored, with hidden gems to be discovered upstairs and in back rooms. Some places cater more to collectors and foreign dealers, pushing prices higher, though not necessarily out of reach. **Nelsons Gallery** [264 C2] (*84 Jln Bazaar*) is a floor-to-ceiling clutter of charm – tribal art, antiques, jewellery – run by members of a prominent family of Kuching art dealers, as is **Art of Dayaks** [264 D3] (*68 Jln Bazaar*). As well as handicraft demonstrations, the **Sarawak Handicraft Centre & Craft Council** [264 C2] (*Courthouse complex;* ☏ *082 425652; www.sarawakhandicraft.com;* ⊕ *08.30–12.30 & 14.00–17.00 Mon–Fri, 08.30–noon w/ends & public holidays*) offers a 'mini bazaar' of Sarawak handicrafts, with different ethnic groups represented each month, and a resource centre with library and handicraft videos. More handicrafts and textiles are on sale at the **Sarakraf Pavilion** [off map, 265 F.6] (*78 Jln Tabuan, near Reservoir Park;* ⊕ *09.00–17.00 daily*); as well as crafts for sale there are demonstrations, and workshops in handicraft and dance. **Perbadanan Kemajuan Kraftangan Malaysia** [264 A1] (*Lot 3057, Block 18, Daerah Salak, Jln Stadium, Petra Jaya;* ☏ *082 444205*) sells indigenous crafts gathered and commissioned at the source.

BOOKS A good range of English-language books and maps are sold at **Bell Books** [265 F3] (Sarawak Plaza).

GENERAL Kuching's fanciest new shopping centre is the atrium-roofed **Plaza Merdeka** [265 F3] (*88 Pearl St; www.plazamerdeka.com;* ⊕ *10.00–22.00 daily*), in the old town centre, opposite the General Post Office and behind the visitor information centre at the Old Courthouse. Opened at the end of 2012, its 152 stores are spread over four floors, along with food and entertainment outlets.

Of the many shopping centres, **Riverside shopping centre** [265 E3] has a department store but also lots of electronic stores etc, plus a supermarket. **Sarawak Plaza** [265 F3] also has a supermarket at basement level.

OTHER PRACTICALITIES

BANKS AND MONEY CHANGERS Banks are generally open 09.30–15.00 Monday–Friday. Money changers are open much longer, including weekends.

$ **Everrise Money Changer** [265 F4] Ground Floor, Bangunan Hin Ann, Jln Padungan; ⊕ 10.00–21.00 Mon–Fri, 10.00–18.00 Sat–Sun
$ **HSBC Bank** [265 H4] 1st Floor, Bangunan Binamas, Jln Padungan

$ **Majid & Sons** [264 B2] 45 Jln India; ⊕ 09.00–19.30 Mon–Sat, 09.00–15.00 Sun. Reputable money changers & bookstore.
$ **Mohamad Yahia & Sons** [265 F3] Lower Ground Floor, Sarawak Plaza; ⊕ 10.00–21.00, closed Fri afternoons. Reputable money changers.

COMMUNICATIONS AND MEDIA
✉ **Post office** [264 C3] Jalan Tunku Haji Openg; ⊕ 08.00–18.00 Mon–Sat, 10.00–13.00 Sun

Tourist press The annual publication Kuching Guide is very handy while the quarterly Kuching Talk has nice cultural background and human-interest stories.

HEALTH AND EMERGENCY

Central Police Station [264 A6] Opposite Padang Merdeka (sports field); ☎ 082 241222; emergency calls ☎ 999

Tourist Police Unit [264 C2] Kuching waterfront; ☎ 082 250522; ⏰ 08.00–noon daily; fire ☎ 994

Hospitals

✚ **Sarawak General Hospital** [off map, 264 B6] Jln Ong Kee Hui, about 2.5km from city centre; ☎ 082 276666. Public accident & emergency dept. Foreign visitors charged RM50 for consultation, payable by cash or credit card.

✚ **Timberland Medical Centre** [off map, 264 B6] Jln Rock; ☎ 082 234466. Private hospital with 24hr emergency facilities.

✚ **Normah Medical Specialist Centre** [264 A1] Jln Tun Abdul Rahman, Petra Jaya; ☎ 082 440055; e inquiry@normah.com; www.normah. com.my. Private hospital in northern Kuching.

Doctors

✚ **The Clinic** [264 D3] Jln Bazaar, opposite Chinese History Museum. Highly reputable & purportedly very experienced in dealing with tourists' complaints.

Pharmacies

✚ **Apex Pharmacy** [265 F3] 1st Floor, Sarawak Plaza; ⏰ 10.00–21.00 daily

✚ **UMH Pharmacy** [265 F4] Jln Song Thian Cheok (opposite Malaysia Airlines office); ⏰ 09.00–18.00 Mon–Sat. Helpful staff.

MISCELLANEOUS

Sarawak State Library [264 A1] ☎ 082 442000; ⏰ 14.00–21.00 Mon, 10.00–21.00 Tue–Sat. Petra Jaya bus No 6.

Spotfree Dry Cleaning [265 E4] 105 Jln Padungan

WHAT TO SEE AND DO

While the greater city spreads out over 50km², the centre accounts for less than 4% (2km²) of that. Being compact, it is easily seen on foot. Kuching feels like a very safe city but there are warnings about pickpockets on the waterfront and in the market area. There is a police booth on the waterfront in case of any problems.

KUCHING CENTRAL

The Waterfront Life ebbs and flows along the banks of the Sungai Sarawak. On one side there are the old Chinese coffee shops, with antique stores in the old town along **Jalan Bazaar** [264 C2–D3] ('Main Bazaar' in English, and the oldest street in Kuching). On the other riverbank is the stroller's esplanade, known as The Waterfront. Official lines say it grew from the pyres of a drab warehouse area in the early 1990s under a programme of 'urban renewal'; critics say some old gems were cleared in the process. From the marketplaces in the west on Jalan Gambier through to the **Golden Triangle** [265 E3] on Jalan Tunku Abdul Rahman, the riverside esplanade is one of the most atmospheric places to stroll, as dozens of tambang slip into the night shadows of the 200m-wide river.

Little India Here, in the pedestrianised area around Jalan India (*adjacent to the open-air market*) and along Jalan Gambier, you can buy spices and textiles while absorbing the atmosphere; ideal for people-watching. Nearby is the 1850s **Masjid India** [264 B2], the city's oldest Indian mosque.

China Town Some places here have historic monumental walls, others have giant modern cat statues. The monument of Kitty Kitschery, the **Great Cat of Kuching** [265 H4], sits at the end of the street that forms the heart of China Town, Jalan Padungan. Most of the buildings here date to the rule of the Third Rajah, Charles Vyner Brooke, around 1910–30; a few even date back to the 1850s. Running parallel to the riverbank it's a hub of hip in the evenings, and a good street for eating out.

Malay *kampungs* [265 E–H1–2] Crossing the river to these four villages (*kampungs*) is like a trip out of the city, without actually leaving. Reached from Batu jetty or Ah Pun jetty, land at Encik Omar jetty in Kampung Boyan.

Petra Jaya [264 A1] This northern side of the river is developing into a visionary hub of high-tech and glistening new government buildings, state libraries and sports centres.

LANDMARKS

Mosques At the western end of the waterfront, **Kuching Mosque** [264 A3] (Masjid) sits like a piece of perfect Arabia on the Kuching skyline; its golden domes and minarets, and milky-walled, aqua-pillared façade are most impressive when viewed from the river. The sound of evening prayer flowing from it through the marketplace and over the river adds to the spiritual high of Kuching's watery sunsets. From 1968 it was the state mosque, until a new mega-mosque with an Italian marble interior was built in Petra Jaya on the northern bank of the river.

The lime-green façade announcing the Masjid Bandar Kuching, the **Indian Mosque** [264 B2] looks like just another shop-house in the rather baubled Jalan Gambier – deceptive first impressions, as it is actually the oldest mosque in the whole of Sarawak. Built in 1837 by Indian Muslims who had migrated from southern India, for a long time it was called Masjid India. The original nipah palm roofs were gradually replaced by *belian* (ironwood), the floors were cemented and the mosque engulfed by new buildings so that you have to pass through a small laneway, Lorong Sempit, to reach the entrance. The sound of a *bedok* (drum) rings out at prayer times and hundreds of the faithful descend upon the mosque. Tired travellers are welcome, in keeping with the mosque's tradition.

Temples At the other end of the Main Bazaar and the spiritual spectrum, the gaudy dragon-embossed pastiche of the **Tua Pek Kong Temple** [264 D3] (*corner of Jln Temple & Jln Padungan*) is, at heart, the city's oldest Chinese temple, dating back to 1843 but with several renovated layers, including the multi-coloured wooden and carved stone façade. The Sarawak Cultural Heritage Ordinance, which protects it, came too late for some other buildings. Many locals believe this temple protected the town from Japanese bombing and saved the whole row of old buildings along Jalan Bazaar from obliteration. The intersection of Jalan Bazaar and Jalan Tabuan opposite the temple has thus been named 'Corner of Good Hope'. Among the shop-houses of Ewe Hai, the small **San Ti Temple** [264 C3] fades into the shadow of the city's most famous Chinese worship house, yet is a picturesque mesh of mythical figurines, ruby-coloured lanterns and baubles. It also dates back to the 1860s and is the soul place of the Teochew Chinese population. As such, it is frequently the nerve centre of celebrations and street festivals.

Colonial relics Among the older buildings in the city – all along the Main Bazaar – are the English-castle-like **Square Tower** [264 C2], built in 1879 as the town's jail, a

275

1912 **Chinese Chamber of Commerce** [264 D3] (now the **Chinese History Museum**), and the colonial **Courthouse complex** [264 C2] – a stunning mix of building styles, New Orleans' pavilions, white colonnades and belian roof tiles, it was built as the seat of Sarawak's government in 1871 and continued that way for just over a century. The colonial Baroque **Clock Tower** was added in 1883, and a 6m-high granite obelisk – the **Charles Brooke Memorial** – erected in front of the courthouse in 1924. The four decorative bronze plaques on the memorial signify the Malay, Iban, Chinese and European cultures of Sarawak. Since 2003, the restored building has housed the Sarawak Tourism complex, visitor information centre and National Park administration.

Two eminent buildings protrude from the dense slopes of greenery on the northern banks of the river. The **Astana** [264 C1] (a slight variation on istana, or palace, in Malay) was built in 1870 by Charles Brooke as a bridal gift to his wife Ranee Margaret. It was the seat of power for the White Rajahs and is now the official residence of the Governor of Sarawak and not open for visiting. The symmetrical cream-coloured citadel, **Fort Margherita** [264 D2], was built in 1879 to ward off pirates. Now on state-owned grounds of the police barracks, it houses the **Police Museum**, although this is frequently closed. Check with the visitors' centre before venturing that way, or just enjoy the view from the water. Alongside the fort is the stunning new spherical structure of the **Sarawak State Legislative Assembly**, the Dewan Undangan Negeri, which lights up like an origami spaceship at night.Opened in 2009, the nine-storey building with its Chinese pagoda-style payung or 'umbrella roof' also incorporates Malay architectural features in its steel-and-glass structure. The highest building in Kuching, its dome roof and pinnacle skylight rise 120m above ground level.

VIEWPOINTS The best 360° bird's-eye view of the whole of Kuching and outlying areas is from the lookout tower on top of the **Civic Centre** [off map, 264 C6]. From its rooftop you can see Mount Serapi and Mount Santubong, and on a clear day even the peaks rising up on the Kalimantan border.

SPORTS AND GREEN SPACES The green lung of Kuching is **Reservoir Park** [264 C5], which is good for jogging. The botanical gardens are in the grounds of the Sarawak Museum. With national parks on its back doorstep, you can go hiking for a morning or afternoon. (See pages 282–86, for more on surrounding national parks.) Most four- and five-star hotels have gyms and tennis courts. The public swimming pool and another recreational ground are off Jalan Padungan by the Kuching South City Council.

MUSEUMS AND GALLERIES Most Sarawak museums have free admission, though some have a small camera (photo and video) fee. Most that 'open daily' are closed on the first day of major festivals and public holidays. The first five museums here come under the umbrella of the **State Museums** (❦ *082 244232; www.museum.sarawak.gov.my;* ⊕ *09.00–17.30 daily; free*).

Sarawak Museum [264 B4] ((*Old Building) Jln Tun Abang Haji Openg*) Built in the style of a Normandy townhouse, this museum was opened by Charles Brooke in 1891 and is the most interesting for its ethnographic collections, artefacts and historical documents and displays of indigenous arts and crafts. The foundations of the collection were put in place by Tom Harrisson, its curator from 1947 up until Sarawak's independence in 1963. Harrisson, distinguished naturalist, archaeologist and anthropologist, is also credited with 'discovering' the 39,000-year-old skull in the Niah Caves. On the other side of the overpass along the same avenue is the **new wing** of the museum in a former state parliament building, named after the second prime minister of Malaysia, Dewan Tun Abdul Razak. This houses special exhibitions and has a museum shop on the ground floor.

Natural History Museum and Sarawak Arts Museum [264 B4] (*opposite Sarawak Museum*) These are two relatively recent additions. The first has vast collections of flora and fauna (some gathered by Alfred Russel Wallace in the 19th century), mounted specimens of Sarawak reptiles, birds and mammals including the near-extinct banteng (*Bos javanicus*), or Asian wild cattle. The second houses historical paintings and photographs.

Sarawak Islamic Museum [264 B4] (*Jln P Ramlee*) Housed in the restored 1930s' building Maderasah Melayu – Malay Islamic School – the Islamic Museum has seven galleries depicting the history and culture of Malay people in Sarawak and the entire Malay–Indonesia Archipelago, from weaponry and religion to literature, architecture and education.

Textile Museum [264 C3] (*Jln Tun Abang Haji Openg;* \ *082 246194*) This offers a fascinating look into the textile history of indigenous Borneans, from bark cloth to Iban pua kumbu weaving, raw materials, textile motifs and accessories.

Pua Kumbu Museum (*4th Floor, Tun Jugah Tower;* \ *082 239672;* ⊕ *09.00–16.30 Mon–Fri, closed Sat, Sun & public holidays; free*) Another must for textile buffs, this museum goes a few steps further in the hands-on experience of Iban pua kumbu textiles – you can watch the weavers in action and take lessons, plus see antique and modern pua kumbu, Iban silverware and jewellery.

Cat Museum [264 A1] (*Lobby Floor, Kuching North City Hall;* \ *082 446688; www.dbku.gov.my/catmuseum;* ⊕ *09.00–17.00 Tue–Sun; free; RM4 photo fee*) Cat kitsch or kitty consecration, depending on your taste. The dedicated museum of meows plays on the rumour that Kuching's name comes from the Chinese word for 'cat' (see page 259). It houses 2,000 cat-fetish exhibits, including a mummified cat said to have been discovered in Egypt sometime between 3000BC and 3500BC. The museum is on the hilltop Bukit Siol, a RM15 taxi ride from the city centre, or take Petra Jaya bus No 2C and walk 15 minutes up the hill to the museum from the bus stop.

Chinese History Museum [264 D3] (*Kuching Waterfront, near Tua Pek Kong Temple;* \ *082 244232; www.museum.sarawak.gov.my;* ⊕ *09.00–17.30 daily; free*) In the old Chinese courthouse building, this museum shows the historical power of the Chinese as a trading people, from early trade routes and migration to modern times.

Timber Museum [264 A1] (*Wisma Sumber Alam, Petra Jaya;* ⊕ *08.00–13.00 & 14.00–17.00 Mon–Thu, 08.00–11.40 & 14.00–17.00 Fri; free*) A forest resources and timber industry showcase.

Timber Product and Bamboo Museum [264 A1] (⌕ *082 368575; www. sarawakforestry.com;* ⊕ *on request 09.00–16.30 Mon–Fri; free)* Another forestry promotional point, displaying some 82 species of wood found in Sarawak and a collection of bamboo products. It's located in the Sama Jaya Nature Reserve in Stutong, 15 minutes from the city, along with the **Forest Biology Museum**.

EXCURSIONS FROM KUCHING

Easy day or half-day trips include Santubong Peninsula, the Sarawak Cultural Village and Damai Beach; Bako, Kubah and Gunung Gading national parks; and Semenggoh Wildlife Centre. All are detailed in the following chapter.

borneo
adventure

55 Main Bazaar
93000 Kuching, Sarawak,
Malaysia

+60-82-245175
info@borneoadventure.com
www.borneoadventure.com

• *Tours* • *Treks* • *Travel*

10

Southern Sarawak

From the Santubong Peninsula and Damai Beach area north of Kuching south to the Borneo Highlands, and west towards the cape of Tanjung Datu nudging Indonesia, much of southern Sarawak falls within the vast Kuching Division. One of 11 Sarawak districts, it takes in six national parks. Stretching east of the capital along the Indonesian border, the Samarahan Division gives way to Sri Aman, gateway to some of the deepest forests and most moving river journeys into Iban territory.

NORTH OF KUCHING

Travelling north towards the Santubong Peninsula, the summit of **Gunung Santubong** (810m) rises up through a swirl of clouds beyond the wide Sungai Santubong River. Rimmed by beaches and bays, the majority of lodgings on Semanjung Santubong Peninsula are concentrated around the resort area of **Pantai Damai** (Damai Beach).

A popular beach getaway for Kuchingites, Damai – meaning 'peaceful' – is still just that, and one of Sarawak's special places. The big tourist beacon here is the Sarawak Cultural Village. With more time, go hiking in the jungle-thick landscape, visit the Malay fishing villages, and explore the wetlands and mangrove environments. Some repeat visitors love it so much, they prefer to base themselves here and visit Kuching for the day.

The much-talked-up retail and leisure strip, **Damai Bay Bazaar**, is taking shape, but only slowly. Extending for 658m along the foreshore, opposite the Sarawak Cultural Village, it will eventually include parks and children's playgrounds, shops, restaurants, food stalls, bicycle-rental and sea-sport centres, as well as business centres, prayer halls and public toilets. An arts and crafts gallery and evening cultural performances are also planned, in the hope of bringing the Damai area alive by night. The crowning centrepiece will be Sarawak's answer to Australia's Big Pineapple – a Big Hornbill. The 9m-wide, 7.4m-long and 6.8m-high sculpture of the rhinoceros hornbill – Sarawak's state emblem – is to be depicted 'in flight', authorities say. A tribute to the precious bird and largest of the hornbill species – so large that the Iban people believed it was a messenger of the gods. Let's hope the sculpture, together with the whole plan, don't prove to be just pie in the sky.

GETTING THERE AND AWAY

By car Kampong Santubong village is 32km north of Kuching; Pantai Damai (Damai Beach) slightly further at 35km. The roads are quite bumpy over the mangroves.

By taxi A one-way fare from Kuching will cost around RM60, from the airport RM70–80.

By bus A Kuching–Damai shuttle-bus service operates from outside the Hotel Grand Margherita, with stops at the Damai Beach Holiday Inn Resort and Sarawak

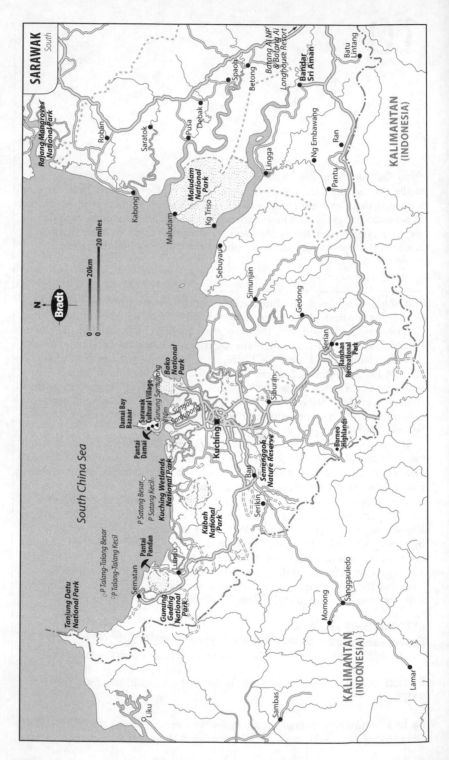

SARAWAK
South

Bradt

South China Sea

Rajang Mangroves National Park
Roban
Saratok
Kabong
Maludam National Park
Kg Triso
Maludam
Pusa
Debak
Spaoh
Betong
Batang Ai NP & Batang Ai Longhouse Resort
Bandar Sri Aman
Batu Lintang
Lingga
Ng Embawang
Ran
Pantu
KALIMANTAN (INDONESIA)
Sebuyau
Simunjan
Gedong
Serian
Ranchan Recreational Park
Siburan
Borneo Highlands
Damai Bay Bazaar
Sarawak Cultural Village
Gunung Santubong
Bako National Park
Pantai Damai
Sungai Santubong
Kuching
Kubah National Park
Kuching Wetlands National Park
P Satang Besar
P Satang Kecil
Semenggoh Nature Reserve
Bau
Serikin
Pantai Pandan
P Talang-Talang Besar
P Talang-Talang Kecil
Sematan
Lundu
Gunung Gading National Park
Tanjung Datu National Park
Momong
Sanggauledo
Liku
Sambas
KALIMANTAN (INDONESIA)
Lamar

N

0   20km
0   20 miles

Cultural Village (SCV). The journey takes about 40 minutes, and a one-way fare is RM12 for adults, or RM6 for children under 12. The first bus from Kuching is 07.30, the last bus back from Damai 21.00.

Petra Jaya Transport bus No 2D heads to Kampung Buntal, the first fishing village on the eastern side of the peninsula where there are beaches and seafood restaurants. The bus departs from Jalan Khoo Hun Yeang, not far from the open-air market, hourly between 07.00 and 18.00, returning hourly from 08.00 to 18.00. One-way fares are approximately RM4.

WHERE TO STAY

Damai Beach Resort (224 rooms) Teluk Bandung Santubong; 082 846999; e general@damaibeachresort.com; www. damaibeachresort.com. Renovation in hardware & service urgently required – that's unfortunately the overwhelming message here in 2014, with little improvement since my previous stay in 2011. In a leafy beach location, the place has everything going for it to be a top resort, but lack of upkeep, attention to detail, & dated, dirty presentation are giving it a bad name. The newer wing of hilltop rooms & suites, built in longhouse Malay & 'Baruk' roundhouse style, have private pool, water views & jacuzzi. Decent dining & entertainment – cocktail bars, pubs & cafés. Treez Café has good Malaysian cuisine at mid-range prices, though there are some complaints of slow service. **$$$$$–$$$**

Damai Puri Resort & Spa (207 rooms) Teluk Penyuk; 082 846900; e info@ damaipuriresort.com; www.damaipuriresort. com. Current reviews of this supposedly top-class resort after a US$10 million facelift in 2007 are alarming, across the board. Things have rapidly gone downhill since its switch from a Holiday Inn, & old fans are disappointed. Rather than exclude it from this edition, I urge you to check the latest ratings across several websites to form a view. The secluded beach location on Teluk Penyuk Bay has everything going for it. The revamp added a spa village with yoga pavilion, a speciality teahouse & club floor. All rooms & suites have AC, satellite TV, kettle, safe, hairdryer, & minibar. Tennis courts, pool, fitness centre, children's club & meeting rooms. 6 restaurants including Asian & international. **$$$$$–$$$**

Nanga Damai (6 rooms) Jln Sultan Tengah; Mob: 019 887 1017; e polseb@pc.jaring.my; www. nangadamai.com. Its name means 'home of peace' in Iban, & both the rainforest location & eco-rustic design of this homestay are wonderfully peaceful.

Service & feedback during its 15 years in business have been consistent, & the number of fans of Nanga Damai has snowballed as a result.

Run by Polycarp Teo Sebom, he makes his guests feel at home in this relaxed jungle house, whose wooden doors open on to a large deck. 4 double AC rooms on upper floors have phone, TV & jungle views. 2 cottage suites with small kitchen & forest-edge veranda. B/fast is rye bread & freshly brewed coffee. Minimum 2 nights' stay for B&B. Considered unsuitable for children due to poolside sculptures, & best for peace-loving singles & couples. Polycarp is an expert 'freelance trekker' if you are ready for an off-the-beaten-track jungle adventure on Mt Santubong. **$$**

Sarawak Cultural Village 082 846411; e info@scv.com.my. Basic but clean longhouse rooms with threadbare facilities yet high on natural setting and ethnic colour. Choose from Iban, Bidayuh, Orang Ulu or Melanau style. **$$**

Permai Rainforest Resort (39 cabins plus a longhouse) 082 846487; e reserve@ permairainforest.com; www.permairainforest. com. Back-to-jungle experience for trekkers, nature enthusiasts & families, with minimum creature comforts, this rustic rainforest resort has risen up the reviewer scales. While clearly too basic for some (who prefer to sleep in their hire car than this 'shed'), many Asians & Westerners love the experience & setting, particularly from the bird-chiming tree houses. Jungle pool, Wi-Fi & Rainforest Café; the 2-person, AC tree houses are located at canopy level, not in the trees themselves, with balconies overlooking the water & b/fast included; also cabins sleeping 6–10 with fans & mosquito nets, & a 6-bed longhouse for a family/group; the Outdoor Activity Centre organises climbing & trekking. Be warned: the resort attracts many school & team-building groups, so if leafy calm is important, avoid peak 'camp' periods. **$$–$**

⌂ **The Village House** (12 rooms) Off Jln Pantai Puteri, Kampung Santubong; ☎ 082 846166; e info@villagehouse.com.my; www.villagehouse.com.my. The first boutique newcomer to Damai in a decade is this good place to chill, with nice ethnic, art-decked atmosphere, food, pool, outdoor spaces & cocktails. Paintings by local artist, Ramsay Ong, & hand-woven Ikat textiles on the walls. Nice touches including his & her sarongs. Accommodation ranges from 6-bed dorms to luxury suites – the 2 'Rajah rooms' have private balconies, high-tech fittings, Nespresso machine & upmarket price tags. Village doubles/twins have four-poster beds & views over the pool. There's a 'No children below 12' policy, but that, say some, doesn't stop a noisy ambiance. The Village House Restaurant has international food. **$$–$**

✖ **WHERE TO EAT AND DRINK** There are many small seafood and other restaurants on the peninsula, along the main road and in the villages. The new hub of eating and nightlife – when completed – will be the Damai Bay Bazaar (see page 279). In Kampung Buntal (you will need to take a car or taxi from hotels), there are at least half-a-dozen inexpensive restaurants including **Lim Hock Ann** and **Teo Seafood**; all under RM40 per person for a good feed. Many people point towards the **Palm Garden Seafood Restaurant** (*Jln Kampung Santubong*). Personally, I found the big metal structure lacking charm, and there was a strong smell of diesel; the food was average. In Kampung Santubong, **Dayang Seafood** is recommended. **Green Paradise Café** on the Jalan Santubong–Kuching road at the entrance to the Santubong mountain trek has simple but healthy rice and noodle dishes. At the Sarawak Cultural Village, the **Budaya Sarawak Restaurant** (☎ *082 846411*) has a buffet lunch and menu, including ethnic specialities such as manok pansoh (chicken cooked in bamboo and served in banana stem). **Damai Lookout Point Seafood** restaurant has a good selection of dishes.

WHAT TO SEE AND DO

Trekking Though Gunung (Mount) Santubong is not yet a national park or reserve its dense lush beauty should not be underestimated. A mountain guide is not necessary, but can be arranged through hotel recreation desks. From the trail head on the main Kuching–Santubong road, the **Red Trail** to the summit is about a five-hour return trip; the **Blue Trail** an easy 2km trek around the foothills of the mountain. On all walks, caution should be taken with spiders, scorpions and snakes.

Birdwatching Buntal is an important wintering ground for migratory birds. Birdlife International has registered the whole area between Teluk Buntal and Teluk Bako bays as an 'Important Bird Area'. Between October and March many migratory birds including terns, egrets, sandpipers and godwits are sighted in the estuary of the Buntal River, as well as the resident white-bellied sea eagles and collared kingfishers. Pacific reef egrets frequently stop over on the rocky outcrop of Pulau Tokong Ara in Santubong Bay.

Kuching Wetlands National Park Damai is a good springboard for navigating the mangroves, within the marine estuaries and tidal creeks of the Sungai Salak and Sungai Sibu rivers. Critter-sightings include estuarine crocodiles, Irrawaddy dolphins (see box, page 283), kingfishers, storks, silver leaf monkeys, proboscis monkeys, macaques and fireflies. Designated a 'wetlands of international importance' in 2002, the giant stretch of mangrove forest is a shadow of its former self, whittled down from 17,000ha to 6,600ha through deforestation. At 15km from Kuching and 5km from Damai Beach, several tour operators offer coastal and river cruises, starting from either Damai Beach or the boat club in Kampung Santubong.

The 'Santubong Wildlife Cruises' operated by **CPH Travel** (✆ *082 243708;* ✉ *cphtrvl@ streamyx.com; www.cphtravel.com.my*) leave Santubong jetty daily at 16.00 and return around 19.30. Transfers from Kuching can be included.

Sarawak Cultural Village (*Kampung Budaya Sarawak, Pantai Damai;* ✆ *082 8464111;* ✉ *info@scv.com.my; www.scv.com.my;* ⏰ *09.00–16.45 daily; dance performances 11.30 & 16.00; adult RM60, children RM30, under 6 free*) Beyond the veneer, Santubong's hit attraction offers a deep gaze into Sarawak's rich ethno-cultural history. As you wander between the re-created Melanau tall house, Chinese pagoda and Orang Ulu longhouse, the setting brings greater vitality to the museum, with its girth of trees, and lakes reflecting the peaks of Mount Santubong. The experience is more authentic than the hyperbole suggests. The traditional dwellings are decorated with artefacts and peopled by tribes doing craftwork, cooking or chatting with visitors. The 45-minute dance show – of Bidayuh, Malay, Orang Ulu, Iban and Chinese dances performed by the SCV staff – is genuinely and impeccably presented. The SCV is also home to the annual **Rainforest Musical Festival** (*www. rainforestmusic-borneo.com*) every July.

Sports and leisure The **Damai Golf Course** (*Jln Santubong;* ✆ *082 846088*) has a Mountain Nine below the foothills of Mount Santubong. The Damai Lagoon Resort and Holiday Inn Resort offer a range of **watersports** – snorkelling, sailing, windsurfing, canoeing – and the Permai Rainforest Resort rents **sea kayaks**. **Mountain bikes** can be hired to do a whirl of the 3.5km Damai Cross Country Track.

BAKO NATIONAL PARK

Sarawak's oldest national park and Malaysia's second oldest, Bako National Park (Taman Bako) was established in 1957. Covering 27km² at the end of the Muara Tebas Peninsula, adjacent to Santubong, the park has a spellbinding quality – no doubt due to its astounding diversity of landscapes. Bako has 25 distinct kinds of plant life and seven ecosystems. From Tanjung (Cape) Rhu to Tanjung Po, and all the beaches and bays in between, it sweeps through mangrove, heath, peat swamp and mixed dipterocarp forest, grasslands, sandstone cliffs and sea-eroded coastal formations. With a population of some 280 proboscis monkeys, the chances of sightings as you wander along the many well-marked trails are high, particularly early morning or towards dusk. Big-headed, bristly snouted pigs often wander right in front of the park

IRRAWADDY DOLPHINS

These shy cetaceans live in the coastal, brackish and fresh waters of the tropical and sub-tropical Indo-Pacific region. Their bulging forehead and snubbed beak give them a distinctive, sweet appearance, and they are known for their friendliness towards people, helping Burmese fishermen by herding fish towards their boats. In return, many fishermen tap their oars against the boat to attract the dolphins and share with them their catch. Not all Irrawaddy–human relations are so exemplary. By-catch is a major threat, along with habitat degradation, and with an estimated population of just 100 individuals, the species is critically endangered. The best time to see them in the Kuching Wetlands is from April to October, though their timid nature means they are not easily spotted, even by the guides.

HQ, scavenging for scrap food or wallowing in mangrove mud. The animals to be most wary of are the audacious macaque monkeys – known to raid many an unlocked room, as well as the canteen and dustbins, and even confront guests for food they might be carrying. 'Compulsive thieves' is how they are not-so-fondly described!

GETTING THERE AND AWAY Kampung Bako, the propeller-point for the boat trip to the park, is 37km northeast of Kuching along Jalan Bako. Petra Jaya Transport bus No 6 runs there hourly from 07.00 to 17.00. The journey takes about 45 minutes. From the jetty, you must charter a motorboat to take you to the park HQ. Organise this at the National Parks boat ticketing booth next to the jetty. A one-way fare is roughly RM50, which can be shared by up to five people. The 30-minute boat trip out of the estuary of the Sungai Bako into the bay is half of the fun.

OTHER PRACTICALITIES Park accommodation is basic: two- and three-bedroom chalets with a fan and attached or shared bathrooms, four-bedroom hostels, and a camping ground. The rustic nature of the lodgings satisfies most nature-lovers, though there are occasional complaints of poor maintenance/cleanliness and dampness. 'Cooking facilities' means barbecue pits, and there is a canteen at the park HQ, with prices deemed by some visitors as a bit high. The park registration desk and the Kampung Bako boat-ticketing counter are open daily (⏱ *08.00–16.15*), including public holidays. A conservation fee must be paid (*adult RM10, children & students with international/ Malaysian student card RM5*). The information centre in the park shows films and slide shows on Bako's wildlife and provides pamphlets on all the trails, flora and fauna. The boatmen's canteen at Kampung Bako has cheap meals, snacks and refreshments. Bring all other food and other items with you if you plan to stay.

WHAT TO SEE AND DO
Wildlife Bako is often tipped as the best park in Sarawak for wildlife experiences. Apart from the monkeys, there are otters, crabs, frogs and lots of lizards and snakes – lime-green whip snakes, green spotted paradise snakes, and Borneo's only dangerous snake, the triangular-headed pit viper. The wildlife experience starts among the mangroves of Telok Assam, park HQ area, where many of the 150 locally listed birds can be sighted.

Treks Bako boasts one of Borneo's best networks of park trails – 16 well-signed walks from hour-long forest strolls (1.6km return) to full-day treks (21km return). Pick up a map and flora-and-fauna guide at the park HQ, where you must also register for longer forest forays. You may find one or more of the trails closed for maintenance. It's amazing how many kinds of vegetation you will pass in an hour as you climb up a couple of cliffs, and circumnavigate the inland of a bay. Both of the supposedly best trails for seeing the proboscis monkey – **Telok Delima** and **Telok Paku** – are about 2km return from Telok Assam (park HQ), with sightings also frequent in the mangroves near the park HQ. Pitcher plants are found along the red-arrowed **Lintang Loop Trail** (10.8km return).

Beach, bay and boat Telok Pandan Kecil, reached via the 2.5km yellow-arrowed trail, is one of the nicest beaches, nestled within a secluded bay and rocky headland. To cut the journey, or to visit bays and coves further afield, you can charter a boat at park HQ and organise a pickup time with a boatman for a return journey. On the way, you will get to see the casuarina-topped limestone and sandstone cliffs and some of the coast's fascinating eroded rock features like the Sea Stack.

West of Kuching there are three national parks: first up is Kubah, then Gunung Gading, and finally Tanjung Datu, on the end of the peninsula. As many in the Sarawak tourism industry declare quite openly, the coasts – and beaches – along this stretch are not on the same level, in beauty or infrastructure, as those of Santubong and Bako. Others love its relaxed, undeveloped nature. The main road passes some sleepy coastal and inland towns from Lundu to Sematan. Accommodation is threadbare, and mostly geared to the low end of the domestic market. On weekends, it will be hard to avoid the karaoke and coastal exodus from Kuching. On weekdays, you might get more of a chance to discover a relaxed beach atmosphere on the flat 'Gold-Coast-like' beaches of Pantai Pandan and Patai Siar. The main attraction to the Lundu area – unless you are really into silkworms – might be the close-to-Kuching outdoor escape, or rafflesia flower pursuit, in the form of Gunung Gading National Park.

GETTING THERE AND AWAY
By car The road heads west of Kuching to Lundu and Sematan, 100km from Kuching.

By bus Matang Transport buses go to Kubah Park from outside the Saujana car park in Kuching. STC buses go to Lundu four-times daily from the long-distance bus terminal. From Lundu there is a connecting bus to Gunung Gading National Park or a taxi for under RM10. There are onward buses to Sematan from Lundu.

By boat There is no road access to the Tanjung Datu National Park. To get there, you must first take a boat from Sematan to the village of Telok Melano, then either another boat to the park HQ (a 15-minute trip), or a 2½-hour walk along the Telok Melano–Telok Upas trail. The boats are infrequent, unscheduled and cater to local communities, so it is best to rely on your feet or on a tour operator departing from Kuching. The whole area is inaccessible by boat during monsoon season (*October to February*).

WHERE TO STAY AND EAT Aside from the national park accommodation, there are slim pickings in the area, and the 'resorts' are rather downmarket and overpriced for the services they offer.

National park accommodation
Kubah Park HQ The Park HQ has five bungalows that sleep six, a ten-bed resthouse and a 12-bed hostel, all with air conditioning, TV, hot water, a veranda, full kitchen facilities and a barbecue area (**$**). The nearby **Matang Wildlife Centre** has more basic chalets and a hostel 'longhouse'.

Gunung Gading National Park The infrastructure here is not in the same league as Kubah Park HQ: there are campsites, three-bedroom chalets and hostel accommodation (**$**), but neither a canteen nor cooking facilities – so stock up on ready-to-eat provisions, or come and go from Lundu 2km away.

Tanjung Datu There are no park lodgings, but a community homestay in the fishing village of Teluk Melano. Call or visit the park office in Kuching for details (see page 266).

Other accommodation

🏠 **Sematan Palm Beach Resort** No 295 Kampung Sungai Kilong, Jln Seacom; 📞082 712388; ℮ enquiry@spbresort.com; www. spbresort.com. The resort is now revamped with new management, but still needs greater attention to detail to make it a more uplifting stay. Nice location. Plainly furnished chalets (sleeping 2–6) with AC, TV & en-suite bathroom; individual & family rates include b/fast & dinner; swimming pool, beach, bikes & kayak rental. Sand flies, jellyfish & loud music in the restaurant are potential nuisances. **$$**

WHAT TO SEE AND DO
Kubah National Park

The massive sandstone ridge in this park can be seen from Kuching, 22km away – notably the 911m peak of Gunung Serapi. The limestone ridges of the Serapi range, rising between 150m and 450m, are forested predominantly by mixed dipterocarp and over 100 different palm species. Punctuated by limestone-gouged waterfalls, the park's six marked trails range from the 255m 'Palmetum' to a 5km summit trail. The 1,429m 'Belian' Trail takes in Bornean ironwoods and many fruit trees. The 3,830m 'Rayu' Trail passes by several bintangor trees, which for two decades have been tapped for their sap as a hopeful cure for AIDS (the chemical costatolide is extracted from the substance). The **Matang Wildlife Centre** is adjacent to the park; orphaned orangutans are prepped up here before graduating to Semenggoh's more open jungle.

Lundu An hour's drive from Kuching, Lundu is a small, scenic, sleepy town with a thriving ikan pusu (anchovy) industry. With just a couple of rows of shop-houses and a local market, it spreads along the riverbank in the shadow of Gunung Gading Mountain. Nearby are the beaches of Patai Siah and Patai Pandan.

Gunung Gading National Park Every park has its own signature rafflesia species: Gunung Gading hosts Rafflesia tuanmudae. A plank walk leads to a common blooming ground (*guiding fees RM20 per hour per group with ranger*). For rafflesia-blooming checks, ring the National Parks Office in Kuching (📞 *082 248088*), or the park HQ (📞 *082 735714*). The park's three trails include a light two-hour trek and a six–eight-hour return 'Gunung Gading' summit walk.

Sematan Half an hour from Lundu on the South China Sea, Sematan is a hobby barramundi fishing area – the fish were introduced by the Agriculture Department. It also has a **Silk Farm** (📞 *082 320130; www.sematansilk.com; RM5*), where you can purchase silk quilts. In the 14km² **Tanjung Datu National Park** on the Datu Peninsula, Sarawak meets Indonesia, land meets sea and rainforest meets coral reef – and turtle conservation territory. Lack of regular viable transport makes independent travel here difficult – the boats from Sematan to Telok Melano cater to local communities and are unscheduled, but that can be an adventure in itself. Tour operators in Kuching organise transport and guided tours to the park. The area is totally off-limits during the October–February monsoon. Extreme mountain biker Hans Rey says the Sematan area is a **mountain-bike** paradise with 'an estimated 60–80km of all types of trails, with covered single-tracks, waterfalls, desert-heat, killer climbs and screaming downhills'. For tours, contact **Outdoor Trek** (📞 *082 363344; ℮ best@bikcloud.com; www.bikcloud.com*).

SOUTH OF KUCHING

From the small market town of Serikin to the village of Anah Rais, the foothills of the Borneo Highlands, along the Indonesian border, are Bidayuh homeland.

Fleeing the coast for the hinterland – where they built longhouses and baruk warrior houses from bamboo – earned these timid people the name of the 'land Dayaks'. The region is punctuated by a series of peaks, rippled between 400m and 1,400m, perfect for an off-the-beaten-track adventure. Sarawak's answer to the wildlife sanctuary of Sabah is in the neighbourhood, as are some lively Chinese market towns, caves and kayaking.

GETTING THERE AND AWAY

By car Take the Kuching–Serian road south from Kuching; for Bau (60km) veer right into Jalan Batu Kitang; for the Borneo Highlands, Jalan Penrissen.

By bus STC buses travel to Semenggoh from the city bus stand on Jalan Tun Abang Haji Openg. Take bus Nos 6, 6A, 6B or 6C and alight at the Forestry Department Botanical Research Centre in Semenggoh, from which there is a short stroll to the centre through the forest. Buses leave Kuching at 08.20, 10.30, 11.00 and 13.30. The last return bus leaves Semenggoh at 17.00. The journey time is roughly 30 minutes and the fares are about RM2.

Buses to Bau leave from the Kuching Regional Bus Terminal (*Jln Penrissen*). Operated by both STC and Bau Transport, buses leave every half hour between 06.20 and 18.00; the journey costs RM4.50–5.

WHERE TO STAY AND EAT

Borneo Highlands Resort (62 rooms) Jln Borneo Heights, Padawan, Kuching; m 016 886 0790/019 829 0790; e enquiry@borneohighlands.com.my; www. borneohighlands.com. The resort has loads of potential as a highland haven of ecotourism, organic horticulture, rainforest & golf, but work needs to be done to ensure the standards of service, food & maintenance match the location. Jungle spa, 18-hole golf course, rooms, suites & secluded chalets with ethnically refined décor. The Annah Rais Café serves organic, vegetarian, local & international food. The Hornbill's Nest is a lounge-cum-tea parlour with highland organics. The entry road is extremely steep (upgrades are planned), requiring a 4x4 to reach it. The resort organises this for RM50 return. In my mind, there is no way they should be charging guests for that trip; if they must, best build it into the room price. Good 'Jungle Spa' & other packages available online at www.sarawakresorts.com. **$$$$$–$$**

Kurakura Homestay (4 rooms) Kampung Semadang, Batu 24, Jln Borneo Heights; m (Lars) 012 892 0051; e kurakurahomestay@gmail.com; http://kurakura.asia. Wildlife-watching, culture-soaking rustic eco-experience, a remote upriver jungle home guesthouse, with organic garden, solar energy. 50mins from Kuching, then no road; only river access (*25min trip*). Good-for-the-soul simplicity. 2-night stay min, including stay in basic huts, mosquito-netted bed, no AC, meals, tea/coffee with a host of guided activities as optional add-ons. **$$**

Annah Rais Longhouse Adventure 71 Kampung Annah Rais, Jln Padawan/Borneo Heights, 60km from Kuching; ☏ 082 457941; www. longhouseadventure.com. In a traditional Bidayuh longhouse village, longhouse rooms, jungle treks, waterfalls & traditional food. 2-night packages include transfers, accommodation, meals & activities from RM398 adult/RM198 child. Take any additional requirements – no major shops close by. Full itinerary on website. **$**

WHAT TO SEE AND DO
Semenggoh Wildlife Rehabilitation Centre (*20km from Kuching;* ☏ *082 618423;* ⊕ *08.00–12.30 & 14.00–16.00; adult RM3, child RM1.50*) Sarawak's first forest reserve, established in 1920, was converted into a rehabilitation centre for orangutans, honey bears and hornbills in 1975. 'Semi-wild' orangutans inhabit the sanctuary, having graduated up from the infant-oriented Matang Wildlife Centre. Visits revolve around feeding times (*half an hour at 08.30 and 15.00*). The viewing

area is a 1km walk from the entrance, where a series of graphic images warn of the dangers of serious injury from inappropriate behaviour with the orangutans. Such interaction most commonly includes goading and teasing the animals with food, and simply getting too close for comfort. Morning visits can be better, when the apes roam free prior to the afternoon feed. It is not uncommon to run into some on the reserve's pathways – but keep in mind the previous caution and do not wander alone. The rehabilitation centre is part of the **Semenggoh Nature Reserve**, whose arboretum and botanical research centre displays fernariums, ethnobotanic and other gardens. Visits to the latter must be booked in advance.

Bidayuh longhouses

Tour operators visit longhouses as a day trip but you can also visit several independently, including those in Kampung Annah Rais: at Kampung Benuk (*off Jln Penrissen, 50km from Kuching*) there are about 80 families in a longhouse; Kampung Pelaman Dunuk is 62km from Kuching. Admission with or without a guide is RM5. If you are visiting in June, the Bidayuh villages celebrate the rice festival **Gawai Padi** (Gawai Sawa'a in Bidayuh dialect) in their own special way, with lots of shamanistic rituals, priestesses, trance dancers and music.

Borneo Highlands trekking

From Annah Rais, there is a three-hour trek into the Kalimantan border region, where a large community of some 200 Bidayuh families live traditionally in four longhouses, strung each side of a suspension bridge. Two- to three-day trekking excursions are available, taking in Gunung Penrissen (1,329m) and the surrounding landscapes, longhouses and villages along small trails, giving views over Kalimantan, Kuching and the South China Sea.

Bau

The Bau region bears scars from 19th-century mining – both on the land and in the memories of the people. Antimony was discovered here in the 1820s, and the area later became a hotspot of rebellion against oppressive Brunei rulers, who forced the Bidayuh to work in the mines for a pittance and sold the women and children as slaves. Local Malays and natives rebelled in 1836, proclaiming Sarawak's independence. The rebellion dragged on, with James Brooke apparently playing the role of peacemaker when he arrived on the scene in 1839. In subsequent decades the gold rush began and migrants, mostly Hakka people, came from China and Dutch Kalimantan. In 1857, there was another uprising, this time by Chinese miners against Brooke. In a massacre that is rarely spoken of, some 2,000 Chinese men, women and children were killed by the rajah's forces, smothered in caves they took shelter in while their mining settlement was set alight. On the way to Bau is the small market town of **Siniawan**. Composed of 1920s double-storey wooden shop-houses, it was once the rebels' headquarters. Strong on local history is Borneo Adventure's founder and guide Philip Yong (✆ *082 245175; e info@borneoadventure.com*), also Honorary Secretary-General of the Sarawak Tourism Federation and son of the late Sarawak minister Stephen Yong. The opencast mine in Bau has created a small blue lake, **Tasik Biru**.

Caves and kayaking

Caves, rivers and limestone ridges make the highlands area a magnet for outdoor activities. The **Wind Cave** reserve towards the border is a pleasant picnic spot; **Fairy Cave** – which has some Chinese shrines at the entrance and interior – is also an **abseiling** destination. Buses travel on from Bau to here.

Serikin

At the left of the fork in the road towards the border, this is a modern Bidayuh town. You won't find longhouses here but you can buy Indonesian crafts – bags, baskets and kasah floormats – at the gerai stalls.

Southeast of Kuching, the sinewy Sri Aman Division skirts the Indonesian border. Over 90% of the population are Iban, and their rice paddy, rubber and pepper cash crops thread the river-lined landscape. The longhouses that start appearing in fields after the town of Serian are a mix of traditional wooden and modern cement structures. Deeper inland, the rivers that run through national parks and longhouse communities can only be experienced by boat trip. Allow at least a two-night stay in this area whichever way you tackle it.

GETTING THERE AND AWAY

By car   Head southeast along the Serian–Kuching road.

By bus   From Kuching's regional bus express terminal on Jalan Penrissen, Sarawak Transport Company/STC bus 3A leaves every hour for Serian from 06.15 to around 19.00 and costs RM6.60. From Serian there are local buses to Ranchan Pools. STC bus No EP09 make the three-hour journey to Sri Aman (*RM19*), with departures at 07.30, 09.45, noon, 15.15 and 19.45. Some of the Eva Express coaches that ply the route between Kuching, Sibu and Miri also pass through Serian, Sri Aman and Betong.

By boat   Longboats and speedboats are used for river journeys and to cross the Batang Ai.

WHERE TO STAY

Saloma Villagestay   75 Kampung Sadir, Jln Puncak, Siburan; m 016 868 2525; e saloma.lisa@gmail.com; www.salomavillagestay.org. A Mass Communication graduate is host at this new homestay. A Bidayuh native, she renovated her father's house for this hospitable venture. Count on jungle treks, Bidayuh culture & food, & a bamboo immersion (the Bidayuh use it for furniture making, cooking, house building & more). Package of 2 days/1 night from RM450 including transfer to/from Kuching, 3 meals & bed, jungle adventure, Semenggoh entrance, & Bidayuh handicraft. **$$**

KC Inn   Jln Alamanda, Serian. Recommended if you need a room mid journey. Spotless, spacious rooms & hot showers. **$**

WHERE TO EAT AND DRINK
In the 200km between Kuching and Batang Ai, standard food stops are at Serian (which has fantastic market food), Lachau and Sri Aman. Lachau – a small car and coach rest-stop – is referred to as 'cowboy town'. The once-widespread cross-border barter continues among travelling traders who arrive in town from Indonesia. The Chinese coffee shops along the main street are a good place to have a drink and some noodles – **Lee Chong Café** is recommended.

WHAT TO SEE AND DO
At **Siburan**, 30km from Kuching, is **Jong's Crocodile Farm** and mini zoo (*off Serian Rd;* 082 863570; ① *09.00–17.00 daily, feeding times 11.00 & 15.00; adult RM8, child RM4*). Here you will learn a lot about Sarawak's saltwater crocodiles (Crocodylus porosus), particularly the deadly 'happy bachelor' (see page 58). The skull of the 6m-long killer is on display here.

Another 40km east, **Serian** is a small but sparkling market town of 85,000 – nearly two-thirds of the population are Bidayuh, the rest a mix of Malay, Iban and Chinese. In the middle of the market square is the **Big Durian** – a monument to the king of local fruits. The under-cover farmers' market is a maze of culinary forms: chillies, freshly picked peanuts, snake fruit and squirming sago worms. There are plenty of stalls for *pisang goreng* (fried banana) and savoury snacks. The **Taman**

A few handy words to have up your sleeve for longhouse visits are:

Nama berita nuan?	How are you? (used as a general greeting instead of hello)
Berita akumana	I am well
Nyamai	It's delicious (a good one to comment on the rice wine)
Terima kasih	Thank you (the same as in Malay)

Danu recreational park is pretty at night, when its lights cast on the lake, over a couple of restaurants and some food stalls. Near Serian, the **Ranchan Recreational Park** comprises a waterfall, rainforest picnic spot and swimming pool. The park facilities and trails have been criticised for being run-down and seem set for an upgrade; on the other hand, the canteen and park chalets are relatively new and in a lovely setting.

BANDAR SRI AMAN At 194km from Kuching, 9km from the main road turn-off, Bandar Sri Aman on the banks of the Batang Lupar River is the district trading hub for the timber, oil palm, rubber and pepper industries, and gateway to the Batang Ai National Park. The city's main claim to fame is its *benak* or 'tidal bore', which rolls in through the river mouth and fills the riverbed within minutes. The tidal bore is actually a daily occurrence, on such a small scale that it is unnoticeable. A couple of times a year, however, it reaches speeds of 7–18km/h, and heights of up to 3m. The phenomenon was immortalised by Somerset Maugham in the short story *The Yellow Streak* after he visited and nearly drowned in 1921 while boating on the river with his companion. Sri Aman is trying to build up its tourism power with the **Pesta Benak** – tidal bore festival. Amid lots of merriment, food and dance, people even try surfing the bores. The only historical building of note, **Fort Alice**, was built out of belian wood in 1864, after Rajah Charles Brooke's declared 'defeat' of the last of the great Iban chieftains, Rentap.

Batang Ai Nantional Park For wildlife research more than orangutan spotting, the park is accessed after a three–four-hour longboat journey. Mapped out with the assistance of the local Iban communities, the arduously challenging **Red Ape Trail** has the endorsement of the Orangutan Foundation. The full trek is 11 days, but shorter walks can be arranged. In November 2010, I felt I had come as close as possible to reliving a slice of Redmond O'Hanlon's classic adventure *Into the Heart of Borneo*, heading way upriver and into the jungle to tackle part of this trail, accompanied by Borneo Adventure's local Iban guides and foragers. To try it for yourself, contact **Borneo Adventure** (*55 Main Bazaar, Kuching;* ✆ *082 245175;* e *info@borneoadventure.com; www.borneoadventure.com*).

BATANG AI The water catchment of **Batang Ai Reservoir** was formed when the valley and some 30 longhouses in it were submerged in the 1980s – a controversial move in which hundreds of locals were forcibly relocated. The power station provides half of Sarawak's daily energy needs. The area is the starting point for excursions deep along the Sungai Batang Ai and Sungai Engkari rivers, leading to huge longhouses where Iban communities live isolated existences, somewhere between tradition and modernity.

Getting there and away Reaching Batang Ai Reservoir is remarkably inexpensive for the distance involved (*275km*), yet is difficult, time-consuming and ill advised. First, take the STC express bus No EP09 to Sri Aman from Kuching's regional bus terminal, a three-hour trip costing RM19, then a local bus to Lubock Antu (*2hrs*). For the remaining 5km to the dam, the only option is to hitch a ride. If you get stuck in Lubok Antu, you will require a private longboat charter to continue your journey – an expensive option unless pre-organised as part of a tour.

Where to stay and eat

Longhouse experiences Most longhouses that accept guests are located in the Skrang and Lemanak river areas near Bandar Sri Aman, and the Batang Ai River and its tributaries. On the whole, these are remote areas, reached only by longboat. The easiest option is to visit on a tour. One possible alternative for the independent adventurer is to travel to Betong, and once there organise a trip to Batang Skrang directly with local Ibans. The most popular longhouse stays and tours are:

Nanga Ukum Longhouse www. borneoecotours.com. Borneo Eco Tours do a luxury safari, 3 days/2 nights from Kuching, stopping on the way at Semenggoh Orangutan Centre & Serian Town, staying at the Hilton Batang Ai & visiting Nanga Ukum longhouse by longboat. **$$$$**

Nanga Sumpa Borneo Adventure Longhouse 55 Main Bazaar, Kuching; ✆082 245175; e info@borneoadventure.com; www. borneoadventure.com. Kuching-based Borneo Adventure's longhouse is located way up the Batang Ai River in the Sri Aman District's Iban longhouse community of the same name. The ethically run lodge offers a rustic nature experience with mattresses & mosquito nets & excellent food prepared by village women. The Nanga Sampa lodge will also be your first night's stay for embarking on various jungle escapades including treks along the Red Ape Trail. It was first mapped out in 2002, with a UK group & local Iban trekkers, & is endorsed by the UK's Orangutan Foundation. Walk it with Iban guides employed by Borneo Adventure on a 5–11-day adventure. This is a tough, challenging trek, with plenty of mud, leeches, humidity, wading through rivers, & roughing it up. Very rewarding, it offers an unparalleled insight into Iban traditions (from food foraging to fishing & longhouse life), & hopefully a rare view of the orangutan in the wild. Interaction with the local longhouse community is a vital part of the trip, & the company has worked closely with them over the past 2 decades, contributing greatly to sustainable tourism development in the region. Borneo Adventure also has a new 6 day 5 night tour, In Search of

Orangutans, which covers three different areas of orangutan habitat at Batang Ai, so the chances of seeing orangutans are apparently higher. On the volunteer side, the company runs several community projects at Ulu Ai in the heart of the park, where guests get to participate in community rebuilding projects with the Iban. These projects involve light construction work (e.g. helping to build a new sceptic tank, rebuilding the longhouse, etc) or land clearing. The Ulu Ai Volunteer Project is a 7D6N programme in which visitors work on maintaining the traditional jungle trail network. Similar shorter volunteer trips are available for school groups. 2-night packages from RM1,250. **$$$$–$$$**

Hilton Batang Ai Longhouse Resort (100 rooms) ✆083 584388, or via Kuching Hilton, ✆082 248200. A 15min boat journey from the Batang Ai Dam, the only hotel in the area is this 3-star longhouse construction on the banks of the reservoir. Wood-panelled rooms with rattan & belian furnishings are arranged in several inward-facing longhouses, while the veranda & outdoor dining areas overlook the water. Nice swimming pool, tennis court & ample buffet spread. The $31m^2$ rooms are on the small side; the $71m^2$ duplex suites have a separate living room & are very comfortable. Good base for excursions to longhouses, jungle treks, boating & fishing. Also good to wind up here after some heavy-duty jungle trekking. **$$$–$$**

Nanga Sumpa Community Batang Ai, Sri Aman. It is also possible to organise a simple longhouse stay at the Nanga Sumpa's community longhouse. Shared by some 10 families, it was modernised in 2009. Expect an authentic stay in simple, clean rooms, participating in local life & subsisting on fresh fish & vegetables. Contact the visitor information centre in Kuching (see page 266) or one of the tour operators to organise this budget trip. **$$**

Longhouse visits Reached either by self-chartered longboat trip or on a tour, some of the upriver longhouse communities still live a relatively isolated and traditional life that's fascinating to observe. At **Kampung Mengkak Longhouse** (*Rumah Burau, Mengkak;* m *013 286 7451*) on the Sungai Engkari, you can mingle with some of the 26 families who live in the 200m-long structure as they sit in the *ruai* (communal veranda), drinking *tuak* (rice wine) and making handicrafts. The locals demonstrate their blowpipe skills, perform dances and play music in traditional dress on request, but with far more personality and passion than you could ever expect in a city cultural show. Indeed, the best visits can be those that just experience 'life as usual' rather than extravaganza shows. The key to making such a visit as enriching as possible is to be humble and respectful, learn a couple of Iban greetings and mingle gently with the people. Get acquainted with the chief (*Tuai Rumah*), and get ready to feel your face all smiled out as the whole community turns out to welcome you. Another important lesson I have learned – don't ever blatantly turn down an offering, even if you don't want anything, whether it be food or rice wine. Simply accept smilingly and then try to offload it subtly (as I once did, on to my accompanying Iban guide!).

FOLLOW BRADT

For the latest news, special offers and competitions, subscribe to the Bradt newsletter via the website www.bradtguides.com and follow Bradt on:

f www.facebook.com/BradtTravelGuides
◆ @BradtGuides
◯ @bradtguides
◉ www.pinterest.com/bradtguides

11

Central Sarawak

Intersected by the mighty Batang Rejang and its tributaries, the journey through this vast region from the South China Sea to remote inland areas is a compelling mix of tribal traditions, coastal modernity and mountainous isolation. River transport is as vital for getting around the area, as reaching it. Long river trips open a fascinating window on to the complex cultural landscape of the Rejang, whose lower reaches are peppered by Iban and Melanau settlements, while way inland, is home to nomadic Penan hunter-gatherers and other Orang Ulu upriver dwellers.

SIBU

At the confluence of the Rejang and the Igan, 130km from the South China Sea, river geography has played a major hand in Sibu's history. A major transport hub for the whole Rejang Basin, parts of Sibu's massive harbour are over 1km wide. Sarawak's affluent second-biggest city – with a population of 180,000 – it was pushed to modernity by a former mayor, backed by powerful Chinese community associations. About 60% of Sibuan are Chinese, the rest Malay, Melanau, Iban and Orang Ulu. Propelled by religious persecution and poverty, the Chinese started arriving in 1901, led by Methodist missionary Reverend Wong Nai Siong, heralded as the town's founder. He persuaded Charles Brooke to give land to the Chinese in the Lower Rejang region for farming paddy, pepper and rubber. Sibu rebounded in the post-World War II years as a centre of the timber industry, and maintained a booming trade in timber, sawmilling and shipbuilding throughout the 1980s. Named after the Iban word for rambutan – buah sibau – one Malaysian observer sums it up well, as a town 'full of can do attitude'.

GETTING THERE AND AWAY

By air The airport is 23km from town. A taxi costs RM28 with a coupon purchased at a desk inside the arrival hall. (This system is in place to help protect you from unscrupulous practices rather widespread in Malaysia owing, unfortunately, to the lack of regulation of fares.) There is no highly reliable public transport service to the airport, though Lanang Bus 3A does the trip about every 90 minutes between 06.00 and 18.00. Malaysia Airlines' MASwings has two daily flights each way between Sibu and Kuching ('Promo Fares' from RM88), as does AirAsia ('Low Fare' from RM75). Both MAS (not its regional carrier) and AirAsia also connect Sibu with Kuala Lumpur, though AirAsia's fares here are significantly cheaper, starting from RM154 – almost half Malaysia Airlines' lowest ticket prices for the route. MASwings also connects Sibu with Bintulu, Miri and Kota Kinabalu. In the past, AirAsia's flights from Kuching to Sibu were renowned for delays but those problems seem to be diminishing, though an estimated 30% of flights on the route still experience some kind of holdup, on average 14 minutes.

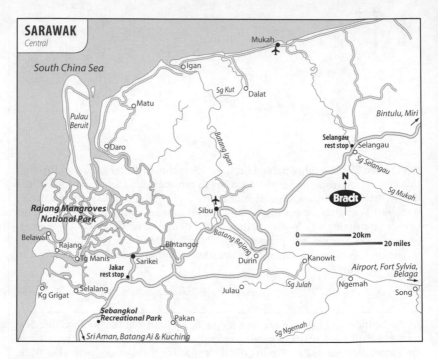

Airlines

✈ **AirAsia** Jln Tuanku Osman; ☎ 084 307808
✈ **Malaysia Airlines** Jln Tuanku Osman; ☎ 084
321055. Town office.

By car Sibu is roughly midway between Kuching (*462km*) and Miri (*380km*).

By bus The long-distance bus hub, the Sibu New Bus Terminal, is on Jalan Pahlawan, 3km from the city centre. Several bus companies operate from here. **Biaramas Express** has daily buses to Kuching, Bintulu (*RM20*) and Miri (*RM40*), as well as to Pontianak in Indonesia. **Borneo Amalgamated Transport** serves Bintulu, Kuching, Sarikei, Sri Aman and Kanowit. **Trans Borneo Resources** also goes to coastal and inland towns to the north in Mukah Division, including Mukah (*RM16*), Oya and Dalat (*RM17*). Bus 21 links the long-distance bus station to the city bus 'Transit Point' in about 20 minutes.

By boat Longer-distance express boats come and go from the Express Wharf for Kuching, Belaga, Dalat, Daro, Kapit, Kanowit, Sarikei and Song. Tickets are sold at the passenger terminal at the wharf. During peak holiday periods it's best to book in advance, otherwise arrive 30 minutes before departure. For up-to-date schedules, contact the **Sarawak Rivers Board** (☎ *084 339936*).

GETTING AROUND The city centre is small, and pleasant to walk around.

By car For car hire, contact the Visitor Information Centre (see page 295). They warn of unlicensed drivers and advise tourists to contact them for the latest details of recommended car-hire companies.

By taxi Taxis do not use meters; shorter trips cost between RM6 and RM12. Taxis are easily flagged outside the big hotels, at the taxi stand opposite the Express Wharf, and on Jalan Lintang – or call the station (☎ *084 320773*). Official long-distance fares (one-way) are: Mukah RM200; Bawang Assan longhouse settlement RM50; Sarikei RM100; Kanowit RM50; and Bintangor RM90.

By bus The city Transit Point is opposite the Express Wharf on Jalan Khoo Peng Loong, with buses bound for the town area, Sibu region and neighbouring Sarikei. The destination is generally marked on the front of the bus. Prices for local trips range from RM1 for city destinations to RM10 to Sarikei.

TOURIST INFORMATION

⒤ Sibu Visitor Information Centre 32 Jln Tukang Besi; ☎ 084 340980; e vic-sibu@ sarawaktourism.com; ⊙ 08.00–17.00 Mon–Fri, closed Sat, Sun & public holidays. Brochures,

guidebooks & maps available. The helpful staff can advise on travel plans & national park accommodation bookings in the district & the whole Rejang River Basin area, as well as car hire.

WHERE TO STAY *See map, below.*

Hotels There are a handful of very good international class **hotels** in Sibu, and some excellent mid-range hotels – usually lacking pools and gyms, but often with free Wi-Fi. Some three- to four-star establishments offer budget, mid-range

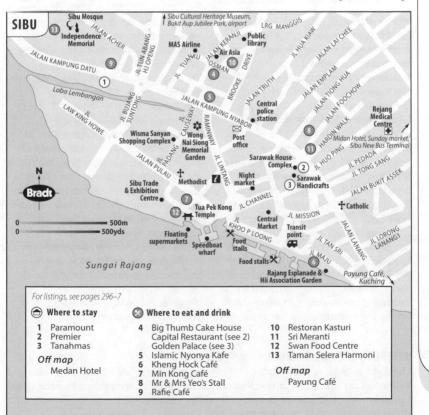

SIBU

For listings, see pages 296–7

🛏 **Where to stay**
1 Paramount
2 Premier
3 Tanahmas

Off map
Medan Hotel

✖ **Where to eat and drink**
4 Big Thumb Cake House
   Capital Restaurant (see 2)
   Golden Palace (see 3)
5 Islamic Nyonya Kafe
6 Kheng Hock Café
7 Min Kong Café
8 Mr & Mrs Yeo's Stall
9 Rafie Café

10 Restoran Kasturi
11 Sri Meranti
12 Swan Food Centre
13 Taman Selera Harmoni

Off map
Payung Café

and suite-level luxury options under one roof. There is a big crossover of **budget/ shoestring** prices in Sibu. In a three-star hotel, it is possible to have a large double room for RM100–150; this will cost around RM100 in a two-star hotel. Meanwhile, standard rooms in some of the hotels listed below cost RM60–100 and come with bathroom, television and fan or air conditioning; some also have a fridge and kettle.

All the following hotels have a great range of room prices, from standard doubles at budget prices to hyper-luxurious river-plunging suites. I personally find it far preferable to stay in a budget room in a classy, central establishment than an often small and poky cheap hotel. For this reason I have eliminated a couple of previously listed shoestring-budget hotels as they really did not make the grade, on any budget. Just because you are paying half the price or less for a no-frills double, doesn't mean you can't expect absolute cleanliness, a nice atmosphere, good dining choices and shopping location, as these long-lasting Sibu stars attest.

At several star-less small hotels and lodging houses, you will pay RM80–90 for a room with fan, television and phone, possibly even free Wi-Fi, mini fridge and air conditioning. Those costing less are most likely dodgy in cleanliness and management, some doubling up as brothels. Among the most respectable bunch is the **Medan Hotel** near the bus terminal (*No 20, Lorong Pahlawan 7D, Jln Pahlawan;* \ *084 216161;* e *hotel@mymedan.com; www.hockpeng.com.my/web2/node/679*). Outside of that, contact the Sibu Visitor Information Centre (for contact details, see page 295) for the latest recommendations.

Premier Hotel (189 rooms) Sarawak Hse Complex, Jln Kampung Nyabor; \ 084 323222; e reservation@premierh.com.my; www.premierh. com.my. A business-oriented 4-star, with restaurant, music lounge, karaoke room, Wi-Fi, 24hr business centre, flanking shopping malls & Cineplex. A refurbishment has left a stark contrast between the new- & old-style (slightly tired for some) rooms. Still, the standard deluxe rooms, at budget prices, are spacious & comfy; the service welcoming & efficient; & the internet remarkably fast (& free, as is the parking). Newly added rooms on the 11th–13th floors are home to the 'Riverview' & executive suites – with great views over the Rejang River, & superior furnishings. Many of the suites offer very good value for money, with their mid-range price tags. The Premier Suites are luxury category & up in price. **$$** (suite **$$$$**)

Tanahmas Hotel (120 rooms) Lot 277, Block 5, Jln Kampung Nyabor; \ 084 333188; e enquiries@tanahmas.com.my; www.tanahmas. com.my. A very swish revamp for this central hotel,

with Sibu's high-tech savvy & small-city amiability reflected in the services & the staff. One of the best 3-stars in town, located near the waterfront market strip with swimming pool, karaoke & restaurant. Fast internet & very friendly staff seem to be Sibu hallmarks. **$$** (suite **$$$$**)

Paramount Hotel (95 rooms) 3 Lorong 9A, Jln Kampung Dato (1km from town); \ 084 331122; e paramount_hotel@yahoo.com; www.paramountsibu.com. Budget-priced 3-star property with courteous Malay service, 600m from the town centre in the riverside zone of Kampung Datu. Many Malay café & food stalls nearby. One of few hotels with a non-smoking policy in lobby & on some floors though recent complaints have focused on smoky non-smoking rooms – as well as slow Wi-Fi. Spacious comfortable rooms & unbeatable value, budget-priced family & executive suites, with b/fast included. Only downside is a lack of sports & leisure facilities, though there's a landscaped riverside area fit for jogging & sports alongside. **$$$–$$**

✖ WHERE TO EAT AND DRINK *See map, page 295.*

The food in Sibu is probably the best value in the whole of Sarawak. Food is of a high quality and most of the restaurants are as spotless as the rest of the town. Local specials include: *kam pua mee* – noodles tossed in pork lard, chilli, onion and sliced pork; *mee sua* – longevity noodles in a tub of rich herbal soup with chunks of boiled chicken; *konpia* – the local 'bagel', yeast buns sandwiched together with spicy minced pork (or chicken in Muslim restaurants); and *mee udang* – river prawns with noodles in a bowl of spicy broth.

Restaurants More upmarket Chinese restaurants with mostly mid-range prices are found at leading hotels: **Golden Palace** (☏ *084 333188*) at Tanahmas Hotel and **New Capital Restaurant** in the Premier Hotel, renowned for its Hainanese chicken rice. (See page 296 for their addresses.)

✖ **Sri Meranti** 1 Jln Hardin; ⊕ evenings only. This Chinese Muslim (halal) seafood restaurant is bright & clean with an AC section & outdoor tables. Its famous fish-head curry, tapah, is made with fresh river fish.

✖ **Restoran Kasturi** 18 Jln Tuanku Osman. Sibu's leading Malay/Melanau eatery serves spicy curries & Malay seafood dishes, as well as Melanau *tebaloi* – sago crackers – & *umai* fish salad.

Coffee shops From early morning onwards the streets are alive with coffee shops serving the aforementioned specialities. Nearly all are open for breakfast, lunch and dinner, so from around 06.30 to late evening.

🖳 **Kheng Hock Café** 49 Jln Maju (facing the Rejang Esplanade). Moderately priced noodle dishes, steamed buns, dumplings, seafood, & barbecued pork & duck are on the menu here. $$$–$$
🖳 **Islamic Nyonya Kafe** 141 Jln Kampung Nyabor. Recommended for its cosy ambience & *roti canai* – reportedly 'the largest in the Rejang Basin'. $$–$
🖳 **Min Kong Café** 13 Jln Bank. Cheap-&-cheerful Chinese café for *mee udang* foochow-style (noodles pre-fried before being dunked in soup), & other delights. $$–$

🖳 **Payung Café** 20F Jln Lanang. Worth going the distance, this café lies 2km east of town on the Rejang River skirting road. The odd mix of Malay, Indonesian & Nyonya dishes includes satays, rojak, chicken Marsala, guava salad, *otak-otak* fish in banana leaf, the signature mushroom roll, durian drinks & ice cream, and fresh coconut juice. $$–$
🖳 **Rafie Café** Jln Tun Abang Haji Openg. Opposite the Paramount Hotel in Kampung Dato, cheap good-quality Malay food & Chinese halal dishes. $$–$

Stalls and market food The first floor of the Sibu Central Market has around 30 (mostly Chinese) stalls, offering cheap, fresh food from 06.00 to 14.00. Some are also open in the evenings. Food stalls also unfurl on Jalan Market and at the **pasar malam** night market on Jalan Lebuh Tinggi. The **Swan Food Centre** (*Jln Temple, next to Sibu Trade & Exhibition Centre; ⊕ morning to evening*) has mostly Chinese food stalls with lots of chicken rice and roasted pork. For food on the go, there is a food court on the first floor of Express Boat Wharf, and Malay food to go from stalls next to the wharf. **Taman Selera Harmoni** (near the Sibu mosque) is a vast under-roof pavilion with several Malay *restoran*, each with its own section of tables and chairs, and, in most cases, a television screen. A hotspot for breakfast *konpia* is **Mr & Mrs Yeo's Stall** (*Lorong Tiong Hua 26, 15mins' walk or take a taxi*), where they serve pork buns in a pork broth, with slices of stewed pork.

Bakery A fantastic bakery, **Big Thumb Cake House** (*71–73 Jln Tuanku Osman;* ☏ *084 339829*), is a family business specialising in cakes, bread and Hong Kong *cha siew pau* (mini steamed bun).

ENTERTAINMENT AND NIGHTLIFE Sibu has several pubs and clubs, and even a few Iban karaoke pubs. For cocktails and sophistication, head to the international hotels – **Club Emas** at the Tanahmas Hotel (*Lot 277, Block 5, Jln Kampung Nyabor*) for cocktails and karaoke or the hotel's **Blowpipe Lounge** for music. Apparently pulling in the more in-crowd of late with its cocktails, beer and high teas, is the **E S Bar** (*34 Jln Merdeka Barat*), though it is hardly central, over 1km north of the main hotel and market area.

SHOPPING If you're travelling by car, the **Durin Handicraft Shop** (*35km southeast from Sibu, near the Rejang's Durin ferry terminal*) sells handicrafts from all over the central region. Chinese potteries are produced at several workshops near Sibu. The narrow crowded streets of the town centre are packed with clothing and high-tech stores. The 28-storey **Wisma Sanyan** shopping complex is Sibu's largest retail mall – and Sarawak's tallest building. On the fourth floor is the cyber café, **Forever Link**.

Markets With 1,200 stalls selling everything from fish, fruits, handicrafts and live ducks, Sibu's **central market** is one of the biggest trading markets in Malaysia, combining the former 'wet market' and indigenous Lembangan market. Good, moderately priced handcrafts are found here and at night market stalls, often direct from the source. The tamu is also held in the Central Market district on Sundays. The **night bazaar** (🕑 *17.00–22.00 daily*) on Leboh Market has a colourful melange of stalls selling household goods, fashion and footwear, and a variety of foods from steamed buns to satay.

OTHER PRACTICALITIES
Health and emergency There are several downtown clinics, a public hospital out of town and two modern and central private hospitals including the **Rejang Medical Centre** (*29 Jln Pedada;* ☎ *084 330733*).

Miscellaneous The website of **Sibu Municipal Council** (*www.smc.gov.my*) is a good source of local information.

WHAT TO SEE AND DO
Around town Sibu is a compact town easily explored on foot, with taxis or buses available for out-of-town locations. The climb to the top floor of the seven-storey **Kuan Yin** ('Goddess of Mercy') **Pagoda** is undoubtedly the icing on the city sights cake. Towering above the 100-year-old **Tua Pek Kong Temple**, it's a great viewing spot for the day-to-day river activity and huddle of colourful '**floating supermarkets**' – wooden boats servicing Rejang longhouse communities anchored in the port. The **heritage walk** links several public places and memorial gardens. One of the prettiest is the Hokkien community's **Chiang Chung Immigration Garden** on the riverside, in front of the temple. The **Rejang Esplanade** starts from the Express Boat passenger terminal and ends near the emblematic **Swan statue**. Sibu's swans symbolise its ugly-duckling transformation, drawing on Chinese folklore about a town saved from starvation by a sago-drinking swan. The vast **Town Square** – the largest urban square in Malaysia – is the venue for the **Borneo Cultural Festival** held every July, with performances from all of Sarawak's major ethnic groups as well as some from Sabah and Kalimantan. **Bukit Aup Jubilee Park** (*Tekub bus No 2/3;* 🕑 *08.00–18.00 daily; free*) is a great place for strolling, picnicking and jogging, with views from its 60m tower over the Igan River and nearby longhouses. The Iban bring offerings to the top of the hill for the benevolent spirit Naga

Bari, believed to help people in need. Another workout-friendly place is the **Sungai Merah (Red River) Heritage Walk** (*Sungai Merah bus*), a landscaped river promenade area on the site of the original Chinese settlement in Sibu. True to its name, the water is rusty red in colour because of the tidal action on peat soils from upriver forests. The walk leads to the **Wong Nai Siong Memorial Garden**, which is graced by a dour statue of the town's revolutionary father.

Museums and galleries

Sibu Cultural Heritage Museum (*In the Civic Centre, Jln Tun Abang Haji Openg; 2km from city, take Sungai Merah bus No 1A; ⊕ 10.30–17.30 Tue–Sun; free*) Dull, yet interesting presentation of antiques, artefacts and photos on the town's history, Chinese migration and the various ethnic groups of the Rejang River Basin. The Foochow presence in Sibu is elucidated at the **World Fuzou Heritage Gallery** on Jalan Salim.

EXCURSIONS FROM SIBU

LONGHOUSES Day or overnight trips to **Kampung Bawang Assan**, a settlement of eight Iban longhouses both modern and old (*taxi RM50, vans from central market every 2hrs*), are available. Andy Austin, the son of one of the longhouse chiefs, acts as a guide and can be contacted via the visitors' centre (see page 295). Frankie Ting from **Sazhong Trading & Travel Service** (*4 Jln Central;* ✎ *084 336017;* e *sazhong@ tm.net.my*) does tours to nearby longhouse settlements such as Bawang Assan, upriver trips and treks (for longer trips book at least one week in advance).

SARIKEI In 1856, the town was burnt down in an uprising against the Brooke administration, waged by Iban people from the Sungai Julau River area. At 122km southwest of Sibu (buses leave the city station every 30 minutes), Sarikei is now an agro-industry hub: home of the *ananas* (curiously locals use the French name for pineapple); oranges, pomelo and avocado also thrive in the area's acidic soils. Malaysia owes its ranking as the world's fifth-biggest pepper exporter to Sarikei Division, which produces more than 80% of Sarawak's crop. Government-subsidised tiger prawn farms and shrimp-processing factories are part of a move to diversify from pepper. The town lies about 40km from the mouth of the Rejang. At the river's delta is the largest mangrove swamp in Sarawak. The coast is both a timber-processing zone and developing deep-sea port.

About 15km from Sarikei, at the heart of the district's fruit production zone, **Bintangor** is a small market town renowned for its green oranges. These agrumes infuse Malay rojak, a spicy salad of fruits and vegetables. **Sebangkoi Forest Park**, 25km from Sarikei, may be small but the 13ha reserve makes a good mid-journey rest spot for those travelling along the Pan-Borneo Highway.

⌂ **Where to stay and eat** If you're travelling independently, try Sarakei's **Dragon Inn** (*60 Jln Masjid Lama;* ✎ *084 651799;* e *hotelbahagia@gmail.com; http:// dragoninnsarikei.blogspot.com;* $$–$). This plain but clean two-star hotel also has a coffee shop serving noodle and rice dishes. The prices suit shoestring to budget travellers. An inexpensive Chinese eatery is **Golden Happiness Restaurant** (*Jln Masjid Lama;* $$) – a good coffee shop serving seafood and venison specialities. **Hung Kiew Kee Restaurant** (*Jln Masjid Lama;* $$) also serves up Malay and Chinese standards. Two fast-food options in this same street are the **Sugar Bun bakery** ($) and **KFC** ($).

Tours For an organised tour of Sarikei and surrounding areas, contact Ling How Kang at **Greatown Travel** (☏ *084 211243;* m *019 856 5041;* e *greatown@gmail.com*) – on regional knowledge he is second to none. The trip focuses on Sarikei's agricultural attractions: dragon fruit and orange orchards, pineapple farms and pepper gardens, as well as visits to Kampung Rejang to see songket weavers, and Kampung Belawai – the heart of the smoked prawn (*sesar unjur*) processing industry. You can meet him in Sibu or in Sarikei.

MUKAH Originally from Mindanao Island in the Philippines, the Melanau people have lived in Borneo since the 16th century. Mukah is their heartland. Around 130,000 Melanau live along the coast between the Rejang Estuary and city of Bintulu, marked by six distinct groups and 11 different dialects. The Melanau's distinctive signature dish, *umai*, is a spicy salad of raw shredded fish marinated with lime, ginger and chilli.

Brooke dynasty rajahs and Brunei sultans competed with each other to control the trade in rumbia (*sago*) in the late 1800s. Sago still underpins the economy, local customs and cottage industries, but fishing and oil palm are zooming ahead. The South China Sea coastline adjacent to town still sports only one resort, several years after claims of a pending Riviera-effect, with more developments to come. Melanau and Iban *kampungs* dot riversides and mangrove swamp edges around the coast.

Getting there and away

By air MASwings' Twin Otters link Mukah with Kuching (*1hr 10mins flight; from RM130*), and Miri (*1hr 10mins; RM120*).

By car It's a 156km (*about 2hrs*) drive from Sibu – works on the formerly pot-holed Sibu–Matadeng Road have finally been completed. Tourism and overall driving safety in the region stands to benefit from improvements to coastal area roads, which have been ongoing since at least my first visit in 2005. In 2014, Malaysia's *Business Times* (part of the New Straits Times Press), reported 'RM216.68 million (US$64 million) was spent on road projects in the area covering a stretch of about 944.29km', since 2011. According to Kuching-based Naim Holdings' Berhad investment and engineering company who straightened and flattened the Sibu–Mukah stretch, it provides 'fast and direct access to one of Sarawak's fastest growing regions, (and)... will help to release the economic potential of Sarawak's coastal heartland'. Media reports now claim another new road, linking Kuala Serupai to Kuala Tatau, will shorten the distance north between Mukah and Bintulu by an impressive 120km when completed 'in two to three years' time'.

By bus Express buses from Sibu take about 3½ hours (see page 294).

By boat The most riveting way to reach the 'Melanau Heartland' if you have time on your hands, is by speedboat, travelling from Sibu to Dalat, about 40km from Mukah township. The journey across the Batang Igan Dam, down the tree-lined Sungai Kut River, into the Sungai Oya River at Dalat takes up to two hours, depending on how many village-stops it makes en route. The boats leave from the jetty on Jalan Khoo Peng Loong (at the junction with Jalan Temple), roughly every hour from 07.00 to 14.30. Be sure to get there at least 15 minutes ahead of time, as boats leave when they are full. The journey costs approximately RM20. (Only two boats leave from Dalat to Sibu, at 06.30 and 12.30.) For the onward connection to

Mukah, buses leave from the station behind the Hiap Leong Mini Market, and cost around RM5, compared with RM30–40 for a taxi.

Getting around The best way to visit the coastal and inland kampung is by car. A mixture of boat and bus travel is possible, if you are determined to see the area on a budget, but ensure that there are food options near your accommodation.

Where to stay

Kingwood Resort (99 rooms) Lot 96, Block 17, Mukah Land District; 084 873888; e kingwoodresort_mukah@yahoo.com; no website. Located 12km from town, 15km from the airport, facing the South China Sea, the pillared, nouveau-Chinese structure stands pretty much on its own between the oil plantations & the ocean, with totally uninterrupted 180° views to the horizon. A vigorous promoter of the culture of the area. Friendly & incredible value for money, modern, spacious, light & bright, full of high-tech & leisure facilities. $$ (suite $$$$)

King Ing (19 rooms) 1–2 Jln Boyan, Mukah; 084 871400. Best choice if you want to be in Mukah Town itself, surrounded by shops & eateries. AC, TV, bathroom, plain but spic-&-span standard & superior rooms. Some rooms have river views, Wi-Fi throughout, laundry service; personable place. $$–$

Homestays Sarawak Tourism describes homestays in the Mukah area as 'culture-based accommodation'. Other than the well-managed Lamin Dana, the following are best arranged through the Sibu Visitor Information Centre (e vic-sibu@ sarawaktourism.com).

Oya Homestay Kampung Senau, Oya; 084 871416. About 19km from Mukah Town in sago-growing territory, this Melanau homestay programme centres on 10 village houses run by the Malaysian Fisheries Development Board as a rural development initiative. Locals will cook traditional Melanau food for you & perform *bermukun*, which involves playing drums, dancing & reciting poetry, & give healing Melanau massages. $$

Lamin Dana (12 rooms) Kampung Tellian (4km from Mukah); 084 871543; e genistarose@ gmail.com (contact manager Diana Rose); http:// lamindana.blogspot.com. Part riverside lodge, part cultural centre, Lamin Dana is built in Melanau style at the end of a village boardwalk through mangroves. Rustically alluring, it is much like a longhouse homestay without the crowds. Earthy décor with beautiful crafts on display; twin & family rooms, fans, games/computer room; Melanau meals; & Mangrove tours, boat trips, bike hire. $$–$

Pantai Harmoni Resort Km 4, Jln Mukah-Oya (4km south of Mukah on the coast); 084 872566. Family-run, simple beach chalet, 2 bedrooms with double bed, sitting room & restaurant. $$–$

Where to eat and drink Mukah's streets are packed with Chinese and Malay coffee shops serving cheap and charming food. Several makeshift kitchens are clustered around a large open-air space. For more upmarket food (and mid-range prices) try **JS Seafood** and **River View Restaurant**, both situated near the Tua Pek Kong Temple and serving authentic Melanau food, including tasty umai, or **Nibong House** (Jln Orang Kaya Setia Raja, opposite the Civic Centre). The (halal) **Palm Beach Restaurant** (⊕ *06.30–22.45 last order*) in the Kingwood Resort (see above) serves Malaysian and Melanau specialities as well as Western food. In Dalat there are several Chinese coffee shops opposite the riverfront and a Melanau restaurant, **Taku Café**, serving local specialities.

What to see and do Mukah has a new and old town – the fishing harbour is in the latter. The wet market is a fascinating affair, with fresh and river fish on sale, fruit, sago worms and other fresh foodstuffs.

The modern **mosque** and **civic centre** both sport emblematic terendak roofs – made in the form of the conical Melanau palm-leaf sunhat. Melanau traditions are on full show during the **Pesta Kaul**, held at the beginning of the fishing season (usually the fourth week of April) to appease the spirits. A three-day taboo on leaving and entering the town precedes the festivities and feasting. During the seraheng procession, food is carried up the Batang Mukah River by canoe – raised on bamboo poles by mask-wearing Melanau. **Fireflies** thrive in the mangroves of Mukah and one prime firefly territory is **Tanjung Pedada**, a cape in **Kampung Pedada**, just across the narrow stretch of river from Mukah Town. Head here near sunset, for the Tanjung Pedada Mangrove Walk along a belian wood boardwalk.

The award-winning **Lamin Dana Handicraft Centre** (*Kampung Tellian Tengah, 4km from Mukah Town;* \ *084 871543*) is the offspring of a Melanau performing arts and youth development project, launched in 1999 to preserve Melanau heritage. In the first two years, 50 weavers were trained. The handicrafts are mostly woven from sago fronds. The seven villages involved each focus on one craft industry, and receive RM1,000–2,000 per month for their produce. The only original **Melanau longhouse**, dating to 1872, is in Kampung Sok, Matu. Vans go there from Daro wharf. Arrange visits through the Mukah Resident's office (\ *084 872596*). **Kelidieng** are ornately carved wooden burial poles made out of hollowed ironwood (*belian*) tree trunks. One of the finest is in Dalat, opposite the wharf and Chinese temple.

KAPIT AND THE UPPER REJANG The Rejang flows across administrative borders into Kapit Division, a river-ribbed area the size of Switzerland, yet with a population density under three people per square kilometre. Unfurling for another 120km between Kapit and Belaga, the Upper Rejang area is one of the last Bornean frontiers for rugged, remote adventure and deeper ethnographic encounters. A collection of peaks averaging 1,200m altitude frame dozens of rivers: major tributaries' of the Rejang criss-cross the region and provide the main means of transport. Thick carpets of forest have been heavily pockmarked by logging, mining and slash-and-burn agriculture; in the last case to make way for hill paddy, pepper, rubber, cocoa, fruit and vegetable crops, and increasingly for oil palm plantations.

Getting there and away

By boat Express boats run by various companies ply the Rejang daily between Kanowit, Sibu, Song and Kapit, from as early as 05.30, through to mid afternoon. The direct Sibu to Kapit boat takes two–three hours. After RM2–10 fare hikes in November 2014, economy tickets now cost RM25, business class RM30, and first class (in a massage chair) RM35. Other boats stop in Kanowit (*a 40-min trip*) and Song (*2½hrs*). There's also a daily service from Kapit to Belaga, leaving at 09.30. The journey takes 4½ hrs and costs RM45.

Practicalities Foreign visitors require a permit to travel beyond Kapit to Belaga or up the Baleh River, so an overnight stay in Kapit Town is mandatory. One- and two-week permits are issued at the **Kapit Resident's office** (*9th Floor, New State Office Complex, Beleteh Commercial Centre;* ⊕ *08.00–13.00 & 14.00–17.00 Mon–Thu, 08.00–11.45 & 14.15–17.00 Fri, closed Sat, Sun & public holidays*). Take a van from Jalan Airport to reach the office. You can view and request information via their website (*www.kapitro.sarawak.gov.my*). Belaga is not accessible by boat when water levels are low so services may not operate during the dry season from July to September. Air conditioning in the boats (as on many forms of Malaysian transport) can be icy-cold, so bring a long-sleeved top.

▲ Where to stay

The accommodation in Kapit is appalling. Back in 2010, there were complaints of cockroaches running over people's feet in the supposedly flashiest of the town's hotels. The same establishment today is described invariably as run-down, 'scary' and very basic. Sadly, no hotel of whatever kind in or out of town any longer makes the grade. Closure in 2012 of the **Regency Pelagus** riverside resort put a major damper on nature-based tourism to the area – indeed on any kind of tourism. Within months, the RV *Orient Pandaw* made its final Rejang River/ *Into the Heart of Borneo* expedition, before heading to more promising horizons in Myanmar. Apparently safety and cost considerations came into the decision. A tour company is supposedly building an 18-cabin cruise boat to fill the gap. In the meantime, the only option is to arrange, either independently or via an agent, an adventure tour to the Upper Rejang longhouses.

Longhouse stays The Kapit Resident's office can give you an up-to-date list of longhouses accepting visitors for day/overnight visits (it often changes). An overnight stay including longboat trip will cost around RM320 per person, plus a minimum of RM30 for meals. Those upstream from Kapit on the Sungai Tisa, Sungai Kain and Sungai Mujong require overnight stays. More adventurous trips to consider are week-long outings to Long Singut, a remote Kenyah longhouse on the Sungai Baleh, and more arduous jungle treks and expeditions to the remote peak of Batu Tiban (*12–14 days; physical fitness required*). The latter is evoked in Redmond O'Hanlon's classic book *Into the Heart of Borneo* (see page 332).

✗ Where to eat and drink

River prawns and fish dishes are big in Kapit. Try them at the air-conditioned **Jade Garden** (*Jln Lapangan Terbang, opposite the Meligai Hotel;* ⊕ *lunch & dinner*). **Orchard Restaurant** (*64 Jln Tlong Ung Hong;* ⊕ *09.00– 23.00*), is also air conditioned, and has many pork dishes. Cheap coffee shops with good noodles and rice dishes are all over town. There are outdoor food stalls every evening in the **Taman Selera Empurau**, near the Eon Bank, and by day on the first floor of the **Pasar Teresang** town market – a good place to buy fresh food and fruits, sweets and cakes (*kuih*). It is possible to try the Iban cooking style pansuh at some local restaurants, though it's best to request ahead: chicken and fish are cooked in bamboo stems over an open fire.

What to see and do

Kapit A lively trading centre and transport hub for the upper river regions, Express boats, longboats and steamboats converge on the wharf. Kapit was settled by Charles Brooke as a garrison town in the 1880s, using **Fort Sylvia** (⊕ *10.00– noon & 14.00–17.00 Tue–Sun; free*) to crack down on Iban warriors who were moving upriver to fight other tribes. A peacekeeping ceremony between the Iban and Orang Ulu was held at the fort in 1924. Originally called Kapit Fort, Brooke changed the name to honour his wife Ranee Sylvia. A former district office and courthouse, the fort is now a small museum. A bigger historical picture is offered at the **Kapit Museum** (*Kapit Civic Centre;* ⊕ *09.00–13.00 & 14.00–16.15 Mon–Thu, closes 11.45 Fri; free*).

Belaga Beyond Kapit through to Belaga, boat journeys on the Rejang and Baleh rivers are a unique experience, with the greatest chance of traditional Kayan and Kenyah longhouse stays along the riverbanks. It's mandatory to do such trips with a licensed nature guide. Contact the Kapit Resident's office (see page 302 for contact information) for details. Belaga is the last trading post on the Rejang – it sprang up in the early 1900s when some Chinese traders set up shop to supply goods such as kerosene, salt and cooking utensils to the Orang Ulu people upriver.

Warning There have been reports of alcoholism being rife among Belaga guides; do not use guides unless the operator can promise they will be sober. Women are advised not to travel alone.

Kanowit About 50km southeast of Sibu, Kanowit is the furthest point along the river accessible by road. A small riverside town of 1930s Chinese shop-houses, the main landmark is **Fort Emma**, a 19th-century Brooke-era wooden stockade. The area has one of the greatest concentrations of Iban longhouses in Sarawak, particularly along the Sungai Julau and the Sungai Katibas near Song.

SEND US YOUR SNAPS!

We'd love to follow your adventures using our *Borneo* guide – why not send us your photos and stories via Twitter (@BradtGuides) and Instagram (@bradtguides) using the hashtag #borneo. Alternatively, you can upload your photos directly to the gallery on the borneo destination page via our website (*www.bradtguides.com/borneo*).

12

Northern Sarawak

Stunning beaches no, but the coastline stretching north from Bintulu to Miri has some beautiful coastal geology and vegetation. As oil, petroleum and gas hubs, the northern cities have traditionally attracted mostly business travellers, foreign investors and workers. Sarawak Tourism continues to portray Bintulu as a 'transit point' for the Niah Caves and Miri, a 'gateway' to Gunung Mulu National Park and sometimes disproportional interest is pinned on these must-sees, to the exclusion of other gems such as the coastal national parks. Deep inland towards the Indonesian border, the temperate Kelabit Highlands are a haven for independent trekkers – subsisting on Bario rice and vegetables and living in basic accommodation.

BINTULU

'Boom-town Bintulu' got a real economic boost from the large natural gas and oil deposits found near its shores in the 1970s. Today, the city is a monument to the power of Petronas, the Malaysian government's oil corporation, whose subsidiary – the Malaysia Liquefied Natural Gas Corporation – owns Bintulu's natural gas processing plant, the largest in the world. Annexed as part of Sarawak by James Brooke in 1861, the town of Bintulu grew up along the banks of the Sungai Kemena River, which flows into the South China Sea. Until oil was discovered in the region, Bintulu's port was primarily a centre of the fishing and timber trades, with export wood sent downstream from the forests. Said to be the most wonderfully planned city in Sarawak, the city continues to prosper and grow in an independent fashion.

GETTING THERE AND AWAY

By air Bintulu Airport is about 20km from town. MASwings connects Bintulu with various regional towns: Kuching in an hour (*3 daily departures each way; promotional fares from RM88*); Sibu in 35 minutes (*2 daily flights each way; from RM88*); Miri in 35 minutes (*2 daily flights each way; from RM88*); and Kota Kinabalu in 75 minutes (*1 daily flight each way; RM200 – plus 1 indirect flight, 2hrs 5mins*).

From Kuala Lumpur, AirAsia operates twice-daily flights (*from RM164*), which take just over two hours. AirAsia also flies between Kuching and Bintulu (*from RM94*).

By car Bintulu is about 644km north of Kuching, 192km north of Sibu, 214km south of Miri and 124km south of Niah National Park.

By bus Long-distance buses depart several times daily for Kuching (*11hrs; RM70*), Miri (*4½hrs; RM25*), Mukah, Sri Aman and Sibu (*3½hrs; RM25*), and Sarikei from the Medan Jaya express bus terminal on Jalan Tun Hussein Onn, 3km north of the

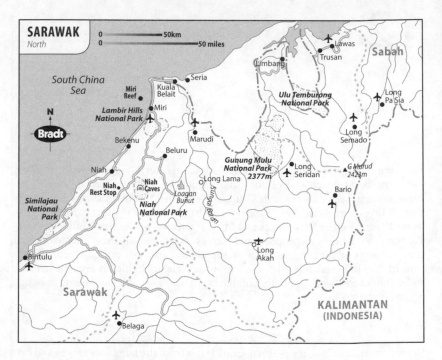

civic centre, at the Medan Jaya shopping centre. Major bus companies operating
from here include Biaramas/Bus Asia, Bintang Jaya Express and the Miri-based
deluxe coach set-up MTC Express (*www.mtcmiri.com*). A taxi to reach the terminal
costs RM10–15.

GETTING AROUND Local buses leave from the town bus station near the markets
off Main Bazaar.

TOURIST INFORMATION
Bintulu Information Centre
Jln Keppel. Walk-in office only.

WHERE TO STAY *See maps, opposite and page 308.*
Most of the budget hotels are found in the downtown area of Jalan Keppel and
Jalan Abang Galau, which run parallel to the riverbank for over 0.5km. A couple
of three-star establishments are located a few hundred metres out of the CBD
(Central Business District) towards the river's entrance and landscaped area of
Bintulu Park City. Contact Sarawak Tourism for help with arranging hotels.

ParkCity Everly (228 rooms) Lot 3062, Jln
Tun Razak; 086 318888; e reservation.pehb@
everlygroup.com; http://bintulu.theeverlyhotel.
com. The ParkCity Everly is situated on the
attractive, landscaped waterfront esplanade
that runs for a couple of kilometres along the
shoreline. It is the top business hotel in town,
and has AC, satellite TV, deluxe rooms & suites,
a swimming pool & gym, a coffee shop, a
restaurant & a pub. **$$$** (suite **$$$$**)

Kemena Plaza Hotel (161 rooms)
116 Taman Sri Dagang, Jln Abang Galau; 086
335111; e kemenaplazahotel@yahoo.com; http://
kemenahotelgroup.com/kemena-plaza-hotel-
home. The former Regency Plaza Hotel has come
up with a modern concept & attitude, matched by

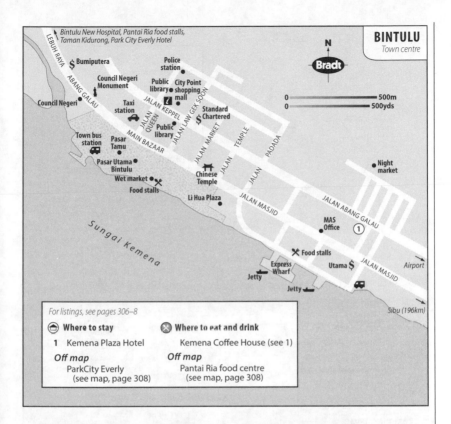

BINTULU
Town centre

Bintulu New Hospital, Pantai Ria food stalls,
Taman Kidurong, Park City Everly Hotel

Bumiputera
Police station
Council Negeri Monument
Public library
City Point shopping mall
Council Negeri
Taxi station
Standard Chartered
Public library
Town bus station
Pasar Tamu
Pasar Utama Bintulu
Wet market
Food stalls
Chinese Temple
Li Hua Plaza
JALAN MASJID
Night market
MAS Office
JALAN ABANG GALAU
Food stalls
Express Wharf
Jetty
Utama
Jetty
JALAN MASJID
Airport
Sibu (196km)

LEBUH RAYA
ABANG GALAU
JALAN KEPPEL
JALAN LAW GEK SOON
JALAN QUEEN
MAIN BAZAAR
JALAN MARKET
JALAN TEMPLE
JALAN PADADA

N

Bradt

0   500m
0   500yds

Sungai Kemena

For listings, see pages 306–8

🛏 **Where to stay**

1   Kemena Plaza Hotel

Off map
    ParkCity Everly
    (see map, page 308)

✖ **Where to eat and drink**

Kemena Coffee House (see 1)

Off map
    Pantai Ria food centre
    (see map, page 308)

its website. Rooftop swimming pool, sauna, Wi-Fi & 23hr reception round off the standard 3-star offerings: satellite TV, AC, bath & fridge. Family & executive suites & standard, deluxe & twin rooms are wood-floored & furnished. Local & Western food at L A Bistro coffee house. **$$** (suite **$$$$**)

🏠 **Li Hua** Lot 36, Berjaya Commercial Centre, Jln Sultan Iskandar (1km north of town, near the civic centre & temple); ✆086 335000; e bintulu@lihua.com.my; www.ihua.com.my. With its pink musk & slick, bright, new (though basic) website, this good-value, friendly, standard but solid 1-star has pool, rooftop lounge, AC, family rooms & suites, free Wi-Fi, halal coffee house & restaurant. Buffet meals RM10–15. **$$**

🏠 **101 Hotel Bintulu Hotel** (101 rooms) No 203, Lot 7932, Assyakirin Commercial Square; ✆086 314172; www.101hotelbtu.com. Far better reports have already shot this new, budget AirAsia hotel to the top of TripAdvisor's hotel hit list, across price brackets. Located in the same shopping centre as the previous listing, the much-loved zone is close to town but in its own hive of shops, restaurants & cafés. Hard-to-beat prices meet sparkling clean, nicely decorated rooms, comfy beds & friendly service. The only complaint is about noise levels from a nearby Karaoke lounge. Note there are just 2 single rooms up for grabs; the rest a near-equal share of doubles/twins. **$**

✖ **WHERE TO EAT AND DRINK** *See maps, above and page 308.*

Restaurants/coffee shops More chic and air-conditioned places with mid-range prices are found in the top hotels (see pages 306–7 for contact details). **M&D's Restaurant** (🕐 *06.00–midnight daily*) at the ParkCity Everly has an open kitchen and international food, while there are lighter snacks and drinks at its **Luconia Bay Coffee Terrace** (🕐 *10.00–01.00*). The **Kemena Coffee House** (*in the Kemena Plaza Hotel*) has good local as well as Western dishes.

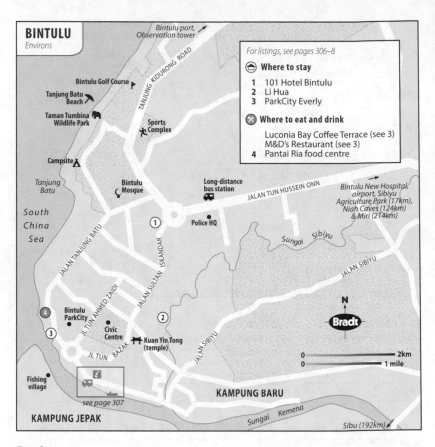

see page 307

BINTULU
Environs

Bintulu port,
Observation tower

For listings, see pages 306–8

Where to stay
1. 101 Hotel Bintulu
2. Li Hua
3. ParkCity Everly

Where to eat and drink
Luconia Bay Coffee Terrace (see 3)
M&D's Restaurant (see 3)
4. Pantai Ria food centre

Bintulu Golf Course

Tanjung Batu Beach

Taman Tumbina Wildlife Park

Sports Complex

Campsite

Tanjung Batu

South China Sea

Bintulu Mosque

Long-distance bus station

JALAN KIDURONG ROAD

JALAN TUN HUSSEIN ONN

Police HQ

Bintulu New Hospital, airport, Sibiyu Agriculture Park (17km), Niah Caves (124km) & Miri (214km)

Sungai Sibiyu

JALAN SIBIYU

JALAN TANJUNG BATU

JALAN SULTAN ISKANDAR

JL TUN AHMED ZAIDI

Bintulu ParkCity

Civic Centre

Kuan Yin Tong (temple)

JL TUN BAZAR

JALAN SIBIYU

Fishing village

KAMPUNG BARU

KAMPUNG JEPAK

Sungai Kemena

Sibu (192km)

0 ――――― 2km
0 ――――― 1 mile

Food to go **Pantai Ria food centre** (*2km from the city, by the sea*) has evening food stalls. A ten-minute walk from most hotels is the night market – medan pasar malam. Many other food stalls are clustered around the market place and Express Wharf on Main Bazaar.

SHOPPING City Point shopping mall on Jalan Keppel is the most central. The *pasar utama*, central market and *pasar tamu* handicrafts market are held by the riverside under a *terendak* (conical hat) shaped roof.

OTHER PRACTICALITIES
Banks
$ **Standard Chartered Bank** Jln Keppel
$ **Utama Bank** Near the jetty area off Jln Masjid

Health and emergency
Police station Jln Queen, off Jln Keppel

✚ **Bintulu New Hospital** Jln Nyabau, north of town

Miscellaneous
Public library Jln Queen, off Jln Keppel

WHAT TO SEE AND DO The main spiritual landmark is the modern **Bintulu Mosque**, Masjid *Assyakirin* – meaning 'gratefulness to God' – set in landscaped surrounds on Tanjung Batu headland. The **Kuan Yin Tong Temple** is located on Jalan Sultan Iskandar, 2km north of the CBD. **Kampung Jepak**, a traditional Melanau fishing village, lies on the other side of Sungai Kemena near the river mouth – take a short ride over on a bot tambang riverboat to see fish-drying and sago-processing activities. The **Council Negeri** (State Council) **Monument** in the **civic centre** commemorates Sarawak's 1867-convened legislative assembly, the oldest parliament in Malaysia, composed of five British officers and 18 Malay and Melanau chiefs. The best city view is from the **Observation Tower** in Tanjung Kidurong, where you can gaze up the coast over the Bintulu Port area.

Two connecting coastal parks, **Taman Tumbina** and **Taman Kidurong**, unfurl 3km north of the town centre from the headland and beach area of Tanjung Batu. **Taman Tumbina Wildlife Park** has a small zoo, botanical garden and butterfly world. The second-biggest port in Malaysia and an industrial port for agro-food, petrochemical and timber industries, the **Bintulu deep-sea port** and container terminal covers an area of 320 acres with a total quay length of nearly 0.5km.

Sports The sports complex in Taman Tumbina parklands has a swimming pool and tennis courts while the **Bintulu Golf Course** is located on the headland of Tanjung Kidurong.

EXCURSION FROM BINTULU

SIMILAJAU NATIONAL PARK Some 30km north of Bintulu on an unsealed road, with no regular bus service, this park lives largely in the shadow of the Niah Caves, but is really a great nature getaway, with lovely brackish water beaches, skirted in kerangas and rainforest. Stretching 32km up the coast in a 1.5km-wide strip, the park covers an area of over 9,000ha. There is just one main trail with a few possible deviations along the coast to various beaches, where turtles come ashore to lay eggs. You could easily spend a day here. The park is home to saltwater crocodiles and, though there have been no attacks reported, stay alert and avoid swimming.

Where to stay Park accommodation is disappointing – the chalets (which sleep four) have electricity and running water but not much more. There is also a campsite and barbecue pits. Despite the basic facilities, holiday periods can be particularly busy. Book accommodation online, through the Miri National Park office, or by calling or turning up at the park HQ registration and information desk (where there is also a canteen) (\\ *086 391284; www.forestry.sarawak.gov.my/forweb/homepage/contact.htm;* ◔ *08.00–12.30 & 13.30–17.15 daily*).

NIAH NATIONAL PARK

Rising up dramatically behind the small township of Batu Niah, the 388m massif of Gunung Subis dominates Niah National Park, enfolding the famous archaeological site of the Niah Caves within its limestone outcrops. First gazetted as a National Historic Monument in 1958, after the find of a 44,000-year-old skull at the entrance to the caves, 3,100ha of surrounding rainforest and limestone hills were swept into the park's realm when it was created in 1974. Most people visit for the day from either Miri or Bintulu, though the visitors' accommodation facilities are among the better maintained of Sarawak's parks. The discovery of coffins, urns, pottery, paintings, textiles, tools and ornaments in Niah show consistent habitation over thousands of years – the area within and around the caves is full of archaeological, cultural and natural history.

12

GETTING THERE AND AWAY

By car The Niah National Park HQ is located at Pengkalan Batu, 109km south of Miri and 131km north of Bintulu. The closest town is Batu Niah, public transport hub for the caves.

By bus Syarikat Bas Suria buses travel to Batu Niah from Miri's express bus terminal (Pujut Corner) (1hr 40mins), and from Bintulu (approximately three hours). Fares for both trips are about RM10. The park office is 3km from Batu Niah, reached either by foot – a 45-minute plank walk along the riverbank – by motorised longboat, or taxi. Tour buses and hire cars continue to the park HQ. The above bus services have been known to be disrupted for long periods so check with

---

THE GREAT CAVE OF NIAH – A BRIEF HISTORY   *Dr Huw Barton*

The Great Cave of Niah is enormous by any measure. The floor area of the cave has been calculated at almost 10ha, and in places, the majestic cave roof rises 75m above the rubble-strewn floor. As well as being home to multitudes of bats, darting swiftlets (their nests are the famous ingredient of Chinese bird's nest soup) and the occasional snake, it is also the site of human occupation dating back at least 46,000 years. The richness of the deposits at Niah, and the great span of time they encompass, marks the site as one of the most important archaeological sites in Southeast Asia.

The site was first excavated by the brilliant but cantankerous Tom Harrisson, a self-trained archaeologist, curator and ethnologist of the Sarawak Museum, who realised the enormous potential of the site and began excavation in 1954. In 1958 came the discovery of a 44,000-year-old human skull at the front of the West Mouth (an area affectionately referred to as 'Hell' – due to the working conditions in the heat of the day). The skull has since been determined to belong to a 15–17 year old, probably female. Flaked stone and other evidence of human activity were found as well.

Food remains recovered more recently show people had a fairly broad diet, using a wide range of plant and animal foods from the forest and nearby freshwater streams. Recent analysis of bone fragments shows evidence that people were hunting arboreal primates, butchering them on-site, and manufacturing bone tools. A favoured food appears to have been the bearded pig, *sus barbatus* – still a popular food today. Fabulous preservation of plant remains at Niah has shed new light on ancient diet and foraging knowledge. Charred remains of edible but toxic tubers and nuts have been recovered, indicating a degree of sophistication in food processing not previously believed to occur this early. We have also found evidence that these early foragers knew how to make complex multi-component tools: some of these tools included jagged stingray spines and bone splinters finely worked to make spears or arrows.

Use of the cave changed over time. At one time used occasionally by roaming foragers, it later became a major repository of the dead around 4,000 years ago. At this time, there is evidence for the use of pottery as funerary gifts and burial jars, with later evidence of imported metals, ceramics and glass. Remarkably, even textiles were recovered from some graves. Some of the recovered material is on display at the site museum at Niah Cave, and also in the Sarawak Museum in Kuching.

the Miri Visitor Information Centre beforehand or telephone the bus company (☎ 085 424311/430417). Another option is the unmarked 4x4s, which leave from opposite the Miri Visitor Information Centre to various destinations including Niah. It's a bit of a potluck situation, however, as drivers only leave if and when there are six passengers. They generally charge RM15–20 and take you right to the park entrance, though the tariff will rise if passenger numbers are low. Many express buses heading south to Bintulu, Sibu and Kuching will let you off along the highway, at the village of Simpang Ngu, near the Batu Niah turn-off. The ticket costs about RM10. The **taxi** for the remaining 12–15km will cost about three-times more.

PRACTICALITIES The park has a visitors' centre and canteen. An extensive network of plank walks leads to and through the caves, about a 3km walk from park HQ. A torch and good walking shoes are recommended as the caves are unlit and the plank walk can be slippery. Conservation fee is RM10.

🏠 **WHERE TO STAY AND EAT** There's accommodation available in the park itself, but if you choose to stay in Batu Niah, the one-street township boasts some basic lodging houses and coffee shops.

🏠 **National Park accommodation** (9 chalets) ☎ 085 737450. Basic 2-room chalets (4-beds), with attached bathroom, some with AC, plus a 'Forest Hostel' sleeping 16 in 4 rooms, & a 30-site campsite. All have 24hr electricity & piped water, but no cooking facilities. Common park facilities include washrooms, a canteen, an AV room & Information centre. **$**

🏠 **Niah Cave Inn** Lot 621, Batu Niah Bazaar; ☎ 085 737333. TV, AC. **$**

WHAT TO SEE AND DO About 3km from the park HQ, along a path buttressed with huge tapang trees, pandanus plants, orchids and fungi – sightings of monkeys, lizards, butterflies, hornbills and squirrels are likely on your way to **Great Cave**. Its spectacular entrance (West Mouth) is over 60m high and 250m wide – inside, *guano* collectors gather bat excrement to sell as fertiliser. The walls of nearby **Painted Cave** feature a set of etchings in red hematite depicting boat journeys of the dead into the afterlife. The wall paintings tie in with the discovery of a number of 'death ships' in the cave – boat-shaped coffins containing human remains and a selection of 'grave goods' considered useful in the afterlife, such as Chinese ceramics, ornaments and glass beads. The death ships date to sometime between AD1 and AD780, although local Penan folklore tells of death-ship burials as late as the 19th century. Some birdwatching enthusiasts come just to witness the sunset 'changing of the guard', which happens when up to half a million swiftlets return to their nests and the bats swarm out to forage in the forest.

From the park HQ there are two other well-marked but short trails of 2–3km: the **Bukit Kasut Trail** through rainforest and Kerangas forest to the top of a hill, and the **Madu Trail** along the Sungai Subis River through peat and alluvial swamp forest to the base of Bukit Kasut.

MIRI

Determined to shake its reputation as an industrial oil town, Miri has become an important leisure stretch for the local expat community, and a weekend playground for escaping Bruneians.

If you are seeking a bit of a beach atmosphere before, between or after backcountry trips, 'Miri Resort City' is the best place for it, with its big choice of classy-to-budget

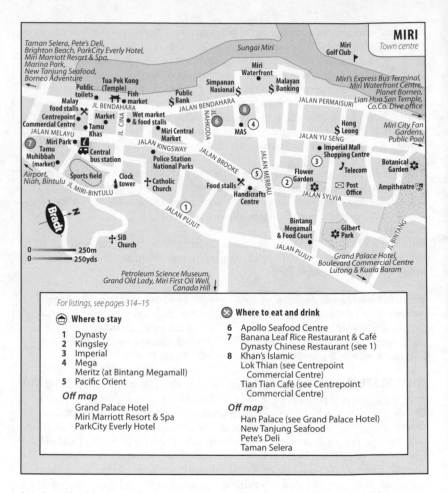

MIRI
Town centre

Taman Selera, Pete's Deli,
Brighton Beach, ParkCity Everly Hotel,
Miri Marriott Resort & Spa,
Marina Park,
New Tanjung Seafood,
Borneo Adventure

Sungai Miri

Miri
Golf Club

Miri
Waterfront

Miri's Express Bus Terminal,
Miri Waterfront Centre,
Planet Borneo,
Lian Hua San Temple,
Co.Co. Dive office

Public
toilets
Malay
food stalls
Centrepoint
Commercial Centre
JALAN MELAYU
Miri Park
Tamu
Muhibbah
(market)

Tua Pek Kong
(Temple)
Fish
market
Market
Tamu
Khas

Simpanan
Nasional
Malayan
Banking
JALAN PERMAISURI

Public
Bank
JALAN BENDAHARA
Wet market
& food stalls
Miri Central
Market
JALAN KINGSWAY

MAS
JALAN BROOKE

Hong
Leong
JALAN YU SENG

Miri City Fan
Gardens,
Public Pool

Imperial Mall
Shopping Centre
Telecom

Botanical
Garden

JL BENDAHARA
JL CINA
JL NAHKODA

Central
bus station
Police Station
National Parks

JALAN MERBAU

Flower
Garden
Post
Office
JALAN SYLVIA

Ampitheatre

Airport,
Niah, Bintulu
Sports field
Clock
tower
Catholic
Church
JL MIRI-BINTULU

Food stalls
Handicrafts
Centre

JALAN PUJUT

SIB
Church

0   250m
0   250yds

Bintang
Megamall
& Food Court
JALAN PUJUT

Gilbert
Park

JL BINTANG

Grand Palace Hotel,
Boulevard Commercial Centre
Lutong & Kuala Baram

Petroleum Science Museum,
Grand Old Lady, Miri First Oil Well,
Canada Hill

For listings, see pages 314–15

Where to stay
1 Dynasty
2 Kingsley
3 Imperial
4 Mega
  Meritz (at Bintang Megamall)
5 Pacific Orient

Off map
  Grand Palace Hotel
  Miri Marriott Resort & Spa
  ParkCity Everly Hotel

Where to eat and drink
6 Apollo Seafood Centre
7 Banana Leaf Rice Restaurant & Café
  Dynasty Chinese Restaurant (see 1)
8 Khan's Islamic
  Lok Thian (see Centrepoint
    Commercial Centre)
  Tian Tian Café (see Centrepoint
    Commercial Centre)

Off map
  Han Palace (see Grand Palace Hotel)
  New Tanjung Seafood
  Pete's Deli
  Taman Selera

hotels and relaxed social buzz. Evolving from the oil slick of its past, its future as a self-made resort town is positively glowing with the rise of coastal condominiums and luxury hotels. In Sarawak's second metropolis, with a population of 300,000, locals live, eat, work and play hard. Chinese and Iban form the bulk of the rich cultural infusion, topped up with Malay and Orang Ulu.

GETTING THERE AND AWAY
By air Miri's modern airport is developing into a major northern Borneo hub. AirAsia and Malaysia Airlines fly direct between Miri and Kuala Lumpur several times a day (*from RM94/RM191 respectively*); MAS actually operates a couple-of-dozen daily flights in both directions Miri–KL. Both airlines also fly to/from Johor Baru in southern Malaysia and Singapore (*2hrs 10mins; from RM684 for MH Basic fare, from RM153 with AirAsia*), as well as smoothly hooking up with many other of their destinations via KL. Royal Brunei Airlines connect Miri with the Brunei capital Bandar Seri Begawan. AirAsia and MASwings operate intra-Borneo routes between Miri and Kuching, and Miri and Kota Kinabalu.

MASwings also operates rural air services from Miri to Sarawak's interior on both Fokker 50s and Twin Otters: to Gunung Mulu National Park, Ba Kelalan and

Bario (Kelabit Highlands), Marudi, Lawas, Limbang and Labuan, Sibu and Bintulu. Most of these 30–60-minute flights cost from around RM100 one-way. Since 2011, ATR 72-500 planes ply some routes, with a carrying capacity of 68 passengers, compared with the Fokker's 50, and 19 on the Twin Otters. Luggage limits for the smaller planes are 10kg.

Airlines There are AirAsia and MAS counters at the airport.

By car Miri lies 800km north of Sarawak's capital Kuching, 215km north of Bintulu, along the Pan-Borneo Highway. The supposedly smooth stretch is far from that in places – indeed its notoriously pot-holed surface has at times earned it a very bad name. In 2011, cries of 'killer highway' followed a spate of fatal accidents, some of them involving foreigners and express bus services.

Some 30km north of Miri, the Sungai Tujuh immigration checkpoint at Kuala Belait marks the entry point to Brunei, a journey that can take over two hours depending on the queues. Make sure you have your passport and money for a visa – there are no ATMs or credit-card facilities.

By bus Express air-conditioned buses link Miri with Kuching (14 hours; RM80), Sibu (7¼ hrs; RM40), and Bintulu (4½hrs; RM25). They travel to and from Miri's edge-of-town express bus terminal (Terminal Bas Pujut), at the location known as 'Pujut Corner'. Its precise location is opposite the Boulevard Commercial Centre on Jalan Miri Pujut, near the intersection with the Miri Bypass. Minibuses connect Pujut Corner with the city's central bus station on Jalan Padang. The main companies operating from here include Biaramas/Bus Asia (*www.ba.my*), Suria Bus Express, and MTC Express (*www.mtcmiri.com*). MTC's six daily departures for Kuching pass through Bintulu, Sibu and Serian. For those heading to Brunei, Borneo Explore Green (*www.borneoexploregreen.com*) is the new operator with two services departing Miri at 08.45 and 15.45; one-way tickets cost B$18.

GETTING AROUND Miri spreads out and walking around can be tiring. Buses for the city area and surrounds leave from the central bus station on Jalan Padang, a couple of hundred metres from the visitor information centre on Jalan Melayu. Average prices for local journeys are RM1 or less. The Taman Selera/Hawaii Beach buses Nos 11/13 go towards the marina, beach and luxury resort area.

TOURIST INFORMATION

🄸 **Visitor Information Centre** Lot 452, Jln Melayu (entry off Jln Padang); 📞085 434180/1; e vic-miri@sarawaktourism.com. The national park booking office is also located here.

TOUR OPERATORS

Borneo Adventure Lot 1344, 1st Floor, Miri Waterfront Commercial Centre; 📞085 424332; e info@borneoadventure.com; www.borneoadventure.com. The award-winning Kuching-based company also has a Miri office, for launching its excellent, top-of-the-range but well-priced tours to the Niah & Mulu caves (*2 nights; RM530*), northern Sarawak's Headhunters' Trail (*4 nights; RM1,870*), for jungle trekking in the Bario Highlands & trips to Brunei. Tailor-made trips are also common ground. See ad on page 278.

Minda Travel Offices On the waterfront, & at the Miri Marriott & ParkCity Everly; 📞085 414433; www.mindatravel.com.my. From Miri city tours to reasonably priced day tours to Niah & Similajau national parks, Brunei's Seria oil coast & Brunei city & water tours (*RM158–258*).

Planet Borneo Tours & Travels Lot 273, Ground Floor, Brighton Centre, Jln Temenggong Datuk Oyong Lawai; 📞085 415582; e info@

planetborneotours.com; www.planetborneotours.
com. For local city tours as well as trips outside of
Miri (to Brunei & Sabah, as well as Sarawak-wide).
Formerly known as Seridan Mulu.

🏠 WHERE TO STAY *See map, page 312.*

Ever-tougher competition is pushing standards higher and higher, with reasonable prices still available across the board. Talk of a new five-star hotel in the Miri Marina Park over the past three years has unfortunately not materialised, along with the rest of the development. The top five-star hotels are located 2km south of the city, overlooking the South China Sea, off the main Miri–Bintulu road.

Upmarket

🏠 **Meritz** (290 rooms) Bintang Megamall; e reservation@meritzhotel.com; www. meritzhotel.com. Great to average reports of this new '4-star business-class hotel', which falls short of that according to several reviews on service & presentation. Adjoining the Bintang Megamall 500m east of the town centre, 800m from the river, pleasant staff, large rooms, & impressive city views from the 17th-floor Sky Garden outdoor venue. Business centre, gym, pool, several food outlets – lobby bar, Chinese & revolving bar/restaurant. Enclosed by a frantic commercial zone, & the mall's myriad international brands, shops & cafés. **$$$$–$$$**

🏠 **ParkCity Everly Hotel** (168 rooms) Jln Temenggong, Datuk Oyong Lawai; 085 440288; e reservation.pehm@theeverlyhotel. com; http://miri.theeverlyhotel.com. This 4-star is more business-oriented than the Marriott, but bright, upbeat, & with a beachside location near Miri Marina. Well-furnished rooms with balcony & Executive Club floor. Very affordable Malay & international food at Melinau Terrace Coffee House with indoor/outdoor dining & entertainment. Shuttle service to city. **$$$$–$$**

Mid range and budget

🏠 **Miri Marriott Resort & Spa** (220 rooms) Lot 779, Jln Temenggong Datuk Oyong Lawai, 2km from city; 085 421121; e sales@mirimarriott. com; www.marriott.com. A comfortable luxury hotel. Spacious, well-furnished garden & sea-facing rooms, with balconies arranged in breezy wings, well away from lobby area. Possibly the best hotel b/fast in Borneo. Large pool, gym, spa, free parking. **$$$** (suite **$$$$$**)

🏠 **Grand Palace Hotel** (125 rooms) Km 2 (north of city centre) Pelita Commercial Centre, Jln Miri-Pujut; 085 428888; e gpalace@po.jaring. my. A big pink hotel in popular shopping/
entertainment complex. Family-run 4-star; large rooms with elegant Chinese-style furnishings, free broadband, satellite TV, coffee house & Han Palace Cantonese restaurant, pool terrace. **$$** (suite **$$$$**)

🏠 **Imperial Hotel** (96 rooms, 144 apts) Jln Pos; 085 431133; e enquiries@imperialhotel.com.my; www.imperialhotel.com.my. In Imperial Mall, stylish rooms & self-catering apartment suites, good online promotional rates of up to 40% off. Fitness centre, sauna & swimming pool. **$$** (suite **$$$$**)

🏠 **Mega Hotel** (293 rooms) Lot 907, Jln Merbau; 085 432432; e info@megahotel.com. my; www.megahotel.com.my. Standard & deluxe rooms are budget-priced, large junior & executive suites mid range. Free Wi-Fi, AC, satellite TV, non-smoking floor, babysitting service, business centre, fitness & sauna, plus its own bakery, coffee house (🕐 05.00–midnight) Chinese restaurant & pub. **$$** (suite **$$$**)

🏠 **Dynasty Hotel** (130 rooms) Lot 683, Town Centre, Block 9, Jln Pujut-Lutong; 085 421111; e dyhlmyy@streamyx.com; www. dynastyhotelmiri.com. 3-star, eastern edge of town, comfortable well-equipped rooms, satellite TV, AC, 2 non-smoking floors, coffee house & gym. **$$**

🏠 **Kingsley Hotel** (43 rooms) Lot 2167, Jln Sylvia; 085 423988; e kingsleyhotel.miri@ gmail.com; www.kingsleyhotel.my. Good reports for this new central hotel near Bintang Plaza. Clean & comfortable, with family rooms – though apparently only the deluxe king-side rooms benefit from windows. Free parking, 24hr front office & CCTV security; LCD TV/Astro channels, coffee & tea making, complimentary bottled water. **$$**

🏠 **Pacific Orient Hotel** (66 rooms) 49 Jln Brooke; 085 413333; e info@pacificorienthotel. com; www.pacificorienthotel.com. 2-star with AC, cable TV, free Wi-Fi, fridge, central location. Free secure parking, decent in-house Chinese café (called The Rainforest Café in English). **$$–$**

✕ WHERE TO EAT AND DRINK *See map, page 312.*

There are food stalls in roads and at markets everywhere, though the waterfront's messy streets can make them less appealing. Some riverfront restaurants do not display prices, so enquire ahead of eating.

Seafood In the city, the **Apollo Seafood Centre** (*4 Jln South Yu Seng*) is a hit among locals and foreigners alike for simple but excellent steamed fish, prawns and black pepper crabs, at budget prices in a popular setting. The open-air **Taman Selera** food park (*3km from city past Marina Park, Jln Temenggong Datuk; bus Taman Selera No 11; ⊕ about 17.00–late*) has about 12 stalls serving seafood by weight, and Chinese and Malay dishes at cheap to mid-range prices. The outside and under-cover seating overlooks Brighton Beach. On the same stretch (opposite Miri Marriott) is a cluster of seafood restaurants, with indoor/outdoor seating, where you can pick your fish from the aquarium. The last restaurant is perhaps the best, **New Tanjung Seafood** (*Jln Temenggong Datuk;* \ *085 433401*); look out for its big lantern with Carlsberg sign. It serves cheap to mid-range Chinese seafood, game and noodle dishes. Loitering dogs have troubled some diners of late.

Chinese The **Boulevard Restaurant** (*Bd Commercial Centre, not city centre;* \ *085 436936*) serves excellent, mid-priced Chinese food, a favourite with locals. **Dynasty Chinese Restaurant** at the Dynasty Hotel and the **Han Palace** in the Grand Palace Hotel (see page 314 for details) are good for their air-conditioned environments, big choice and mid-range prices. The Chinese coffee shops clustered in street-level shop-lots of **Centre Point Commercial Centre** (*the southern end of the city, off Jalan Melayu*) have excellent cheap local dishes cooked on the spot. **Tian Tian Café** has lots of *laksa, mee sua, kolok mee* and other noodle dishes. **Lok Thian Restaurant** (*Jln Merbau*) is part of a chain, and makes great fresh buns.

Western and Asian snacks, food courts, cafés and bakeries The out-of-

town **Boulevard Shopping Complex** and **Bintang Megamall** are the places to head for pizza, burgers and other Asian and international fast-food chains. **KFC, SugarBun, Big Apple Donuts and Coffee, Sushi King, Starbucks** and **Coffee Bean and Tea Leaf** are all on the ground floor of Bintang Megamall, while the mezzanine-floor **Food Court** has some far more authentic Malay and Chinese quick eats.

The **Boulevard** also has Japanese and Korean restaurants and a huge **food court** with Chinese, Malay, clay-pot dishes, Western meals, steaks and snacks. A good chain bakery is **Hot Cross Buns** (*Jln Kubu*). If you're craving brownies or apple pie, head to **Pete's Deli** (*Lot 284, Ground Floor, Brighton Centre*), in the Brighton Beach area. The café-restaurant also whips up fresh homemade ravioli, taco bakes, Caesar salads and pizzas in a parlour decked with Elvis photos and other Americana.

Indian Dirty to some, heaven for others, **Khan's Islamic Restaurant** (*229 Jln Maju*), is a basic Muslim–Indian eatery with curries, tandoori chicken, *roti cani, aloo gobi* (potato and cauliflower), naan and plenty of veg options. **Banana Leaf Rice Restaurant and Café** (*Lot 1136, Jln Kubu; ⊕ 11.00–22.00*) serves spicy southern Indian banana-leaf meals and fish-head curry.

Markets The *Pasar Raya* central market stalls on Jalan Brooke are excellent. The opening hours of different eateries vary – some operate from dawn to midnight, others evening only. The *pasar malam* night market off Jalan Abang Galau is the place to stroll for typical Malay snacks, grilled meats and fish, and delicious local *kuih* (cakes).

12

ENTERTAINMENT AND SHOPPING Miri is set out between shopping centres. The most central are the **Imperial Mall** in Jalan Merpati, and **Bintang Megamall** off Jalan Merbau and Jalan Miri-Pujut highway (*www.bintangmegamall.com*). Also referred to as the Bintang Plaza Shopping Complex, it has 200 stores, many cafés and the Parkson department store from the ground to the third floors. **Sarawak Handicraft** is located on Jalan Merbau (*Lot 96, Block 9, 5B, Ground Floor;* ⊕ *09.00–18.00 daily*), while the main multi-store **Miri Handicraft Centre** lies near the intersection of Jalan Merbau and Jalan Brooke. The **Boulevard Shopping Complex** about 5km north of town is also a favourite among locals for its nightspots, bars and lounges.

OTHER PRACTICALITIES

Police Central Police Station, Balai Polis Sentral, Jln Kingsway; ☏ 085 433730/222

✉ **Post office** Corner of Jln Post & Jln Sylvia, towards Miri City Fan

WHAT TO SEE AND DO Miri is raffish and relaxed. Stretching in a thin lip along the estuary of the Sungai Miri for over 2km, some of the prettiest parts such as gardens and recreational areas lie at either extreme. Though billed as a 'resort town', the beach is out of sight from the city centre.

Many attractions lie just out of town. For the best 360° view of the city, head to Canada Hill, a ridge above town where the '**Grand Old Lady**' – an endearing term for Malaysia's first oil well – struck good in 1910. There's also a **Petroleum Museum** here; on the way up you will see a couple of giant sea horses – Miri's mascot.

About 3km from the city, people stop to walk around a geological marvel – a cliff face of multiple dimensions and myriad colours known rather unromantically as the **Airport Road Outcrop**, exposed during the road's construction. The large **public park** is located in the same zone. Modern Miri has a multitude of parks, underpinning its vision to become a health-resort city. At the city's northern end, the **City Fan** is a 10.5ha green space with promenades, fountains, public pools, amphitheatres, Islamic and Chinese cultural gardens, botanical gardens and IT library. Even some temples are relatively far-flung – the **Lian Hua San** (Lotus Hill) **Temple** is a strange apparition planted in the nouveau residential area of Krokop in 2000. Far more charming, **Tua Pek Kong Temple** graces the old town near the river on Jalan Bendahara. The central market, fish market and spice-laden Malay *tamu lama* are all huddled in this waterfront area. A few hundred meters back from the river, Orang Ulu people bring all kinds of Bario rice, highland fruit and vegetables, wild ferns and fruit, rattan mats and baskets to the fascinating under-cover **Tamu Muhibbah** and **Tamu Khas** (*opposite the visitor information centre, Jln Padang*).

At 2km south of Miri, the **beach** area begins. Along the sandy strip of Tanjung Lobang, the 'Miri Resort City' tag is unfurling along with an ever-so-slowly developing marina, coastal promenades and condominiums. Brighton Beach (the English moniker for Tanung Lobang), is the best sunset-watching spot, according to Gustino Basuan from Sarawak Tourism. 'The city's oldest recreational park is popular with joggers, anglers and t'ai chi enthusiasts. From the piers there are great views of the Marina lighthouse, shaped like the city's emblematic seahorse.'

By night, locals, expats and visitors gather at the Taman Selera, a casual outdoor dining spot overlooking the South China Sea. The **Marina Park Project** (*www.mirimarina.com*) is clearly a work in progress. After rechannelling the river to create a 3km canal, plans for a world-class marina, festival park, business and retail zone, leisure strip and new luxury accommodation have progressed at a snail's pace since 2008. So far, all that has materialised from the drawing board is a marina with 78 wet berths, connected by nicely designed pontoons and pathways. There's also a

MARINE MAGIC

From soft corals and elephant's ear sponges to massive sea fans, the Miri-Sibuti Coral Reef National Park is making big ripples among scuba fans.

'Some of the sights on the Miri Reef are as good as I have ever seen in many years of diving all over the world,' says Miri dive master Voo. Coming from a man who has four decades of diving under his belt, or rather wet suit, including sorties with French explorer Jacques-Yves Cousteau, that is saying something.

Founder of Co.Co. Dive (*www.cocodive.com.my*), Voo is a pioneer in diving exploration in Miri. 'I discovered most of the dive sites and gave the naming,' he says. He also pushed hard for the establishment of a marine park. Fully protected since 2007, it extends over an area equivalent to 470,000 football fields, through depths ranging from 7 to 30m, and visibility of 10–30m. Water temperatures hover around 29°C in the peak season of May–October.

Just ten minutes' boat ride from the Marina you can tumble among the 6–12m carpets of soft leather corals at Eve's Garden. 'Giant anemones and clownfish (Nemos) dominate this reef,' says Voo.

Things start get more interesting further out in both species diversity and reef drop-off. VHK Reef takes its name from the Miri dive star's full name – Voo Heng Kong. 'At around 17m depth, purple sea-whips sway among its hard coral, and schools of small barracudas sail overhead.' Miri's long-unheard of reefs, says Voo, are now starting to get the attention they deserve. Note the Miri Reef can be rough. Not necessarily rough enough to turn back, but the turbulence can make life hell for those prone to seasickness. I got my PADI Open Water Diver certificate on the reef, between heaves into the big blue and descents to pass successive technical tests. Take some Novomin or other motion tablets along with you, or try a natural cure. Among them, reportedly, are ginger capsules and crystallised ginger, eating a banana, and blocking one ear during the boat ride. This stops the balancing liquid near your ears moving around, preventing the brain from sensing you are motion sick – even if you are! Another vital tip Voo shares with me, is to fix your eyes firmly on a spot on the horizon the whole way.

pier-end restaurant. Developers give no idea on the timing to complete the fancy-on-paper marina – the 'Marina Quay' retail site, the 'Marina Market', serviced apartments, a clubhouse and kilometre-long boardwalk and linear park. Some 9km south is the **Luak Bay Esplanade** picnic spot.

Diving Miri Reef is a developing dive area – within the 150km² triangle offshore are drop-offs, reefs and shipwrecks. There is good beginner and advanced diving in the patch reefs: 7–22m depth, few currents and visibility of 10–30m. The further out you go, the better it gets. (See box *Marine magic*, above.)

The best local operation to contact is **Co.Co. Dive** (*Lot 2117, Block 9, Jln Miri-Pujut;* \ 085 417053; e *miri.cocodive@gmail.com; www.cocodive.com.my*).

EXCURSIONS FROM MIRI

Miri is the most common departure point for locals and tourists heading inland to the mountainous area of Sarawak: the Kelabit Highlands, Bario region and Gunung Mulu National Park.

12

LAMBIR HILL NATIONAL PARK The waterfalls, rainforest and low-lying peaks of this park lie 30km south of the city along the Miri–Bintulu road. The dozen trails include 20-minute forest strolls, the 7km Pancur Waterfall walk, and 6km Summit Trail to Bukit Lambir. The 25m **Latak Waterfalls** is a popular bathing spot less than 200m from park HQ. The park has basic accommodation (✆ *085 491030*). Local buses connect it to Batu Niah Caves and Bintulu.

LOAGAN BUNUT NATIONAL PARK Some 120km southeast of Miri via Beluru, the park centres on Sarawak's largest natural lake, which sometimes dries up into an expanse of cracked mud, surrounded by mixed peat swamp forest. There are many wading birds, reptiles and small mammals here. The lake is fished by Berawan people, with whom you can charter rides on the lake and Baram River (RM60/hr for 4 people). The forest hostel has seven bunk beds, a small canteen, and generator electricity from 06.00 to midnight. A Berawan family run the **Mutiara Hostel** (m *011 292164, or reserve via Miri's national park office*), with nine twin bedrooms, simple cooking facilities, and a floating grocery nearby. Buses from Miri go to Lapok Bridge, 15km before the park HQ. Head to the coffee shops to organise a lift, or pre-arrange with the Mutiara Hostel.

MARUDI Commercial centre of the Sungai Baram River District, Marudi was the usual starting point for river trips to Gunung Mulu National Park and other remote highland areas, well before the advent of plane services. It's still a base for off-the-beaten-track adventures and longhouse safaris. Some people trek from Marudi to the Kelabit Highlands over four days, or do the 'old-fashioned' river trip starting from Kuala Baram (see *Getting there and away*, page 320). For all such trips, approach the Miri Visitor Information Centre for information on tours, besides those listed in the *Tour operators* section (see pages 313–14). If you do stay in Marudi overnight, visit the Chinese Temple and belian-roofed Fort Hose. Now the Baram District Museum, the fort was home of 'Resident' colonial administrator, Charles Hose, from the late 1890s. For a workout, head to the hilltop Taman Tasik Recreation Park with its suspended bridges, walkways and Baram River views. At the end of September or early October, the two-day **Baram Regatta** is an annual tradition carried on since 1899, when Charles Hose organised the race of war canoes in an effort to create a worthy diversion from headhunting and tribal warring. For overnight stays in Marudi, the **Mount Mulu Hotel** (*60 rooms*; ✆ *085 756671; $$*) is a one-star establishment, with air conditioning and television; the **Mayland Hotel** (✆ *085 755106*) and **Grand Hotel** (✆ *085 755711*) also have plain but clean shoestring-to-budget-priced rooms. Many coffee shops for Chinese eats are concentrated around the main street and Jalan Cinema. Buy food to go from the stalls of the **Pasar Rakyat** food centre on Jalan Merpati. The **Boon Kee Restaurant** on Jalan Newshop gets good reports for a more substantial meal.

GUNUNG MULU NATIONAL PARK

Approaching the Malaysian–Indonesian border, the deep northern Sarawak interior is an isolated area of rivers and mountains. Encircled by pinnacles and peaks, the World Heritage Site of Gunung Mulu National Park lies in a corridor of lowland rainforest criss-crossed by rivers and streams.

The 53,000ha park contains the largest limestone cave system in the world, formed from thousands of years of erosion. Since the beginning of a National Geographic expedition in 1977, over 300km of caves have been surveyed, though it

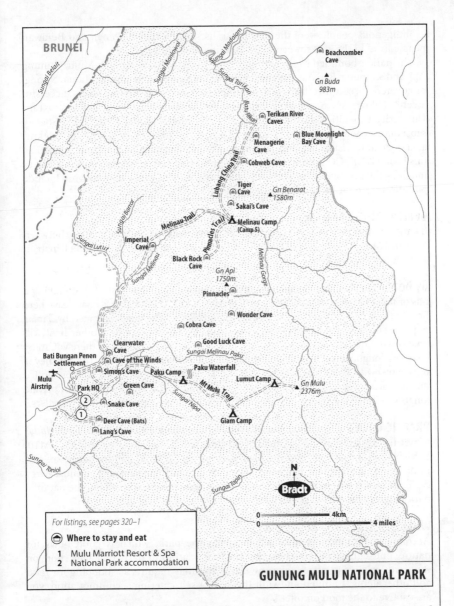

GUNUNG MULU NATIONAL PARK

For listings, see pages 320–1

🏠 **Where to stay and eat**

1 Mulu Marriott Resort & Spa
2 National Park accommodation

is believed there could be at least twice as many more. Only four of the 25 caves and passages discovered are open to the public.

The park's 17 different habitats enclose primary lowland rainforest, limestone forest, alluvial forest, tropical heath forest, peat swamp and riparian forest. Between altitudes of 35m and 2,375m, it contains a staggering 3,500 plant species, 4,000 types of fungi, 80 mammals, 270 birds, 130 reptiles and amphibians, 50 fish types and 2,000 different bugs, beetles and butterflies. Like Gunung Kinabalu National Park, it's an entomologist's dream, with hundreds of distinctive insect species including stick insects (Phasmids), camouflaged crawlies and butterflies (including *Trogonoptera brookiana* – Brooke's birdwing butterfly).

12

Indigenous people were the first naturalists of the region. Penan and Berawan people lived in the area for centuries, hunting and gathering.

The park is bounded by three mountains – its namesake Gunung Mulu, Gunung Api and Gunung Benarat. In the 1920s, a Berawan rhino hunter, Tama Nilong, discovered the southwest ridge of Gunung Mulu, opening the way for its successful ascent. Nilong led South-Pole explorer Sir Ernest Shackleton and an Oxford University expedition to the summit in 1932. The National Geographic Society subsequently lobbied for the creation of a national park in 1976, and the 544km² area opened to visitors in 1985. Listed as a World Heritage Site in December 2000, this is one UNESCO natural treasure where the negative effects are on show just as much as the positive ones. Threats to the environment other than logging include pollution from locals, tourist hordes, and slack tour companies.

GETTING THERE AND AWAY
By air MASwings operates a couple of flights daily, in both directions, between Miri and Mulu (*30mins; from RM88*), and once-daily flights between Kota Kinabalu and Mulu (*50mins; from RM192*).

By boat The adventurous and potentially tedious day-long trip starts with taking a bus or taxi to Kuala Baram (*15km north of Miri, taxi RM40*). Express boats leave here hourly from 07.30 to Marudi, along the Baram River. The boats operated by Tinjar Express take 2½–3 hours and tickets cost RM30. From Marudi, another boat will take you to Long Terawan – a four-hour journey costing RM20. From there you must charter a longboat to take you up the Sungai Tutoh River to the park. This journey is unreliable, with boats between Marudi and Long Terawan cancelled at short notice due to water levels or inadequate passenger numbers. The prohibitive cost of private longboat hire (*RM400 for a 30–60-min trip*) excludes this option for most travellers.

PRACTICALITIES On arrival, head to the National Park HQ (⊕ *08.00–17.00 daily*) for visitor registration and payment of **entrance fees**. Single entry per adult is RM10. Students, senior citizens and disabled persons get 50% off; children aged six and under are free. The park has no ATM or credit-card facilities so you must carry cash. Transport within the park is by longboat, van or foot, with all but the national park lodgings 3km from park HQ.

🏠 **WHERE TO STAY AND EAT** *See map, page 319.*
Accommodation choices are limited within the park, which is good news for nature, but higher-end, privately run accommodation in particular falls short on standards relative to price. Take any extras you may require, as shopping for food and other items is limited and with the lack of self-catering accommodation, you are captive to the food on offer.

🏠 **Mulu Marriott Resort & Spa** (101 rooms) ☎ 085 790100; e sales@royalmuluresort.com; www.royalmuluresort.com. By Mar 2015, the fully fledged Mulu Marriott Resort & Spa will morph out of the old-timer Royal Mulu Resort. Great news for the park & its high-end visitors, with the tired old lodgings hopefully taken to a truly international 5-star standard, together with food & beverage outlets & other services. The resort's activities did not cease, but were scaled down, during the refurbishment, whose results I am yet to witness firsthand. Early accounts confirm that the rebranding has already produced a far more modern, luxurious feel, with enhanced management & staff. The rather dated wood-panelled chalets have a smart & ethnic-stylish new look arranged like a cluster of longhouses, 6m above the forest, & linked up by walkways.

Each room has a Melinau River-facing balcony, flat-screen TV, & internet. On top of that, the Marriott has a new lobby lounge, pool & spa, a bakery/deli & riverside bar, plus brand hallmarks such as a business centre, library, activity centre, & Marriott Kids' Club. Hopefully prices (on package tours as well as internet deals) will be accessible to mid-budget travellers too. The resort is adjacent to park HQ (a 5min van journey), & about a 3km (45min) walk to the caves. All guests make use of the free shuttle service to/from the airport. **$$$$–$$$**

⌂ **National park accommodation** ╲085 792301; e enquiries@mulupark.com; www.

mulupark.com. Located at the entrance of the park, lodgings here include rattan-clad longhouse rooms sleeping 2–4, with fans & en-suite bathrooms with b/fast included. The most upmarket are the wood-floored 'Garden Bungalow Rooms', actually small chalets sleeping up to 3 with tasteful Malay décor & edge-of-the-forest setting. They still come at budget prices. The 20-bed hostel dorm is equipped with fans, bed linen (but not towels) & storage lockers (RM43 pp for a bed, including b/fast). Check-in at 14.00, check-out at 10.00. Reservation essential. Cheap basic local & Western food at the open-air Café Mulu (⊕ 07.30–21.00). **$$$–$**

WHAT TO SEE AND DO A cave trip and longer jungle trek or river safari will allow you to experience the incredibly beautiful forest world. Freedom to enjoy the park in a more independent manner is limited due to a highly bureaucratised park service. Definitely look beyond the caves and lap up some of the encompassing rainforest, local people and traditions.

Caves All caves are reached along solid timber-plank walks, and are visited by way of eco-lit cement paths. The 3km duckboard walk to reach **Deer Cave** and neighbouring **Lang's Cave** is a lovely experience in itself, passing rainforest, peat swamp, alluvial flats, streams and some spectacular limestone outcrops. Two-hour return treks led by park guides leave daily at 13.45 and 14.30 from park HQ. **Clearwater Cave** and **Cave of the Winds** are reached from park HQ by longboat along the Melinau River in about 15 minutes (*RM27 pp return*), or via the 4km Moonmilk Walk that hugs the riverbanks much of the way. Park guides lead tours into the Cave of the Winds at 09.45 and 10.30 from the entrance. The most impressive site for stalactites and other formations is Lang's Cave; the most amazing overall for its size and cavernous pit is Deer Cave (Gua Rusa). At a staggering 2km in length, this is the largest cave passage in the world – its main chamber has enough room for five St Paul's Cathedrals!

Caving Speak with the park HQ or a tour organiser about adventure caving at Mulu. A park brochure outlines eight cave escapades from beginner to advanced level, lasting from 45 minutes to ten hours. Some popular caves have been fitted with fixed ropes on the short descents and traverses, but you are advised to bring your own equipment for anything beyond that. The **Sarawak Chamber** – on the way to Gunung Api – is compared to an aircraft hanger that could house 40 Boeing 747s. The day trip starts at 07.30, tracing the Summit Trail for about three hours.

Trekking Without a doubt, trekking away from the park's HQ and hotels is the best way to feel the wonder of nature and get up close with the wildlife. There are many treks in the park: some require a guide, others can be done independently. Inform park officers before you do an unguided walk, as they are aware of weather conditions, including dangerously high water levels. Unguided treks include the four-hour **Paku Waterfall** through rainforest to a good swimming spot and the three-hour **Long Lansat River Walk** (*RM180 for the longboat return transfer; 3 people minimum*). The day walk to 'Camp 1' (guided) follows part of the **Mulu Summit Trail** and concludes at one of the camps used during the 1977 Royal

12

Geographical Society expedition. The **summit** (guided) trek to the top of solitary-standing **Gunung Mulu** (2,376m) – Sarawak's second-highest peak – is a 24km climb, conducted over two to three nights, lodging in forest huts with basic cooking facilities (*park guide costs are RM1,000 for 1–5 people*). En route to Gunung Api (1,750m) the **Pinnacles** is a 50m-high series of razor-shaped limestone outcrops, pointing skyward and interlinked with several caves. This tough, guided climb requires at least one overnight stay at Melinau Camp ('Camp 5'). Most people stay two nights, depending largely on fitness levels. The first day's trekking takes in visits to a couple of Mulu's caves. Lodgings consist of sleeping mats in five open rooms, a self-catering kitchen (cooking equipment and utensils provided), and a dining room. You have to carry all of your own food, a sleeping bag and appropriate clothing. It costs RM250–800, depending on numbers. Accommodation costs RM22 per person per night; park guide RM400 for one to five people; longboat return RM370 for a group of one to four.

The popular tour-operated **Headhunters' Trail** combines 15km of deep jungle trekking over two days with longboat journeys and an optional longhouse stay. The route taken is that of Kayan headhunting parties who paddled up the Melinau River to Melinau Gorge before launching raids against the people of the Limbang area. This trip can also be done from Limbang to Mulu Park HQ. Another option is to add a night and include the Pinnacles climb (from Camp 5) in the trip.

Longboat safaris A couple of trips visit Penan settlements along the Sungai Tutoh and Sungai Melinau rivers. These are very prescriptive though, so if you prefer to explore more independently then take your own day trip on the rivers.

KELABIT HIGHLANDS

The isolation of the Kelabit Highlands did not save them from the snowballing appropriation of Sarawak territory by Rajah Brooke, whose corps claimed it in 1911. It was nonetheless one of the only Bornean regions that didn't fall into Japanese hands during World War II. Allied troops led by Tom Harrisson, the future curator of the Sarawak Museum in Kuching, had bases in the area. Along the Indonesian border, the Tama Abu range skirts Kalimantan's Apo Duat range. During the Konfrontasi with Indonesian militants in the 1960s, people from border settlements fled inland and **Bario** came into existence. Geographical isolation continues to play a big hand in shaping the region's culture – until early 2000, there was very little in the way of telecommunications or reliable power sources, and there are still no paved roads. All this translates into a great sense of remoteness and peace for the highland trekker. Rounded, velvet upholstered peaks roll into valleys of temperate crops – Bario rice, oranges, pineapples, highland coffee and sugarcane. Scattered among them are villages and longhouse settlements of Kelabit, Kenyah, Kayan and Penan peoples. Hopefully the area will retain its secluded charm with the increasing onset of tourism and technology.

GETTING THERE AND AWAY MASwings has up to three daily flights each way between Miri and Bario (*50mins; from RM116*), but only once-weekly (*Wed*) flights between Miri and Ba Kelalan (*95mins; from RM110*). Some Bario flights go via Marudi; some Ba Kelalan flights via Lawas.

WHERE TO STAY AND EAT One website with listings and online booking for several lodges, homestays and guides is www.ebario.com. You can also see details of individual lodgings and photos. All are suited to budget travellers. Some offer packages from RM60 a day for airport transfer, bed and three meals. Count on RM30–40 extra for a guide. Others provide rooms only for about RM20–30 per person with many options for guided activities. Among the most recommended of late is the quirky **Junglebluesdream Art Gallery & Homestay** (*4 rooms;* m *019 884 9892;* e *junglebluesdream@gmail.com; junglebluesdream.weebly.com,* **$**). It's run by Bario-born Kelabit artist Stephen Baya and his Danish wife Tine Hjetting. The accommodation is part of the hilltop Ulung Palang longhouse, surrounded by mountains and paddy fields. There are two double rooms, two singles, shared bathrooms/toilets, and a living room-art gallery. RM90 covers three meals a day, made with fresh local ingredients; there are bikes for rent and plenty of hiking advice and maps at hand. Other options include **Nancy Harris Homestay** (*10 rooms;* e *nancyharriss@yahoo.com,* **$**) and **De Plateau Lodge** (*8 rooms;* e *deplateau @hotmail.com,* **$**), staying with Munney and Mille Bala and their four children. **Leminan Lodge** (*7 rooms;* e *jtarawe@bario.com,* **$**) in Bario Town has satellite television, backup solar power and electricity from 18.00 to 23.00. Joanna Joy, a MAS agent and pineapple-grower, runs **Bario Airport Homestay** – reportedly good, but very hard to touch base with.

OTHER PRACTICALITIES
Climate   At 1,000m above sea level, average day temperatures are usually between 21°C and 26°C, whereas nights can be as cool as 15°C. Walking conditions can be muddy, with many leeches, and you need good shoes and protective clothing, including leech socks.

Electricity and communications   The town runs on a diesel generator boosted by solar power. A UNESCO-backed engineering project has helped set up the **E-Bario Telecentre**, a cyber café, which is open about three days a week, with phones and internet provided via solar-powered VSAT.

Shops   Bario's town centre has just a row of small bazaars, coffee shops and grocery stores. Sundries are more expensive because everything is flown in.

WHAT TO SEE AND DO
Treks and walks   Most of the Bario highland treks follow the network of muddy trails and dirt roads that link the community longhouses and villages, so expect to share the trails with locals on foot and on bike, and the odd buffalo. The treks take in the Bario Valley area, longhouse settlements, local markets, rice paddy and some primary and secondary rainforest. Organised trips of four to seven days from Miri rely on longhouses and jungle camps but you can also organise your guide and accommodation independently in either Bario or Ba Kelalan.

Women travellers are said to be in safe hands in Bario, where there is not the same problem with alcohol among guides, as in the Belaga region. Walks include Bario to Pa Ukat and Pa Lungan, four to five hours each way with a stay at the Pa Lungan longhouse. The hardy trek to the small settlement of Ba Kelalan takes two days – some trails go via Pa Rupai in Kalimantan.

Mountaineering   The Kelabit Highlands offer some of the most challenging climbing in Borneo, outside of national parks. The region is flanked by Sarawak's highest mountain, Gunung Murud (2,423m) – the five- to six-hour trail goes from Bario through a couple of longhouse settlements. The Batu Lawi (2,043m) is judged trickier.

12

Separated by a section of Brunei, Limbang Division's two main towns are typical border-town thoroughfares. Both have pasts as small-scale sin-city destinations, full of sleazy pubs, massage parlours and prostitution. Centres for timber, agricultural and oil palm industries, it is rare to hear Sarawak Tourism allude to either town, other than as transit points. Lawas sits prettier, bound by forest and river on one side, and Brunei Bay to the northwest.

GETTING THERE AD AWAY

By air MASwings operates some three to four daily flights from both Limbang and Lawas to Miri as well as other weekly flights. There are flights a couple of times a week from Lawas to Kota Kinabalu and vice versa. Single journey prices start at RM78.

By car Lawas and Limbang are near-border checkpoints with Brunei and Lawas about 20km to the Merapok-Sindumin checkpoint into Sabah. Limbang is a two-hour drive from Miri.

By bus Express buses run to Brunei, Kota Kinabalu and Miri.

WHERE TO STAY With a new website, you can now see the golden bedspreads and Lego-set bright exterior of Limbang's most recommended (though not always highly) lodging, the **Purnama Hotel** (*Jln Buangsiol;* \ *085 216700;* e *sales.purnama@penviewhotel.com; www.penviewhotel.com/purnama;* $). A superior double at the 218-room property costs RM60 more than a double deluxe (RM195/RM135), while a suite is still a budget-priced RM230. There Is Wi-Fi in the lobby, and a hair salon on the second/mezzanine floor. In Lawas, **Hotel Seri Malaysia** (*Jln Gaya;* \ *085 283200; www.serimalaysia.com.my*) has plenty of facilities (24-hour reception/security, coffee house, free parking, pool, and Wi-Fi), but the rooms get mixed reviews.

If you would like information about advertising in
Bradt Travel Guides please contact us on
+44 (0)1753 893444 or email info@bradtguides.com

Appendix 1

LANGUAGE

A good dictionary for reference is the *Periplus Pocket Malay Dictionary* (available online from www.peripluspublishinggroup.com for about €5). Berlian are another publisher (Malaysian) of good Bahasa Melayu–Bahasa Inggeris dictionaries.

Teach yourself CD kits are much harder to come by for Malay than for Indonesian language, but there is a noticeable bolstering under way of Malay learning tools for foreigners. Two courses I have used in the past are *Colloquial Malay: The Complete Course for Beginners* by Zaharah Othman and Sutanto Atnosumarto, and Hodder Education's *Complete Malay (Bahasa Malaysia)* by Christopher Byrnes and Tam Lye Suan with Eva Nyimas as narrator.

Routledge's original *Colloquial Malay* by Zaharah Othman (*www.routledge.com*) published in 1995 was updated in 2012. However, try to get hold of the 1995 edition as it came with audio CDs which included dialogue, reading and grammer points.

The meaty 400-page tome plus CDs of the 2010 edition of *Complete Malay* (*www.hoddereducation.co.uk*) is widely available. Eva Nyimas's accent-less English conceals her Indonesian nationality, but the audio relies on distinctive Malay accents to deliver language units clustered into themes from 'Eating Out' to 'Changing Money'. The interaction between the book and the audio dialogues is very useful, and a constant reminder that the two elements are there to be used together. At times, there appear to be large sections of dialogue with insufficient grammar and vocabulary explanations. That is because the effectiveness of the audio learning relies on you doing lots of textbook homework.

PRONUNCIATION Vowels differ from English pronunciation but words are relatively phonetic and consistent. All vowel sounds are short. Consonants are mostly the same as English, with a couple of exceptions.

a	*apa* (how, what) first a as in father; at the end of a word as in again
e	there are two e sounds, *empat* (four), a low sound like a in about and *mereka* (they/their), a high sound as in met
h	*apa kabah* (how are you?) the h, says Hodder's author, is a 'puff of air'
i	*nasi* (rice) 'ee' sound as in Bali
k	*tuak* (rice wine) at end of word, only just pronounced
o	*orang* (human being) as in not
u	*juga* (also) like oo in too but short
sy	sounds like sh as in shoot (also applies to English words used widely in Malaysia, eg: 'fashion' is spelt *fesyen* to bring it in line with standard Malay pronunciation)
c	ch as in chain/cheese
sy	sh as in shut

ng	sounds like ny – banyan/oignon
t	*selamat* (greeting) barely pronounced at end of word

BASIC GRAMMAR

- There is no verb 'to be' in Malaysian. The word saya means 'I', 'me' and 'my'.
- There is also no word for 'is' in Malay, so for example *apa nama anda* ('What is your name?') literally means 'What name you?'
- There are no gender prounouns – *dia* means both he and she
- Bahasa Malaysia – commonly referred to as BM – is an *agglutinative* language – a word can be changed simply by adding various prefixes and suffixes to root words, both nouns and verbs. Eg: makan is the verb to eat, and can become memakan – eating/is eating … dimakan (eaten), and the noun makanan – food.
- Plurals are formed by repetition though sometimes with slight variations: *rumah-rumah* (houses) from *rumah* (house) and *gunung-gunang* (mountains) from *gunung* (mountain)

VOCABULARY
Greetings

English	Malay	English	Malay
Hello	*hello*	Good evening	*selamat petang*
Goodbye	*selamat tinggal*	Welcome	*selamat dating*
Good morning	*selamat pagi*	See you again	*jumpa lagi*
Good afternoon	*selamat tengahari*	(literally 'meet again')	

Basic vocabulary

English	Malay	English	Malay
Please	*tolong*	I am from England	*saya datang dari England*
Thank you	*terima kasih*		
You are welcome	*sama sama*	How are you?	*apa khabar?*
I am fine	*khabar baik terima*	I am fine	*khabar baik terima kasih*, or simply *baik*
yes	*ya*		
no	*tidak* – also means 'not' *Tak* is an informal abbreviation	Do you understand?	*faham anda?*
		I don't understand	*saya tidak faham*
		Excuse me	*maafkan saya*
What is your name?	*apa nama anda?*	you	*anda*
My name is (eg: Tamara)	*nama saya/ saya Tamara*	we/us/our	*kita*
		they/their	*mereka*
Where are you from?	*kamu datang dari mana?*	Where is the toilet?	*tandas di mana?*

Questions

English	Malay	English	Malay
How?	*bagaimana?*	Who?	*siapa?*
What?	*apa?*	How much?	*berapa?*
Where?	*di mana?*	How long?/ How long will it	*berapa lama?*
What is it/this?	*apa ini?*		
Which?	*yang mana?*	take?	*berapa lama?*
When? (also 'if')	*bila?*	How far?	*berapa jauh?*
Why?	*mengapa?* or *apa sebab?*		

Numbers

English	Malay	English	Malay
one	*satu*	11	*sebelas*
two	*dua*	12	*dua belas*
three	*tiga*	13	*tiga belas* etc
four	*empat*	20	*dua puluh*
five	*lima*	21	*dua puluh satu* etc
six	*enam*	30	*tiga puluh* etc
seven	*tujuh*	99	*sembilan puluh*
eight	*lapan*		*sembilan*
nine	*sembilan*	100	*seratus*
ten	*sepuluh*	1,000	*seribu*

Time

English	Malay	English	Malay
What time is it?	*pukul berapa sekarang?*	tomorrow	*esok*
It is… am/pm	*Sekarang pukul… pagi/ malam*	yesterday	*semalam* or *kelmarin*
		morning	*pagi*
eg: it is 7am/7pm	*Sekarang pukul tujuh pagi/ tujuh malam*	evening	*waktu malam/petang*
		day	*hari*
today	*hari ini*	month	*bulan*
tonight	*malam ini*		

Days of the week

Monday	*Isnin*	Friday	*Jumaat*
Tuesday	*Selasa*	Saturday	*Sabtu*
Wednesday	*Rabu*	Sunday	*Ahad*
Thursday	*Khamis*		

Months

January	*Januari*	July	*Julai*
February	*Februari*	August	*Ogos*
March	*Mac*	September	*September*
April	*April*	October	*Oktober*
May	*Mei*	November	*November*
June	*Jun*	December	*Disember*

Public transport

English	Malay	English	Malay
in 30 minutes	*dalam masa 30 minit*	tour bus	*bas persiaran*
car	*kereta*	bus station	*stesen* or
taxi	*teksi*		*perhentian bas*
minibus	*bas mini*	airport	*lapangan terbang*
boat	*perahu*	fare	*tambang*

Directions

English	Malay	English	Malay
to	*ke*	to the left	*kiri*
from	*dari*	to the right	*kanan*
here	*sini*	north	*utara*
there	*sana*	south	*selatan*

English	Malay	English	Malay
Can you help me?	*bolehkah anda tolong saya?*	east	*timur*
Where is…?	*di manakah…?*	west	*barat*
Where would you like to go?	*anda hendak ke mana?*	behind	*di belakang*
		in front of you	*di hadapan anda*
I would like to go...	*saya hendak ke...*	straight	*ke hadapan*
Can you give me the address of…?	*bolehkah kamu beri saya alamat untuk...?*	near	*dekat*
		far	*jauh*
How far is it from here?	*berapakah jauhnya dari sini?*		

Road signs

English	Malay	English	Malay
stop	*berhenti*	exit	*keluar*
toll	*tol*	street	*jalan*
enter	*masuk*		

Other signs

English	Malay	English	Malay
open	*buka* or *terbuka*	level	*aras*
closed	*tutup*	toilets	*tandas*
floor	*tingkat*	danger	*bahaya*

Food

English	Malay	English	Malay
food	*makanan*	Do you have any vegetarian dishes?	*anda ada makanan vegetarian* or *anda ada makanan sayu sayuran?*
eat	*makan*		
drink	*minum* (v), *minuman* (n)		
menu	*menu*		
drinks price list	*harga minuman*	Please can I have…?	*boleh saya …?*
food price list	*harga makanan*	want	*mahu*
I am a vegetarian	*saya vegetarian*	Please bring the bill	*tolong bawa/ bawakan bil*
don't want	*tak mahu*		
a lot/plenty/many	*banyak*	hot (temperature)	*panas*
a little	*sedikit*	hot (spicy)	*pedas*
more	*lebih banyak labi*	cold	*sejuk*
less	*kurang*	sweet	*manis*
without	*tanpa*	sour	*masam*
What would you like to drink/eat?	*anda hendak minum apa/makan apa?*		

Basics

bread	*roti*	salt	*garam*
cheese	*keju*	pepper	*lada*
rice	*nasi*	sugar	*gula*
noodles	*mee*	cake	*kuih* or *kueh*
oil	*minyak*	curry	*kari*
sago	*sagu*		

Fruit

fruit	*buah*	mango	*buah mangga*
apples	*epal*	mangosteen	*buah manggis*

coconut	*kelapa*	oranges	*limau manis*
bananas	*pisang*	lime	*kapur limau nipis*
lemon	*limau* or *lemon*		

Vegetables

mixed vegetables	*sayur campur*	broccoli	*brokoli*
garlic	*bawang putih*	potato	*ubi kentang*
onion	*bawang*	yam	*ubi keladi*
carrot	*lobak merah*	eggplant/aubergine	*terung*
cabbage	*kubis*		

Fish

fish	*ikan*	prawns/shrimp	*udang*

Meat

beef	*daging lembu*	pork	*daging babi*
chicken	*daging ayam*		

Condiments

chilli	*cabai*	chilli paste	*sambal*
shrimp paste	*sambal belacan*	sauce	*sos*

Drinks

water	*air*	alcohol	*minuman keras* or *alkohol*
fruit juice	*jus*		
coffee	*kopi*	wine	*wain*
tea	*teh*	rice wine	*tuak*
milk	*susu*	beer	*bir minuman*

Shopping

English	Malay	English	Malay
I'd like to buy…	*saya hendak beli…*	It's too expensive	*mahal*
How much is it?	*berapa harga ini?*	cheap	*murah*
Do you have…?	*anda ada…?*	more	*lebih lagi*
I'm just looking	*saya pandang*	less	*kurang*
Can you give it to me a bit cheaper?	*Boleh bagi saya murah sikit?*	rural market	*tamu*
		night market	*pasar malan*
Market	*pasar*		

Communications

English	Malay	English	Malay
I am looking for…	*saya ingin mencari…*	post office	*pos*
I wish to go to …	*saya ingin pergi ke …*	telephone	*telefon*
bank	*bank*	mobile phone	*hand phone* (HP)

Emergency

English	Malay	English	Malay
Help!	*tolong!*	police	*polis*
I'm lost	*saya hilang*	fire	*api*
Leave me alone	*tinggalkan saya sendirian*	ambulance	*ambulans*

NB If you are trying to get rid of peddlers, it suffices to say *tak mahu*, meaning 'I don't want it'.

hospital	*hospital*
doctor	*doktor*
I am ill/in pain	*saya sakit*
thief	*pencuri*

Health/Medical

English	Malay	English	Malay
prescription	*preskripsi*	nausea	*rasa hendak muntah* or *rasa mual*
medicine	*ubat*		
pharmacy	*farmasi*	headache	*(sakit) kepala*
painkiller	*ubat sakit*	stomach ache	*(sakit) perut*
antibiotics	*antibiotik*	fever	*demam*
antiseptic	*antiseptik*	asthma	*asma*
I am ill	*saya sakit*	epilepsy	*epilepsi*
I have...	*sakit...*	diabetes	*diabetes* or *kencing manis*
diarrhoea	*cirit* or *cirit-birit*		
allergic	*alergi*		

Other useful words

English	Malay	English	Malay
my	*saya punya*	forest	*hutan* or *rimba*
mine	*kepunyaan saya*	beach	*pantai*
yours	*kepunyaanmu* or *kepunyaan tuan*	shop	*kedai*
		room	*bilik*
white person	*orang putih*	island	*pulau*
and/but	*dan/tetapi*	great! beautiful, fine	*bagus!*

Since 1993, we've been helping travellers escape the crowds and seek out the most unique cultures, wildlife and activities around the globe.

Wanderlust offers a unique mix of inspiration and practical advice, making it the ultimate magazine for independent-minded, curious travellers.

For more about *Wanderlust* and for travel inspiration visit www.wanderlust.co.uk

Appendix 2

FURTHER INFORMATION

BOOKS
General history/reference

Bellwood, P *Prehistory of the Indo-Malaysian Archipelago* Academic Press, 1986. 'Landmark work in southeast Asian archeology and prehistory'. Peter Bellwood is Professor of Archaeology at the School of Archaeology and Anthropology, Australian National University.

Payne, R *The White Rajahs of Sarawak* Oxford University Press, 1960.

Runciman, S *The White Rajahs: A History of Sarawak from 1841 to 1946* Cambridge University Press, 1960.

Saunders, G E *A History of Brunei* Routledge, 2002.

Turnbull, M C A *A History of Malaysia, Singapore and Brunei* Allen & Unwin, Australia, 1989. Revised sub-edition.

Wallace, A R *The Malay Archipelago: The Land of the Orang-Utan and the Bird of Paradise. A Narrative of Travel, with Studies of Man and Nature.* London, 1869. Newer editions by various publishers. The legendary Alfred Russel Wallace's defining work from his travels around the Malay Archipelago. Stanfords Books (*www.stanfords.co.uk*) have recently republished this as part of their Travel Classics series.

Historic memoirs/biographies

Brooke, C *Ten Years in Sarawak* London, 1866. Available online as a Google book.

Brooke, Ranee M *My Life in Sarawak* Oxford University Press, Singapore, 1913 (reprint 1986).

Brooke, Ranee S *Sylvia of Sarawak: An Autobiography* Hutchinson, 1936, and *Queen of the Headhunters* Oxford University Press, London 1970. The two-volume autobiography of the last Ranee of Sarawak.

Eade, P *Sylvia, Queen of the Headhunters: An Outrageous Woman and Her Lost Kingdom* Weidenfeld & Nicolson, 2007. A biography of Lady Sylvia Brooke.

Keith, A N *White Man Returns* Little Brown and Company, Boston, 1951.

Keith, A N *Three Came Home* Mermaid Books, London, 1955.

Keith, A N *Land Below the Wind* Michael Joseph, London, 1958.

Reece, R H W *The Name of Brooke: The End of White Rajah Rule in Sarawak* Oxford University Press, South East Asia, 1982.

Culture

Ave, J B and King, V T *People of the Weeping Forest: Tradition and Change in Borneo* Leiden, National Museum of Ethnology, 1986. An informative introduction to the region's contemporary cultures.

Davis, W *Nomads of the Dawn: The Penan of the Borneo Rainforest* Pomegranate, 1995. Wade Davis is an anthropologist/ethnobotanist.

Geddes, W R *Nine Dayak Nights* Oxford University Press, 1985. Anthropologist Geddes spent two years in a remote inland village of Sarawak after World War II.

Appendix 2 FURTHER INFORMATION

A2

331

Hose, C and McDougall, W *The Pagan Tribes of Borneo* 1912 (reprinted Oxford University Press, USA 1993). Charles Hose spent 24 years as a civil officer under James Brooke's rajah-ship – mostly in Baram but also in Rejang District – and McDougall was part of the Cambridge anthropological expedition, in Baram area, in 1898. The magnum opus of ethnology can be read as an e-book.

Jones, L V *The Population of Borneo: A Study of the Peoples of Sarawak, Sabah and Brunei;* Athlone Press, 1966.

King, V T *The Peoples of Borneo* Blackwell, 1993. A pace-setting anthropological history.

Lasimbang, R and Moo-Tan, S (eds) *An Introduction to the Traditional Costumes of Sabah* Natural History Publications in association with Department of Sabah Museum, 1997

Munan, H *Beads of Borneo* Editions Didier Millet, Singapore, 2005

Sather, C *The Bajau Laut: Adaptation, History and Fate in a Maritime Fishing Society of South-eastern Sabah* (South-East Asian Social Science Monographs) Oxford University Press, 1997. Interesting cultural and historic portrait of the Bajau Laut peoples.

Travel literature

Hansen, E *Stranger in the Forest: On Foot Across Borneo* 1988, reprinted in 2001 by Methuen, London/Vintage Books, USA. The best classic travel literature on Borneo – an account of Hansen's 4,000km of tripping by foot across Borneo, in the company of Penan hunter-gatherers in 1976.

Hansen, E *Orchid Fever: A Horticultural Tale of Love, Lust and Lunacy* Vintage Books, 2001. Hansen brings his wit to our fascination with orchids, with some of the action set in Borneo.

Hatt, J *The Tropical Traveller: An Essential Guide to Travel in Hot Climates* Penguin Travel Library, London, 1982. Good background on travel in sticky places.

Maugham, S *Borneo Stories* Heinemann Educational Books, Kuala Lumpur, 1976. A collection of stories about expatriate Englishmen and women in exotic settings. Also included in his *Collected Short Stories*.

Munan, H *Culture Shock! A Guide to Customs and Etiquette, Borneo* Times Books International, Singapore, 1988 (revised 1992, reprinted 1996). A personal, engaging account of expat life in Borneo, social etiquette, customs and insider views on subjects as varied as 'Do You Speak Bahasa?', 'Bornean Social Circles' and 'Lo! The Cute Native'. The author was born in Switzerland, brought up in New Zealand and moved to Sarawak in 1965 where she continues to work as a journalist and cultural historian.

O'Hanlon, R *Into the Heart of Borneo* Salamander Press, Edinburgh, 1984. An account of a journey made in 1983 into the mountains of Batu Tiban on the Sarawak–West Kalimantan border, with James Fenton.

St John, S *Life in the Forests of the Far East* Elder Smith, London, 1862.

St John, S *Thirteen Years of Spencer St John's Travels in North and Western Borneo* Elder Smith, London, 1862.

Wassner, J *Espresso with the Headhunters: A Journey Through the Jungles of Borneo* Summersdale, Australia, 2001. A light but personal account of travels in Sarawak, by a Sydney advertising executive turned writer.

Natural history If your interests lie in flora and the fauna, it's worth checking the list of titles published by Sabah-based **Natural History Publications.** The **Sabah Society** *(Kota Kinabalu;* ✆ *088 250443; www.sabahsociety.com)*, responsible for the establishment of the Sabah Museum and Sabah Parks, is an NGO with natural heritage at its heart, and brings together a very interesting circle of local experts – a good source of information.

ARBEC *ASEAN Review of Biodiversity and Environmental Conservation* Available online at www.arbec.com.my. Web journal published by MIMCED in conjunction with the Malaysian University of Science and Technology.

Beaman, J H, Anderson, C and Beaman, R S *The Plants of Mount Kinabalu* Natural History Publications, Borneo, 2001. Fourth volume in a series with sections on the history of plant collecting on Mount Kinabalu and a biographical sketch of two of the most important collectors, Mary Strong and Joseph Clemens. Analysis and indexes of collections, and list of plants. Information on each species on habitat, elevation range, literature and specimens upon which the study is based.

Cranbrook, Earl of (ed) *Wonders of Nature in Southeast Asia* Oxford University Press, 1997. Compilation of excerpts from famous and obscure works by the great explorers, with comments by Cranbrook.

Davidson, G *A Photographic Guide to the Birds of Borneo* New Holland, 4th edition, 2009. Illustrated pocket field guide of 250 species found in Borneo.

Francis, C M *Pocket Guide to the Birds of Borneo* Sabah Society, 1984. Very popular, easy-to-use pocket guide for field reference.

Garbutt, N and Prudente, C *Wild Borneo: The Wildlife and Scenery of Sabah, Sarawak, Brunei and Kalimantan* New Holland, 2006. Illustrated book with 250 colour photographs, preface by Sir David Attenborough and accompanying essays on Borneo's fauna and flora and conservation (including a chapter on the Heart of Borneo project). Published in association with WWF.

Inger, R F and Stuebing, R B *A Field Guide to the Frogs of Borneo* Natural History Publications, Malaysia, 1997.

Myers, S *Birds of Borneo: Brunei, Sabah, Sarawak, and Kalimantan* Princeton Field Guides, 2009 (published in UK by New Holland, 2009). Beautifully illustrated and painstakingly researched book with over 1,500 colour illustrations. A comprehensive field guide to 630 species accompanied by distribution maps, yet not overly cumbersome to carry on a birding trip.

Nais, J *Rafflesia of the World* Natural History Publications, 2001. By the assistant director of Sabah Parks. Can be ordered through Royal Botanic Gardens, Kew Books (*www.kewbooks.com*).

Payne, J and Cubitt, G; *Wild Malaysia: The Wildlife and Scenery of Peninsular Malaysia, Sarawak, and Sabah* 2nd edition, New Holland, 1999. Another coffee-table book with photographs of Malaysian wildlife and natural history.

Smythies, B E *The Birds of Borneo* 4th edition, Natural History Publications, Borneo, 2000. Essential reference on Borneo ornithology; still considered by many to be the most comprehensive guide.

Tweedie, M W F *Malayan Animal Life (and the Common Birds of the Malay Peninsula)* University of Chicago Press, 1954.

Whitehead, J *The Exploration of Mount Kina Balu, North Borneo* Graham Brash, 1993. Revised edition of the classic work published in 1893. Whitehead was the first European to reach the summit of Mount Kinabalu in 1888. The first edition included hand-coloured plates and is now rare and valuable.

Whitmore, T C *An Introduction to Tropical Rain Forests* 2nd edition, Oxford University Press, 1998. Tim Whitmore was a tropical botanist at the Geology Department of the University of Cambridge until his death in 2002. He produced several major reference works on tropical rainforests – see also *Tropical Rainforests of the Far East* Clarendon Press, 1984 and *Palms of Malaya: White Lotus* White Lotus Co Ltd, 2nd edition, 1998.

Conservation

Bevis, W *Borneo Log: The Struggle for Sarawak's Forests* University of Washington Press, 1995. An account of travels in Sarawak; travel narrative and environmental observation.

Harrison, B *Orang-utan* Collins,1962.

Health

Wilson-Howarth, Dr J, and Ellis, Dr M *Your Child Abroad: A Travel Health Guide* Bradt Travel Guides, 2005

Wilson-Howarth, Dr J *Bugs, Bites & Bowels* Cadogan, 2006

WEBSITES

www.brunei.gov.bn Brunei government
www.gov.my Malaysian government
www.sabah.gov.my Sabah State government
www.sarawak.gov.my Sarawak State government

OTHER SOURCES OF INFORMATION

Institute of East Asian Studies (*Universiti Malaysia, Sarawak;* e *aroshima@ieas. unimas.my; www.ieas.unimas.my*) Publishes many books on historical and contemporary culture in Borneo, anthropology and Dayak society. Titles include: *Mapping the Peoples of Sarawak*; *The Malay Population of Sarawak*; *Suket: Penan Folk Stories*; *Changing Borders and Identities in the Kelabit Highlands*; and *Life in the Malay Kampongs of Kuching Fifty Years Ago.*

Natural History Publications (*9th Floor, Wisma Merdeka Kota Kinabalu, Sabah;* ℡ *088 233098;* e *chan@nhpborneo.com; www.nhpborneo.com*) A very active local publisher of nature titles by international experts in their field, headed by C L Chan. Titles include books on rafflesia and rhododendrons of Sabah, the ferns of Mount Kinabalu and the *Nepenthes* (pitcher plants) of Borneo. They have also published historical documents such as *A Botanist in Borneo: Hugh Low's Sarawak Journals from 1844–46*. Some books have been published in conjunction with the Royal Botanic Gardens, Kew, England.

WWF *Terrestrial Ecoregions of the Indo-Pacific: A Conservation Assessment*. WWF report, Island Press, December 2001. WWF reports are available online at www.panda.org. They include *Borneo's New World: Newly Discovered Species in the Heart of Borneo*, 2010.

SEND US YOUR SNAPS!

We'd love to follow your adventures using our *Borneo* guide – why not send us your photos and stories via Twitter (@BradtGuides) and Instagram (@bradtguides) using the hashtag #borneo. Alternatively, you can upload your photos directly to the gallery on the Borneo destination page via our website (*www.bradtguides.com/borneo*).

Index

Page numbers in **bold** indicate main entries; those in *italics* indicate maps.

338

INDEX OF ADVERTISERS

Borneo Adventure 278
Regent Holidays inside front cover
Sticky Rice Travel 3rd colour section
Wanderlust 330